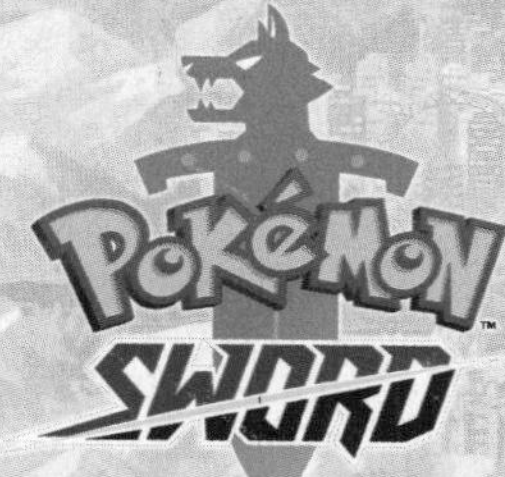

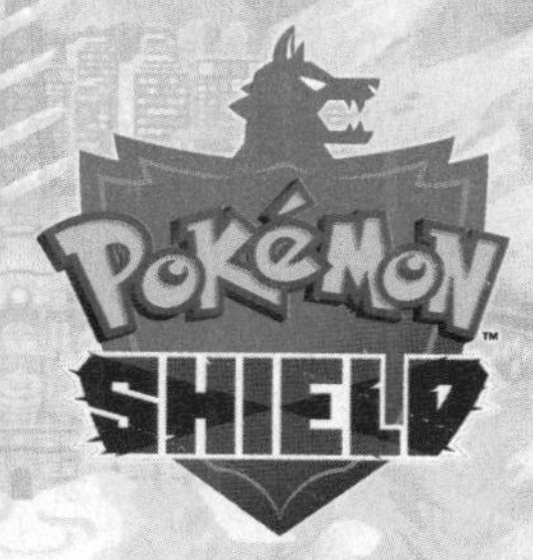

The Official GALAR REGION Strategy Guide

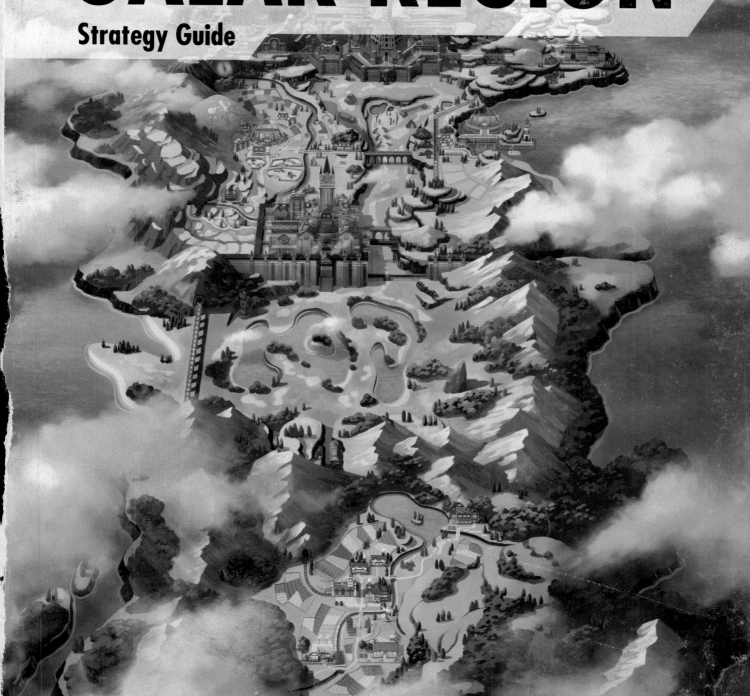

Table of Contents

ALPHABETICAL LIST OF MAJOR MAPS

WILD AREA ZONES

Pokémon in the Galar Pokédex

☐	**001**	Grookey
☐	**002**	Thwackey
☐	**003**	Rillaboom
☐	**004**	Scorbunny
☐	**005**	Raboot
☐	**006**	Cinderace
☐	**007**	Sobble
☐	**008**	Drizzile
☐	**009**	Inteleon
☐	**010**	Blipbug
☐	**011**	Dottler
☐	**012**	Orbeetle
☐	**013**	Caterpie
☐	**014**	Metapod
☐	**015**	Butterfree
☐	**016**	Grubbin
☐	**017**	Charjabug
☐	**018**	Vikavolt
☐	**019**	Hoothoot
☐	**020**	Noctowl
☐	**021**	Rookidee
☐	**022**	Corvisquire
☐	**023**	Corviknight
☐	**024**	Skwovet
☐	**025**	Greedent
☐	**026**	Pidove
☐	**027**	Tranquill
☐	**028**	Unfezant
☐	**029**	Nickit
☐	**030**	Thievul
☐	**031**	Zigzagoon
☐	**032**	Linoone
☐	**033**	Obstagoon
☐	**034**	Wooloo
☐	**035**	Dubwool
☐	**036**	Lotad
☐	**037**	Lombre
☐	**038**	Ludicolo
☐	**039**	Seedot
☐	**040**	Nuzleaf
☐	**041**	Shiftry
☐	**042**	Chewtle
☐	**043**	Drednaw
☐	**044**	Purrloin
☐	**045**	Liepard
☐	**046**	Yamper
☐	**047**	Boltund
☐	**048**	Bunnelby
☐	**049**	Diggersby
☐	**050**	Minccino
☐	**051**	Cinccino
☐	**052**	Bounsweet
☐	**053**	Steenee
☐	**054**	Tsareena
☐	**055**	Oddish
☐	**056**	Gloom
☐	**057**	Vileplume
☐	**058**	Bellossom
☐	**059**	Budew
☐	**060**	Roselia
☐	**061**	Roserade
☐	**062**	Wingull
☐	**063**	Pelipper
☐	**064**	Joltik
☐	**065**	Galvantula
☐	**066**	Electrike
☐	**067**	Manectric
☐	**068**	Vulpix
☐	**069**	Ninetales
☐	**070**	Growlithe
☐	**071**	Arcanine
☐	**072**	Vanillite
☐	**073**	Vanillish
☐	**074**	Vanilluxe
☐	**075**	Swinub
☐	**076**	Piloswine
☐	**077**	Mamoswine
☐	**078**	Delibird
☐	**079**	Snorunt
☐	**080**	Glalie
☐	**081**	Froslass
☐	**082**	Baltoy
☐	**083**	Claydol
☐	**084**	Mudbray
☐	**085**	Mudsdale
☐	**086**	Dwebble
☐	**087**	Crustle
☐	**088**	Golett
☐	**089**	Golurk
☐	**090**	Munna
☐	**091**	Musharna
☐	**092**	Natu
☐	**093**	Xatu
☐	**094**	Stufful
☐	**095**	Bewear
☐	**096**	Snover
☐	**097**	Abomasnow
☐	**098**	Krabby

099	Kingler
100	Wooper
101	Quagsire
102	Corphish
103	Crawdaunt
104	Nincada
105	Ninjask
106	Shedinja
107	Tyrogue
108	Hitmonlee
109	Hitmonchan
110	Hitmontop
111	Pancham
112	Pangoro
113	Klink
114	Klang
115	Klinklang
116	Combee
117	Vespiquen
118	Bronzor
119	Bronzong
120	Ralts
121	Kirlia
122	Gardevoir
123	Gallade
124	Drifloon
125	Drifblim
126	Gossifleur
127	Eldegoss
128	Cherubi
129	Cherrim
130	Stunky
131	Skuntank
132	Tympole
133	Palpitoad
134	Seismitoad
135	Duskull
136	Dusclops
137	Dusknoir
138	Machop
139	Machoke
140	Machamp
141	Gastly
142	Haunter
143	Gengar
144	Magikarp
145	Gyarados
146	Goldeen
147	Seaking
148	Remoraid
149	Octillery
150	Shellder
151	Cloyster
152	Feebas
153	Milotic
154	Basculin
155	Wishiwashi
156	Pyukumuku
157	Trubbish
158	Garbodor
159	Sizzlipede
160	Centiskorch
161	Rolycoly
162	Carkol
163	Coalossal
164	Diglett
165	Dugtrio
166	Drilbur
167	Excadrill
168	Roggenrola
169	Boldore
170	Gigalith
171	Timburr
172	Gurdurr
173	Conkeldurr
174	Woobat
175	Swoobat
176	Noibat
177	Noivern
178	Onix
179	Steelix
180	Arrokuda
181	Barraskewda
182	Meowth
183	Perrserker
184	Persian
185	Milcery
186	Alcremie
187	Cutiefly
188	Ribombee
189	Ferroseed
190	Ferrothorn
191	Pumpkaboo
192	Gourgeist
193	Pichu
194	Pikachu
195	Raichu
196	Eevee
197	Vaporeon
198	Jolteon
199	Flareon
200	Espeon
201	Umbreon
202	Leafeon
203	Glaceon
204	Sylveon
205	Applin
206	Flapple
207	Appletun
208	Espurr
209	Meowstic
210	Swirlix
211	Slurpuff
212	Spritzee
213	Aromatisse
214	Dewpider
215	Araquanid
216	Wynaut
217	Wobbuffet
218	Farfetch'd
219	Sirfetch'd
220	Chinchou
221	Lanturn
222	Croagunk
223	Toxicroak
224	Scraggy
225	Scrafty
226	Stunfisk
227	Shuckle
228	Barboach
229	Whiscash
230	Shellos
231	Gastrodon
232	Wimpod
233	Golisopod
234	Binacle
235	Barbaracle
236	Corsola
237	Cursola
238	Impidimp
239	Morgrem
240	Grimmsnarl
241	Hatenna
242	Hattrem
243	Hatterene
244	Salandit
245	Salazzle
246	Pawniard
247	Bisharp
248	Throh
249	Sawk
250	Koffing
251	Weezing

252 Bonsly
253 Sudowoodo
254 Cleffa
255 Clefairy
256 Clefable
257 Togepi
258 Togetic
259 Togekiss
260 Munchlax
261 Snorlax
262 Cottonee
263 Whimsicott
264 Rhyhorn
265 Rhydon
266 Rhyperior
267 Gothita
268 Gothorita
269 Gothitelle
270 Solosis
271 Duosion
272 Reuniclus
273 Karrablast
274 Escavalier
275 Shelmet
276 Accelgor
277 Elgyem
278 Beheeyem
279 Cubchoo
280 Beartic
281 Rufflet
282 Braviary
283 Vullaby
284 Mandibuzz
285 Skorupi
286 Drapion
287 Litwick
288 Lampent
289 Chandelure
290 Inkay
291 Malamar
292 Sneasel
293 Weavile
294 Sableye
295 Mawile
296 Maractus
297 Sigilyph
298 Riolu
299 Lucario
300 Torkoal
301 Mimikyu
302 Cufant
303 Copperajah
304 Qwilfish
305 Frillish
306 Jellicent
307 Mareanie
308 Toxapex
309 Cramorant
310 Toxel
311 Toxtricity
312 Silicobra
313 Sandaconda
314 Hippopotas
315 Hippowdon
316 Durant
317 Heatmor
318 Helioptile
319 Heliolisk
320 Hawlucha
321 Trapinch
322 Vibrava
323 Flygon
324 Axew
325 Fraxure
326 Haxorus
327 Yamask
328 Runerigus
329 Cofagrigus
330 Honedge
331 Doublade
332 Aegislash
333 Ponyta
334 Rapidash
335 Sinistea
336 Polteageist
337 Indeedee
338 Phantump
339 Trevenant
340 Morelull
341 Shiinotic
342 Oranguru
343 Passimian
344 Morpeko
345 Falinks
346 Drampa
347 Turtonator
348 Togedemaru
349 Snom
350 Frosmoth
351 Clobbopus
352 Grapploct
353 Pincurchin
354 Mantyke
355 Mantine
356 Wailmer
357 Wailord
358 Bergmite
359 Avalugg
360 Dhelmise
361 Lapras
362 Lunatone
363 Solrock
364 Mime Jr.
365 Mr. Mime
366 Mr. Rime
367 Darumaka
368 Darmanitan
369 Stonjourner
370 Eiscue
371 Duraludon
372 Rotom
373 Ditto
374 Dracozolt
375 Arctozolt
376 Dracovish
377 Arctovish
378 Charmander
379 Charmeleon
380 Charizard
381 Type: Null
382 Silvally
383 Larvitar
384 Pupitar
385 Tyranitar
386 Deino
387 Zweilous
388 Hydreigon
389 Goomy
390 Sliggoo
391 Goodra
392 Jangmo-o
393 Hakamo-o
394 Kommo-o
395 Dreepy
396 Drakloak
397 Dragapult
398 Zacian
399 Zamazenta
400 ???

What's New in the Galar Region?

Some of you reading this are probably seasoned Pokémon veterans. You already know what to expect—catching Pokémon, training them, battling them, all the basics. But the Galar region is a new region to explore, and there will be things you've never seen before! Here's just a preview of what you'll find covered in this guide.

The Gym Challenge

The Gym Challenge is an annual event in the Galar region, where endorsed Trainers can try to defeat eight Gym Leaders, make their way through the Semifinals and Finals tournaments, and ultimately defeat the Champion! Learn more about this unique sporting event on page 11, or dive right into it with the walkthrough starting on page 31.

Poké Jobs

Pokémon have a very active role in Galarian society. You can experience this yourself with Poké Jobs—job postings from companies across Galar that you can send your Pokémon to help out on. Have Pokémon in your Boxes go lend a hand (or tail, or tentacle, or claw), and they'll earn rewards ranging from cash and items to Exp. Points and base points! For more info, head to page 241.

Y-Comm

Y-Comm is the easy communication hub where you can find other players to trade Pokémon or League Cards with, have Link Battles against, or join for Max Raid Battles. Connect to the internet or play with others nearby, and you'll see stamps pop up on your screen whenever other Trainers are looking for someone to connect with so they can play together (p. 298).

The Wild Area

Another defining feature of Galar is the massive uninhabited wilderness known as the Wild Area. You'll visit this wide, open expanse often on your adventure. It's a great place to explore, catch Pokémon, camp, and take part in Max Raid Battles against Dynamax Pokémon with up to three other players! If you want to find out more about the Wild Area and what you can do there, turn to page 249.

Camping

You saw we mentioned camping up there? That's right—in the Galar region, camping is pretty common! Pitch your tent in the Wild Area or on routes, and you might just run into other Trainers who've decided to set up camp, too! To learn more about all you can do at camp (including playing with Pokémon or cooking up restorative curries), turn to page 280.

The Dynamax phenomenon

If there's one thing that makes the Pokémon of the Galar region unique, it's that they can Dynamax. Once Dynamaxed, Pokémon become massive, get a huge boost to their HP, and gain access to new Max Moves. If that sounds a little intimidating, don't worry—you'll be able to Dynamax your own Pokémon in time! But so will some opponents you face, so turn to page 14 to start studying up!

!

This certainly isn't all that's new! Explore this guide to learn about marks and special titles your Pokémon can get in battle, your nifty new Rotom Bike, how weather plays a role in catching Pokémon in the Galar region, and more. There are plenty of new functions for expert players, too, like Nature mints to change your Pokémon's stats, new ways to get Egg Moves and evolve certain Pokémon, new online battle systems, and so much more waiting for you in *Pokémon Sword* and *Pokémon Shield*!

Quick Start to This Guide

We're all new to the Galar region, but maybe some of you reading this are new to the world of Pokémon itself! Perhaps you're feeling a bit overwhelmed already with everything that you can do and find. Well, not to worry! This section is to help you get a smooth start and point you to some areas of this book that will be particularly helpful for newcomers to the series!

Getting a hang of the basics

If you've already had a look at the table of contents, you've probably noticed this guide is divided into a variety of sections. They've all got useful data for Trainers, but a few will be particularly relevant to newcomers. First and foremost, check out the section titled Welcome to the World of Pokémon! (p. 10) for a breakdown of what it means to be a Pokémon Trainer, from catching Pokémon to trading and battling them. Read on from there, and you'll learn about the world you're going to explore, including tips on how to obtain useful items or earn money, descriptions of the various shops and facilities around Galar, and lots more to feel right at home!

> **!** If you're already familiar with the world of Pokémon but want to see what's new in the Galar region, check out the previous page!

Walkthrough

The walkthrough, beginning from page 31, is probably the section you'll use most—at least initially. In it, you'll find detailed maps for every area of Galar you'll visit, along with what items you'll find, which Pokémon you can encounter, and where Trainers might be waiting to challenge you. You'll also find advice on how to prepare for and triumph over key battles. And if you're in the mood for a little sidetracking, there'll also be callouts for subevents and the rewards they offer, so you don't have to worry about missing out on anything!

You took the time to talk to a Poké Ball, so you deserve a little reward!

Advanced Trainer Handbook

After the walkthrough, you'll find this section starting on page 161. This is where we dive deeper into the game. You'll turn to it again and again once you're ready to explore different ways to play in more depth. Here are just a few of the key things you'll find there:

- How to catch and raise Pokémon and master everything you need to know for battle (p. 162), such as type matchups (p. 164) or how to build a balanced team (p.166)
- How to complete your Pokédex (p. 207) if you're up to the challenge, including how to find Pokémon Eggs to get new Pokémon for your teams (p. 234)
- What you can do in the Wild Area (p. 249), a wide, open expanse where you can find tons of different Pokémon species, camp out, take on Max Raid Battles, and so much more
- How to make and collect League Cards (p. 301), plus all the different ways you can customize your character (p. 313), if you want to go through your adventure in your own style

Adventure Data

Adventure data, beginning on page 335, is exactly what the name implies—data about all the items, moves, Abilities, and more that you'll come across during your adventure. If you find an item that you don't know how to use, or if there's an item you want but you don't know how to get it, you can look it up by its name here. Moves and Abilities will also be described in detail, down to any secondary or hidden effects they might have, so browse through them to build new strategies. This section is where you can find detailed information on many of the more complicated aspects of training Pokémon, so once you're ready for it, dive right in!

> **Becoming a Real Champion Trainer**
>
> The handbook sections get pretty detailed, so don't feel like you need to master everything immediately. You'll keep coming back here again and again, and you'll probably pick up a bit more each time you do—especially from the advice boxes like these! They sometimes highlight more-advanced strategies or functions that aren't needed when you're just starting out. As you gain experience, pay closer attention to them!

Map of the Galar Region

To the right is the map of the Galar region, where you'll embark on your adventure as a Gym Challenger aiming for victory in the Champion Cup. Cities, towns, and other key locations are labeled on this map, and routes are labeled in red. You'll also see that train tracks connect a few locations. Information about some of the key facilities you'll want to recognize around Galar can be found below, followed by a summary of what you can find in each town and city in this region. Places where you can shop for items or clothes are listed following the 🛍 symbol.

Gym Stadiums

Challenge the leaders of Pokémon Gyms at these stadiums to collect eight Gym Badges and become a Gym Medalist.

Pokémon Centers

Visit these centers to heal your Pokémon, buy essential items at the Poké Mart counter, and more (p. 16).

Pokémon Nurseries

Leave two Pokémon at the Nurseries on Route 5 or in the Wild Area, and you may find a Pokémon Egg (p. 234)!

Postwick

- Your house
- Hop and Leon's house

Wedgehurst

- Pokémon Research Lab
- Pokémon Center
- Wedgehurst Station

🛍 Poké Mart clerk, boutique, Berry shop

Motostoke

- Pokémon Center ×2
- Motostoke Stadium
- Hair salon
- Battle Café
- Budew Drop Inn
- Motostoke Station
- Move tutor

🛍 Poké Mart clerk, Poké Ball and battle item clerk, TM clerk, boutique, uniform shop, vending machine

Turffield

- Pokémon Center
- Turffield Stadium
- Geoglyph

🛍 Poké Mart clerk, uniform shop

Hulbury

- Pokémon Center
- Hulbury Stadium
- The Captain's Table seafood restaurant
- Hulbury Station

🛍 Poké Mart clerk, Incense Merchant, Herb Shop, uniform shop

Hammerlocke

- Pokémon Center ×3
- Hammerlocke Stadium
- Hair salon
- Battle Café
- Hammerlocke Station
- Friendship rater
- Move tutor

🛍 Poké Mart clerk, Poké Ball and battle item clerk, TM clerk, boutique, BP Shop, uniform shop, vending machine

Stow-on-Side

- Pokémon Center
- Stow-on-Side Stadium
- Historical mural

🛍 Poké Mart clerk, uniform shop, bargain stall, buyer stall

Ballonlea

- Pokémon Center
- Ballonlea Stadium

🛍 Poké Mart clerk, uniform shop

Circhester

- Pokémon Center
- Circhester Stadium
- Hair salon
- Hotel Ionia
- Bob's Your Uncle restaurant
- Circhester Bath
- Move tutor

🛍 Poké Mart clerk, boutique, uniform shop

Spikemuth

- Pokémon Center
- Spikemuth Gym

🛍 Poké Mart clerk

Wyndon

- Pokémon Center ×2
- Wyndon Stadium
- Hair salon
- Battle Café
- The Rose of the Rondelands hotel
- Rose Tower
- Wyndon Monorail
- Wyndon Station
- Move tutor

🛍 Poké Mart clerk, Poké Ball and battle item clerk, TM clerk, BP Shop, boutique, vending machine

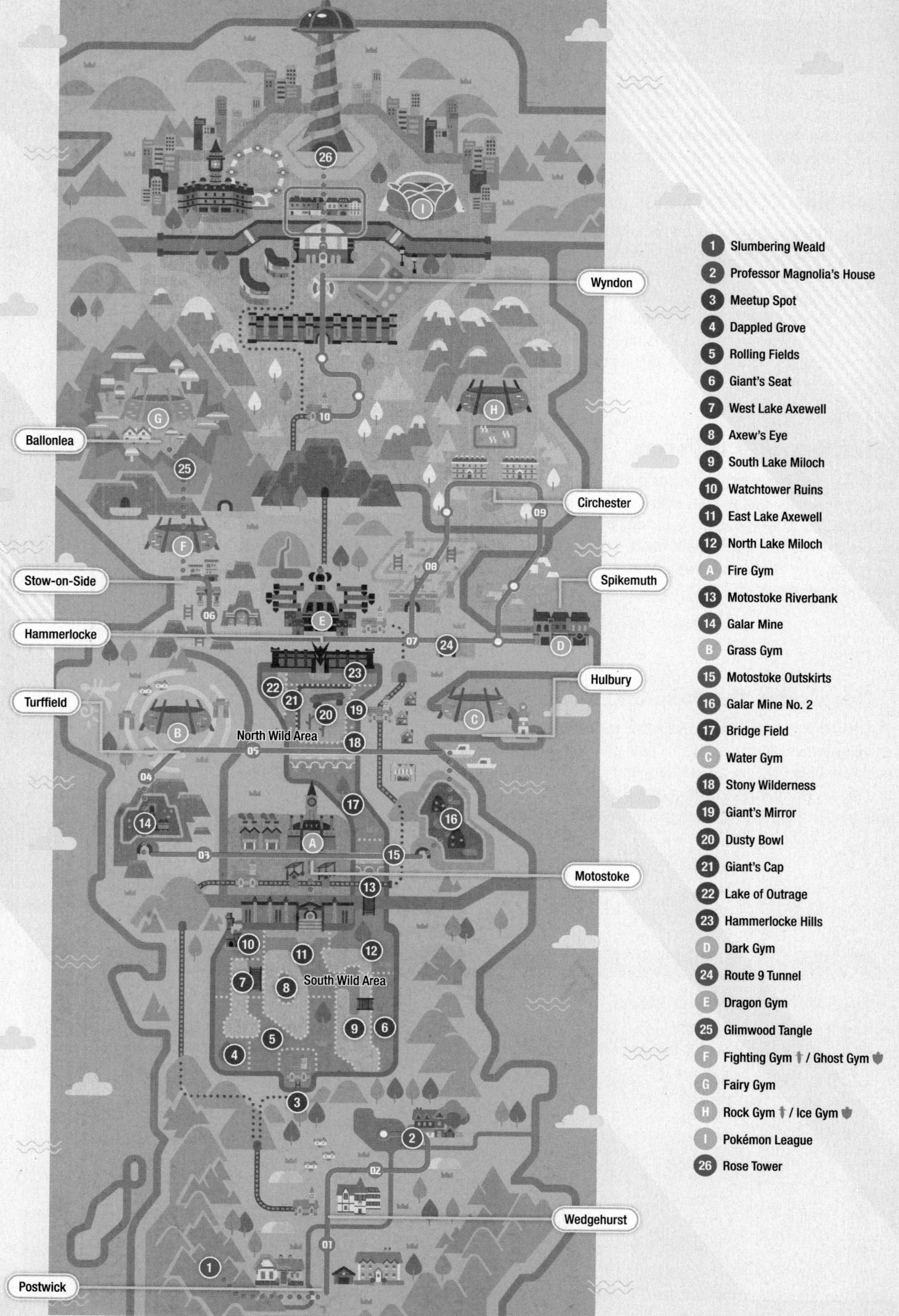
Wyndon
Ballonlea
Circhester
Stow-on-Side
Spikemuth
Hammerlocke
Hulbury
Turffield
North Wild Area
Motostoke
South Wild Area
Wedgehurst
Postwick
1 Slumbering Weald
2 Professor Magnolia's House
3 Meetup Spot
4 Dappled Grove
5 Rolling Fields
6 Giant's Seat
7 West Lake Axewell
8 Axew's Eye
9 South Lake Miloch
10 Watchtower Ruins
11 East Lake Axewell
12 North Lake Miloch
A Fire Gym
13 Motostoke Riverbank
14 Galar Mine
B Grass Gym
15 Motostoke Outskirts
16 Galar Mine No. 2
17 Bridge Field
C Water Gym
18 Stony Wilderness
19 Giant's Mirror
20 Dusty Bowl
21 Giant's Cap
22 Lake of Outrage
23 Hammerlocke Hills
D Dark Gym
24 Route 9 Tunnel
E Dragon Gym
25 Glimwood Tangle
F Fighting Gym / Ghost Gym
G Fairy Gym
H Rock Gym / Ice Gym
I Pokémon League
26 Rose Tower

Welcome to the World of Pokémon!

The Pokémon world is similar to ours in many ways, but it has one huge difference—the existence of creatures called Pokémon! Pokémon are found in just about every corner of this world—in vast plains, sandy wastes, and snowy mountains! Humans and Pokémon live together and help each other thrive, but people who call themselves Pokémon Trainers take things even further. They're dedicated to catching, raising, and battling Pokémon as they work to complete their Pokédex!

Catching Pokémon

Pokémon Trainers are always on the lookout for new Pokémon in the wild to catch. Pokémon can be caught in special devices called Poké Balls, which comfortably hold them. You can keep up to six Pokémon in your party to use in battle. The rest will be stored in your Boxes, accessible from the Rotom Information (or Rotomi) terminal (p. 16) and from the Pokémon option in the X menu once you have the Pokémon Box Link item.

Battling with Pokémon

When two Trainers meet, it's tradition that they have a battle. Usually, Pokémon battles start with each Trainer sending out one Pokémon at a time, and the Pokémon take turns using moves to try to win. Moves have many different effects, and becoming a great Trainer means learning how and when to use the right moves (p. 183).

Completing the Pokédex

The Pokédex is a high-tech device that records data about each Pokémon you catch. It is the goal of many Trainers to complete their Pokédex by catching every last Pokémon found in a region. But this isn't always an easy goal! If you think you're up to the challenge, you can learn more on page 207.

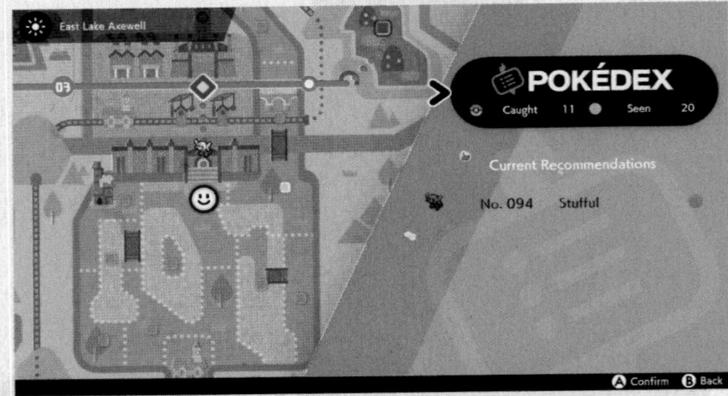

You Don't Have to Do It Alone!

Trading Pokémon with other Trainers is a key part of any Pokémon adventure, whether you trade with characters found in the game or other players in the real world. Not only is it great fun to see what you get, but trading Pokémon can also be necessary for completing your Pokédex, since some species are only found in one version of the game (p. 24). Using Y-Comm (p. 298), you can connect with nearby people, trade with others online, and even trade with people you pass by in the real world. And that's not all you can do together—you can also battle other players using Y-Comm, or you can take on more competitively minded Trainers from the VS option in the X menu (p. 202)!

> **!** Traded Pokémon also grow a bit quicker than Pokémon you catch yourself, gaining more experience after every battle!

The Gym Challenge

In the Galar region, the best and brightest Trainers can try to prove themselves in the Gym Challenge! The Gym Challenge and the Champion Cup that follows are renowned sporting events held each year to help crown a single Champion for the region. People come from all over Galar—and some even come from other regions—to watch the spectacle. Strong Gym Challengers are practically celebrities in Galar!

But not just anyone can take part. To become a Gym Challenger, you must be endorsed by one of the Gym Leaders or another high-ranking member of the Pokémon League, such as the chairman or the current Champion.

The Pokémon League

The Galarian Pokémon League organizes the annual Gym Challenge. It's helmed by Chairman Rose, a self-made businessman who has transformed the Galar region with his numerous successful companies. The League and the Gym Challenge exist to promote Galarian Trainers, helping them become as strong as they can be.

Pokémon Gyms and Gym Leaders

Galar is home to numerous Pokémon Gyms—powerful teams of Trainers that each specialize in a different Pokémon type. A Gym Challenger must take on and defeat eight of these Gyms in a specific order set by the Pokémon League, earning a Gym Badge from the Gym Leader of each. The journey will take you from the southern end of Galar all the way to Wyndon in the north of the region, if you manage to collect all eight Gym Badges.

> **!** Because all the Gym Challengers must earn their Gym Badges in the same order, you're probably going to keep running into at least a few other challengers on your adventure. And they'll definitely want to test their skills against yours!

The Champion Cup

If a Gym Challenger collects all eight Gym Badges, they will be recognized as a Gym Medalist. That means they're eligible to enter the Champion Cup! On the first day, all of the Gym Medalists who made it through the Gym Challenge face off in elimination rounds until only one remains. That Gym Challenger then moves on to the Finals, where they face the true strength of the Gym Leaders in elimination rounds. The last Trainer standing wins the honor of one last battle against the reigning Champion in the Championship Match. If the challenger wins, they'll take the throne and become the new Champion of the Galar region!

Champion Cup

Gym Challenge

Endorsed Trainers can try to earn eight Gym Badges by defeating Gym Leaders throughout Galar to gain entry into the Champion Cup!

Semifinals

Eligible Gym Medalists compete in elimination rounds, till only one remains!

Finals

The victorious challenger faces off against the Gym Leaders in elimination rounds—and they're not holding back this time!

Championship Match

Face the reigning champ in a battle, and if you win, you'll become the region's new Champion!

Pokémon Basics

If you hope to snag your spot in the Gym Challenge, you'll need to master the basics of Pokémon training first! Once you're ready for more, turn to page 161 or follow the references below for more in-depth guides to making the strongest team you can.

Help your team grow

More on p. 180!

Once you're out there battling your Pokémon against others, your Pokémon will start earning Experience Points (Exp. Points). As they earn more and more, your Pokémon will level up, and they'll grow even stronger. Helping your team of Pokémon level up is the most basic of basics for any Trainer.

> Your whole team will earn some Exp. Points from battles—even those that don't take part. But they'll earn more Exp. Points if they join the battle, even if they don't use any moves. Pokémon in your Boxes won't earn any Exp. Points.

> Evolution can open the door to new moves your Pokémon can learn—but it can also shut the door on some others. Pokémon may lose the chance to learn certain moves after evolving. If they're evolving after a level-up, you can press Ⓑ during the Evolution process if you want to make it stop. Don't worry about missing out on evolving—your Pokémon will start to evolve again the next time it goes up a level!

Help your team evolve

More on p. 211!

When one of your Pokémon levels up, you might be surprised to see it evolve! Pokémon Evolution can be triggered by many different things, but the most common way is by leveling up. When Pokémon evolve, their stats go up—even more than they do from a normal level-up. They may also gain new types or new Abilities.

It's not just their stats that change. Pokémon's appearances change, too!

Understand how stats stack up

More on p. 168!

So, stats can go up from leveling up or Evolution, but what are they? There is a total of six stats—HP, Attack, Defense, Sp. Atk, Sp. Def, and Speed. Each one has a big effect on how a Pokémon does in battle.

HP

HP (hit points) indicates a Pokémon's health. If HP drops to zero, the Pokémon will faint, meaning it's too tired to battle anymore.

Attack

High Attack will make a Pokémon's **physical** moves deal more damage.

Defense

High Defense will reduce the damage a Pokémon takes from **physical** moves.

Sp. Atk

High Sp. Atk (Special Attack) will make a Pokémon's **special** moves deal more damage.

Sp. Def

High Sp. Def (Special Defense) will reduce the damage a Pokémon takes from **special** moves.

Speed

Speed affects which Pokémon will probably get to use its move first each turn.

Skwovet uses Tackle

Wooloo has high Defense

Skwovet uses Tackle

Hoothoot has low Defense

> Stats can be raised in ways other than simply leveling up your Pokémon. You can do a lot to affect them, as you'll learn on page 168.

Master new moves

More on p. 183!

Your Pokémon can learn up to four moves at a time to be used in battle, generally by leveling up or by using items like TMs or TRs. There are hundreds of moves out there, so you'll want to try different ones to see which four you'll stick with. Each time your Pokémon has the option to learn a new move, check out the move's description, consider its category, and definitely think about its type.

	Physical moves	Deal physical damage. Teach them to Pokémon with high Attack, and use them against Pokémon with low Defense.
	Special moves	Deal special damage. Teach them to Pokémon with high Sp. Atk, and use them against Pokémon with low Sp. Def.
	Status moves	Have other effects, such as causing status conditions or affecting the battlefield.

!

On the previous page, you can see how different stats affect physical and special moves. No stats affect the amount of damage status moves do, because they generally don't deal direct damage. Using them wisely can be the key to more-advanced strategies!

Factor in types

More on p. 164!

Having Pokémon with high Attack learn physical moves—or those with high Sp. Atk learn special moves—is one thing to keep in mind. But just as important (or even more so) is the type of your Pokémon's moves. First of all, when a Pokémon uses a move that shares a type with it, the move's power goes up by 50%. This is called the **same-type attack bonus**. But this isn't the only way to increase the damage dealt by a Pokémon's moves!

Your opponent's type will have a huge impact on how much damage your Pokémon's moves can deal. Every Pokémon can have one or two of 18 possible types. Each has different weaknesses and strengths. If your Pokémon uses a move of a type that the opponent is weak to, your move will do much more damage than usual. These relationships are called **type matchups**, and such a move would be **super effective**.

An easy way to think of it is like a game of rock-paper-scissors. Fire-type moves are strong against Grass-type Pokémon because fire burns up grass. However, Fire-type moves aren't very effective against Water-type Pokémon, because water puts fire out. On page 383, you'll find the full type matchup chart, but there's also a preview below to the right.

Battle text	Effect on the opponent
Super effective	Deals 2× the regular damage or more!
Effective	Deals the regular amount of damage
Not very effective	Deals 1/2 the regular damage or less
No effect	Has no effect on the Pokémon

See the different symbols here? They show how the type of a move being used by an attacking Pokémon will stack up against each type an opponent could have. If you see ◉, the move will be super effective (2× damage). If you see ▲, it will be not very effective (1/2 damage). An × means the move will do no damage at all. And if you see nothing at all in a square, the damage dealt will just be the regular amount.

Attacking Pokémon's Move Type \ Defending Pokémon's Type	NORMAL	FIRE	WATER	GRASS	ELECTRIC	ICE	FIGHTING	POISON	GROUND	FLYING	PSYCHIC	BUG	ROCK	GHOST	DRAGON	DARK	STEEL	FAIRY
NORMAL													▲	×			▲	
FIRE		▲	▲	◉		◉						◉	▲		▲		◉	
WATER		◉	▲	▲					◉				◉		▲			
GRASS		▲	◉	▲				▲	◉	▲		▲	◉		▲		▲	
ELECTRIC			◉	▲	▲				×	◉					▲			
ICE		▲	▲	◉		▲			◉	◉					◉		▲	
FIGHTING	◉					◉		▲		▲	▲	▲	◉	×		◉	◉	▲
POISON				◉				▲	▲				▲	▲			×	◉
GROUND		◉		▲	◉			◉		×		▲	◉				◉	
FLYING				◉	▲		◉					◉	▲				▲	
PSYCHIC							◉	◉			▲					×	▲	
BUG		▲		◉			▲	▲		▲	◉			▲		◉	▲	▲
ROCK		◉				◉	▲		▲	◉		◉					▲	
GHOST	×										◉			◉		▲		
DRAGON															◉		▲	×
DARK							▲				◉			◉		▲		▲
STEEL		▲	▲		▲	◉							◉				▲	◉
FAIRY		▲					◉	▲							◉	◉	▲	

Strategize with Abilities and held items

Abilities can also have a key part to play in battle, and each Pokémon has one. Check the Ability of each Pokémon you catch, and think about how you could use it to your advantage. You can learn more about Abilities on page 181. There are also items you can use on your Pokémon and have your Pokémon hold for special effects. Learn more about those on page 185. There's a great deal of depth in Pokémon battling if you choose to embrace it—and you'll want to if you hope to be the very best!

The Power of Dynamaxing

In the Galar region, Pokémon are able to Dynamax! Only Pokémon caught in this region have been found to undergo this transformation, which makes them appear as giant forms of themselves. Professor Magnolia, a Pokémon Professor in the region, has spent a long time unraveling the secrets of this phenomenon, and here are just a few of her key findings:

- Pokémon can only Dynamax at Power Spots.
- A Pokémon Trainer must possess a Dynamax Band in order to Dynamax their Pokémon.
- Dynamaxing transforms a Pokémon's moves into Max Moves.
- The power of Max Moves is so great, it can change the entire battlefield.
- A Trainer's Pokémon can only hold their Dynamax form for three turns.
- Only one of your Pokémon can Dynamax during a regular battle, and they can only do this once.
- Dynamaxing can be powered up further by raising a Pokémon's Dynamax Level.

!

This transformation has a number of surprising effects in battle. Dynamax Pokémon will never flinch, and they can't be forced out of battle (by moves like Dragon Tail, for example). They're also immune to moves that are based on a Pokémon's weight, like Grass Knot and Low Kick.

What Are Max Moves?

While a Pokémon is Dynamaxed, its moves will change into moves only Dynamax Pokémon can use. The Max Move a particular move becomes is based on the original move's type and whether or not it's a status move. These moves gain special additional effects, ranging from changing the weather condition to boosting certain stats. There are even moves that may have extra effects for certain Pokémon, too! Learn more on page 353.

Pokémon can Dynamax in the stadiums where most battles with Gym Leaders are held. This is because they've been built over Power Spots. Dynamaxing is also possible during Max Raid Battles in the Wild Area, as well as in Link Battles against other Trainers!

Certain Pokémon can also take on special forms when they Dynamax. This phenomenon is known as **Gigantamaxing**. It isn't yet known why these certain Pokémon change in appearance when they Dynamax, but they are an awesome sight to behold! If you want a little preview, you can turn to page 216!

Getting Around Galar

You'll spend a lot of time exploring the Galar region, especially its vast Wild Area. The going can be slow on foot, but through your adventure, you'll gain access to various modes of transportation that'll help get you where you need to go in a flash!

Rotom Bike (Land Mode)

Riding your Rotom Bike will get you around faster than running on foot. Hop on and off using the ⊕ or ⊖ button, and move using the Left Stick. You can also trigger the turbo boost by pressing Ⓛ, Ⓡ, or Ⓑ. This mode allows you to blast off at high speed for a few seconds, letting you travel farther and also making it less likely you'll encounter wild Pokémon! You'll have to let it recharge between uses, though. Once you see green sparks flash across your bike, you'll be ready to blast off again!

Trigger the turbo boost, and you'll be in for an extra burst of power that'll propel you forward faster than usual!

Rotom Bike (Water Mode)

You'll sometimes encounter bodies of water that you can't cross on your own. In time, though, you'll be able to use your Rotom Bike to paddle across them! Once you unlock this feature, consider revisiting lakes, rivers, and pools to see what might lie on the other side of them. The controls, including the turbo boost, remain the same as when riding on land.

Once you've unlocked Water Mode, ride your bike right onto the water and it will transform into Water Mode automatically!

Getting Past Pokémon

You'll often spot Pokémon moving about in the tall grass throughout the Galar region. If you want to try to sneak by them without attracting their notice, you can crouch down and move about slowly through tall grass by gently tilting the control stick in the direction you want to go. You'll generally go undetected. On the other hand, if you wish to get the attention of Pokémon that are walking about, you can whistle at them—or ring your bell if on your Rotom Bike—by pressing the Left Stick.

Rail and monorail

The extensive rail network can help you move between a number of the cities and towns in the Galar region. There's also a monorail system in the sprawling city of Wyndon, which will help you navigate it if you're feeling lost or just want to get around more quickly. There's no charge!

Flying Taxis

Flying Taxis let the people of the Galar region call Corviknight to carry them around the region, zipping them straight to other towns, cities, and routes—and certain spots in the Wild Area. The version that Gym Challengers get free access to has a special restriction placed on it, though—it can only be used to fly back to locations you've already visited before. You have to prove your skill by reaching each new location under your own power the first time! Once you have access to the Flying Taxi service, you can call one by choosing a location you'd like to go to from the Town Map in the X menu.

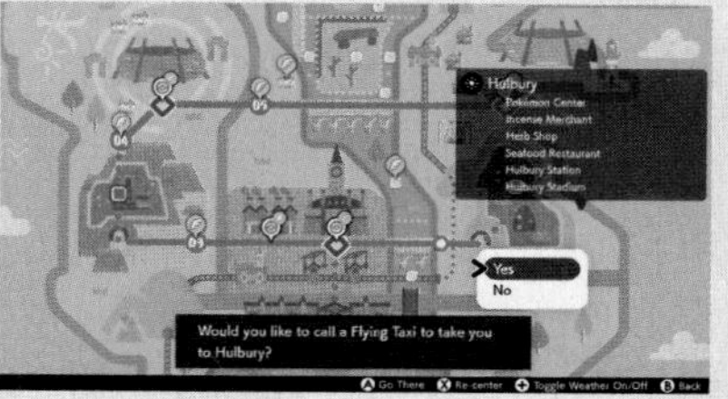

Finding items while out and about

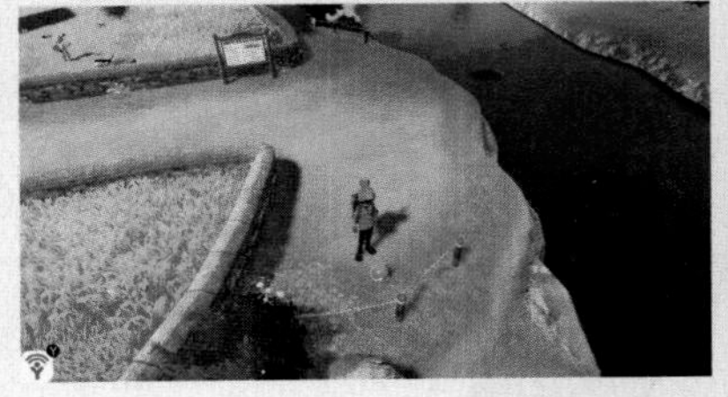

Pokémon aren't all you can find in the field—keep an eye out, and you'll come across handy items, too! Some items will be easy to spot, appearing like Poké Balls that have fallen on the ground. The red ones hold regular items, such as Potions to heal your Pokémon or X Attacks to help them hit harder in battle. Yellow ones contain TMs, which are items you can use over and over to teach Pokémon moves! More about TMs on page 356.

There are more items lying about than just the ones in Poké Balls, though. As you explore the Galar region, keep your eyes peeled for little sparkles on the ground—they mark the locations of hidden items! These can be rare items that are useful for battles or training or that can be sold to Poké Mart clerks for a high price.

Notice a sparkle flash once in the field? Hunt around to pinpoint its location...

There it is! When you see the sparkle flashing, you've hit pay dirt!

Press Ⓐ and claim your prize!

> **!** Generally, once you've found an item in a certain spot, you won't see any sparkles there again. But in some spots, you may find more items the next day. This happens in places such as on routes and especially in the Wild Area! Hidden items in the Wild Area will keep appearing again and again—though they might not always be the same item you found before! Perhaps the many people out exploring there keep dropping things over time? Learn more about the Wild Area starting on page 249.

Shops and other facilities

Pokémon Centers

The reassuring glow of these red-roofed buildings is a welcome sight to any Trainer! These centers are popular hubs where Trainers pop in to have their party taken care of, stock up on supplies, pick up Poké Jobs, get help with training, or simply catch the latest Gym Challenge matches on the big screens.

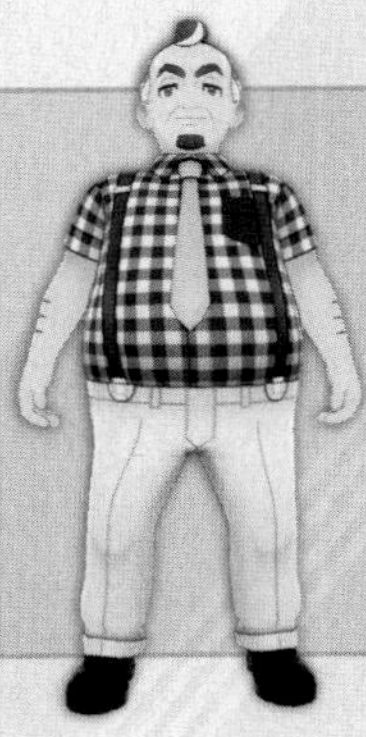

Jack

Meet Jack, the jack-of-all-trades (see what we did there?) who has his own setup in Pokémon Centers. Talk to this fellow to have your Pokémon remember or forget moves or to change their nicknames. If you've won at least three Gym Badges, he'll even tell you about memories your Pokémon have!

Rotomi

The Rotom Information terminal, which everyone just calls Rotomi, is where you can check your Pokémon Boxes, take on Poké Jobs (p. 241), edit your League Card (p. 301), and try your luck in the Loto-ID!

Poké Mart

Essential items for Trainers are sold at this counter. Some Poké Marts have a second clerk, who sells items such as rare Poké Balls and TMs! Check out a full list of what these different clerks sell on page 381.

Healing

Talk to the nurse here to have all your Pokémon's HP and PP restored and any status conditions cured. And don't worry about payment—it doesn't cost a thing!

Boutiques, hair salons, and uniform shops

Find boutiques in Wedgehurst, Motostoke, Hammerlocke, Circhester, and Wyndon to try out new looks. Each of these shops offers different lineups—check them out starting on page 324. You can also visit the hair salons in all the big cities if you feel like changing your hairstyle and hair color. They'll even give you a fresh cosmetic look and change your color contacts for just a small fee! More about that on page 313. Finally, if you love that Gym Trainer style, head to the left-hand counter inside most stadiums to browse their stock of uniforms from minor-division Gyms.

BP Shops and Watt Traders

The BP Shops in Hammerlocke and Wyndon will be your go-to spots for advanced items to help you raise strong Pokémon and pull off complex battle strategies. Turn to page 200 to find out how you can earn BP. And if you find yourself with an abundance of Watts from exploring the Wild Area or participating in the Rotom Rally (p. 274), the Rotom Rallyists found throughout the Wild Area can serve as Watt Traders, too! They have rare items, such as TRs or even Wishing Pieces, which can attract Dynamax Pokémon to Pokémon Dens (p. 270).

Other shops

You'll find other small shops here and there around the region, selling specialized goods. For example, the Herb Shop in Hulbury sells bitter herbs that will heal your Pokémon but reduce their friendship toward you. The nearby Incense Merchant stocks items handy for both battles and Egg hatching! The marketplace in Stow-on-Side is also well worth a visit for its daily bargains.

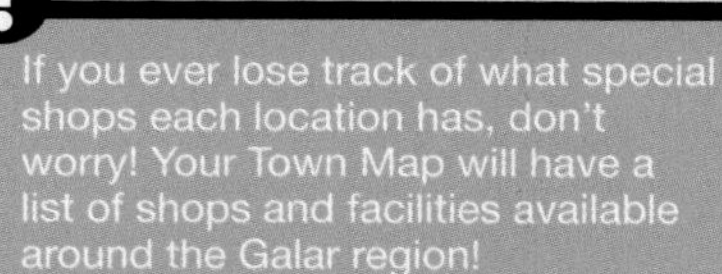

If you ever lose track of what special shops each location has, don't worry! Your Town Map will have a list of shops and facilities available around the Galar region!

Start Making Some Money!

It's probably clear by now that there's plenty for you to spend your hard-earned pocket money on in the Galar region. Here are some ways you can help fill your wallet to ensure you never run short on cash!

- Use the move Pay Day. In addition to dealing damage to the opponent, it lets you pick up a little more cash after the battle! This move can be learned using TM02, so turn to page 356 for more info on where to get it.
- Have your Pokémon hold an Amulet Coin or a Luck Incense. If the Pokémon holding either of these items participates in a Trainer battle, you'll get double the prize money when you win. Check out how to find items like these in the items list starting on page 370.
- Take advantage of Poké Jobs! Poké Jobs will provide you with all sorts of rewards, such as items, Exp. Points, and yes, sometimes money! If you have some Pokémon in your Boxes that you don't immediately need, it's not a bad idea to have them help out with Poké Jobs. Turn to page 241 to learn more.
- Sell items—but sell them smartly! During your adventure, you'll come across items that sell for a hefty amount of money, like Nuggets or Pearls. You can reliably get some of them from people in the Wild Area each day, too (p. 279). You could sell these items at any Poké Mart for some quick cash, but if you've made it to Stow-on-Side, you have a better option. Talk to the man at the buyer stall (p. 89), and if you're lucky, he'll buy items from you at a much higher price than the Poké Marts!

Camping

The Galar region isn't all fancy cities and boutiques! You'll spend a lot of time wandering through its wilderness and many routes. Along the way, you can set up camp or pop into the camps of other Trainers. Camping is a major part of your experience in these games, so there's a detailed guide to it starting on page 280, but here are a few basics.

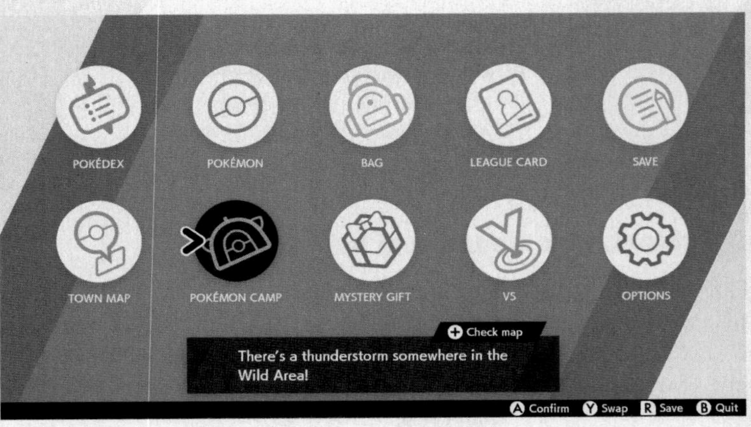

Setting up your own camp

You'll be able to set up your own camp as soon as you get the Camping Gear from your mom. This happens pretty early on in your adventure, just before you set out from Wedgehurst Station. If you want to find out exactly when you get your gear, check out the walkthrough starting on page 31. Once you have your Camping Gear, you'll see the Pokémon Camp icon appear in the X menu—just select that, and you'll be able to set up camp almost anywhere!

Playing with Pokémon (p. 282)

You can play with your Pokémon as they relax at your campsite by using a Poké Toy or throwing a bouncy ball. Playing can help make your team more friendly toward you and grant them some Exp. Points. There's even a chance they might find items to give you as they roam around the campsite!

Cooking curries (p. 285)

Nothing says "camping" like cooking over the old campfire! You can cook up a variety of curries, alone or with visitors, through a special little game. When your Pokémon dig in, they'll gain Exp. Points and become more friendly. They can also have their HP restored, status conditions healed, and even PP restored to their moves if the curry is tasty enough!

Visiting other campsites (p. 295)

During your adventure, you'll find plenty of other happy campers in Galar. Trainers and other Galarians have set up camping spots along the region's various routes, and if you're connected to the internet, you'll see players from the real world camped out in the Wild Area. Other Trainers will appear in the Wild Area over local wireless, too. Pop by other people's camps to share in the fun!

Watch out for the weather

No one wants to go camping in a downpour, but the weather in the Galar region affects a lot more than just that. The changing weather you face as you travel can affect the wild Pokémon you'll encounter in the Wild Area in the center of the region. Some types of Pokémon tend to appear more frequently in one kind of weather than in another, and some Pokémon only appear in the right weather. Keeping an eye on the weather will be key to completing your Pokédex! But some of the rarest weather patterns won't appear in the Wild Area early in your adventure. You won't run into blizzards or sandstorms until you've reached Hammerlocke for the first time. And fog won't come rolling in until you've become Champion!

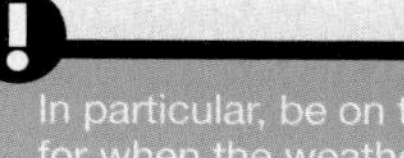

In particular, be on the lookout for when the weather turns to a thunderstorm, blizzard, sandstorm, or fog. These are rare weather patterns that can help you encounter rare Pokémon to match! When they occur in the Wild Area, you'll see a notification on your X menu, so you can call a Flying Taxi to take you to the nearest stop at once.

Battle also gets affected by certain weather conditions, whether they're caused by Galar's fickle climate or a tricky opponent. Learn all about how weather conditions and terrains affect the battlefield on page 189 if you hope to turn a spot of nasty weather back to your team's advantage!

Weather	Pokémon types more likely to appear in the Wild Area	Effects on battles
Clear	Normal, Grass, Flying	—
Cloudy	Fighting, Poison, Dark	—
Rain	Water, Bug	**Rain** Boosts the power of Water-type moves and reduces the power of Fire-type moves, among other effects
Thunderstorm	Water, Electric, Dragon	**Rain** Boosts the power of Water-type moves and reduces the power of Fire-type moves, among other effects **Electric Terrain** Boosts the power of Electric-type moves for Pokémon on the ground and prevents them from falling asleep
Snow	Ice	**Hail** Damages all Pokémon that aren't Ice types, among other effects
Blizzard	Ice, Steel	**Hail** Damages all Pokémon that aren't Ice types, among other effects
Harsh sunlight	Fire, Ground	**Harsh sunlight** Boosts the power of Fire-type moves and reduces the power of Water-type moves, among other effects
Sandstorm	Ground, Rock	**Sandstorm** Damages all Pokémon that aren't Ground, Rock, or Steel types, among other effects
Fog	Psychic, Ghost, Fairy	**Misty Terrain** Halves the damage taken from Dragon-type moves for Pokémon on the ground and protects them from status conditions and confusion

Not long into your adventure, you'll be given access to the Flying Taxi service, which will allow you to zip back to certain places you've visited before, such as towns. It's free and a good way to get around quickly—handy if you want to get back somewhere to try to catch a rare Pokémon before the weather turns!

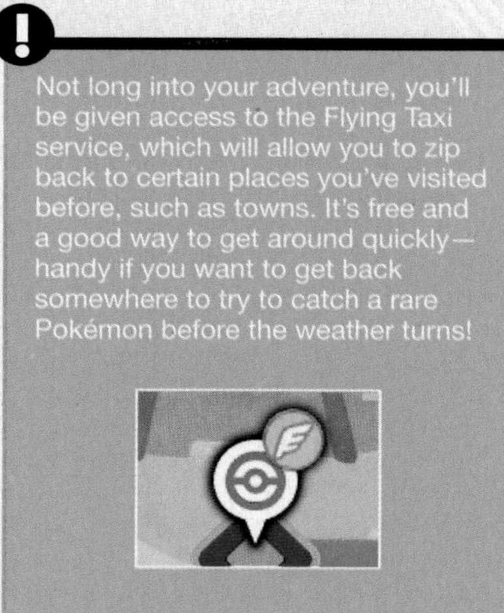

Look for these little wing icons on your Town Map to see which areas you can fly to!

Speeding Things Up

Sometimes, maybe all you really want is for battles to go a bit quicker so that you can finish the Gym Challenge or for dialogue to move faster so that you can get back to exploring the Wild Area. If you want your adventure to move along at top speed, check out the Options screen. From there, you can set text speed to fast and enable movie skipping to zip past certain scenes—though keep in mind you might miss out on chunks of the story if you do! Here you can also disable battle effects so moves are carried out in an instant. Luckily, "battle effects" don't include weather conditions, so you can still keep an eye on that pesky sandstorm while it rages on the battlefield!

Another battle setting you can change is whether you'll be asked to switch Pokémon when you knock out an opponent's Pokémon. If you set Battle Style to Set, you won't have to answer that question after each opponent falls—and you'll find that battles are tougher, too, since you don't get the extra leg up of switching in a Pokémon with a type advantage!

How to Play

You can take *Pokémon Sword* and *Pokémon Shield* on Nintendo Switch™ everywhere you go. You can play on the big screen at home or in handheld mode on the move! Just choose the play mode and controller setup that suits you and dive into your adventure!

Handheld mode

You can always play on the go if you play in handheld mode! In this mode, you'll attach the two Joy-Con™ controllers to your system and use the buttons on both Joy-Con controllers to play.

Tabletop mode / TV mode

If you want to play with a little less wrist effort, you can always pull out the system's stand, slide off both Joy-Con controllers (or just one—we'll get to that in a bit), and play in tabletop mode! You can also experience the wondrous world of *Pokémon Sword* and *Pokémon Shield* on the big screen by docking your Nintendo Switch to play in TV mode. When playing in either of these two modes, you have the choice of playing either with one or both of your Joy-Con controllers, and you can change your style by turning on or off the Casual Controls mode in the Options menu. You can also use a Pro Controller!

Below, you'll find the basic controls for each style of playing the game. These are the most common functions of the various buttons, but it's not a complete list. If you're ever in doubt about what a specific button does, you can also refer to the info bar on the bottom of the screen, which often gives you a clue!

! The instructions throughout this guide use the default buttons for handheld mode or playing with a right Joy-Con, but you can use whichever button is appropriate for your controller settings.

Handheld Mode / Using Two Joy-Con Controllers / Pro Controller

Move/Select (Gentle tilt: Crouch in tall grass / Full tilt: Run)	L stick
Whistle / Ring bell (while on bike)	Press L stick
Move camera when in the Wild Area	R stick
Zoom in/out when in the Wild Area	Press R stick
Get on/off bike	+ / −
Accelerate on bike / Save / Navigate menus and more (L can also reset the camera in the Wild Area, too!)	L / R
Talk/Confirm	ZL / ZR
Open the X menu	X
Talk/Confirm	A
Back/Quit/Cancel	B
Open the Y-Comm menu (p. 298)	Y

Casual Controls

Casual Controls let you play with just one hand. To play this way, you'll need to go to Options in the X menu and enable Casual Controls. Then choose a Joy-Con to use, slide it off your system, and you're ready to go. You can do almost anything with Casual Controls—but you won't be able to control the camera in the Wild Area!

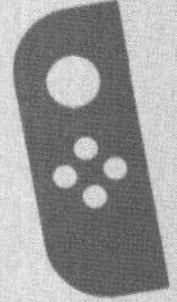

	Left Joy-Con	Right Joy-Con
Move/Select (Gentle tilt: Crouch in tall grass / Full tilt: Run)	L stick	R stick
Whistle / Ring bell (while on bike)	Press L stick	Press R stick
Get on/off bike	−	+
Accelerate on bike / Save / Navigate menus and more	L	R
Talk/Confirm	ZL	ZR
Open the X menu	▲	X
Talk/Confirm	▶	A
Back/Quit/Cancel	▼	B
Open the Y-Comm menu	◀	Y

Starting your game

When you start up *Pokémon Sword* or *Pokémon Shield* the first time, you'll have to decide a few things. First, you'll need to pick the language you want to play in—English, Spanish, French, German, Italian, Japanese, Korean, Simplified Chinese, or Traditional Chinese. Once you choose a language, you won't be able to change it for that save file. If you want to try out another language, create another user account (explained below), and you can choose different settings when you start the game with that account.

After you set your language, you'll need to decide what you'd like to look like in your game. You can choose from eight different appearances to start with. Later on, you'll be able to change your hair color and eye color, but you won't be able to change your physical features, such as your skin tone, from what you first select here. Choose whichever feels right to you, then enter the name you'll use throughout your adventure!

English
にほんご
Español
日本語
Français
한국어
Deutsch
简体中文
Italiano
繁體中文

01 Select the language you would like to play in

02 Choose your photo from the lineup

Can't wait to customize your look? You can take a peek ahead at page 313, which is where coverage starts on all the different hairstyles, cosmetics, and clothes you'll eventually have access to.

Multiple save files

There are plenty of ways to play together with others in *Pokémon Sword* and *Pokémon Shield*, especially using Y-Comm (p. 298) and when out camping (p. 280). But you can also share the game with your family by creating multiple save files. You can create a new game on each of the user accounts on your Nintendo Switch.

Creating new user accounts

1. Select **System Settings** on the HOME Menu.
2. Scroll down to find **Users**, then select **Add User** on the right side of the screen and click **Create New User**.
3. Select an icon to represent your new account, or create a Mii.
4. When prompted, enter your nickname and select **OK** twice to finish.
5. Choose to link an existing Nintendo Account or create a new one—or press **Later** to create a user without using a Nintendo Account.

Autosave

Pokémon Sword and *Pokémon Shield* have a handy autosave feature. With autosave enabled, your progress will automatically be saved after certain events, whenever you enter or leave a building or area, and when using communication features. If you've ever lost your progress because you forget to save often, keep this feature on! But if you'd rather choose when you save, you can turn autosave off in the Options menu.

How to delete a save file

So, what if you want to delete your game data for any reason? You'll do that through System Settings on your Nintendo Switch. But once you delete your data for any user account, it and everything from your game for that account will be gone forever—so think carefully before you do!

1. From the HOME Menu, select **System Settings**.
2. Scroll down to **Data Management**.
3. Select **Delete Save Data** on the right side of the screen.
4. Choose the game, then choose to either delete the save data linked to a specific user account or delete all save data for the software.

If you want to enjoy all of the online features of these games, you'll have to link your Nintendo Account to your user profile and have a Nintendo Switch Online membership. Learn more on page 206. Don't worry if you aren't a member, though—you can use your system's local wireless connection to enjoy most communication features with other players nearby!

Know your menus

Your X menu has most everything you need on your adventure, and you can open it by pressing Ⓧ anytime that you're not in a battle or a scene. Not all the options below will be available from the start, but they'll be unlocked as you continue your adventure. You can get started rearranging them to your liking by pressing Ⓨ when you're viewing the X menu.

Pokédex Open your Pokédex to get a quick view on recommended Pokémon that can be found for you to catch as well as to check the details of Pokémon you've seen or obtained (p. 207).

Pokémon Check your active party of Pokémon you've chosen to bring into battle with you. Use Ⓛ or Ⓡ to access the Box menu, once you have a Pokémon Box Link. You can also access your Boxes from the Rotomi terminal at any Pokémon Center (p. 16).

Bag Find all the items you've obtained here, including items to heal your Pokémon, TMs that can teach them moves, Key Items (like your Rotom Bike), and lots more.

League Card View your League Card, which records your progress and can be shared with others. You can also check your League Card Collection from here (p. 308).

Save Save your progress often, especially if you've turned off autosave, to be sure you don't have to retrace your steps or take on tough opponents again!

Town Map Pop open the Town Map to view the region, check the weather in different areas (p. 19), and eventually use Flying Taxis to go back to places you've been before.

Pokémon Camp Select this icon to set up your own camp whenever you're on dry land. Play with your Pokémon (p. 282) or whip up a fortifying curry (p. 285).

Mystery Gift Claim special gifts when they are distributed through codes, online distributions, or other means! Keep an eye on www.pokemon.com for announcements.

VS Battle other players online, taking part in Ranked Battles and more to keep pushing yourself and your team to new heights (p. 202).

Options Adjust the way you experience the game by changing settings that will affect your gameplay, including the autosave function and many settings to speed up your game.

Y-Comm

When out exploring, you'll see alerts on your screen from Y-Comm. These pop-ups, called stamps, let you know what other players are up to in the nearby area—or from all over, if you're connected to the internet. You can open the Y-Comm menu by pressing Ⓨ in most locations. Learn more starting on page 298, and keep an eye out for these stamps if you don't want to miss out on all the buzz!

The battle screen

The battle screen is another screen you'll spend a lot of time looking at. There are four main options to select from, as outlined below, and a couple of handy shortcuts you'll want to know. Plus, key information on your team and your opponent will be visible on this screen.

Battles against wild Pokémon

On the next page, you can see an example of what the battle screen will usually look like in battles against wild Pokémon. This is also pretty similar to the battle screen you'll see when taking on Trainers—but you won't be able to use Poké Balls to try to catch another Trainer's Pokémon! That's not very sporting! On these battle screens, you'll see the four options illustrated here on the right. These are the actions you can take in battle, and you can only choose one each turn.

Fight Choose a move to use during the turn from among the moves your current Pokémon knows, or select Dynamax if you're in a Power Spot.

Pokémon View the details of the other Pokémon on your team. You can choose to switch one in, but it will use up your turn.

Bag Open up your Bag to use medicine, Poké Balls, battle items, or Berries, which will count as your turn in battle.

Run You can try to run away from battles against wild Pokémon, though it won't always succeed—and you can't run from Trainers!

❶ Your current Pokémon's name, gender, and level are shown here.

❷ This bar and the numbers below it show your Pokémon's HP.

❸ This bar indicates how close your Pokémon is to leveling up.

❹ These icons show your team's condition. A gray Poké Ball shows that a Pokémon has fainted, while a yellow Poké Ball means a Pokémon has a status condition.

❺ Up here you can see mostly the same details for a wild Pokémon or an opponent's team.

❻ A Poké Ball image will appear here if you're battling a wild Pokémon you've already caught.

Use Ⓧ to quickly select a Poké Ball to use in a wild Pokémon encounter, switching between different types using your Control Stick or the ▶ and ◀ buttons.

Press Ⓨ to view all kinds of useful information about the battle, such as the effects of an Ability or whether any Pokémon's stats have been boosted or lowered (p. 187).

Max Raid Battles

The battle screen looks a bit different when you're taking on a Dynamax Pokémon in a Max Raid Battle! Since you'll be joined by three allies, you can get some hint of what they intend to do by checking the upper-left corner of the screen. There's no option to run from a Max Raid Battle, and if you want to use a Poké Ball, you'll have to earn the chance by reducing the Dynamax Pokémon's HP to zero!

❶ Your current Pokémon's information is here, just like in a regular battle.

❷ This bar shows the HP of the Dynamax Pokémon you're battling against. If it's protected by a mysterious barrier, you'll see its gauge beneath the HP bar.

❸ These boxes show the Pokémon your allies have sent out and what kind of action they're planning to take this turn. You can also tell how much HP they have left by looking at the bars beneath each.

❹ When the gauge is full and it starts to glow, selecting the Dynamax button before you choose a move will let you Dynamax your Pokémon!

! The Dynamax button will appear in certain Trainer battles as well, when you are battling in a Power Spot, such as a stadium! And in these battles, you won't have to wait for your turn to Dynamax as you do in Max Raid Battles!

Signs from your allies

 This ally hasn't yet chosen an action for the turn.

 This ally is going to use a status move this turn.

 This ally is going to use a damage-dealing move this turn.

 This ally is going to use an item this turn.

Version Differences

What's in a name? Perhaps more than you might think! There are a few differences to be discovered between *Pokémon Sword* and *Pokémon Shield*. The most traditional difference is, of course, which Pokémon you can encounter in the wild and catch.

Pokémon only found in *Pokémon Sword*

There are over 30 Pokémon that are exclusive to *Pokémon Sword*, meaning that they only appear in the wild in that game. If you want them in *Pokémon Shield*, you'll have to trade with other players!

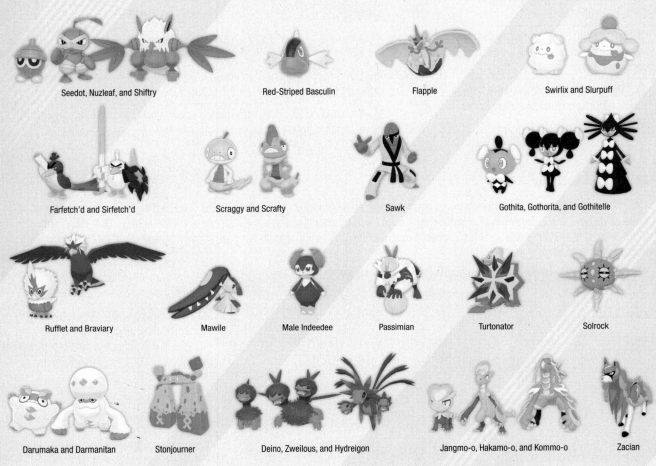

Seedot, Nuzleaf, and Shiftry

Red-Striped Basculin

Flapple

Swirlix and Slurpuff

Farfetch'd and Sirfetch'd

Scraggy and Scrafty

Sawk

Gothita, Gothorita, and Gothitelle

Rufflet and Braviary

Mawile

Male Indeedee

Passimian

Turtonator

Solrock

Darumaka and Darmanitan

Stonjourner

Deino, Zweilous, and Hydreigon

Jangmo-o, Hakamo-o, and Kommo-o

Zacian

Different challenges

Some of the trials you'll face along the way to the Champion Cup differ depending on the game you're playing. Only in *Pokémon Sword* will you have to take on Fighting- and Rock-type Gym Leaders in order to clear the Gym Challenge.

Bea, Leader of the Fighting Gym

Gordie, Leader of the Rock Gym

There's a nice man in Circhester who's willing to trade his Throh in *Pokémon Sword* or his Sawk in *Pokémon Shield* for your Vanillish. That means you can obtain at least one of each of these Pokémon in both versions!

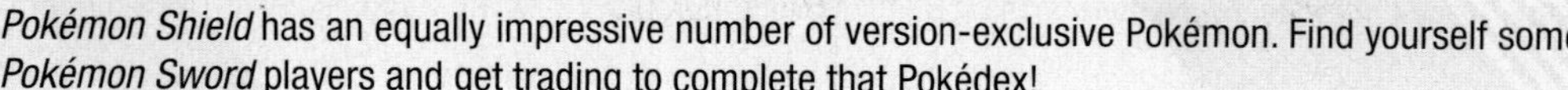

Pokémon only found in *Pokémon Shield*

Pokémon Shield has an equally impressive number of version-exclusive Pokémon. Find yourself some *Pokémon Sword* players and get trading to complete that Pokédex!

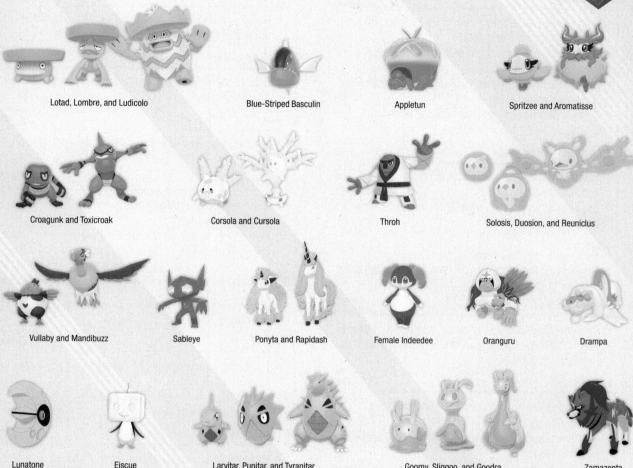

Lotad, Lombre, and Ludicolo

Blue-Striped Basculin

Appletun

Spritzee and Aromatisse

Croagunk and Toxicroak

Corsola and Cursola

Throh

Solosis, Duosion, and Reuniclus

Vullaby and Mandibuzz

Sableye

Ponyta and Rapidash

Female Indeedee

Oranguru

Drampa

Lunatone

Eiscue

Larvitar, Pupitar, and Tyranitar

Goomy, Sliggoo, and Goodra

Zamazenta

Different challenges

If you're playing *Pokémon Shield*, a couple of different Pokémon Gyms have qualified for this year's Gym Challenge than in *Pokémon Sword*. Ghost- and Ice-type Gym Leaders will be the ones standing in the way of your chance to participate in the Champion Cup in this version.

Allister
You are challenged by Gym Leader Allister!

Allister, Leader of the Ghost Gym

Melony
You are challenged by Gym Leader Melony!

Melony, Leader of the Ice Gym

Your Recommended Route

Whether you want to avoid any spoilers you might stumble across in the detailed walkthrough or you just want a quick reminder of where you're at in your game, this recommended route will keep you on track to make progress through the main adventure of *Pokémon Sword* and *Pokémon Shield*. It covers all the main events you must complete on the path to the Champion Cup, but it skips over tons of subevents and extra guidance, so be sure to explore every nook and cranny of the Galar region on your own if you're using these pages as your main guide!

POSTWICK p. 34

- Start your adventure by meeting up with Hop to go along with him to Wedgehurst
- Travel north on Route 1 out of Postwick to reach Wedgehurst and meet Leon
- Back in Postwick, choose your first partner Pokémon and battle against Hop
- On your way back home, get dragged into some trouble in the Slumbering Weald

SLUMBERING WEALD p. 37

- Navigate the misty forest to try to rescue a lost Pokémon
- Check in at home, then head to Route 1 to start your adventure at last!

ROUTE 1 p. 39

- Travel north up Route 1 again, this time through the patches of tall grass

WEDGEHURST p. 40

- Go to the Pokémon Research Lab to get your Pokédex
- Visit a Pokémon Center and check out the town, then move on to Route 2

ROUTE 2 p. 42

- Meet up with Hop and Leon, then battle across Route 2 on your own
- Visit Professor Magnolia's home, and battle against Hop once more
- Get an endorsement and a Dynamax Band, then set off to return to Wedgehurst Station
- Join up with Hop again, then board the train from Wedgehurst Station

SOUTH WILD AREA p. 46

- Explore the southern half of the Wild Area (or more!) on your way to Motostoke

MOTOSTOKE p. 50

- Meet Sonia then Leon as you make your way to Motostoke Stadium
- Register for the Gym Challenge, and meet your fellow challengers and Team Yell!
- Join the opening ceremony and then meet Chairman Rose
- Head toward Route 3 and run into Hop for another battle

ROUTE 3 p. 56

- Make your way west across the route to reach the tunnels of Galar Mine

GALAR MINE p. 58

- Explore the twisted shafts of the mine, and battle Bede on your way out

ROUTE 4 p. 60

- Meet Milo on your way down the hill to reach the town of Turffield

TURFFIELD p. 62

- Run into Hop soon after arriving and get a message from him
- Meet Sonia on the hill to check out the old geoglyph together

Challenge the Grass Gym .... p. 64

- After claiming your first Gym Badge, move on to Route 5

ROUTE 5 p. 66

- Head east, checking out the Pokémon Nursery as you go
- Defeat Team Yell to get a bike, and ride ahead for another battle with Hop

HULBURY p. 69

- Run into Chairman Rose and Oleana, and get an invite for a fancy dinner
- Go to Hulbury Stadium, then find the Gym Leader at the lighthouse

Challenge the Water Gym .... p. 71

- Head to the Captain's Table for your dinner plans with Chairman Rose, then head to Galar Mine No. 2

GALAR MINE NO. 2 p. 73

- Make your way through Galar Mine No. 2, battling Bede and Team Yell on the way
- Find the Fire Gym Leader, then exit the mine toward Motostoke

MOTOSTOKE OUTSKIRTS p. 75

- Pass through this short path on your way back to the city

MOTOSTOKE (REVISITED) p. 76

- Battle Marnie to get fired up, then it's on to the stadium again

Challenge the Fire Gym .... p. 77

- When you're done in Motostoke, head back into the Wild Area

NORTH WILD AREA p. 78

- Travel all the way to the north end of the Wild Area to reach Hammerlocke

HAMMERLOCKE p. 80

- Find Chairman Rose, and learn a bit about his company's energy plant
- Run into Leon, then visit the vault to learn more of Galar's history
- Turn to Route 6 on the west when you're done with Hammerlocke!

ROUTE 6 p. 85

- Run into Team Yell again for yet another series of battles
- Meet Opal along the route, then continue on to Stow-on-Side

STOW-ON-SIDE p. 88

- Check out the town, battle Hop, and then head to the stadium for your next mission

Challenge the Fighting Gym† .... p. 91

Challenge the Ghost Gym .... p. 91

- Head up the stairs to check out the ancient mural on the cliff face
- Have a Pokémon battle against Bede in front of the mural
- When the dust settles after the excitement, head for Glimwood Tangle

GLIMWOOD TANGLE p. 95

- Navigate the dark with the guiding light of the mushrooms

BALLONLEA p. 97

- Meet Marnie in the stadium lobby, then head inside if you're ready

Challenge the Fairy Gym .... p. 98

- After the battle, take Opal's offer to return to Hammerlocke

HAMMERLOCKE (REVISITED) p. 100

- Run into Bede again, then head east to meet up with Sonia
- After catching up with Sonia, Leon, and Hop, it's off to Route 7 for you!

ROUTE 7 p. 101

- Hop will spring another battle on you before you get far

ROUTE 8 p. 103

- Climb through the ruins that choke Route 8 on your way north
- Pass through Steamdrift Way on your way to reach Circhester

CIRCHESTER p. 106

- Head to the stadium once ready, and get a League Card from Hop

Challenge the Rock Gym† .... p. 108

Challenge the Ice Gym .... p. 108

- Defeat the Gym Leader, and head outside to meet Sonia
- Share a meal and more with Sonia at Bob's Your Uncle
- Visit the Hero's Bath, and have a battle against Hop
- Head southeast out of town to reach Route 9

ROUTE 9 p. 112

- Fight off Team Yell to unlock Water Mode for your Rotom Bike
- Explore the many surprising nooks of Circhester Bay
- Cross Outer Spikemuth, and meet Marnie for a battle and some help

SPIKEMUTH p. 116

- After you and Marnie part ways, battle your way across the town

Challenge the Dark Gym .... p. 116

- Head out to Route 9, then carry on to the west

RETURNING TO HAMMERLOCKE p. 118

- Pass through the Route 9 Tunnel to get back to Route 7
- Run into Hop on Route 7, and then continue west to Hammerlocke
- Meet up with Hop and the others, then head to the stadium

Challenge the Dragon Gym .... p. 120

- Run into Sonia and her grandmother, Professor Magnolia, then head to the train station
- With one last farewell from Raihan, take the train north toward Wyndon

ROUTE 10 p. 122

- Overcome snowy Route 10 to head into Wyndon!

WYNDON

p. 124

- Explore the metropolis, then head to Wyndon Stadium!
- Do your best to win your way through the Semifinals
- Find your way to Rose Tower, then battle your way to the top
- Head to the stadium once more for the Finals

SLUMBERING WEALD (REVISITED)

p. 140

- Search the forest for some way to help out Leon

HAMMERLOCKE (REVISITED)

p. 142

- Return to Hammerlocke, and try to lend a hand at the stadium
- Descend into the Energy Plant, and be ready for another battle
- Take the lift up to the roof to find Leon and a whole lot of trouble!

WYNDON (REVISITED)

p. 144

- Back in Wyndon, bring the Champion Cup to a close at last!

CHAMPION'S GUIDE

p. 145

- Find out about the further adventures (and more!) that await you if you manage to become Champion of the Galar region!

Subevents and Things to Do Daily

On your journey across Galar to compete in the Gym Challenge, you'll discover many other tasks for you to do that may not advance your progress in the Gym Challenge but will get you rewards. You can earn Exp. Points from some extra battles or get unique special items you won't be able to get anywhere else in Galar! Take a look below at the list of subevents to see where they are and what you can get from them. Some events you'll be able to complete as soon as you arrive in a new location, while others can only be completed after you've fulfilled certain conditions, like defeating the Champion. Keep an eye out for events that can be repeated over and over, which are listed up at the end of this section!

Location	Page	Subevent
Wild Area	47	If you have save data on your Nintendo Switch from *Pokémon: Let's Go, Pikachu!*, then get a special Pikachu capable of Gigantamaxing from a girl on the west side of the Wild Area Station.
Wild Area	47	If you have save data on your Nintendo Switch from *Pokémon: Let's Go, Eevee!*, then get a special Eevee capable of Gigantamaxing from a boy on the west side of the Wild Area Station.
Wild Area	47	Talk to a backpacker inside the Wild Area Station for five Poké Dolls.
Motostoke	51	Talk to a girl in the lower-level Pokémon Center. You can trade a Bunnelby for her Skwovet.
Motostoke	52	Talk to a man outside the first record shop on the west side of the main street for TR13 Focus Energy. So retro!
Motostoke	52	Talk to an old man outside the record shop on the east side of the main street to receive the Hi-tech Earbuds.
Motostoke	52	Talk to the Ball Guy outside Motostoke Stadium for a Poké Ball.
Motostoke	55	Talk to a man in the leftmost room upstairs in the Budew Drop Inn to receive a Star Piece.
Motostoke	55	Help a child by the Pokémon Center on the higher level of Motostoke find his Minccino to get a Throat Spray.
Route 3	57	Talk to a woman by the tent for a Berry.
Turffield	63	Talk to a girl standing by the area that overlooks the geoglyph. Follow the clues to find the treasure—an Expert Belt!
Turffield	64	Talk to the Ball Guy inside Turffield Stadium for a Friend Ball.
Turffield	64	Talk to a boy in Turffield Stadium. You can trade a Galarian Meowth for his Meowth, which is a Normal-type Meowth sometimes seen in other regions.
Route 5	67	Stop by the nursery on Route 5, and receive a recently-hatched Toxel—and five pieces of Exp. Candy XS to help raise it!
Hulbury	70	Talk to a woman sitting alone on a bench in the market. You can trade a Minccino for her Cottonee.
Hulbury	71	Talk to the Ball Guy inside Hulbury Stadium for a Lure Ball.
Hammerlocke	81	Talk to the Ball Guy inside Hammerlocke Stadium for a Level Ball.
Hammerlocke	82	Talk to a girl in the house across the street from the Pokémon Center by the stadium for a Soothe Bell.
Hammerlocke	82	Talk to a boy in the house across the street from the Pokémon Center, and show him a Pokémon with high friendship. He'll give it a Best Friends Ribbon.

Location	Page	Subevent
✓ Hammerlocke	82	Talk to a woman in the house across the street from the Pokémon Center, and show her a Pokémon with maxed-out base points. She'll give it an Effort Ribbon.
✓ Hammerlocke	82	Talk to a man in the third house to the right of the Pokémon Center once per day for five days to learn about weather effects, and get a different item each day—a Heat Rock, a Damp Rock, an Icy Rock, a Smooth Rock, and a Utility Umbrella.
✓ Hammerlocke	82	Deliver an old letter from a strange girl on the far-upper-east side of Hammerlocke to the old man in the first house on the left in Ballonlea for a Choice Scarf. Return to where the little girl was to find a piece of Reaper Cloth.
✓ Hammerlocke	83	Battle and defeat Mr. Focus in the house to the left of the Pokémon Center by the stadium for a Focus Sash.
✓ Hammerlocke	83	Talk to a woman across the street from the vault entrance. You can trade a Toxel for her Togepi.
✓ Hammerlocke	83	Talk to a boy on the far-west side of Hammerlocke, and let him borrow an Applin you've caught so he can express his feelings to a girl. In exchange, you'll get a Tart Apple in *Pokémon Sword* or a Sweet Apple in *Pokémon Shield*.
✓ Stow-on-Side	89	Head into the Pokémon Center and speak to the man by the left side table to receive two Fossilized Birds in *Pokémon Sword* or two Fossilized Drakes in *Pokémon Shield*.
✓ Stow-on-Side	90	Talk to a man sitting on a rooftop. You can trade a Maractus for his Hatenna (*Pokémon Sword*) or Impidimp (*Pokémon Shield*).
✓ Stow-on-Side	90	Talk to a cabbie in the house to the west of the stairs leading up to the stadium for TM06 Fly.
✓ Stow-on-Side	90	Talk to the Ball Guy inside Stow-on-Side Stadium for a Heavy Ball.
✓ Ballonlea	97	Help a man on the west side of Ballonlea by the pile of wood feel like a Pokémon by showing him some fiery clothes for TM78 Acrobatics.
✓ Ballonlea	97	Speak to an old lady in the last house before the tree arch in front of the stadium to receive TM77 Hex in *Pokémon Sword* or TM42 Revenge in *Pokémon Shield*.
✓ Ballonlea	97	Battle and defeat a woman in the same house for an Eviolite.
✓ Ballonlea	98	Talk to the Ball Guy inside Ballonlea Stadium for a Love Ball.
✓ Ballonlea	98	Talk to a Poké kid near the counter in the stadium. You can trade a Galarian Yamask for her Yamask, which seems to have come from another region.
✓ Circhester	106	Stop by the first house behind the Pokémon Center and speak to the man inside, and he'll give you TM27 Icy Wind in *Pokémon Sword* or TM48 Rock Tomb in *Pokémon Shield*.
✓ Circhester	106	Talk to a man behind a food stand. You can trade a Vanillish for his Throh (*Pokémon Sword*) or Sawk (*Pokémon Shield*).
✓ Circhester	107	Help a bumbling detective solve the case of the stolen Berries in the first upstairs room to the left of the elevator in the east Hotel Ionia building for a Wide Lens.
✓ Circhester	107	Talk to a man in the first upstairs room on the right of the elevator in the east Hotel Ionia building for TM16 Screech.
✓ Circhester	107	Talk to a man in the last upstairs room to the right of the elevator in the east Hotel Ionia building for TM47 Fake Tears.
✓ Circhester	107	Talk to the GAME FREAK Director in the last upstairs room to the left of the elevator in the west Hotel Ionia building for a Catching Charm.
✓ Circhester	107	Talk to the Ball Guy inside Circhester Stadium for a Moon Ball.
✓ Route 9	115	Talk to the lady at a little private getaway for two to receive TM45 Dive.
✓ Spikemuth	117	Talk to a male Team Yell Grunt by the stall near the stage. You can trade an Obstagoon for his Mr. Mime, which looks different than it normally does in Galar.
✓ Wyndon	125	Talk to an artist in the first turquoise building down across the bridge from the stadium. You can trade a Frosmoth for his Duraludon.
✓ Wyndon	126	Battle and defeat a man in the first orange building down across the bridge from the stadium for a Rotom Catalog.
✓ Wyndon	127	Talk to the Ball Guy inside Wyndon Stadium for a Dream Ball.
		After Becoming Champion
✓ Postwick	146	Pick up the Poké Ball in Leon's room for a very special Charmander. Try Dynamaxing it once it's evolved from Charmeleon to Charizard for a champion time!
✓ Motostoke	146	Talk to the Ball Guy after becoming the Champion, and they'll give you their League Card!
✓ Galar Mine	146	Find Oleana and talk to her for Chairman Rose's rare League Card.

GETTING STARTED

Location	Page	Subevent
Hulbury	146	Talk to a cook in the Captain's Table to help out with three deliveries and get an Exp. Candy L, five Nuggets, two Big Nuggets, and a Lucky Egg.
Stow-on-Side	147	Talk to the man running the stall on the right to get a Beast Ball.
Circhester	147	Battle and defeat Morimoto in the first room to the left of the elevator in the west Hotel Ionia building for an Oval Charm.
Circhester	147	Talk to the GAME FREAK Director after you've completed your Pokédex to upgrade your League Card and receive a Shiny Charm.
Wyndon	148	Talk to a League staff member in the Battle Tower to get a Type: Null and all the memories for Silvally.
Wyndon	148	Advance from Beginner Tier to Poké Ball Tier in the Battle Tower (p. 200) by defeating Leon to receive his rare League Card.
Spikemuth	148	After your final battle with Hop in the Slumbering Weald, defeat Marnie to get her rare League Card. Come back and battle her once per day.

In addition to the things you can find on this list, there are a few people hidden across Galar who can teach certain Pokémon unique and powerful moves! You may want to visit them over and over, too, so learn more on page 354.

Things to Do Daily

Even after you've completed the subevents listed above, there are plenty of things to do every day to reap rewards and get more from your game. Check out these lists for a reminder of all the things you might want to give a try each and every day that you're playing *Pokémon Sword* or *Pokémon Shield*!

Outside the Wild Area

- Collect hidden items that may have appeared on the bridges spanning the Wild Area, and shake down Berry trees (p. 290) to add more to your collection
- Check out new Poké Jobs at the Rotomi in any Pokémon Center once you've reached Motostoke, and welcome back any Pokémon that have finished jobs (p. 241)
- Try your luck at the Loto-ID once you've reached Turffield for the first time—today could be your lucky day! (p. 63)
- Have battles at the Battle Cafés in Motostoke, Hammerlocke, and Wyndon for sweet treats and other rewards (p. 194)
- Check out the daily bargains in Stow-on-Side's Street Market and maybe sell a treasure for profit there, too (p. 89)
- Once Champion, battle in Champion tournaments (p. 196) and at the Battle Tower (p. 200) as many times as you like for rewards

In the Wild Area

- Collect new hidden items that may have appeared each day (p. 252), and shake down Berry trees to add more to your collection
- Visit Pokémon Dens in the Wild Area to collect Watts and take part in Max Raid Battles—and maybe even find Gigantamax Pokémon (p. 271)
- Take part in the Rotom Rally to gather lots of Watts to get TRs and Wishing Pieces, which can be used to activate more Pokémon Dens (p. 274)
- Check out the daily offerings from Rotom Rallyists, Ingredients Sellers, and other Galar residents (p. 277)—or maybe have a battle against Chloe (p. 279)
- Check for rare weather patterns in the Wild Area, and catch Pokémon that only appear in certain weather conditions to fill your Pokédex (p. 207)
- Check for Wild Area news from the Mystery Gift option on your X menu—new Pokémon might appear in the Wild Area as a result!

WALKTHROUGH

How to Read the Walkthrough Pages

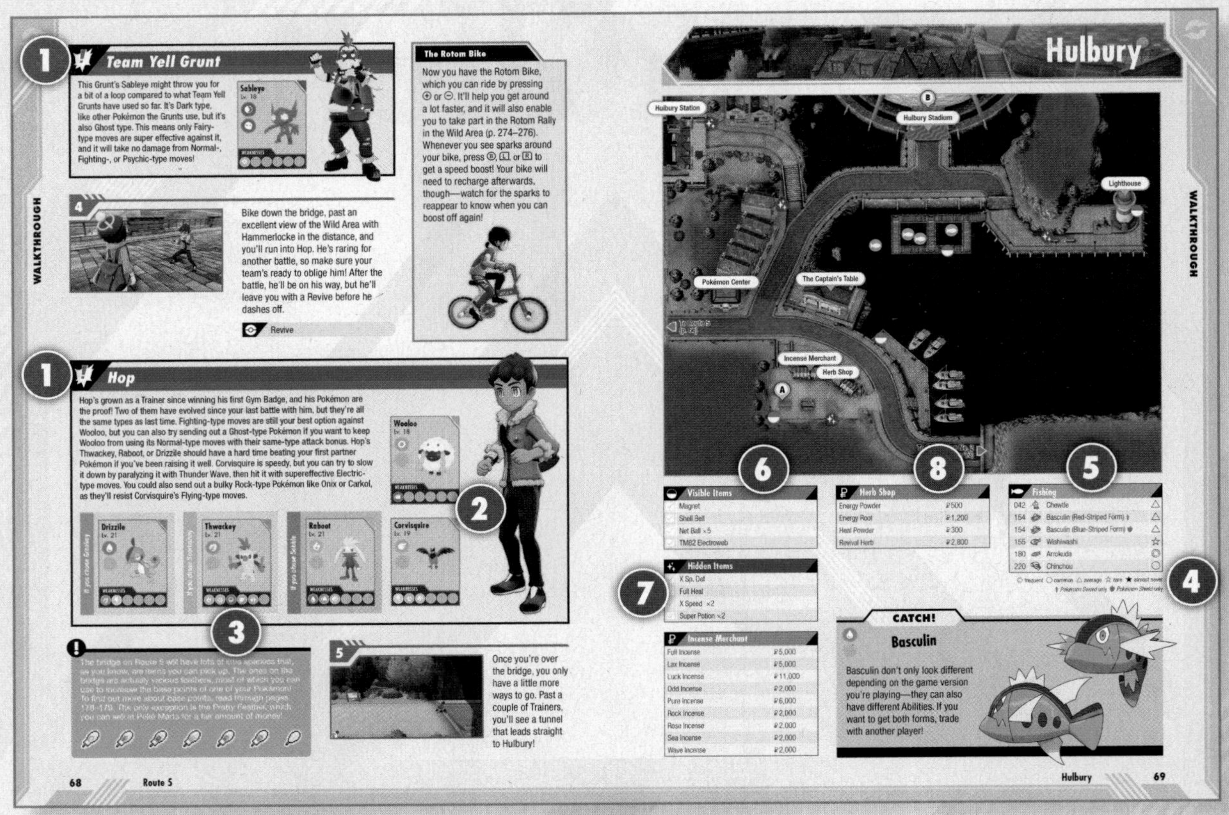

The following pages will lead you through your adventure as you take on the Gym Challenge and what lies beyond it! Before you dive in headfirst, you may want to review this quick guide to understanding the information you'll typically find on each walkthrough page.

- Items that you'll be able to see on the ground, which look like either red or yellow Poké Balls
- Locations where you'll see sparkles that indicate a hidden item is nearby
- Spots where you can use your Fishing Rod to fish up Pokémon
- Berry trees that you can shake for Berries and wild Pokémon encounters (p. 290)

A Trainer who will challenge you to battle if they spot you—the number shows how many Pokémon they have

A duo of Trainers ready to spring a Double Battle (p. 163) on you—the number shows their combined number of Pokémon

Locations where you can complete subevents (described on the surrounding pages)

Campsites set up by other Galarians that you can join for fun activities (p. 295)

Key facilities such as shops, Pokémon Centers, or other buildings you'll probably want to check out

1 Whenever there are key battles you need to get through to continue your journey, these battle boxes will give you the lowdown on your opponents' Pokémon and some advice on effective battle strategies.

2 These boxes show your opponents' Pokémon, including their names, levels, types, and what move types they'll be weak to. But be warned—your opponent could send out their Pokémon in a different order than what you see here, so be ready for anything!

3 Certain Trainers may have different teams depending on which Pokémon you choose to start your adventure with. In those cases, these boxes will show you which Pokémon you'll face based on your first partner Pokémon.

4 This key here explains what the symbols you might see in an encounter table mean. Don't worry about needing to memorize them all—the key will be repeated wherever they appear!

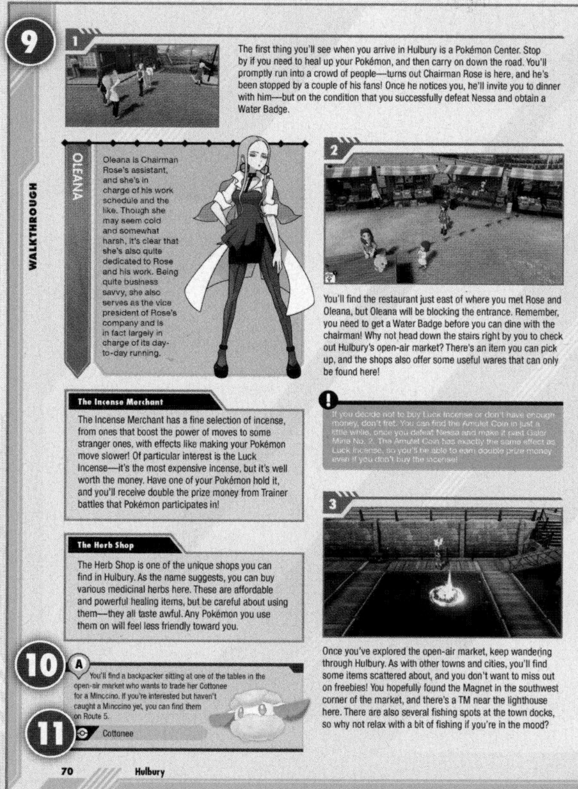
9

1

The first thing you'll see when you arrive in Hulbury is a Pokémon Center. Stop by if you need to heal up your Pokémon, and then carry on down the road. You'll promptly run into a crowd of people—turns out Chairman Rose is here, and he's been stopped by a couple of his fans! Once he notices you, he'll invite you to dinner with him—but on the condition that you successfully defeat Nessa and obtain a Water Badge.

OLEANA

Oleana is Chairman Rose's assistant, and she's in charge of his work schedule and the like. Though she may seem cold and somewhat harsh, it's clear that she's also quite dedicated to Rose and his work. Being quite business savvy, she also serves as the vice president of Rose's company and is in fact largely in charge of its day-to-day running.

2

You'll find the restaurant just east of where you met Rose and Oleana, but Oleana will be blocking the entrance. Remember, you need to get a Water Badge before you can dine with the chairman! Why not head down the stairs right by you to check out Hulbury's open-air market? There's an item you can pick up, and the shops also offer some useful wares that can only be found here!

The Incense Merchant

The Incense Merchant has a fine selection of incense, from ones that boost the power of moves to some stranger ones, with effects like making your Pokémon move slower! Of particular interest is the Luck Incense—it's the most expensive incense, but it's well worth the money. Have one of your Pokémon hold it, and you'll receive double the prize money from Trainer battles that Pokémon participates in!

If you decide not to buy Luck Incense or don't have enough money, don't fret. You can find the Amulet Coin in just a little while, once you defeat Nessa and make it past Galar Mine No. 2. The Amulet Coin has exactly the same effect as Luck Incense, so you'll be able to earn double prize money even if you don't buy the incense!

The Herb Shop

The Herb Shop is one of the unique shops you can find in Hulbury. As the name suggests, you can buy various medicinal herbs here. These are affordable and powerful healing items, but be careful about using them—they all taste awful. Any Pokémon you use them on will feel less friendly toward you.

3

Once you've explored the open-air market, keep wandering through Hulbury. As with other towns and cities, you'll find some items scattered about, and you don't want to miss out on freebies! You hopefully found the Magnet in the southwest corner of the market, and there's a TM near the lighthouse here. There are also several fishing spots at the town docks, so why not relax with a bit of fishing if you're in the mood?

10 A

You'll find a backpacker sitting at one of the tables in the open-air market who wants to trade her Cottonee for a Minccino. If you're interested but haven't caught a Minccino yet, you can find them on Route 5.

11 Cottonee

70 Hulbury

5

These tables list the wild Pokémon you can encounter as you explore each area. Pokémon can appear in a number of different ways, as you'll see below, but bumping into them will always trigger a battle with a chance to catch that Pokémon!

Random Encounters Pokémon you can't see lurking in the tall grass. A ! will appear where you may run into them, so avoid it if you don't want a battle.

Tall Grass Pokémon you can see moving about in the tall grass. They might approach you or try to run away.

Ground Pokémon you can see on the ground in places like caves.

Flying Pokémon you can see flying or floating overhead.

Water Surface Pokémon you can see swimming on the surface of certain bodies of water.

Wanderers Pokémon you can see wandering about in unusual ways and that don't simply stick to the tall grass.

Berry Trees Pokémon that might attack you when you shake a Berry tree one too many times.

Fishing Pokémon you can fish up from the water using the Fishing Rod in your Bag.

6

These tables list all the visible items you can find in the area, with check boxes beside each item so that you can keep track of them until you've found them all. When you pick up an item ball, you may sometimes find it has more than one item in it! Because of that, you'll see some items listed in multiples, like "Poké Ball ×3". If some items can't be reached without special means, they'll be separated out with a header.

7

Likewise, these tables list any of the items hiding around the area and waiting to be found. As explained on page 16, these items can be found if you keep your eyes peeled for flashing sparkles. They'll twinkle for a moment when you move nearby and twinkle again when you draw closer. Tick each off as you find them!

8

Shop tables always have teal headers. You'll find them whenever an area has unique shops that stock items you can often only find there. There are also Poké Marts all over the Galar region, but since they all offer the same basic Trainer goods, you'll normally only find tables for the Poké Marts in cities where rarer goods are sold by a second clerk. For a complete lineup of all Poké Mart wares, you can always check page 381.

The clothes available in boutiques aren't listed in each town either, but they are covered in great detail starting on page 324, if fashion strikes your fancy! This is a tip box, by the way—as is the green box at the bottom of this page. Look for these boxes throughout the guide!

9

These steps will lead you through tasks you'll need to complete to make progress on your adventure.

10

Subevents are featured in boxes like these. These events don't have to be completed, but they'll provide you with rewards and can even teach you more about life in the Galar region or being a Pokémon Trainer. Look for the matching icon on the map for a clue where to trigger each subevent! Flip back to page 28 for the complete list of subevents.

11

These reward boxes show any items or Pokémon you'll receive at certain stages of your adventure or after completing a subevent.

These icons indicate Pokémon encounters that happen only once. Though the Pokémon won't appear again in this spot, don't worry—it may appear elsewhere in the region!

  Yamper

Postwick

1

There's no time to waste sitting around! Grab your Bag from your bedroom at the other end of the house, then head outside to follow Hop to his house on the east side of Postwick. Exciting things are afoot, and you won't want to miss out on the action.

 Potion ×3, Adventure Guide, Fishing Rod

2

After talking to Hop's mom, it seems you and Hop are off for the town of Wedgehurst. Head to Route 1, which leads north out of Postwick. Without a Pokémon to call your own, you'll want to avoid the tall grass on the east side of the route. Wild Pokémon could be there, and you'd have no way to fight them off, so Hop will keep you on the straight path this time.

HOP

Your friend and neighbor, Hop, lives right down the road in the other large home you'll find in Postwick. He's an outgoing fellow and is always up for the chance to compete. He's got high hopes to become a top-tier Pokémon Trainer and catch up to his elder brother, who has made quite the name for himself in the Galar region!

3

You'll hardly arrive in Wedgehurst before you run smack into Hop's elder brother, Leon, surrounded by his adoring fans. Even though you don't get to explore the town now, fret not—you'll get the chance soon enough.

LEON

Leon is Hop's older brother, and he's the undefeated Champion of the Galar region! He's an amazingly strong Trainer who has defended his position as Champion for a number of years against every challenger that's come at him. He's a real star in the region as a result, larger-than-life and known far and wide. That's quite the example that Hop has got to live up to.

4

Back at Hop and Leon's family home, get to know the Champion and especially the three Pokémon he's brought with him. You'll be given the chance to choose one to keep as your very first partner! If you need help choosing the best match for you, read more about these three in the section to the right.

Grookey, Scorbunny, or Sobble

! Note that you can save your game at this point. The Save option is on the X menu, which you can open by pressing Ⓧ. If you'd really like your first partner to have a particular gender or Nature (p. 172), save before you make your selection to be able to try your luck again!

Grookey

ABILITY: Overgrow

Grookey is a Grass-type Pokémon that grows to have high HP and Attack. Focus on training it to use physical moves for a chunky damage-dealing Pokémon that can take hits. Grookey may be slower than other Pokémon, but its high HP will keep it on the field.

Scorbunny

ABILITY: Blaze

The Fire-type Pokémon Scorbunny's Attack and Speed grow more quickly than its other stats. Train Scorbunny to develop it into a fast Pokémon that can deal high damage in quick bursts to compensate for Scorbunny's lower Defense and Sp. Def.

Sobble

ABILITY: Torrent

Sobble, a Water-type Pokémon, excels in Sp. Atk and Speed. During your adventure, training it to build on its strength in these two stats will help it deal big damage to opposing Pokémon before they know what hit them. You'll want quick KO's since Sobble is a bit lacking in HP.

5

After you choose your new partner and enjoy a nice family barbecue, the next day will dawn and bring with it your first-ever Trainer battle! Pokémon battling is the most popular sport in the Galar region, and there will be plenty of it in your future. Dive in and get to know your way around the battle screen, or turn back to page 22 if you're feeling a bit lost.

> Many Pokémon have access to status moves early in the game. Status moves might seem like a letdown, since they don't deal direct damage in battle, but they can actually have a big impact on how much damage Pokémon dish out or take. Turn to page 187 to learn more about how stat-altering moves like Growl can affect Pokémon in battle.

Hop

Hop is ready to take you on in your first battle, and he even seems like he has the upper hand with two Pokémon to your one. But things aren't always as simple as they seem in Pokémon battles! Your first partner has a type advantage against the new Pokémon Hop just chose. After you knock out his Wooloo, your partner will even learn a new move that'll be super effective against Hop's second Pokémon. Give it a try!

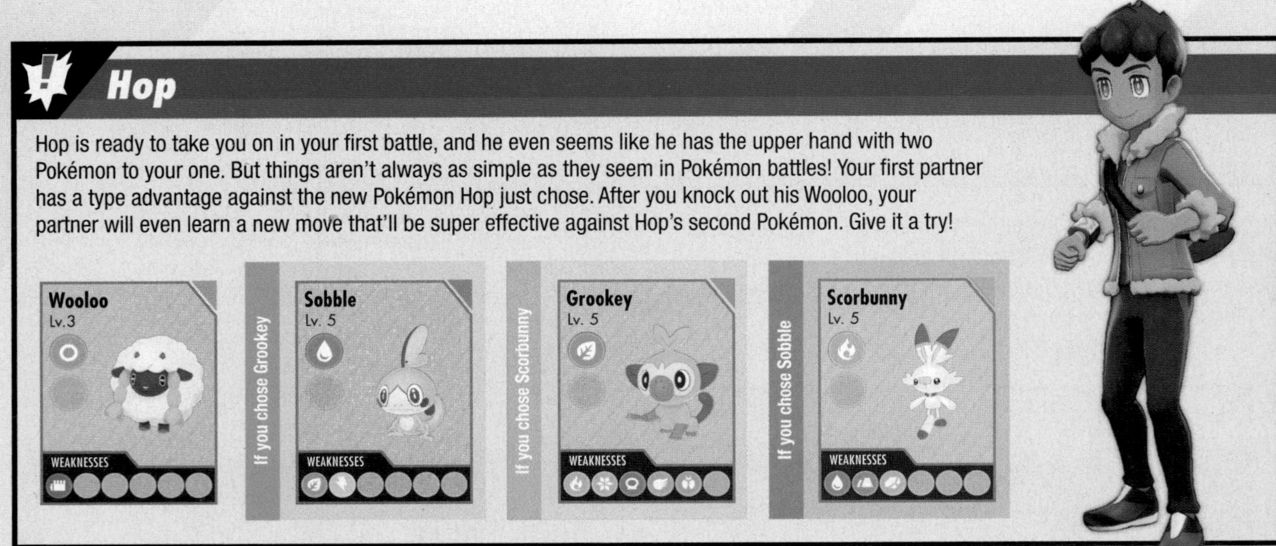

6

After your battle, Hop tries to convince his brother that he's ready to take part in the Gym Challenge, but he is told by Leon to get a Pokédex first. It seems another trip to Wedgehurst is in your future, so turn your feet toward home to go tell your mom you'll be off again.

7

Before you can make it to your front door, your plans are interrupted! It seems one of the local Pokémon might be in trouble. If you and Hop want to do the right thing and rescue it, you'll have to venture into the off-limits Slumbering Weald to try to bring it back home safe!

Slumbering Weald

The Slumbering Weald conceals many different wild Pokémon as well as numerous visible and hidden items within its foggy interior, but you won't be able to catch or access these on your first visit. In fact, you won't return to this mysterious forest until quite a bit later in your journey! Flip way ahead to page 140 if you want to check out the encounter tables and items for this area.

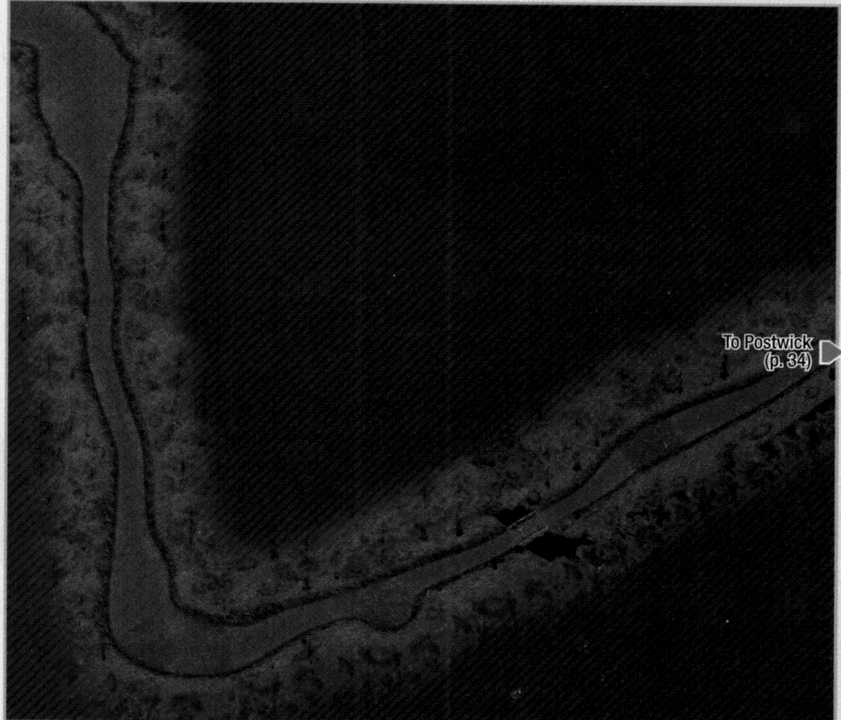

1

Make your way through the forest in the thickening fog. You'll run into a wild Pokémon in each of the three patches of tall grass you enter, so put your new partner through its paces as you head west. If its HP starts to get a bit low, talk to Hop and he'll see it sorted—restoring your partner to full health in a flash.

You've got some Potions in your Bag, too. But better to save them for when you really need them, since you've got Hop around to help you out this time!

BATTLE! Skwovet

Get ready for your very first wild Pokémon encounter! Skwovet is a Normal-type Pokémon that can come at you with Tackle or Tail Whip, but your Pokémon's higher level gives you an advantage. Dish out some damage-dealing moves to easily win the day!

BATTLE! Rookidee

The Flying-type Pokémon Rookidee will be next to ambush you in the Slumbering Weald. You can always choose to run instead of battle, but you'll miss out on Exp. Points if you do! Like Skwovet, Rookidee is a few levels lower than your first partner Pokémon, but watch out for its Peck attack nonetheless—it's super effective against Grass types, like Grookey!

2

Carry on through the woods, following the strange cries and heading deeper into the fog...until you run into trouble. You're under attack by a fearsome Pokémon unlike any of the others you've seen so far in the Slumbering Weald!

Mysterious Pokémon

If you're playing *Pokémon Sword*, you'll face a mysterious blue-colored Pokémon, and if you're playing *Pokémon Shield*, you'll face a mysterious red-colored Pokémon. Whatever the unknown Pokémon is, it has a powerful presence. You can try to use your best damage-dealing moves and take advantage of the same-type attack bonus (p. 165). Or maybe you might try a status move like Tail Whip to lower its Defense. Yet something strange is going on in this battle. Don't give up—you'll make it through as long as you keep at it!

3

In the aftermath of this mysterious event, you and Hop are found by Leon and his trusty Charizard. After you tell Leon about your strange encounter, it seems it's time to get back on track—which means on to Wedgehurst at last. Swing by home to tell your mom and get a few last things so you're well outfitted for the start of your adventure. Then it's back to Route 1!

 ₽30,000, Poké Ball ×5

Route 1

1

Hit the road again with Hop, but this time, the tall grass is all yours to explore! In fact, you've got no choice but to explore it, since some Wooloo are blocking the path. Dive right in to see what the tall grass holds for you.

2

There are many reasons to battle as many wild Pokémon as you can. Not only will it make your Pokémon stronger—it will also help set you up favorably for future battles by collecting information on what moves will be more or less effective against a given species. Learn more on page 164, and as you build your team, use this info to help you decide which of your team members you want to switch in to battle most effectively.

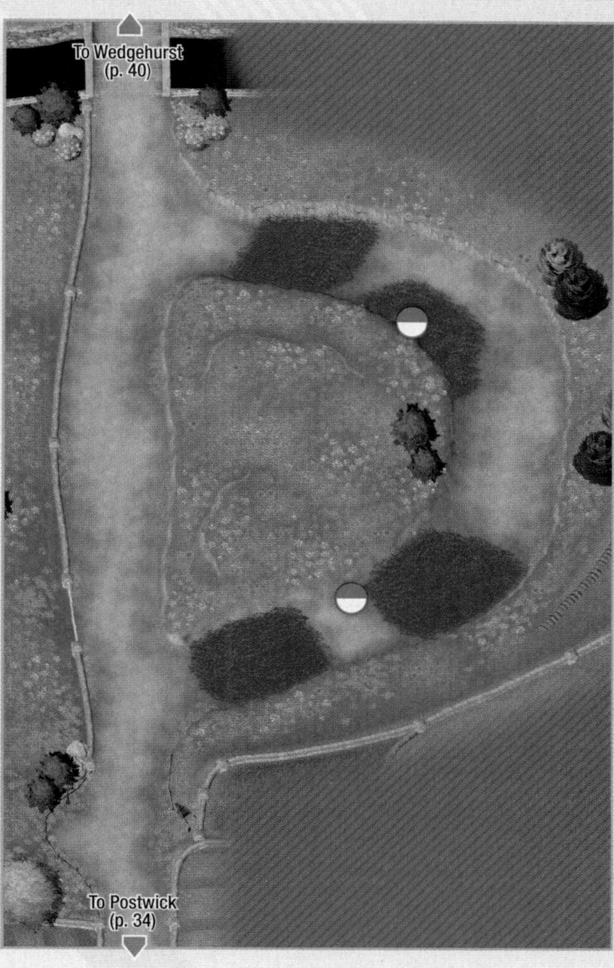

! You actually got some Poké Balls from your mom, if you want to flesh out your team right away. Simply whittle a wild Pokémon's HP down low, then throw a Poké Ball at it and hope for the best! You can easily select a Poké Ball to use during battles with wild Pokémon by pressing ⓧ!

3

Pick up a Potion between the patches of tall grass. You'll find items dropped here and there along routes and in towns and other places if you keep your eyes peeled. You'll find each of these items listed around the maps in this guide, so tick them off as you collect them to be sure you don't miss any—like the Paralyze Heals that lie a bit farther ahead!

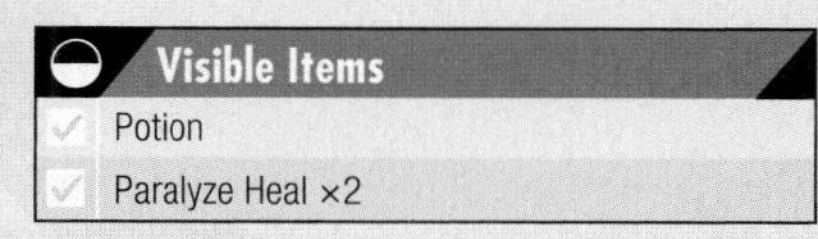

Visible Items
Potion
Paralyze Heal ×2

Tall Grass		
021	Rookidee	◯
024	Skwovet	◎
029	Nickit	☆
034	Wooloo	△

Random Encounters		
010	Blipbug	◯
013	Caterpie	△
016	Grubbin	△
019	Hoothoot	☆
024	Skwovet	◎

◎ frequent ◯ common △ average ☆ rare ★ almost never

Wedgehurst

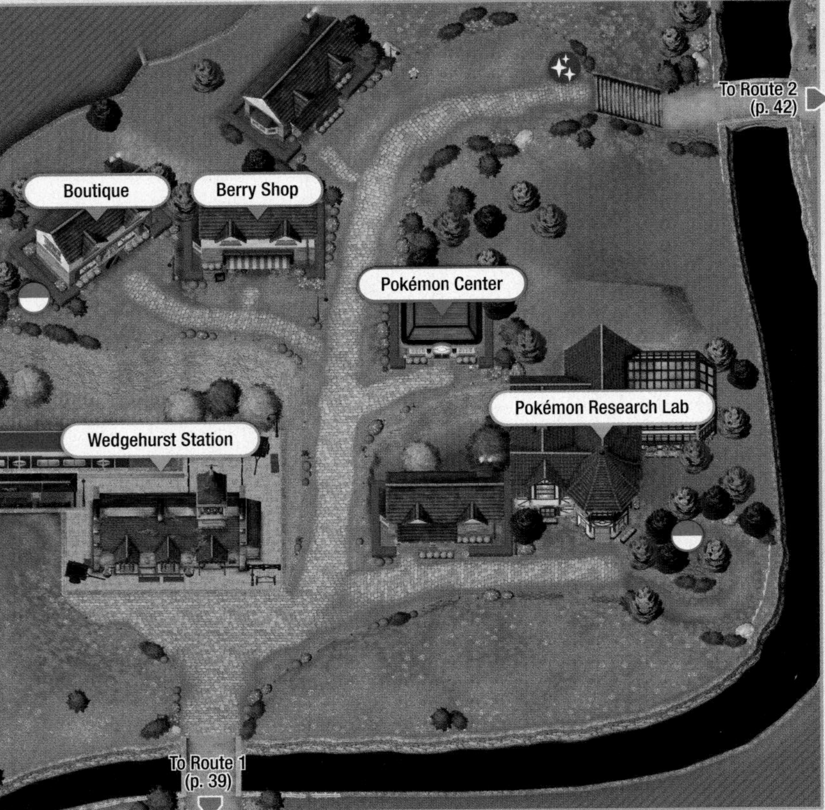

Visible Items
Rare Candy
Poké Doll

Hidden Items
Revive

Poké Mart	
Antidote	₽200
Awakening	₽200
Burn Heal	₽200
Ice Heal	₽200
Paralyze Heal	₽200
Poké Ball*	₽200
Potion	₽200
Revive	₽2,000

*This item will become available after you meet up with Leon on Route 2 (p. 42)!

Berry Shop	
Cheri Berry	₽80
Oran Berry	₽80
Pecha Berry	₽80

Every Pokémon Center has a counter where you'll find a Poké Mart clerk and sometimes another specialty service, such as a TM seller. The specialty services vary from location to location, so their wares will be listed up each time they appear. You can also find a full list of them on page 381. The regular Poké Mart clerks also offer different items throughout your adventure, but this isn't based on location. Instead, their lineup will change based on the number of Gym Badges you've earned. The goods they sell won't be listed for every town and city, but know that regular Poké Mart offerings can always be found in Pokémon Centers and in some train stations and stadiums.

1

It may be your second visit to Wedgehurst, but this is your first chance to really explore it! Your goal is to reach the Pokémon Research Lab in the southeast corner of the town. It's easy to spot with its pointed purple roof and the red and white Poké Ball mark on its front. After your visit, don't forget to pick up the Rare Candy found in the trees to the east of the building. This item can be used to level up a Pokémon in a flash!

2

Meet Leon outside the lab, and you'll head inside with him. You'll get to meet Sonia and an interesting new Pokémon. Sonia will teach you about your Rotom Phone—and will even add the Pokédex to it for you! She then sends you on a mission down Route 2 to tell her grandmother what a fine job she's done.

Pokédex

SONIA

Sonia is the granddaughter of one of Galar's greatest Pokémon Professors. Don't let her stylish look deceive you—she's quite the prodigy! She and Leon have been friends since they were both children and even took part in the Gym Challenge together, years ago. After Leon became Champion, she decided to give up on battling with Pokémon and focus more on studying them.

3 Outside again, a friendly stranger gives you a Potion. If you open your X menu, you'll notice that you now have access to your Pokédex! Give it a whirl to start getting familiar with its various functions. You can also flip to page 207 for some tips on how to get the most from this amazing feature!

Potion

! Don't forget that you have a lot of other handy resources available in the X menu! Open up the Town Map for useful information on your current destination and surroundings, or choose Options to customize things like battle settings and text speed. Page 22 offers a quick summary of all the X menu can offer you.

4

Head up the hill to where you can see Hop in the distance. Follow him to the Pokémon Center, and let him tell you more about what the various people and stations can do for you, if you desire. And if you want even more details about all you can do at Pokémon Centers, turn back to page 16.

! When you leave the Pokémon Center, talk to a young lady outside the entrance who is quite into horoscopes. If you tell her your birthday, you may not get the fortune you were hoping for, but you will see a special celebration in any Pokémon Center in the game when your big day rolls around!

5

Hop is dead set on reaching the professor's house at the end of Route 2, but why not shop a bit first? There's a Berry shop here where you can buy Berries for your Pokémon to hold. Pokémon can't use most items, like Potions, on their own. But give them a Berry to hold and their instincts will kick in, causing them to eat the Berry during battle when they need its effect.

There's also a boutique past the Berry shop—and another item lying on the ground near it. If a style shake-up sounds like your cup of tea, turn to page 315. You also may find you have some clothes already. Guess your mom really did think of everything! If you want to get changed, just head into a fitting room found in any boutique in the region. You'll be able to change into anything you've got already. To buy new clothes, talk to the woman behind the counter!

6

Once you've bought everything you want (or can afford) in town, move on to Route 2 and the next step of your adventure! Did you see a little something sparkle on your way? Remember to seek out such sparkles, as described on page 16, since the items hidden around them are often useful—like the Revive here!

Route 2

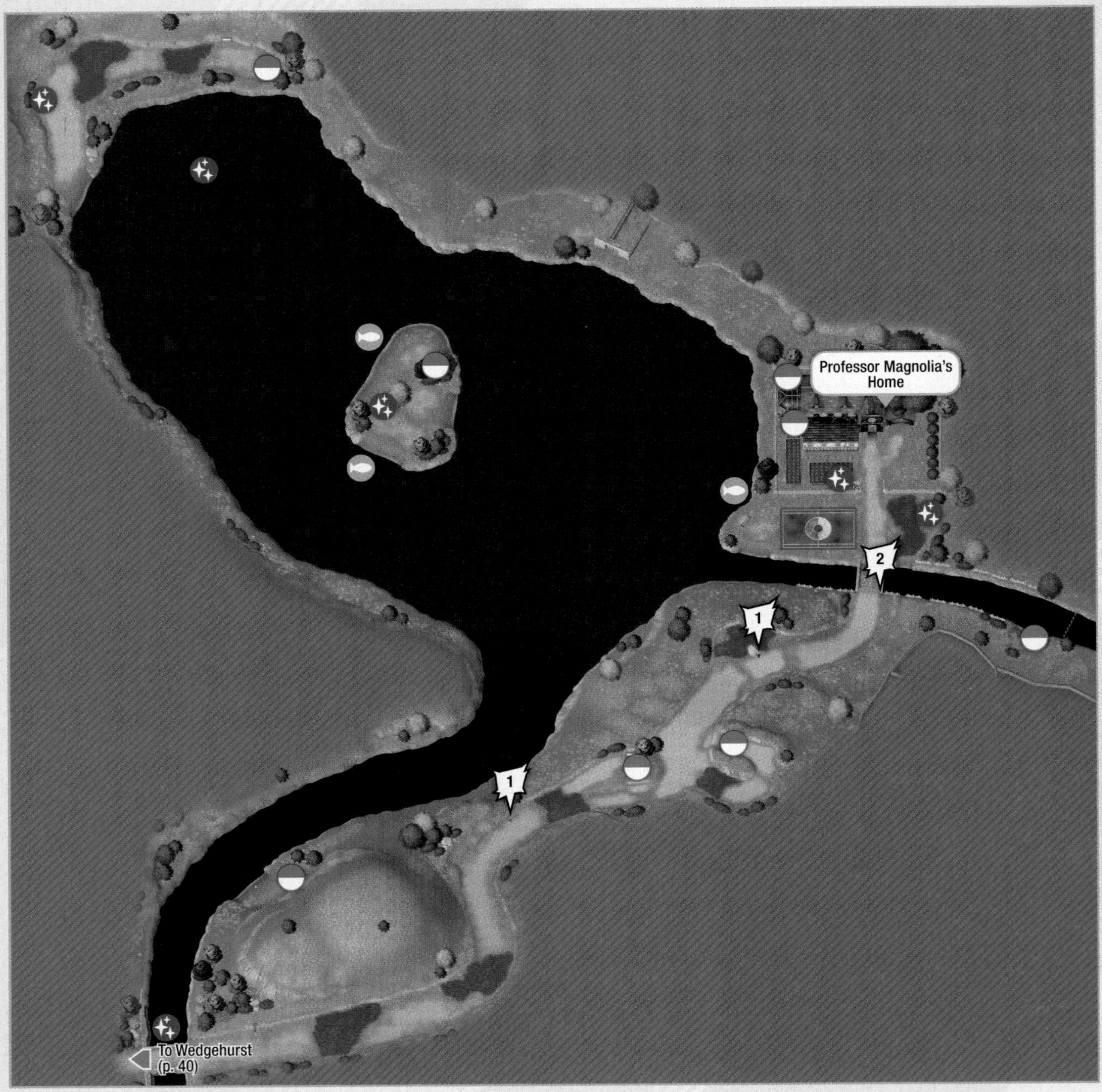

Professor Magnolia's Home

To Wedgehurst (p. 40)

1

You won't get far at all before Leon's caught up with you yet again! He'll make sure you know the ropes of catching Pokémon if you didn't catch some already on Route 1, and he'll give you some Poké Balls, too. Time to start filling in that shiny new Pokédex!

 Poké Ball ×20

You can now buy more Poké Balls from the Pokémon Center back in Wedgehurst. Stock up if you think you might run out!

Visible Items

	Item
✓	Potion ×2
✓	Poké Ball ×3
✓	Great Ball
✓	TM57 Payback
	With Water Mode Rotom Bike
✓	Choice Band
✓	PP Max
✓	TM69 Psycho Cut
✓	Psychic Seed

Hidden Items

	Item
✓	Repel
✓	Fresh Water
	With Water Mode Rotom Bike
✓	Rare Candy
✓	Prism Scale
✓	Max Ether
✓	Water Stone

Tall Grass

No.	Pokémon	Rate
021	Rookidee	○
024	Skwovet	○
029	Nickit	△
031	Zigzagoon	☆
042	Chewtle	△
046	Yamper	☆
	Across the lake	
010	Blipbug	○
029	Nickit	△
031	Zigzagoon	◎
046	Yamper	☆

Random Encounters

No.	Pokémon	Rate
010	Blipbug	◎
019	Hoothoot	☆
021	Rookidee	○
036	Lotad (*Pokémon Shield* only)	○
039	Seedot †	○
044	Purrloin	△
	Across the lake	
010	Blipbug	△
036	Lotad (*Pokémon Shield* only)	○
039	Seedot †	○
042	Chewtle	☆
044	Purrloin	○
126	Gossifleur	○

Wanderers

No.	Pokémon	Rate
◆ 042	Chewtle	◎
◆ 046	Yamper	◎
	Across the lake	
◆ 033	Obstagoon	◎
◆ 043	Drednaw	◎

Water Surface

No.	Pokémon	Rate
145	Gyarados	☆
180	Arrokuda	◎
181	Barraskewda	○
◆ 361	Lapras	◎

Fishing

No.	Pokémon	Rate
042	Chewtle	△
144	Magikarp	◎
180	Arrokuda	☆
	Across the lake	
042	Chewtle	◎
144	Magikarp	△
152	Feebas	★

◎ frequent ○ common △ average ☆ rare ★ almost never

† *Pokémon Sword* only (*Pokémon Shield* only)

!

Pokémon can live in the water, too! But you won't be able to encounter all of them just yet. Any Pokémon you can see swimming on the surface of the lake are still out of reach until you can find some way to travel across the water yourself... But the same can't be said for all the Pokémon living *under* the water! You've got a Fishing Rod in your Bag, so pull it out and press Ⓐ wherever you see a dark shadow and bubbles in the water. You'll cast your line, and when you feel your Joy-Con rumble or when you see the **!** mark appear above your head, press Ⓐ once more to reel in a Pokémon!

2

There's more than just wild Pokémon on Route 2. You'll start encountering other Trainers who are out and about training their teams. If they catch sight of you, fellow Trainers will always demand a battle, and there's no refusing them. Be ready whenever you see people hanging around, especially with a Poké Ball in hand.

!

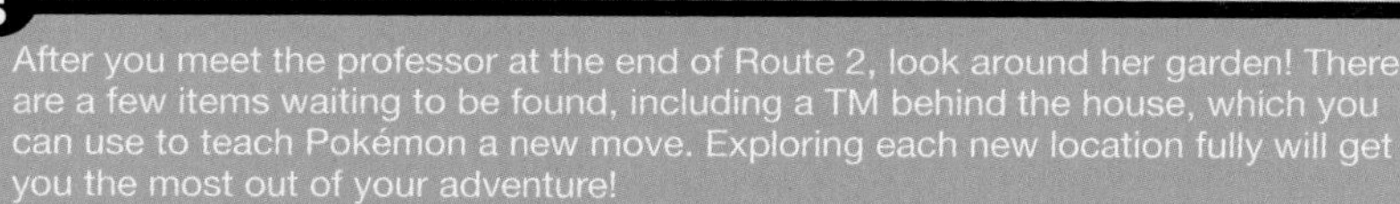

After you meet the professor at the end of Route 2, look around her garden! There are a few items waiting to be found, including a TM behind the house, which you can use to teach Pokémon a new move. Exploring each new location fully will get you the most out of your adventure!

3

Arrive at the house at the end of Route 2 and meet Professor Magnolia. With a bit of gentle encouragement from the professor, Leon seems willing to consider endorsing you and Hop for the Gym Challenge...if the two of you can wow him in battle!

PROFESSOR MAGNOLIA

Professor Magnolia is a greatly accomplished Pokémon Professor in the Galar region. She's spent years unraveling the secrets of the Dynamax phenomenon, and it's thanks to her research and discoveries (much of it conducted in partnership with Chairman Rose) that Trainers around the region can now harness the power of Dynamaxing for themselves.

WALKTHROUGH

4

You'll need to take on Hop for a second time to earn your shot at an entry in the Gym Challenge! You've got plenty of time to prepare, so ready your Pokémon as much as possible. Then talk to Hop when you're ready for action.

Hop

Hop still leads with his Wooloo, and it's only weak to Fighting-type moves, which you likely don't have yet. Focus on dealing damage with moves that get a same-type attack bonus (p. 165). When he sends out his Rookidee, try using Electric-type moves if you happen to have any Pokémon that know them. Finally, he'll send in his Grookey, Scorbunny, or Sobble, depending on which Pokémon you chose as your first partner. Just like in your first battle, your first partner Pokémon should know a move that's super effective against this one, so focus on that to get Hop's strongest Pokémon off the field. Don't forget to use Potions if your Pokémon's HP gets low, and you should be all set!

Wooloo
Lv.6
WEAKNESSES

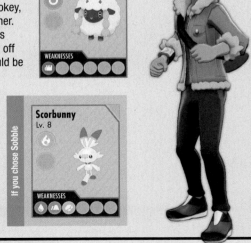

Rookidee
Lv. 5
WEAKNESSES

If you chose Grookey

Sobble
Lv. 8
WEAKNESSES

If you chose Scorbunny

Grookey
Lv. 8
WEAKNESSES

If you chose Sobble

Scorbunny
Lv. 8
WEAKNESSES

5

Leon gives you his endorsement, and then you get a Wishing Star of your own! Stay the night at the professor's house, and she'll make that Wishing Star into a Dynamax Band for you, allowing you to Dynamax your Pokémon around Power Spots. With your new prizes in hand, it'll be time to return to the train station to start out on the challenge of a lifetime!

 Endorsement, Dynamax Band, Wishing Star

Want to be ready to Dynamax as soon as you hit your first Power Spot? Turn to page 14 to learn the basics of this dynamic new twist on Pokémon battles!

6

With some last advice from Hop, try crouching and whistling your way back along Route 2! Take note of how Pokémon react, and see if you can sneak up on some of the more skittish Pokémon. You've got a competition with Hop, after all, to see who can catch more Pokémon!

CATCH!

Yamper

Yamper is more than just an adorable partner to Sonia! It evolves into Boltund, one of our top recommendations for the Electric type (p. 170). You may have luck finding one wandering around by the Trainer Tips board, or by searching about in the tall grass.

7

Once you get back to town, you may want to head into the Pokémon Center on your way down the hill to heal up your team. You'll nearly catch up to Hop, but it seems he's still going to win the race to the station! When you get there, compare your success at catching Pokémon, and no matter which one of you comes out on top, he'll be generous enough to give you a TM for your collection!

 TM40 Swift

8

If you're ready to move on to the next chapter in your adventure, head into Wedgehurst Station and say good-bye to your mom, and off you and Hop will go with some new gear in your Bags. Hope you're ready for what comes next, because it's going to be wild!

 Camping Gear

South Wild Area

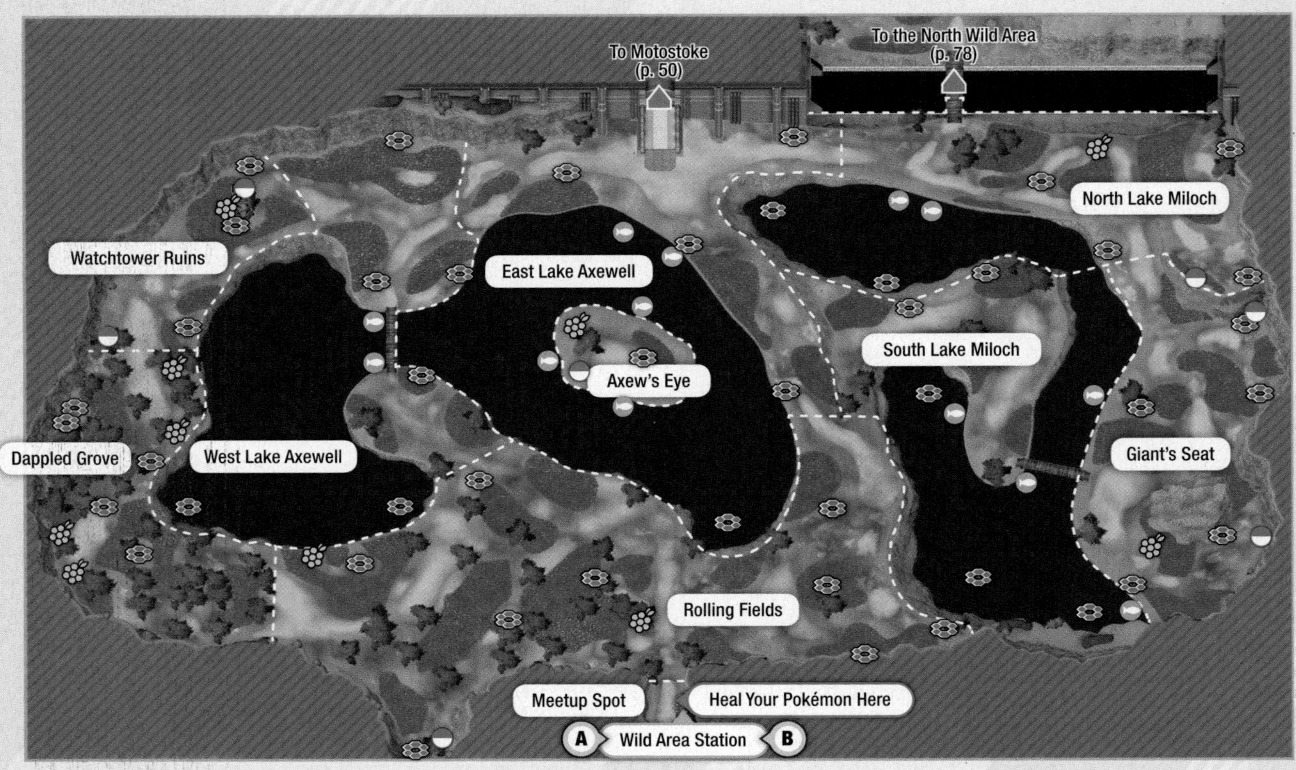

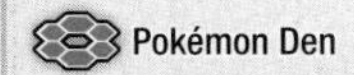

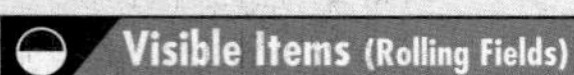

Visible Items (Rolling Fields)
TM84 Tail Slap

Visible Items (Watchtower Ruins)
White Herb
Max Revive

Visible Items (North Lake Miloch)
Thunder Stone

Visible Items (Giant's Seat)
Leftovers
TM81 Bulldoze

Visible Items (Axew's Eye)
With Water Mode Rotom Bike
TM95 Air Slash

There's Much More to Find in the Wild Area

The item tables to the left only show you the items you might spot lying around in the southern half of the Wild Area, but there is so much more you can find here! There are plenty of hidden items and Pokémon to find in the Wild Area—too many to list on one page, in fact! Random items appear again and again in the Wild Area, so turn to page 252 to get an idea what they can be and where you might look for them. The Pokémon you can encounter will also change depending on the zone you're in and the current weather. If you want to try to track down a particular species, the tables beginning on page 254 should help you out. And there are also plenty of people to talk to in the Wild Area, as you'll start to learn about in the following pages. If you want to skip right ahead to the in-depth guide, turn to page 249!

1

Once you get off the train, the first thing you'll probably notice is that you're definitely not in Motostoke. Some Wooloo have blocked the tracks, so you have to walk the rest of the way—across the massive Wild Area! While you might be eager to go out and explore, take a moment to speak to the various people in the Wild Area Station. There's also a Poké Mart, where you can stock up on supplies, and some of the people standing around might have some goodies for you, too.

A

Inside the Wild Area Station, you'll see these two waiting just to the left of the gates to the tracks. If you happen to have save data from *Pokémon: Let's Go, Pikachu!* on your Nintendo Switch, you'll want to speak to the girl. If you have *Pokémon: Let's Go, Eevee!* save data, speak to the guy. You can receive a Pikachu or Eevee, respectively, but these aren't just normal Pokémon. Try Dynamaxing them in battle to see what happens!

- Pikachu (if you have *Pokémon: Let's Go, Pikachu!* save data)
- Eevee (if you have *Pokémon: Let's Go, Eevee!* save data)

!

There are loads of Pokémon to encounter and catch in the Wild Area, so you might want to stock up on Poké Balls before heading on out!

B

You'll want to have a chat with this backpacker near the exit of the station, since she has some good advice for navigating the Wild Area. She'll also give you some Poké Dolls, just in case you run into a Pokémon that's too strong for your team to handle!

- Poké Doll ×5

WALKTHROUGH

2

Once you've done everything you want to in the station, step outside—you'll be greeted by the wide expanses of the Wild Area! You're in an area known as the Meetup Spot, and Hop will be waiting for you to take the name of this place to heart and meet up with him near the exit that leads to the Wild Area. Talk with him, and he'll show you your next destination—Motostoke. You'll also be joined by Sonia, who'll teach you about the Pokémon Dens (p. 270) and also give you the Pokémon Box Link. Now you can access your Boxes while you're on the road!

 Pokémon Box Link

3

You're now free to roam the Wild Area. The most direct path to Motostoke starts by heading slightly east through the Rolling Fields, then turning north to follow the eastern shore of the lake before you, making your way through East Lake Axewell to reach the brick city in the distance. Be careful turning east or west around the lake. You'll reach an area known as the Giant's Seat if you head east, and going west through the Dappled Grove leads to the Watchtower Ruins. Both are filled with tough Pokémon! Explore, gather items, catch Pokémon, and train up your team as you go.

Tips for catching Pokémon in the Wild Area

If you're setting out to explore the Wild Area in search of Pokémon, there are a few things you'll want to remember.

Weather changes as you progress

More and more weather patterns will appear as you progress in your game. Remember that you won't see blizzards or sandstorms until you've reached Hammerlocke for the first time. You won't see fog until you've become Champion. You'll have to be an experienced Trainer to run into some of the rarest Pokémon that only appear in these weather conditions!

Weather changes daily

The weather in each zone of the Wild Area will change at the end of each day (when the time on your system reaches midnight, that is). If you're looking for a certain weather pattern that isn't appearing on a given day, there's no need to keep coming back thinking it might have changed. Focus your attentions somewhere else and try again the next day.

Wandering Pokémon change as you progress

While it isn't as extreme an effect as new weather patterns appearing, many zones of the Wild Area have wandering Pokémon that only appear after you become Champion. Read the encounter tables (p. 254-269) for each zone carefully to check for any conditions that might prevent you from running into that Pokémon you want to catch so much.

Battling Pokémon reaps many rewards

Of course you know that battling and defeating or catching wild Pokémon can help your team level up by gaining Exp. Points. But that's not all! You'll also increase the count that makes it more likely you'll encounter a Brilliant Pokémon (p. 174) of that species, with great individual strengths and rare moves.

Progress means fewer limitations

There are even more reasons to celebrate your victories over Galar's Gym Leaders! Each Gym Badge you obtain will allow you to catch wild Pokémon of a higher level, and the cap on Exp. Points you earn from battling high-level Pokémon will be raised too.

Don't forget those Pokémon Dens

In addition to the Pokémon roaming around in the Wild Area, there are also the Dynamax Pokémon you can encounter in Pokémon Dens! These Pokémon won't necessarily be the same Pokémon you would encounter aboveground in the same zone. In fact, there are some species that can only be found in Max Raid Battles, as listed on page 215.

Den difficulty changes with your progress

Like some other elements described here, the types of encounters you may find in Pokémon Dens also depend on how many Gym Badges you have collected. At first, you will only see one-star Max Raid Battles appear, but as you collect more Gym Badges, you'll see the number of these stars increase until you reach five stars, which might indicate rare Pokémon!

More stars on a Max Raid Battle means that the Pokémon you're facing will also have more individual strengths maxed out! Any Dynamax Pokémon you catch in a Max Raid Battle should have at least one stat with the best individual strength possible. But in the more difficult levels of these encounters, you may start encountering Pokémon with two or even four stats with the best possible individual strengths.

Plenty of reasons for Max Raid Battles

Max Raid Battles don't only reward you with the chance to catch some promising Pokémon. You also earn reward items, as outlined on page 273, and these battles can be a great way to level up your team, too! You'll also want to keep checking in for the latest Wild Area news from the Mystery Gift menu for the chance to encounter new Pokémon species in these dens.

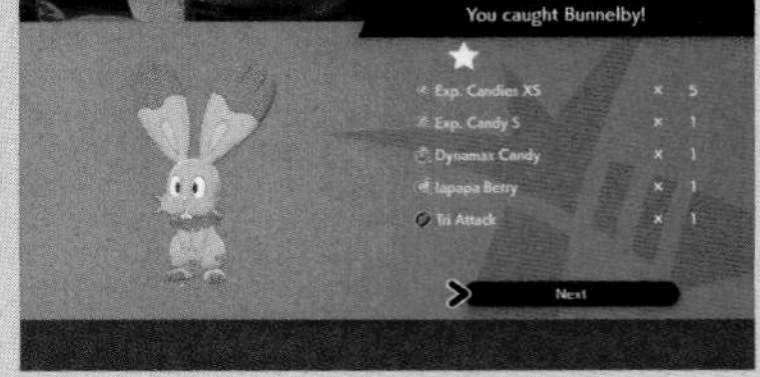

4

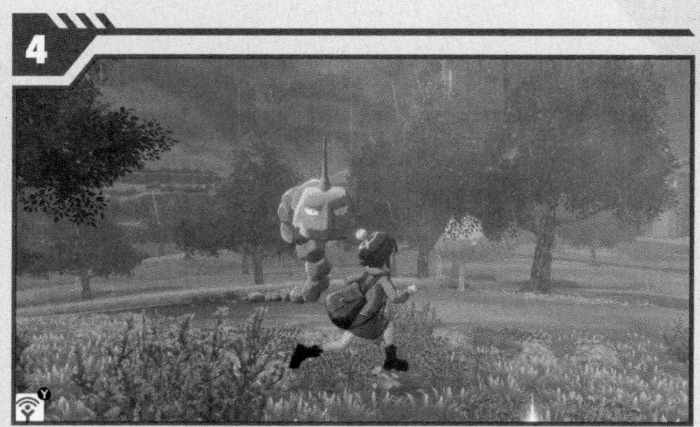

If you see wild Pokémon wandering outside of the tall grass, they're likely to be stronger than the other Pokémon in that area, so be careful! If you ever run into a Pokémon you feel is too strong for you, don't forget about those Poké Dolls you might have received at the Wild Area Station. You can also talk to the lady standing outside the station to fully heal your team if you're ever in a pinch, or you can set up your camp and cook up some restoring curry! To learn about camping alone and visiting the camps of other players in the Wild Area, turn to pages 280 and 296 respectively.

5

Don't hesitate to talk to the various people you'll meet throughout the Wild Area. Some will sell you ingredients for cooking up curries (p. 285), while others might want to trade items they've found for Watts. You may even run into someone who claims to be a strong Trainer—it's best to take her word for it right now. Her party is likely stronger than yours at the moment, so come back once you've trained up a bit more! For more information on the people you'll encounter and what you can do, flip to page 277 and read on.

6

As you wander around the Wild Area, you'll probably notice these odd-looking trees here and there. These are Berry trees, and you can find a variety of Berries by giving them a shake! There's also a chance that a Pokémon will drop down and battle you, too—keep an eye on the rustling of the leaves to see if you should give the tree another shake or not. Lots of rustling in the leaves means that a Pokémon's about to drop down! There's more about them on page 290.

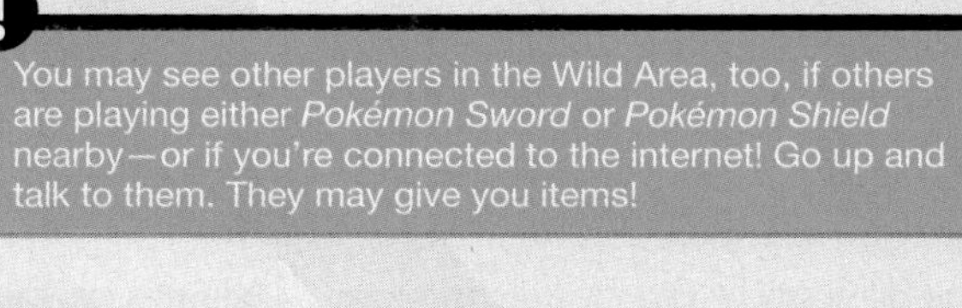

You may see other players in the Wild Area, too, if others are playing either *Pokémon Sword* or *Pokémon Shield* nearby—or if you're connected to the internet! Go up and talk to them. They may give you items!

7

This is also the first place you can try out Dynamaxing your own Pokémon if you're up for a Max Raid Battle! You can trigger Max Raid Battles by examining Pokémon Dens that are emitting pillars of light. You can also join the Max Raid Battles other players are starting if you see them searching for allies on Y-Comm (p. 298). Learn all about these exciting battles on page 271!

8

Once you've had your fill of exploring the Wild Area, head to the giant staircase that leads into Motostoke. You may notice that down the hill to the right of the stairs is a bridge that leads into an even greater section of the Wild Area—but don't go that way yet. The Pokémon across the bridge will be much stronger than yours right now, and you won't even be able to catch them until you've gathered enough Gym Badges!

Motostoke

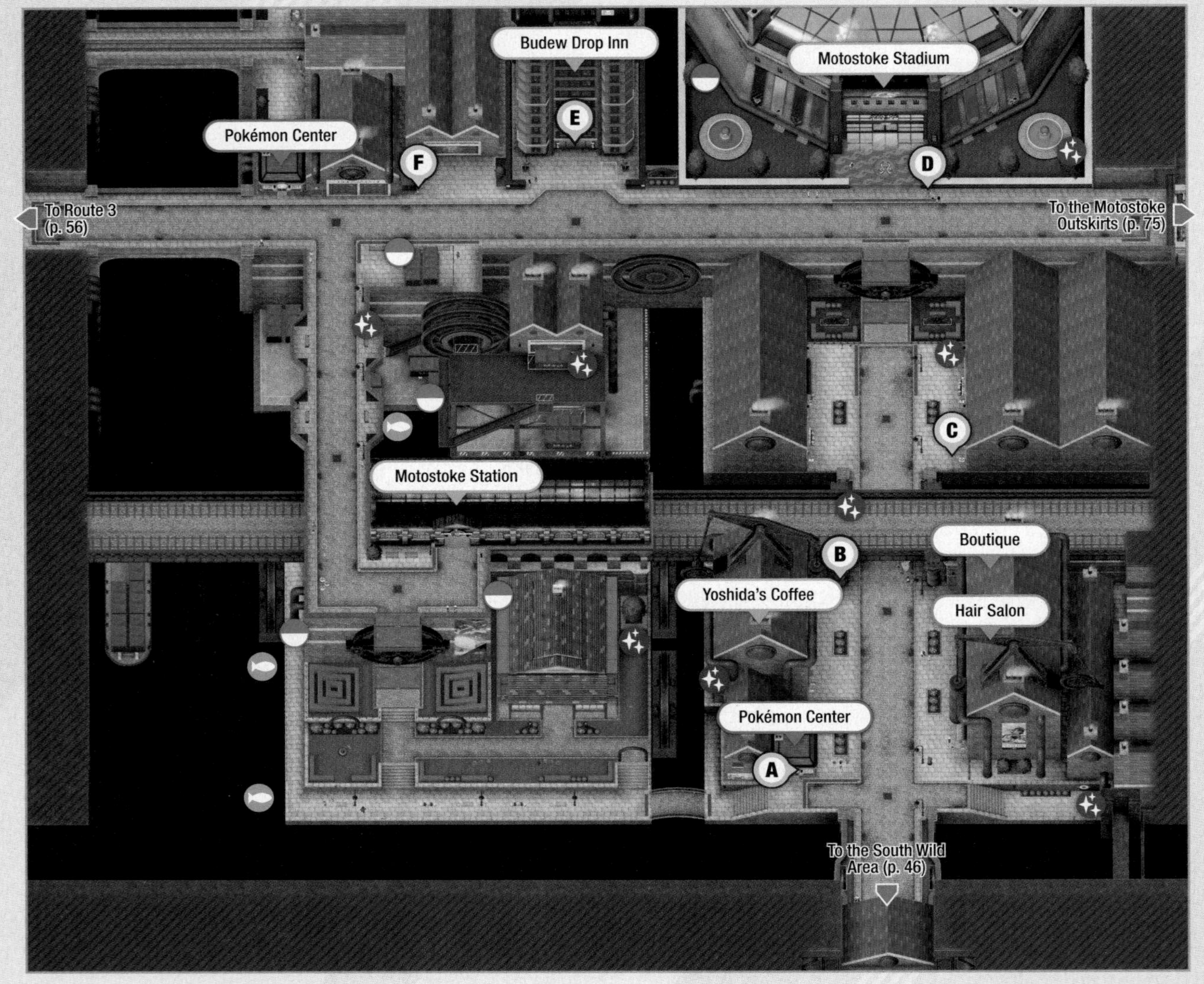

Budew Drop Inn
Motostoke Stadium
Pokémon Center
To Route 3 (p. 56)
To the Motostoke Outskirts (p. 75)
Motostoke Station
Boutique
Yoshida's Coffee
Hair Salon
Pokémon Center
To the South Wild Area (p. 46)

Visible Items

✓	Item
✓	Black Glasses
✓	Great Ball ×3
✓	Silk Scarf
✓	TM02 Pay Day
✓	Burn Heal ×3

Hidden Items

✓	Item
✓	Poké Ball
✓	Nugget
✓	Revival Herb
✓	Super Potion
✓	Paralyze Heal ×2
✓	Poké Doll
✓	X Accuracy
✓	Repel

Poké Mart (lower level)

Heal Ball	₽300
Nest Ball	₽1,000
Net Ball	₽1,000
X Attack	₽1,000
X Defense	₽2,000
X Sp. Atk	₽1,000
X Sp. Def	₽2,000

Poké Mart (upper level)

TM17 Light Screen	₽10,000
TM18 Reflect	₽10,000
TM19 Safeguard	₽10,000
TM25 Protect	₽10,000
TM41 Helping Hand	₽10,000
TM76 Round	₽10,000
TM94 False Swipe	₽10,000

Vending Machine (Motostoke Station)

Fresh Water	₽200
Lemonade	₽350
Soda Pop	₽300

Fishing

No.	Pokémon	Rate
042	Chewtle	◎
144	Magikarp	◎
228	Barboach	△

◎ frequent ○ common △ average ☆ rare ★ almost never

1

After a panoramic view of the city, you'll be free to move around, so just head straight—you'll bump into Sonia again! She'll introduce you to the Rotomi inside the Pokémon Center and give you one of Leon's League Cards. You can edit your own League Card, too, so why not play around with it a bit? For more on what you can do with your League Card, check out the info starting on page 301.

 Leon's League Card

You'll no doubt notice that there are two clerks at the Poké Mart counters inside Motostoke's Pokémon Centers. The one on the left has the usual lineup of Potions and the like, but the one on the right will sell either TMs or battle items and rare Poké Balls! Check this counter whenever you visit a new Pokémon Center to see what different items they sell!

2

You'll also be able to access Poké Jobs from the Rotomi! Check out what jobs are available, and send out Pokémon from your Boxes if you want to complete any of them. For a full breakdown of Poké Jobs, check out pages 241–248! They're a great way to earn cash and items, and they can also help your Pokémon level up and gain base points (p. 178)!

A

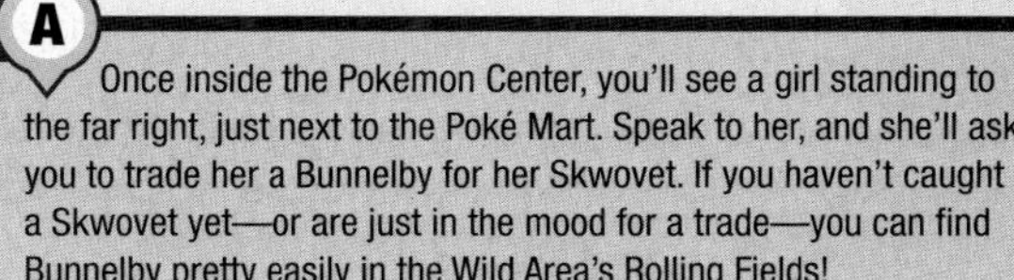

Once inside the Pokémon Center, you'll see a girl standing to the far right, just next to the Poké Mart. Speak to her, and she'll ask you to trade her a Bunnelby for her Skwovet. If you haven't caught a Skwovet yet—or are just in the mood for a trade—you can find Bunnelby pretty easily in the Wild Area's Rolling Fields!

 Skwovet

3

When you head outside again, Sonia will remind you why you came to Motostoke in the first place—to register for the Gym Challenge! But you can also take the time to explore Motostoke a bit. This is the first chance you'll have to visit a hair salon if you want to rock a new hairdo or makeover, and there's also a boutique if you want to check out clothing. There's even a café where each day you can take part in a battle to earn rewards (p. 194)! Once you're done exploring, head toward the lift that Sonia mentioned!

B

On your way to the lift, look to your left just before going under the bridge—you'll see a record shop with a man standing out front. Speak to him, and this nice gent will give you a TR, as well as a bit of info about them!

 TR13 Focus Energy

C

Once you pass under the bridge, look to the right—there will be a kind older man standing near another record shop who'll give you Hi-tech Earbuds! These advanced earbuds allow you to adjust the sounds around you. Just go to Options in the X menu and scroll down to see the sound adjustments you can make!

 Hi-tech Earbuds 

4

Just as you're about to get on the lift, you'll hear a roar. Don't worry—it's just Leon's Charizard. Leon himself isn't far behind, and he'll be so impressed by how far you've already come that he'll give you an item! Which item he gives you changes depending on which Pokémon you chose to be your first partner. Letting your partner hold the item will help it deal more damage during battle. The next step is to get on the lift and head to Motostoke Stadium!

 Charcoal (if you chose Scorbunny) / Miracle Seed (if you chose Grookey) / Mystic Water (if you chose Sobble)

D

After you get off the lift, you'll probably see a strange figure that's dressed up as the official mascot of the Gym Challenge, Ball Guy. This Ball Guy's identity is a mystery, but have a chat anyway. You'll be rewarded with a Poké Ball! But this isn't the last you'll see of the Ball Guy... Keep your eyes peeled for this enigmatic person as you continue on your adventure!

 Poké Ball

5

It looks like Hop's already made it to the stadium and has been waiting for you. Follow him into Motostoke Stadium, and you two will run into another Gym Challenger who doesn't seem very friendly. Don't let that bring you down, because now you can finally register for the Gym Challenge yourself! Pick your uniform number and receive your Challenge Band, and you'll be all set. Since the opening ceremony isn't until tomorrow, your next stop is the Budew Drop Inn!

6

You don't have to worry about finding your way to the inn. A kind League staff member will show you the way, so just follow him. Head inside, and you'll run into Sonia yet again. She's here to have a look at the statue in the hotel lobby, and she'll give you a brief lesson on the history of the Galar region.

Legends of Galar: The Lone Hero

Long ago, the entire Galar region was endangered by an unknown threat. The only stories that live on today talk of black storms, gigantic Pokémon, and the phrase "the Darkest Day." Whatever truly happened in those ancient days, a single young hero, bearing a sword and shield, is said to have saved the region and turned back the Darkest Day. The statue here in Motostoke is one artist's idea of what this hero might have looked like, wielding his sword and shield against any peril.

7

It's time to check in to the hotel and get some well-deserved rest. But wait! There are some rowdy-looking people jamming up the front desk! Meet Team Yell—they say they want to cheer on Gym Challengers, but they'll challenge you to a battle if you try to make it past them. Make sure your team's ready, because they'll come at you one after another!

Team Yell Grunt

If you caught any Pokémon with Fighting-, Bug-, or Fairy-type moves, try sending them out in battle here, as those are the types of moves Dark-type Pokémon are weak to.

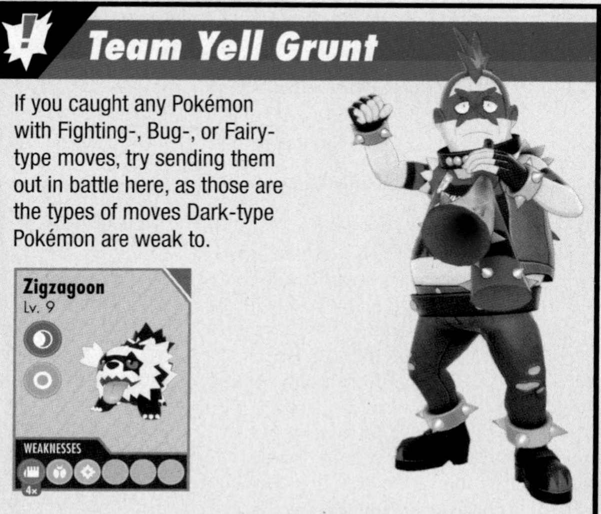

Team Yell Grunt

Just like the first Grunt's Zigzagoon, Nickit is a Dark-type Pokémon, so if you've got a move that was super effective in the last battle, use it again here for a quick win!

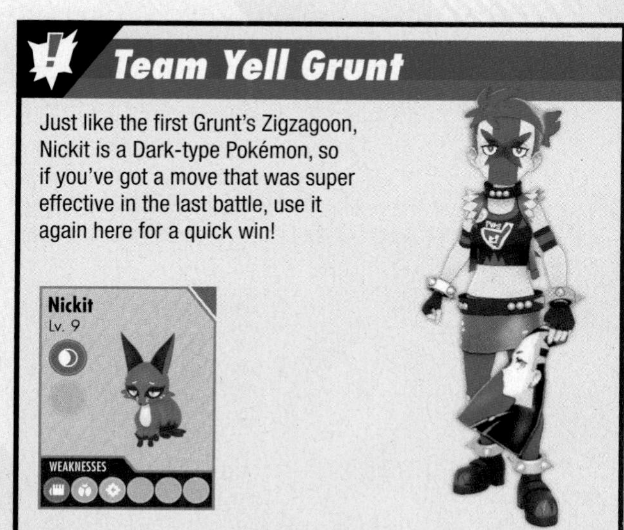

Team Yell Grunts

Your very first Double Battle! With a reliable Trainer like Hop at your side, you shouldn't have too much trouble. The two Grunts use a Zigzagoon and Nickit, Pokémon you should be pretty familiar with battling by now. Bust out a supereffective move, like Low Sweep or Double Kick, to get these pesky hooligans out of your way fast!

8

Successfully defeat Team Yell, and you'll be properly introduced to Marnie. Perhaps you spotted her once already when registering for the Gym Challenge at the stadium. That's right—she's a fellow Gym Challenger! And it turns out that Team Yell is actually a group of her fans. All it takes is some sharp words from her to clear them out, and then you can finally talk to the desk clerk to get checked in. What a day!

MARNIE AND TEAM YELL

Marnie will be taking part in the Gym Challenge just like you and Hop, so you'll probably be running into her again and again as you make your way to each of the Gyms. That means you'll see more of her devoted Team Yell fans, too. Marnie can be a bit gruff but has a good heart, as you can see when she scolds Team Yell for getting in your way. Make no mistake, though—she's a talented Trainer and will always battle to win!

9

After a good night's sleep, it's time to head to Motostoke Stadium again for the opening ceremony of the Gym Challenge. A League staff member will be waiting for you outside the inn, so you can have him escort you to the stadium if you want. Once inside, speak to the League staff member behind the front desk, and he'll ask you to go get changed into your uniform. Then the ceremony begins! Check out (almost) all the Gym Leaders you'll face—and you'll even get to meet Chairman Rose himself after the ceremony!

ROSE

Chairman Rose is the head of the Galar Pokémon League and the man responsible for organizing the Gym Challenge. And not just that—he's also behind the Macro Cosmos group, which provides energy, entertainment, banking, transit, and so much more to the Galar region. It was his company that supported Professor Magnolia's research into the Dynamax phenomenon and helped develop the Dynamax Band!

10

ahem Excuse me.
The gift is access to the Flying Taxis!

Head out from the stadium, and there'll be a League staff member waiting for you outside again. She's here to give you a gift from Chairman Rose—access to the Flying Taxis! You can use this service to travel back to places you've visited before, including various locations in the Wild Area! Now you're free to head to Route 3 and then on to Turffield—or head back down into the Wild Area, where there's always more to do!

You may have noticed that you can actually use the elevators inside the Budew Drop Inn. Once you're on the upper floor, head to the room on the far left and speak to the man inside—apparently he's found a whole bunch of Star Pieces, and he's more than happy to share one with you!

Star Piece

There's quite a bit to find in Motostoke, and now you'll be able to explore areas you couldn't enter before the opening ceremony. It's good practice to thoroughly explore each new location you arrive at before moving on. You never know what you might discover! Of particular interest in Motostoke is TM02 Pay Day, which you can find by heading down the long staircase in the upper level of the city, southeast of the western Pokémon Center. The map of each area will show you where you can find items, so be sure to check it out to collect them all!

To the left of the Budew Drop Inn, you'll come across two young boys with their mother. One of them is upset because his Minccino's gone missing. Why not give him a hand and help look for it? He'll give you a few clues about where and how to look for it, but it hasn't wandered far. The Minccino's hiding in the fountain to the left of Motostoke Stadium, so just whistle (that is, push the Left Stick!) there to find it, and then return to the boy! You could also whistle at the fountain to the right first. You'll get an extra reward!

Fresh Water, Throat Spray

WALKTHROUGH

11

Just before the exit to Route 3, you'll run into Hop again. He's been waiting for you and is apparently itching to have a battle before you both set out on the Gym Challenge. If you feel your team is ready, accept his challenge and test your skills against your rival! After the battle, Hop will give you one of his League Cards to add to your album. Have a look at the back of the card if you want to learn more about your best mate. Now it's on to Route 3 and Galar Mine beyond!

Hop's League Card

Hop

Hop's first partner, Wooloo, is up first. If you caught a Machop in the Wild Area, its Fighting-type moves should be able to knock out this Pokémon without a lot of trouble. You could also try using a Ghost-type Pokémon like Golett, as Ghost-type Pokémon take no damage from Normal-type moves. But remember that Ghost-type moves can't touch Normal-type Pokémon, either! Next up should be either Grookey, Scorbunny, or Sobble. Your first partner Pokémon will have the type advantage over this one, so send it out and use a move that matches your partner's type for that same-type attack bonus! Last comes Rookidee, with plenty of weaknesses. If you have a Yamper from Route 2, try one of its Electric-type moves!

Route 3

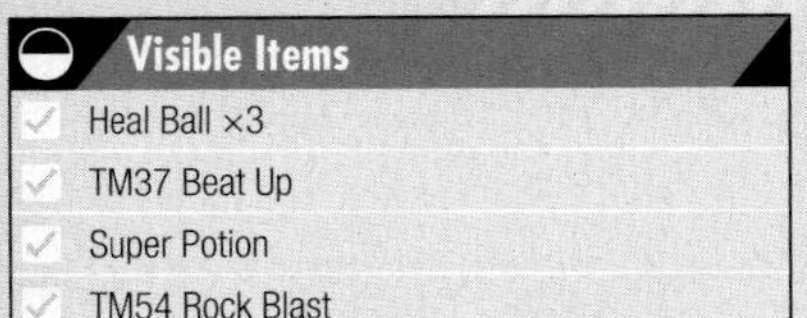

Visible Items
Heal Ball ×3
TM37 Beat Up
Super Potion
TM54 Rock Blast

Hidden Items
Big Mushroom
Burn Heal
Revive
X Defense ×2

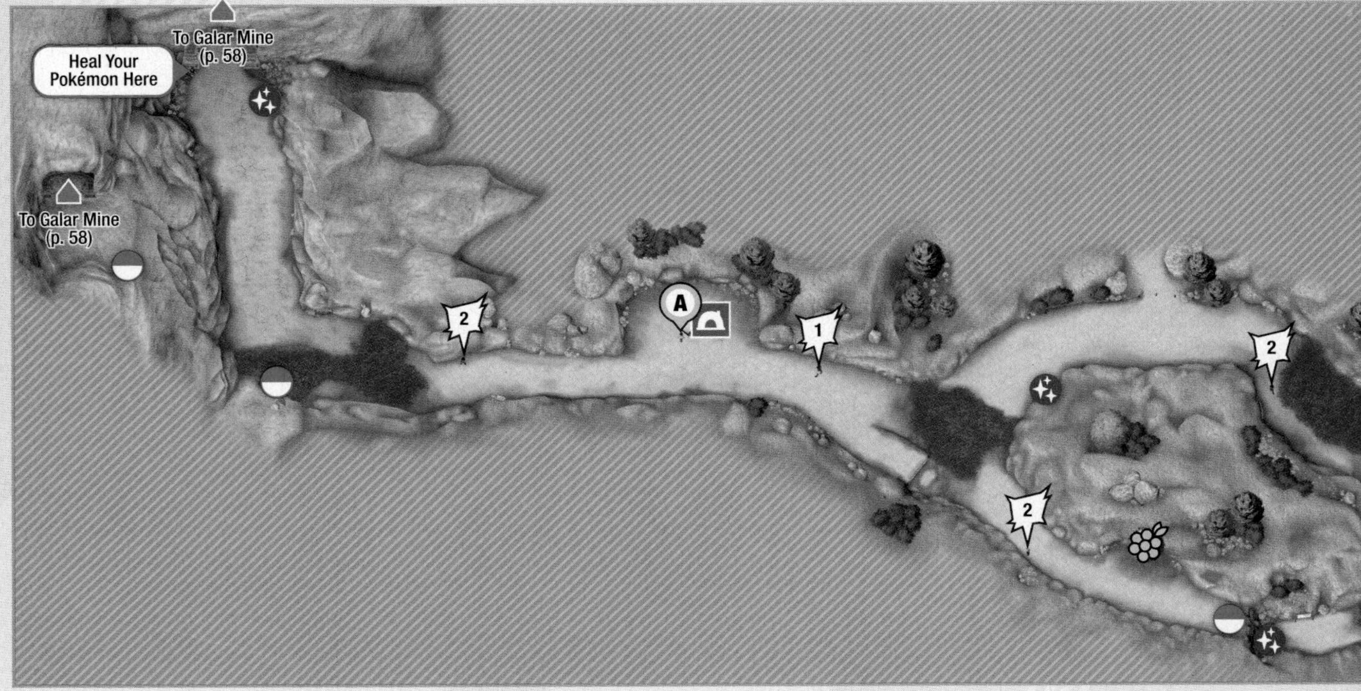

1 It's up to you whether you try to sneak around or run straight toward the new species of Pokémon you'll find here on Route 3. Catch as many as you'd like to help fill your Pokédex or increase your odds of encountering Brilliant Pokémon (p. 174) that have great individual strengths. Running low on Poké Balls? Return to the Pokémon Center on the west edge of Motostoke and stock up, because you're about to head through several areas full of new species to catch!

2

There are plenty of Trainers to battle here, but you'll find some friendly faces as well. Sonia is out enjoying the scenery, so talk to her to learn a bit more about Chairman Rose and his role in the Galar region. She'll give you an Escape Rope before healing up your Pokémon and sending you on your way. That Escape Rope might come in handy to help you get out of places like caves or forests. Select it from the Key Items pocket in your Bag!

 Escape Rope

Tall Grass		
031	Zigzagoon	○
068	Vulpix †	△
070	Growlithe (Shield)	△
107	Tyrogue	☆
126	Gossifleur	○
130	Stunky	△
157	Trubbish	☆
West		
157	Trubbish	★
161	Rolycoly	◎

Random Encounters		
021	Rookidee	○
084	Mudbray	△
111	Pancham	○
113	Klink	△
138	Machop	○
159	Sizzlipede	★

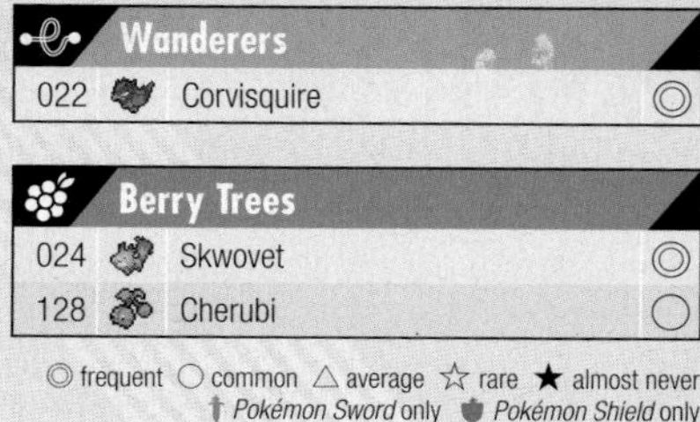

Wanderers		
022	Corvisquire	◎

Berry Trees		
024	Skwovet	◎
128	Cherubi	○

◎ frequent ○ common △ average ☆ rare ★ almost never
† *Pokémon Sword* only (Shield) *Pokémon Shield* only

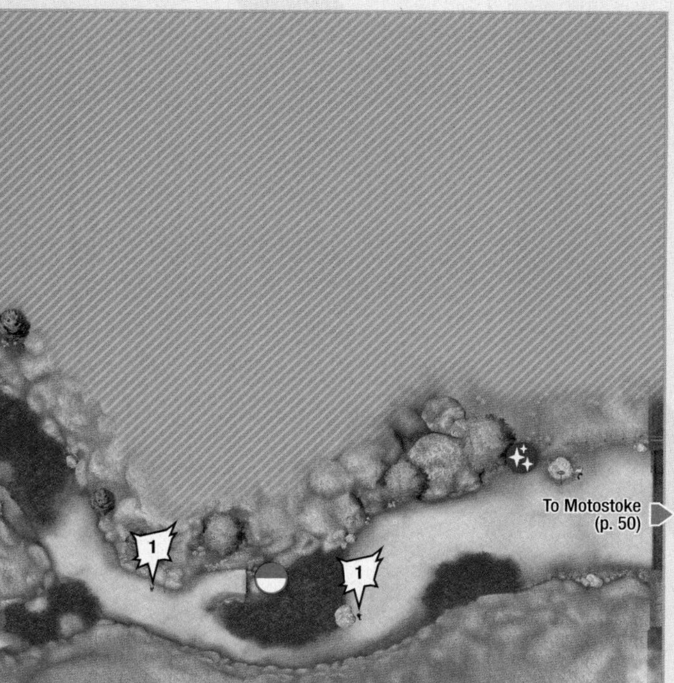

A Along the way to Galar Mine, you'll come across a tent with a young lady standing out front. You're free to visit her camp, and she'll give you a Cheri Berry just for speaking to her!

Cheri Berry

! The Galar Mine is home to many Rock- and Ground-type Pokémon. It may be a good idea to have a Water- or Grass-type Pokémon in your party. There are several fishing spots in Motostoke where you can try to reel in a Water-type Pokémon if you don't have one. And you can always head back to the Wild Area if you want tons more options!

CATCH!

Gossifleur

You can catch the Grass-type Gossifleur right here on Route 3, too!

3

Carry on along Route 3, and keep your eyes open for items. You don't want to miss TM37 Beat Up! You can also shake a few more Berries loose from the Berry tree here. With the long trek ahead, you'll probably want a nice stock of Berries in case you want to whip up curries to heal your team while you make your way through Galar Mine.

4

Eventually, you'll come to a tunnel at the end of the route that leads into the mine. If your team could use some healing, save your Berries for now and speak to the lady standing next to the tunnel. She's set up an impromptu Pokémon Center service and will get your team in tip-top shape whenever you need. It's time to head into the mine!

Galar Mine

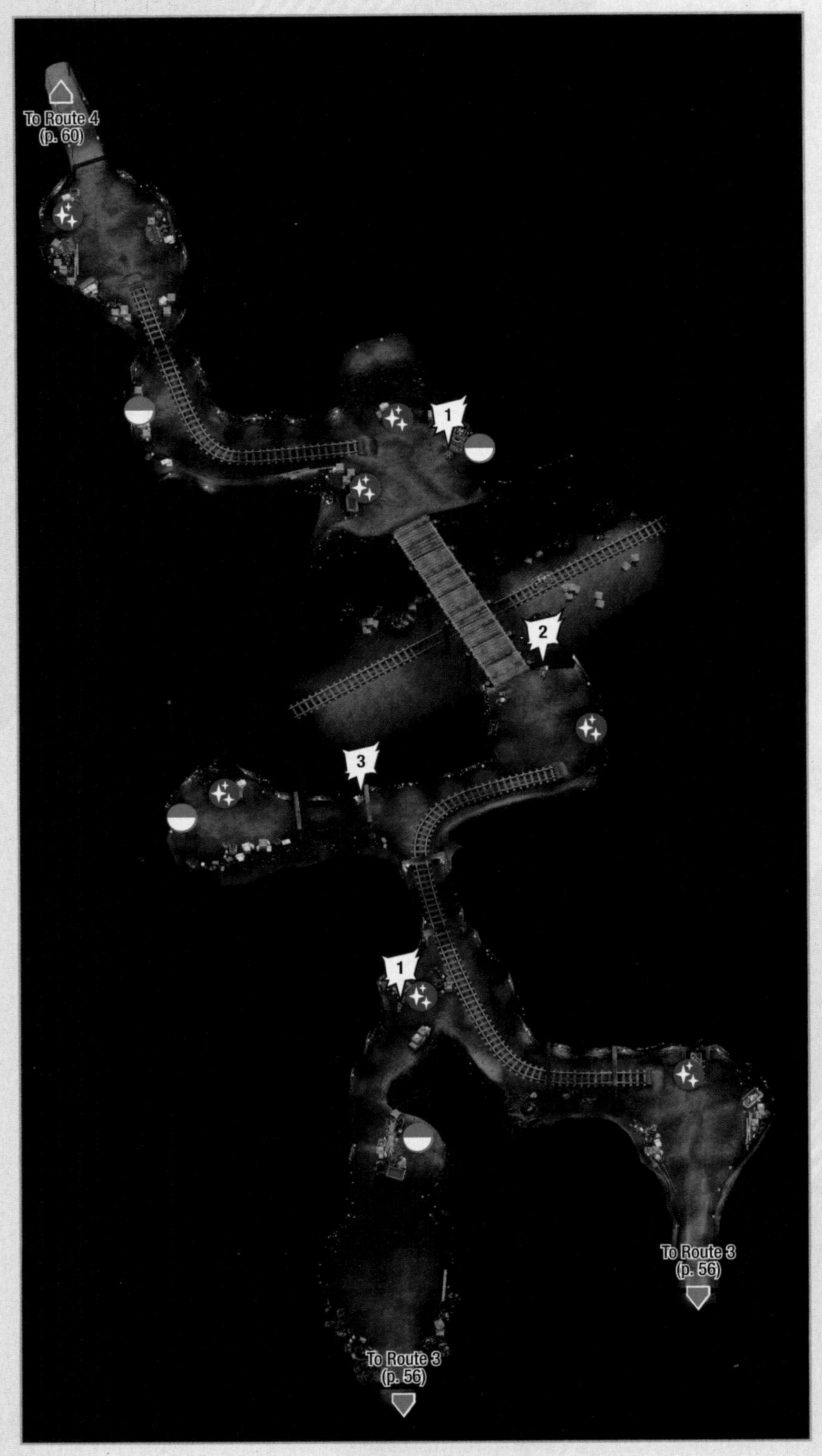

To Route 4 (p. 60)

To Route 3 (p. 56)

To Route 3 (p. 56)

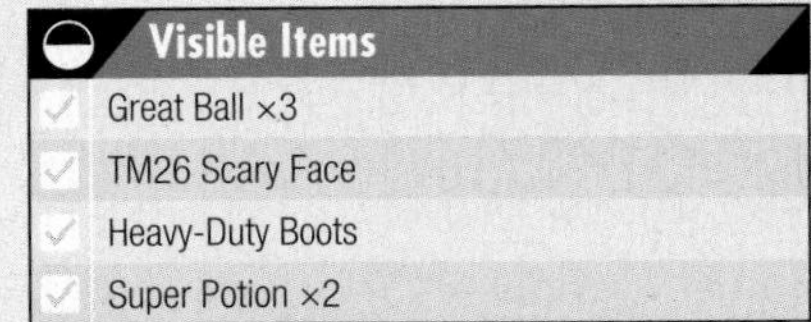

Visible Items
Great Ball ×3
TM26 Scary Face
Heavy-Duty Boots
Super Potion ×2

Hidden Items
Star Piece
Revive
Stardust
Hard Stone
Ether
Revive
Stardust

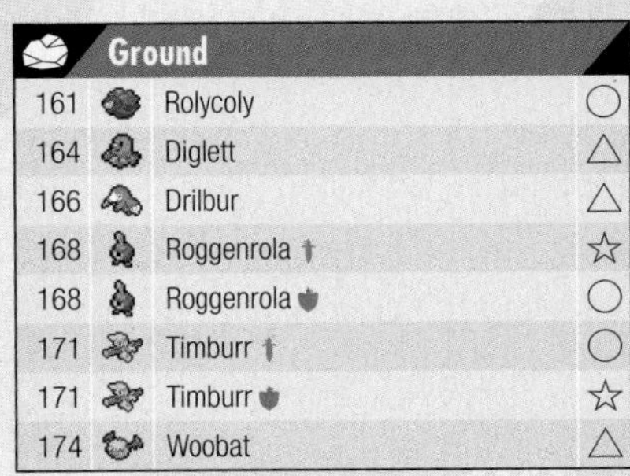

Ground		
161	Rolycoly	○
164	Diglett	△
166	Drilbur	△
168	Roggenrola †	☆
168	Roggenrola 🛡	○
171	Timburr †	○
171	Timburr 🛡	☆
174	Woobat	△

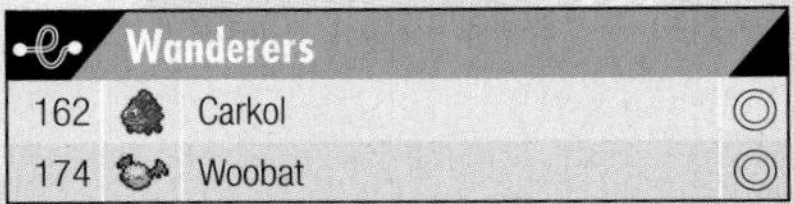

Wanderers		
162	Carkol	◎
174	Woobat	◎

◎ frequent ○ common △ average ☆ rare ★ almost never
† *Pokémon Sword* only 🛡 *Pokémon Shield* only

1

Many Pokémon make the glistening Galar Mine their home, and they can be a bit trickier to tackle than the Pokémon you faced on Route 3. Be on the lookout for them while also hunting for the sparkle of hidden items. With all the sparkling gems in the walls, it would be easy to overlook those items!

2

As you follow the tracks, don't miss the side path that turns to the west—it'll lead to some items and an extra Trainer. In fact, it goes all the way back out to Route 3, to a ledge that you couldn't reach before. There you'll find TM54 Rock Blast, bringing you one step closer to completing your TM collection.

!

Follow the tracks within the mine to find your way to the exit. But watch out—there's a chance you'll run into a Carkol on the tracks that's at a higher level than the other Pokémon in the mine!

3

At the end of the tracks, cross the bridge and follow the next set of tracks. They'll take you to the exit—but someone's standing in the way and looking for a battle. If you spoke to this Trainer in Motostoke, you'll know that he's a Gym Challenger endorsed by Chairman Rose himself—and if you missed it, don't worry. He'll be happy to remind you every chance he gets!

BEDE

Though you ran into him at Motostoke Stadium (or was it the other way around?), this is where you'll first be really introduced to Bede. He's another Gym Challenger and seems eager to prove his superiority to all other challengers. He's also collecting Wishing Stars for some reason. He obviously expects you to be impressed that he's endorsed by Rose. Why not show him that the Champion also endorses great Trainers? But be ready for a good fight. He might be prideful, but he's got some strength as a Trainer to back it up!

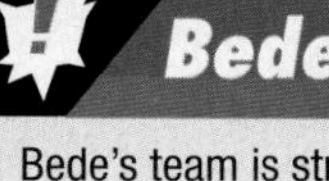

Bede

Bede's team is stronger overall than Hop's team was in your last battle. But luckily, all three of his Pokémon are Psychic type, meaning they all have the same weaknesses for you to take advantage of. Using Dark-type Pokémon is a particularly great choice against Bede. Psychic-type moves have no effect on Dark-type Pokémon, and Psychic-type Pokémon are weak to Dark-type moves. If you caught a Zigzagoon on Route 3, its Snarl move will be perfect for this battle. Don't be afraid to use healing items like Potions or Revives if you find yourself in a tight spot.

Solosis
Lv. 13

WEAKNESSES

Gothita
Lv. 15

WEAKNESSES

Hatenna
Lv. 16

WEAKNESSES

4

Once you defeat Bede, your path forward will be clear. As beautiful as the mines may be in their own way, at last it's time for some sunlight and fresh air again. Head toward the exit and onward to Route 4. Beyond it waits Turffield, which is both a new town to explore and the site of Turffield Stadium, where you'll get to challenge your first Gym!

Route 4

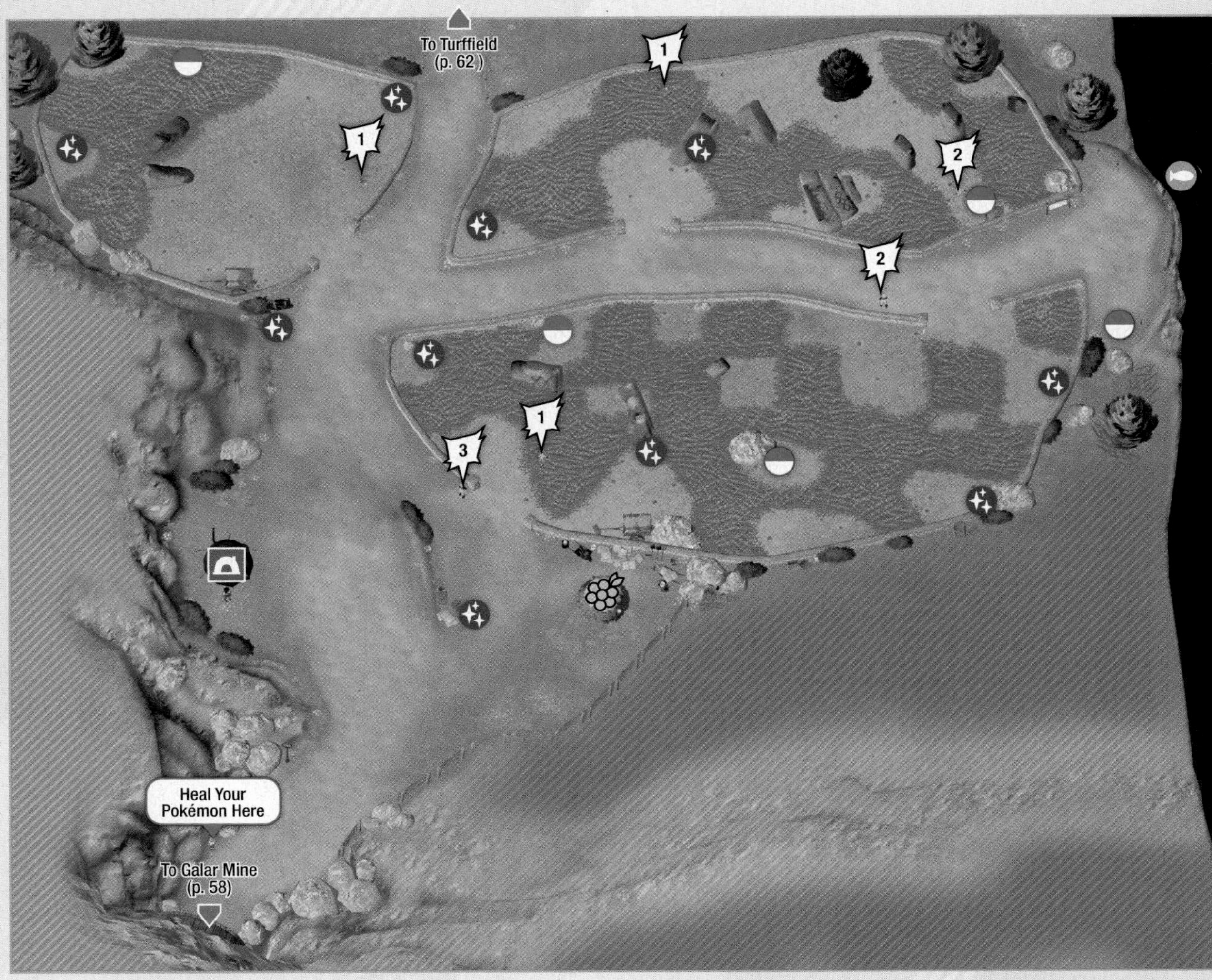

Visible Items

Visible Items
Cleanse Tag
Nest Ball ×3
Sharp Beak
TM07 Pin Missile
Silver Powder

Hidden Items

Hidden Items
Energy Powder
Ether
Paralyze Heal
Rare Candy
Energy Powder ×2
Repel
Paralyze Heal
Revival Herb
X Accuracy ×2
Energy Root

Tall Grass

No.	Pokémon	Rate
046	Yamper	○
066	Electrike	○
182	Meowth	○
191	Pumpkaboo (Average Size)	△
191	Pumpkaboo (Small Size)	☆
191	Pumpkaboo (Large Size)	☆
191	Pumpkaboo (Super Size)	★
194	Pikachu †	☆
194	Pikachu (Shield)	★
196	Eevee †	★
196	Eevee (Shield)	☆

Random Encounters

No.	Pokémon	Rate
034	Wooloo	○
059	Budew	☆
064	Joltik	△
182	Meowth	○

Random Encounters

No.	Pokémon	Rate
185	Milcery	○
187	Cutiefly	☆
189	Ferroseed	★

Wanderers

No.	Pokémon	Rate
164	Diglett	◎

Berry Trees

No.	Pokémon	Rate
024	Skwovet	◎

Fishing

No.	Pokémon	Rate
042	Chewtle	○
144	Magikarp	◎
146	Goldeen	△

◎ frequent ○ common △ average ☆ rare ★ almost never
† *Pokémon Sword* only (Shield) *Pokémon Shield* only

1

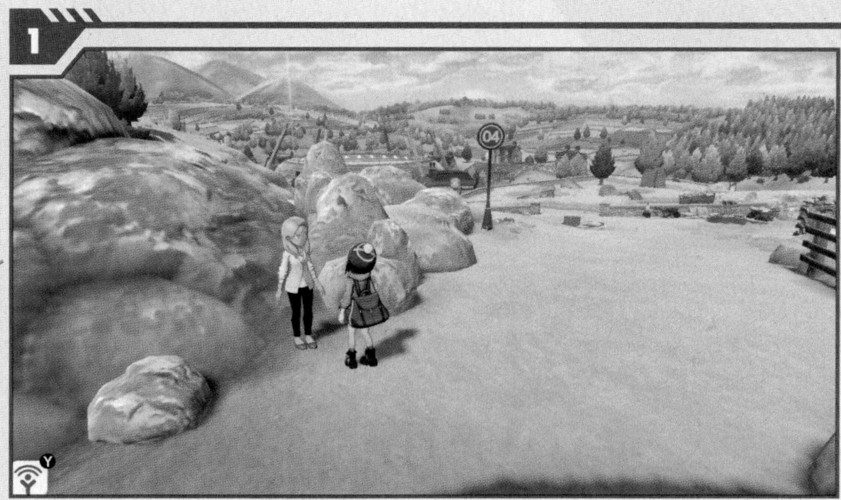

You'll see this woman just outside of Galar Mine. She's the sister of the lady who was at the entrance of the mine and will also provide Pokémon Center services! Now's a great time to get healed up, because though Route 4 may seem short, there's a lot to explore here and plenty of Trainers to battle, if you choose to.

2

Route 4 is characterized by its golden fields, and you'll find plenty of items if you take the time to search for them. Head eastward through the fields, and keep your eyes open for sparkles, since there's a Rare Candy hidden here! Once you reach the river, you'll find a fishing spot, if you'd care to cast a line. You'll also find a Sharp Beak, which boosts the power of Flying-type moves, down the road, among the various other items to be found both east and west of the main path.

3

Once you're done exploring, head north down the road and you'll be tackled by a runaway Wooloo being chased by the Gym Leader of the Grass Gym—Milo. As he puts it himself, he's rather partial to Grass-type Pokémon, so naturally that's what you should expect when you face him. Grass types tend to be weak to Bug-type moves, so make sure to nab a few Pokémon that can use them on Route 4 before you head down into Turffield!

CATCH!

Joltik

Joltik appear as random encounters in the yellow grass. Look out for the telltale ! mark.

Turffield

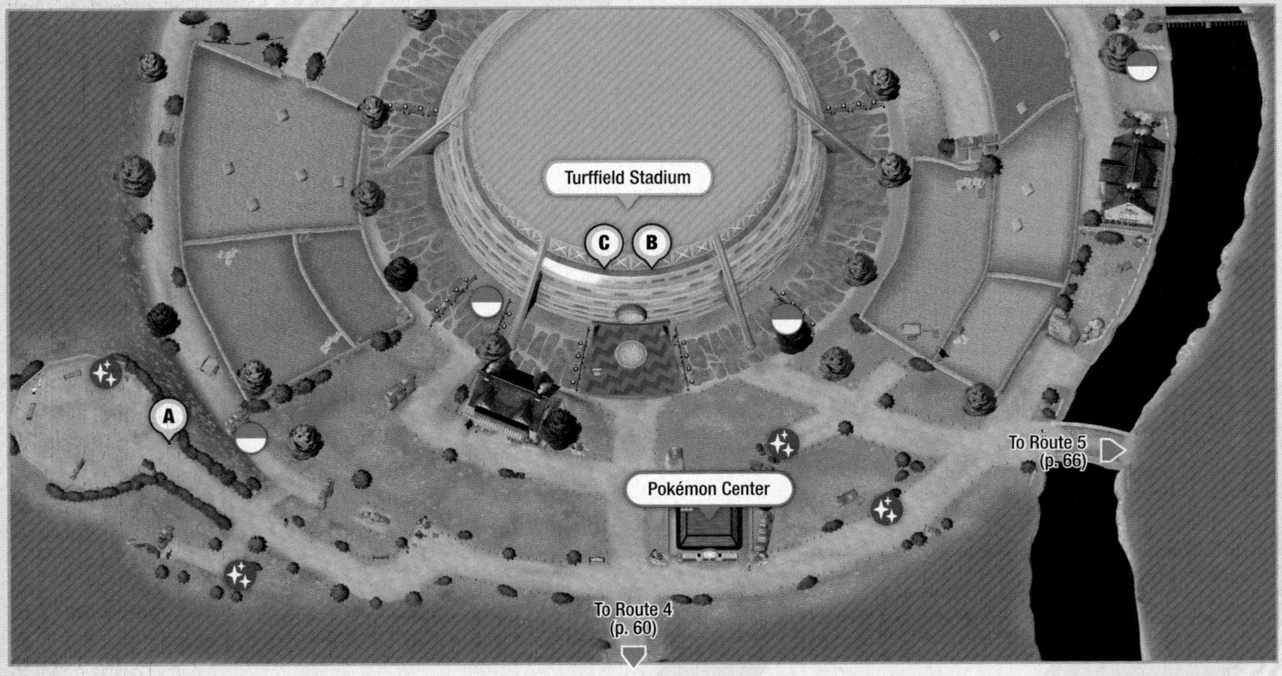

Legends of Galar: The Geoglyph

The great image carved into the hill in Turffield shows a giant figure with many smaller figures tumbling around its feet. What is this depicting? Sonia seems to think it shows the ancient disaster known as the Darkest Day—the catastrophe Sonia mentioned in Motostoke, which may have ties to the Dynamax phenomenon. After all, it seems unlikely that people three thousand years ago would just imagine giant Pokémon!

1

Turffield may seem like a quiet little country town, but there's more going on here than you may think! When you arrive from Route 4, you'll notice Hop waiting for you. He says Sonia was looking for you, but he isn't exactly helpful in telling you where she is now. Thankfully, Sonia's Yamper is here to guide you in the right direction, so just follow it toward the hill on the west side of town.

!

As you wander Turffield and admire the standing stones, keep your eyes open for items, too! There are several items you can find, both visible and hidden. Of particular interest is TM97 Brutal Swing, which you can find by just heading toward the Gym from the northeast stone structure!

Visible Items
X Attack ×3
Max Revive
TM97 Brutal Swing
With Water Mode Rotom Bike
TM11 Solar Beam

Hidden Items
Leaf Stone
Fresh Water
Energy Root
Everstone

Water Surface		
103	Crawdaunt	◎

◎ frequent ○ common △ average ☆ rare ★ almost never

2

At the top of the hill, you'll meet up with Sonia—and also get a fantastic view of the geoglyph! A geoglyph is a work of art using the ground as a giant canvas, and the one in Turffield is said to depict some sort of ancient cataclysm. Sonia will fill you in a bit more on the legend of the Darkest Day, and she'll give you Milo's League Card and some Revives to help you in your battle against him!

 Milo's League Card, Revive ×2

WALKTHROUGH

A

Speak to the little girl at the entrance to the clearing at the top of the hill, and she'll tell you about a treasure buried in Turffield. The standing stones are supposed to guide you to it, but the clue you get is more like a riddle. If you check the various stone structures around Turffield, you'll see that each one is engraved with a type, and the riddle mentions starting with Grass. Find the stone with Grass written on it, and then remember your type matchups—Grass is strong against Water but weak against Fire! Visit the stones in that order, and you'll find an Expert Belt buried at the end of the line!

 Expert Belt

3

When you're done exploring Turffield, head down to the Gym Stadium. It seems Hop's already defeated Milo and obtained a Grass Badge—he'll happily tell you that he managed it on his first try, too! Now it's your turn to get your first Gym Badge, so head into Turffield Stadium!

! Take some time to stop by the Rotomi at the Pokémon Center while you're wandering around Turffield. You'll find that a new function is now available—the Loto-ID! Depending on your luck, you could get a Moomoo Milk, a PP Up, a PP Max, a Rare Candy, or even a Master Ball!

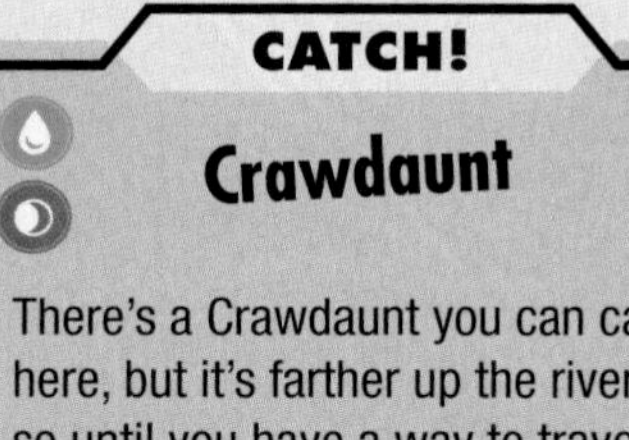

There's a Crawdaunt you can catch here, but it's farther up the river—so until you have a way to travel over water, it's out of your reach!

4

Once inside the Gym Stadium, talk to the various people there. They may have some helpful advice or maybe even an item to give you! As soon as you feel you're ready to start the Gym mission, you can talk to the girl at the far end of the lobby to change into your uniform and get the mission going!

B

It's hard to miss the Ball Guy when you enter the stadium. They have a Poké Ball for you again, but it's a bit more special this time! You'll receive a Friend Ball, which will make the caught Pokémon more friendly toward you!

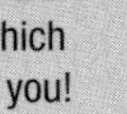

 Friend Ball

C

Just past the Ball Guy, you'll see a young lad in a blue sweater. It seems that he's having trouble catching a Galarian Meowth and is willing to trade his Meowth from another region to get one! You can catch Galarian Meowth on Route 4, so head out there if you haven't caught one already!

 Meowth

Dynamaxing in Gym Battles

You may have seen Dynamax Pokémon out in the Wild Area, but you can also Dynamax your Pokémon during your battle against Milo and other Gym Leaders! Like in the Max Raid Battles in the Wild Area, you can only Dynamax your Pokémon once, and it will only last for three turns. The same restrictions apply to the Gym Leader you're facing, and they won't get to perform multiple moves in one turn or create a mysterious barrier, so you'll largely be on even footing. Gym Leaders choose to Dynamax their Pokémon at different points in the battle, so plan carefully before you decide to Dynamax your own!

Turffield Gym Mission

1 The Gym mission of Turffield Gym is to herd the unruly Wooloo to the blue area at the end of each field. There the Wooloo will bash through the wall of straw bales and let you move forward. Do this four times and you'll reach the end! The Wooloo will stay in the blue area once you get them there, so you don't need to worry about herding them all at once. Herding will get more difficult as you progress—from the second field onward, Gym Trainers will have Yamper running around, which scare the Wooloo and cause them to scatter. Try avoiding the Yamper, or if that's proving difficult, defeat the Gym Trainer. That'll get the Yamper to stop running around!

Herding Wooloo can be a bit tricky, since they can scatter if you get too close to them. We suggest running in a zigzag pattern a bit of a distance behind them—this will help keep them together and make it that much easier to get them all to the blue areas!

2 Once you've herded the Wooloo to the end of the fields, it's time to head up the stairs and face Milo, the Grass-type Gym Leader! Make sure your team's in order and head onto the pitch for your very first battle for a Gym Badge!

Milo

Both of Milo's Pokémon are pure Grass type, which means they have a number of different weaknesses for you to exploit for supereffective damage. Check out the type matchup chart if you need a refresher on them (p. 383). If you don't have a Pokémon with a type advantage over Milo's, try heading back to Galar Mine and catching a Carkol. Milo will Dynamax his Eldegoss the first chance he gets, giving it increased HP and powerful Max Moves, like Max Overgrowth. Make sure you Dynamax a Pokémon that can stand up to it. If you're having trouble with Eldegoss's higher HP, try giving it a status condition like poison or a burn to drain its HP each turn!

3 If you defeat Milo, you'll be rewarded with a Grass Badge. You've now obtained the first Gym Badge for the Gym Challenge and taken your first steps toward facing Leon for the seat of Champion! But that's not all you'll receive for your victory—you'll also be given a replica of Milo's uniform and TM10 Magical Leaf!

 Grass Uniform, TM10 Magical Leaf

The Grass Badge

So now you've obtained the Grass Badge, but what does that mean? Well, as Milo will explain after your battle, Gym Badges allow you to catch more-powerful Pokémon! The Grass Badge will allow you to catch Pokémon of up to Lv. 25. Each Gym Badge will also let you buy more items at Poké Marts and give you access to more Poké Jobs, so make sure to stop by a Pokémon Center whenever you get a new Badge! The Grass Badge will add Great Balls and Super Potions to the shop lineup!

5

As Milo tells you, your next stop is Hulbury, which lies beyond Route 5. Head out of the Gym Stadium and cross the bridge to the east, and you'll be on your way!

Route 5

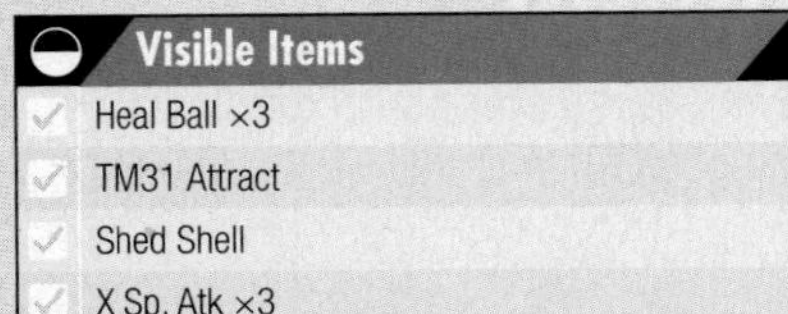

Visible Items
✓ Heal Ball ×3
✓ TM31 Attract
✓ Shed Shell
✓ X Sp. Atk ×3

Hidden Items
✓ Big Mushroom ×2
✓ Health Feather*
✓ Muscle Feather*
✓ Resist Feather*
✓ Genius Feather*
✓ Clever Feather*
✓ Swift Feather*
✓ Pretty Feather*
✓ Absorb Bulb

*You have a chance to randomly find one of these feathers at each spot on the bridge.

Tall Grass		
050	Minccino †	△
050	Minccino 🛡	○
094	Stufful	○
124	Drifloon	☆
210	Swirlix †	○
212	Spritzee 🛡	○
217	Wobbuffet	△
218	Farfetch'd †	☆

Random Encounters		
011	Dottler	○
037	Lombre 🛡	○
040	Nuzleaf †	○
104	Nincada	☆
205	Applin	△

Random Encounters		
208	Espurr	○
210	Swirlix †	△
212	Spritzee 🛡	△
214	Dewpider	☆

Wanderers		
◆127	Eldegoss	◎

Berry Trees		
024	Skwovet	◎

Fishing		
042	Chewtle	○
144	Magikarp	◎
146	Goldeen	△

◎ frequent ○ common △ average ☆ rare ★ almost never
† *Pokémon Sword* only 🛡 *Pokémon Shield* only

1

Route 5 is quite a bit longer than Route 4, and there's a lot going on here. Make it past a battle against a reporter and her cameraman, and you'll see a road splitting off down to the south. There you'll find more Trainers, a Trainer's camp, a Berry tree, a fishing spot, and some items, including TM31 Attract! It's pretty well hidden in the southeast corner of the area, so make sure you don't miss it!

2

Follow the path back up north, and you'll see a rather large house in front of you. This is the Pokémon Nursery, where you can leave your Pokémon to find Eggs—as long as the conditions are right! If you want to learn more about Pokémon Eggs, head inside and speak to the old lady behind the counter or check out the section beginning on page 234!

3

Once you've stopped by the Pokémon Nursery, keep on heading east, and you'll reach a bridge—and a doctor being harassed by two Team Yell Grunts! You'll have to defeat both of them, but if you do, the kind doctor will reward you with the very bike Team Yell was after!

Rotom Bike

A

Inside the Nursery, you'll find a lady with her Toxel. She's eager to have it raised by a proper Trainer, and that means you'll get to take it with you! Toxel is a pretty rare Pokémon, so it doesn't hurt to add it to your Pokédex now. She'll even give you five Exp. Candies XS to make raising it easier!

Toxel, Exp. Candy XS ×5

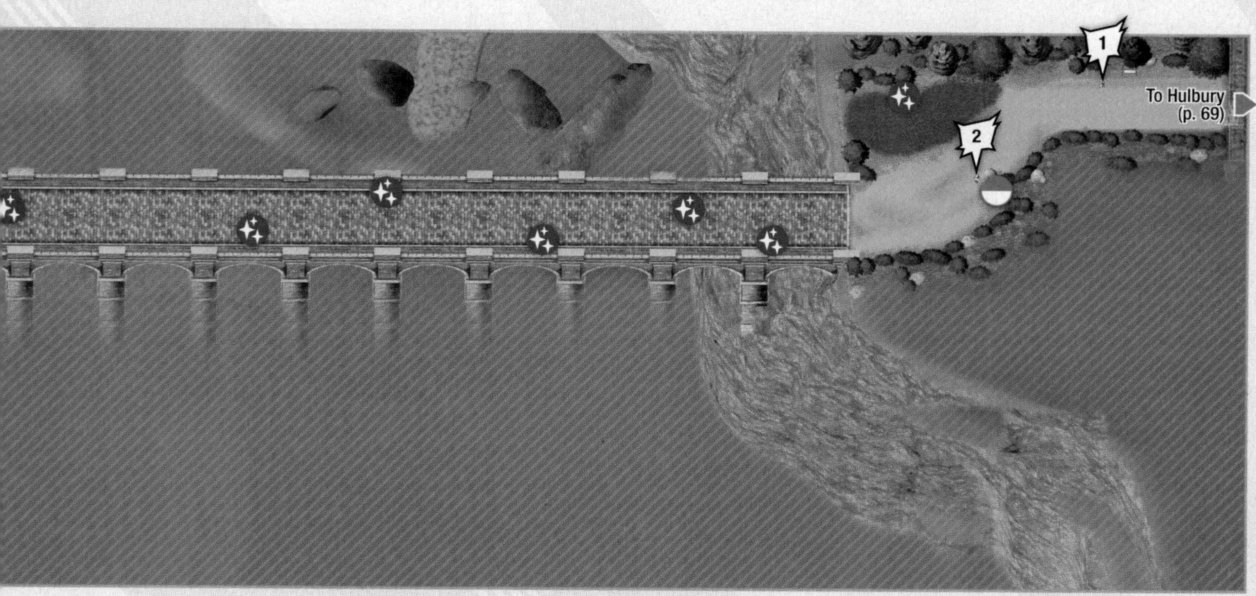

Team Yell Grunt

After battling a Gym Leader, you won't have much trouble battling a Team Yell Grunt. He uses two Dark-type Pokémon, Thievul and Zigzagoon. If you've been raising any Pokémon with Fighting-, Bug-, or Fairy-type moves, they'll easily handle this troublesome Trainer and his Pokémon!

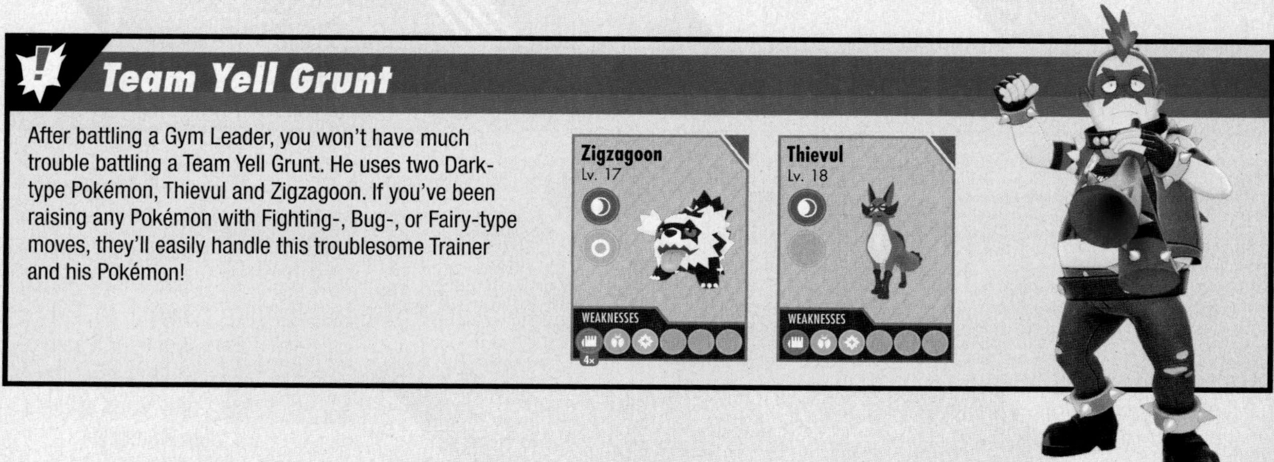

Team Yell Grunt

This Grunt's Sableye might throw you for a bit of a loop compared to what Team Yell Grunts have used so far. It's Dark type, like other Pokémon the Grunts use, but it's also Ghost type. This means only Fairy-type moves are super effective against it, and it will take no damage from Normal-, Fighting-, or Psychic-type moves!

The Rotom Bike

Now you have the Rotom Bike, which you can ride by pressing ⊕ or ⊖. It'll help you get around a lot faster, and it will also enable you to take part in the Rotom Rally in the Wild Area (p. 274–276). Whenever you see sparks around your bike, press Ⓑ, L, or R to get a speed boost! Your bike will need to recharge afterwards, though—watch for the sparks to reappear to know when you can boost off again!

4

Bike down the bridge, past an excellent view of the Wild Area with Hammerlocke in the distance, and you'll run into Hop. He's raring for another battle, so make sure your team's ready to oblige him! After the battle, he'll be on his way, but he'll leave you with a Revive before he dashes off.

Revive

Hop

Hop's grown as a Trainer since winning his first Gym Badge, and his Pokémon are the proof! Two of them have evolved since your last battle with him, but they're all the same types as last time. Fighting-type moves are still your best option against Wooloo, but you can also try sending out a Ghost-type Pokémon if you want to keep Wooloo from using its Normal-type moves with their same-type attack bonus. Hop's Thwackey, Raboot, or Drizzile should have a hard time beating your first partner Pokémon if you've been raising it well. Corvisquire is speedy, but you can try to slow it down by paralyzing it with Thunder Wave, then hit it with supereffective Electric-type moves. You could also send out a bulky Rock-type Pokémon like Onix or Carkol, as they'll resist Corvisquire's Flying-type moves.

If you chose Grookey

If you chose Scorbunny

If you chose Sobble

The bridge on Route 5 will have lots of little sparkles that, as you know, are items you can pick up. The ones on the bridge are actually various feathers, most of which you can use to increase the base points of one of your Pokémon! To find out more about base points, read through pages 178–179. The only exception is the Pretty Feather, which you can sell at Poké Marts for a fair amount of money!

5

Once you're over the bridge, you only have a little more ways to go. Past a couple of Trainers, you'll see a tunnel that leads straight to Hulbury!

Hulbury

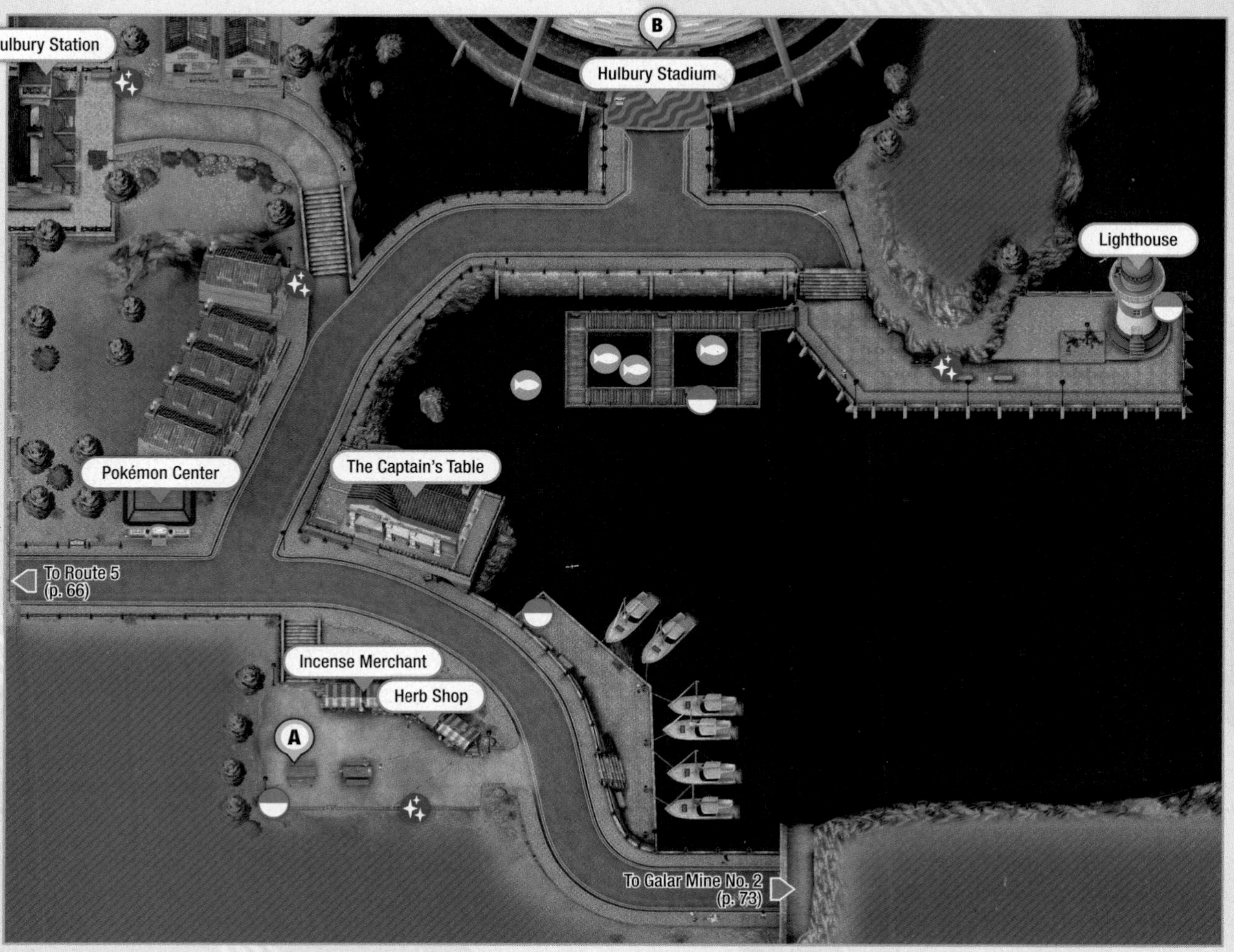

Hulbury Station
B
Hulbury Stadium
Lighthouse
Pokémon Center
The Captain's Table
To Route 5 (p. 66)
Incense Merchant
Herb Shop
A
To Galar Mine No. 2 (p. 73)

Visible Items

Item
Magnet
Shell Bell
Net Ball ×5
TM82 Electroweb

Hidden Items

Item
X Sp. Def
Full Heal
X Speed ×2
Super Potion ×2

Incense Merchant

Item	Price
Full Incense	₽5,000
Lax Incense	₽5,000
Luck Incense	₽11,000
Odd Incense	₽2,000
Pure Incense	₽6,000
Rock Incense	₽2,000
Rose Incense	₽2,000
Sea Incense	₽2,000
Wave Incense	₽2,000

Herb Shop

Item	Price
Energy Powder	₽500
Energy Root	₽1,200
Heal Powder	₽300
Revival Herb	₽2,800

Fishing

No.	Pokémon	Frequency
042	Chewtle	△
154	Basculin (Red-Striped Form) (*Sword* only)	△
154	Basculin (Blue-Striped Form) (*Shield* only)	△
155	Wishiwashi	☆
180	Arrokuda	◎
220	Chinchou	○

◎ frequent ○ common △ average ☆ rare ★ almost never
Pokémon Sword only *Pokémon Shield* only

CATCH!

Basculin

Basculin don't only look different depending on the game version you're playing—they can also have different Abilities. If you want to get both forms, trade with another player!

1

The first thing you'll see when you arrive in Hulbury is a Pokémon Center. Stop by if you need to heal up your Pokémon, and then carry on down the road. You'll promptly run into a crowd of people—turns out Chairman Rose is here, and he's been stopped by a couple of his fans! Once he notices you, he'll invite you to dinner with him—but on the condition that you successfully defeat Nessa and obtain a Water Badge.

OLEANA

Oleana is Chairman Rose's assistant, and she's in charge of his work schedule and the like. Though she may seem cold and somewhat harsh, it's clear that she's also quite dedicated to Rose and his work. Being quite business savvy, she also serves as the vice president of Rose's company and is in fact largely in charge of its day-to-day running.

2

You'll find the restaurant just east of where you met Rose and Oleana, but Oleana will be blocking the entrance. Remember, you need to get a Water Badge before you can dine with the chairman! Why not head down the stairs right by you to check out Hulbury's open-air market? There's an item you can pick up, and the shops also offer some useful wares that can only be found here!

The Incense Merchant

The Incense Merchant has a fine selection of incense, from ones that boost the power of moves to some stranger ones, with effects like making your Pokémon move slower! Of particular interest is the Luck Incense—it's the most expensive incense, but it's well worth the money. Have one of your Pokémon hold it, and you'll receive double the prize money from Trainer battles that Pokémon participates in!

!

If you decide not to buy Luck Incense or don't have enough money, don't fret. You can find the Amulet Coin in just a little while, once you defeat Nessa and make it past Galar Mine No. 2. The Amulet Coin has exactly the same effect as Luck Incense, so you'll be able to earn double prize money even if you don't buy the incense!

The Herb Shop

The Herb Shop is one of the unique shops you can find in Hulbury. As the name suggests, you can buy various medicinal herbs here. These are affordable and powerful healing items, but be careful about using them—they all taste awful. Any Pokémon you use them on will feel less friendly toward you.

3

Once you've explored the open-air market, keep wandering through Hulbury. As with other towns and cities, you'll find some items scattered about, and you don't want to miss out on freebies! You hopefully found the Magnet in the southwest corner of the market, and there's a TM near the lighthouse here. There are also several fishing spots at the town docks, so why not relax with a bit of fishing if you're in the mood?

A

You'll find a backpacker sitting at one of the tables in the open-air market who wants to trade her Cottonee for a Minccino. If you're interested but haven't caught a Minccino yet, you can find them on Route 5.

 Cottonee

While you're at the lighthouse, you'll also likely spot Nessa, too—she's the Hulbury Gym Leader, and apparently she already knows who you are. Speak to her, and she'll give you her League Card before heading back to her Gym. Follow after her to return to Hulbury Stadium, and head inside!

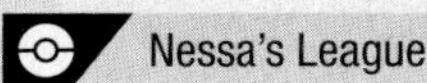

Nessa's League Card

You'll be encountering a lot of Water-type Pokémon during Hulbury's Gym mission and your battle with Nessa. Make sure your team is prepared for this, and then speak to the girl at the far end of the lobby to get the Gym mission started!

B Before you begin the Gym mission, you'll no doubt notice that the Ball Guy's made their way here to Hulbury. Talk to them, and they'll give you another rare Poké Ball—the Lure Ball!

Lure Ball

Hulbury Gym Mission

The Gym mission of Hulbury is a maze made out of various platforms and waterfalls. Look carefully at each waterfall, and you'll see that it's falling through a grate of a specific color—and nearby, there will be another grate of the same color with no waterfall. Pressing a switch causes a waterfall of the corresponding color to change where it falls. If this sounds confusing, don't worry. We'll guide you through which switches you need to press to get to Nessa!

1 Make your way past the Trainer, and then press the red switch, the yellow switch, and the red switch again. This will clear the way to the staircase. Onward to step 2!

2 Once up the stairs, ignore the red switch for now and head up around the outer platform past a Trainer to hit the yellow switch. Then, move on down to hit the red switch, and then go up the second set of stairs and on to step 3!

3 Follow this platform to the west until you can't anymore. Then head straight south down the platform and hit the yellow switch at the very bottom, then make your way up toward the left to hit the red switch. After that, hit the blue switch to the right, then head down the stairs just below it to get back to the central platform. You're now clear to head up to the finish line!

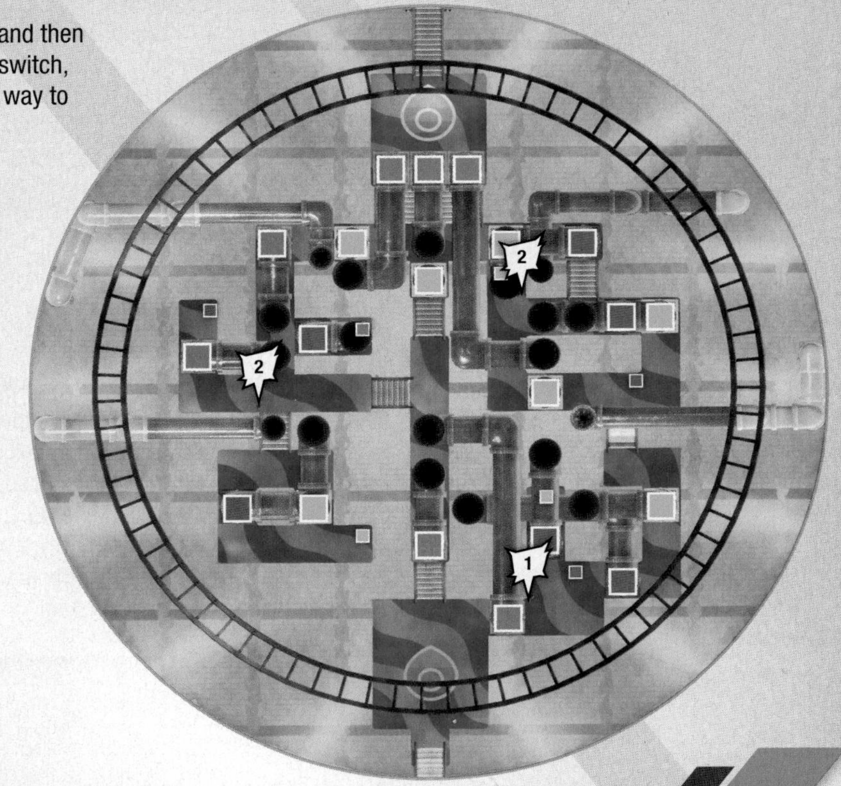

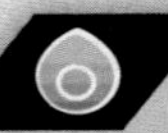

Nessa

Nessa's a pro when it comes to Water-type Pokémon. Make sure your team is packing some Grass- or Electric-type moves, or you'll get soaked! Grass moves will be especially effective against Nessa's Drednaw, which is both Water and Rock type. Remember that if Nessa's Drednaw uses Max Geyser, it will change the weather to rain, strengthening Water-type moves. If you don't want that to happen, you'll need to plan your own Dynamax carefully and use a Max Move to change the weather to something more favorable for your team. If you've been battling often, a few Pokémon on your team should have evolved by now, so Drednaw should be the only opponent that might give you trouble. But don't underestimate Goldeen or Arrokuda! Both have good Attack and Speed for unevolved Pokémon.

4 After you defeat Nessa and receive your Water Badge, you'll also get TM36 Whirlpool and a replica of Nessa's uniform once you're back in the lobby! Now you're ready to have that celebratory dinner with Chairman Rose, so leave the Gym and head to the restaurant to the east of the Pokémon Center!

 Water Uniform, TM36 Whirlpool

The Water Badge

You've now obtained your second Gym Badge—the Water Badge! It'll allow you to catch Pokémon of up to Lv. 30 and will also add Poké Dolls to the stock of Poké Marts!

6

Oleana will be right outside once you leave the Gym Stadium. She'll tell you to get a move on to the restaurant, and she'll also give you one of Chairman Rose's League Cards just in case you forgot what he looked like. You might as well go now so you don't keep the esteemed businessman waiting too long!

 Rose's League Card

7 Once you get to the restaurant, head to the back and you'll see Rose, Oleana...and, surprisingly, Sonia! It seems that she was invited to dinner with Rose, too. Once you sit down, you'll be treated to a bit of discussion about Professor Magnolia's research, but sadly the chairman will need to be on his way shortly. Sonia will also head off, but she'll give you TM79 Retaliate as her own way of celebrating your victory over Nessa!

 TM79 Retaliate

8 Leave the restaurant, and Hop will let you know where your next stop will be. Though the next Gym is back in Motostoke, apparently the Motostoke Gym Leader is in Galar Mine No. 2 doing some special training. You can't get his Gym Badge if he's not in his Gym, so head to Galar Mine No. 2 via the tunnel in the southeast of Hulbury and see if you can find him!

Kabu is a Fire-type specialist, so you may want to take a look at your team and add Water-, Ground-, or Rock-type Pokémon. Luckily, you can find wild Pokémon of all these types in Galar Mine No. 2, or you can fish up some Water-type Pokémon before leaving Hulbury!

Galar Mine No. 2

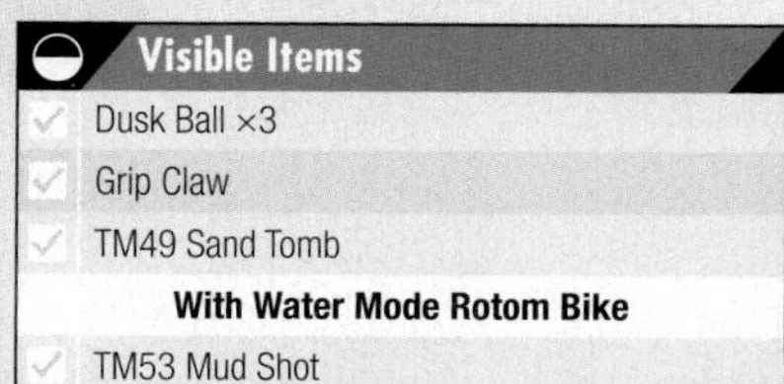

Visible Items
Dusk Ball ×3
Grip Claw
TM49 Sand Tomb
With Water Mode Rotom Bike
TM53 Mud Shot

Hidden Items
Star Piece
Soft Sand

Ground		
042	Chewtle	☆
176	Noibat	△
222	Croagunk (Pokémon Shield only)	△
224	Scraggy (Pokémon Sword only)	△
227	Shuckle	☆
230	Shellos (East Sea)	○
232	Wimpod	○
234	Binacle	△

Water Surface		
◇231	Gastrodon (East Sea)	◎

Wanderers		
◇043	Drednaw	◎
226	Stunfisk	◎

Fishing		
042	Chewtle	○
102	Corphish	△
228	Barboach	◎

◎ frequent ○ common △ average ☆ rare ★ almost never

† *Pokémon Sword* only ● *Pokémon Shield* only

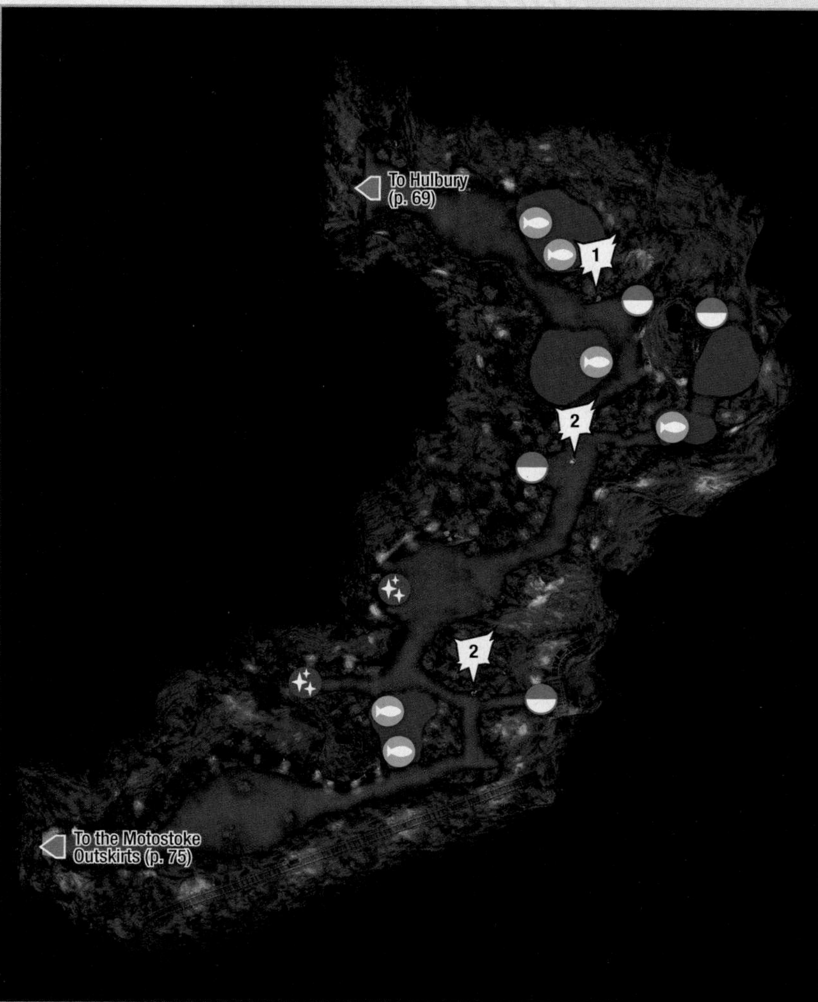

1

You won't get too far into Galar Mine No. 2 before you're running into Bede again. He certainly seems to enjoy hanging out in mines and challenging passersby to battles! You can ask him to wait a moment if you need some time to prepare, but if you want to keep going, you'll need to defeat him!

 Bede's League Card

Bede

Bede apparently hasn't taken his loss to you very well. His team has grown much stronger, and he's added another Pokémon to it. Thankfully, they all still share the same type as last time—Psychic. This means that if you've got a Pokémon with a powerful Bug-, Ghost-, or Dark-type move, you should more than stand a chance. Sending out a Dark-type Pokémon in battle against Bede is still a great strategy, since it means he can't use any Psychic-type moves to deal damage to your Pokémon.

2

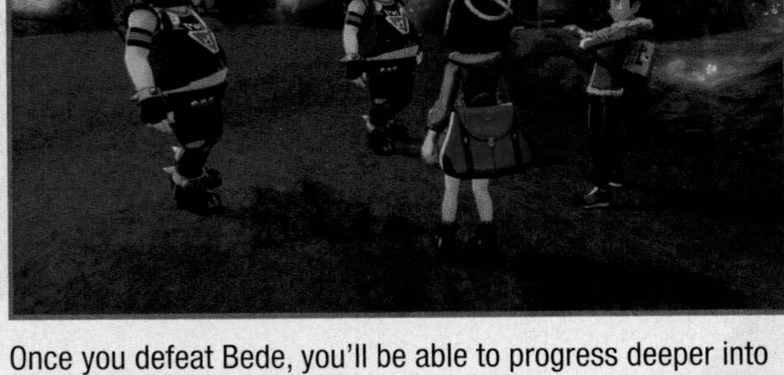

Once you defeat Bede, you'll be able to progress deeper into the mine. Follow the path, and you'll eventually run into a pair of Team Yell Grunts blocking your path. They'll act polite at first, but you should know by now they're probably up to no good. Thankfully, you'll be joined by Hop (how'd he get behind you?), so get ready for a Double Battle!

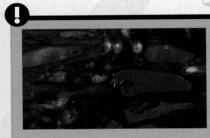

! You might notice that there are sections of the mine that you can't reach right now—you'll need to get the bike upgrade that lets you ride over water to fully explore the area!

! Be careful when walking over what look like tiny Poké Balls on the ground—these are actually the lips of Stunfisk! They're trying to lure you over, only to surprise you by leaping out of the ground!

Team Yell Grunts

Time for another Double Battle with Hop at your side. While Team Yell's Linoone, Thievul, and Liepard are all Dark-type Pokémon, Pancham is Fighting type. The only shared weakness across all four of these Pokémon is Fairy-type moves, but if you don't happen to have any Pokémon that knows one, don't be afraid to swap out your Pokémon as needed.

3

Send Team Yell packing, and it's back to exploring the mines! Take a moment to pick up TM49 Sand Tomb, which you can find just past the area where you faced Team Yell, and then keep going along the path. You'll soon meet Kabu, who's apparently just finished teaching Team Yell a lesson of his own. Once the Team Yell Grunts run off again, Kabu will introduce himself and give you directions back to Motostoke. Now it's just a short run to the Motostoke Outskirts for you and Hop!

Motostoke Outskirts

Visible Items
Amulet Coin
Great Ball ×3

Hidden Items
PP Up
Health Feather*
Muscle Feather*
Resist Feather*
Genius Feather*
Clever Feather*
Swift Feather*
Pretty Feather*

*You have a chance to randomly find one of these feathers at each spot on the bridge.

Tall Grass		
020	Noctowl †	◎
020	Noctowl (Shield)	○
241	Hatenna	△
244	Salandit (Shield)	☆
248	Throh (Shield)	☆
249	Sawk †	☆
250	Koffing	△
253	Sudowoodo	○

Random Encounters		
042	Chewtle	△
168	Roggenrola	○
222	Croagunk (Shield)	○
224	Scraggy †	○
238	Impidimp	☆
246	Pawniard	○

◎ frequent ○ common △ average ☆ rare ★ almost never
† *Pokémon Sword* only (Shield) *Pokémon Shield* only

1

Leaving Galar Mine No. 2 brings you to the Motostoke Outskirts, which lie right by Motostoke itself. As Kabu said, it's a fairly straight shot to reach the big city—but there are still a couple of Trainers along the way, so don't let your guard down!

! Don't miss the Amulet Coin behind the sign you'll find to the northwest of the mine exit. This works much like the Luck Incense you can obtain in Hulbury—it will double any prize money you earn if a Pokémon holding it participates in the battle! The effect won't stack with Luck Incense, but it's still nice to be able to choose between two Pokémon to send out.

2

Soon you'll come to a bridge that leads directly to the east side of upper Motostoke. Much like the bridge on Route 5, you can find various feathers here, too. Cross the bridge, and you're back in Motostoke again!

Motostoke (Revisited)

1

Here you are, back in Motostoke. Kabu's regarded as the first real roadblock for Gym Challengers, so you'd better rest up before facing him. Head to the Budew Drop Inn to catch some shut-eye with your Pokémon! It's the same inn you stayed at when you first came to Motostoke—the one to the west of the stadium!

2

Inside the inn, you'll see Marnie gazing at the statue. She apparently wants to see if she's ready for the next part of the Gym Challenge—and that means a battle! It's a good chance for you to find out how good she is, too, so make sure your party is ready and accept her challenge!

Marnie

While Marnie does use Dark-type Pokémon like her personal cheering squad, Team Yell, she has a bit more type diversity than they do. Her first Pokémon, Croagunk, isn't even Dark type! It's a Poison- and Fighting-type Pokémon, meaning that it's doubly weak to Psychic-type moves. Don't forget to use an Antidote if Croagunk poisons your Pokémon, and make sure to switch out any Psychic-type Pokémon after Croagunk faints. You don't want a Psychic type going up against Scraggy or Morpeko! They're both Dark types, so they share a couple of common weaknesses. Aim for these and don't let your guard down, especially against Marnie's Morpeko. It may look cute, but its Attack and Speed are no joke!

3

After the battle, you'll both get some much-needed rest. The next morning, Marnie will be waiting for you in the lobby, and she'll give you Kabu's League Card! Have a look at it if you want to find out a bit more about what to expect when you face the Fire-type Gym Leader. Marnie will also give you two Burn Heals, just to make sure you're extra prepared!

 Kabu's League Card, Burn Heal ×2

4

Now you're free to roam around Motostoke. If there are any items or events you missed, now's another chance to get them! You may also want to stop by a Pokémon Center to stock up on Potions and Burn Heals—and maybe purchase a TM or two, if any strike your fancy. Some extra Poké Balls will also be handy for the Gym mission. When you're ready, get changed into your uniform as always and get the Gym mission started!

You might consider visiting the Battle Café in lower Motostoke. It's a good way to get items that heal status conditions, but don't get too confident—the Café Master's strengthened his team, and you'll be facing him in a Double Battle now (p. 194)!

The wild Pokémon you encounter in Kabu's mission are actually pretty unusual. You can catch Vulpix, Litwick, and Sizzlipede, which are all difficult to find elsewhere. If you were looking for a Fire-type Pokémon to add to your team, this is a good place to find one!

Motostoke Gym Mission

1 As Dan explains, your goal is to earn five points—you'll earn 1 point for defeating a wild Pokémon and 2 points for catching each of them. This is why having Quick Balls is a good idea. Once the battle begins, immediately throw a Quick Ball, and if you're lucky, that'll be 2 points in the bag for you. Do that three times, and you'll be done with the mission!

2 Now it's time to face the Man-of-Fire himself, Gym Leader Kabu! There's a reason why so many Gym Challengers don't make it past him—make sure your team is ready!

Kabu

Kabu and his Pokémon might be red-hot, but you'll keep your cool as long as you go in prepared with a few Burn Heals and some Water-, Ground-, or Rock-type Pokémon. Remember that the burn status condition reduces a Pokémon's Attack stat until it's cured. If you can't heal the condition, make sure that the burned Pokémon isn't using physical moves! While Water- and Ground-type moves are good choices for this battle, Rock-type moves will be especially helpful. Kabu's ace Pokémon is a Centiskorch that can Gigantamax! Its signature G-Max Move is the fearsome G-Max Centiferno, which prevents the target from fleeing and deals damage to the target every turn for up to five turns! Centiskorch is both Fire and Bug type, so it will take four times the damage from Rock-type moves. This is why Rock-type moves are a great choice, especially Max Rockfall. Take out Kabu's Centiskorch quickly to ensure its G-Max Move doesn't burn you to a crisp. If you want to play more defensively, you could also try to stall with your Dynamax Pokémon by using Max Guard until Kabu's Pokémon runs out of Dynamax turns, but remember that Max Guard has a higher chance of failing the more turns in a row you use it!

3 You've now successfully obtained three Gym Badges—nobody can call you a rookie Trainer anymore! Hop will be waiting for you in the lobby of Motostoke Stadium to celebrate your victory, and Dan will give you both TM38 Will-O-Wisp and a Fire Uniform as rewards.

Fire Uniform, TM38 Will-O-Wisp

The Fire Badge

If you manage to defeat Kabu, you'll earn a Fire Badge! Now you'll be able to catch wild Pokémon of up to Lv. 35, and Repels will be available at Poké Marts!

5

You've proven yourself good enough to brave the northern section of the Wild Area and the strong Pokémon there. You'll also now be able to enter your next destination: Hammerlocke! Milo, Nessa, and Kabu will meet up with you at Motostoke's entrance to give you a proper send-off, and then it'll be time to explore the Wild Area once more. But you barely set foot outside Motostoke before Bede shows up with his usual charming attitude. This time he'll push Hop just a little too far, and the two will head off to engage in a Pokémon battle, leaving you to your own devices.

North Wild Area

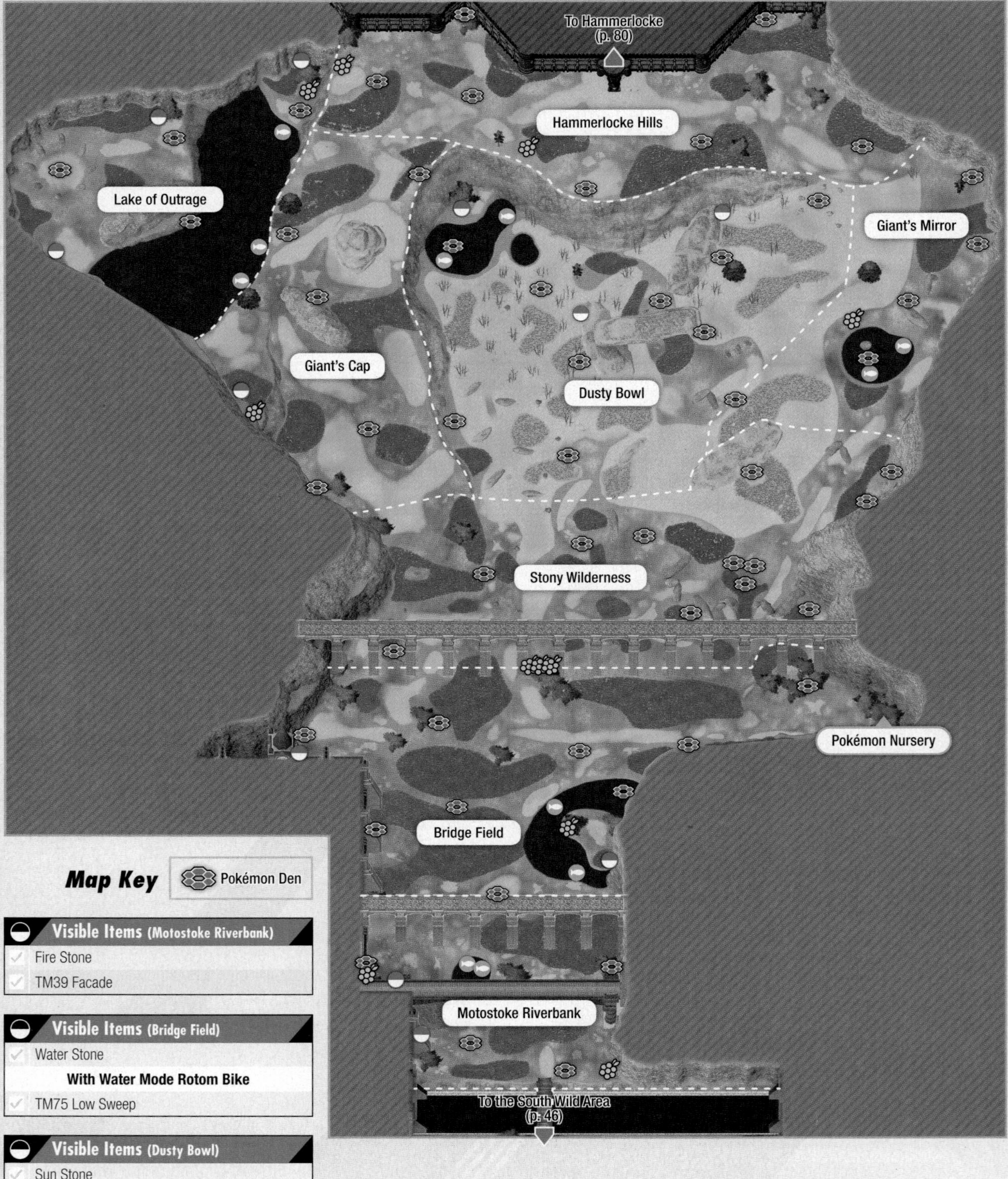

Map Key

Pokémon Den

Visible Items (Motostoke Riverbank)
Fire Stone
TM39 Facade

Visible Items (Bridge Field)
Water Stone
With Water Mode Rotom Bike
TM75 Low Sweep

Visible Items (Dusty Bowl)
Sun Stone
Moon Stone
With Water Mode Rotom Bike
TM73 Cross Poison

Visible Items (Giant's Cap)
Dawn Stone

Visible Items (Lake of Outrage)
With Water Mode Rotom Bike
Focus Sash
Assault Vest
TM65 Shadow Claw

Remember that detailed breakdowns of the Wild Area, including all the Pokémon you can encounter, are covered in the special section beginning on page 249.

1

While it's possible to visit the northern section of the Wild Area at any point after your first visit, now you'll be able to take full advantage of everything you can find. You'll be able to catch stronger Pokémon there, including ones in Max Raid Battles! You could just head straight to Hammerlocke—it's clearly visible in the distance, after all—but there are lots of goodies hidden around the north side of the Wild Area, as well as some helpful people you can meet!

Now is also a good time to explore the Giant's Seat, on the east side of the Wild Area's southern zones, since the Pokémon there will be more manageable now. It's worth searching around, since you can find TM81 Bulldoze behind the giant rock. You can find another, TM39 Facade, nestled behind some pipes just after the bridge leading to the north portion of the Wild Area.

2

If you've had enough of the Wild Area for now, head up to Hammerlocke and speak to the League staff member in front of the entrance. He'll check to make sure you have three Gym Badges, but before you can move on inside, Bede will show up to give you some more attitude. It sounds like he managed to defeat Hop in their battle—hopefully your rival didn't take it too hard. Bede will make his way into Hammerlocke, so follow him up the stairs!

The Pokémon Nursery

In the area called Bridge Field, you'll find a branch of the Pokémon Nursery to the east! Leave your Pokémon here as you explore the Wild Area, and you won't have to go to Route 5 each time you want to check for an Egg (p. 234)!

More Rotom Rallyists

Near the Nursery, you'll find yet another Rotom Rallyist (p. 274). There will also be one near the Lake of Outrage and another by the entrance to Hammerlocke, too. That means new Rotom Rally courses for you to try out and more places to spend your Watts!

The Digging Duo

Just before the Nursery, you'll find the Digging Duo (p. 278), twins who excel in digging up unusual items! You can pay either of them 500 W to do some digging for you—one brother can keep digging over and over, while the other brother is more likely to dig up rare items!

Hammerlocke

Visible Items
Strawberry Sweet
Wise Glasses
Hyper Potion ×2
Muscle Band
TM29 Charm

Hidden Items
Nugget
Dire Hit
Rare Candy
Super Repel
X Attack ×2

Poké Mart (west)	
TM13 Fire Spin	₽10,000
TM23 Thief	₽10,000
TM32 Sandstorm	₽10,000
TM33 Rain Dance	₽10,000
TM34 Sunny Day	₽10,000
TM35 Hail	₽10,000
TM50 Bullet Seed	₽10,000
TM55 Brine	₽10,000

Poké Mart (central)	
Dire Hit	₽1,000
Dive Ball	₽1,000
Dusk Ball	₽1,000
Guard Spec.	₽1,500
Timer Ball	₽1,000
X Accuracy	₽1,000
X Speed	₽1,000

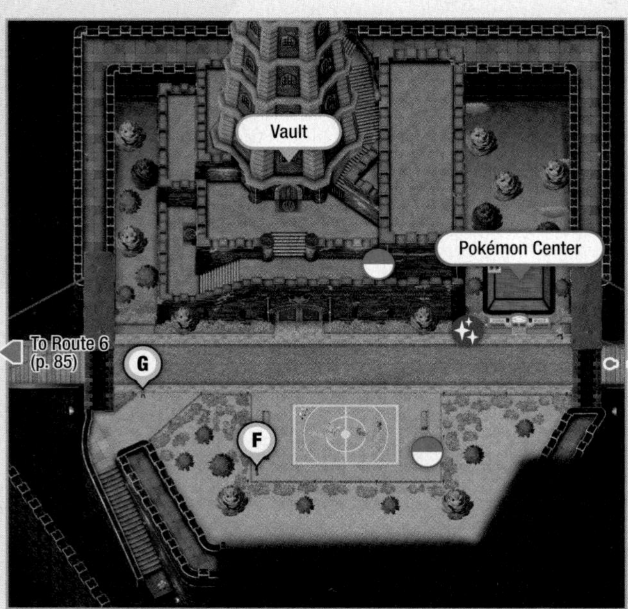

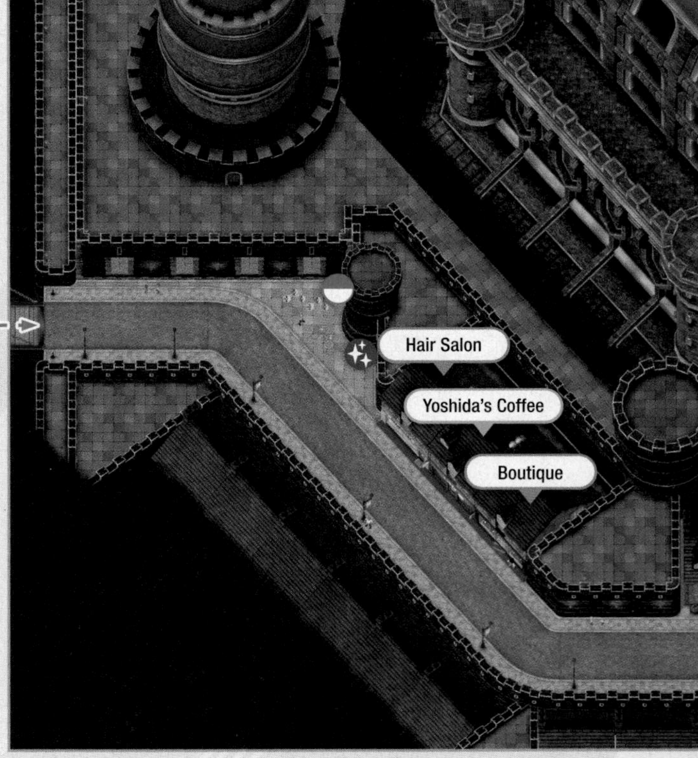

1

Welcome to Hammerlocke, the second major city in the Galar region. This is where Chairman Rose has set up a power plant to provide the entire region with energy, and it's also where you'll face the Dragon-type Gym Leader Raihan—but not just yet! You can only face him once you collect the other seven Gym Badges. So for now, head on toward the Gym Stadium and see what Rose and Bede are talking about!

₽ Poké Mart (east)	
After you defeat the fifth Gym	
TM00 Mega Punch	₽10,000
TM01 Mega Kick	₽40,000
TM46 Weather Ball	₽30,000
TM66 Thunder Fang	₽30,000
TM67 Ice Fang	₽30,000
TM68 Fire Fang	₽30,000
TM88 Grassy Terrain	₽20,000
TM89 Misty Terrain	₽20,000
TM90 Electric Terrain	₽20,000
TM91 Psychic Terrain	₽20,000

BP BP Shop (central Pokémon Center)	
Calcium	2 BP
Carbos	2 BP
Destiny Knot	10 BP
HP Up	2 BP
Iron	2 BP
Macho Brace	10 BP
Power Anklet	10 BP
Power Band	10 BP
Power Belt	10 BP
Power Bracer	10 BP
Power Lens	10 BP
Power Weight	10 BP
PP Up	10 BP
Protector	10 BP
Protein	2 BP
Rare Candy	20 BP
Razor Claw	10 BP
Reaper Cloth	10 BP
Sachet	10 BP
Whipped Dream	10 BP
Zinc	2 BP

₽ Vending Machine (Hammerlocke Station)	
Fresh Water	₽200
Lemonade	₽350
Soda Pop	₽300

2

After his conversation with Bede, the chairman will discuss a few things with you, too. Clearly, the energy of the Galar region is his passion—follow him into the stadium, and he'll give you a little lecture on how the region gets its juice! But it's not long before the chairman has to head off again, and you'll now be free to explore Hammerlocke!

A Once the chairman leaves, take a good look around the lobby of the stadium—though actually, all it should take is a quick look for you to spot the Ball Guy once again. Go and speak to them, and this time around, they'll give you a Level Ball!

Level Ball

B

In the first house to the east of the stadium (the one with the reddish door), you'll find a very interesting family. They're all about making sure you and your Pokémon are getting along, and they'll give you a few things if you're doing a good job!

First things first—speak to the girl in the back of the house. She'll give you a Soothe Bell—it will help a Pokémon holding it become more friendly toward you!

If you speak to the woman on the sofa, she'll ask if you want to see if your Pokémon are giving their "best effort." What she means is that she'll check to see if a Pokémon's base points (p.178–179) are maxed out! Show her a Pokémon with maxed base points, and she'll give that Pokémon an Effort Ribbon!

Last but not least, the little boy can tell how friendly a Pokémon is with you. Once you're best buddies with one of your Pokémon, show him. He'll give your companionable Pokémon a Best Friends Ribbon!

 Soothe Bell, Effort Ribbon, Best Friends Ribbon

3

You could immediately go have a look at the vault as Rose suggested, but you may also want to spend some time roaming Hammerlocke. If you head to the east, there are items you can find, plus plenty of people to talk to! You can also visit Hammerlocke Station, but you won't be able to go all the way to Route 7 yet. Team Yell's decided to practice their cheers in the middle of the road!

C

Continue east past the house with the red door, and you'll come to a row of three houses. In the house in the middle, you'll find a gentleman who's quite knowledgeable about various weather conditions! If you stick around to hear him out, he'll thank you by giving you an item that'll help you take full advantage of weather conditions—but all the excitement of talking about the weather will tire him out. You'll have to come back another day if you want to hear what else he has to say next. You can receive a total of five items from him, so why not pay him a visit every day until he's happy?

 Heat Rock, Damp Rock, Icy Rock, Smooth Rock, Utility Umbrella

D

Past the weather man's house, you'll see a staircase leading up to a small area with a Poké Ball statue. This is the famous Hammerlocke University—and you'll find a small girl out front. She'll ask you to deliver a letter to a boy named Frank, who apparently lives in Ballonlea. Ballonlea's a bit of a way off, but we'll be sure to remind you once you get there!

4

Once you've explored the east side of town, come back and head west. Lo and behold, Leon's waiting right there for you! He's apparently run into Hop, and it sounds like your rival took his defeat against Bede pretty hard. Maybe you should try to cheer him up next time you run into him. After a brief conversation, Leon will be off to meet with the chairman, and you can now see what the west side of the city has to offer! You'll find a new Battle Café and boutique here, as well as a hair salon!

E

In the house just to the west of the Pokémon Center, you'll find a black belt who is apparently known as Mr. Focus. He'll challenge you to a battle, and it might seem very underwhelming at first—all he has is a Lv. 2 Cottonee. But true to his name, Mr. Focus has given his Cottonee a Focus Sash, an item that allows the holder to withstand a potential KO attack so long as it has full HP, leaving it with 1 HP. Cottonee can also unleash Endeavor, a move that causes the target's HP to equal the user's current HP. If you manage to defeat Mr. Focus, he'll give you a Focus Sash of your very own!

Focus Sash

!

You may not need to heal up at this point, but it's worth stopping by the Pokémon Center in central Hammerlocke just to have a look at a BP Shop! BP Shops are rare little shops where you can spend BP to buy items that'll be helpful if you want to get super serious about battles. The League staff member in the right-hand corner of the Pokémon Center runs the BP Shop here, so see what she has to offer. You can earn BP by participating in Ranked Battles or Online Competitions from the VS option in your X menu (p. 202) or at the Battle Tower (p. 200) after you've become Champion.

F

Keep heading west, and you'll pass a second Pokémon Center. Past that, there will be a little park where people can have Pokémon battles or make trades—and it just so happens that the lady standing in the corner wants to trade her Togepi for a Toxel. Toxel may be hard to find in the wild, but so is Togepi. Now's a great chance to register one for your Pokédex if you're in the mood!

Togepi

G

You might notice Raihan waiting in front of the vault, but head past him for now, and you'll find a young man wearing a red hoodie. Talk to him, and he'll ask for an Applin to give to a lady as a gift before she travels abroad. Applin are hard to find, but don't worry that giving him one means losing a Pokémon permanently. You'll get it back later, and he'll give you an item that'll allow it to evolve, too!

Tart Apple, Sweet Apple

Battle-Combo Move Tutor

Past the boy in the red hoodie, there's a somewhat hidden staircase leading down. At the bottom, you'll find someone who can teach your Pokémon battle-combo moves. There are three such moves—Grass Pledge, Fire Pledge, and Water Pledge. When two of them are used by allies on the same turn in a Double Battle, they have a variety of effects! For more information on these moves, check out the move list starting on page 336!

5

You've kept Raihan waiting long enough, so head on over to say hi. Raihan's the Gym Leader of Hammerlocke, but as he'll tell you, you can't face him just yet. For the time being, let him know you're here to see the vault and the treasures within. He'll give you access, and he'll also give you his League Card!

 Raihan's League Card

6

Now you can head up the stairs to the left, which lead up to the vault, but don't miss TM29 Charm on the way! It's outside the vault itself, just below the small steps leading up to it. Once inside the vault, you'll find Sonia—seems like she took the advice of Chairman Rose after all. The vault contains several tapestries showing a tale from Galar's past, so now's your chance to learn even more about the legends! Sonia will also give you two Revives, just to make sure you're set for the next section of your challenge.

 Revive ×2

7

Head back down the stairs for another quick chat with Raihan. He'll let you know where you should head next—Route 6 and then Stow-on-Side. If you're done exploring Hammerlocke, then you can get to Route 6 through the western exit!

Legends of Galar: The Two Youths

The tapestries in the vault depict two youths and how they came to be crowned kings. The story starts with the youths witnessing a Wishing Star falling from the sky and then the coming of a mysterious black storm. It seems safe to say that this storm and the Darkest Day are one and the same... The tapestries then show that the youths used a sword and a shield to repel the storm and thus were crowned as kings. But why are there two heroes shown here when the statue in Motostoke only featured one? And there's still not much information on what exactly caused the Darkest Day...

Route 6

To Stow-on-Side (p. 88)

To Hammerlocke (p. 80)

Visible Items

✓	Item
✓	Ultra Ball ×3
✓	Light Clay
✓	TM15 Dig
✓	TM30 Steel Wing

Hidden Items

✓	Item
✓	Rare Bone ×2
✓	Rare Candy
✓	† Fossilized Dino ×2
✓	🛡 Fossilized Fish ×2

Shortest route

If you've already noticed that blue line on the map to the left, that's the shortest path you can take through Route 6! But if you follow the steps outlined on the following pages instead of taking the shortest route, you'll find plenty to reward your efforts!

Tall Grass

No.	Pokémon	Rate
165	Dugtrio	○
296	Maractus	△
318	Helioptile	○
321	Trapinch †	★
321	Trapinch 🛡	☆
324	Axew †	☆
324	Axew 🛡	★
327	Yamask	○

Random Encounters

No.	Pokémon	Rate
135	Duskull	○
285	Skorupi	△
300	Torkoal	☆
312	Silicobra	○
314	Hippopotas	△
316	Durant †	○
316	Durant 🛡	☆

Random Encounters

No.	Pokémon	Rate
317	Heatmor †	☆
317	Heatmor 🛡	○
320	Hawlucha	☆

Berry Trees

No.	Pokémon	Rate
025	Greedent	◎

Fishing

No.	Pokémon	Rate
043	Drednaw	○
144	Magikarp	◎
146	Goldeen	△

◎ frequent ○ common △ average ☆ rare ★ almost never

† *Pokémon Sword* only 🛡 *Pokémon Shield* only

CATCH!

Yamask

Yamask appear only on Route 6. So don't forget to catch one here!

WALKTHROUGH

1

Just out of Hammerlocke's western gate is Route 6, but you won't be able to get far before you run into Team Yell getting up to their usual shenanigans. This time, they say they won't let you pass because you might wake up a Silicobra! You'll be joined by Hop, but it seems he's not his usual self. You'll have to defeat the two Team Yell Grunts on your own if you want to get through!

Team Yell Grunt

Team Yell's teams might be getting stronger, but Dark-type Pokémon are still clearly their favorite. This Grunt sends out a Stunky and a Linoone. Ground-type moves will work best against Stunky, while Fighting-type moves deal 400 percent damage against Linoone.

Team Yell Grunt

Liepard's not an exceptionally powerful damage dealer, but it is quite fast. If you want to outspeed it, try using high-priority moves like Quick Attack or Shadow Sneak! If Speed isn't your main concern, then you can focus on high-damage supereffective Fighting-, Bug-, or Fairy-type moves.

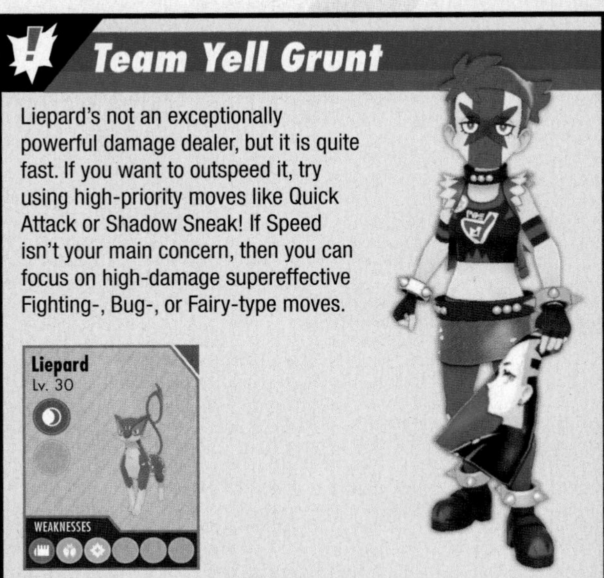

2

Once you send Team Yell on their merry way, Hop will tell you about what's been eating him—but it seems he needs some more time to process things and will go dashing off. Before you can go after him, you'll be called by Opal, the Fairy-type Gym Leader. She'll introduce herself by giving you her League Card, and she says she'll keep an eye on you before heading on her way. You'll face her eventually, but for now, you should focus on getting to Stow-on-Side!

 Opal's League Card

3

Route 6 is a maze of cliffs and ladders, with quite a few Trainers waiting for you. Follow the path marked on the map if you want to get to the next town as soon as possible, but be aware that this route is worth exploring thoroughly. There are plenty of items to find, a Berry Tree, and even a fishing spot! Check the map, and make sure you pick up TM15 Dig and TM30 Steel Wing. Near the end of the route, you'll also find a campsite. This would be a great place to make some curry and get your team shipshape before pushing on to Stow-on-Side.

Professor Cara Liss

If you've been keeping a lookout for sparkles along the ground, chances are you've come across several Fossils by now. Professor Cara Liss, whom you can find near the campsite on Route 6, is studying the Fossils of the Galar region and can restore them for you! It's a little different from how Fossils are restored in other regions, though. Two Fossils will need to be combined to restore a full Pokémon! There is a total of four types of Fossils you can find—Fossilized Birds, Fossilized Fish, Fossilized Drakes, and Fossilized Dinos. Mix and match these as you find them to have new Pokémon restored!

Dracozolt

Dracozolt can be revived from a Fossilized Drake and a Fossilized Bird.

Arctozolt

Arctozolt can be revived from a Fossilized Dino and a Fossilized Bird.

Dracovish

Dracovish can be revived from a Fossilized Drake and a Fossilized Fish.

Arctovish

Arctovish can be revived from a Fossilized Dino and a Fossilized Fish.

!

There are a few ways you can find Fossils. They can be found by checking out sparkles in the Wild Area and Route 6, but they may be hard to come by this way. The easiest way to get them is to have the Digging Duo (p. 278) do some excavation! Both of them have a chance to dig up Fossils, but the skilled brother can find rarer ones!

4

From the campsite, take the east ladder down, and then keep heading to the east until you find another ladder. Climb up that and head through a natural tunnel, and you'll reach some impressive Diglett carvings. Just past them is Stow-on-Side!

Stow-on-Side

Visible Items
Dusk Stone
Cracked Pot
Rocky Helmet
TM74 Venoshock

Hidden Items
X Sp. Atk ×2
Rare Bone ×3
Metal Coat
Max Revive

The Street Market

The Street Market in Stow-on-Side is made up of the bargain stall and the buyer stall. Each day, the bargain stall will be selling one item from the table to the far right at the reasonable price of ₽3,000! The item offered changes every day. You'll still have a chance to buy the previous day's bargain if you missed out on it—but it'll cost you a little bit extra.

The man at the buyer stall is willing to buy items from you at a premium, if you can bring him what he wants! Each day, he'll want a random item from the table to the right, and you can find all of these items in the Wild Area. Check in with him after doing some exploring, and always keep a few of these items in your Bag for a rainy day!

Buyer Stall	
Tiny Mushroom	₽2,000
Pearl	₽3,000
Stardust	₽4,000
Big Mushroom	₽10,000
Rare Bone	₽11,111
Big Pearl	₽12,000
Star Piece	₽14,000
Balm Mushroom	₽25,000
Pearl String	₽27,500
Comet Shard	₽30,000

Bargain Stall	
Cracked Pot	◎
Protector	○
Razor Claw	○
Reaper Cloth	○
Metal Coat	△
Quick Claw	△
Binding Band	☆
Black Sludge	☆
Charcoal	☆
Chipped Pot	☆
Dragon Fang	☆
Focus Band	☆
Metronome	☆
Miracle Seed	☆
Mystic Water	☆
Poison Barb	☆
Protective Pads	☆
Ring Target	☆

Bargain Stall	
Spell Tag	☆
Twisted Spoon	☆
Black Belt	★
Black Glasses	★
Magnet	★
Never-Melt Ice	★
Pixie Plate	★
Sharp Beak	★
Silk Scarf	★
Silver Powder	★

◎ frequent ○ common △ average ☆ rare ★ almost never

WALKTHROUGH

1

Once you arrive safely in Stow-on-Side, you'll see a Pokémon Center to your right. Heal up your team if you need, because Hop is waiting for you at the far end of the market. Be ready for another battle against your rival!

A

The man standing by the left-hand table inside the Pokémon Center apparently found some treasures, and he'll give some to you! You'll receive two Fossilized Birds in *Pokémon Sword* or two Fossilized Drakes in *Pokémon Shield*. He'll also give you some pointers on how to find more, too!

- Fossilized Bird ×2
- Fossilized Drake ×2

Hop

Hop might have lost to Bede, but it's only pushed him to keep growing and experimenting with his team of Pokémon. His team is almost completely different from other times you've battled him, and most of his team members don't share weaknesses. Hop will lead with Cramorant. Since it's both Flying and Water type, Electric-type moves are a great choice. But if Cramorant uses Dive, watch out! Its Gulp Missile Ability will allow it to fish up an Arrokuda or a Pikachu, and it'll spit this prize at your Pokémon when hit with a damage-dealing move. This will damage your Pokémon in return—and either lower its Defense or paralyze it to boot! Toxel's unique type combination makes sending out a Ground- or Psychic-type Pokémon to battle it a great choice. Silicobra shouldn't be too difficult if you've got a Flying-type Pokémon to dodge its Ground-type moves or Pokémon with Water-, Grass-, or Ice-type moves to deal supereffective damage. His strongest Pokémon is still the partner he chose when you chose your first partner Pokémon. If you've been raising your first partner Pokémon well and you battle smart, his ace Pokémon shouldn't give you too much trouble.

2

Hop will go dashing off after your battle, but you'll be stopped by Opal approaching once again—it seems she meant it when she said she'd keep an eye on you. Apparently she was watching your battle with Hop, and she'll give you the League Card of Stow-on-Side's Gym Leader as thanks for the spectacle!

- Bea's League Card 
- Allister's League Card

3

As Opal says, your next challenge is Stow-on-Side's Gym. But the town is a pretty fun place to explore—it's much like Route 6 in that it's a convoluted maze with lots of ups and downs. Keep your eyes open for ladders that can lead up to rooftops or down to previously hidden ledges! In particular, head behind the houses in the west, and you'll find a ladder leading up to the roof—here you'll find TM74 Venoshock!

B Enter the house just to the west of the staircase where you faced Hop, and you'll see a Flying Taxi driver. Talk to him, and he'll give you TM06 Fly!

- TM06 Fly

C On the same roof where you find TM74 Venoshock, you'll pass by a man sitting there enjoying the scenery. He's looking to trade his Hatenna in *Pokémon Sword* or Impidimp in *Pokémon Shield* for a Maractus. You can find Maractus on Route 6, so if you're interested in adding Hatenna or Impidimp to your Pokédex, this is a great opportunity!

- Hatenna, Impidimp

4

Once you're done exploring, it's time to head to the Gym Stadium and get the next Gym mission started!

D You should be expecting them at this point, but once inside the stadium, you'll likely notice the Ball Guy immediately! This time, they've got a nice little Heavy Ball for you!

- Heavy Ball

Stow-on-Side Gym Mission

1 Stow-on-Side is a bit special in that you'll be facing different Gyms depending on which version of the game you're playing. In *Pokémon Sword*, it will be a Fighting-type Gym led by the Galar karate prodigy Bea, while in *Pokémon Shield*, you'll be facing Ghost-type specialists headed by Allister. But first things first—speak to the League staff member at the front desk in the lobby to get changed into your uniform!

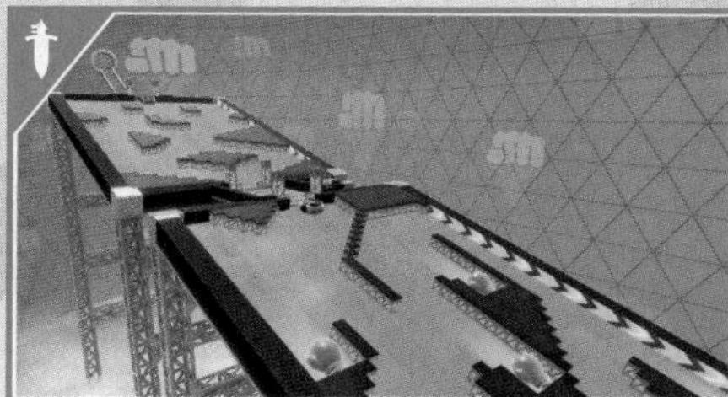

2 The Gym mission of the Stow-on-Side Gym is navigating mazes using a rotating cup! You can control the cup by rotating your Control Stick—rotate it to the right, and the cup will start to move to the right. Rotate it to the left, and the cup will start to move to the left. It's a bit tricky, but you'll have plenty of time to practice. Check the map to see our recommendations for making your way through the mazes!

! After each maze segment, there will be a little platform with a Trainer and a glowing pad on the floor. The glowing pad is a warp panel—get on it, and you'll be transported back to the entrance!

3 Starting from the second segment of the maze, you'll notice giant spring-loaded bumpers throughout the maze. These will push your cup in the direction they're pointing, which can sometimes help you navigate the maze and sometimes send you back a bit. Bigger bumpers have more kick to them than the little ones. Just keep an eye on our recommended routes, and you should get a clear idea of where the bumpers are and which ones to use!

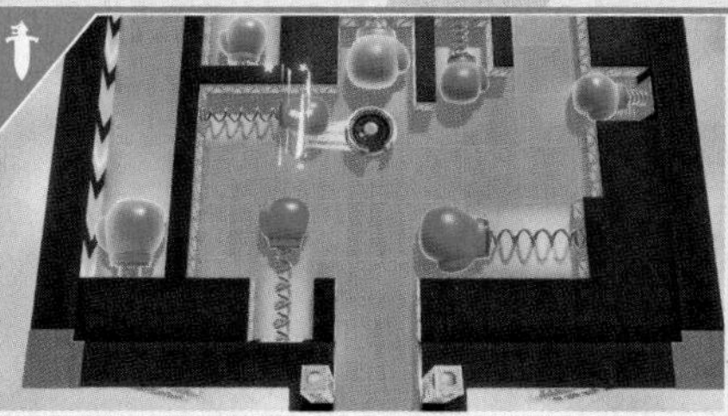

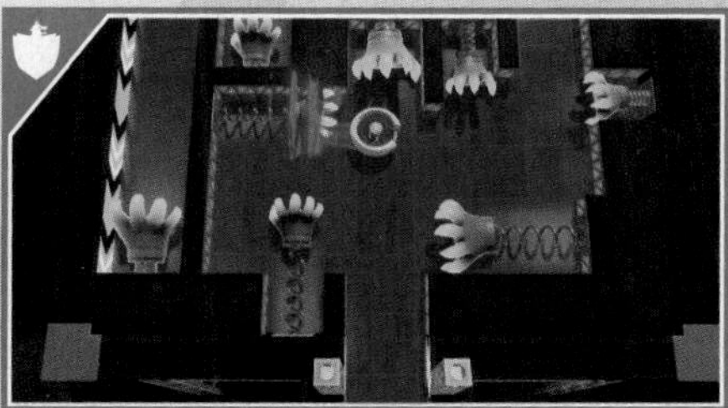

⟶ Shortest route

*The map shown is from *Pokémon Sword*. The colors will look different if you are playing *Pokémon Shield*, but the basic layout is the same.

†In *Pokémon Shield*, the first Trainer you run into will have three Pokémon. This is more Pokémon than the Trainer in *Pokémon Sword* has, but some of them will have slightly lower levels.

4 After making your way through three mazes in your cup, you'll finally reach the end—which means it's time to face the Gym Leader!

Bea

Bea's Fighting-type Pokémon all pack a punch with their high Attack stats. You can try to counter this by battling her with Pokémon that have high Defense to reduce damage. If you're feeling a bit braver, you could also go for a more offensive strategy by using Pokémon with supereffective Flying-, Psychic-, or Fairy-type moves. Most of her Pokémon have fairly good Defense and Sp. Def, though, so make sure your Pokémon can take a hit or two if you can't knock out Bea's Pokémon in one attack. A trickier strategy is sending out Ghost-type Pokémon, since Ghost-type Pokémon can't be hit by Fighting-type moves. But if you go this route, watch out for Pangoro, as its Dark-type moves are super effective against Ghost-type Pokémon. Bea will Gigantamax her Machamp as soon as she sends it out, so make sure you're ready. Its signature move, G-Max Chi Strike, will increase its critical-hit ratio! You'd better be ready with Pokémon that can withstand such might or with one that can dish out enough damage to take this Gigantamax Machamp down quickly.

Allister

Allister might be a little creepy, but he's got more than scare tactics up his sleeve! His Ghost-type Pokémon can't be touched by Normal- or Fighting-type moves, so don't waste time trying to use them here. While all his team members are Ghost type, most have a different secondary type, giving them a few different weaknesses and resistances compared to their teammates. Ironically, all Allister's Pokémon are weak to Ghost-type moves, so if one of your Pokémon happens to know a particularly powerful one, it's not a bad option for this battle. Remember to watch out for Mimikyu's unique Disguise Ability. It will prevent the damage from the first damage-dealing move used on it, so don't waste a Max Move or anything else powerful just to bust Mimikyu's decoy! Allister will Gigantamax his Gengar right after he sends it out. Unlike with other Dynamax Pokémon, you won't be able to rely on poison to help you lower its increased HP—Gengar is Poison type, so it can't be poisoned. Gigantamax Gengar's signature move is G-Max Terror. It prevents the target Pokémon from switching out! Make sure the Pokémon you send out against it is up to the challenge of battling Allister's Gengar, or you're in for a fright!

Fighting Badge / Ghost Badge

Once you defeat the Gym Leader of Stow-on-Side, you'll be given the Fighting Badge if you're playing *Pokémon Sword* or the Ghost Badge if you're playing *Pokémon Shield*. Whichever Gym Badge you receive, it will let you catch Pokémon of up to Lv. 40 and add Hyper Potions to the Poké Mart lineup!

5 Now you've earned your fourth Gym Badge, and that means you're at the halfway point of the Gym Challenge! Now it's time to move on, so head out of the stadium for the next step in your adventure!

 Fighting Uniform, TM42 Revenge

 Ghost Uniform, TM77 Hex

5

After you leave the stadium, you'll be greeted by Sonia's Yamper. Naturally, Sonia will be right behind it, and it sounds like she came to Stow-on-Side to check out the mural. But before she gets a chance to explain much more, your conversation will be interrupted by a huge noise! Head up the staircase to the west to see what happened!

6

Once you reach the mural, you'll find the cause of all the commotion—it's Bede. He's here with the chairman's Copperajah, and he's trying to destroy the mural! Maybe it's not the most impressive work of art, but it's still part of Galar's history—you've got to stop him!

Bede

Bede talks a big game, but unlike Hop, he's hardly learned anything from his losses. He uses the same four Pokémon he did in your last battle with him, though they've grown a few levels and some have evolved. His entire team is still pure Psychic type, which means his team is extremely weak against any Dark-type Pokémon you may have. Be careful, though, as his Hattrem and Ponyta know Fairy-type moves. If you don't happen to have any Dark-type Pokémon on your team, try using Bug- or Ghost-type moves. You could also try Pokémon with high Sp. Def—Bede's Pokémon tend to focus on special moves.

Duosion
Lv. 32

WEAKNESSES

Hattrem
Lv. 35

WEAKNESSES

Gothorita
Lv. 32

WEAKNESSES

Ponyta
Lv. 33

WEAKNESSES

7

Once you defeat Bede, the chairman himself will appear and personally disqualify Bede from the Gym Challenge. Unfortunately, it's all too late—the mural crumbles before your eyes. But wait! There is a statue hidden behind it, depicting two heroes and two Pokémon wielding a sword and a shield!

Legends of Galar: Two Pokémon

This hidden statue seems to tell the oldest and truest story of all—two heroes, yes, but also two Pokémon! The Pokémon were the ones to wield the sword and shield that were shown on the statue in Motostoke and in the tapestries of Hammerlocke. These two Pokémon must have helped the two youths avert the cataclysm known as the Darkest Day.

8

Sonia is understandably excited about the new discovery, and she'll ask your opinion, too. Give her some feedback, and she'll reward you with some Revives! Now you're free to be on your way. Next stop, Ballonlea—via the glowing maze that is Glimwood Tangle!

 Revive ×2

Glimwood Tangle

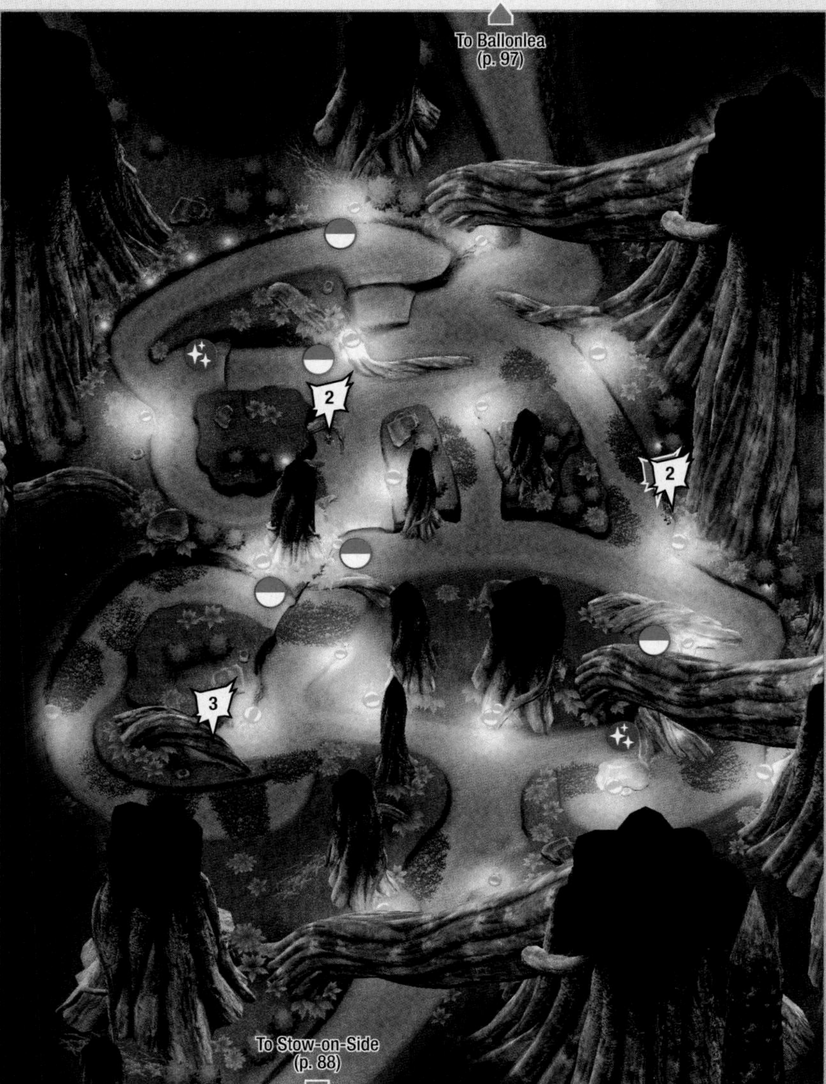

Visible Items
Bright Powder
Big Root
Hyper Potion ×2
TM56 U-turn
TM24 Snore

Hidden Items
Full Heal ×2
Luminous Moss

Random Encounters		
210	Swirlix †	△
212	Spritzee (Shield)	△
239	Morgrem	○
242	Hattrem	△
333	Ponyta (Shield)	△
335	Sinistea (Phony Form)	△
335	Sinistea (Antique Form)	★
337	Indeedee (Male) †	☆
337	Indeedee (Female) (Shield)	☆
338	Phantump	△
341	Shiinotic †	○
341	Shiinotic (Shield)	△
342	Oranguru (Shield)	△
343	Passimian †	△

Wanderers		
238	Impidimp	◎
239	Morgrem	◎

◎ frequent ○ common △ average ☆ rare ★ almost never
† *Pokémon Sword* only (Shield) *Pokémon Shield* only

1

Welcome to the softly glowing Glimwood Tangle, a natural maze shrouded in darkness. It might be hard to figure out where you're going at first, but don't worry—we'll make sure you reach Ballonlea! For starters, walk north until you come to the roads branching to the west and east!

!

Notice the big glowing mushrooms that line the path? Go up and touch one, and it'll help illuminate your path, though only for a little while! But be careful—sometimes a Pokémon will be hiding near the mushroom!

2

At the fork in the road, head to the west first. You'll come to another crossroads, but going north will only lead to a dead end with tall grass. Instead, go south past a cook, follow the path, and you'll find a bag of Bright Powder! Jump down and head south, and you'll be back at the crossroads before the cook.

3

Now you want to go east, past the path to Stow-on-Side and deeper into the forest. If you run into a dead end, take a few steps back and you'll find a path leading south—take that and keep going. It'll soon turn back north, and there'll be a little branch to the west that'll have an item at the end of it. Pick up the item and keep heading north, and you'll reach another set of branching paths.

4

Head north past the Trainer couple and then west again. You'll see that there are actually two paths heading west. One is blocked off by a root with a mushroom, while the other leads deeper into the forest. Just at the mushroom on the root, the path will branch yet again—head south this time after picking up an item, and you'll see a woman waiting for a battle. It might be hard to spot, but there's actually a westward path just in front of her! Keep your eyes peeled for the small golden mushrooms that mark the entrance to this path.

5

Follow the path up as far as it goes, looking for another series of those small golden mushrooms. They'll lead you all the way north to get TM56 U-turn! From there, jump down two ledges, and you'll find yourself back where you started. Head west toward the woman again, but instead of taking the hidden path, go south—you'll find TM24 Snore!

6

From where you found TM24 Snore, head east, and you'll be back where you battled the couple. By now you should have found most items in Glimwood Tangle, so go north—you'll see Ballonlea through the trees in no time!

CATCH!

Ponyta

Ponyta is a Pokémon exclusive to *Pokémon Shield*, and it only appears here in Glimwood Tangle!

Ballonlea

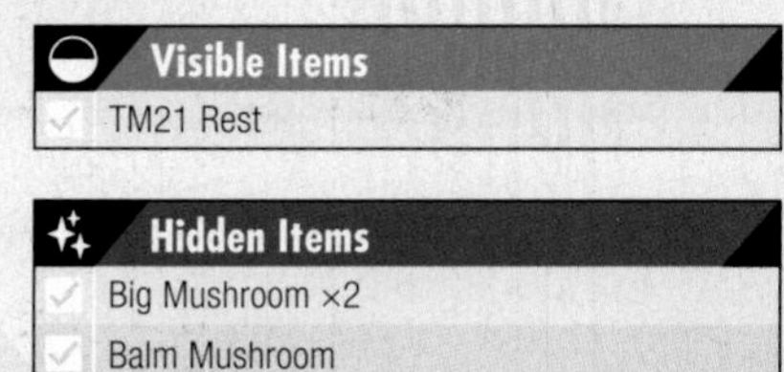

Visible Items
TM21 Rest

Hidden Items
Big Mushroom ×2
Balm Mushroom

1

The first thing you'll see upon arriving in Ballonlea is the Pokémon Center. Stop by if you need to heal up your team, and then get to exploring the town! It's a small place, but the glowing mushrooms give it a mysterious air—and there are still a few things you might want to take care of before heading to the stadium! Talk to the people around town, nab TM21 Rest behind the Pokémon Center, and then when you're ready, it'll be time to pay Opal a visit in Ballonlea Stadium!

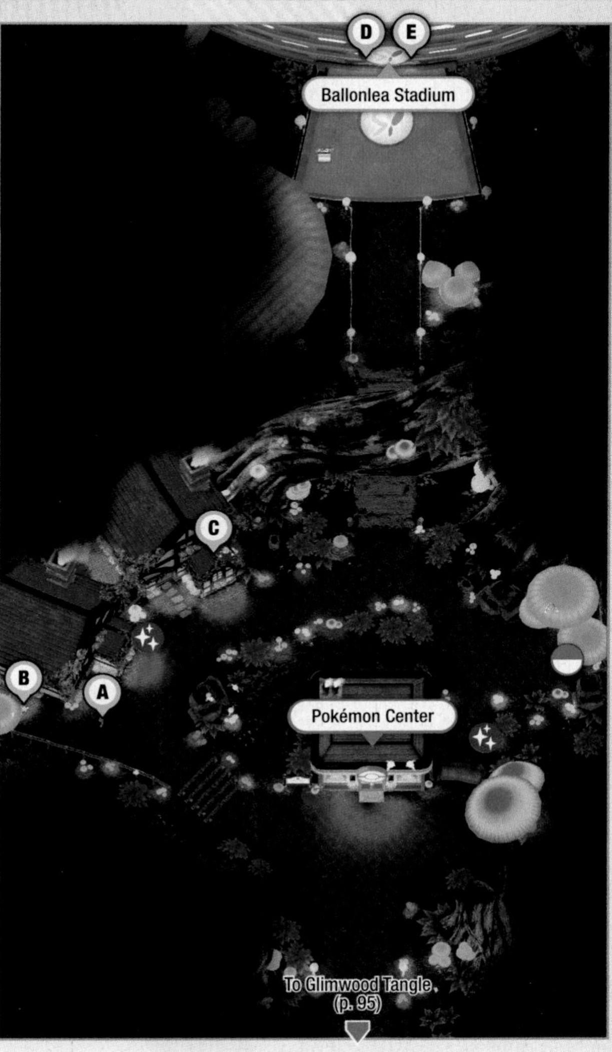

A

Near the house west of the Pokémon Center, you'll find a young boy. If you picked up a certain love letter in Hammerlocke (p. 82), he'll tell you his grandfather's name is Frank—that's the person the girl wanted you to give the letter to. Head into the home right nearby, and speak to the old man inside. It seems that the letter is from someone he knew as a child... Something strange seems to be going on, but Frank will give you a Choice Scarf for delivering the letter. You can also revisit Hammerlocke and check the area where Paula was, even if you don't see anything, to find a Reaper Cloth! While you're in Hammerlocke, you may also want to stop by the boutique to pick up a Fire-type Tracksuit Jacket. You'll see why in the next section.

Choice Scarf, Reaper Cloth

C

In the last house before the tree arch in front of the stadium, there will be an old lady who'll give you a TM—TM77 Hex if you're playing *Pokémon Sword* or TM42 Revenge if you're playing *Pokémon Shield*. You can also speak to the Pokémon Breeder in the living room for a battle, after which she'll give you an Eviolite!

 TM77 Hex / TM42 Revenge, Eviolite

B

Right next to Frank's house, you'll find an artist who wants to become a Pokémon. He'll ask you to show him fiery fashion that reflects his burning passion—this means you need to show him the Fire-type Tracksuit Jacket! As mentioned in the previous subevent, you can get one in the Hammerlocke boutique. Speak to the artist while wearing the Fire-type Tracksuit Jacket, and he'll be so moved that he'll give you a TM!

 TM78 Acrobatics

2

Upon entering Ballonlea Stadium, you'll be greeted by Marnie. After some banter, she'll give you her League Card and declare that she now thinks of you as a rival. Looks like Hop isn't the only one you've got to worry about now!

Marnie's League Card

D

And of course the Ball Guy is here to greet you at Ballonlea Stadium, too. They'll give you a Love Ball this time—kind of fitting for the charming atmosphere of Ballonlea!

Love Ball

E

Notice the little girl wearing an Eevee costume in the corner of the Gym? She's looking for a Galarian Yamask and will trade her own Yamask for one—but her Yamask is one found in another region!

Yamask

3

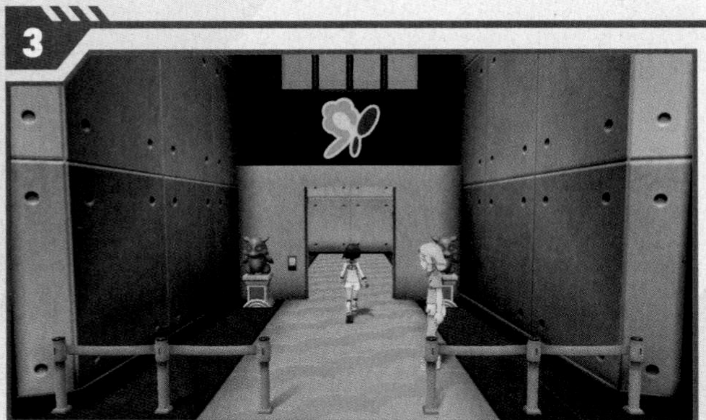

If you're done speaking to everyone in the lobby, stocking up on items from the Poké Mart, and the like, it's time to get changed into your uniform and start the Gym mission of Ballonlea!

Ballonlea Gym Mission

1

The Gym mission of Ballonlea is a bit different from the ones of other Gyms—it serves as an audition for Opal to find a worthy successor as Gym Leader! You, of course, have the Gym Challenge to complete, but it seems like humoring Opal is the only way to get her Badge, so...we hope you're prepared for some trivia!

2

You'll have to battle the Gym Trainers and also answer questions they'll ask during the battle. Answer correctly, and your Pokémon will get a stat boost. Answer incorrectly, and your Pokémon's stats will be lowered instead! If you need a cheat sheet, the correct answers are at the bottom of the page. Each of the Trainers you face will have two Pokémon, so be ready for them!

Q1. Do you know about Fairy type's weaknesses?

Q2. What was the previous Trainer's name?

Q3. What do I eat for breakfast every morning?

Defeat the three Gym Trainers, and it will be time for you to finally face Opal! Let's see if you've met her standards...

A1. Both Poison type and Steel type are Fairy type's weaknesses! **A2.** The correct answer here is Annette, with an *e* at the end!
A3. Don't ask us how you'd know this, but the correct answer is omelets.

Opal

Opal's been a Gym Leader since before you were born and has mastered using Fairy-type Pokémon. Don't even think about using Dragon-type moves in this battle, since they can't deal any damage to Fairy types! Poison- and Steel-type moves will deal supereffective damage against most of Opal's team, but be prepared to switch up your strategy against certain Pokémon. Opal's Weezing is both Poison and Fairy type, so Poison-type moves will only deal an average amount of damage. Mawile is Steel and Fairy type, so Poison-type moves won't affect it! One thing that's common among all Opal's Pokémon is how strong their defensive stats are. They can have high Defense, Sp. Def, and even HP. Her Weezing and Mawile have pretty high Defense, and her Togekiss has exceptionally high Sp. Def. Make sure you pay attention to whether you're using physical or special moves in battle—you can check out page 12 if you need a refresher on these. Opal will Gigantamax her Alcremie on the first turn she sends it out. Not only does Gigantamax Alcremie have the signature G-Max Finale move, but it also has a massive amount of HP. While you've faced Gigantamax Pokémon in Gym Battles before, you may find this one particularly challenging, as its immense HP makes it very hard to knock out before the Gigantamax effects wear off. If you can poison or burn Alcremie to drain its HP each turn, it'll be a great help. You could also try giving it the paralysis or asleep status conditions to try to keep it from acting.

Weezing
Lv. 36

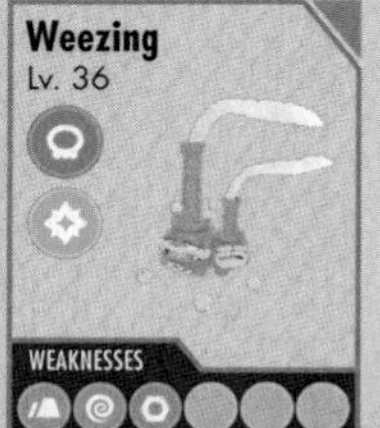

WEAKNESSES

Mawile
Lv. 36

WEAKNESSES

Togekiss
Lv. 37

WEAKNESSES

GIGANTAMAX
Alcremie
Lv. 38

WEAKNESSES

One more thing! During battle, Opal will ask you questions like what her nickname is, what her favorite color is, and how old you think she is. The thing to know about Opal is she can be a bit contrary. Don't assume the obvious answer is the one she wants to hear. Sometimes it's better to pick the wrong answer, because it's kinder than the right answer.

The Fairy Badge

The Fairy Badge is the fifth Badge for the Gym Challenge, and it will allow you to catch Pokémon of up to Lv. 45! It'll also add Ultra Balls and Super Repels to the Poké Marts, so stop by if you want to pick some up!

3 You've defeated five Gym Leaders now, with three more to go—but they'll only get tougher from here! Get your rewards for defeating Opal, and then head out of the stadium!

 Fairy Uniform, TM87 Draining Kiss

4

Opal
I've got a few errands to run in Hammerlocke.
Care to join me for the journey?

Once outside Ballonlea Stadium, Opal will call you once again—she's got a few errands to run in Hammerlocke and offers to take you there directly! You can accept her offer and go back to Hammerlocke immediately, or you can turn it down if you want to explore Ballonlea and its surroundings. Once you've had your fill of exploring, your next stop is—you guessed it—Hammerlocke!

Hammerlocke (Revisited)

1

Once you arrive back in Hammerlocke, you can stop by a Pokémon Center if you need to heal up, and then head toward the stadium. You'll run into Bede, and Opal will take quite a liking to him! Seems she's willing to give Bede a chance...or something. You can leave them to sort things out between themselves. You need to head to Route 7!

2

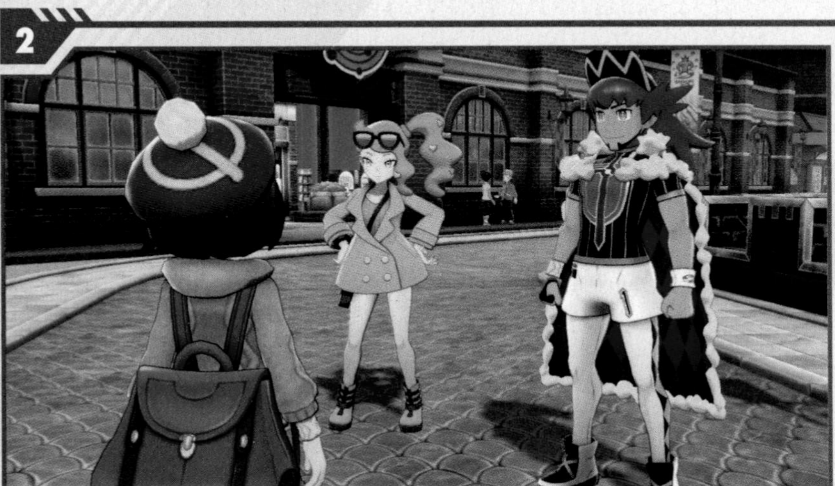

Route 7 is past the eastern exit of Hammerlocke, so keep heading east—but once again you'll see a familiar face along the way! Sonia apparently came back to Hammerlocke so she could get another look at the tapestries, but your conversation will be interrupted by a loud noise. Thankfully, Leon's in town, too. He and Sonia dash off to warn Chairman Rose that there seems to be some trouble.

3

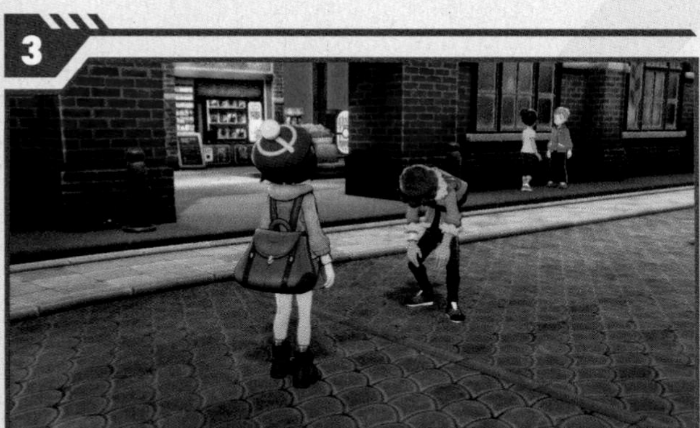

Head up toward the station to greet your rival. Seems he had his share of trouble with Glimwood Tangle and Opal's Gym mission, and he asks you to join him on Route 7 for some motivation! You can head right there, knowing another battle is in store. But no need to rush. Hop won't be going anywhere until he gets that battle out of you!

If you haven't done so already, don't forget to check the location where you met the little girl that gave you the letter for Frank (p. 82). You'll find a scrap of Reaper Cloth!

See Some More of Hammerlocke

This is your second stop by Hammerlocke, but it surely won't be your last. You'll still have to visit again to challenge Hammerlocke's Gym Leader, Raihan! But that's not until a while from now, since you need two more Gym Badges before he'll see you as a worthy challenger. Still, there's a bit more to do here in Hammerlocke and nearby, if you want to, before you hit the road on Route 7!

Start by considering a visit to the east Pokémon Center in Hammerlocke. It was blocked by some Team Yell Grunts when you first passed by, but it has a TM Seller who will be happy to sell you TMs for some high-powered moves! And it's not just power that's on offer here. The TMs for triggering terrains could help you set up some trickier strategies. Learn about terrains on page 189, if you haven't already!

And if you haven't been back in Hammerlocke for a while, you could go to the boutique to spend some more of the cash you may have picked up while battling Trainers. Maybe make a quick stop in a salon, too, then update your League Card with all your latest and greatest stats! Also, don't forget about the Battle Café if you want to get some practice with Double Battles! Or you could even pop down to the Wild Area to go on another spree catching wild Pokémon, collecting and swapping Watts, or hunting for hidden items. There's always more to do in the Wild Area!

Route 7

Visible Items

Item
Quick Ball ×3
After visiting Spikemuth
TM58 Assurance
Safety Goggles

Hidden Items

Item
Ether
Balm Mushroom
After visiting Spikemuth
PP Up

Tall Grass

No.	Pokémon	Frequency
030	Thievul	○
045	Liepard	△
065	Galvantula	○
183	Perrserker	○
290	Inkay	△
344	Morpeko	☆

Random Encounters

No.	Pokémon	Frequency
023	Corviknight	○
045	Liepard	△
134	Seismitoad	☆
209	Meowstic (Male) †	△
209	Meowstic (Female) (Shield)	△
273	Karrablast †	○
273	Karrablast (Shield)	☆
275	Shelmet †	☆
275	Shelmet (Shield)	○
310	Toxel	○

Berry Trees

No.	Pokémon	Frequency
025	Greedent	◎

◎ frequent ○ common △ average ☆ rare ★ almost never

† *Pokémon Sword* only (Shield) *Pokémon Shield* only

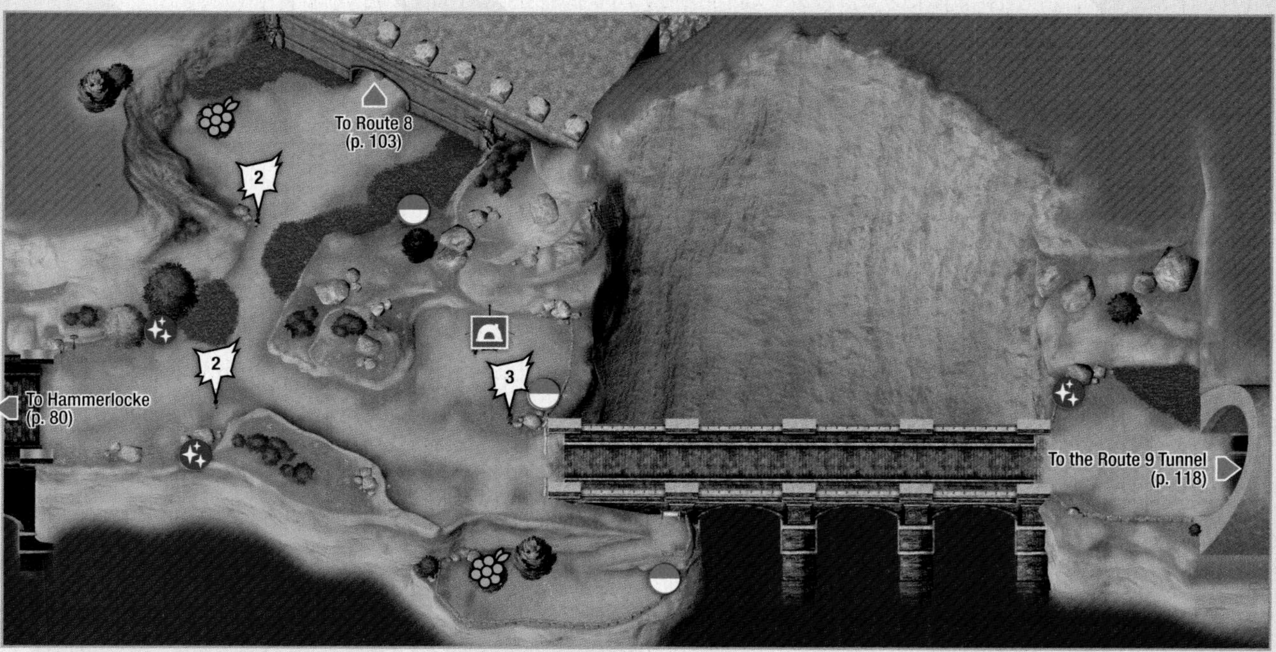

1

Once you get to Route 7, keep pressing on across the bridge—at the end you'll see Hop, who's itching for another battle with you! He won't give you a chance to decline and prepare this time, so if you need to get ready, make sure you do so before you get to him!

Hop

Hop continues to experiment with his team, raising all kinds of different Pokémon. His team has changed considerably and has grown much stronger since your battle in Stow-on-Side. Hop's diverse team means that there aren't too many shared weaknesses, though Heatmor, Boltund, and Cinderace (if you chose Sobble) are all weak to Ground-type moves. Hopefully you've been raising a team that's just as varied to counter Hop's new strategies. Trevenant has particularly high Attack, but its speed is low. Try to knock it out quickly using supereffective moves. Heatmor's got fairly good Attack and Sp. Atk, but its Defense and Sp. Def aren't as high. Try using either a Pokémon with high defensive stats to withstand Heatmor's attacks or a Pokémon with high Speed that can get a quick KO before Heatmor can deal damage. A Ground-type Pokémon may be a good idea against Boltund, as Ground types will be immune to Electric-type moves and paralysis. Snorlax is a Pokémon that's popular among many skilled Trainers, so it's no wonder Hop's added one to his team. It's only weak to Fighting-type moves and has very high HP, Attack, and Sp. Def. Hop's ace Pokémon is now fully evolved and powerful at Lv. 37. Your strategy may vary based on whether you're going up against Inteleon's high Sp. Atk, Rillaboom's high Attack, or Cinderace's mix of high Attack and Speed.

Snorlax
Lv. 35
WEAKNESSES

Boltund
Lv. 35
WEAKNESSES

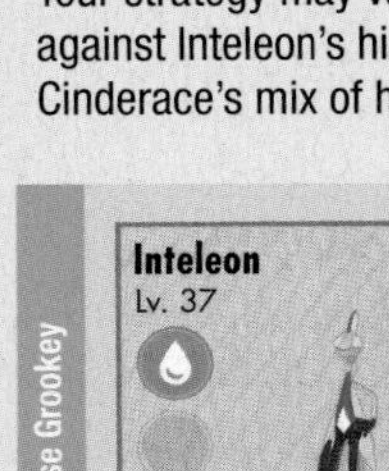

If you chose Grookey

If you chose Scorbunny

If you chose Sobble

2

Hop will see your team healed up after you battle him, so you'll be ready for Route 7 and what lies beyond it. Since the only way open to you is the northern path, turn that way next. Catch some more Pokémon for your team or for your Pokédex, including Perrserker, a new Evolution of Meowth found in the Galar region! This might be your first time seeing one in the wild, unless you've been exploring the Wild Area. And once Perrserker sees you, it'll come running right at you!

!

Route 7 was never going to be a very long trek but it's even shorter on this first visit, because you'll find that Team Yell is blocking the eastern half of it! If you go up to talk to them, they won't even bother you for a battle. They'll just carry on with their cheering. You'll have to give up on collecting the items on the eastern half of the route for now. But if it's any consolation, the Pokémon you can encounter are the same on both the west and east sides of Route 7, so you aren't missing out on any chance to build up your team!

3

Route 8 lies ahead, and it's a pretty convoluted route that's teeming with Pokémon. Grab a few last Berries from the Berry tree, if your stock for cooking fortifying curries is running low. And consider adding some of the Pokémon from Route 7 to your team. Inkay's Dark-type and Fighting-type moves can help against Pokémon you'll face soon, and it appears at a high enough level that you can evolve it into Malamar the very next time it levels up. Just rotate your Nintendo Switch upside down when Inkay is leveling up to see it evolve. Next, it's on to Route 8!

Route 8

Shortest route

Hidden Items
X Defense ×3
Elixir
Pixie Plate
Big Nugget
Nugget

Tall Grass		
088	Golett	○
169	Boldore (Sword)	△
169	Boldore (Shield)	○
172	Gurdurr (Sword)	○
172	Gurdurr (Shield)	△
246	Pawniard	○
281	Rufflet (Sword)	△
283	Vullaby (Shield)	△
348	Togedemaru	☆
362	Lunatone (Shield)	☆
363	Solrock (Sword)	☆

Random Encounters		
119	Bronzong	△
136	Dusclops	△
142	Haunter	△
264	Rhyhorn	○
286	Drapion	☆
313	Sandaconda	○
315	Hippowdon	△
345	Falinks	☆

Wanderers		
◇ 087	Crustle	◎
345	Falinks	◎

◎ frequent ○ common △ average ☆ rare ★ almost never

† *Pokémon Sword* only *Pokémon Shield* only

Visible Items
Shiny Stone
TM96 Smart Strike
Hyper Potion ×3
Luxury Ball ×3

Visible Items
Max Revive
King's Rock
TM43 Brick Break
Terrain Extender

Steamdrift Way

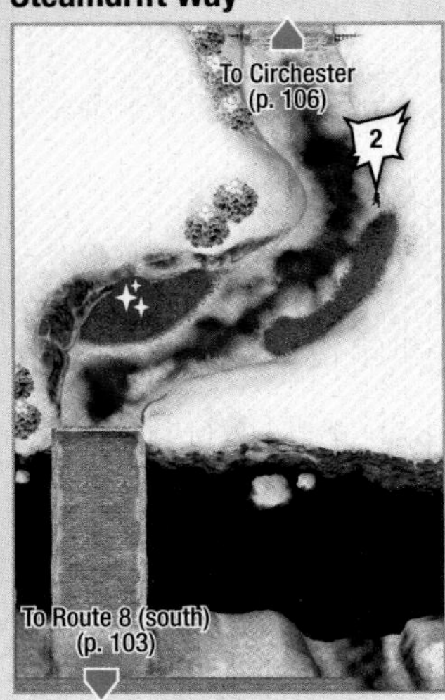

Hidden Items
Star Piece ×2

Tall Grass		
073	Vanillish	△
079	Snorunt	○
248	Throh (Pokémon Shield only)	☆
249	Sawk (Pokémon Sword only)	☆
292	Sneasel	○
349	Snom	◎

Random Encounters		
078	Delibird	△
096	Snover	○
292	Sneasel	○
349	Snom	◎
367	Darumaka (Pokémon Sword only)	☆

◎ frequent ○ common △ average ☆ rare ★ almost never
† *Pokémon Sword* only ● *Pokémon Shield* only

! The steps here will help you explore the area pretty thoroughly, but if you just want to get to Circhester, then follow the path shown on the map on the previous page. It's the shortest way through Route 8!

1

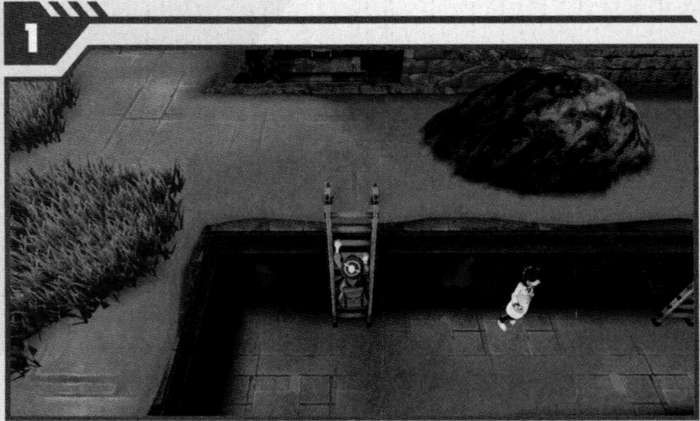

Route 8 is a maze of ruins and ladders, so we hope you're ready for some ups and downs! You can head up the ladder to the northwest, but that'll just get you to a Trainer Tips sign and a view of a TM. You can't get the TM until later, so for now just head down the first ladder you find on Route 8 to get to the lower level!

2

Get past a Trainer and climb back to the upper level. Before heading north, try taking the detour to the east and then south to pick up an item! You can then go north, down some stairs, and up a ladder to get to the next part of Route 8. From here, head to the west and up a ladder to pick up that TM behind the sign—TM96 Smart Strike!

3

Now you can proceed all the way east until you come to another ladder. Climb down, pick up an item, and then go up the next ladder you come to. You'll find yourself on yet another small platform with a ladder on its northeast corner, so climb down again. Go north through the tall grass until you reach the lip of the platform, then move on to the west to jump down a ledge!

4

You found a Big Nugget!

Head south, then east to grab an item, and then west past caves that Pokémon might jump out of. Keep going west to get another item, then turn north to where the road branches into a staircase continuing north and a path leading to the east. Climb up the stairs first to take on a Trainer and find a Big Nugget, then double back to the east.

5

Make your way past a musician and down yet another ladder. In this area you'll find a King's Rock—and a Nugget if you're attentive to the sparkle! Keep an eye out for the Falinks that pop out of the caves (and catch one if you'd like), and head up the stairs to the far east and up the ladder. The path to Circhester will be straight ahead—but first, take a westward path hidden behind a wall to nab TM43 Brick Break!

6

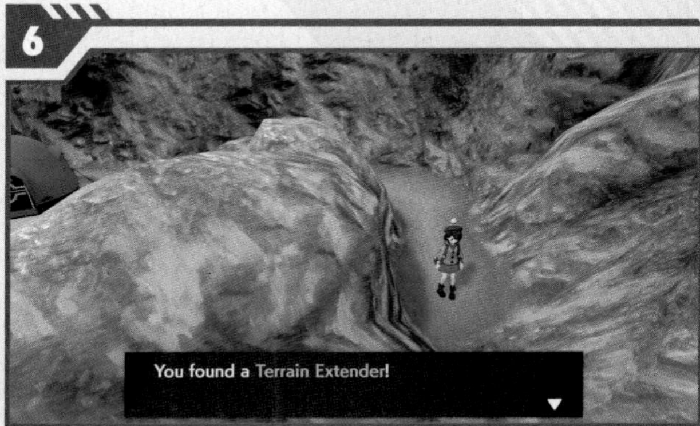
You found a Terrain Extender!

Now you have a choice: you can head back and go through the tunnel leading north toward Circhester, or you can go farther east first and pass some Trainers to find a campsite and—down another small path—a Terrain Extender!

7

After the hot, baked ruins of the southern part of Route 8, Steamdrift Way may come as a shock. The temperature seems to have dropped significantly, and amid the falling snowflakes, you'll find a Trainer and some new Pokémon to battle. Spend as much or as little time as you like in this new environment, because Circhester is just around the bend!

Circhester

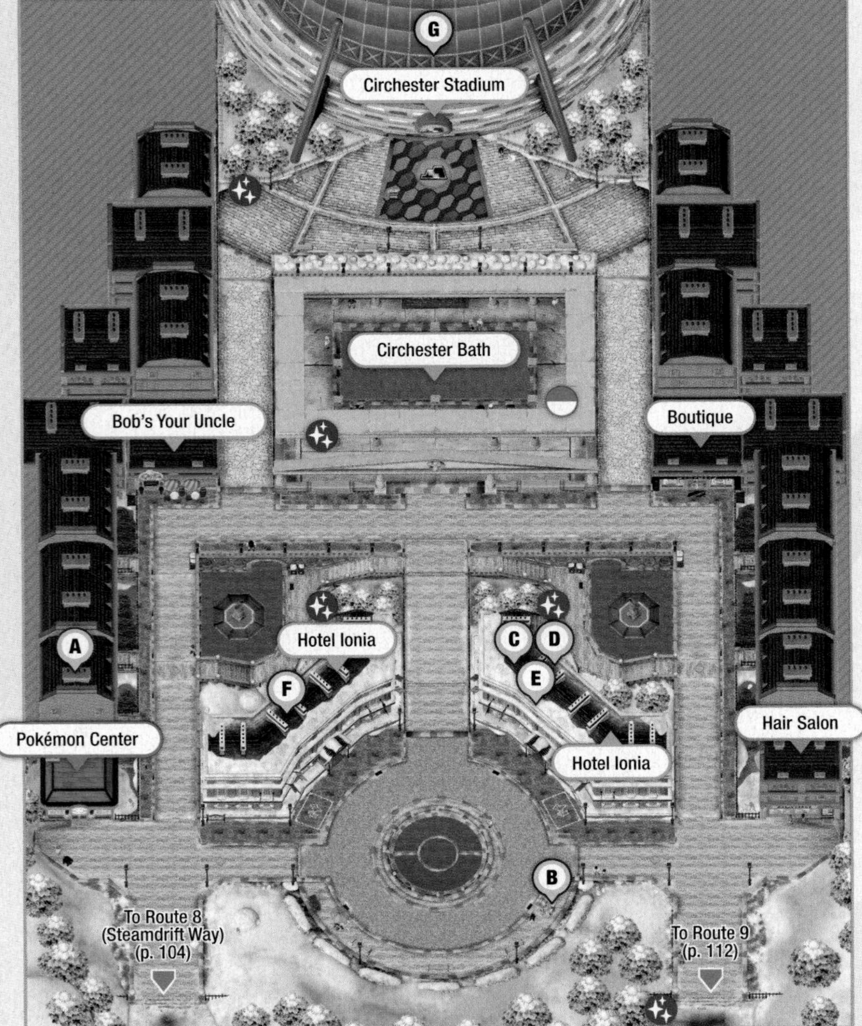

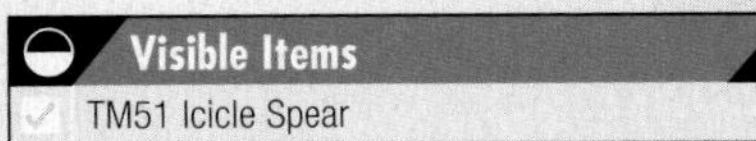

Visible Items

- TM51 Icicle Spear

Hidden Items

- Full Heal ×3
- Poké Doll
- Snowball
- Lemonade
- X Sp. Atk ×2

A

Stop by the house behind the Pokémon Center, and speak to the young man inside to receive TM27 Icy Wind in *Pokémon Sword* or TM48 Rock Tomb in *Pokémon Shield*, as well as some advice on how to find TRs!

- TM27 Icy Wind
- TM48 Rock Tomb

B

On the east side of the main square, you'll find a man at a vending stall who wants a Vanillish in exchange for his Throh in *Pokémon Sword* or Sawk in *Pokémon Shield*. This is a good trade if you're looking to fill your Pokédex, since Throh can't be found in the wild in *Pokémon Sword*, while Sawk is similarly elusive in *Pokémon Shield*! Having a Fighting-type Pokémon on your team can also come in handy when you face the Circhester Gym Leader. You can catch Vanillish on Route 8's Steamdrift Way, just outside Circhester, so why not make this old man happy?

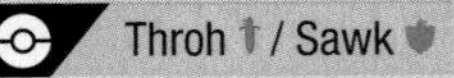

Throh / Sawk

1

Welcome to the snowy town of Circhester! This place is full of history, including an ancient hot-spring bath where it is said that heroes healed and rested. For now, why not take some time to look around? There's plenty to explore in this chilly town—up ahead from the entrance, there's the restaurant Bob's Your Uncle, and to the east, you'll find a boutique and hair salon!

Draco Meteor Move Tutor

At the end of the central street, you'll find a large hot-spring bath with quite a few people standing around it. Of particular interest is the old man on the left side of the bath, who'll teach your Pokémon the powerful Dragon-type move Draco Meteor!

2

While you're exploring, don't forget to stop by the two buildings of Hotel Ionia, located on the east and west of the main square! You can head up the elevators inside and visit the guest rooms, too, where you can get some more items from the people inside!

> **!** While exploring Circhester, don't miss TM51 Icicle Spear near the bath! You can find it on the opposite side from the Move Tutor.

C

Go up the elevator in the eastern Hotel Ionia building, and enter the first room on the left—you'll run into what appears to be a detective solving a crime. Help him find the culprit, and you'll receive a Wide Lens!

- Wide Lens

D

You're not done yet! Go into the first room on the right, and speak to the hiker inside—he'll give you TM16 Screech!

- TM16 Screech

E

But wait, there's more! Go to the room all the way to the right, where you'll find a musician who'll give you TM47 Fake Tears!

- TM47 Fake Tears

F

Now it's time to head over to the western building of Hotel Ionia. Take the elevator, and enter the room on the far left—there'll be a bunch of people here, but you'll especially want to speak to the man dressed up like a doctor near the windows. He'll give you a Catching Charm for now, but remember where he is! You're going to want to come back once you complete your Pokédex.

- Catching Charm

> **!** There's also a police officer nearby who wants you to come back when you're as strong as a Champion. We'll remind you when it's time to come back and speak to him again!

3

If you're done poking around and getting a feel for the town, head to Circhester Stadium. Just like in Stow-on-Side, you'll face different Gym Leaders in Circhester depending on which version of the game you're playing. If you're playing *Pokémon Sword*, you'll be facing down the Rock-type specialist Gordie, while in *Pokémon Shield*, you'll have to brave the cold fury of Melony. You'll get the League Card of the Gym Leader in your version of the game from Hop inside the stadium, so read up before you start the Gym mission!

- Gordie's League Card (Sword) / Melony's League Card (Shield)

G

There they are again, good old Ball Guy! Like clockwork, they've come to Circhester to cheer you on. They'll also give you a Moon Ball to add to your Poké Ball collection.

- Moon Ball

Circhester Gym Mission

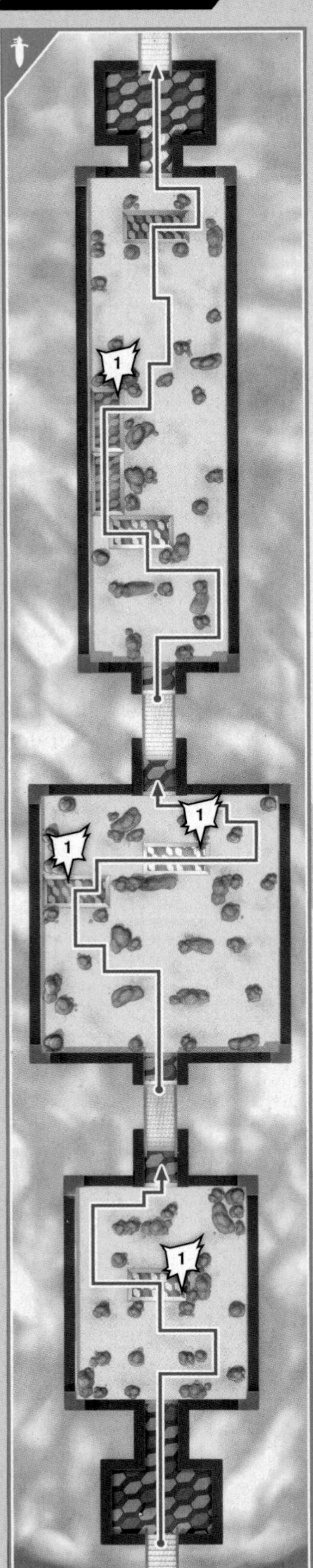

1 Whether you're challenging the Rock- or Ice-type Gym, you'll be facing the same mission—navigating a lengthy maze riddled with pitfalls! Pay attention to the vibrations of the Trap Detector and use the map to make your way to the Leader!

! Even if you keep falling into the holes, don't give up! The holes you fall into will remain open, so sooner or later you'll be able to navigate a clear path to the goal!

2 The first section of the maze isn't too bad. You'll need to head east, then north, then west to reach a checkpoint with a Trainer. Then all you need to do is make your way west around the holes and walls to reach the goal!

3 Now things get trickier. The maze is much more complicated now, so watch your step! You'll first head north—not too far, or you'll fall in a hole—until you're just past the wall, and then west. Next, go north while watching out for the small holes to the sides of your path until you find a safe spot and a Trainer. Then, make your way to the next safe spot (and Trainer) to the east, and then keep going east until you can loop around to the north to the goal!

4 This is the final section of the maze, but also the longest. You'll notice that visibility is greatly reduced—be extra careful where you're going! From the starting point, it's best to head east first to circle around to the checkpoint. Then, stick to the platform until you come to a Trainer. The next section has lots of little holes, so check the map to the left to make it to the next checkpoint. From there, the goal is within your reach! Don't rush right toward it, though—the final pitfall is right in front of you. Head to the east or west to loop around to the finish line.

5 Now it's time to meet the Gym Leader of Circhester. Make sure you adjust your team based on the opponent you're facing! You'll want Water-, Grass-, or Ground-type Pokémon for Gordie, and you'll want Fire-, Fighting-, or Rock-type Pokémon to take down Melony. Let the battle begin!

Shortest route

*The map shown is from *Pokémon Sword*. The colors will look different if you are playing *Pokémon Shield*, but the basic layout is the same.

Gordie

Gordie's built himself a team of rock-solid Pokémon with high Defense. Most of his Pokémon deal damage using physical moves, so countering with Pokémon of your own that have high Defense and Sp. Atk seems like a good choice. While most of his Pokémon have a second type, giving them a few different weaknesses and resistances, they are generally weak to Ground-type moves. Using just Pokémon with high Defense may not work, though. Gordie's Stonjourner uses the move Wonder Room, which swaps the Defense and Sp. Def of all Pokémon! Gordie's ace is a Coalossal that he'll Gigantamax as soon as he sends it out. Its G-Max Volcalith move will cause non-Rock-type Pokémon to lose 1/16 of their HP every round for a few turns. Thankfully, Coalossal is very weak to both Water- and Ground-type moves, taking 400% damage from them! If you can, try to focus on moves of those types to break through Gigantamax Coalossal's high HP.

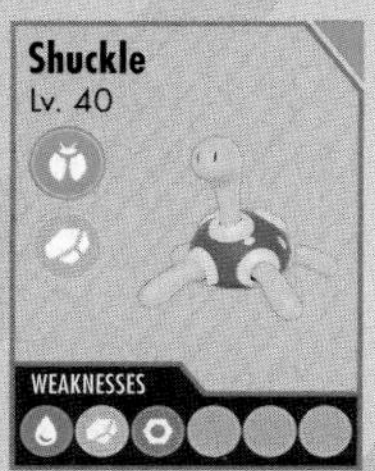

Melony

Like mother, like son. While all of Melony's team members share the Ice type, they have varying weaknesses because most of her Pokémon have different second types—just like Gordie's Pokémon. Ironically, all of Melony's Pokémon share a weakness to Rock-type moves, particularly Frosmoth, which takes 400% damage from them! Melony also makes use of a few Pokémon with very tricky Abilities that can easily alter the pace of the battle. Her Darmanitan starts as an Ice-type Pokémon, but its Zen Mode Ability will change it into an Ice- and Fire-type Pokémon once its HP drops to half or lower. Melony's Eiscue can also be quite troublesome. Its Ice Face Ability will prevent damage from one physical move, similar to Mimikyu's Disguise Ability—except Ice Face reforms in hail and doesn't prevent special moves. Melony will waste no time and Gigantamax her Lapras right after sending it out! Its G-Max Resonance move will reduce any damage from physical or special moves that Lapras would take. This makes Melony's Lapras very defensive and hard to knock out. Don't forget that burning or poisoning a Pokémon with high HP is a great way to give you an advantage against it in battle.

Rock Badge / Ice Badge

You've now obtained your sixth Gym Badge! That medal on your League Card must be looking pretty full now. The Gym Badge from Circhester will allow you to catch Pokémon of up to Lv. 50, and now Poké Marts will offer Full Heals!

6 Now that you've defeated the Circhester Gym Leader, you only need one more Badge before heading back to Hammerlocke and taking on Raihan. But who is the seventh Gym Leader?

 Rock Uniform, TM48 Rock Tomb

 Ice Uniform, TM27 Icy Wind

4

Sonia will be waiting for you once you leave the stadium. She'll invite you for a meal to celebrate your victory, but she wants to bounce some ideas off you, too. Bob's Your Uncle is just down the little hill west of the stadium, so head on over and see what Sonia has to say!

5

Once at the restaurant, you'll see that Hop has joined you as well. Sonia will start talking about how she's hit a wall in her research, but it's not long before she notices the antique tapestry in the back! Somehow, a piece of Galar's legends has ended up here!

Legends of Galar: What happened to the Pokémon?

The tapestry in Bob's Your Uncle seems to continue the story of the tapestries found in Hammerlocke. It shows the two youths, now with their crowns, looking sadly at what appear to be two stones. What happened to the sword and shield Pokémon? Did they meet their end, or were they sealed away by someone? Or something else?

6

There is still a lot of mystery surrounding the ancient legends of Galar. After a meal with Hop and Sonia, follow them to the Hero's Bath for a bit more investigation. Once you're there, Hop will challenge you to a battle. Sonia will heal your Pokémon for you, so make sure to show her a battle worthy of the legends!

Hop

Hop seems to have found a team he's comfortable with—much of it is made up of Pokémon you've seen him use before. He has two Normal-type Pokémon, Dubwool and Snorlax. Both are weak to Fighting-type moves, but their stats are very different. Dubwool has more balanced Defense and Sp. Def, while Snorlax has somewhat low Defense and very high Sp. Def. Pincurchin is an unusual Electric-type Pokémon. It has very high Attack but low HP and Speed. If you can knock it out quickly with a Ground-type move before it has a chance to get in big hits, that's probably best. Corviknight has high Defense, but like Pincurchin, it's not all that fast. Try to focus on special Fire- and Electric-type moves to deal high damage to it. Hop's Inteleon, Rillaboom, or Cinderace is still at a disadvantage against your first partner Pokémon. Even so, you may want to send out a Pokémon with high Sp. Def to counter Inteleon—or one with high Defense to counter Rillaboom or Cinderace. It will be hailing during this battle, so be sure to bring a Pokémon that can change the weather if that's a problem for your team!

If you chose Sobble
Cinderace
Lv. 41
WEAKNESSES

WALKTHROUGH

7

Hop
Then, once I get that Gym Badge, I'll be heading for Route 9 to take on Spikemuth next.

After your battle, Hop will be off to challenge the Gym again. As for you, you need to travel to Route 9 and onward to Spikemuth!

Route 9

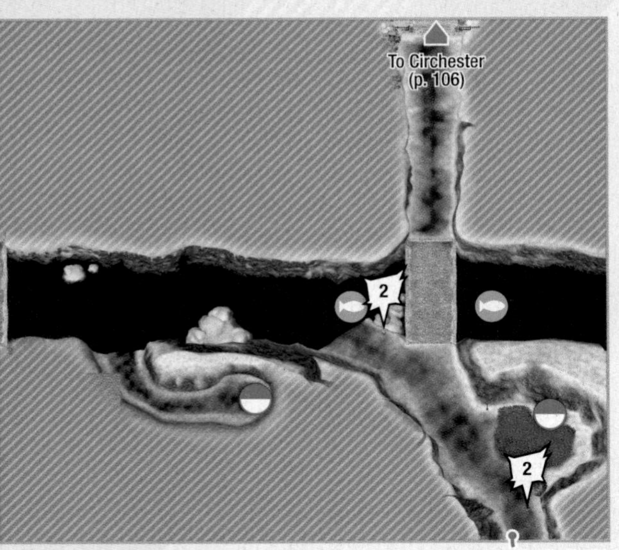

CATCH!

Dhelmise

Catch elusive Dhelmise here—it doesn't appear anywhere else!

Circhester Bay

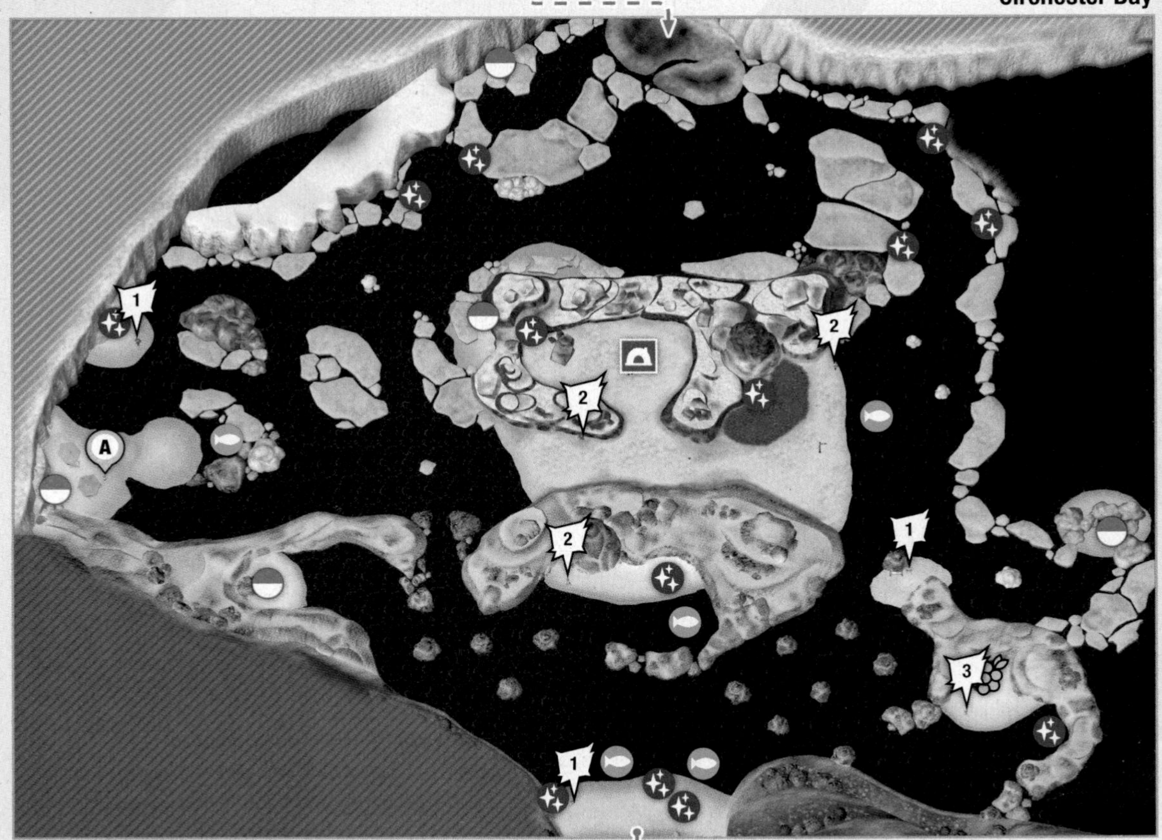

Outer Spikemuth

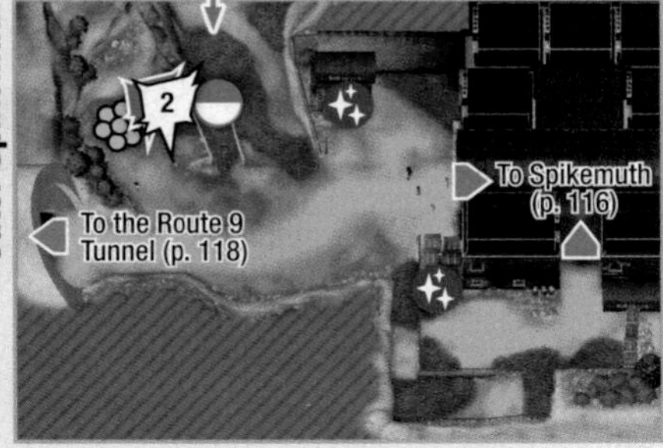

Visible Items
Max Potion
TM64 Avalanche
Circhester Bay
Zoom Lens
Protector
Max Revive
Dive Ball ×3
TM22 Rock Slide
Outer Spikemuth
Scope Lens

Hidden Items
Circhester Bay
Big Pearl
Pearl String
Ice Stone
Never-Melt Ice
Rare Candy
Big Pearl
Pearl
Black Belt
Normal Gem
PP Up
Pearl
Big Pearl
Max Elixir
Outer Spikemuth
Dire Hit ×3
Guard Spec. ×3

Tall Grass		
063	Pelipper	◎
156	Pyukumuku	☆
231	Gastrodon (East Sea)	△
306	Jellicent †	☆
306	Jellicent ⛉	○
307	Mareanie †	○
307	Mareanie ⛉	☆
	Circhester Bay	
149	Octillery	○
235	Barbaracle †	△
235	Barbaracle ⛉	○
308	Toxapex †	○
308	Toxapex ⛉	☆
351	Clobbopus	○
358	Bergmite †	△
358	Bergmite ⛉	○
360	Dhelmise	★
	Outer Spikemuth	
306	Jellicent	☆
307	Mareanie	○
308	Toxapex	☆
351	Clobbopus	○
358	Bergmite	◎
360	Dhelmise	★

Random Encounters		
099	Kingler	○
149	Octillery	○
309	Cramorant	◎
353	Pincurchin	☆
	Circhester Bay	
231	Gastrodon (East Sea)	○
290	Inkay	○
309	Cramorant	◎
353	Pincurchin	☆

Random Encounters		
	Outer Spikemuth	
030	Thievul	○
045	Liepard	○
183	Perrserker	◎
344	Morpeko	☆

Water Surface		
063	Pelipper	◎
304	Qwilfish	○
306	Jellicent	☆
354	Mantyke	○
	Circhester Bay	
148	Remoraid	△
352	Grapploct	◎
354	Mantyke	○
355	Mantine	△
356	Wailmer	◎

Wanderers		
◆ 080	Glalie	◎

Berry Trees		
	Circhester Bay	
025	Greedent	◎
	Outer Spikemuth	
025	Greedent	◎

Fishing		
149	Octillery	◎
155	Wishiwashi	○
156	Pyukumuku	△
	Circhester Bay	
354	Mantyke	◎
355	Mantine	△
356	Wailmer	○
357	Wailord	☆
361	Lapras	★

◎ frequent ○ common △ average ☆ rare ★ almost never
† *Pokémon Sword* only ⛉ *Pokémon Shield* only

1

You can get to Route 9 by leaving Circhester from the eastern exit. From there, carry on down the road, past a few Trainers and an item along the way. Soon you'll see a couple of Team Yell Grunts—what are they up to this time?

2

Get close to them, and you'll see that they're cheering on the Drednaw—but also preventing people from getting to Spikemuth! The doctor who gave you your bike is also there, and it seems he could use some help. Send Team Yell packing, and see what useful reward he has for you this time!

Team Yell Grunt

Team Yell never seems to learn, no matter how many times they lose to you. This Grunt uses a Linoone and a Pangoro. Linoone is particularly weak to Fighting-type moves, taking 400% damage from them. You can also get supereffective hits with Bug- and Fairy-type moves. Linoone isn't particularly powerful, but it does have very high Speed. Pangoro is much slower but is also able to deal a lot more damage with physical moves, as its Attack is very high. Pangoro will take 400% damage from Fairy-type moves, though. So if you have a speedy Pokémon with a good Fairy-type move, try to use it to knock out Pangoro before it can deal too much damage to your team.

3

This time, the doctor will modify your bike so you can ride over water! You can use this to move on to Spikemuth, of course, but it wouldn't hurt to go back to locations you've already visited and check out paths you couldn't explore before—like the little loop that lies west of the bridge you crossed earlier on Route 9. There's a TM waiting for you there!

4

Route 9 is one of the more convoluted routes in the Galar region. Spikemuth is located to the south, but it's worth taking the time to explore the route. There are lots of goodies for you to find!

!

The Wild Area has several bodies of water for you to bike across, as do locations like Galar Mine No. 2. You can also head back northward on Route 9 to bike on the river and find TM64 Avalanche! Don't forget about Route 2, either. You can ride over the big lake near Professor Magnolia's home and catch some interesting Pokémon, like Obstagoon and Drednaw!

5

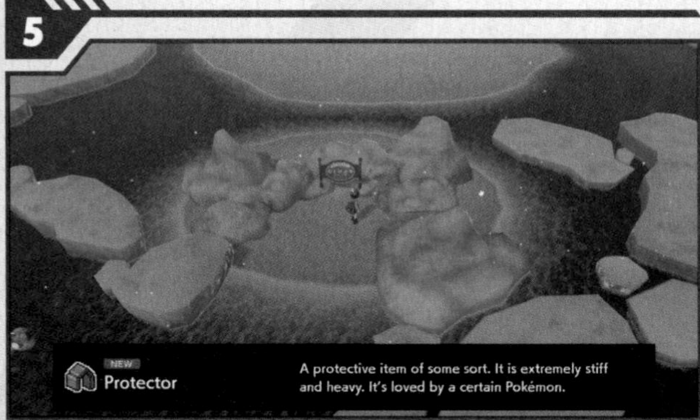

NEW
Protector
A protective item of some sort. It is extremely stiff and heavy. It's loved by a certain Pokémon.

The first path leading to the west from the shore where you got your bike upgraded is a dead end, but you'll find a Zoom Lens there. Then ride back to where you met Team Yell and head east and then south. When a small island with a Trainer Tips sign on it comes into view, turn east and you'll come to another little island with a sign and a Protector.

6

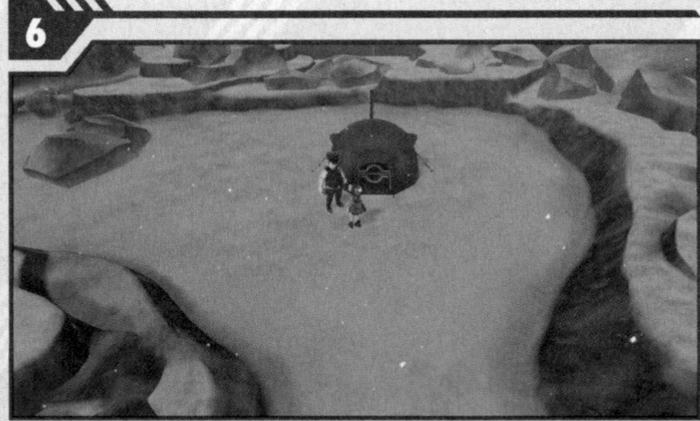

Going west from where you find the Protector will bring you to a large landmass in the center of the route. Here you'll find a campsite, if you want to cook and heal up! And keep your eyes open for sparkles on this landmass. You don't want to miss out on free items, and you'll even find a Rare Candy behind the rocks to the west of the campsite!

7

Keep heading west from the campsite, with a small detour north if you want to grab a Max Revive. Eventually you'll come to a beach where you'll see two people in bathing suits. Behind them you'll find three Dive Balls!

A

The two swimmers apparently treat this little beach as their own little private getaway. It seems a bit cold for swimming, but the lady doesn't seem to mind. In fact, she'll even give you TM45 Dive!

 TM45 Dive

8

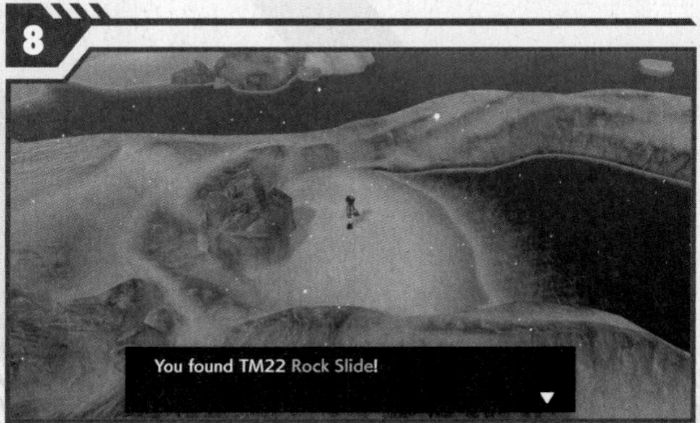

From the little beach, bike east again, then south through the small passage between rocks. From here, you can find a Berry tree to the east and TM22 Rock Slide to the west. If you're happy with your exploration, then just travel south to reach Outer Spikemuth, where you'll find a few more items and another Berry tree.

9

Once you reach Outer Spikemuth, it'll be clear that something's amiss. The city's entrance is shuttered, and Gym Challengers are stuck outside! Thankfully for you, Marnie's in the area, and it turns out Spikemuth is her hometown. She knows another way in, but you'll need to battle her if you want to hear about it!

Marnie

Though Marnie's team has grown much stronger since your first battle with her, she's still using the same Pokémon. Most of her team is weak to Fighting- and Fairy-type moves and specialize in physical moves. However, Fairy-type moves may be a better choice, as her Scrafty will take 400% damage from them. Liepard is quite fast, but it's not a great damage dealer. If you've got a Pokémon even faster, or a slower one that can take a few hits while dealing out high damage, Liepard shouldn't give you too much trouble. Marnie's Scrafty has both high Defense and Sp. Def. If you don't knock it out quickly, it can deal a good amount of damage using physical attacks. This is a good time to use those Fairy-type moves if you've got them! Toxicroak is Marnie's odd one out, being her only non-Dark-type Pokémon. Psychic-type moves are your best choice against it, as they'll deal 400% damage. Morpeko is very much the same as the last time you battled Marnie. Make sure to pay attention to what form it's in, as this affects the type of Morpeko's signature move, Aura Wheel.

Spikemuth

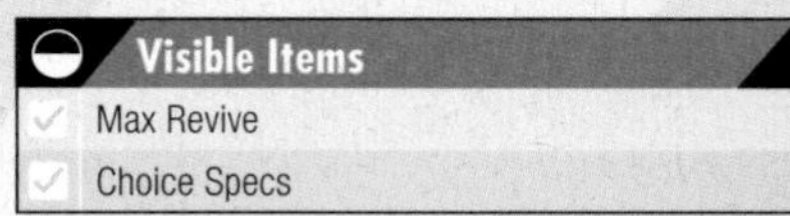

Visible Items
Max Revive
Choice Specs

1

The first thing you'll see once you enter Spikemuth is the Pokémon Center. Stop by if you need to heal up your team, and then go east to talk to Marnie. She'll give you the League Card of the Spikemuth Gym Leader before heading off to figure out what's going on.

 Piers's League Card

2

Once you part ways with Marnie, the Team Yell Grunt will ask that you get changed into your uniform for the Gym mission. It seems that you'll be able to continue on your Gym Challenge—but why is Team Yell involved?

Spikemuth Gym Mission

1 The mission you'll face is actually a gauntlet of Team Yell Grunts trying to prevent you from reaching the Gym Leader! You'll have to defeat a total of six Grunts before you make it to the end, and you'll have to face two of them in a Double Battle! They're not much different from the Grunts you've faced previously, so you should already know how to get them out of your way.

If you run into an invisible wall, try backtracking a little bit. Team Yell won't keep you waiting long!

2 As it turns out, Team Yell Grunts are actually Spikemuth Gym Trainers! They were all trying to help Marnie reach the Champion Cup by removing the competition, but Marnie herself's not too pleased. She'll tell you to go on and face the Gym Leader, while she gives Team Yell a scolding!

A In the corner of the court, there's a Team Yell Grunt in a stall. He wants to trade his Mr. Mime from another region for an Obstagoon! Linoone caught in Galar will evolve into Obstagoon if it reaches Lv. 35 at night, and you can catch Linoone in the Wild Area!

 Mr. Mime

Gym Leader Piers

Piers is Marnie's older brother, so it makes sense that he's just as experienced in using Dark-type Pokémon. He's also the only Gym Leader who doesn't use Dynamax. There's no Power Spot at his Gym, which means you won't be able to use Dynamax, either. He leads with Scrafty, a Pokémon Marnie also used. If you use the same strategy against his Scrafty that you did against Marnie's, you shouldn't have too much trouble knocking it out quickly. Remember, Fairy-type moves deal 400% damage against it. Malamar has a pretty balanced set of stats, but its Sp. Atk and Sp. Def are lower than its Attack and Defense. Bug-type moves are fantastic against Malamar, if you have any. Piers's Skuntank is Poison and Dark type. That means it's only weak to Ground-type moves. Steelix is great for this battle. Obstagoon is the strongest Pokémon on Piers's team and is immune to both Psychic- and Ghost-type moves. It also has a signature move called Obstruct. This move works like Protect, guarding Obstagoon from your moves, but can also lower an attacking Pokémon's Defense!

3 Defeating Piers will grant you the seventh Gym Badge—now you're ready to battle Raihan in Hammerlocke. Leave Marnie to face her big brother, and claim your rewards!

 Dark Uniform, TM85 Snarl

Dark Badge

The seventh Gym Badge of the Gym Challenge will allow you to catch Pokémon of up to Lv. 55 and will also make Max Potions and Max Repels available for you to buy at Poké Marts!

Returning to Hammerlocke

1

Now it's time to return to Hammerlocke, but it seems that some sort of situation's been stirred up outside of the city. You'll hear what sounds like explosions, and you'll run into Leon himself—he's come out to investigate and see if he can get things under control. He'll head toward the Route 9 Tunnel, so follow him to see if you can help!

2

Enter the tunnel, and you'll see quite a crowd gathered. It sounds like somehow, Pokémon have started Dynamaxing along the route, even though there are no Power Spots nearby! Leon probably has things handled, but go on through the tunnel—after all, you need to get to Hammerlocke to battle your next and last Gym Leader!

3

After you exit the tunnel, you'll be met by Hop. Apparently he was caught up in whatever caused Pokémon to start Dynamaxing, but Leon was able to get things under control pretty quickly. He's also managed to make headlines in the process. After Hop goes off on his own again, you'll be able to have a look around.

4

Now, you may have already noticed that leaving the tunnel brought you to Route 7. You're actually just east of Hammerlocke now, in a little corner of the route you weren't able to reach before. Head west across the bridge and you'll start seeing a more familiar landscape—to the north is Route 8, the route you took to Circhester!

When you first came through Route 7, you may have noticed part of it was inaccessible. That's exactly where you are now! You'll find a campsite here with TM58 Assurance nearby. And make sure you don't miss the slope just after the bridge. Head downward to find an item and a Berry tree! If you want to check the map of Route 7 once more, turn back to page 101.

5

Now that you've got your seven Gym Badges, it's time to challenge the great Raihan himself and bring your Gym Challenge to an end! Raihan is waiting for you in Hammerlocke. Are you sure you're ready for him and his mighty team? Dragon types are famously strong, but they're weak to Ice-type moves. Did you nab any great Ice-type Pokémon back around Circhester? If you didn't, you might want to consider going back for one or two and then flying to Hammerlocke once more!

6

Once you reach Hammerlocke, stop by the Pokémon Center if you need to heal, and then head west. You'll find Hop, Leon, and Sonia gathered in front of the stadium. They're discussing what just happened, and Professor Magnolia will join the conversation, too!

7

The professor, Sonia, and Leon all have plenty to work on, and Hop seems eager to help out. But Leon makes it clear he'd prefer for both of you to focus on completing the Gym Challenge for now. After that, everyone will head off on their own way and you'll be free to explore Hammerlocke once more.

Legends of Galar: The Darkest Day and Dynamaxing

Professor Magnolia seems to suspect that the incident on Route 7 and the Darkest Day are connected somehow. It's true that evidence suggests the Darkest Day involved massive Pokémon. Could it be that somehow Pokémon were able to Dynamax without being near Power Spots? Is this how the Darkest Day began, all those years ago? If so, then the Dynamax Pokémon on Route 7 may well be a sign of something far more dire...

8

At this point, you could go talk to the weather man (p. 82) if you haven't heard everything he has to say. Raihan has a fondness for changing the weather condition in battle, so it would be wise to know what each weather condition does! You could also check to see if your Pokémon have become more friendly toward you, but it's best to follow Leon's advice—head into Hammerlocke Stadium.

Hammerlocke Gym Mission

1 You'll need to speak to the Gym Trainer at the far entrance to get the Gym mission started, but before you do, make sure you have at least two battle-ready Pokémon in your team. You'll find out why soon enough...

2 Raihan's Gym mission is actually held in the vault and appears deceptively simple—you only need to defeat three Gym Trainers! But there's a catch, of course. They were all personally trained by Raihan himself, and you'll be facing them in Double Battles! Each one will employ different strategies to throw you off, so make sure your team is set up properly before taking them on!

Gym Trainer Sebastian

Sebastian's Pelipper will trigger the rain weather condition as soon as the battle begins. Don't let him wash you away!

Lv. 45

Lv. 45

Gym Trainer Camilla

Camilla likes things a bit hotter, and she'll trigger harsh sunlight with her Ninetales to try to roast you in this battle.

Lv. 45

Lv. 45

Gym Trainer Aria

Using Ice types against the dragons in this gym? You're not alone! Aria will bring the hail with her Ice-type Abomasnow.

Lv. 45

Lv. 45

3 Once you defeat the three Gym Trainers, it's finally time to face Raihan. He's the only Trainer in all of Galar that Leon considers a rival, and he has skills to match his reputation! Now it's time to show Leon that he's got another rival on the rise!

Raihan

Raihan's battle is very different from those of other Gym Leaders because it's a Double Battle. Thankfully you've already had some practice with Double Battles during his Gym mission. His team is also somewhat unusual—despite being the keeper of the Dragon Badge, he only uses two Dragon-type Pokémon. He starts off with Gigalith and Flygon. Gigalith's Sand Stream Ability will immediately kick up a sandstorm. This means that any Pokémon that isn't Ground, Rock, or Steel type will lose 1/16 of its HP at the end of each turn. If you have a Pokémon that can change the weather to something more favorable to your side, it's best to do so. Many types of moves, including Water- and Grass-type moves, deal 200% damage to Gigalith. Ice-type moves are the best way to deal with Flygon, but make sure your Pokémon can take a hit from Flygon first, as it will probably outspeed them. Raihan will likely send in Sandaconda next. When Sandaconda is hit by a move, its Sand Spit Ability will create a sandstorm, so be careful. Raihan's last Pokémon is Duraludon. He will Gigantamax this fearsome Pokémon right away. Duraludon has massive Defense and Sp. Atk, and its signature G-Max Depletion will take away PP from the moves of Pokémon on your side of the field. It's best to use special moves, as Duraludon has very low Sp. Def.

Dragon Badge

Defeat Raihan, and you'll receive the eighth and final Gym Badge of the Gym Challenge. You'll now be able to catch Pokémon of any level, and you'll also find that Full Restores are now available at Poké Marts!

4 Raihan's the last Gym Leader in the Gym Challenge. You've got all the Gym Badges now, so collect your TM and uniform! Hop will arrive to challenge Raihan, too, after successfully defeating Piers. It sure seems like he's back to his old self, so leave him to his battle and be on your way!

 Dragon Uniform, TM99 Breaking Swipe

9

Once outside the Gym Stadium, you'll find Professor Magnolia and Sonia waiting for you. While you've been busy completing the Gym Challenge, it looks like Sonia's been hard at work, too—and it's paid off! Professor Magnolia will give her lab coat to Sonia as a symbol of trust and acknowledgment. Meet Professor Sonia!

10

Now it's finally time to make your way to Wyndon, where the Champion Cup will be held! Head east toward Route 7 and enter the station. Hop will join you—he certainly made short work of Raihan and his Gym mission! Now, onward to Route 10 and Wyndon for you two!

Route 10 is a great place to catch Ice-type Pokémon, but on the flip side, you won't find many other types of Pokémon there. Since you can now catch Pokémon of all levels—and take part in five-star Max Raid Battles—it's not a bad idea to stop by the Wild Area to see if there are any Pokémon you'd like to add to your team!

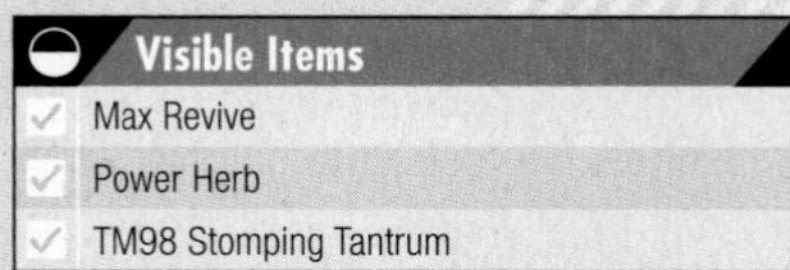

Route 10

Visible Items

Item
Max Revive
Power Herb
TM98 Stomping Tantrum

Hidden Items

Item
X Attack ×2
Comet Shard
PP Up

Tall Grass

No.	Pokémon	Rate
074	Vanilluxe	△
080	Glalie	△
096	Snover	○
279	Cubchoo	○
365	Mr. Mime	○
North		
096	Snover	○
279	Cubchoo	○
292	Sneasel	△
365	Mr. Mime	○
371	Duraludon	★

Random Encounters

No.	Pokémon	Rate
073	Vanillish †	○
073	Vanillish (Shield)	☆
114	Klang	○
265	Rhydon	○
349	Snom	△
367	Darumaka †	☆
North		
073	Vanillish †	○
073	Vanillish (Shield)	☆
097	Abomasnow	○
280	Beartic	○
349	Snom	△
367	Darumaka †	☆
369	Stonjourner †	☆
370	Eiscue (Shield)	☆

Wanderers

No.	Pokémon	Rate
North		
097	Abomasnow	◎
280	Beartic	◎

◎ frequent ○ common △ average ☆ rare ★ almost never

† *Pokémon Sword* only (Shield) *Pokémon Shield* only

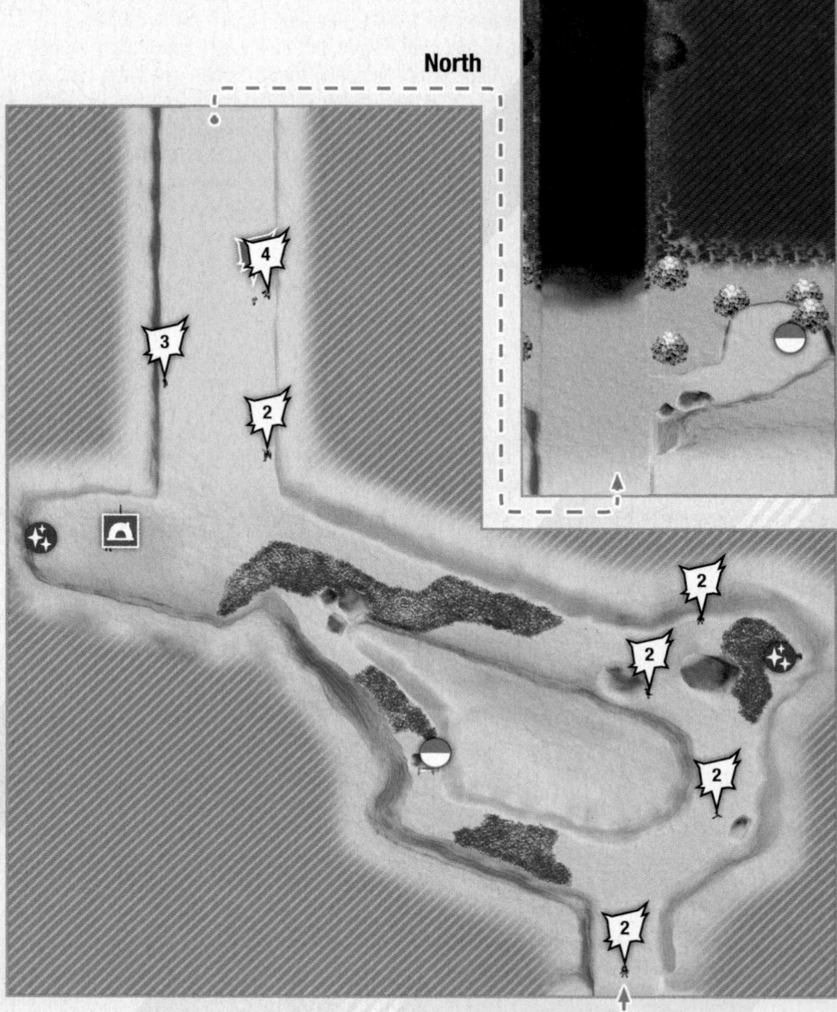

CATCH!
Beartic
You can catch Beartic near the campsite on this route!

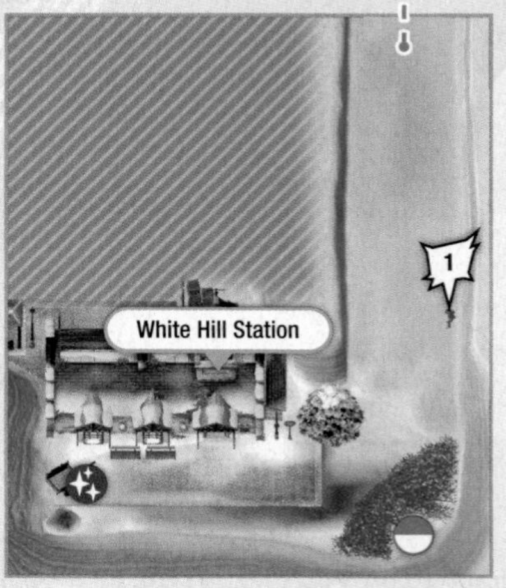

1

Route 10 is a snowy mountain path, with Wyndon located to its north. Reaching Wyndon itself shouldn't be too difficult—you'll run into some Trainers along the way, but they shouldn't prove too much trouble if you've made it this far. But it's worth going off the beaten track to find some good items along the way!

2

The only way you can go at first is north, up the hill by the station. Nab the item at its base first, and then head on up! At the top of the hill, you'll come to branching paths. The path to the west is a dead end with a Trainer Tip there—you can check it out, but the northeastern path is the one you want to take!

3

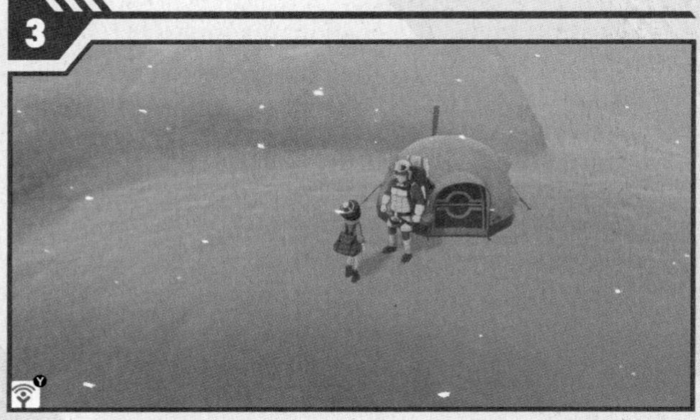

Keep following the path, and you'll come to another set of branching roads. The hill heading north leads to Wyndon, but wait! You'll find a campsite with an item sparkle nearby to the west, and if you take the little road south, you'll find an item at its end!

4

If you're done catching Pokémon and gathering items, go up the hill heading north. Make your way past a gauntlet of Trainers, and you'll see Wyndon just ahead! You're almost there!

!

It may be tempting to head straight toward Wyndon, especially if you need to heal up and resupply, but resist the urge to rush! There's a small hidden path just off the right side of the road that leads to TM98 Stomping Tantrum!

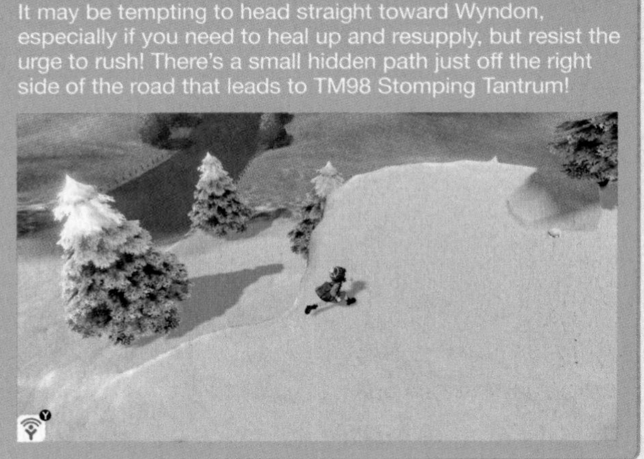

Wyndon

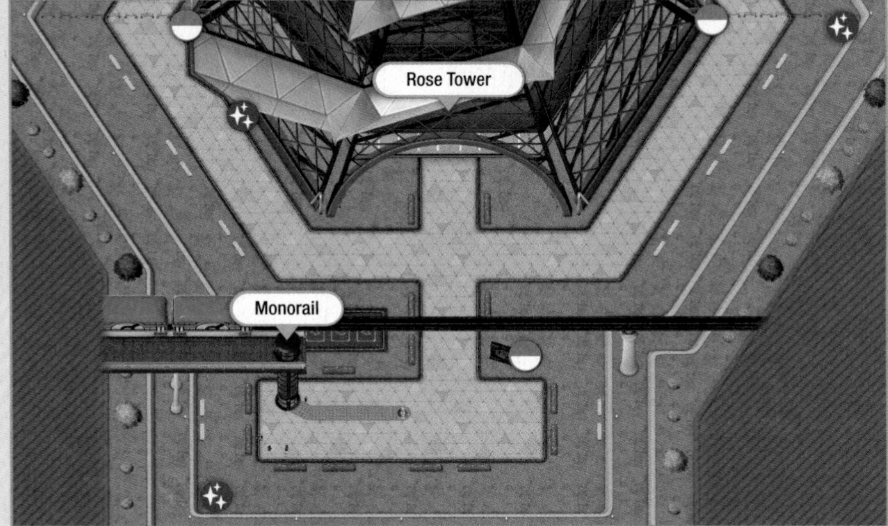
Rose Tower
Monorail

Rose of the Rondelands
Monorail

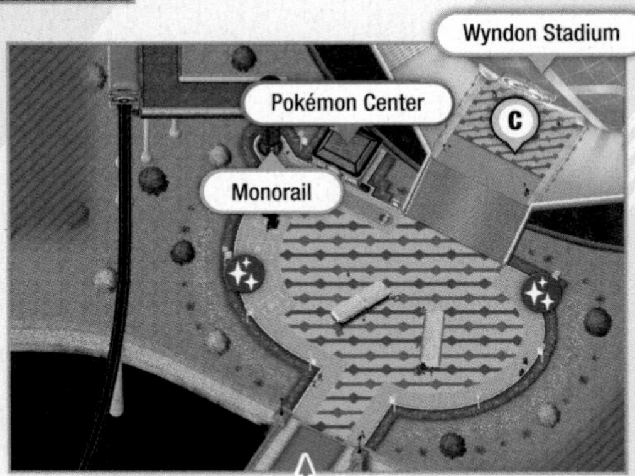
Wyndon Stadium
Pokémon Center
Monorail
C

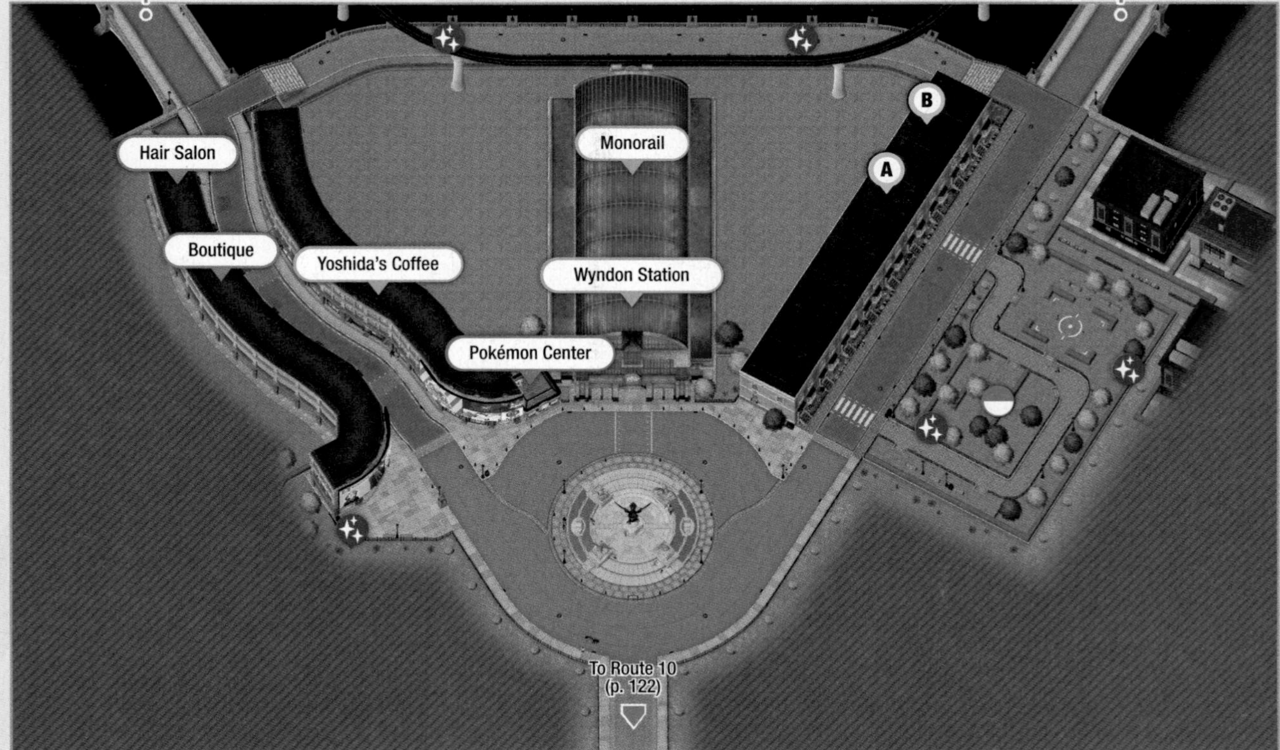
B
A
Hair Salon
Monorail
Boutique
Yoshida's Coffee
Wyndon Station
Pokémon Center
To Route 10
(p. 122)

Visible Items

✓	Grassy Seed
✓	Air Balloon
	Rose Tower
✓	TM93 Eerie Impulse
✓	Cell Battery
✓	Electric Seed

Hidden Items

✓	Max Revive
✓	Rare Candy
✓	Balm Mushroom
✓	Nugget
✓	Black Sludge
✓	Big Nugget
✓	X Speed
✓	X Sp. Atk ×2

Hidden Items

	Rose Tower
✓	Rare Candy
✓	PP Up
✓	Nugget

Poké Mart (south)

Calcium	₽10,000
Carbos	₽10,000
HP Up	₽10,000
Iron	₽10,000
Luxury Ball	₽3,000
Protein	₽10,000
Quick Ball	₽1,000
Repeat Ball	₽1,000
Zinc	₽10,000

Poké Mart (stadium front)

TM03 Fire Punch	₽50,000
TM04 Ice Punch	₽50,000
TM05 Thunder Punch	₽50,000
TM08 Hyper Beam	₽50,000
TM09 Giga Impact	₽50,000
TM12 Solar Blade	₽50,000
TM60 Power Swap	₽30,000
TM61 Guard Swap	₽30,000
TM62 Speed Swap	₽30,000
TM63 Drain Punch	₽50,000

1

The moment you arrive in Wyndon, Hop will dash off toward the stadium, where the Semifinals will be held. You can head over immediately to participate, but there's plenty to see in Wyndon, too! You can pick up some new clothes at the boutique, get a haircut at the salon, and even have a daily battle at the Battle Café!

A

As you walk northeast toward the stadium, you'll pass several colorful houses on your left. Enter the sixth one you pass this way (it's light blue), and you'll find an artist who's looking for a trade! If you have a Frosmoth, he'll be happy to exchange his Duraludon for it! Duraludon are pretty rare, so this is a good chance to get one!

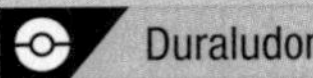

Duraludon

B Next, enter the orange house farther down the road. Inside, you'll find a League staff member who seems to be a huge fan of Rotom! He'll challenge you to a battle, in which he'll show off the various forms Rotom can take. Manage to defeat him, and he'll give you a Rotom Catalog. If you've caught a Rotom, now you'll be able to have it change its form!

Rotom Catalog

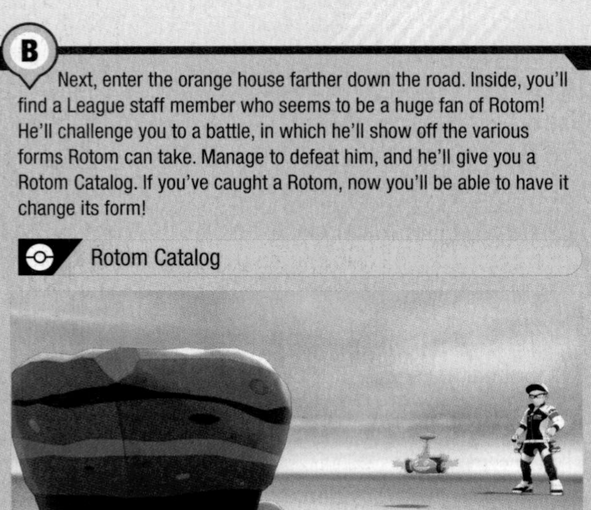

The Ultimate-Move Tutor

In the park opposite the houses, you'll find a man standing by a small pitch. He's the Ultimate-Move Tutor, and he can teach certain Pokémon some very powerful moves! The type of move he teaches depends on the type of the Pokémon you want to learn a move—he'll teach Blast Burn to Fire-type Pokémon, Hydro Cannon to Water-type Pokémon, and Frenzy Plant to Grass-type Pokémon. These are all powerful moves, so if your team needs a little extra kick, this man is the one to see! Turn to page 354 to find out which Pokémon can learn these moves.

2

Once you've had your fill of exploring, head north toward the stadium. There's a Pokémon Center nearby if you need to heal up—and your team needs to be in top shape for the Semifinals! Once you feel you're ready, enter the stadium!

C There they are again—the Ball Guy. And as always, they've got another Poké Ball for you! This time you'll receive a Dream Ball!

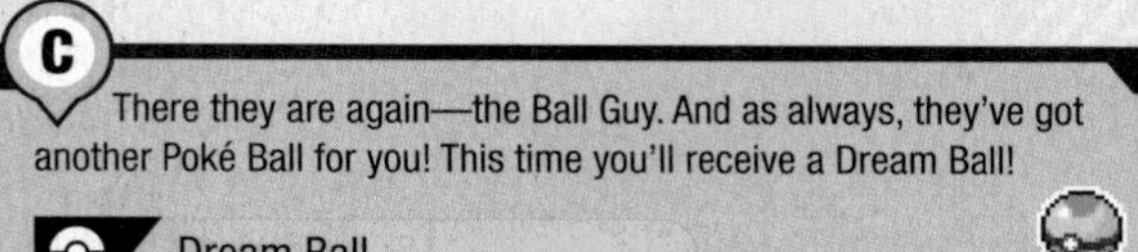

Dream Ball

3

This is it—you traveled the region and faced down eight Gym Leaders so that you could participate in the Champion Cup! Once you're registered, you'll be asked to go to the locker room. The Semifinals are ready to begin just as soon as you're ready for them! Read on for some final tips in the next section, then it will be time to take on the other Gym Challengers who have made it this far. Turn the page if you don't mind some spoilers!

Your Guide to the Champion Cup

Yes, it's true—once you step into the locker room here in Wyndon Stadium, you'll don your official kit and the Champion Cup will begin! Perhaps you're wondering if you've done everything you can to be ready for this ultimate challenge. We'll give you some pointers on that below, but first shake out those jitters, because there are a few key points to know about how the Champion Cup matches function. Knowing them might take some pressure off!

Once you enter the locker room, you'll be changed into your uniform. But it's not as though the doors have been locked forever! In fact, you can leave the locker room between each match, if you need to stock up on some more items or even if you feel like you need to train up your team a bit more before facing the next opponent.

Even if you don't need to go that far, you can access your Pokémon Boxes while you're in the locker room and switch up your team between opponents. If you're looking ahead to the next pages and checking out your opponents' weaknesses before you battle them, you can adjust your team to hit them where they're most vulnerable.

Worried about what happens if you lose a battle? It's not a game over, young challenger! Losing a battle in the Semifinals or the Finals simply means you'll have to try again—you'll be sent back to the stadium's lobby. So if that's where you find yourself, get your head on straight and try once more to tackle the challenge that lies before you.

If you don't want to completely spoil yourself for the coming battles but you also want some idea what you're going to have to make it through, here's a little hint. Thanks to the elimination round format of the Semifinals and Finals, you'll have to face two opponents in the Semifinals and then you'll be facing four opponents in the Finals—if you make it that far!

Last-minute prep

Your team should be quite well trained by this point, but sometimes it's that last finishing touch that can mean the difference between victory and defeat! If you're struggling to beat your opponents or are worried about whether you'll be able to, consider these last-minute tips.

Have you used up all your Exp. Candies and Rare Candies? A few extra levels never hurt anyone, and the Exp. Candies you can get in the Wild Area can be a great way to level up in a hurry. And if you haven't been raising your Pokémon's base points (p. 178), now is the time to do it with some last-minute Poké Jobs!

Raise your Dynamax Levels! You'd better believe that your opponents will all try to Dynamax their Pokémon. If you haven't been raising your team members' Dynamax Levels by using Dynamax Candies on them, now's the time! That extra boost to a Pokémon's HP just might see it through a hard hit.

Make sure every one of your Pokémon is holding an item that can help it when it goes into battle. Whether they prep something as simple as Leftovers to keep getting back HP or something sneaky like a Rocky Helmet, savvy Trainers know that sending their Pokémon into battle empty-handed is a rookie mistake.

When all fails, look to your Bag! Perhaps you've got some TMs or TRs that could teach your Pokémon a move with higher power than any they've currently got. And while you're rummaging around in there, be sure that you have some Max Revives—or at the very least some Revives, Max Potions, and Full Restores!

CHAMPION CUP SEMIFINALS

1 Once you've changed into your uniform, step out onto the pitch. Your first opponent is none other than Marnie—time to see once and for all who the better Trainer is!

! Did you register and get changed only to realize you forgot a step in your preparation, like buying items? Well, you actually can leave the locker room—just head to the elevator in the right corner, and it'll take you back down to the stadium lobby! This isn't the case once you're in the tunnel to the pitch, though. Once you're through the doors to the field, there's no turning back!

Marnie

Marnie's team hasn't changed too much since you last battled her. Fairy-type moves are a fairly safe choice to use in this battle, as all Marnie's Dark-type Pokémon are weak to them, especially Scrafty. But you'll need to watch out for her Toxicroak, with its Poison-type moves that are super effective against Fairy-type Pokémon. Psychic-type moves will make short work of Toxicroak. The biggest change to Marnie's team since your last battle is the addition of a Grimmsnarl. Grimmsnarl has exceptionally high Attack, making its physical moves very dangerous. Thankfully, it doesn't have very high Speed, so try to outspeed it and go for a quick KO. Although her brother's not too keen on anything to do with Dynamaxing, Marnie will Gigantamax her Grimmsnarl when she sends it out. Its signature move, G-Max Snooze, will cause its target to fall asleep at the end of the next turn. This means you'll need to switch out your Pokémon if you don't want it to fall asleep!

2 If you manage to defeat Marnie, you'll get a break while the next match takes place—but it won't be a long break! Hop's eager to face you, and he won't waste any time defeating his opponent! Now it's time for you to face your rival. Show him everything you've learned on your journey!

Hop

Hop's team has the same members as in your last battle, but his Pokémon have grown strong, much like Hop himself! Both Hop's Dubwool and Snorlax are Normal-type Pokémon, so you could try sending out a Ghost-type Pokémon against them. Normal-type moves don't work on Ghost types. Just remember that Ghost-type moves can't touch Normal-type Pokémon, either! Pincurchin's high Attack shouldn't be too much of an issue if you can take advantage of its very low Speed. Corviknight's strong Defense can be countered by using supereffective special Fire- or Electric-type moves. Hop's final Pokémon is likely to be the one he chose after you picked your first partner Pokémon. He'll Dynamax that Pokémon as soon as he sends it out. Your own first partner Pokémon is still a reliable counter to his Inteleon, Rillaboom, or Cinderace. However, the increased HP of a Dynamax Pokémon makes things more challenging. You could try countering with a Dynamax Pokémon of your own if you haven't already used one in this battle.

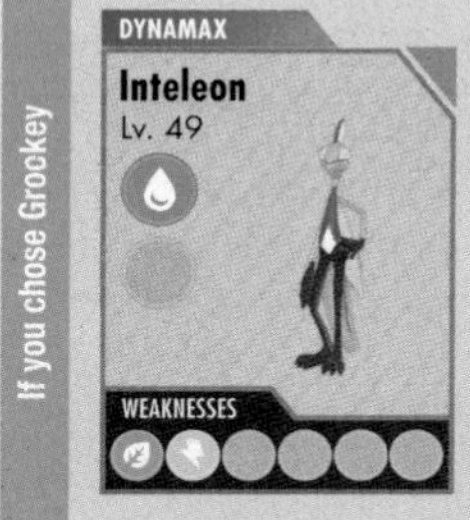

If you chose Grookey
DYNAMAX
Inteleon
Lv. 49
WEAKNESSES

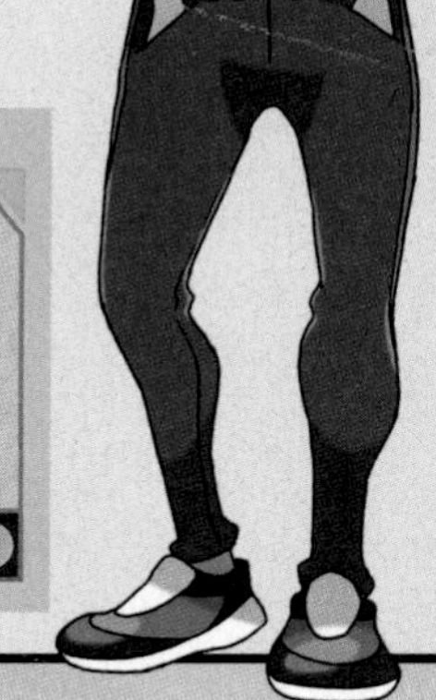

3

Your battle against Hop is the last match of the Semifinals. If you win, you'll be heading to the Finals! But first, Leon's here to invite you out to dinner, so why not have a good meal and get rested up?

You'll go to the hotel with Hop, but Leon's not there yet—in fact, he never shows! Thankfully, Piers was in the neighborhood, and he comes to tell you that he heard Leon was heading to Rose Tower. Now, what could Leon be doing there? Head over with Piers and Team Yell to see what's going on!

Outside the hotel, you'll be met by Oleana. She's intent on keeping you out of the chairman's hair for now and has handpicked a League staff member to lead you on a wild-goose chase! You'll have to chase him down three times and battle him each time you find him—so be ready!

Chasing Down the Bad League Staff Member

1. Once the bad League staff member goes running off, you'll have to chase him down a few times before he gives you the key you need. The first place you'll find him is at the northeast end of the main plaza, facing a wall so you can't see his shades!

Macro Cosmos's Eric

This nasty Macro Cosmos employee is no match for a seasoned Gym Challenger such as yourself! You'll find that Macro Cosmos employees like to use Steel-type Pokémon. Fire-type moves are your best choice in this battle, as Eric's Durant will take four times the damage from them. Marnie will also cheer you on each time you battle Eric, boosting different stats!

Meowth
Lv. 47

WEAKNESSES

Durant
Lv. 47

WEAKNESSES
4x

2. Once you defeat him, he'll flee and go hide somewhere else. This time, he'll try to blend in with the crowd standing around the center of the plaza, but you can spot him standing just to the west, near two other people!

Chasing Down the Bad League Staff Member

Macro Cosmos's Eric

This guy just won't quit! This time, Eric will send out a Mawile and an Excadrill. Both Pokémon are weak to Fire- and Ground-type moves. Focus on those if you have any, and you should beat him in no time. Remember, even though Mawile is Fairy type, it won't take any damage from Poison-type moves, because it's Steel type, too!

3. Defeat him a second time, and he'll dash off again... Now he'll be hiding inside the phone booth at the west side of the plaza!

Macro Cosmos's Eric

One last battle against this troublemaker! In your final battle with Eric, he'll use a Ferroseed and a Steelix. Once again, your best choice for knocking out Eric's Pokémon quickly are Fire-type moves. Steelix will take double damage from them, and Ferroseed will take quadruple damage. Wrap up this battle quickly so you can get on the monorail to Rose Tower and find Leon!

6

Once you've managed to corner the bad League staff member three times, he'll dash off to the monorail station and block your way with some of his pals. Piers will start up a street performance as a distraction, opening the way for you and Hop to get to Rose Tower!

Before heading into the tower, have a look around its exterior. You'll find TM93 Eerie Impulse behind the sign, a Cell Battery to the east, and an Electric Seed to the west!

7

Once inside the tower, you'll need to make your way up to the top. The only way up is the giant elevator at the far end of the lobby, but it won't be a smooth trip! You'll need to defeat a League staff member just to get on, and you'll be stopped several times on your way up by more League staff, who you'll have to face in Double Battles! But fear not—Hop will help you out in these battles, and he'll also heal your team between them!

Macro Cosmos's Elijah

Elijah only uses a Durant, a Pokémon you already defeated not too long ago. Bust out a strong Fire-type move to make quick work of Elijah's Pokémon. You've got to get in that elevator and head to the top floor!

Macro Cosmos's Jane and Mateo

Jane and Mateo send out a Cufant and a Bronzong. Both share the Steel type, which should make both of them weak to Fire- and Ground-type moves. However, Bronzong's Levitate Ability makes it immune to Ground-type moves, so be careful! Fighting-type moves are super effective against Cufant but not Bronzong, since it's both Steel and Psychic type.

Macro Cosmos's Kevin and Carla

Kevin and Carla use Klang and Mawile. By now you should know quite well what works against all these Steel-type Pokémon. Be sure not to send out any Dragon-type Pokémon against Mawile, though! Dragon-type moves have no effect on it.

Macro Cosmos's Adalyn and Justin

The last battle before you reach the roof is against Adalyn and Justin, who use a Steelix and a Stunfisk. Stunfisk's Snap Trap move will trap its target and continuously deal damage for a few turns, so watch out!

8

Make it to the top of Rose Tower, and you'll find that the chairman and Leon are nowhere to be seen! Instead, Oleana is waiting for you—and she's definitely not pleased with your meddling! It sounds like she's trying to get Leon to do something for Rose, and she'll battle you in an attempt to make Leon lose spirit. Don't go easy on her!

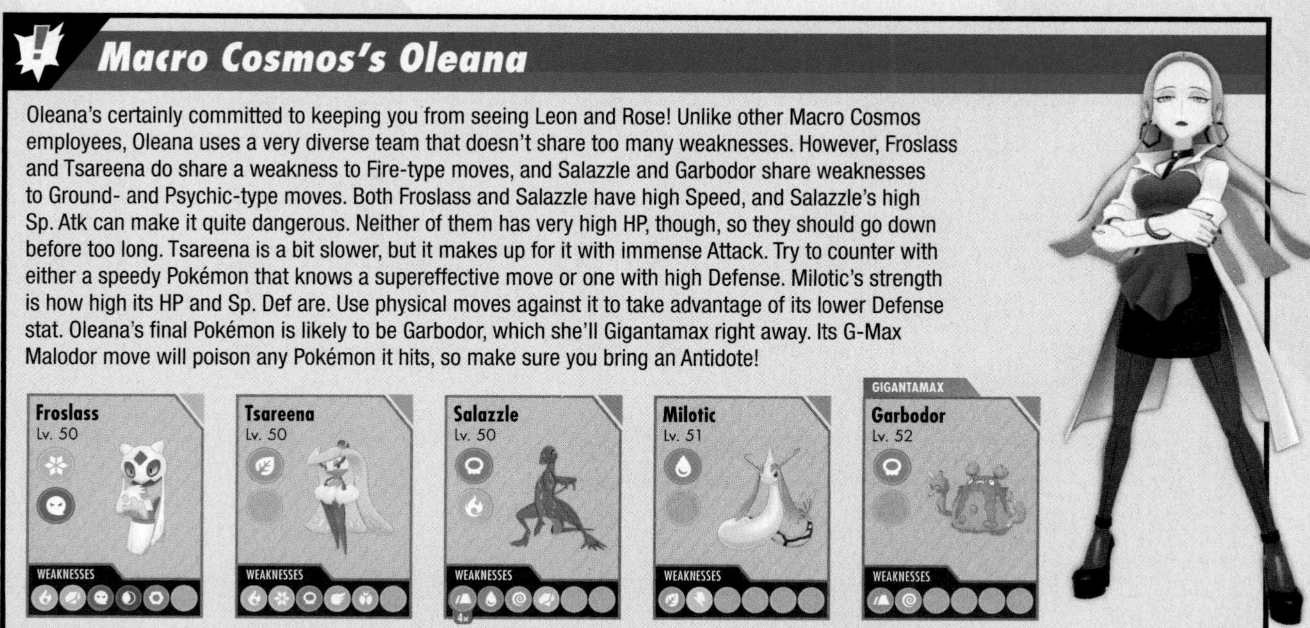

Macro Cosmos's Oleana

Oleana's certainly committed to keeping you from seeing Leon and Rose! Unlike other Macro Cosmos employees, Oleana uses a very diverse team that doesn't share too many weaknesses. However, Froslass and Tsareena do share a weakness to Fire-type moves, and Salazzle and Garbodor share weaknesses to Ground- and Psychic-type moves. Both Froslass and Salazzle have high Speed, and Salazzle's high Sp. Atk can make it quite dangerous. Neither of them has very high HP, though, so they should go down before too long. Tsareena is a bit slower, but it makes up for it with immense Attack. Try to counter with either a speedy Pokémon that knows a supereffective move or one with high Defense. Milotic's strength is how high its HP and Sp. Def are. Use physical moves against it to take advantage of its lower Defense stat. Oleana's final Pokémon is likely to be Garbodor, which she'll Gigantamax right away. Its G-Max Malodor move will poison any Pokémon it hits, so make sure you bring an Antidote!

9

Once you defeat Oleana, you'll be able to make your way to where the chairman and Leon are. As it turns out, they were just having a talk about Galar's future—and it looks like they're just about to wrap things up! Now you can finally head back for a nice supper and some well-earned rest!

10

The next evening is the big event—the Finals of the Champion Cup! A League staff member will come to escort you to the stadium, so if you don't feel like heading over on your own, you can go with her. Once you're there, get checked in and prepare to face the Gym Leaders once again!

1 After a brief opening ceremony, the Finals will finally begin! Your first opponent is...a surprise battle with none other than Bede! It seems he's gone through some special training with Opal so that he can replace her as the Fairy Gym Leader, and he's here to prove his worth once more. Let's see what he's got in store!

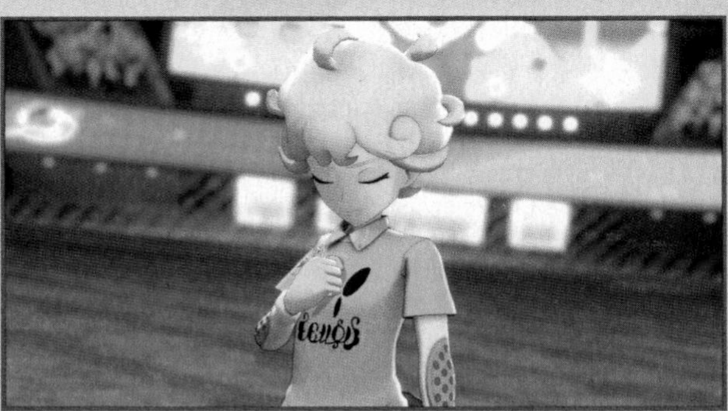

Bede

It's been a while since you've faced Bede in battle, and his team's grown much stronger from training with Opal. He now has a bigger focus on Fairy-type Pokémon. He'll probably lead off with his Mawile. You've faced a few of these Pokémon already while battling the Macro Cosmos employees. Remember that Mawile is immune to both Poison- and Dragon-type moves. When Bede sends out Gardevoir is when things get tough. It has very high Sp. Atk and Sp. Def, and if it gets an opportunity to attack, there's a good chance your Pokémon could be knocked out in one hit! Bede's Rapidash will require a different strategy. Its Attack and Speed are quite high, but its defensive stats are fairly low. Last is Bede's Hatterene, which he'll Gigantamax as soon as he sends it out. Like Gardevoir, Hatterene has high Sp. Atk and Sp. Def. Plus, when it's Gigantamaxed, it gains the signature move G-Max Smite, which will confuse any target it hits! Even Gigantamaxed, though, Hatterene still has very low Speed. Outspeeding it and hitting with supereffective moves is the way to win here!

Mawile
Lv. 51

WEAKNESSES

Gardevoir
Lv. 51

WEAKNESSES

Rapidash
Lv. 52

WEAKNESSES

GIGANTAMAX
Hatterene
Lv. 53

WEAKNESSES

2 After the match against Bede, the Finals will begin in earnest. You'll be facing Nessa in the first round, so make sure your party is prepared for a dousing!

Nessa

Nessa's team shares a common weakness to Electric-type moves. She'll probably lead off with Golisopod, a powerful Pokémon when it comes to Attack and Defense but not when it comes to Speed. Focus on special moves to knock it out. Pelipper shouldn't be too much of an issue if you've got a damage-dealing Electric-type move. However, when Pelipper enters the field, its Drizzle Ability will cause it to rain, increasing the power of Water-type moves. Counter by using a Pokémon of your own that can change the weather with a move like Sunny Day or an Ability like Sand Stream. Barraskewda has incredible Speed and Attack, but the rest of its stats are fairly low. Seaking's stats aren't too threatening aside from its higher Attack. Don't underestimate its Water-type moves if it's attacking in the rain, though! Last is Nessa's Drednaw—she'll Gigantamax it as soon as it's on the battlefield, so make sure you're ready! Its G-Max Stonesurge will create the same effect as Stealth Rock while also dealing damage, so think carefully if you need to switch in any Pokémon, since they'll take Rock-type damage when they enter the field!

Golisopod
Lv. 51

WEAKNESSES

Pelipper
Lv. 51

WEAKNESSES
4×

Barraskewda
Lv. 52

WEAKNESSES

Seaking
Lv. 52

WEAKNESSES

GIGANTAMAX
Drednaw
Lv. 53

WEAKNESSES
4×

3 Your next opponent will change depending on which version of the game you're playing. In *Pokémon Sword*, you'll take on Bea once again!

Bea 

Most of Bea's Pokémon focus on physical moves, so any of your Pokémon with good Defense will be useful, as long as they aren't weak to Fighting-type moves. Hawlucha's biggest strength is its high Speed stat. Its Sp. Def is particularly low, though. Hit it with a powerful supereffective special move to knock it out quickly. Grapploct is much slower but has higher Attack. If it's giving you trouble, try to counter with a Pokémon that has a high Speed stat. Sirfetch'd battles much like Grapploct, with high Attack and low Speed. The odd little Pokémon Falinks also has high Attack, and it has equally high Defense. Try to avoid using physical moves when battling it. Last is Bea's Machamp. Just like in your first battle with her, she'll Gigantamax it as soon as she can. G-Max Chi Strike raises Machamp's critical hit ratio, so make sure you take it out quickly before it can take advantage of that!

3 Your next opponent will change depending on which version of the game you're playing. In *Pokémon Shield*, you'll be up against Allister!

Allister

Allister's Dusknoir is very bulky, with high Attack, Defense, and Sp. Def. Thankfully, its other stats are very low, so try to hit as hard as you can with speedy Pokémon to knock it out quickly. Chandelure is a very powerful Pokémon in terms of Sp. Atk, so try to counter with a Pokémon that has high Sp. Def, like Snorlax. Similar to Chandelure, Cursola has immense Sp. Atk, but its Sp. Def far outweighs its Defense, so focus on physical supereffective moves. Polteageist's stats are quite similar to Cursola's, so the strategy you used to beat Cursola should also work on Polteageist. Allister's ace Pokémon is his Gengar, which you should remember from your first battle with it back in Stow-on-Side. Allister will Gigantamax Gengar right away, giving it access to the signature move G-Max Terror, which will prevent the Pokémon hit by it from switching out. Make sure you don't have the wrong Pokémon on the field when battling Gengar, or it might get trapped there!

Dusknoir
Lv. 52

WEAKNESSES

Chandelure
Lv. 52

WEAKNESSES

Cursola
Lv. 53

WEAKNESSES

Polteageist
Lv. 53

WEAKNESSES

GIGANTAMAX
Gengar
Lv. 54

WEAKNESSES

4 True to his reputation as the strongest Gym Leader, Raihan has managed to crush all opposition and now waits to face you in the last match! You'll need to defeat him again if you want to face Leon!

Raihan

Raihan's team has changed, but his love of altering the weather in battle hasn't. He'll probably lead with Torkoal, and its Drought Ability will immediately turn the sunlight harsh, boosting the power of Fire-type moves. If you've got a Pokémon that can counter this by changing the weather again, it's a good idea to do so. Goodra has high Attack, Sp. Atk, and Sp. Def, making it a tough Pokémon to battle. It's best to use a Fairy-type Pokémon against it, as it will be immune to Goodra's Dragon-type moves. Turtonator has incredible Defense, but the rest of its stats aren't too threatening, particularly its extremely low Speed. If the sunlight is still harsh when you battle Turtonator, be very careful of its Fire-type moves. Flygon's Attack and Speed are fairly high, but the rest of its stats don't make it too tough. Raihan's ace Pokémon is still his Duraludon, and he'll Gigantamax it right after he sends it onto the field. Duraludon has noticeably low Sp. Def, so focus on special moves when battling it. Remember that its G-Max Depletion move can reduce the PP of the move last used by the target Pokémon.

11

If you defeat Raihan, you'll have made it to the Championship Match—and Leon! But before you can even get the battle started, the event is hijacked by Chairman Rose. He was so intent on saving Galar's future that he says he went ahead and triggered the Darkest Day. Whatever he meant by that, it seems things have quickly gotten out of his control!

12

Hop
That's it, Gloria!
I'm sure it's got to be the Slumbering Weald!

Leon will go dashing off to see if he can contain the issue, and Hop wants to help out in any way he can. After discussing what you know about the legends surrounding the Darkest Day, you both decide to head back to where it all began—the Slumbering Weald!

13

You'll run into Sonia once you make it back to Postwick. She's been researching the Slumbering Weald, too, and will give you some Max Revives before sending you off. Now it's time to head into the forest once more to see if the Pokémon of the legends actually are there!

 Max Revive ×3

Slumbering Weald (Revisited)

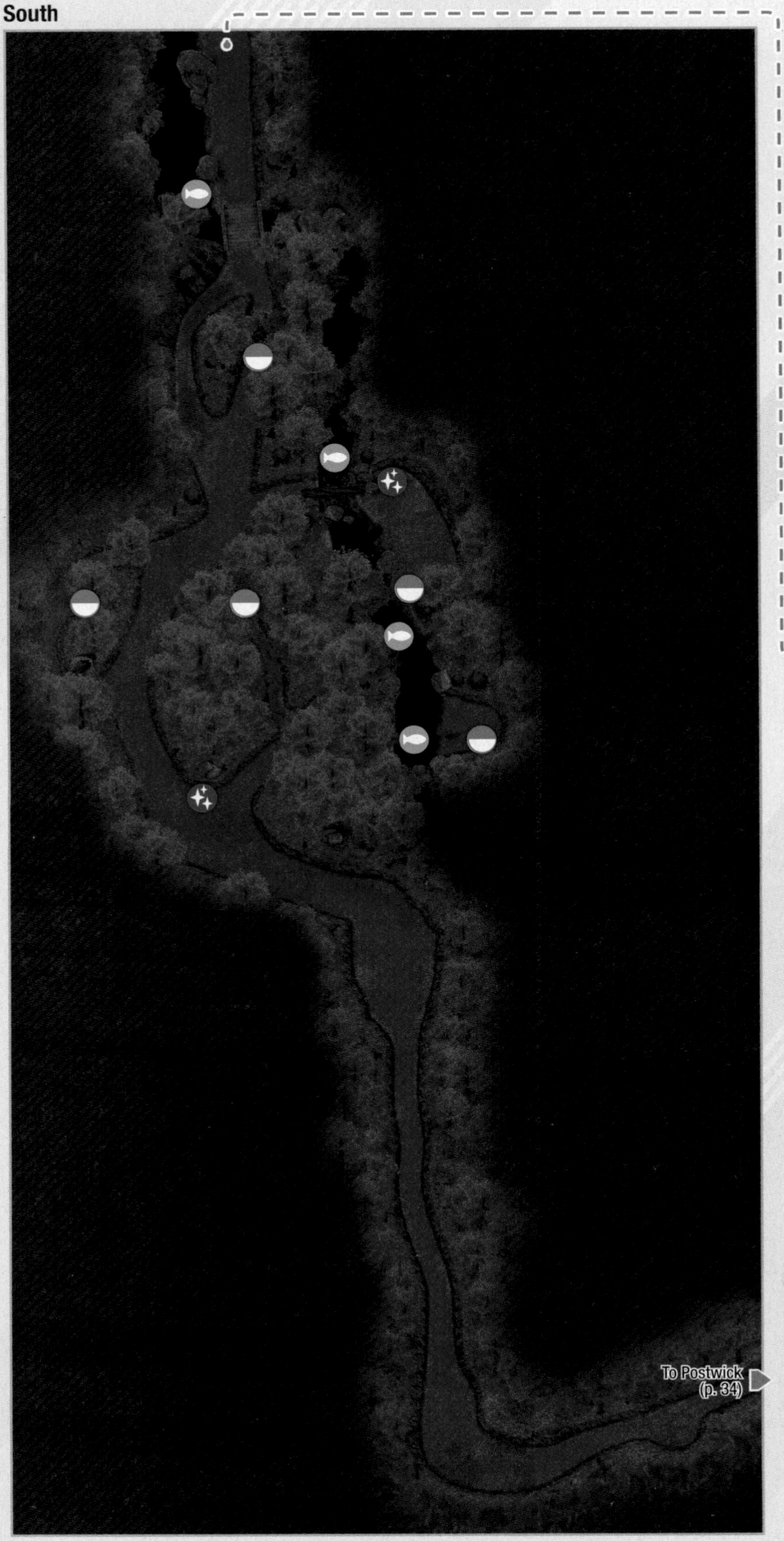

South

To Postwick (p. 34)

North

CATCH!

Weezing

The only other place Weezing appear is at the Lake of Outrage, and they can pop up much more frequently here in the Slumbering Weald. If you haven't caught Weezing yet, here's your chance!

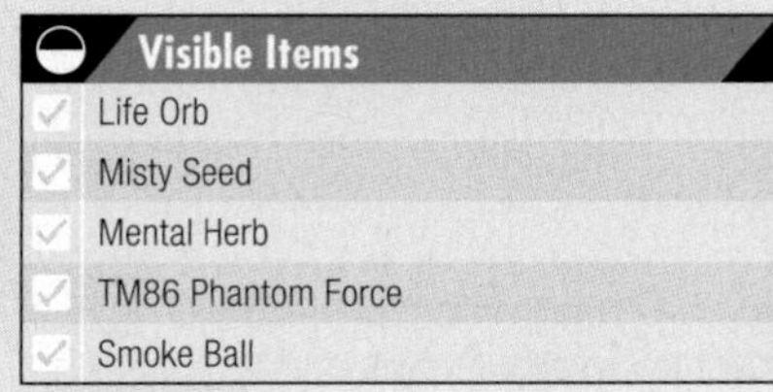

Visible Items
Life Orb
Misty Seed
Mental Herb
TM86 Phantom Force
Smoke Ball

Hidden Items
Full Restore
Elixir

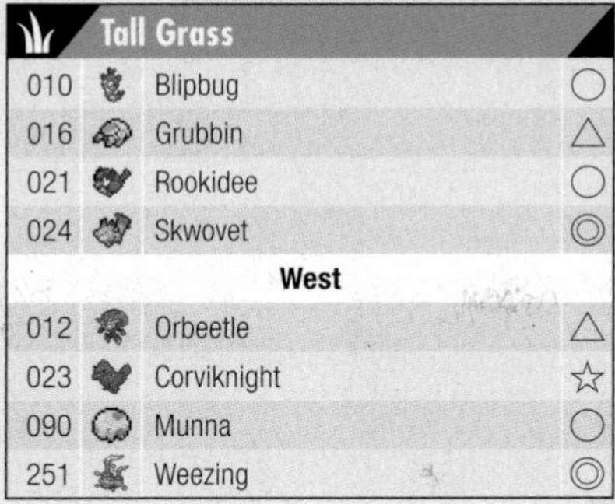

Tall Grass		
010	Blipbug	○
016	Grubbin	△
021	Rookidee	○
024	Skwovet	◎
West		
012	Orbeetle	△
023	Corviknight	☆
090	Munna	○
251	Weezing	◎

Ground		
226	Stunfisk	◎

Random Encounters		
010	Blipbug	△
016	Grubbin	☆
019	Hoothoot	△
021	Rookidee	○
024	Skwovet	◎
West		
012	Orbeetle	△
015	Butterfree	☆
023	Corviknight	○
090	Munna	○
226	Stunfisk	☆
251	Weezing	○

Fishing		
West		
144	Magikarp	○
228	Barboach	○
229	Whiscash	◎

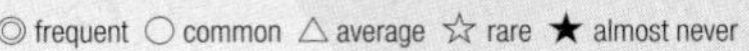

◎ frequent ○ common △ average ☆ rare ★ almost never

1

Once you're in the Slumbering Weald, head on straight until you come to where you passed out before. This time, there's no wall of mist, and you can explore deeper into the forest! There are lots of winding paths up ahead and several items you'll want to collect. In particular, head northeast and across a log to find TM86 Phantom Force!

2

Keep going north through the forest until you meet up with Hop again in front of a bridge. The mist will come rolling in, and with it are two Pokémon. Are these the Pokémon mentioned in the legends? The mist will soon recede, and Sonia will catch up with you to share a little more information. Now it's time to keep pressing onward!

3

Deep inside the Slumbering Weald, you'll come to a small lake and what appears to be some sort of shrine. The mysterious Pokémon are nowhere to be seen—all that you find is a rusty sword and shield. There's nothing more you can do here, so pick up the items and go to Hammerlocke to see what help you can give Leon!

Rusted Sword / Rusted Shield

Hammerlocke (Revisited)

1

Once back in Hammerlocke, you should see Raihan standing in front of the stadium. He's as confused as you are about what the chairman's goals are, but it seems that Leon's up ahead. Hop will dash off like he always does. Follow once you feel you're ready!

2

Once inside the stadium, who do you run into but Oleana! This time, her attitude is far from her previous aggressiveness—she seems to be on the verge of panic. Apparently, even she's been taken off guard by how much things have gotten out of hand, and she'll beg you to save Chairman Rose. Head toward the elevator to see exactly what's going on!

3

Once you're underneath the stadium, follow the path until you come to a brightly lit area, where Hop will be waiting for you. Whatever this place is, it almost looks like something's broken out of a shell... Approach the center of the platform, and you'll find Chairman Rose. And he clearly has no intention of letting you interfere with whatever his plans are, even if you're trying to help!

Macro Cosmos's Rose

Like many of his employees, Rose uses a team focused on Steel types. Fire-type moves are your best option, as all Rose's Pokémon are weak to them—they even deal 400% damage to a couple. Escavalier can hit very hard, but it's extremely slow. KO it quickly with a Fire-type move. Ferrothorn has high defensive stats, but it isn't capable of dealing too much damage. Watch out for its Iron Barbs Ability, which deals damage if your Pokémon makes contact! Perrserker battles much like Escavalier—high Attack but low Speed. Klinklang is actually not too slow, so try to take advantage of its lower Sp. Def. Rose will Gigantamax his trusty Copperajah as soon as he sends it out. Its G-Max Steelsurge will set a trap on the field that deals Steel-type damage to your Pokémon that switch in!

4

5

Rose seems to calm down a little once you defeat him. He expresses confidence that Leon has done all that Rose wanted him to do. He'll let you pass to go up to the roof. Leave the big dome you're in now, and you'll find that the elevator to the left is now open to you. Talk to Hop if you're ready to check on Leon!

Once the elevator reaches the top of the tower, take the stairs to find Leon—and the disaster he seems embroiled in! He's doing his best to get things back under control, but this is one gigantic problem that Rose has created! You'll have to help. Get ready to have a battle fit for the legends!

The Darkest Day

This is what was behind the Darkest Day?! Leon might've weakened it, but it certainly doesn't seem any less intimidating for it. Its power is so immense that it begins to warp space around the battle! (Is that Postwick?) It might even seem that this thing's powers are preventing moves from working, but don't give up! Focus on Ice-, Ground-, Psychic-, and Dragon-type moves as best you can—they're super effective against the challenge you're facing. Think back on all you've learned in regular battles as well as in Max Raid Battles, and use your moves and items wisely! You have to push through to save the Galar region from disaster!

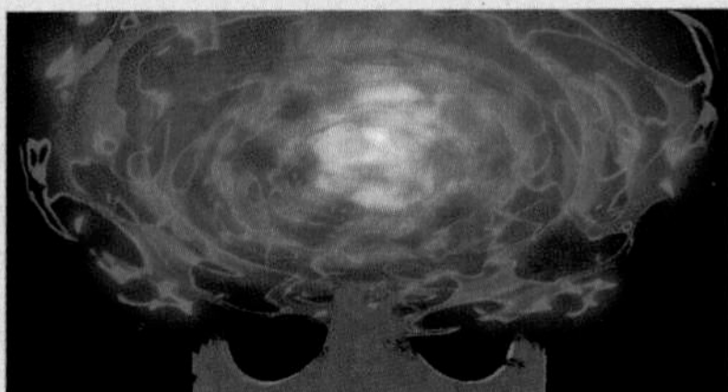

6

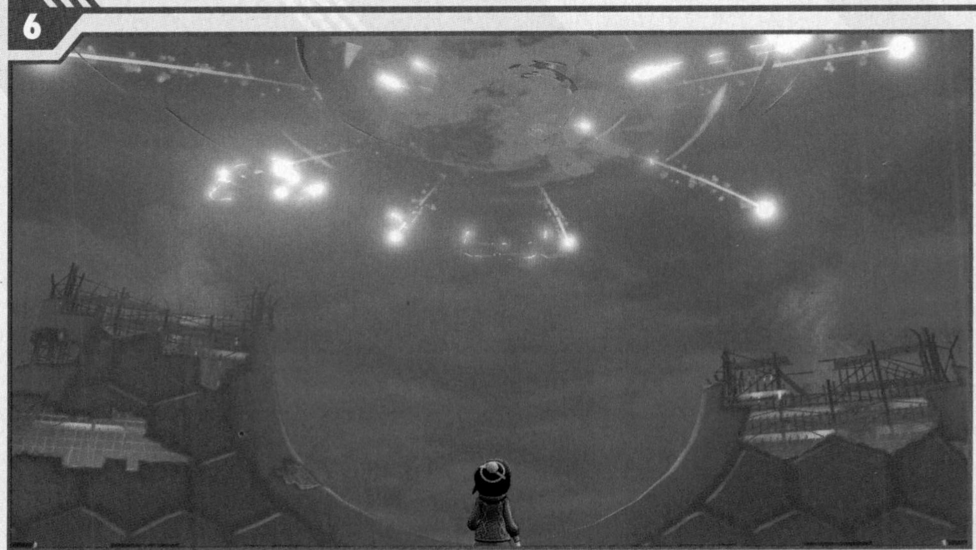

At last, things settle down and peace is restored. That's that, right? Well, actually, there's one last thing you need to do. Did you forget the entire reason you started this adventure? You still need to face Leon in the Championship Match!

Wyndon (Revisited)

1

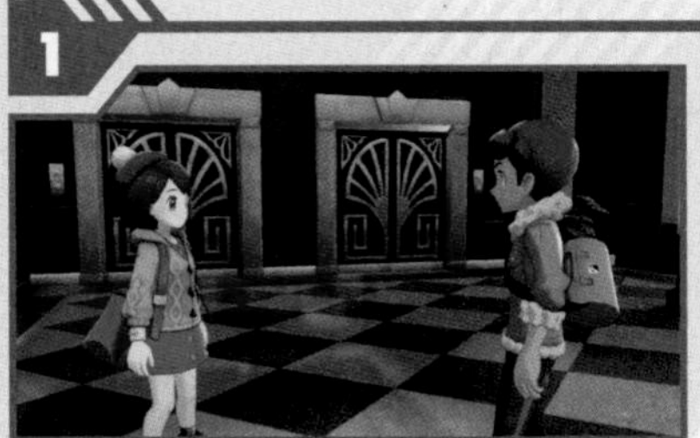

After a relaxing three days at the hotel in Wyndon, you'll finally be recovered enough for your big match! Hop will meet you in the hotel lobby and let you know that the final match is going to be held in Wyndon Stadium. Check your party, maybe save your progress, and then make your way to the stadium and speak to the League staff member at the counter!

CHAMPIONSHIP MATCH

Leon

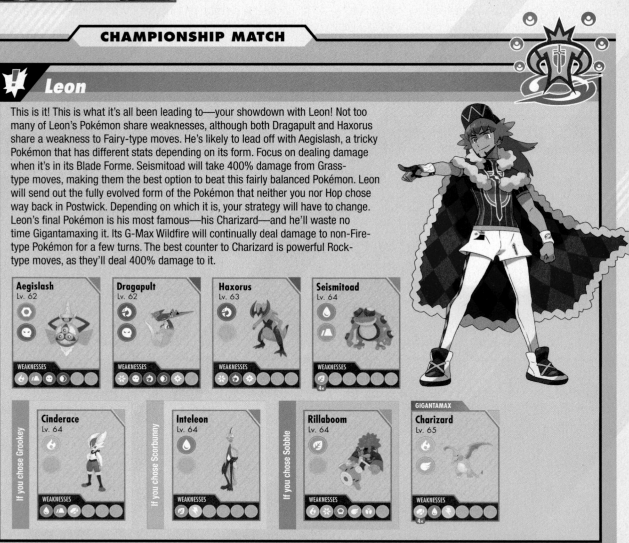

This is it! This is what it's all been leading to—your showdown with Leon! Not too many of Leon's Pokémon share weaknesses, although both Dragapult and Haxorus share a weakness to Fairy-type moves. He's likely to lead off with Aegislash, a tricky Pokémon that has different stats depending on its form. Focus on dealing damage when it's in its Blade Forme. Seismitoad will take 400% damage from Grass-type moves, making them the best option to beat this fairly balanced Pokémon. Leon will send out the fully evolved form of the Pokémon that neither you nor Hop chose way back in Postwick. Depending on which it is, your strategy will have to change. Leon's final Pokémon is his most famous—his Charizard—and he'll waste no time Gigantamaxing it. Its G-Max Wildfire will continually deal damage to non-Fire-type Pokémon for a few turns. The best counter to Charizard is powerful Rock-type moves, as they'll deal 400% damage to it.

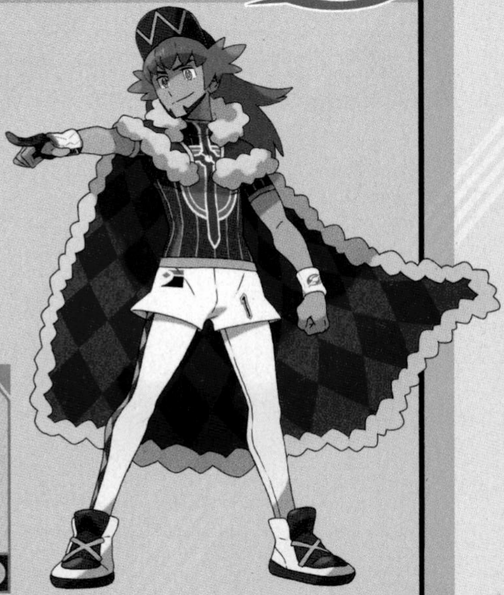

Aegislash Lv. 62 — WEAKNESSES

Dragapult Lv. 62 — WEAKNESSES

Haxorus Lv. 63 — WEAKNESSES

Seismitoad Lv. 64 — WEAKNESSES (4×)

If you chose Grookey: **Cinderace** Lv. 64 — WEAKNESSES

If you chose Scorbunny: **Inteleon** Lv. 64 — WEAKNESSES

If you chose Sobble: **Rillaboom** Lv. 64 — WEAKNESSES

GIGANTAMAX **Charizard** Lv. 65 — WEAKNESSES (4×)

2

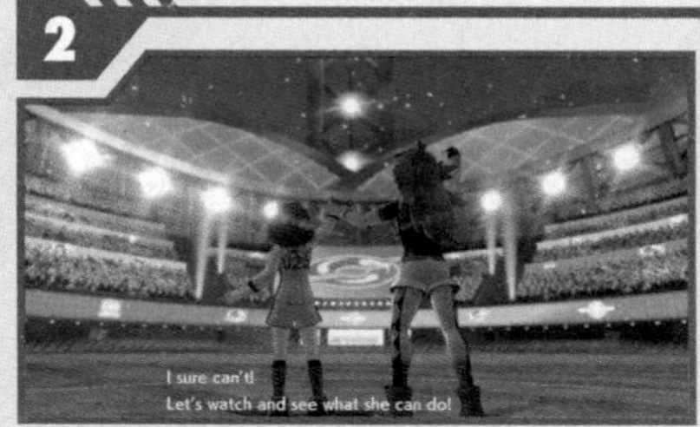

Defeat the unbeatable Champion, and you'll have made history a second time in a week—you're now the new Champion of the Galar region! Congratulations to you and your team!

1

After becoming Champion, you'll be taken back to the title screen, where you can continue your adventure. You'll have a brief vision of the altar in the Slumbering Weald before finding yourself in your room again. Is something new afoot?

Once you become Champion, the day and night cycle of the Galar region will follow real-world time. If the internal clock of your Nintendo Switch says it's daytime, it'll be daytime for you in Galar as well. The same goes for nighttime!

2

You obtained a Master Ball!

In the kitchen, you'll find that Professor Magnolia has come to visit! She's here to celebrate your becoming Champion, and she has something very special for the occasion—a Master Ball! This amazing Poké Ball is sure to catch any wild Pokémon, so use it wisely!

 Master Ball

3

After your conversation with Professor Magnolia, you're free to explore the Galar region as you wish. You can head to the Wild Area or visit the various towns again—there's still plenty to do as Champion! Or if you've got nothing specific on your mind, you could follow the vision you had and check out the Slumbering Weald!

It's worth revisiting the Wild Area once you become Champion. You'll encounter stronger Pokémon, the fog weather condition will have a chance of occurring, and you'll earn more Watts when investigating Pokémon Dens!

Steel Beam Move Tutor

Now you've become the Champion, a Move Tutor in Motostoke can teach your Pokémon a very powerful move called Steel Beam. Take the path between Budew Drop Inn and the upper-level Pokémon Center and go all the way down the stairs to find him. He'll teach your Steel-type Pokémon—and a few other special Pokémon—the powerful move.

Things to Do as Champion

These events can all be done whenever you like, so feel free to jump straight ahead to the events beginning on page 149 first if you want to. But remember to come back to this list eventually to make sure you've done everything you can do now as Champion of the Galar region!

If you do decide to do some exploring first, why not take the time to stop by Hop and Leon's home? Up in Leon's room on the second floor, you'll come across a Poké Ball with a note from Leon. Inside it you'll find a Charmander—and a very special one at that. Once you raise it into a Charizard, you'll be able to Gigantamax it!

 Charmander

Surely you haven't forgotten about your old buddy the Ball Guy! They'll be waiting for you where you first met—out in front of Motostoke Stadium. Have a chat with them to get their League Card!

 Ball Guy's League Card

If you happen to stop by Galar Mine again, explore the side paths. You'll run into somebody you probably won't expect—Oleana! She's doing some community service on behalf of Rose (don't ask us why he isn't doing it himself) and seems to be enjoying the experience. She's in such a good mood that she'll actually give you Rose's rare League Card!

 Rose's rare League Card

Do you remember the Captain's Table in Hulbury? It's where you had a meal with Sonia and Chairman Rose just after you'd gotten your Water Badge. Well, it seems like they could use a hand—the delivery guy's off sick and can't make the deliveries! The chef behind the counter will ask if you can help, so why not give food delivery a shot?

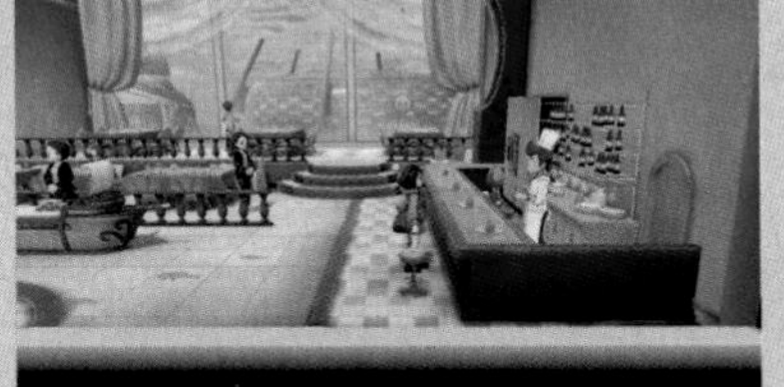

Unfortunately, the chef forgot to ask for an address for your first delivery—but he does say that he heard a clickity-clack sound over the phone. If you guessed that was the sound of trains, you'd be right! Head to the grayish home closest to the train station to drop off the meal, and then return to the Captain's Table to inform the chef of a job well done!

 Exp. Candy L, Nugget ×5

Speak to the chef again, and he'll have another delivery ready for you. He's forgotten to ask for an address again, but he did hear a distinctive Pokémon cry over the phone. This is actually the cry of a Swirlix, and the only house with a Swirlix is the fourth house down the road to the west of the Captain's Table! Drop off the order, and head back to let the chef know you're done.

 Big Nugget ×2

It was easy to spot the green roof, wasn't it?

The chef's got one last order for you to deliver, but—you guessed it—he forgot to ask for an address. The customer did apparently say to look for a green roof, but none of the houses in Hulbury have a roof of that color. But there is a stall in the open-air market that has green stripes on its roof, and this is where you need to drop off the food! Afterward, let the chef know everything's been handled.

 Lucky Egg

Near the lighthouse in Hulbury, you'll run into the Pokémon band known as the Maximizers! You may remember seeing their performance after you defeated Leon in the Championship Match. If you stick around to watch them perform, you'll be able to relive that experience all over again!

Next stop: Stow-on-Side! The bargain stall will have something special to give you once you become Champion—a Beast Ball!

 Beast Ball

There are a few things you can do in Circhester. For starters, enter Hotel Ionia's west building, and go up the elevator. Then enter the second room from the left end of the hall, and you'll find Morimoto of GAME FREAK! He'll challenge you to a Double Battle, and make no mistake—he's a tough opponent. If you manage to beat him, he'll give you an Oval Charm!

 Oval Charm

Morimoto

Morimoto might look like a police officer, but he's a battle expert, and he'll offer you the most difficult Double Battle in the game! His team is somewhat diverse, although he does use two Ghost-type Pokémon and two Rock-type Pokémon. This means that there are a few shared weaknesses among his team, if you want to take advantage of them. A lot of his team tend to favor Attack over Sp. Atk, so using Pokémon with high Defense isn't a bad idea. You'll especially want to watch out for Stonjourner in this battle. Its Power Spot Ability strengthens allied Pokémon in battle, so you'll really want to knock it out quickly! Morimoto will Dynamax his Snorlax immediately, so make sure you're ready! Snorlax has low Defense, so hit it hard with physical Fighting-type moves for big damage to get through that increased HP!

Cursola
Lv. 65

WEAKNESSES

Grapploct
Lv. 65

WEAKNESSES

Stonjourner
Lv. 65

WEAKNESSES

Coalossal
Lv. 65

WEAKNESSES
4× 4×

Dragapult
Lv. 65

WEAKNESSES

DYNAMAX
Snorlax
Lv. 65

WEAKNESSES

Don't forget about the room to the far left of the hall. You were told to return once you complete your Pokédex, and if you accomplish that incredible feat, you'll receive a Shiny Charm!

 Shiny Charm

You obtained a Shiny Charm!

WALKTHROUGH

Once you sort out the whole situation with Sordward and Shielbert (covered on the following pages), you may be wondering what Marnie's been up to. Why don't you head over to Spikemuth and pay her a visit? She's taken over as the Spikemuth Gym Leader from Piers, and she'll even offer to have an exhibition match with you! The first time you defeat her, she'll give you her rare League Card to add to your collection. While her rare League Card's a one-time gift, you can come back to have a battle with her once every day!

 Marnie's rare League Card

Marnie

Marnie's team hasn't changed since your battle with her in the semifinals, and after defeating Leon, she shouldn't give you too much of a challenge. Most of her team is still quite vulnerable to Fairy-type moves. Psychic-type moves will knock out Toxicroak fairly quickly, as it will take 400% damage from them. Unlike your last battle, you won't be able to use Dynamax—but neither will Marnie, so you don't need to worry about her Grimmsnarl changing to its Gigantamax form. Even so, it's still her strongest Pokémon, with a very high Attack. You'll want to either take advantage of its low Speed or counter by sending out a Pokémon with high Defense.

Liepard Lv. 59

WEAKNESSES

Toxicroak Lv. 59

WEAKNESSES 4x

Scrafty Lv. 59

WEAKNESSES 4x

Morpeko Lv. 60

WEAKNESSES

Grimmsnarl Lv. 60

WEAKNESSES

The big city of Wyndon has plenty going on, too! First, you can return to Rose Tower (now the Battle Tower—more on that in a bit) and speak to the League staff member on the left side of the lobby to receive Type: Null. You'll also get a bunch of memory items, but these won't be useful until Type: Null evolves. If you want it to evolve, you'll need to become best friends with it!

 Type: Null, All memories

The Battle Tower

As we briefly mentioned above, Rose Tower has been repurposed by Leon as the Battle Tower, a facility dedicated to Pokémon battles! Come here if you want to participate in tough battles and earn BP. If you perform well enough, you'll even get to face Leon again! For more information on the Battle Tower and things you can do here, check out pages 200–201.

Champion Tournaments

Another thing you can do in Wyndon is host Champion tournaments! You can get these set up from Wyndon Stadium. Speak to the League staff member at the front desk, and you'll be asked if you want to enter a tournament. Then it's time to let the actual battles begin, so make sure your team is ready. For more information on Champion tournaments and the rewards you can earn, flip to pages 196–199.

The tournaments here are always open to you, of course! Give one a try, won't you?

A New Mystery Begins

1

Make your way to the altar in the Slumbering Weald, and you'll run into Hop. It seems he's come here to do some thinking. He'll ask to battle you to really experience your full strength. If you're ready, it's time for you to face your rival once again!

Hop

You've seen Hop use all these Pokémon at one point or another during your adventure, but they're all considerably stronger than the last time Hop battled with them. Hop's team is as diverse as ever, so relying on one move type is a bad idea. There are a few shared weaknesses, though. Corviknight and Cramorant are weak to Electric-type moves, while Dubwool and Snorlax are weak to Fighting-type moves. You should be fairly experienced in battling Hop's team by now, so the real challenge is their higher level and stats. If you don't think you're ready to face him, you can always train your team against the stronger Pokémon in the Slumbering Weald.

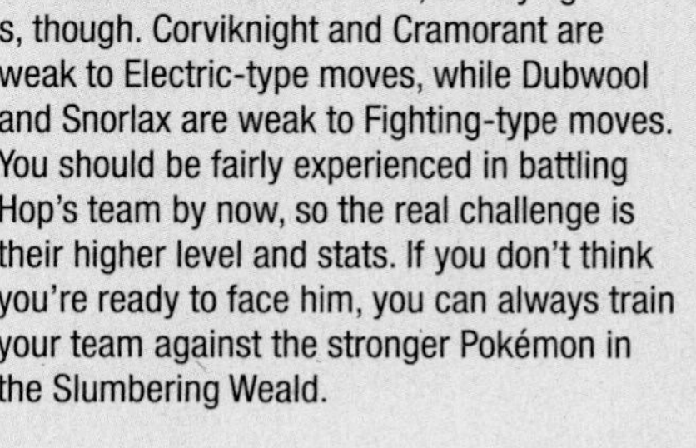

2

After the battle, Sonia will show up, having heard the noise you and Hop were making. She's taken a renewed interest in the history of Galar, and she'll even give you an autographed copy of a book she wrote on the topic! She says you should return the Rusted Sword and Rusted Shield to the altar, which you were totally about to do anyway!

 Sonia's Book

3

No sooner do you return the two artifacts than a strange duo with outrageous hairdos show up. They introduce themselves as Sordward and Shielbert, and they claim to be the new kings of Galar! After rudely insulting Sonia's new book, they'll try to make off with the sword and shield! You can't just let them do as they please, so it's time for a Pokémon battle! You'll face Sordward in *Pokémon Sword*, while in *Pokémon Shield*, you'll have to tackle Shielbert.

Sordward

This weirdo's stolen the Rusted Sword! Sordward uses a diverse team, but two of his Pokémon share the Steel type. His team favors physical moves over special moves, so sending out Pokémon with high Defense isn't a bad idea. Remember that while Fighting-type moves are usually strong against Steel-type Pokémon, Doublade won't take any damage from them because it's also Ghost type. But Fighting-type moves are great against Bisharp, as that Pokémon will take 400% damage from them. Watch out for Golisopod's signature move, First Impression. It has increased priority and deals a good amount of damage!

Shielbert

This weirdo's stolen the Rusted Shield! Shielbert uses Fighting- and Steel-type Pokémon, bringing two of each to this battle. Only his Bronzong has a secondary type, so what's strong against his Sirfetch'd will be good for battling Falinks as well. Bronzong and Klinklang have a few different weaknesses, but both are vulnerable to Fire-type moves. His Fighting-type Pokémon focus more on physical moves, while his Steel-type Pokémon tend to use more special moves. Watch out for Sirfetch'd's powerful signature move, Meteor Assault. It will deal a high amount of damage, but Sirfetch'd will need to recharge after using it, leaving it vulnerable!

These two stuck-up buffoons are Sordward and Shielbert. They claim to be celebrities and, even more audaciously, the kings of the Galar region! Their interpretation of history seems to be... different, to say the least. They even say that the mural at Stow-on-Side was somehow tied to their family! What in the world do they want with the Rusted Sword and Rusted Shield?

4

Though you may be able to take down your opponent, Hop doesn't fare so well. There's something on his mind, and it clearly caused him some distraction during the battle. As a result, Shielbert will make off with the Rusted Shield if you're playing *Pokémon Sword*, or Sordward will nab the Rusted Sword in *Pokémon Shield*. Hop will give chase, leaving you with Sonia.

5

Sonia will mention that she has some idea where Sordward and Shielbert could have headed. Meet her at the Pokémon Lab in Wedgehurst to see what she has in mind and figure out your next steps!

A Dynamax-Sized Disaster

1

Once you make your way to the Pokémon Lab, you'll be greeted by Sonia's new assistant and then Sonia herself. Sonia says that she can use the Power Spot Detector to find out where Sordward and Shielbert went! And the device is already showing some unusual readings—it seems that something's afoot in Turffield!

Incident at Turffield

1

You can take a Flying Taxi to Turffield and then check the stadium to see what's going on—after all, that's the only place that should contain a Power Spot! Inside, you'll find Milo, of course, but more surprisingly, you'll also see Piers. The sword and shield weirdos indeed seem to have come here, and now there's a Dynamax Pokémon causing havoc in the stadium. It's time to settle things down!

2

Four skilled Trainers should have no trouble getting the situation under control, but there's still something very strange going on. How was a Pokémon able to Dynamax in the stadium without a Trainer nearby? Soon enough, Sordward and Shielbert will show up and make it clear that they caused the whole thing before running off. Exit the stadium to see where they went next!

Milo's rare League Card

Tsareena

Hop, Piers, and Milo will join you in this battle against a Dynamax Tsareena. Try to focus on supereffective moves, and don't be afraid to Dynamax your Pokémon right away to dish out some high damage to end this battle quickly! Tsareena has high Attack, so you could send out a Pokémon with high Defense to counter if you're having trouble.

2

Sonia will meet you outside Turffield Stadium. Her Power Spot Detector is picking up even more disturbances, this time in two locations—Hulbury Stadium and Motostoke Stadium. It's your choice where to go next, so pick a destination and get ready to have your very own champion time!

Incident at Hulbury

We'll cover Hulbury first. Grab a Flying Taxi there, and then head to the Gym Stadium. Nessa will be there, and she'll tell you that events much like what happened in Turffield are happening here, too. It's time for another battle against a Dynamax Pokémon!

You got Nessa's rare League Card!

Help calm the Pokémon down, and Nessa will give you her rare League Card before heading off to get everything back in order!

Nessa joins you, Hop, and Piers in this battle. Gyarados will take 400% damage from Electric-type moves, so they're your best choice for dealing damage to this fearsome Dynamax Pokémon! Gyarados has exceptionally high Attack, so sending out a Pokémon with high Defense to battle it isn't a bad idea if you don't have Pokémon that know supereffective moves.

Nessa's rare League Card

Incident at Motostoke

Once in Motostoke, go to the stadium to meet Kabu and assess the situation. Kabu's experiencing the same phenomenon as the one that went down in Turffield—a Pokémon has Dynamaxed and is now causing trouble on the pitch! Time to do your duty as Champion and help bring back the peace!

You got Kabu's rare League Card!

Help Kabu get a handle on things, and he'll thank you by giving you his rare League Card!

You'll have Kabu join you, along with Hop and Piers, in this battle against a Dynamax Torkoal. It doesn't have incredible Attack or Sp. Def, but it does have massive Defense. Try to damage it with supereffective special moves for high damage. If you're having trouble, remember that inflicting the poisoned status is a great way to drain a Pokémon's HP steadily each turn!

Kabu's rare League Card

Sonia
Gloria! We've got trouble! Those two weirdos have showed up at the Pokémon Lab!

Help settle things down at both Hulbury and Motostoke, and you'll get a call from Sonia. The weird duo had the audacity to show up at her Pokémon Lab while you were away, and they're after Wishing Stars! Head back to Wedgehurst to make sure Sonia's OK!

An Audacious Attack

1

Back at the Pokémon Lab, Sordward and Shielbert are in the process of making a scene again, demanding the Wishing Stars that Sonia retrieved from Chairman Rose. Naturally, she has no intent of giving them over, but the two weirdos don't take kindly to being inconvenienced—or being called weirdos, for that matter. It's time to show them the door, whether they want to leave or not!

Sordward and Shielbert

Each of the two brothers uses three Pokémon, both choosing not to use their Sirfetch'd. Hop joins you to help out in this battle. The brothers use a good number of Steel-type Pokémon, so Fire- or Ground-type moves are a good choice. Both Sordward's Golisopod and Shielbert's Falinks are weak to Flying-type moves. A powerful Corviknight using a move like Brave Bird should have no problem knocking them out. Hop might even send a Corviknight out himself if his Dubwool faints during the battle. Remember what you learned from battling either Sordward or Shielbert the first time, and you won't have too much trouble now.

Sordward's Pokémon

Golisopod
Lv. 62

WEAKNESSES

Doublade
Lv. 62

WEAKNESSES

Bisharp
Lv. 62

WEAKNESSES
4×

Shielbert's Pokémon

Bronzong
Lv. 62

WEAKNESSES

Falinks
Lv. 62

WEAKNESSES

Klinklang
Lv. 62

WEAKNESSES

2

Give Sordward and Shielbert a good trouncing, and that should wrap things up nicely... But what's this? Sonia's new assistant was on the side of the two weirdos all along! They were just causing a scene to buy her time to steal the Wishing Stars for them! Sonia's understandably upset, but she's also grown strong. She'll pull herself together and catch up to you as soon as you head out of the lab!

From this point onward, each Gym Stadium will have multiple Dynamax Pokémon causing problems. This means your little troupe will be forced to split up to handle the situation, and you'll have to face a Dynamax Pokémon alone! Make sure your team is prepared to handle this!

3

Once outside, you'll be promptly joined by both Professor Sonia and Magnolia! They have some theories on what Sordward and Shielbert plan to do with the Wishing Stars, but there's little time for speculation—the Power Spot Detector is picking up unusual readings again, and this time at four different stadiums! As before, you get to choose where to go. Time to get busy!

Incident at Hammerlocke

Let's say you start with Hammerlocke. Make your way to the stadium, and Raihan will be very happy for the reinforcements! Multiple Dynamax Pokémon are too much even for a Trainer like him to handle alone. But with four of you here, there's nothing you can't do!

Raihan will be grateful for your assistance. One Dynamax Pokémon is tough enough, but having to take on several would have been dangerous even for him! He'll give you his rare League Card before leaving to take care of the Pokémon that were forcibly Dynamaxed.

Haxorus

Haxorus is a powerful Dragon-type Pokémon with high Attack and Speed. The best option for battling it is a Fairy-type Pokémon, which will be immune to any Dragon-type moves Haxorus tries to use on it. While Haxorus is unable to deal damage, hit it hard with supereffective Fairy-type moves boosted by a same-type attack bonus for big damage!

Raihan's rare League Card

Incident at Stow-on-Side

Stow-on-Side is another spot that's run into some trouble. If you're playing *Pokémon Sword*, you'll meet Bea in the stadium, while in *Pokémon Shield*, you'll need to help out Allister. The Pokémon you must deal with will also be different, so make sure your party's prepared for the right encounter!

Conkeldurr

Conkeldurr has high HP, Attack, and Defense, but its Sp. Def and Speed are very low. Do your best to exploit this by outspeeding Conkeldurr and hitting it with powerful supereffective moves, like Psychic or Dazzling Gleam.

Dusknoir

Dusknoir's a Ghost-type Pokémon, so don't bother using Normal- or Fighting-type moves in this battle. It also has immense Defense and Sp. Def, making it difficult to damage. Don't forget about moves like Toxic to drain Dusknoir's HP. Try lowering its stats with a status move and then hitting with supereffective moves to knock this Pokémon out!

Once you've done your duty as Champion and brought the stadium under control, you'll get a token of thanks from the Gym Leader. You'll get Bea's rare League Card in *Pokémon Sword* or Allister's rare League Card in *Pokémon Shield*, so add it to your album and be on your way!

Bea's rare League Card

Allister's rare League Card

WALKTHROUGH

Incident at Ballonlea

Ballonlea is another spot that had unusual readings, but by the time you get there, Bede himself has already taken care of things. Say what you will about his attitude, but he's definitely a talented Trainer! Seems he's still a bit salty about you becoming the Champion, though, and he'll challenge you to a battle. Since the Dynamax Pokémon are no longer a threat here, surely you have the time to oblige him!

Bede

Bede's already taken care of the Dynamax problem at his stadium, but he's just itching for a rematch with you! His team has grown stronger since he barged into the Champion Cup, but he still uses the same four Pokémon. Poison- or Steel-type moves will help out a lot in this battle, except against Bede's Mawile. It's only weak to Fire- or Ground-type moves. Mawile is also the only one of his Pokémon that doesn't excel in Sp. Atk, so using Pokémon with high Sp. Def against the rest of his team is a good strategy, too. Most of his team has high Speed—if that's giving you trouble, you could try using the move Trick Room. This will let slower Pokémon act first for five turns.

After your battle, Bede seems finally able to accept that you're a fitting Champion. He'll show his respect by giving you his rare League Card before heading off to clean up the stadium. And what do you know—your battle even managed to please Opal, who'll give you her rare League Card, too!

Bede's rare League Card, Opal's rare League Card

Incident at Circhester

1

Much like in Stow-on-Side, the challenge you'll face in Circhester will change depending on which version of the game you're playing. In *Pokémon Sword*, you'll need to help Gordie by taking on a Dynamax Rock-type Pokémon, while in *Pokémon Shield*, you'll be lending a hand to Melony, helping calm an Ice-type Pokémon!

Gigalith

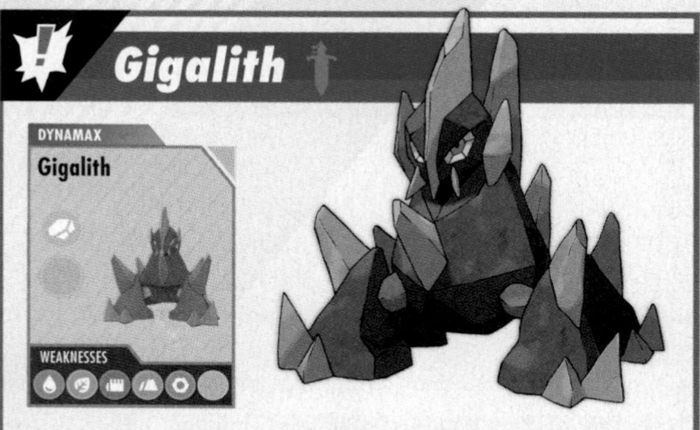

Another solo battle against a Dynamax Pokémon. Rock-type Pokémon have a lot of weaknesses, so you'll likely have a Pokémon on your team with a move that will be good during this battle. Gigalith has very high Defense but poor Sp. Def, so make use of that as best you can.

Froslass

Froslass has a number of weaknesses, but remember that it won't take any damage from Normal- or Fighting-type moves. Froslass has particularly high Speed, but the rest of its stats aren't too much to handle. Use a tough Pokémon that can take a few quick attacks from Froslass and hit hard with supereffective moves.

2

You got Gordie's rare League Card!

You got Melony's rare League Card!

Show the Dynamax Pokémon what the Galar Champion can do, and as before, you'll be thanked by the Gym Leader and given their rare League Card. You should be building up quite the collection now!

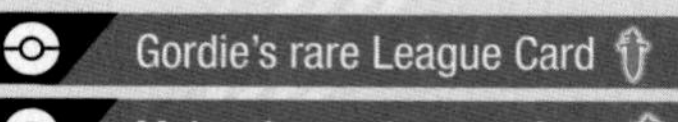

Gordie's rare League Card

Melony's rare League Card

4

Sonia
Gloria? It's me! Sonia!

Once you've taken care of all four stadiums, you'll receive a call from Sonia. She says Sordward and Shielbert are headed to the Energy Plant in Hammerlocke Stadium—this can only mean trouble! Rush back to Hammerlocke to stop them!

Legendary Endings and Beginnings

1

Once you make it back to Hammerlocke, head into the stadium and speak to Sonia—you'll see her by the elevator. She'll get it up and running with a little help from Yamper so you can get going to the Energy Plant!

2

Down the hall from the elevator, you'll find Sordward in *Pokémon Sword* or Shielbert in *Pokémon Shield* and some of the brothers' followers. Now whichever one you encounter will finally explain their motives—they're upset that Sonia claimed that the hero of Galar was, in fact, two Pokémon. They intend to discredit her by forcing Zacian and Zamazenta to run amok. You can't let that happen!

3

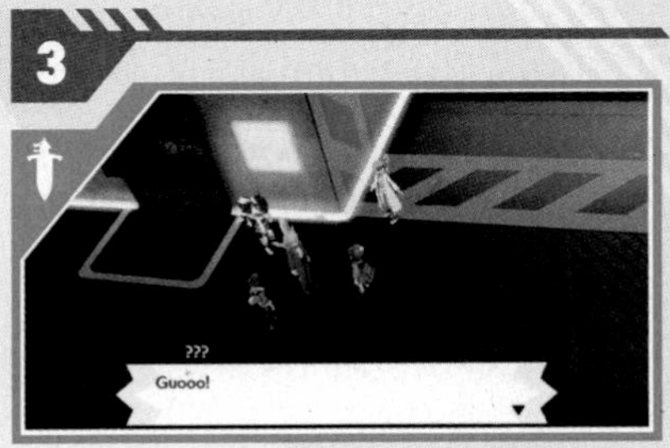

Hop and Piers help take care of the rabble while you take on the weirdo, and soon you'll have a clear path to an elevator heading up. But it seems the bothersome brother you faced bought his sibling enough time—you hear a roar from above. Hopefully you're not too late!

Sordward

Sordward just won't learn! He's still using the same four Pokémon he did when he first battled you. They may have gained a few levels, but their weaknesses are still the same. If his team didn't give you much trouble before, it won't here either. His Attack-focused team is still countered fairly easily by sending out a Pokémon with high Defense. His Sirfetch'd and Golisopod share a weakness to Flying-type moves, while his Doublade and Bisharp share weaknesses to Fire- and Ground-type moves.

Shielbert

Shielbert's team hasn't changed much since you last saw it. His Pokémon are a few levels higher, but they've still got all the same weaknesses. If your battle strategy soundly defeated Shielbert's team during your last battle with him, the same strategy will likely serve you well in this one. Sending out a Pokémon with high Defense is still a good answer to Shielbert's Attack-focused team. Sirfetch'd and Falinks are both weak to Flying-, Psychic-, and Fairy-type moves, and Bronzong and Klinklang are both weak to Fire-type moves. You might note that Bronzong and Klinklang also share a weakness to Ground-type moves just based on their types, but Shielbert's Bronzong is one that has Levitate, nullifying that particular weakness.

WALKTHROUGH

4

Ride the elevator up to the rooftop where you stopped the Darkest Day, and this time you'll find Zamazenta in *Pokémon Sword* or Zacian in *Pokémon Shield*. The other weirdo has already showered it with Galar particles, and it looks like the Legendary Pokémon can't control itself! It's up to you to calm it down!

Zamazenta

The Legendary Pokémon Zamazenta has high stats almost entirely across the board. It favors physical moves over special ones, so Pokémon with high Defense may prove helpful. It's purely a Fighting-type Pokémon, so try to hit hard with Flying-, Psychic-, or Fairy-type moves. If you're having trouble, don't forget you can cut its Attack by inflicting it with the burned status condition, which will also slowly drain its HP each turn!

Zacian

With high scores for nearly all its stats, the Legendary Pokémon Zacian will be a challenging opponent. Pokémon with high Defense will be helpful here to ward off the physical moves Zacian favors. If Zacian's high Attack is a bit much for your team to deal with, you can try to inflict the burned status condition, which will cut Zacian's Attack and drain some of its HP every turn, too! As for Zacian's weaknesses, strong Poison- or Steel-type moves will hit this pure Fairy-type Pokémon hard.

5

Defeating the Legendary Pokémon in battle still wasn't enough—even its counterpart showing up won't calm it completely. It will flee the tower, and Hop will give chase. The remaining Legendary Pokémon is understandably peeved at the two brothers who caused all this trouble...

6

If you're playing *Pokémon Sword*, Zacian will corner the two brothers, while in *Pokémon Shield*, they will be faced with a very angry Zamazenta. The Legendary Pokémon will respond to you if you engage it, but it will still want to battle you. Is it out for revenge, or is it seeking something else from you?

Zacian

While holding the Rusted Sword, Zacian changes to its Crowned Sword form in battle. Its stats have risen tremendously, giving it one of the highest Attack stats in the game! Its Attack rises even higher thanks to its Intrepid Sword Ability. It's only weak to Fire- and Ground-type moves, and even then, this Pokémon is sure to push you to your limits. Cutting Zacian's Attack by inflicting the burned status condition is one of the best things you can do in this battle. Don't be afraid to make use of healing or stat-boosting items. The Legendary Pokémon won't be satisfied until you've proven you can catch it, so weaken it as best you can before throwing a Poké Ball. This is also a great time to use that Master Ball that Professor Magnolia gave you!

Zamazenta

Holding the Rusted Shield causes Zamazenta to take on its Crowned Shield form, giving its already-impressive stats a boost. In this form, Zamazenta has extremely high Defense and Sp. Def, and its Dauntless Shield Ability will make its Defense even more formidable. It's highly recommended that you try to weaken Zamazenta's defenses with status moves before targeting the Legendary Pokémon's weaknesses to Fire-, Fighting-, and Ground-type moves. This is a good time to make use of any healing or stat-boosting items you might have been hanging on to for tough battles, too, because this Legendary Pokémon seems determined for you to prove you can catch it. If you can weaken it first, you'll have a better chance of catching it—or you could make it a sure thing by using the Master Ball you got from Professor Magnolia!

7

Seeing you battle and catch the great Pokémon seems to have shown Sordward and Shielbert the errors of their ways, too. Piers will grudgingly escort them off to the proper authorities but not before giving you his rare League Card!

 Piers's rare League Card

8

As soon as Piers leaves, you'll get a call from Hop. Apparently, he chased the other Legendary Pokémon all the way to the heart of the Slumbering Weald! It's time to return there once more and help bring this whole ordeal to a close!

9

Once you're back in the Slumbering Weald, you can speak to Sonia and have her take you to where Hop is waiting, if you don't feel like making the trek by yourself. Either way, you need to lend Hop a hand!

10

Once at the center of the woods, you'll see Hop and either Zamazenta (in *Pokémon Sword*) or Zacian (in *Pokémon Shield*). And Hop's just succeeded in calming the Legendary Pokémon down, too! It's clear that Hop is worthy of having a Pokémon like this on his team. He truly is your rival, through and through!

11

Once he catches the living legend, Hop will have one more request for you—he wants to battle you one more time, here where your adventures began. You've been through so much together. It would be rude for you to hold back now! Show him the full strength of the new Galar Champion!

Hop

It's time for a climactic showdown where it all began. Hop uses mostly the same Pokémon as the last time you battled him, but they've all grown stronger by ten levels, and he's swapped out Cramorant for either his Zamazenta or Zacian. There's no Dynamaxing here in the Slumbering Weald, so you'll have to rely on other strategies to take down his team. You should know how to handle most of the Pokémon he'll send out by now. The real trouble is his Zamazenta or Zacian, which will take on its Crowned Shield or Crowned Sword form, respectively. This form change makes the Legendary Pokémon extremely powerful, with Zamazenta having boosted Defense and Sp. Def and Zacian having higher Attack. Lower their stats with status moves or by inflicting a status condition like a burn. You could also pad your own Pokémon's stats by raising them with status moves. Either way, use all that you've learned on your adventure and put everything you've got into this! Don't forget—if Hop's team seems too strong, you can always do some training first and come back to battle him again later.

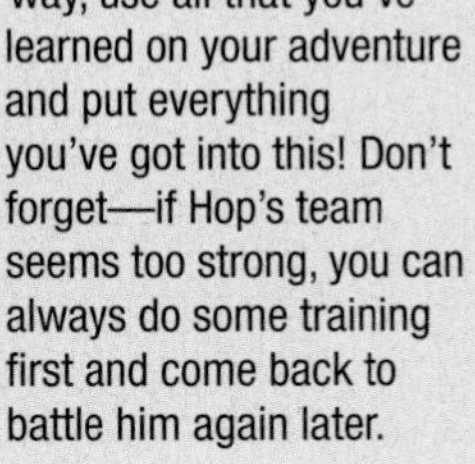

If you're playing Pokémon Shield
Zacian
Lv. 70
WEAKNESSES

12

Your battle seems to have helped Hop find his path—he wants to become a Pokémon Professor! And as luck would have it, Sonia needs a new lab assistant to help out with her research. You'll still be Hop's rival, though, and as proof, he'll give you his rare League Card!

 Hop's rare League Card

13

Just as you and Hop are reaffirming your rivalry, who should show up but Sordward and Shielbert, along with Piers and Leon! With everything settled, this long adventure is finally at a close, and it's time for all of you to head home—but not for long! Your time in the Galar region doesn't have to end, so keep exploring, battling, growing, and finding new partners to journey on with you!

ADVANCED TRAINER HANDBOOK

The Road to Becoming a Champion

If you want to become a true Champion, you'll have to master the complicated art of Pokémon battle! Think there's nothing to it except using hard-hitting moves each turn? Then you're about to get schooled in how to become a master Pokémon Trainer!

Your stops on the path to greatness

Advanced Battle Practice

Think you're ready for anything? Find out by challenging yourself to battles against tough Trainers in-game and the best Trainers the world has to offer online. Flip ahead to these pages if you're interested in more ways to battle.

- Battle Cafés .... p. 194
- Champion tournaments .... p. 196
- The Battle Tower .... p. 200
- Victory Station .... p. 202

Know the Battle Formats

Whether you're running into Trainers along the routes of the Galar region or battling with other players, you'll encounter a few types of battle formats.

Single Battles

Single Battles are the most common kind of battle you'll find during your adventure. Single Battles are exactly what they sound like—each Trainer sends out a single Pokémon at a time to have it out in a turn-based battle. The Pokémon that has the higher Speed generally gets to go first each turn.

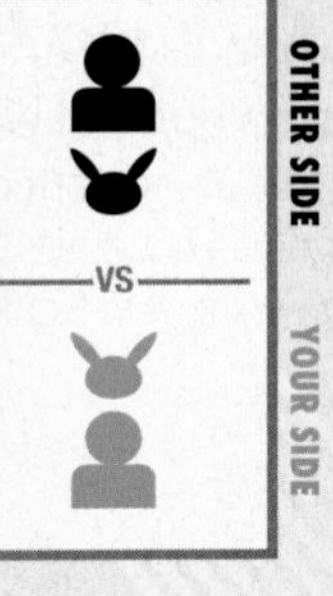

Double Battles

Double Battles can come in a few different formats, but the basics for all of them are the same—two Pokémon on your side battling against another two Pokémon on the opposing side. Sometimes the two Pokémon on your side will both be from your party and under your control, but at other times you might join forces with another Trainer so that each of you sends out one Pokémon to use in the battle. Double Battles are where things start really getting complicated, as you start factoring in complex combos (p.191) or moves that can target multiple opponents.

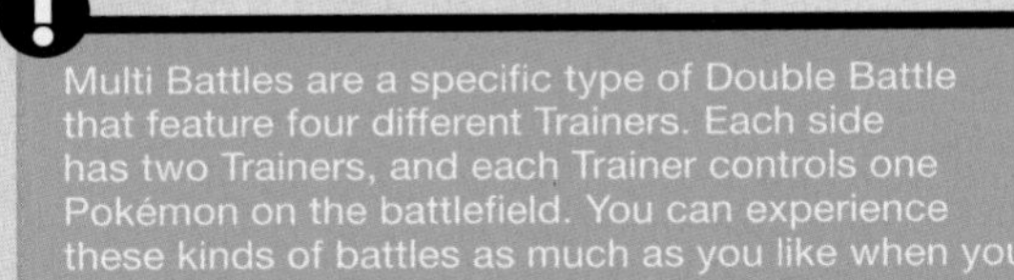

Multi Battles are a specific type of Double Battle that feature four different Trainers. Each side has two Trainers, and each Trainer controls one Pokémon on the battlefield. You can experience these kinds of battles as much as you like when you connect with other players to battle together via Y-Comm (p. 298).

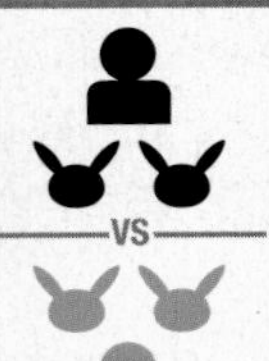

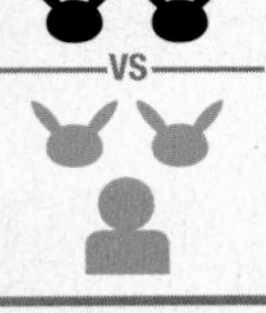

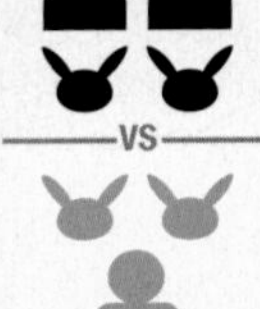

Max Raid Battles

Max Raid Battles are a major new way to battle in the Galar region. They pit four Trainers against a single gigantic opponent—a Dynamax Pokémon! You need to consider how your moves will interact with those of the other Trainers joining you in a Max Raid Battle. Not only that, you also have to negotiate when best to use the power of Dynamaxing and how to break down the Dynamax Pokémon's mysterious barriers. But you'll also have the reassuring support of several other Trainers to help you bring down and catch these tricky opponents!

There's a lot to learn to master Max Raid Battles, and it's covered in detail starting on page 271.

Master Type Matchups

No matter which battle format you're taking part in, understanding how types interact is the first key to success when it comes to Pokémon battling. The amount of damage a move does depends on type matchups, making the same move capable of doing 400% the usual damage to one opponent...and doing no damage at all on a different target.

Look out for move types

Remember that weaknesses and resistances are calculated based on the type of move used against a Pokémon, not the type of Pokémon performing the move. Think you're probably safe just because your Rock-type Rolycoly is facing Greedent? Think again—because Greedent can learn a Ground-type move like Dig and leave your Rolycoly in the dirt! Let's look at how some moves would work in battle.

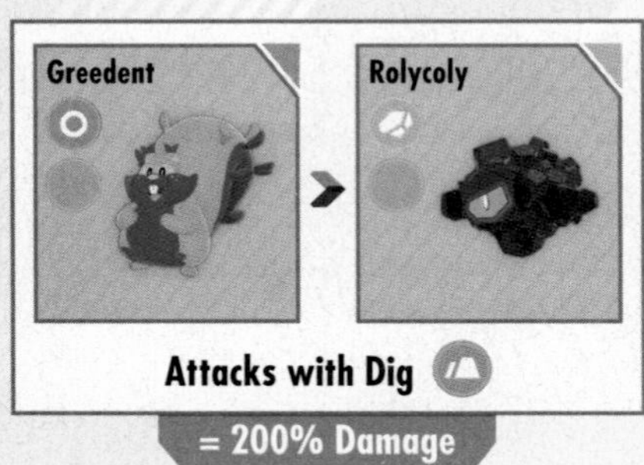

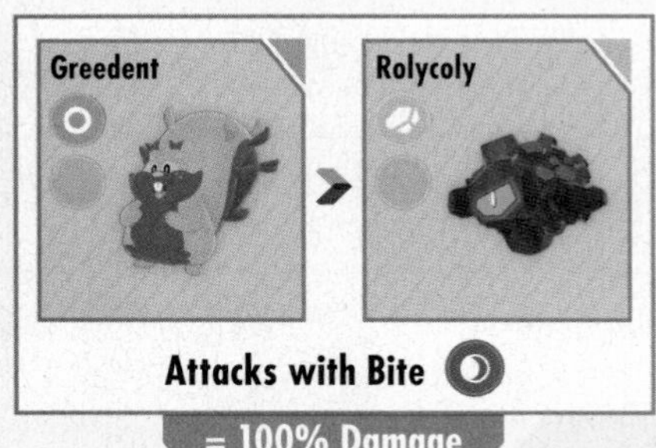

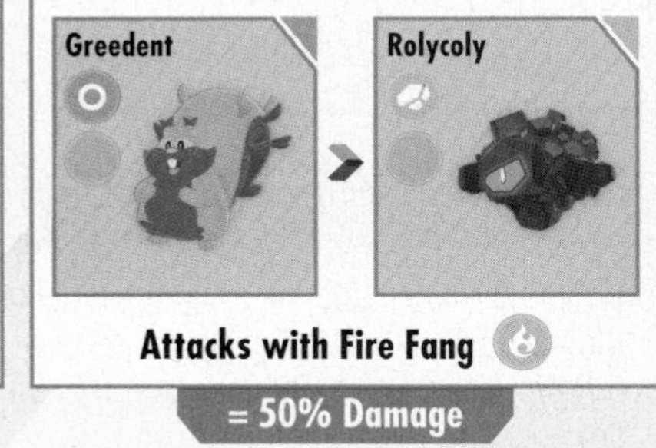

Double Types Mean Double Trouble

What about Pokémon with two types? A Pokémon with two types has all the weaknesses and resistances of both types, meaning they can be doubly weak to some types, be doubly resistant to some types, or have the weaknesses and resistances of their two types cancel each other out so they receive the regular amount of damage.

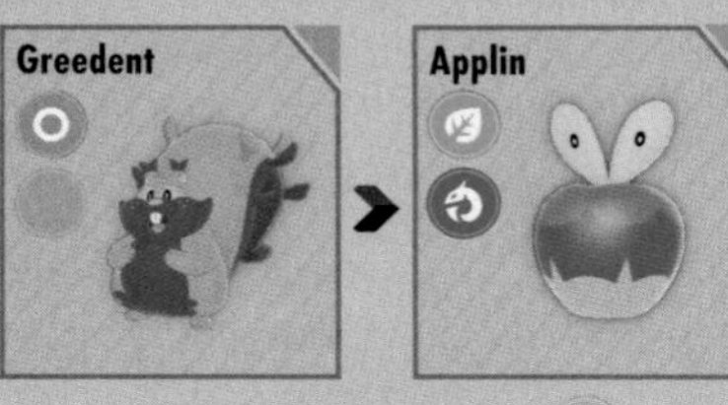

Attacks with Ice Fang

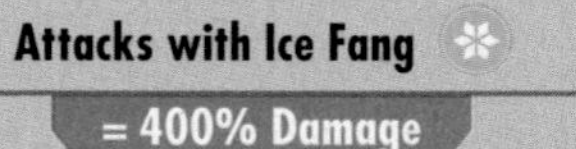

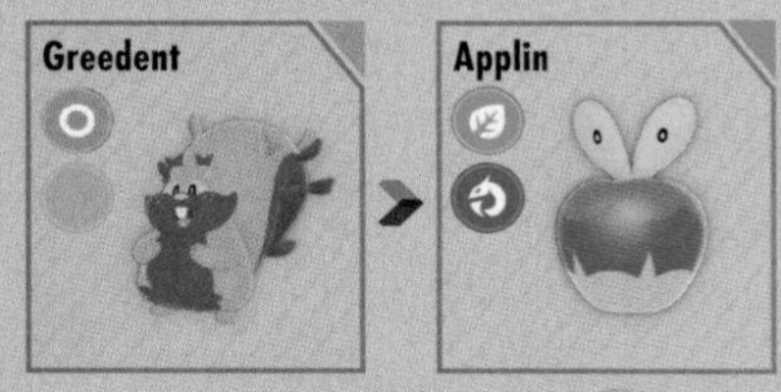

Attacks with Fire Fang

= 100% Damage

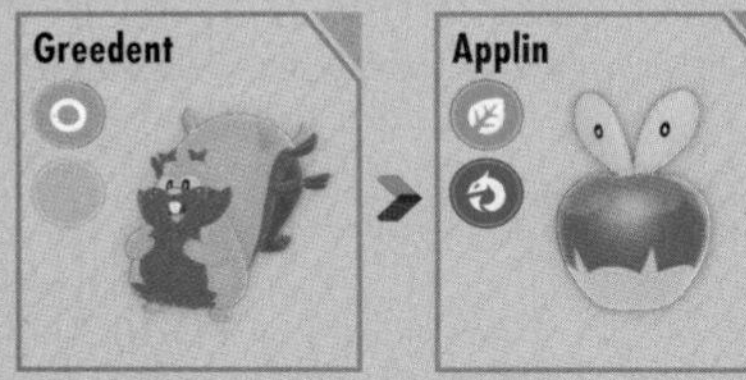

Attacks with Thunder Fang

= 25% Damage

After you've battled a species at least once, you'll be able to see in future battles if your Pokémon's moves will be super effective or not very effective against other Pokémon of that same species. You'll also be able to see if your Pokémon's move will have no effect at all on the target due to its type matchup.

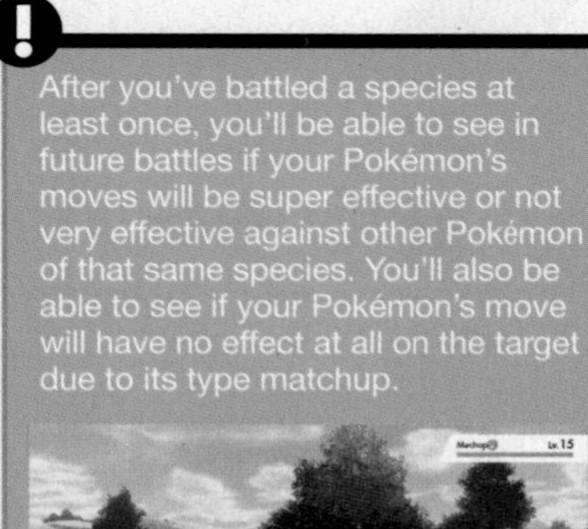

Type-based immunities

Some types of Pokémon also are completely immune to damage from certain types of moves. Ghost-type Pokémon have a rather well-known immunity to Normal- and Fighting-type moves, meaning that any Normal- or Fighting-type move used on a Sinistea will deal no damage! To review how all the types stack up against one another, including immunities like this one, check out the chart on page 383.

Same-Type Attack Bonus

Type matchups don't stop at weaknesses and resistances! Skilled Trainers also know that moves get powered up when they're used by Pokémon of the same type as the move. A Skwovet using Bullet Seed against a Wooloo will deal regular damage, but a Gossifleur using Bullet Seed against a Wooloo will deal 150% the regular amount of damage. This might make it tempting to use moves that match your Pokémon's type all the time, but that's not always the best choice. Remember that even Gossifleur's boosted Bullet Seed will see its effectiveness cut in half against any Pokémon that's strong against Grass-type moves, such as a Fire-type Pokémon. A great Trainer always picks their moves carefully!

Go beyond the basics

Now that you know how a Pokémon's one or two types affect how much damage it takes, it's time to move on to some more advanced ways that you can control the damage dealt by certain types of moves, whether they're used by your Pokémon—or on it!

Reduce a type's damage with Abilities

You'll learn more about Abilities on page 181, but some can have surprising effects on type matchups. There are Abilities like Thick Fat, which reduces the damage a Pokémon takes from Fire- and Ice-type moves. There are also Abilities that completely absorb moves of a certain type, often boosting a stat in return, like the way that Croagunk's Dry Skin Ability absorbs Water-type moves and restores one-quarter of its max HP!

Croagunk's Dry Skin

Boost a type's damage with Abilities

Some Abilities can boost the power of moves of a certain type, stacking on top of the effects of the same-type attack bonus. Steely Spirit is one example of this, and it boosts the power of any Steel-type moves used by a Pokémon or its allies on the battlefield by 50%. Perrserker can have this Ability as a Hidden Ability (p. 182).

Perrserker's Steely Spirit

Reduce supereffective damage with held items

Held items are another topic you can learn more about later on page 185, but some of them can help you reduce the supereffective damage your Pokémon takes. These items are all Berries, which you can find listed on page 372, but here are the basics to know: When held by a Pokémon, certain Berries can reduce the damage taken from a supereffective attack—but only a single time. They are consumed once they are used, and then they're gone!

A Babiri Berry reduces damage from one Steel-type move

Boost a type's damage with held items

There are also a number of items you can give a Pokémon to hold that give a little boost to its moves of a certain type. These are items like the Silk Scarf, which increases the power of Normal-type moves. But the boost is relatively small (just 20%), and other held items might have more meaningful effects in battle, so give some thought to which items you give to each of your Pokémon to hold (p. 374).

Silver Powder increases the power of Bug-type moves

Damage from certain move types is also affected by weather and terrains, which you can control to your advantage! Read more about these battlefield states on p. 189.

Build a Balanced Team

Now that you know how much or how little damage a Pokémon takes from moves based on type matchups, you'll want to have a good mix of types to swap in and out depending on the opponents you face. Let's have a look at how getting a team of diverse Pokémon can aid you on your quest to be the next Champion.

There's no one perfect team, but here are some example teams you could put together pretty early in the game, depending on which Pokémon you chose as your first partner—and an explanation of why it would make sense to do so.

A Grookey-centric team

Grookey

Let's say you started your adventure with the Grass-type Pokémon Grookey...

+

Rookidee

Grookey is weak to Bug-type moves, so we might add Rookidee because Flying-type moves are super effective against Bug-type Pokémon.

+

Sizzlipede

To cover Rookidee's weakness to Ice-type moves, we can catch a Sizzlipede. Its Fire-type moves will work well on Ice-type Pokémon if they show up in battle.

+

Mudbray

Sizzlipede is very weak to Rock-type moves, though, so in comes Mudbray. Its Ground-type moves will defeat Rock-type Pokémon, no problem.

+

Yamper

But Mudbray's weak to Water-type moves, so next we'll add Yamper to our party. Its Electric-type moves will handle pesky Water-type Pokémon!

+

Chewtle

Lastly, we add Chewtle to fill out our team. Yamper is weak to Ground-type moves. However, Chewtle's Water-type moves will fend off Ground types.

A Scorbunny-centric team

Scorbunny

Let's say you started your adventure with the Fire-type Pokémon Scorbunny...

+

Gossifleur

Scorbunny is weak to Ground-type moves, so a great choice for our team is Gossifleur. Its Grass-type moves are super effective against Ground-type Pokémon.

+

Pidove

We'll want to cover Gossifleur's weakness to Bug-type moves, and Pidove is perfect. Its Flying-type moves will work great on Bug-type Pokémon.

+

Klink

However, Pidove is weak to Rock-type moves, so why not add Klink to our team? It resists Rock-type moves, and its Steel-type moves are super effective against Rock-type Pokémon.

+

Woobat

Fighting-type moves can do a lot of damage to Steel-type Pokémon, which is why we bring in Woobat. Its Flying- and Psychic-type moves can easily handle Fighting-type Pokémon in battle.

+

Tyrogue

Our last Pokémon is Tyrogue. Woobat is weak to Ice-, Rock-, and Dark-type moves, but Tyrogue's Fighting-type moves are super effective against Pokémon of all three of those types!

A Sobble-centric team

Sobble

Let's say you started your adventure with the Water-type Pokémon Sobble...

+

Blipbug

Sobble is weak to Grass-type moves. Thankfully, we can easily add Blipbug to our team to help out! Its Bug-type moves will do a lot of damage against any Grass-type Pokémon.

+

Machop

To cover Blipbug's weakness to Rock-type moves, we'll catch Machop and add it to our party. Machop's Fighting-type moves are strong against Rock-type Pokémon. Hi-yah!

+

Stunky

Machop's weak against Psychic-type moves, so we'll catch a Stunky. It's immune to Psychic-type moves. Plus, its Dark-type moves are super effective against Psychic-type Pokémon.

+

Hoothoot

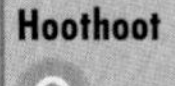

Next we add Hoothoot to our team. Stunky is weak to Ground-type moves, but Hoothoot is a Flying-type Pokémon, and Flying types are immune to Ground-type moves!

+

Drilbur

We finish our team with Drilbur. While Hoothoot is weak to Electric-type moves, they won't do any damage at all to Drilbur, and Drilbur's Ground-type moves will take down Electric types in a flash!

Balance your team's Attack and Sp. Atk

While putting together a team with a diverse number of types, you'll also want to make sure you've got some Pokémon with high Attack and some with high Sp. Atk to make sure your Pokémon can deal lots of damage in any battle.

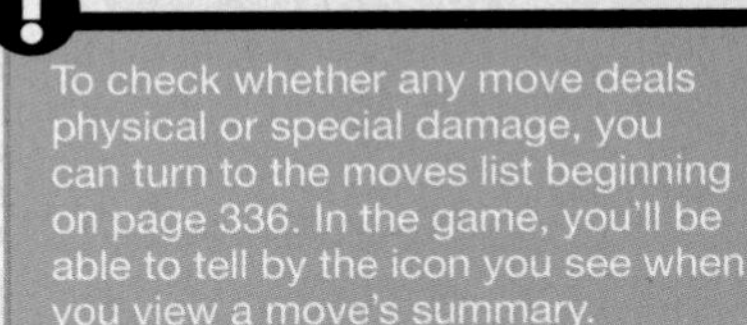

To check whether any move deals physical or special damage, you can turn to the moves list beginning on page 336. In the game, you'll be able to tell by the icon you see when you view a move's summary.

Physical and special moves

Moves that deal damage can be either physical moves or special moves. Physical moves get stronger the higher the user's Attack stat is. Special moves get stronger the higher the user's Sp. Atk stat is. It's the same for defending, too! Physical moves deal less damage to a Pokémon with higher Defense, and special moves are similarly weakened by a high Sp. Def. Check out the chart below for easy reference, and try to make sure you always use physical moves against Pokémon with low Defense and special moves against ones with low Sp. Def.

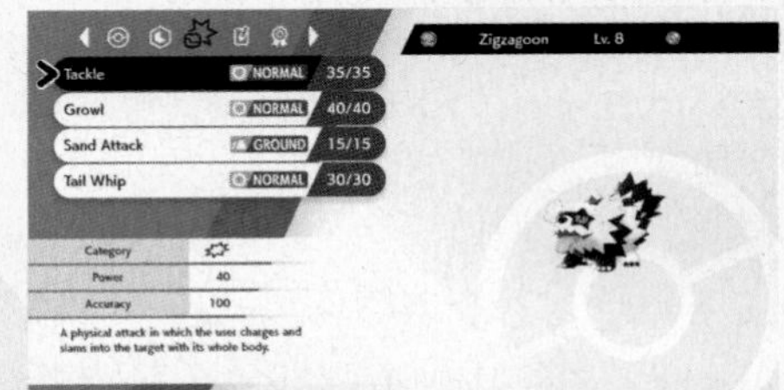

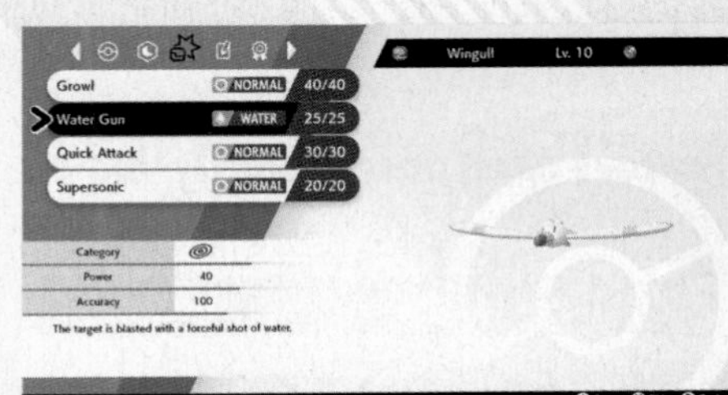

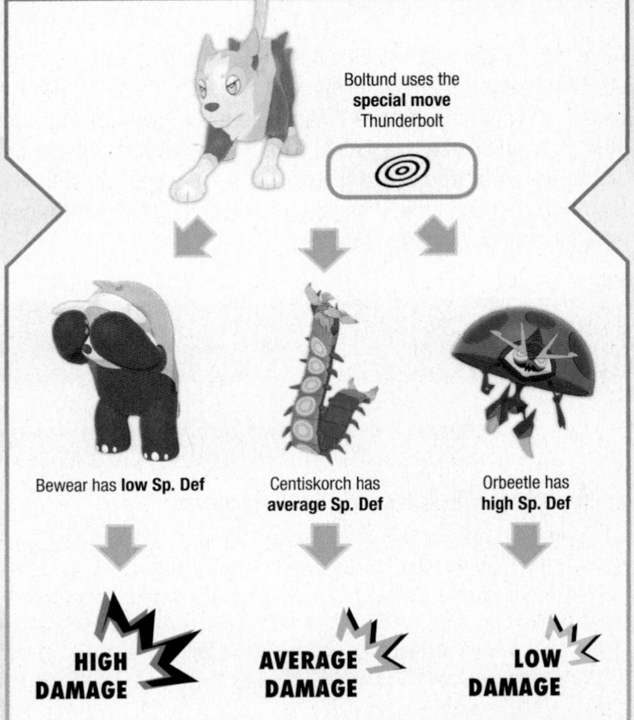

Try Out Different Teams with Battle Teams

Maybe you've got your tried-and-true party that stays by your side throughout your adventure. But what if you want to try out something completely different? That's where Battle Teams can come into play. You can set up to six different Battle Teams from your Boxes. Then select from among them when you're battling in Victory Station (p. 202) or elsewhere.

There are also Rental Teams, which you can borrow to see the kinds of teams other Trainers might use. They can be used in the Battle Tower (p. 200) or in battles in Victory Station (p. 202).

Choose the Right Pokémon

You've got the idea of how to balance different types of Pokémon on your team, but there are many Pokémon of each type. You can choose based on looks and personality, of course. Some Pokémon may simply be too tempting to pass up, but you've also gotten a taste already of how much stats can matter. So if you want to optimize your team for battle, especially against other players, it's time to understand stats and species strengths.

Pokémon stats and what goes into them

The very basics of Pokémon's stats were covered back on page 12, where you learned that Pokémon have six stats that increase as a Pokémon levels up and can affect how much damage they give and take from moves used in battle. Having high stats is a key to success, but leveling up isn't all that affects your Pokémon's stats.

Factors that permanently increase stats

All of these factors can have a huge effect on how your Pokémon's stats shape up. For example, take two Pikachu, both raised up to Lv. 100 from the many battles on your adventure. A Pikachu with a not very helpful Nature, poor individual strengths, and no base points added to its Sp. Atk might end up with a Sp. Atk stat of 94. A Pikachu with a helpful Nature, the best individual strengths, and max Sp. Atk base points might have a Sp. Atk stat of 218. Which one do you think stands a better chance of winning a battle?

> You'll learn about the things you can do to temporarily boost stats for the length of one battle on page 187!

Checking a Pokémon's Stat Growth

Your Pokémon's stat growth can be viewed when you check its summary. Press ⊙ while on the summary screen to see a Pokémon's stat graph, Dynamax Level, and Ability. A blue graph is displayed by default, which shows how your Pokémon's stats are growing. Press ⊗, and the graph will change. This orange and yellow graph shows two things—the yellow section shows your Pokémon's species strengths and the orange section shows which stats have had their base points increased. If the orange chart turns a light blue, that means the base points of that Pokémon have been maxed out. You'll learn more about base points on page 178.

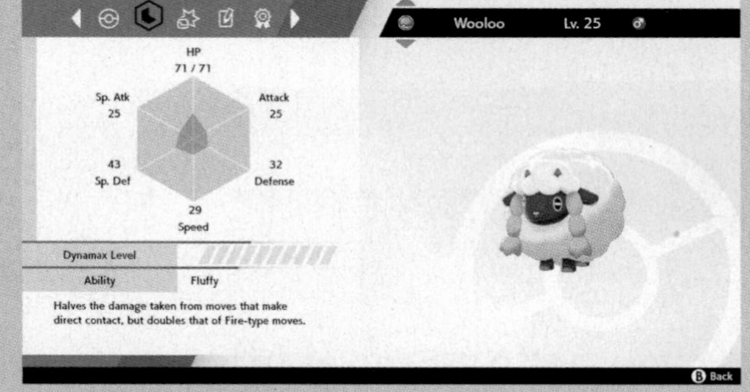

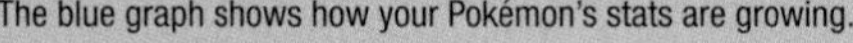

The blue graph shows how your Pokémon's stats are growing.

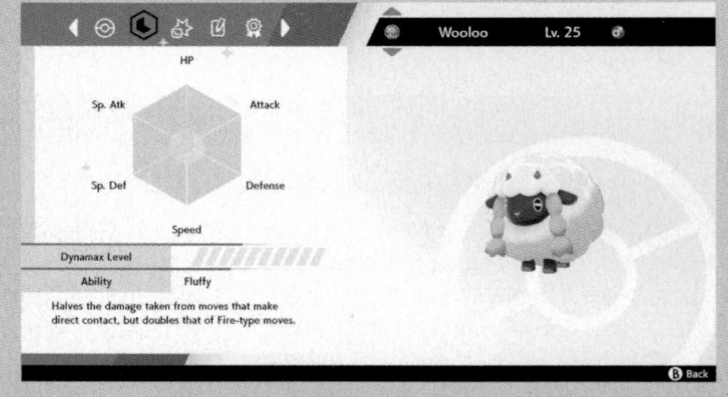

When a particular stat is maxed, it also sparkles!

Species strengths

At the top of the list of things that permanently affect stats, you'll find species strengths—and they're up top for a reason. A Pokémon's species strengths are the one factor that you cannot change for your Pokémon. Each species of Pokémon excels with some stats and not with others, and it'll be true for every Pokémon you catch of that species. All the training in the world won't change these species strengths.

Species strengths are the foundation for determining your Pokémon's stats, so the higher the species strength, the more that stat will increase each time a Pokémon levels up. Choose each species wisely and play to its strengths, whether you're raising your Pokémon to be a quick hitter with high Speed and Attack, a hardy ally with high HP and Defense, or whatever other strategy you find fits on your team.

How to Check Species Strengths

SPECIES STRENGTHS
HP
ATTACK
DEFENSE
SP. ATK
SP. DEF
SPEED

It's a bit hard to compare species strengths in your game, but you can find a breakdown in official Pokédexes. When you check a Pokémon's entry, you'll see a box like the one on the left. The number of colored boxes beside each stat name shows how high that Pokémon's species strengths are for that stat. In the game, you'll have to flip between different Pokémon's summaries if you want to compare one species to another.

Weighing balance and brawn

You can pick a species with off-the-charts species strengths for one or two stats, or you can choose a species that doesn't reach the same heights but is overall more well-rounded. Compare Barraskewda and Sandaconda below, for example. Barraskewda has an exceptionally high Attack stat, but its HP, Defense, and Sp. Def are very low. Sandaconda doesn't have quite as high of an Attack stat, but it has high Defense and most of its other stats are more balanced. Which one is right for you depends on the kind of battle strategy you prefer.

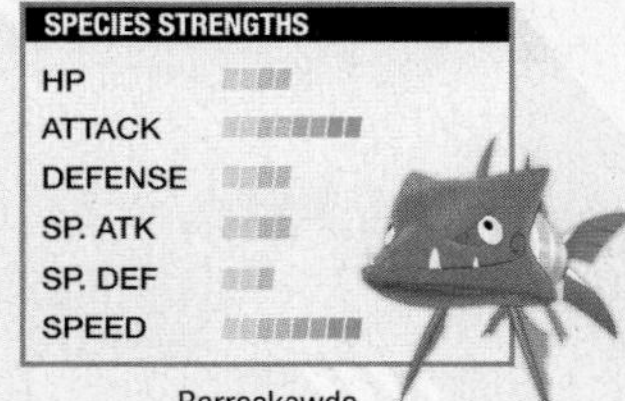

Barraskewda

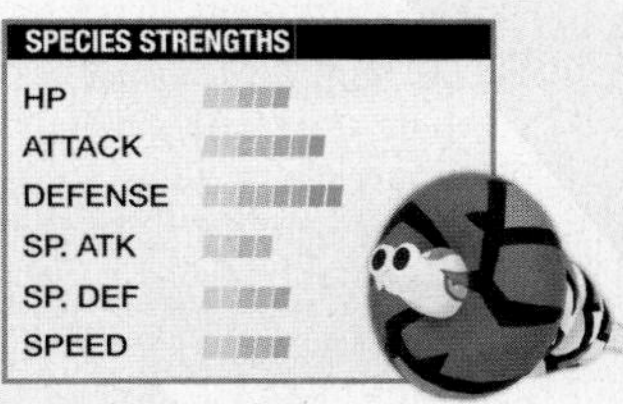

Sandaconda

! Sandaconda and Barraskewda can both be great attackers, but the way you use them in battle, the held items you give them, and the types of moves you teach them will probably be quite different. Perhaps you'd teach Barraskewda high-priority moves, like Aqua Jet, so it can quickly land some hits before it takes too much damage. Sandaconda, however, is much more burly and able to take more hits thanks to its high Defense. You could consider a status move like Toxic, which slowly deals more damage each turn to the affected Pokémon, or Giga Impact, which does high damage but also prevents the user from acting on the next turn.

Recommendations to get you started

Even with an understanding of species strengths, you might still need a leg up in selecting Pokémon from among the hundreds of species you can obtain in the Galar region. So check out these good choices of Pokémon species for each stat depending on where you are in your adventure!

Pokémon with great species strengths per stat

	◀ Obtainable early in the game				Obtainable later in the game ▶
HP	Greedent	Drifblim	Wobbuffet	Musharna	Lapras
Attack	Centiskorch	Crawdaunt	Sirfetch'd	Excadrill	Copperajah
Defense	Dubwool	Cloyster	Coalossal	Sandaconda	Avalugg
Sp. Atk	Eldegoss	Vikavolt	Hatterene	Chandelure	Frosmoth
Sp. Def	Hitmontop	Orbeetle	Alcremie	Cursola	Goodra
Speed	Boltund	Ribombee	Barraskewda	Weavile	Dragapult

Recommended Pokémon for each type

Looking for a good Pokémon for a particular type? Here's a quick guide to solid picks for each type that you might want to track down for your teams!

Some of these Pokémon are version exclusives, meaning that you can only catch them in one version of the game or the other. Look out for the sword and shield icons on their boxes to spot them. If a Pokémon you'd really love to have on your team doesn't appear in your game, then you know what to do—look for someone to trade with who is playing the other version of the game! Using Y-Comm (p. 298), you can connect with other players to trade Pokémon. But it's also worth remembering that you don't have to stick with these recommendations. There are plenty of amazing Pokémon out there for each type, so find your own favorites!

Normal

Snorlax's high Attack is great when combined with a strong Normal-type move like Giga Impact. Its high HP and Sp. Def also allow Snorlax to use Belly Drum to boost its Attack without having to worry too much about getting knocked out early.

Fire

While Coalossal has fairly high HP and Defense, its real strength is its unique Ability, Steam Engine. When hit by Fire- or Water-type moves, this Ability drastically boosts Coalossal's Speed. This extra boost can make the difference between victory and defeat! Send Coalossal out to throw off opponents who send out Fire-type Pokémon.

Water

Barraskewda has high Attack and Speed but low defensive stats. So you'll want to focus on fast hits that can knock out an opponent's Pokémon in one hit. A Barraskewda with the move Liquidation and held items like Choice Band for extra damage or Choice Scarf for extra Speed can really hit hard.

Grass

Eldegoss has high Sp. Def but very low Speed. Its Ability, Cotton Down, slows down other Pokémon when Eldegoss is hit by a move, so your opponent's Pokémon will keep getting slower if they attack Eldegoss. Take advantage of its high Sp. Atk with Giga Drain. Combine it with Leech Seed, which Gossifleur can have as an Egg Move (p. 235), to drain opposing Pokémon, all while slowing them down!

Electric

Boltund is all about Speed. Its Attack and Sp. Atk species strengths are equal, so you could even go for a mix of the two to create a speedy attacker that can handle both high Defense and high Sp. Def Pokémon. Wild Charge and Thunderbolt are both great moves for Boltund.

Ice

Eiscue is a tricky Pokémon. Its Ice Face Ability stops a physical hit and swaps the Pokémon between two forms, one having higher Defense and Sp. Def and the other having high Speed. You'll definitely want Eiscue to use the move Hail to keep the Ice Face Ability going, along with stall moves like Protect. You could also teach Blizzard to Eiscue. It's a powerful Ice-type move that's a sure hit as long as it's hailing!

Fighting

Falinks has an interesting spread of moves that it can learn to take advantage of its high Attack. It can use Protect to stall a turn or two and assess what moves the opposing Pokémon has, then strike with Close Combat for a powerful move with a same-type attack bonus. But Falinks can also learn very powerful Bug-type moves like First Impression and Megahorn, meaning it can defend itself against Psychic-type Pokémon!

Poison

Toxtricity's most interesting quality is definitely its Ability. Punk Rock boosts the power of the user's sound-based moves. Added to Toxtricity's fairly high Sp. Atk, this makes moves like Overdrive amazing for it to use alongside powerful Poison-type moves like Sludge Bomb. Toxtricity is weak to Ground-type moves, so giving it an Air Balloon will help keep it on the battlefield.

Ground

Sandaconda is a fairly balanced Pokémon, with high Attack and Defense. Its only downside is its low Speed. As such, you'll want to take full advantage of its Sand Spit Ability, which creates a sandstorm when Sandaconda takes damage. Using the sandstorm to whittle down the opponent in conjunction with moves like Toxic and Protect is a good strategy. Earthquake is also always a great choice for any Ground-type Pokémon!

Flying

Braviary's high Attack and HP allow it to use moves that deal recoil damage, like Brave Bird, against high Defense Pokémon. It can also learn Bulk Up if you want a little more oomph in your damage-dealing moves. Braviary's Hidden Ability, Defiant, also makes it great for switching in against Pokémon that lower stats, as Defiant will raise Braviary's Attack by two stages in response to such a move!

Psychic

Reuniclus's high HP and respectable defenses make it a perfect Pokémon to stall with—it can take a lot of hits and outlast its opponents. You can't go wrong teaching a Psychic-type Pokémon the move Psychic, and teaching this one Calm Mind to boost its already sky-high Sp. Atk and its Sp. Def would be a good choice, too! Then give it Leftovers to hold to really make it hard to get off the battlefield.

Bug

While very slow, Golisopod has high Attack and the move First Impression, which has high priority and power for a quick knockout. If an ally isn't supporting Golisopod's low Speed with Trick Room, adding another high-priority move, like Aqua Jet—which Wimpod can get as an Egg Move (p. 235)—is smart. High Defense means you can use a stat-boosting move, like Swords Dance, against an Attack-focused foe.

Rock

Stonjourner is a great Pokémon for Double Battles because of its Ability, Power Spot. It boosts the power of adjacent Pokémon's moves by 30%! Stonjourner also has very high HP, Attack, and Defense, though you'll want to avoid sending it out against Pokémon with high Sp. Atk. Stone Edge is a great damage-dealing move for Stonjourner to use, as the physical move has a high critical-hit chance and gets a same-type attack bonus.

Ghost

Runerigus is a great chunky attacker. While its Speed is low, its other stats are high enough that it can take hits without too much problem. Its Attack is higher than its Sp. Atk, so focus on moves like Shadow Claw and Earthquake. Runerigus's Wandering Spirit Ability will also swap around Abilities of Pokémon in battle, further helping to hinder the opponent while you pile on the damage.

Dragon

Duraludon is an interesting Dragon-type Pokémon since it also has the Steel type, making it less vulnerable against Fairy-type moves. And with high Sp. Atk, it can make perfect use of powerful moves like Flash Cannon and Draco Meteor. It even has good Attack and decent Defense, too, for some added versatility!

Dark

Grimmsnarl has very high Attack and good Sp. Atk, but most of its other species strengths aren't great. With that in mind, Sucker Punch is a great choice for Grimmsnarl. It gets a same-type attack bonus and will hit first if the opponent chooses a damage-dealing move. Since Grimmsnarl can have the Prankster Ability, helpful status moves like Thunder Wave will have higher priority and help it act first!

Steel

Copperajah is all about dealing as much damage as you can in one hit, as only its HP and Attack are particularly high. Thanks to its Sheer Force Ability, its moves that have any added effects will lose those effects but deal 30% more damage. Iron Head is a great move to use together with this Ability. Depending on how you train your Copperajah, you could give it a Choice Scarf for some higher Speed or a Life Orb for more damage.

Fairy

Hatterene has very high Sp. Atk, so Fairy-type moves like Dazzling Gleam are great, especially in Double Battles where the move will hit both opposing Pokémon. Hatterene's Hidden Ability Telepathy is also great for Double Battles, as it will prevent Hatterene from being hit by moves like Earthquake when used by allies. Take advantage of its high Defense and Sp. Def with Leftovers to help keep it on the battlefield, since its HP is on the low side.

Catch the Best Pokémon

Let's assume you've decided which species you'd like to catch for a team you're building. The next step will be to catch the best specimen you can. This is where we start considering things like Nature and individual strengths to understand how every individual Pokémon is unique—even if they're the same species.

Nature

Each Pokémon has an innate Nature, which usually makes one stat grow more quickly than average. For example, an Adamant Nature makes a Pokémon's Attack grow faster. If you catch two Dhelmise because you know that species has a good species strength for Attack but one of them has an Adamant Nature and the other has a Timid Nature, the one with the Adamant Nature will see its Attack stat grow much faster.

Natures can be a double-edged sword, though. Any Nature that makes one stat grow faster will make a different stat grow slower than usual. You'll have to decide which stats you want to focus on and which you can sacrifice. Here are some of the most popular Natures used in competitive battles.

Nature	Boosted stat	Suppressed stat	Good for
Adamant	Attack	Sp. Atk	Pokémon that only use physical moves
Jolly	Speed	Sp. Atk	Physical move users that need to be fast
Modest	Sp. Atk	Attack	Pokémon that only use special moves
Timid	Speed	Attack	Special move users that need to be fast

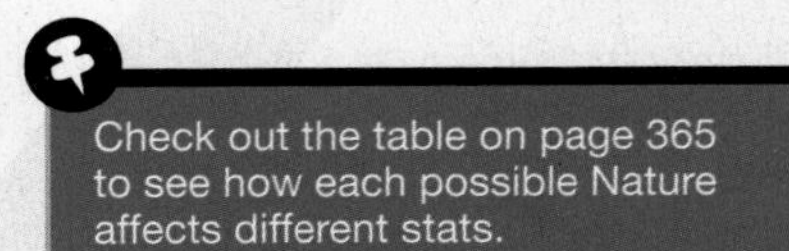

Check out the table on page 365 to see how each possible Nature affects different stats.

Check the effects of your Pokémon's Nature

In addition to the table on page 365, you can also check the effects of your Pokémon's Nature in the game by looking at your Pokémon's summary screen. Any pink stat will increase more quickly than average upon leveling up, while any blue stat will increase more slowly than average. Make sure the stat you want to focus on is pink and that no stat your Pokémon really needs is blue.

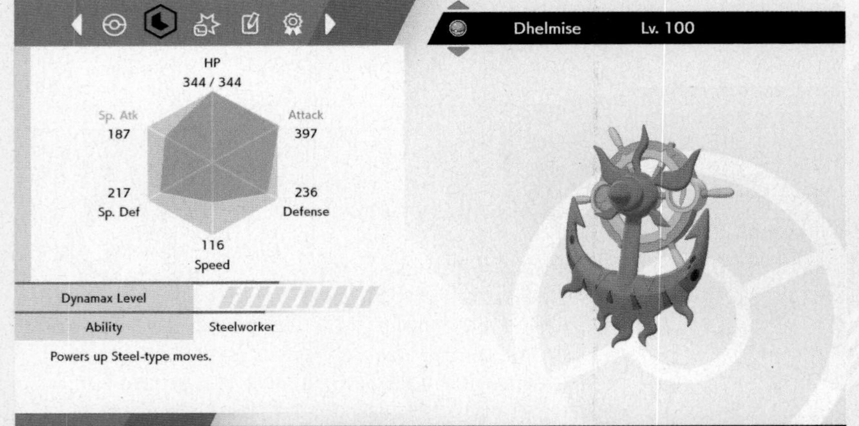

Get the Right Nature

You can try to encounter Pokémon with the Nature you want in the wild, hoping you'll get lucky. You could use the Synchronize Ability (see the Abilities list starting on page 359) or try to pass along a Nature when hatching Pokémon Eggs (p. 234). But expert Trainers can use mints to help their Pokémon gain the effects of a Nature best suited to their stats. You can get these mints at a special BP Shop (p. 382) or earn them at the Battle Tower (p. 200) or in Ranked Battles (p. 202).

Individual strengths

Each Pokémon you catch, even in the same species, will have different individual strengths. Yes, you can assume that all Pincurchin will have a good Attack stat because of their species strengths. And maybe you even catch two Pincurchin with the same Nature. But one of them still might end up with a higher Attack than the other, because of its individual strengths. Along with Natures, these individual strengths are what make each individual Pokémon a bit different from the next.

Individual strengths affect all six stats—HP, Attack, Defense, Sp. Atk, Sp. Def, and Speed. Each varies as well, so your Pokémon might have great individual strengths (and thus great stats!) for Attack and Sp. Def but terrible ones for Sp. Atk and Speed. You'll be able to judge how each of your Pokémon measures up once you unlock the Judge function.

The Judge Function

This function is unlocked once you reach the Poké Ball tier in the Battle Tower (p. 200). Once it's unlocked, you'll be able to see how your Pokémon's individual strengths stack up by moving the cursor to the Pokémon you want to check in the Box screen, and then pressing ⊕ twice. If you see "Best," then you can rest assured your Pokémon has the best possible individual strength for a stat!

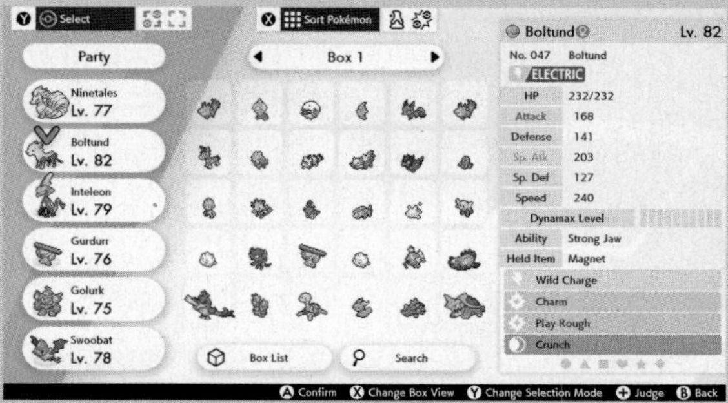

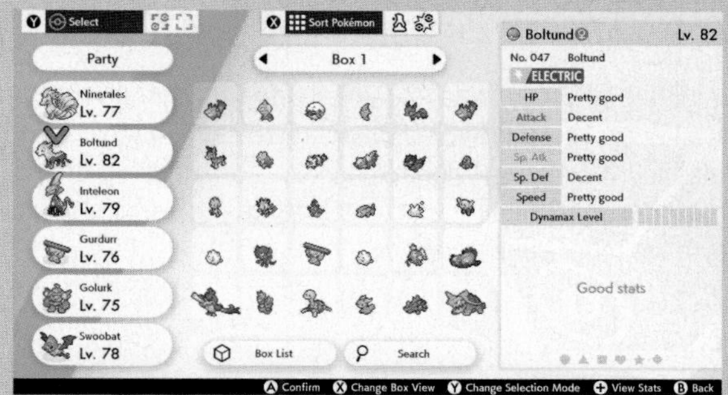

Encounter Pokémon with great individual strengths

Obviously, you want to find Pokémon with as many great individual strengths as possible. Leave it to luck, and you'll be searching for a very long time for that perfect specimen. But you can increase your chance of encountering Pokémon with two, three, or more maxed individual strengths if you find Brilliant Pokémon in the wild! The details of how to find these brilliant specimens and what other benefits they offer are covered on the next page.

Another way to encounter Pokémon with excellent individual strengths is in Max Raid Battles. Pokémon encountered in higher difficulty Max Raid Battles are more likely to have more of their individual strengths maxed, so do your best to catch the Pokémon you encounter in five-star Max Raid Battles!

Hatch Pokémon with great individual strengths from Eggs

Trainers can also try to find Pokémon Eggs that will hatch into Pokémon with great individual strengths. Pokémon Eggs are covered in detail starting on page 234, but for now know that Pokémon that hatch from Eggs can inherit things like individual strengths from the Pokémon you had at the Nursery when the Egg was found.

You'll learn more about inheriting individual strengths on page 236, but be warned! Any increases to your Pokémon's individual strengths from Hyper Training won't be passed along to Pokémon Eggs.

Get great Pokémon from Ranked Battles

If you win your way through Ranked Battles in Victory Station, you'll sometimes be rewarded with the gift of a Pokémon. These Pokémon tend to have as many as five or six individual strengths as high as they can go. Savvy Trainers can use this route to snag some top-notch Pokémon for themselves.

Hyper Training to the Rescue!

Don't despair if you already have a Pokémon you love but its individual strengths aren't the best. Become the Champion of the Galar region and keep on training that Pokémon all the way to Lv. 100, and you'll be able to use Hyper Training! Find the person who can hyper train your Pokémon in the Battle Tower (p. 200). They'll hyper train your Pokémon in return for a Bottle Cap or Gold Bottle Cap, instantly boosting one or all of your Pokémon's individual strengths to the max!

Ways to get Bottle Caps

- Wyndon BP Shop .... p. 124
- Battle Tower victories .... p. 200
- Ranked Battles .... p. 202
- Max Raid Battles .... p. 271
- The Digging Duo .... p. 278
- The Pickup Ability .... p. 364

Stats to prioritize

If you have to pick one stat to improve your Pokémon's individual strengths for, most Trainers would probably choose Speed. A few points' difference in Attack may not make or break a battle, but having a Speed stat even a single point greater than an opponent will mean that your Pokémon gets to use its move first.

Brilliant Pokémon

There's more to catching Pokémon than simply wearing them down and throwing a Poké Ball. If you master the art of catching Pokémon, you'll be rewarded in a variety of ways! One of these is the chance to encounter Pokémon with special auras, when you are catching visible Pokémon in the field or fishing up Pokémon in bodies of water. These specimens are known as Brilliant Pokémon!

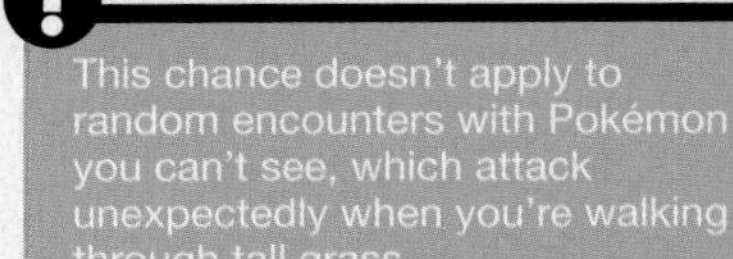

This chance doesn't apply to random encounters with Pokémon you can't see, which attack unexpectedly when you're walking through tall grass.

The benefits of Brilliant Pokémon

Sometimes you may see Pokémon in the wild that give off a special aura. These Brilliant Pokémon will tend to have higher levels than the average Pokémon in the area, making them a bit harder to battle but also strong allies if you catch them. They have other benefits as well, though!

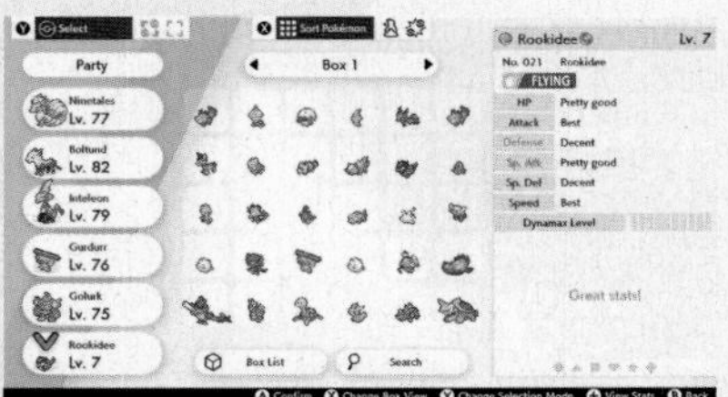

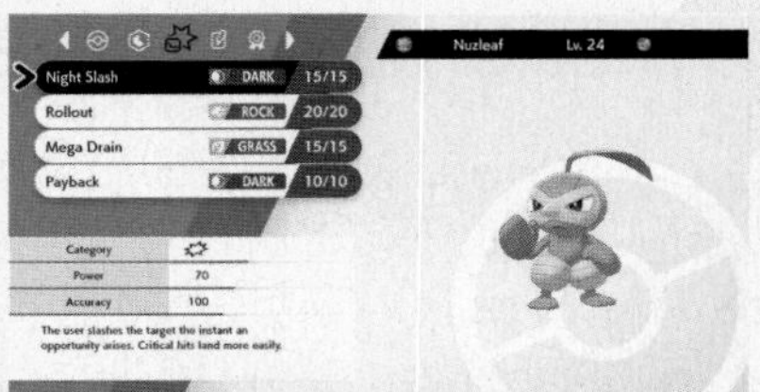

Great individual strengths

A Brilliant Pokémon will have the highest possible individual strengths for at least two or three of its stats, so seeking them out is a great way to get Pokémon with excellent stats.

Unusual moves

Egg Moves aren't learned by leveling up—they're moves a Pokémon could inherit from other Pokémon if it is hatched from an Egg (p. 234). When you catch a Brilliant Pokémon, it will already know one of these rare moves!

Winning Watts

When you catch or defeat a Brilliant Pokémon, you will also earn Watts that can be exchanged for various goodies (p. 275). The number of Watts you receive will be based on the level of the Pokémon!

This all sounds pretty tempting, so how can you increase your chances of encountering these Brilliant Pokémon? The answer lies in battling a Pokémon species over and over. The more times you catch or defeat a species in battle, the more likely you'll be to encounter Brilliant Pokémon in the future.

Number of times you battled a species	Effects on future encounters with that species	
At least one time	Becomes possible to encounter Brilliant Pokémon	+ Chance of encountering Shiny Pokémon does not change
At least 20 times	Around 1.3× the usual chance of encountering Brilliant Pokémon	+ Chance of encountering Shiny Pokémon does not change
At least 50 times	Around 1.6× the usual chance of encountering Brilliant Pokémon	+ 2× the usual chance of encountering Shiny Pokémon
At least 100 times	2× the usual chance of encountering Brilliant Pokémon	+ 3× the usual chance of encountering Shiny Pokémon
At least 200 times	2× the usual chance of encountering Brilliant Pokémon	+ 4× the usual chance of encountering Shiny Pokémon
At least 300 times	2× the usual chance of encountering Brilliant Pokémon	+ 5× the usual chance of encountering Shiny Pokémon
At least 500 times	2× the usual chance of encountering Brilliant Pokémon	+ 6× the usual chance of encountering Shiny Pokémon

Check Your Numbers!

Look at that high-tech Pokédex of yours, and you can see how many times you've caught or defeated a species. The number is listed right there, beside the words "Number Battled."

Look for the Link!

Every time you defeat a Pokémon you can see in the wild, look around! You'll be much more likely than usual to see more Pokémon of that same species appear. Use this trick to keep encountering the same Pokémon again and again, building up the total count for their Evolutionary line and improving your chances at finding a Brilliant Pokémon or a Shiny Pokémon! It can also help out with increasing your Pokémon's base points, as you can read about on page 178. If you run away from a battle or catch a Pokémon instead of defeating it, you won't see this boost in encounter rate.

Fishing chains

When it comes to fishing up Brilliant Pokémon, it's not the times you've battled a particular species that matters most. Instead, the likelihood of reeling in such a Pokémon will be tied to the number of times you're successful in hooking a bite in a row—no matter what species you fish up. If you can keep getting bites and defeating whatever you've hooked, you'll become more likely to fish up Pokémon with auras—and get all the benefits that come along with them. But if you fail to reel anything in, you leave the area, or you turn off your game, then your chain will break! Catching the Pokémon, being defeated, or running from battle will also break a chain. You've got to defeat the Pokémon you fish up to reap these rewards.

Number of successful hooks in a row	Effects on future fishing encounters
0–2	Roughly the usual chance of encountering Brilliant Pokémon
3–6	About 1.3× the usual chance of encountering Brilliant Pokémon
7–14	About 3.3× the usual chance of encountering Brilliant Pokémon
15–24	About 6.6× the usual chance of encountering Brilliant Pokémon
25+	About 16.6× the usual chance of encountering Brilliant Pokémon

Shiny Pokémon

Shiny Pokémon are super rare, which is why everyone wants to get them! They are differently colored than normal specimens of their species, sometimes in subtle ways and sometimes in fantastic ways! But just because they look different doesn't guarantee their stats will be any better than their regularly colored counterparts.

Nickit — Shiny Nickit

Wooloo — Shiny Wooloo

Chewtle — Shiny Chewtle

Increasing or Decreasing Wild Pokémon Encounters

Defeating a Pokémon you can see in the field may make it more likely you'll see the same species again, but what if you just want to see more Pokémon in general? Or fewer? Read on to learn how you can increase and decrease your run-ins with wild Pokémon.

Crouching down and calling out to Pokémon you can see

As you wander through routes, caves, and the Wild Area in the center of the Galar region, you'll see many wild Pokémon going about their daily business. Each species acts a bit differently, with some fleeing if they spot you, some simply ignoring you, and others running right at you full speed! They're not the only ones with a mind of their own, though—you can also do your part to avoid these visible Pokémon or try to encounter them.

! Random encounters with Pokémon you can't see in the tall grass are a little different. Crouching and whistling won't have the same effect on them, though the items and Abilities described below still will.

Tilt the Left Stick slowly to crouch through tall grass
When you're walking through patches of tall grass, you can creep about in a crouch by tilting the Left Stick just a little. Use this to try to sneak by aggressive Pokémon that might otherwise rush to attack you once they spot you. Unfortunately, this trick only works in the tall grass and not anywhere else!

Press down on the Left Stick to whistle
Whistling will catch the attention of nearby Pokémon that haven't noticed you yet. The aggressive ones will immediately hustle over to you, but shy Pokémon that usually run away will pause and let you draw closer. This can be a useful trick for catching these elusive species.

! When you're on your bike, you can ring its bell by pressing on the Left Stick, too. It will have the same effects!

Reducing your encounters with wild Pokémon

There are some strategies that will help you reduce the number of random encounters you have with Pokémon you can't see. For the ones you can see, you'll simply need to crouch down and try to avoid their notice—or run like the wind!

Items that repel Pokémon

You can use Repels, Super Repels, and Max Repels to avoid random encounters with Pokémon hiding in the tall grass. The effects wear off eventually, but you can always buy more of these items at Poké Marts.

The Cleanse Tag and Pure Incense items will also reduce random encounters if held by your lead Pokémon. You can find the first on Route 4 (p. 60) and purchase the second from the market in Hulbury (p. 69)!

! In addition to the other strategies described here, the way you travel can also affect how many wild Pokémon spring out of nowhere at you. Riding your Rotom Bike reduces your chances of random encounters, and using its turbo boost makes those encounters even less likely! Creeping through the grass in a crouch will also completely prevent random encounters, even if it may not get you away from all of the Pokémon you see.

Abilities that repel Pokémon

There are Abilities (p. 359) that make you less likely to run into wild Pokémon in random encounters if you put a Pokémon with such an Ability at the head of your party.

Infiltrator
Noibat, Espurr, Cottonee

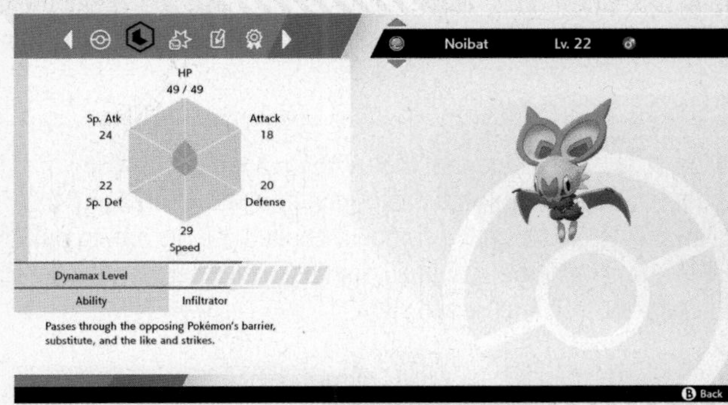

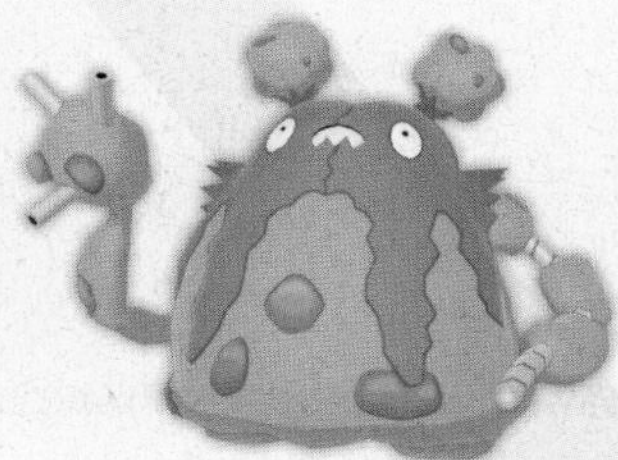

Stench
Skuntank, Garbodor

White Smoke
Torkoal, Sizzlipede

Abilities that attract Pokémon

You can also increase wild Pokémon encounters if you want to train your team or work on filling your Pokédex. Like the Abilities that decrease random encounters, these Abilities also take effect if the Pokémon at the head of your party has one of them.

Arena Trap
Diglett, Trapinch

Illuminate
Chinchou, Morelull

No Guard
Machop, Honedge

Abilities That Attract Certain Types

With Abilities, you can do more than attract random encounters with just any Pokémon. Some Abilities can make it much more likely you'll encounter Pokémon of a certain type, whether they're walking about or hiding in a random encounter.

Ability	Type it attracts
Flash Fire	Fire
Storm Drain	Water
Harvest	Grass
Lightning Rod, Static	Electric
Magnet Pull	Steel

ADVANCED TRAINER HANDBOOK

Train Your Pokémon Right

Once you've decided on your Pokémon team and caught some great specimens using the advice in the previous sections, it's time to knuckle down and get training! By now, you've got the basics down. But you can't count yourself among the best until you know how to get the most out of your Pokémon's base points and how to raise them quickly!

Base points

Base points are points that increase each time your team wins a battle. Every opposing Pokémon your Pokémon defeat will give them base points for particular stats, gradually increasing their HP, Attack, Defense, Sp. Atk, Sp. Def, or Speed. Your Pokémon accumulate points until they have reached the maximum number of total base points that any Pokémon can earn (510 points, to be exact). The number of base points your Pokémon has gained for each stat is used to calculate its final HP, Attack, Defense, Sp. Atk, Sp. Def, and Speed stats.

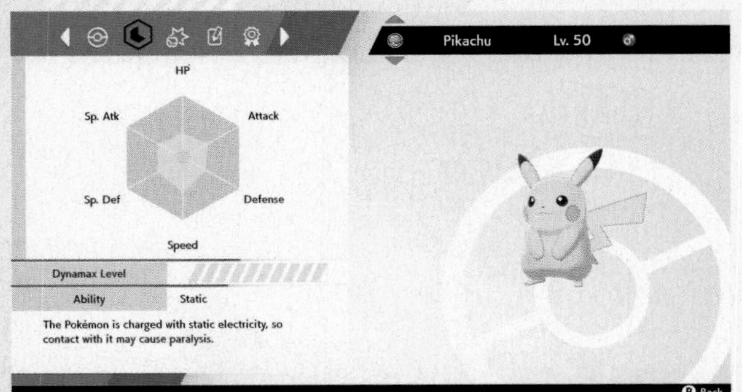

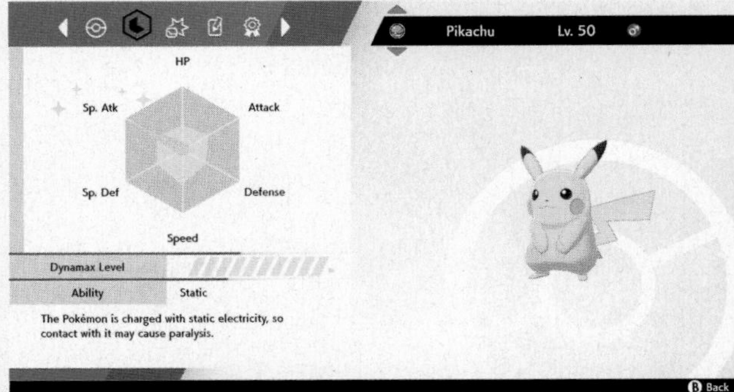

The Pikachu on the left has no base points in its Sp. Atk, while the one on the right has the maximum 252 points given to its Sp. Atk. What a difference!

When you've maxed out a Pokémon's base points, visit a lady in the house in front of Hammerlocke Stadium's drawbridge (p. 82), and she'll give your Pokémon an Effort Ribbon!

Lowering Base Points

Base points don't go down naturally, but you can lower them if you try. Why would anyone want to lower their Pokémon's base points? Because each stat can only be raised by a certain number of base points—252. And since your Pokémon can only earn 510 points total, you can only max the base points of two stats. If your Pokémon has been battling a lot and gained base points in random stats, it might not be able to max out the stats you'd like to emphasize—which could cause trouble if it's up against another Pokémon that *has* maxed the same stats. *That* is why you might want to lower base points for stats you're not focusing on. Don't feel like you have to max out the points of two stats to win, though! There are lots of strategies where base points will be spread across three or even four stats.

Battle to increase base points

When your Pokémon takes part in battles against opposing Pokémon, it earns base points. Which stat these base points will go to depends on the species of Pokémon it battled against, but it's often a stat that species excels in. To check which stat any species found in the wild in Galar will give base points for, check the table beginning on page 366.

For extra efficiency when raising your Pokémon's base points in battle, you'll want to make use of items that help certain base points increase much faster than normal. Most of these items also allow you to gain base points in a stat of your choice, regardless of the Pokémon you're battling! Keep in mind that all these items will reduce your Pokémon's Speed as long as they're held, though.

Apart from the Macho Brace, all items in the table to the right can also help you pass on individual strengths to Pokémon Eggs (p. 234)!

Item	Effect
Power Weight	Increases HP base points every time you defeat or catch a Pokémon but reduces Speed while held
Power Bracer	Increases Attack base points every time you defeat or catch a Pokémon but reduces Speed while held
Power Belt	Increases Defense base points every time you defeat or catch a Pokémon but reduces Speed while held
Power Lens	Increases Sp. Atk base points every time you defeat or catch a Pokémon but reduces Speed while held
Power Band	Increases Sp. Def base points every time you defeat or catch a Pokémon but reduces Speed while held
Power Anklet	Increases Speed base points every time you defeat or catch a Pokémon but reduces Speed while held
Macho Brace	Doubles all base points earned from battles but reduces Speed while held

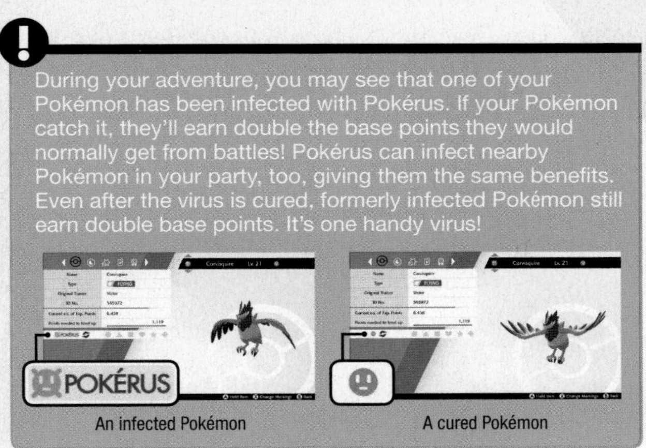

During your adventure, you may see that one of your Pokémon has been infected with Pokérus. If your Pokémon catch it, they'll earn double the base points they would normally get from battles! Pokérus can infect nearby Pokémon in your party, too, giving them the same benefits. Even after the virus is cured, formerly infected Pokémon still earn double base points. It's one handy virus!

An infected Pokémon

A cured Pokémon

Use Poké Jobs to increase base points

A great way to build up a Pokémon's base points while it's not in your party or while you aren't playing the game is to use Poké Jobs. Poké Jobs are tasks you can send Pokémon on to help people all around Galar, and the Pokémon will get rewarded for it! When the job is done, the Pokémon can earn things like money or items, but they can also gain some base points depending on the job they did. The number of points they gain is even affected by Pokérus and base-point-increasing items like the Macho Brace, so you can earn tons of base points this way! Check out page 241 for the full scoop on Poké Jobs.

Use items to instantly increase base points

Certain items can also give your Pokémon's base points an instant lift! The first set of these are nutritious drinks, which can be purchased in exchange for your hard-earned Battle Points (p. 200) at the BP Shop in one of Hammerlocke's Pokémon Centers. BP is hard to come by, though, so you may not want to use it on these items when there are so many other ways to increase base points.

Feather items—the Health, Muscle, Resist, Genius, Clever, and Swift Feathers—can also raise base points by a lesser amount. These can be found as hidden items on Route 5, but they won't give your Pokémon's base points a huge boost. Still, if you happen to have any of these Feather items in your Bag, feel free to use them!

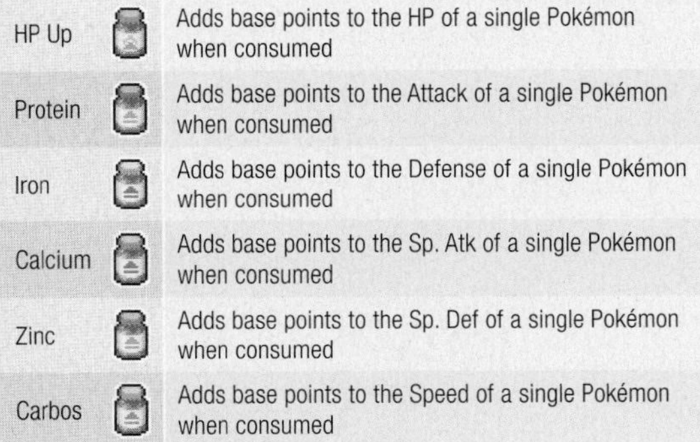

Item	Effect
HP Up	Adds base points to the HP of a single Pokémon when consumed
Protein	Adds base points to the Attack of a single Pokémon when consumed
Iron	Adds base points to the Defense of a single Pokémon when consumed
Calcium	Adds base points to the Sp. Atk of a single Pokémon when consumed
Zinc	Adds base points to the Sp. Def of a single Pokémon when consumed
Carbos	Adds base points to the Speed of a single Pokémon when consumed

Increasing Dynamax Levels

The Dynamax phenomenon increases a Pokémon's HP to gigantic proportions! But did you know that you can increase the multiplier that affects a Pokémon's HP when it Dynamaxes? You can earn Dynamax Candies from battling Dynamax or Gigantamax Pokémon in Max Raid Battles in the Wild Area. Use these candies to max out your Pokémon's Dynamax Level and turn it into a fearsome force! You can check your Pokémon's Dynamax Level anytime from its Summary.

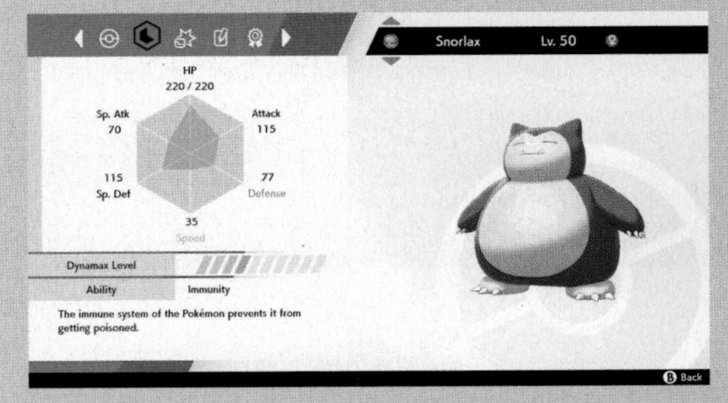

Use Berries to lower base points

If you want to lower a Pokémon's base points so you can start fresh with its training, consider using specific Berries that can be found on Berry trees in the Wild Area's Bridge Field. They lower a Pokémon's base points when consumed. But don't worry about your Pokémon being upset about their lower stats, since these Berries make Pokémon friendlier, too (p. 283)! Learn more about Berry trees and gathering Berries on page 290.

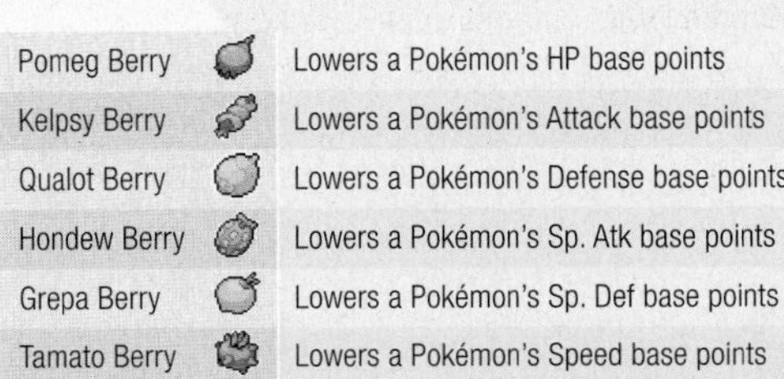

Pomeg Berry	Lowers a Pokémon's HP base points
Kelpsy Berry	Lowers a Pokémon's Attack base points
Qualot Berry	Lowers a Pokémon's Defense base points
Hondew Berry	Lowers a Pokémon's Sp. Atk base points
Grepa Berry	Lowers a Pokémon's Sp. Def base points
Tamato Berry	Lowers a Pokémon's Speed base points

Pokémon hatched from Pokémon Eggs have no base points in their stats at all, letting you start fresh with a clean slate. Oh, to be young!

What about Characteristics?

A Characteristic is another bit of information that appears on your Pokémon's Summary page. Wondering what it means? Characteristics don't actually affect how your Pokémon's stats grow. They just give you a clue about where your Pokémon's individual strengths might be. The full table of Characteristics and the stats each one matches up with can be found on page 365.

Leveling Up Your Pokémon

Leveling up the Pokémon on your team is important during your journey, especially to make sure you're ready to battle the Gym Leaders and challenge your rivals. To level Pokémon up, you're going to need Exp. Points—a lot of them! Usually these are gained by defeating Pokémon in battle or catching them, but there are a few other methods and some tricks to help you earn Exp. Points a little quicker.

Get boosted Exp. Points

Pokémon that meet certain conditions will gain a boosted amount of Exp. Points when an opposing Pokémon is defeated or caught. Pokémon that originally belonged to another Trainer and were traded to you, Pokémon that would normally have evolved at their current level but haven't yet (remember to press Ⓑ to stop Evolution!), and Pokémon with exceptionally high friendship all gain boosted amounts of Exp. Points.

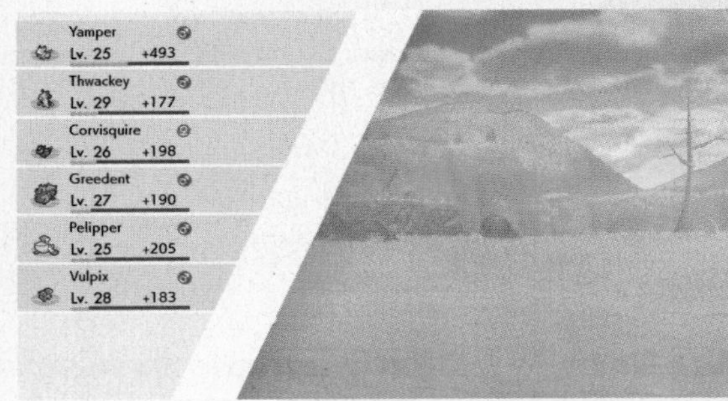

Battle stronger Pokémon

This may seem obvious, but it's easy to forget that a good way to get more Exp. Points is simply to battle stronger Pokémon. The higher the level of the opposing Pokémon compared to your own, the more Exp. Points you'll gain when you defeat or catch it! Evolved Pokémon also give out more Exp. Points. In other words, beating a Boltund will yield more Exp. Points than beating a Yamper!

Exp. Point Caps

Think you can find some strong evolved Pokémon to battle deep in the Wild Area and level up your team in no time at all? You might have to think again, because the amount of Exp. Points you can get from higher-level Pokémon is restricted by how many Gym Badges you have. If you haven't proven yourself by earning enough Badges, you'll find those battles aren't nearly as rewarding as you might've hoped.

No Badges	Any opposing Pokémon over Lv. 25 will give Exp. Points as if they were a Lv. 25 Pokémon.
1 Badge	Any opposing Pokémon over Lv. 30 will give Exp. Points as if they were a Lv. 30 Pokémon.
2 Badges	Any opposing Pokémon over Lv. 35 will give Exp. Points as if they were a Lv. 35 Pokémon.
3 Badges	Any opposing Pokémon over Lv. 40 will give Exp. Points as if they were a Lv. 40 Pokémon.
4 Badges	Any opposing Pokémon over Lv. 45 will give Exp. Points as if they were a Lv. 45 Pokémon.
5 Badges	Any opposing Pokémon over Lv. 50 will give Exp. Points as if they were a Lv. 50 Pokémon.
6 Badges	Any opposing Pokémon over Lv. 55 will give Exp. Points as if they were a Lv. 55 Pokémon.
7 Badges	Any opposing Pokémon over Lv. 60 will give Exp. Points as if they were a Lv. 60 Pokémon.
8 Badges	No restrictions!

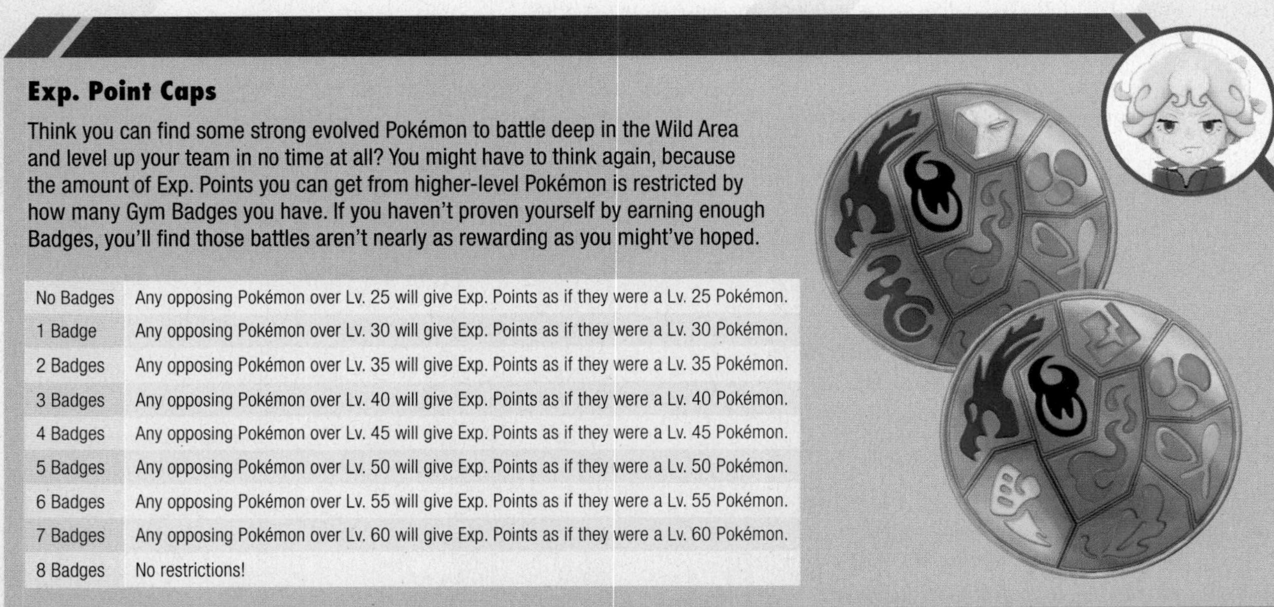

Use items effectively

There are a few different kinds of items that can help your Pokémon gain Exp. Points more quickly. Having a Pokémon hold the item Lucky Egg will increase the Exp. Points it receives from battle by 50%. Rare Candies will instantly raise a Pokémon to its next level, so make sure to use them before that Pokémon has gained a lot of points toward its next level. And then there are Exp. Candies—they're similar to Rare Candies but easier to come by. They give varying amounts of Exp. Points, instead of automatically leveling up your Pokémon. You can get Exp. Candies from Max Raid Battles, so flip to page 271 to learn more about them!

Take part in Poké Jobs

Just like with gaining base points, Poké Jobs can also give Pokémon Exp. Points to help them level up faster. One effective method would be to train a Pokémon against wild Pokémon or in Trainer battles while you play the game and then send that Pokémon off on a job when you're ready to stop playing. The time it takes to complete a Poké Job will keep counting down even when your system is off. Don't forget to have your Pokémon hold a Lucky Egg when it's sent on its job, and it'll earn even more Exp. Points!

> Your Pokémon can also earn Exp. Points when you play with them or cook them tasty curries at your Pokémon Camp (p. 280)!

Use Abilities to Their Fullest

When you look at any Pokémon's Summary, you can check its Ability. Each Pokémon has one, and they can form a vital part of your battle strategy. Unlike moves, Abilities generally trigger on their own in battle. And they can help in a surprising number of ways. Some major categories are included below, along with a few example Abilities, to start giving you ideas for your own Pokémon team!

Pelipper's
Drizzle
It started to rain!

The Element of Surprise

Each Pokémon in your team will have just one Ability—but which Ability it has depends on its species. It's not like any Pokémon can have any Ability! Most species only have one or two Abilities available to them. But if you're battling against a species that can have two different Abilities, you may not know which one your opponent has until it's triggered. Does that opponent's Litwick have Flash Fire or Flame Body as its Ability? One will boost the power of Litwick's Fire-type moves if it's hit by a Fire-type move itself, while the other could burn a Pokémon if it makes contact with Litwick! Experienced Trainers should have a good grip on what Abilities different Pokémon can have and what their effects are.

! If a Pokémon's species can have one of two different Abilities, you can switch which one it has by using an Ability Capsule. This valuable item can be obtained at the Hammerlocke BP Shop (p. 382).

Abilities that affect attacks

Some Abilities can affect moves, such as by boosting their power or increasing the chances of landing a critical hit. If your Pokémon has one of these Abilities, teach it moves that take advantage of its Ability's effects! For example, the Ability No Guard makes all moves hit their target, which is perfect for a Pokémon that has high-power yet low-accuracy moves!

Other such Abilities found in Galar
Compound Eyes, Iron Fist, Mold Breaker, Punk Rock, Technician

Abilities that affect type matchups

Some Abilities affect types and type matchups. They might enable moves of a certain type to deal more damage than usual or to connect even when they would usually have no effect against opposing Pokémon of a certain type. For example, Pokémon with the Ability Scrappy can hit Ghost-type Pokémon with Normal- and Fighting-type moves, which they're usually immune to!

Other such Abilities found in Galar
Adaptability, Blaze, Dry Skin, Levitate, Swarm, Thick Fat

Abilities that help your Pokémon defend themselves

Abilities can raise a Pokémon's Defense stat, protect it from damage, or even completely nullify or absorb certain moves. These kinds of Abilities are great for throwing off an opponent's strategy. For example, the Ability Sturdy prevents a Pokémon at full health from being knocked out in a single hit.

Other such Abilities found in Galar
Dry Skin, Fluffy, Lightning Rod, Shell Armor, Storm Drain

Hidden Abilities

It's true that each Pokémon species usually has one or two Abilities available. When you catch a wild Pokémon in a normal encounter, it'll have one of these common Abilities. But some Pokémon species can instead have something called a Hidden Ability—a rare Ability that can be found in Pokémon caught in Max Raid Battles. A Hidden Ability can be passed on to Pokémon hatched from Eggs (p. 234), but using an Ability Capsule won't change your Pokémon's common Ability to a rare Hidden Ability, so don't get any ideas...

Abilities that cause or interact with negative conditions

Status conditions (p. 186) can quickly turn a battle to your advantage, or they can send your strategy into a tailspin. That's why it's important to know about Abilities that interact with status conditions in different ways. For example, Corrosion lets a Pokémon inflict poison on Poison- and Steel-type Pokémon, which are normally immune to poisoning.

Other such Abilities found in Galar
Effect Spore, Hydration, Insomnia, Pastel Veil, Static

Abilities that cause or protect from stat changes

Stat changes are a central part of battle. You can use them to boost your Pokémon's stats by at least 50%—all the way up to a whopping 400% (p. 187)! Use Abilities to either give your Pokémon these boosts or help keep their stats unaltered. For example, Clear Body protects a Pokémon from having its stats lowered by opponents' moves or Abilities.

Other such Abilities found in Galar
Cotton Down, Hustle, Hyper Cutter, Mirror Armor, Sand Rush, Swift Swim

Abilities that activate at specific times

Some interesting Abilities have an effect when a Pokémon enters or leaves battle. For example, when a Pokémon with Frisk enters the battlefield, it'll let you know what item, if any, an opposing Pokémon is holding. Other Abilities trigger when your Pokémon is hit, most often by direct-contact moves (p. 336). For example, if a Pokémon with the Cursed Body Ability is hit by a move, it has a chance of disabling that move so your opponent can't use it again.

Other such Abilities found in Galar
Aftermath, Cute Charm, Intimidate, Perish Body, Static

Abilities related to the weather and terrain

Weather and terrain influence battles in various important ways (p. 189). You could affect the weather with moves, but Abilities can do the same without using up a turn! Abilities can also give Pokémon an edge in certain weather conditions. One example is the Snow Cloak Ability, which raises the evasiveness of the Pokémon when there's a hailstorm going on—great for lengthy battles!

Other such Abilities found in Galar
Cloud Nine, Drought, Electric Surge, Hydration, Ice Body

Abilities that work outside of battle

Some Abilities have effects that extend outside the battlefield, even if they aren't always any good in battles. For example, the Ability Ball Fetch allows a Pokémon to retrieve the first Poké Ball you throw at a wild Pokémon if the catch fails. It's a handy skill when you're running low on Poké Balls during a catching spree!

Other such Abilities found in Galar
Arena Trap, Flame Body, Infiltrator, Pickup, Stench, Super Luck

!

Some Abilities can fall into more than one of these categories! Sandaconda has the Sand Spit Ability, which calls up a sandstorm that rages for five turns if Sandaconda is hit with a move. Rolycoly's Steam Engine will boost its Speed stat when it is hit by Fire- and Water-type moves—and it helps Pokémon Eggs hatch faster, too (p. 234)!

Learn Moves for Battle

Teaching your team the right moves can be just as important as training them. There are a number of different ways Pokémon can learn new moves, and you'll want to use them all to make sure your Pokémon have the right tools for battle!

Leveling up

Your Pokémon may have the chance to learn a new move or moves when it levels up. Check the new move's description to decide whether it's worth replacing one of the four moves your Pokémon already knows.

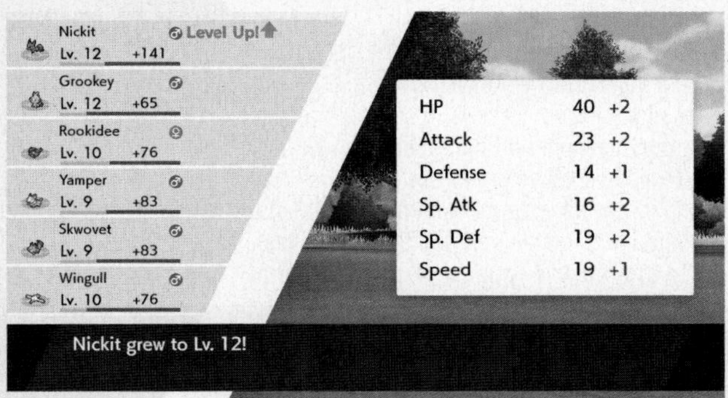

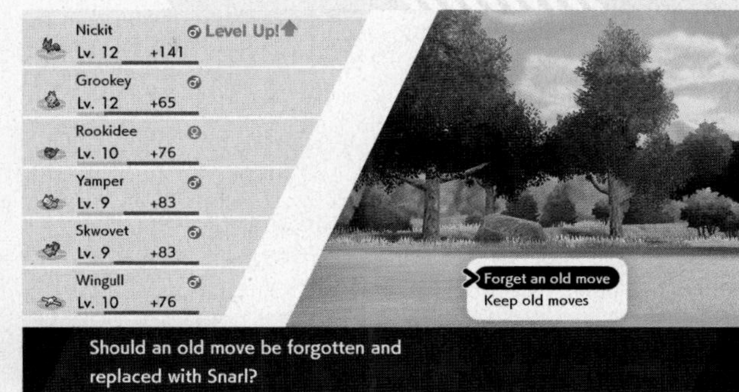

Evolving

Some Pokémon also have the chance to learn certain moves when they evolve. Evolved Pokémon you catch in the wild will often already know these moves.

Egg Moves

When Pokémon are hatched from Eggs or left at the Pokémon Nursery under certain conditions, they may learn unique moves that their species would normally never learn by leveling up or evolving. Learn more on page 235.

Brilliant Pokémon may know Egg Moves when you catch them. More about these rare Pokémon on page 174!

Jack

The jack-of-all-trades you find behind the left counter at every Pokémon Center (p. 16) can teach your Pokémon moves they forgot or had the chance to learn before. Not only that, they can also have your Pokémon forget a move you don't need anymore!

TMs

Technical Machines (TMs) can be used to teach powerful moves to many different Pokémon. You can use them as many times as you want. Select them from the TM pocket in your Bag to use them on the Pokémon in your party. Turn to page 356 to find out how to get them all!

TRs

Technical Records (TRs) are like TMs, but there's one key difference—each TR can only be used once, so think carefully before using them! TRs can be bought from Rotom Rallyists (p. 276) for Watts (you can check prices on page 358). You can also obtain them as rewards for successfully completing Max Raid Battles—turn to page 271 and onward for more information!

Evolution Cancel and Moves

You can stop a Pokémon from evolving by pressing Ⓑ when Evolution starts. This is known as an Evolution cancel. Some Pokémon learn different moves than their Evolutions do, which can be a reason to keep your Pokémon from evolving until they've learned all the moves you're interested in. Even Jack can't help your Pokémon learn missed moves from previous Evolutions!

There are also Move Tutors who can teach certain Pokémon some rare moves! They're all listed on page 354.

Know how to use your moves

With moves, you can do more than just attack your opponent and deal damage to them. Each time one of your Pokémon can learn a new move or you get a new TM or TR, consider the ways you could use it to mix up your battle strategies!

Moves can inflict status conditions

Some moves inflict status conditions, which can disable your opponent temporarily. Others may slowly drain opponents of HP. Turn to page 186 to learn more about status conditions.

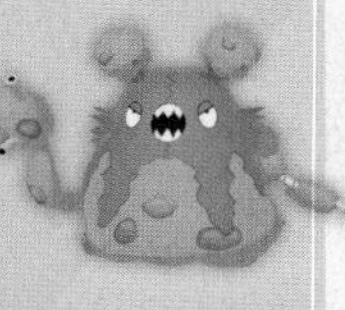

Example move: Toxic

Moves can protect your Pokémon from damage

Some moves can protect Pokémon from certain moves or even from all damage entirely. They don't protect against every possible move, but they can help your team tough it out a bit longer.

Example move: Obstruct

Moves can have an effect on stats

Some moves can be used to boost your Pokémon's stats temporarily or to lower the stats of opponents. Use these to make your attacks hit twice as hard or break down an opponent's defenses to seize victory!

Example move: No Retreat

Moves can help you get the drop on an opponent

The Speed stat of each Pokémon normally decides which one gets to act first, but priority moves strike first even when your Pokémon is slower than an opponent's. If you're close to a win, consider these quick hitters to end the battle before your opponent can strike back. Learn more about Speed and priority on page 188.

Example move: Aqua Jet

> If two Pokémon use moves with the same priority, the one with the higher Speed stat goes first!

Moves can make sure you hit an evasive opponent

Sometimes it can be hard to hit an opponent that has boosted its evasiveness or one that has lowered your Pokémon's accuracy. In these cases, try moves that are guaranteed to hit.

Example move: False Surrender

> Try using Body Slam, Dragon Rush, Flying Press, Heat Crash, Heavy Slam, Steamroller, or Stomp against any opponent that has used Minimize. They'll never miss and they'll deal double the regular damage!

> Some moves make contact with their target, which can set off the effects of an Ability or held item. Check which moves make contact on the move list, starting on page 336.

Moves can interact with held items

Held items are the key to success for many expert Trainers. You can throw opponents off their game by using a move that takes or knocks away their held item! You might also have your Pokémon hold a negative-effect item, like an Iron Ball to lower Speed, so you can swap it with your opponent's held item!

Example move: Knock Off

Moves can do a guaranteed amount of damage

If you're facing an opponent with strong defenses, consider using moves that always do a set amount of damage. They're not the most powerful, but they'll let you keep chipping away at your opponent, regardless of their stats.

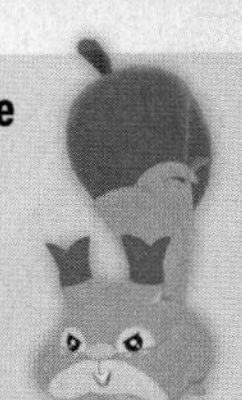

Example move: Super Fang

Moves can guarantee a knockout

These moves are extremely powerful, but most of them have low accuracy. They're generally more likely to hit the lower the level of the target is compared to your Pokémon. They're ideal for quickly ending battles against low-level wild Pokémon. Other moves guarantee that your own Pokémon will faint—but in return, they might heal their allies or deal some serious damage!

Example move: Horn Drill

Moves can help your Pokémon get out of a tight spot

Not all moves do damage to an opponent. Some moves can restore HP, cure status conditions, or reset lowered stats. Note that the example below shows just one of the potentially useful moves in this category. There are many others that can help your Pokémon out in a pinch and keep them in the battle longer.

Example move: Rest

Moves can interact with the battlefield

Moves can change the weather conditions in a battle—helping or hindering certain types of Pokémon. Other moves can change the terrain, affecting Pokémon in a particular way and possibly causing additional effects as well. Some move effects can also be changed by weather conditions, as you can see on page 189.

Example move: Hail

Use Items Wisely

Items are essential tools for any Trainer, whether you use them for battle strategies or out in the field. Below is a breakdown of what you'll find in each pocket of your Bag.

You can use multiple items from your Bag during battle, but each item you use takes up a turn (preventing your Pokémon from using a move). Held items, however, can be triggered automatically when their conditions are met, so you don't have to sacrifice a turn to benefit from them.

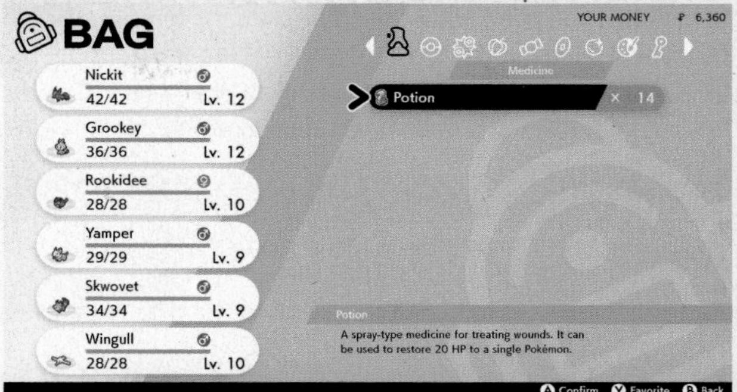

Medicine OUT OF BATTLE /// IN BATTLE ///

This pocket holds items you can use on your Pokémon, either in or out of battle, to restore their HP, restore their PP, or heal their status conditions (p. 186). Before you set out from each town or city, you'll want to be sure that this pocket is well stocked!

Poké Balls IN BATTLE ///

This pocket holds all the Poké Balls you acquire during your adventure. As you can see in the table on page 371, different Poké Balls are better for catching particular kinds of Pokémon. Try to use the right kind of Poké Ball to improve your catching odds!

Battle Items IN BATTLE ///

Items here can be used in battles to do things like boost your Pokémon's stats (p. 187) or help you flee from wild Pokémon. You can view them in your Bag outside of battle, too. But don't give them to your Pokémon as held items, since they won't have any effect.

Berries OUT OF BATTLE /// IN BATTLE ///

Berries you obtain from Berry trees (p. 290) or at the Berry Grocer (p. 40) will go into this pocket. They have various effects, which are listed in the table on page 372. Berries can also be added to curries that you cook up at camp (p. 285), so you'll want plenty of them!

Other Items OUT OF BATTLE ///

This is the pocket where serious battle fanatics come to play. It holds all sorts of items related to in-depth Pokémon battling. The effects of these items and other details are listed in the tables starting on page 374. Below is a quick breakdown.

Category	Example items	What they can do
Training items	Rare Candy, PP Up, Protein, Adamant Mint	Help your Pokémon level up, increase their stats, and increase the PP of their moves
Repels	Repel, Super Repel, Max Repel	Keep away random encounters with wild Pokémon for a time
Wishing items	Wishing Piece	Activate Pokémon Dens to encounter Dynamax Pokémon (p. 271)
Evolution items	Leaf Stone, Metal Coat	Cause certain Pokémon to evolve (p. 375)
Held items	Black Sludge, Choice Specs, Heat Rock, Red Card, Heavy-Duty Boots	Boost stats, protect or heal your Pokémon, reflect damage, foil your opponent's strategy, and much more! Check the whole table beginning on page 376.
Nursery items	Destiny Knot, Everstone, Full Incense	Find Pokémon Eggs that hatch into Pokémon of rare species or that inherit desirable Natures or stats (p. 379)

TMs OUT OF BATTLE ///

This pocket contains TMs and TRs for teaching moves to Pokémon. As mentioned previously, TMs can be used over and over on as many Pokémon as you like—but TRs disappear after one use, so use them wisely!

Treasures OUT OF BATTLE ///

Here you'll find items that can be sold at shops for pocket money! There'll be many opportunities for you to find or earn bags of Stardust, Nuggets, and other such items, so remember that they're here whenever you're in need of a cash boost.

Ingredients OUT OF BATTLE ///

This pocket holds the special key ingredients you can use when whipping up tasty curries at your camp. Turn to page 285 to start on your path to becoming a top chef—you'll find guidance on which ingredient to use for each curry.

Key Items OUT OF BATTLE ///

Most Key Items don't ever need to be selected from your Bag. Some, like your Rotom Bike, you can use in the field. Others give you benefits just by sitting in your Bag, like the Shiny Charm does. Note that this pocket is also where you'll find an Escape Rope—handy in a pinch!

!

Some held items can usually only be used once in battle, and then they're gone (unless you know a tricky move like Recycle). Save them for battles against tough opponents like Gym Leaders! But these items don't disappear from your Bag after Link Battles or in the Battle Tower, so use these places to test out different item strategies!

Capitalize on Status Conditions

Sometimes you need more than pure damage to take out a tough opponent, and status conditions can help. Inflict them on opposing Pokémon, but be prepared for them to return the favor! Thankfully, a Pokémon can only have one status condition at a time and some status conditions go away after a few turns. For those that don't go away until they're cured, take care of them by healing your team at a Pokémon Center, cooking up a tasty curry (p. 285), or using some of the methods below.

Status	Effect	Specific items for curing in battle
POISONED	Deals damage each turn. If badly poisoned, the damage increases each turn. Lasts until cured.	Use an Antidote or a Pecha Berry
PARALYSIS	Halves Speed and causes moves to fail 25% of the time. Lasts until cured.	Use a Paralyze Heal or a Cheri Berry
ASLEEP	Prevents usage of all moves except Sleep Talk and Snore. Lasts 1–3 turns.	Use an Awakening or a Chesto Berry
BURNED	Halves the power of the burned Pokémon's physical moves (p. 12). Deals damage each turn. Lasts until cured.	Use a Burn Heal or a Rawst Berry
FROZEN	Prevents usage of all moves except select, mostly Fire-type moves. Generally lasts several turns, but goes away if the Pokémon is hit with a Fire-type move or Scald.	Use an Ice Heal or an Aspear Berry

During battle, you'll see an icon on a Pokémon's HP gauge if it has a status condition.

In addition to the specific items listed on the left, there are some pricier or rare items that can cure any status condition. A Full Heal or Full Restore will do the trick, as would a Lum Berry! Find out more about them in the Items lists beginning on page 370.

Use moves to inflict conditions

Some moves do damage and also have a small chance of inflicting a status condition. And then there are status moves that do no damage but are guaranteed to inflict a condition (unless the target is immune or the move misses). Browse the Moves list (p. 336) for even more options than the examples here.

Deals damage and might inflict a condition

Thunderbolt PARALYSIS
Flare Blitz BURNED
Ice Punch FROZEN
Sludge Bomb POISONED

Guaranteed to inflict a condition if it hits

Poison Gas POISONED
Sleep Powder ASLEEP
Will-O-Wisp BURNED
Zap Cannon PARALYSIS

Use Abilities to inflict conditions

Another great option is to free up a move slot by using Abilities (p. 181) to inflict negative conditions instead. Such Abilities generally trigger when your Pokémon is hit by a direct-contact move (p. 336), but a Pokémon with Poison Touch can inflict poison when it's the attacker!

Example Abilities that can inflict conditions

Effect Spore POISONED / ASLEEP / PARALYSIS
Flame Body BURNED
Poison Touch POISONED
Static PARALYSIS

Activate Abilities to defend against conditions

Certain Abilities can cure conditions that are afflicting your Pokémon, while others prevent them altogether. There are even some Abilities—like the Healer Ability—that can help heal an ally's status condition in a Double Battle!

Example Abilities to combat conditions

Insomnia ASLEEP
Limber PARALYSIS
Magic Guard POISONED BURNED
Shed Skin BURNED FROZEN PARALYSIS POISONED ASLEEP

Don't Forget All the Other Conditions Out There!

There are other conditions that can affect Pokémon, though they never last longer than a single battle. And these conditions can all affect Pokémon at the same time, unlike the status conditions in the table above, so don't let your guard down! Here are a few of the more common ones:

Confusion: Has a 33% chance of causing moves to fail and damaging the user instead. Lasts 1–4 turns or until the affected Pokémon switches out.

Infatuation: Has a 50% chance of causing moves to fail. Lasts until the Pokémon that inflicted the condition leaves the battlefield or the affected Pokémon switches out.

Flinching: Prevents the Pokémon from using a move that turn. Lasts only one turn.

You can also use Berries when cooking at your camp (p. 285), where a fantastic curry will not only restore your Pokémon's HP but also cure their status conditions! And you can use Berries directly on Pokémon at any time or give them a Berry to hold when they go into battle so they can eat that Berry on their own if it's needed. This strategy allows for some interesting combos, too (p. 190).

Boost and Lower Stats in Battle

During battles, it can be tempting to only pick moves that deal high damage, but this isn't always the best strategy. Some opponents may be faster than any of your Pokémon, while others may have such high Defense or Sp. Def that your moves barely make a dent. When facing opponents like that, remember that some moves, Abilities, and items can boost your Pokémon's stats or lower the opponent's stats. You can affect the Attack, Defense, Sp. Atk, Sp. Def, and Speed stats, plus two variables you might sometimes overlook—evasiveness and accuracy.

At this point, you might be wondering about ways to boost or lower the HP stat. As it turns out, the only way to change the max HP of your Pokémon during a battle is to have it level up or Dynamax (p. 14)!

See and understand stat changes

When you boost or lower a Pokémon's stats, the change is measured in stages. You can tell how many stages your Pokémon's stats have been raised or lowered by the number of pink or blue arrows you see when viewing that Pokémon's information during a battle by pressing Ⓨ.

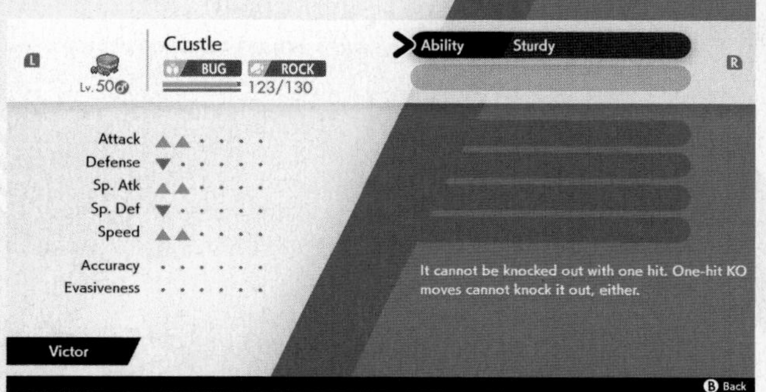

Each pink arrow indicates a one-stage boost to a stat, while blue arrows show how many stages stats have been lowered.

Boosting stats will increase them by as much as 50% per stage. If you want even more of an advantage, you can also lower an opponent's stats (though it's a bit less effective than boosting stats). It's also worth noting that the effects of lowering stats decrease slightly with each stage—each stat can only go so low! So many Trainers choose to focus on boosting stats instead.

Accuracy Matters More Than You Think

You can see the accuracy of each move when you view its description. If it's less than 100%, there's a real chance your move might miss the target. If your target has boosted its evasiveness, this becomes even more likely. But if you boost your Pokémon's accuracy, it can help you land powerful moves that are otherwise likely to miss, like Inferno or Zap Cannon. Just remember—boosting or lowering accuracy and evasiveness works a bit differently than with stats like Attack or Speed, as you'll see below.

Message you see in battle	What it means	Actual increase or decrease
[Pokémon's stat] rose!	Stat or variable was boosted by one stage	50% increase for stats or about 30% for evasiveness or accuracy
[Pokémon's stat] rose sharply!	Stat or variable was boosted by two stages	100% increase for stats or about 60% for evasiveness or accuracy
[Pokémon's stat] fell!	Stat or variable was reduced by one stage	About 30% decrease for stats or 25% for evasiveness or accuracy
[Pokémon's stat] harshly fell!	Stat or variable was reduced by two stages	50% decrease for stats or 40% for evasiveness or accuracy

Stat boosts and reductions add up, meaning you could boost your Pokémon's stats all the way up to 400% of their original value. Use the same move over and over to give your Pokémon a huge boost or to severely weaken an opponent—but don't get careless! If your Pokémon faints, or if you swap it out with another Pokémon without using a move like Baton Pass, all its stat boosts will be lost!

Using moves

Pokémon have many moves that can boost or lower stats. Growl and Tail Whip are probably the first ones you'll come across. Some moves can also affect two stats at once, like Dragon Dance and Noble Roar. Some moves even do damage in addition to affecting a stat, like Rock Tomb. Or some moves lower one stat while potentially boosting others, like Curse. For more details on the various effects of moves, go to page 336.

Using items

As you travel, you'll likely find items with names like X Attack or X Speed. You can use these items in battle to boost the stat in the item's name. These can be handy if you want to give your Pokémon a boost without using up a move slot. Certain held items can also give similar boosts in battle, although some of them, like the Choice Band, may also come with restrictions. Find the list of all items and their effects starting on page 370.

Using Abilities

Certain Abilities can affect stats depending on the situation. Some, like Intimidate, trigger as soon as a Pokémon enters battle, while others, like Gooey, require certain conditions before they do. Check the Abilities list beginning on page 359 to read up on Abilities and put together a strategy that keeps your Pokémon's move slots open for other things.

Play with Speed and Priority

Speed control is key to competitive play because the fastest Pokémon on the battlefield gets to attack first! If a Pokémon is too slow, it could get knocked out before it can even move. Species strengths, Nature, base points, and individual strengths determine a Pokémon's Speed. You can affect some of these with training, but it still might not be fast enough to outspeed certain other Pokémon. That's when you'd want to consider some Speed control!

Inflict paralysis

Paralysis significantly lowers the Speed of the afflicted Pokémon and has a chance to immobilize it, making its moves fail! Paralysis doesn't wear off or go away when a Pokémon is switched out.

Remember to look for unusual ways to inflict Paralysis, like the Static Ability!

Use Speed-reducing moves

You can also use moves that lower your opponent's Speed for as long as they're on the battlefield. If your goal is to significantly lower your opponent's Speed real quick, String Shot lowers the Speed of opposing Pokémon by two stages (p. 187)! Moves like Icy Wind and Electroweb deal damage as well as lower Speed, and all these moves hit all opposing Pokémon!

Moves like Quash can force an opposing Pokémon to go last if they hit!

Use Speed-boosting moves

Tailwind is a popular way to boost your Pokémon's Speed in competitive battles, as it boosts your whole team's Speed stat for four turns! You could also try moves that increase the Speed of only one Pokémon but with greater effect! Dragon Dance can increase both Speed and Attack in one turn, and Agility can increase a Pokémon's Speed by two stages!

Use Speed-boosting Abilities

Some Abilities allow Pokémon to move faster. Pokémon with Speed Boost increase their Speed by one stage at the end of each turn. Also check out Abilities that increase Speed in certain conditions, like Chlorophyll, Sand Rush, Slush Rush, and Swift Swim.

Use Speed-boosting items

Certain held items can increase a Pokémon's Speed in battle, too! Choice Scarf is a popular competitive item that will increase Speed significantly when held, but it forces your Pokémon to keep using the same move over and over. Adrenaline Orb increases a holder's Speed by one stage when it's affected by the often-used Intimidate Ability!

Use priority moves

You can teach your Pokémon a few priority moves (p. 352), like Extreme Speed or Fake Out. Priority moves are always used first in battle, regardless of your Pokémon's Speed. They can be a good tool to equip your slower Pokémon with.

Figuring out priority can be a headache on its own, and it can be even more complicated than you might think. Priority moves won't work if the battlefield's been changed to Psychic Terrain (p. 189), for example. Then there's the Prankster Ability, which gives a Pokémon's status moves priority, unless the target is a Dark-type Pokémon!

Twist the Dimensions with Trick Room

The move Trick Room is a Psychic-type move that reverses the turn order for five turns. So the slowest Pokémon on the battlefield will move first and the fastest Pokémon will move last. This move can really stump your opponents, especially if they tend to rely too much on the Speed of their Pokémon. It also lets slow heavy hitters like Snorlax move before faster Pokémon and hit them for big damage. Try having a Pokémon hold the new item Room Service when using Trick Room—it will lower the Speed of the Pokémon holding it!

The only trouble with Trick Room is that it has negative priority, so it'll be the last move used during the turn. This means you'll need to make sure your Pokémon lasts long enough to set Trick Room successfully. Mimikyu is really popular for this purpose. Its Disguise Ability allows it to soak up a hit without taking any damage, making it a great Trick Room setter! Other Pokémon that are popular to use with Trick Room include Whimsicott and Oranguru.

The move Curse usually lowers Speed, but under Trick Room, this will effectively make the Pokémon faster—on top of getting bonuses to Attack and Defense!

Take Advantage of Weather and Terrains

The battlefield state can have a huge influence on your Pokémon and on battle! There are two main mechanics that can affect it—weather and terrain.

Weather conditions

Certain Pokémon can cause weather conditions through moves or Abilities, and you may also find weather conditions naturally occurring in different places in the Galar region. Any new weather effect that comes onto the battlefield will replace the old one.

Changing the weather in battle won't influence the wild Pokémon you encounter outside of battle!

Make your own weather

	Harsh sunlight	Rain	Sandstorm	Hail
Moves that cause it	Sunny Day, Max Flare	Rain Dance, Max Geyser	Sandstorm, Max Rockfall	Hail, Max Hailstorm
Ability that causes it	Drought	Drizzle	Sand Stream	Snow Warning
Major effects	• Boosts the power of Fire-type moves • Lowers the power of Water-type moves • Lowers the accuracy of the moves Hurricane and Thunder • The HP-restoring moves Moonlight, Morning Sun, and Synthesis restore more HP • Prevents Pokémon from becoming frozen	• Boosts the power of Water-type moves • Lowers the power of Fire-type moves • The moves Hurricane and Thunder become 100% accurate • The HP-restoring moves Moonlight, Morning Sun, and Synthesis restore less HP	• Damages all non-Ground-, Rock-, or Steel-type Pokémon each turn • Boosts the Sp. Def of Rock-type Pokémon • The HP-restoring moves Moonlight, Morning Sun, and Synthesis restore less HP, and Shore Up restores more HP	• Damages all non-Ice-type Pokémon each turn • The move Blizzard becomes 100% accurate • The HP-restoring moves Moonlight, Morning Sun, and Synthesis restore much less HP

Weather and Abilities

On top of their universal effects, weather conditions can also activate Pokémon Abilities with various additional effects! To learn more about the Abilities listed here, turn to the Abilities list starting on page 359.

	Boosts Speed	Restores HP	Boosts power	Various bonuses
Harsh sunlight	Chlorophyll	—	Solar Power	Leaf Guard
Rain	Swift Swim	Rain Dish, Dry Skin*	—	Hydration
Sandstorm	Sand Rush	—	Sand Force**	Sand Veil
Hail	Slush Rush	Ice Body	—	Snow Cloak

*In harsh sunlight, a Pokémon with the Ability Dry Skin will lose HP every turn.
**Sand Force boosts the power of Ground-, Rock-, and Steel-type moves only.

Weather conditions last five turns, but you can make them last eight by having your Pokémon hold certain rocks! Get those rocks in a subevent in Hammerlocke (p. 82).

Terrains

Terrains work like weather—only one can exist on the battlefield at a time, they last for five turns, and they have various effects on the battling Pokémon. But terrains don't affect Flying-type Pokémon or Pokémon with the Levitate Ability, unless Pokémon are brought down to the ground with effects such as Gravity.

You can extend the duration of a terrain from five turns to eight by giving a Terrain Extender to the Pokémon that sets it! Get one at the BP Shop in the Battle Tower (p. 200)!

Setting terrains

	Electric Terrain	Psychic Terrain	Grassy Terrain	Misty Terrain
Moves that cause it	Electric Terrain, Max Lightning	Psychic Terrain, Max Mindstorm	Grassy Terrain, Max Overgrowth	Misty Terrain, Max Starfall
Ability that causes it	Electric Surge	Psychic Surge	Grassy Surge	Misty Surge
Effects	• Boosts the power of Electric-type moves • Pokémon on the ground can't fall asleep	• Boosts the power of Psychic-type moves • Protects Pokémon on the ground from priority moves	• Boosts the power of Grass-type moves • Restores a little HP to Pokémon on the ground each turn	• Halves the damage taken from Dragon-type moves • Protects Pokémon on the ground from status conditions and confusion

Try Your Hand at Combos

Pokémon battles might seem somewhat simple at first glance—just choose a powerful move with the right type matchup, and you should be good, right? Well, not exactly. Choosing the correct move for the situation is definitely important, but you can pull off some amazing battle strategies if you take the time to come up with clever combinations of moves, Abilities, and held items!

In this section, we'll discuss some combos for the various battle formats you'll experience while on your adventure. These aren't the only combos out there, of course. These are just to give you an idea of what combos look like and to give you a start in coming up with your own devastating strategies!

Boost move power with an Ability

First, let's start simple. We'll begin with a combo that will increase the power of moves, letting your Pokémon deal more damage. Dhelmise has the Ability Steelworker. This Ability boosts the power of Steel-type moves, essentially giving Dhelmise a same-type attack bonus (p. 165) for an extra type! Dhelmise can learn Anchor Shot, a pretty hard-hitting Steel-type move, allowing it to take full advantage of this Ability.

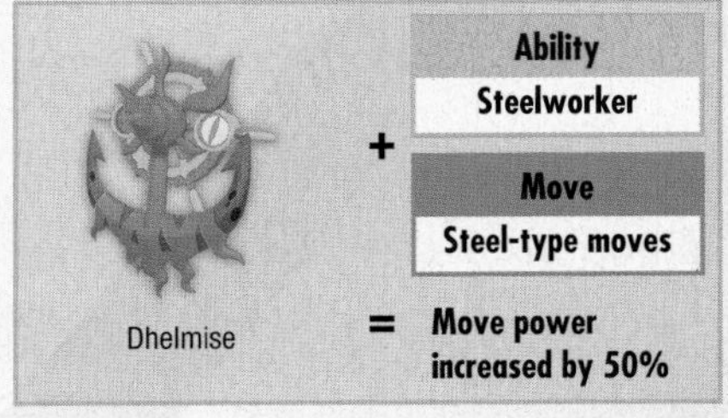

Give moves priority with an Ability

Some combos are more subtle, like those built on the Prankster Ability. It gives status moves priority, meaning a Pokémon with Prankster can likely use its status moves before the opponent has a chance to act! That may not seem as impressive as extra power, but it can be more strategic. For example, Impidimp can have the Prankster Ability, and it learns useful status moves, too. Have Impidimp outmaneuver faster opponents and confuse them with the move Flatter or sharply decrease their Sp. Def with Fake Tears!

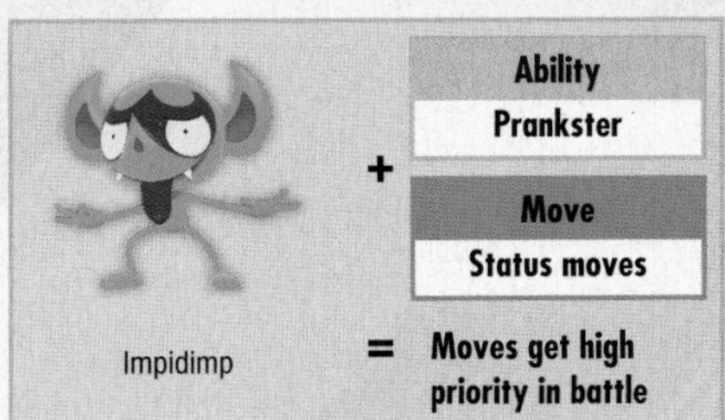

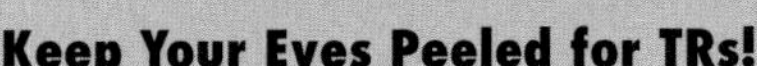

Keep Your Eyes Peeled for TRs!

As you continue along your adventure, you'll come across items known as Technical Records or TRs (p. 358). TRs are similar to TMs in that each one contains one move that you can teach to your Pokémon. The difference is that each TR can be used only once, meaning that you'll need to think carefully before using one on a Pokémon! On the other hand, TRs tend to contain moves that are more powerful or versatile than the ones found in TMs, making them perfect tools to help build useful combos in battle!

TR00 Swords Dance

TR05 Ice Beam

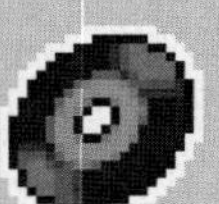

TR10 Earthquake

TR38 Trick

TR48 Bulk Up

Combine moves and items

There's more to combos than just moves and Abilities. You can also combine moves and held items to increase their usefulness! Take the move Thrash, for example. This is a powerful Normal-type move that has a negative effect on the user—once the move is finished, the user becomes confused. Outrage is a Dragon-type move with a similar drawback. But there's an easy way to counter the negative effects of these moves. Simply have your Pokémon hold a Persim Berry, and their confusion will be cured as soon as it's inflicted!

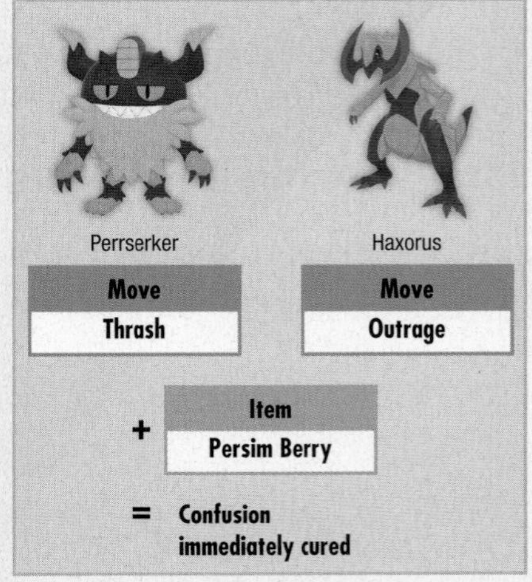

There are similar combos that work for other moves that cause negative status effects. For example, Rest will fully restore the user's HP and remove all status conditions, but the user will fall asleep. Normally, this would almost certainly negate any advantage you'd gain by healing up, but not if the Pokémon is holding a Chesto Berry! A Chesto Berry will instantly wake up the Pokémon, allowing them to jump right back into the action!

Combos to use in Double Battles

The examples so far have all been things a Pokémon can make use of in Single Battles. Needless to say, the possibilities for combos increase greatly when you start taking part in Double Battles. For instance, the move Decorate might seem useless at first glance—it sharply raises the Attack and Sp. Atk stats of the target, and it can't target the user. That means in Single Battles, you'd be giving the opponent a hefty boost! But in Double Battles, you'll be able to target your ally, allowing a Pokémon like Alcremie to give the stat boosts to an ally instead!

= Ally gets stat boost

Alcremie used Decorate!

Choose Your Ally Wisely!

This combo works best if Alcremie has a higher Speed than its ally, allowing Alcremie to use Decorate first. Then its ally can immediately take advantage of the increased stats! Pokémon like Aegislash make a great partner for Alcremie. Aegislash is relatively slow and has very high Defense and Sp. Def in its Shield Forme, meaning it can likely withstand attacks long enough to use a move. Once it switches to its Blade Forme, it gains very high Attack and Sp. Atk, letting it take full advantage of the stat boosts provided by Decorate!

Change the types of other Pokémon

Some moves, like Magic Powder and Soak, can change the type of the opposing Pokémon. These moves can be useful in Single Battles, but where they really shine is in Double Battles. Let's say you send out a Hatterene that can use Magic Powder and a Thievul that knows Night Slash, and you are facing a Fairy-type Pokémon and a Fighting-type Pokémon.

This is not a good matchup in the beginning—the opponents' Fighting- and Fairy-type moves would not only be super effective against Thievul, but they would get the same-type attack bonus, too. Plus, Thievul's Night Slash would not be very effective against either of them. The battle takes a dramatic turn if Hatterene uses Magic Powder. When used on either of the opponents, Magic Powder changes that opponent's type to Psychic, causing it to lose the same-type attack bonus and become vulnerable to the Dark-type move Night Slash!

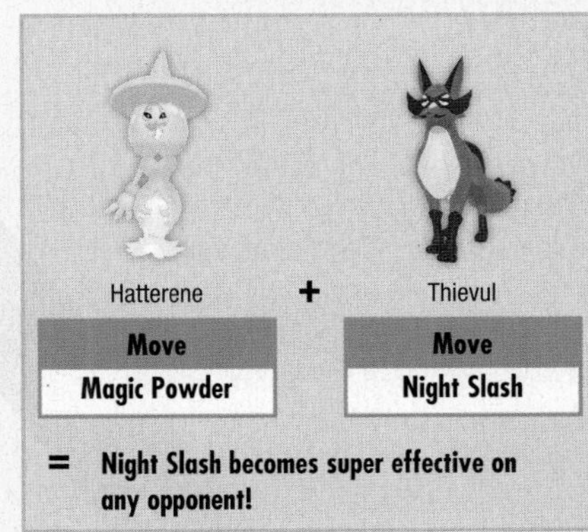

Hatterene
+
Thievul
Move
Magic Powder
Move
Night Slash
= Night Slash becomes super effective on any opponent!

!

Thievul used Night Slash!

One fun thing to remember about moves like Magic Powder is that they can also be used on allies. In the above example, if you would rather give Thievul a better chance of lasting through the battle, use Magic Powder on it instead of the opponents. This will change its type to Psychic, removing its weakness against Fighting- and Fairy-type moves! Note that it will also lose the same-type attack bonus for Night Slash, so think carefully about how you want to mix up the types during battle!

Use combos wisely in Max Raid Battles

In Max Raid Battles, you will team up with three other Trainers to take on a Dynamax Pokémon. If you want to triumph, you'll need to think carefully about what Pokémon to send into battle, as well as what moves to use and when! Dynamax Pokémon are no pushovers—they have huge amounts of HP and can often dish out heavy damage. So how can you best deal with these massive opponents?

To reduce that high HP, you could give your allies' moves more power. You could also use moves that protect your allies from incoming damage. Or why not both? The Pokémon Stonjourner has the Ability Power Spot, which increases the power of moves for adjacent allies. Stonjourner can also learn the move Wide Guard, which protects allies from regular moves that target multiple Pokémon and even reduces the damage received from Max Moves! This makes it a very dependable Pokémon to send out in Max Raid Battles.

Stonjourner

Ability: Power Spot
+
Move: Wide Guard
= Full support in Max Raid Battles

Give your whole team a speed boost

Another Pokémon that can excel in assisting your allies during a Max Raid Battle is Frosmoth. This Pokémon can learn a variety of moves that will provide valuable aid to other Pokémon when facing a Dynamax Pokémon. It can also have the Hidden Ability Ice Scales, which can help it withstand special moves from the opponent.

One very useful move that Frosmoth can learn is Tailwind. We highly recommend using this move in Max Raid Battles, because it will increase the Speed of all Pokémon on your side! This could very well be the key to outmaneuvering a wild Dynamax Pokémon. Frosmoth can also learn Helping Hand, which can give an ally's move a power boost. Definitely try to use this move on an ally that has Dynamaxed, as Helping Hand will make your ally's Max Moves even more powerful! You can see what kind of move an ally is going to use by checking the top left of the screen. If you see they're using a damage-dealing move, it's time to lend them a Helping Hand!

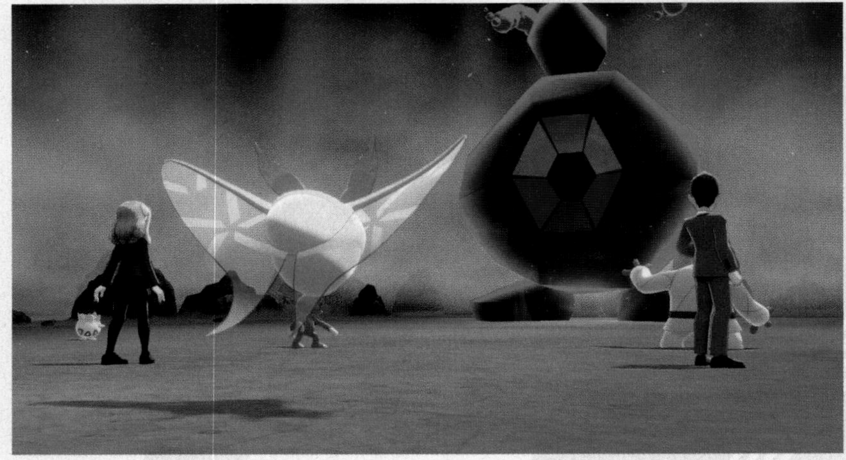

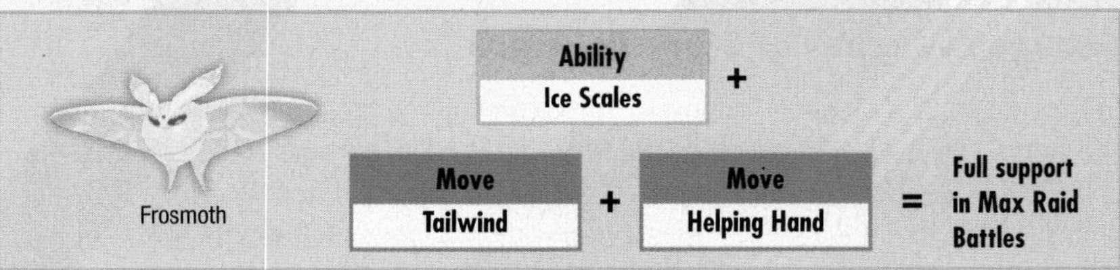

! Another interesting thing about Helping Hand is that its effect will stack—in other words, if Helping Hand is used on the same target multiple times during the same turn, the power boost will keep growing! If three Pokémon on your side all use Helping Hand on a Dynamaxed ally, you could boost the power of its damage-dealing Max Move to over three times its original strength and deal some truly mind-blowing damage!

More Battle Practice

In the previous sections, we've discussed how to build up a powerful team of Pokémon—how types work, how to build a balanced team, how to train them right, and even how to use various combos. In this section, we're going to introduce how you can put your ultimate team to the test. There are many different ways you can get more battle practice in the Galar region—each offers different rewards!

Build Up Your Battle Teams

As you try out new team formations, make use of your Battle Teams! Battle Teams let you put together teams of up to six Pokémon separate from the party that you're using during your main adventure. You can have up to six teams, and the same Pokémon can be placed in more than one team at a time. But you won't be able to have a Pokémon in both your main party and a Battle Team—the Pokémon for your Battle Teams need to be in your Boxes!

In order to set up Battle Teams, you'll need to access your Pokémon Boxes, either by visiting Rotomi at a Pokémon Center or from the Pokémon option in the X menu once you obtain the Pokémon Box Link. Once you've accessed your Boxes, press ⓧ twice to get to the Battle Team setup screen. Now you're ready to register your Pokémon for Battle Teams! Select the Pokémon you want on your team, then move them to the slot you want them in. If you do, ⚙ will show up above them, showing they've been successfully added to your Battle Team.

Battle Cafés BEFORE CLEARING THE GAME

Challenge yourself to daily battles at the Battle Cafés found in Motostoke, Hammerlocke, and Wyndon. It's a handy way to earn some extra money and items during your adventure—plus, you can practice the complex art of Double Battles. We'll go into more detail on Battle Café rewards and strategies on the next page.

Champion tournaments AFTER CLEARING THE GAME

Becoming the Champion doesn't mean the tournaments are over! You'll be able to set up tournaments at Wyndon Stadium to battle against other Trainers whenever you like, making this a good way to earn prize money and level up your team. You'll even get to invite one Trainer you've met during your adventure to participate! Check out pages 196 and onward for more information.

The Battle Tower AFTER CLEARING THE GAME

The Battle Tower is a facility specifically for Trainers who love to battle! You'll earn BP and prizes as you work your way through the ranks—plus, reaching the top will get your Pokémon a Ribbon and a special title (p. 230). The Battle Tower is also a great place to fine-tune a Pokémon team and try out new strategies. You can experiment with various held items worry free, as they won't disappear if used during the battles here. For more information, turn to page 200.

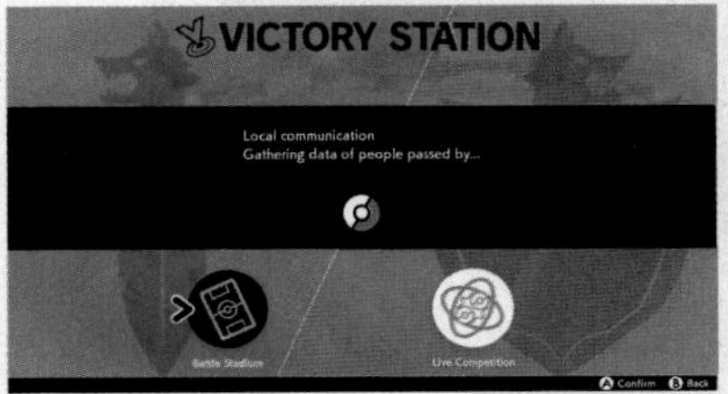

Victory Station BEFORE CLEARING THE GAME

As you refine your team, maybe you'll feel like pitting it against the teams of other players. You can do this from the VS option in the X menu. You'll even be able to face other Trainers from around the world if you have a Nintendo Switch Online membership† (p. 206). Turn to page 202 if you can't wait to get started!

!

If you'd rather just have some casual, no-stakes battles with friends or nearby players, there's also the Link Battle option in Y-Comm. You can search for Link Battles either locally or on the internet, and you can even choose the battle format—Single, Double, or Multi Battles. If you want to play with specific people, just set up a Link Code and have your partner enter the same code. For more on how to use the various features of Y-Comm, flip to pages 298–300!

Battle Cafés

You'll find Yoshida's Coffee shops in Motostoke (p. 50), Hammerlocke (p. 80), and Wyndon (p. 124), and you can recognize them by their dark-red exterior, like in the image here. These coffee shops serve up more than a nice atmosphere—they're also Battle Cafés, where you can battle the proprietor for prizes! Pay them a visit whenever you want to earn some extra money, items, and Exp. Points!

Once inside, just walk right up and speak to the Café Master and answer yes to his question if you're ready for a battle. The Café Masters aren't all the same, and you might find that they're a bit trickier to defeat than you'd initially expect. Below is a guide to each Café Master's team, as well as some tips to take them on!

Motostoke Café Master Dwight

When you first arrive at Motostoke, Dwight will only have a Lv. 10 Combee on his team, with no surprises or tricks up his sleeve. You should be able to defeat him pretty easily if you have a properly leveled-up Rock-type Pokémon or two on your team. But come back after defeating Nessa (p. 72), and he'll take you on in a Double Battle with a Milcery and a Swirlix, both at Lv. 24. He will also have a few tricky status moves, like Attract and Sweet Kiss. Still, as long as you have Poison- or Steel-type Pokémon on your team, you shouldn't have much trouble.

Before defeating Nessa

Combee
Lv. 10
WEAKNESSES
4x

After defeating Nessa

Milcery
Lv. 24
WEAKNESSES

Swirlix
Lv. 24
WEAKNESSES

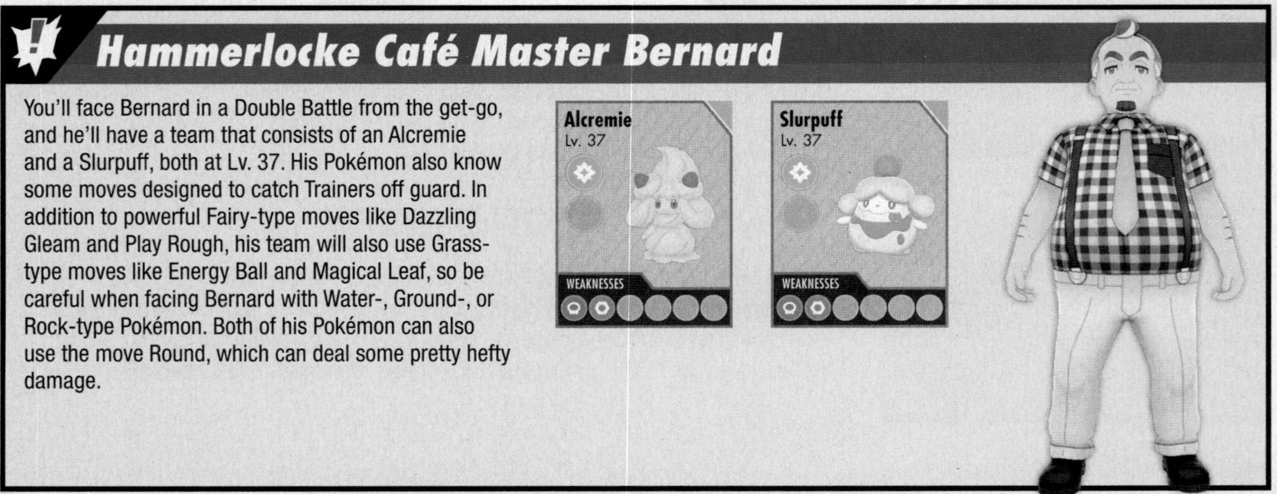

Hammerlocke Café Master Bernard

You'll face Bernard in a Double Battle from the get-go, and he'll have a team that consists of an Alcremie and a Slurpuff, both at Lv. 37. His Pokémon also know some moves designed to catch Trainers off guard. In addition to powerful Fairy-type moves like Dazzling Gleam and Play Rough, his team will also use Grass-type moves like Energy Ball and Magical Leaf, so be careful when facing Bernard with Water-, Ground-, or Rock-type Pokémon. Both of his Pokémon can also use the move Round, which can deal some pretty hefty damage.

Alcremie
Lv. 37
WEAKNESSES

Slurpuff
Lv. 37
WEAKNESSES

Wyndon Café Master Richard

Café Master Richard is the strongest Café Master you'll face. His team is the same as Bernard's, but his Alcremie and Slurpuff are both Lv. 47. He's also taken steps to counter his team's weaknesses—his Slurpuff can use Flamethrower to deal with Steel-type Pokémon, while his Alcremie knows Psychic to take down Poison types. Richard's Pokémon also know moves that will hit opponents weak to Grass-, Electric-, and Fairy-type moves right where it hurts. Your best bet may be to send out Fire-type Pokémon with high Sp. Def in order to withstand the special moves—or maybe Poison-type Pokémon with high Speed to take down Richard's team before they have a chance to attack!

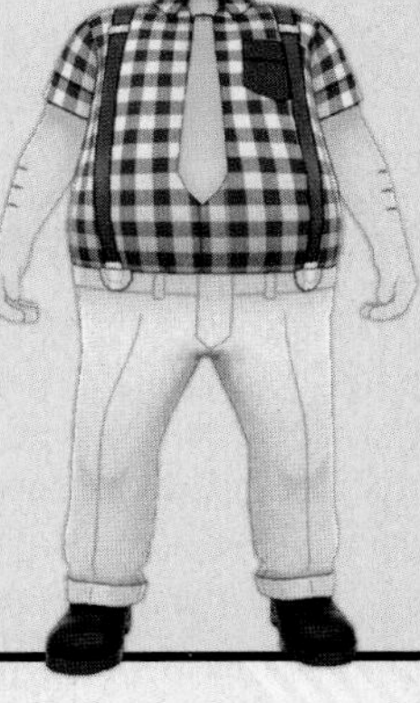

Battle Café rewards

Once you defeat a Café Master, he'll give you a little treat on the house! Check out the table to the right for what exactly you can receive. These items will be awarded to you at random, but since some of them can be pretty hard to come by otherwise, it's well worth the lottery! You can challenge each Battle Café once per day, so be sure to stop by regularly if you want these lovely little snacks!

The various Sweet items that cause Milcery to evolve are especially valuable finds! Most of these can't be found anywhere else in the game, so stock up on them here if you're aiming to obtain all of the numerous different forms of Alcremie.

Keep an Eye Out for the Candies!

While most of the items you can receive are the same between each Battle Café, one important difference is what Exp. Candies you may get. The Battle Café in Motostoke will only give you Exp. Candy XS (worth 100 Exp. Points) and Exp. Candy S (worth 800 Exp. Points), while the café in Hammerlocke gives you Exp. Candy S and Exp. Candy M (worth 3,000 Exp. Points). Wyndon offers the best Exp. Candies, with a chance to receive Exp. Candy M and even Exp. Candy L, which is worth a whopping 10,000 Exp. Points! Each café also has a chance of giving you a Rare Candy, so keep an eye out for these items if you want to level up your Pokémon!

Battle Café rewards	Use
Berry Juice	Restores a Pokémon's HP
Moomoo Milk	Restores a Pokémon's HP
Sweet Heart	Restores a Pokémon's HP
Big Malasada	Cures any status condition
Casteliacone	Cures any status condition
Lava Cookie	Cures any status condition
Lumiose Galette	Cures any status condition
Old Gateau	Cures any status condition
Pewter Crunchies	Cures any status condition
Rage Candy Bar	Cures any status condition
Shalour Sable	Cures any status condition
Exp. Candy	Grants a certain amount of Exp. Points
Rare Candy	Increases a Pokémon's level by one
Sachet	Can cause Spritzee to evolve into Aromatisse under certain circumstances
Whipped Dream	Can cause Swirlix to evolve into Slurpuff under certain circumstances
Berry Sweet	Can cause Milcery to evolve into Alcremie under certain circumstances
Clover Sweet	Can cause Milcery to evolve into Alcremie under certain circumstances
Flower Sweet	Can cause Milcery to evolve into Alcremie under certain circumstances
Love Sweet	Can cause Milcery to evolve into Alcremie under certain circumstances
Strawberry Sweet	Can cause Milcery to evolve into Alcremie under certain circumstances

Champion Tournaments

Don't expect to take it too easy after you've become the Champion. You'll be busier than ever once you're a celebrity across the region! As the Champion, you must carry on Leon's legacy of making the Trainers in Galar the strongest in all the world! Thankfully, you don't have to wait for the next Gym Challenge to gather Galar's strongest Trainers together. You can hold your own tournaments at Wyndon Stadium! Just talk to the League staff member behind the reception desk to get started.

Competitors and how to invite them

Each Champion tournament you hold will have eight competitors (including you!), so that means three elimination rounds of battle to decide a winner. Most Trainers who participate in the tournament are randomly selected—if you knew who you'd be up against every time, it would be too easy. These Trainers are some of Galar's best and brightest. Possible participants include Gym Leaders, Gym Challengers, and high-profile Trainers like Leon and Hop! Some of them may not show if you don't have their rare League Card, though. Read on to see the full list of Trainers that may come to battle and their powerful Pokémon teams.

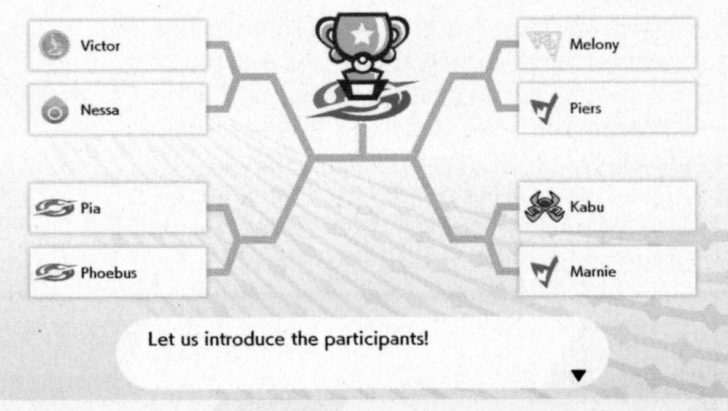

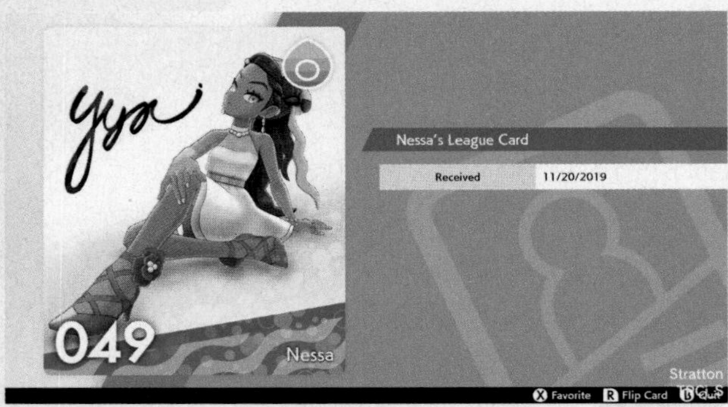

Get a Trainer's rare League Card...

and they may show up when you hold a Champion tournament!

Although you won't be able to choose everyone who participates in the tournament, you can choose to specifically invite one Trainer. However, you'll need their rare League Card to do so. So if there's a Trainer you want to invite, but you haven't gotten their rare League Card yet, make sure you find it! See page 309 if you need help.

Rewards for winning Champion tournaments

You can expect to receive a huge amount of Exp. Points and cash in Champion tournaments as you go about defeating the strongest Trainers in all of Galar. But that's not all! The first time you emerge victorious in a tournament each day, you'll be rewarded with a Wishing Piece that lets you attract Dynamax Pokémon to Pokémon Dens (p. 270). If you keep doing more tournaments in the same day, you'll get one of the rewards from the table below each time you're the final winner.

Item	Rarity
Nugget	◎
Dive Ball ×3	◎
Dusk Ball ×3	◎
Heal Ball ×3	◎
Luxury Ball ×3	◎
Nest Ball ×3	◎
Net Ball ×3	◎
Quick Ball ×3	◎
Repeat Ball ×3	◎
Timer Ball ×3	◎
Great Ball ×5	◎
Ultra Ball ×5	◎
Big Nugget	○
Rare Candy	○
Nugget ×2	○
Nugget ×3	○
Poké Ball ×100	△
Flame Orb	☆
Iron Ball	☆
Life Orb	☆
Toxic Orb	☆
Rare Candy ×3	☆
Beast Ball	★
Fast Ball	★
Friend Ball	★
Heavy Ball	★
Level Ball	★
Love Ball	★
Lure Ball	★
Moon Ball	★

◎ frequent ○ common △ average
☆ rare ★ almost never

Competing Trainers and their teams

On the following pages, you'll find a list of every competitor that can participate in a Champion tournament, along with their team. Any Trainer with  won't join you in a tournament unless you have their rare League Card. Make sure you're ready before starting a tournament, too, as you won't be able to quit midway through, and the Trainers you've faced before are stronger now than they've ever been!

Yue

Yue uses Normal-type Pokémon. They're all weak to Fighting-type moves, but remember that Diggersby is Ground-type too! Don't forget that Ghost-type moves don't work on Normal-type Pokémon.

Lv. 56 | Lv. 56 | Lv. 57 | Lv. 57 | Lv. 58

Polaire

Polaire's team might be all Bug type, but they all have different second types, making his team diverse. Rock-type moves are still great in this battle, though. They're super effective against all of this team.

Lv. 56 | Lv. 56 | Lv. 57 | Lv. 57 | Lv. 58

Kent

All the Pokémon on this team are weak to Electric-type moves, but Rock- and Ice-type moves are strong against a number of them too. Watch out for heavy hitters like Braviary!

Lv. 56 | Lv. 56 | Lv. 57 | Lv. 57 | Lv. 58

Vega

Both Pelipper and Gyarados will take 400% damage from Electric-type moves, but make sure you don't rely on them too much. Seismitoad is Ground type, and immune to Electric-type moves.

Lv. 56 | Lv. 56 | Lv. 57 | Lv. 57 | Lv. 58

Cher

Cher's Rock-type team has pretty high Defense. Try to focus on supereffective special moves to punch through her team. If you're having trouble dealing damage, you could also try inflicting the poisoned status condition.

Lv. 56 | Lv. 56 | Lv. 57 | Lv. 57 | Lv. 58

Deneb

Most of this team is weak to Flying-, Psychic-, and Fairy-type moves, but remember that Lucario is both Fighting and Steel type. That means its weaknesses are totally different from the others in Deneb's party.

Lv. 56 | Lv. 56 | Lv. 57 | Lv. 57 | Lv. 58

Icla

Powerful Ground-type moves like Earthquake are great in this battle, but watch out! Weezing's Levitate makes it immune, so have a Psychic-type move ready to handle it.

Lv. 56 | Lv. 56 | Lv. 57 | Lv. 57 | Lv. 58

Wei

Normal- and Fighting-type moves aren't going to do much in this battle. Ghost- and Dark-type moves are your best bet. Jellicent has a pretty high Sp. Def, so make sure you've got a reliable physical move.

Lv. 56 | Lv. 56 | Lv. 57 | Lv. 57 | Lv. 58

Izar

Ice-type Pokémon have a lot of different weaknesses, but Fire may be your best choice, as Fire-type moves deal 400% damage to Frosmoth while still being super effective against Mamoswine!

Lv. 56 | Lv. 56 | Lv. 57 | Lv. 57 | Lv. 58

Dunne

Try using a Flying-type Pokémon, or one with Levitate, to start this battle with an advantage. Ice-type moves like Ice Beam will be a great help here, especially against the powerful Flygon!

Lv. 56 | Lv. 56 | Lv. 57 | Lv. 57 | Lv. 58

Pia

Fire-type moves will be super effective against all Pokémon on this team. A powerful Poison-type move like Sludge Bomb will work even better against Shiinotic, though. Watch out for Ferrothorn's Iron Barbs Ability!

Lv. 56 | Lv. 56 | Lv. 57 | Lv. 57 | Lv. 58

Terry

Fairy types are great in this battle. They're immune to Dragon-type moves, and Fairy-type moves are super effective against Dragon-type Pokémon. Remember that Turtonator's Fire type means that it will only take regular damage from Fairy-type moves.

Lv. 56 | Lv. 56 | Lv. 57 | Lv. 57 | Lv. 58

Phoebus

All Pokémon on this team are weak to Water-, Ground-, and Rock-type moves, so take your pick! Remember, the burned condition reduces your Pokémon's Attack, so have a Burn Heal or Full Heal ready!

Lv. 56 | Lv. 56 | Lv. 57 | Lv. 57 | Lv. 58

Nessa 

Remember, Quagsire is immune to Electric-type moves, and Pelipper, Golisopod, and Toxapex take only regular damage from Grass-type moves!

Lv. 60 | Lv. 60 | Lv. 61 | Lv. 61 | Lv. 62

Bea 

While they generally don't have moves that do supereffective damage against Fighting types, Ghost-type Pokémon take no damage from Fighting-type moves, making them a good choice when going against Bea's team.

Lv. 60 | Lv. 60 | Lv. 61 | Lv. 61 | Lv. 62

Corvin

Ground-type Pokémon really shine in this battle. They're immune to Electric-type moves, and their moves with a same-type attack bonus deal supereffective damage to all of the Pokémon on this team.

Lv. 56 | Lv. 56 | Lv. 57 | Lv. 57 | Lv. 58

Theemin

All of Theemin's Pokémon share a weakness to Fire-type moves. Steel-type Pokémon tend to have a high Defense, but lower Sp. Def. Use special Fire-type moves like Flamethrower!

Lv. 56 | Lv. 56 | Lv. 57 | Lv. 57 | Lv. 58

Milo

Milo's Grass-type Pokémon share many common weaknesses. Use strong moves like Flamethrower or Ice Beam to handle them.

Lv. 60 | Lv. 60 | Lv. 60 | Lv. 61 | Lv. 61 | Lv. 62 | Lv. 62

Kabu 

Consider bringing your own Pokémon that can change the weather to counter Torkoal's Drought. You don't want Kabu's Fire-type moves getting too hot!

Lv. 60 | Lv. 60 | Lv. 61 | Lv. 61 | Lv. 62

Allister 

Powerful Dark-type moves like Dark Pulse or False Surrender will serve you well in a battle against Allister's best Pokémon.

Lv. 60 | Lv. 60 | Lv. 61 | Lv. 61 | Lv. 62

Bede 

Bede seems to be fitting well in his new role of Fairy-type Gym Leader. His team is a little stronger than you may be used to at this point. You'll want a powerful supereffective move like Flash Cannon or Sludge Bomb.

Lv. 61 | Lv. 61 | Lv. 62 | Lv. 62 | Lv. 63

Gordie 

Despite all being Rock-type Pokémon, Gordie's team is actually somewhat diverse, with different weaknesses. Be ready to switch between a few different types of moves if you want to maximize damage in this battle.

Lv. 60 | Lv. 60 | Lv. 61 | Lv. 61 | Lv. 62

Melony 

Though Melony's Pokémon have some different secondary types, all of her Pokémon are weak to Rock-type moves. Be careful not to get frozen!

Lv. 60 | Lv. 60 | Lv. 61 | Lv. 61 | Lv. 62

Piers  

Piers doesn't actually use only Dark-type Pokémon, making him a bit more of a diverse opponent. Ground-type moves will help against Skuntank and Toxtricity!

    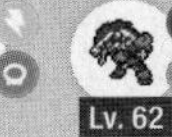

Lv. 60 | Lv. 60 | Lv. 61 | Lv. 61 | Lv. 62

Raihan 

Fairy-type moves can help you take down most of Raihan's Dragon-type team, but keep Fairy-type Pokémon clear of his Torkoal, Goodra, and Duraludon, since they have Poison- and Steel-type moves!

Lv. 60 | Lv. 60 | Lv. 61 | Lv. 61 | Lv. 62

Marnie 

Like her brother, Marnie splashes some Electric- and Poison-type Pokémon into a mainly Dark-type team. Earthquake can make short work of both of these types!

Lv. 59 | Lv. 59 | Lv. 59 | Lv. 60 | Lv. 60

Hop 

Hop's team is just as varied as the other times you've battled him, and he's got a powerful Legendary Pokémon on his team, too! Try using strong Fire- or Ground-type moves against Zacian or Zamazenta.

Lv. 69 | Lv. 68 | Lv. 70

Lv. 70 If you chose Grookey | Lv. 70 If you chose Scorbunny | Lv. 70 If you chose Sobble

Lv. 70 | Lv. 70

Leon  

Leon's team is quite diverse, without too many common weaknesses. Make sure you bring a Pokémon with a strong Rock-type move like Rock Slide to help against his Gigantamax Charizard.

Lv. 70 | Lv. 69 | Lv. 68

Lv. 70 If you chose Grookey | Lv. 70 If you chose Scorbunny | Lv. 70 If you chose Sobble

Lv. 70

The Battle Tower

After you become the Champion, Rose Tower (p. 127) will be revamped into the Battle Tower, a place where many strong Trainers come to battle! Winning against them can earn you BP that can be spent in the lobby for rare and useful items (p. 382)! Clawing your way up the ranking system of the Battle Tower can be tough, but it's a necessity for any Trainer who wants to battle competitively with other Trainers in the real world, as BP is the only way to get certain powerful held items. Plus you can win Bottle Caps and Gold Bottle Caps for Hyper Training (p. 173)!

> **!** Overcoming the Battle Tower is definitely hard, but there is one easy way to advance if you're having a difficult time. Talk to the fellow in the green jacket in the lobby of the Battle Tower, who will be happy to lend you one of his Rental Teams (p. 204). If your own team is struggling, give a Rental Team a try, and then study its composition to see what's different about it!

What you should know before you get started

- You can choose **Single Battle** or **Double Battle** format, and your achievements in each will be tracked separately.
- You can only bring **three** Pokémon to Single Battles or **four** to Double Battles.
- You **can't change** your team's order or composition until you return to the lobby.
- You can choose the Pokémon from your regular party, one of your Battle Teams (p. 193), or a Rental Team (p. 204).
- Your team's **HP**, **PP**, and **held items** will all be restored between each battle.
- Every Pokémon you face in the Battle Tower will be at Lv. 50. Any Pokémon you bring in over Lv. 50 will be set to Lv. 50.

Move up the ranks and tiers as you battle

As you defeat other Trainers in the Battle Tower, you'll climb the ranks from Rank 1 all the way up to MAX. These ranks fall into five tiers, each containing one or three ranks. Moving up through the ranks will also let you move up through the tiers, as you can see in the table to the right.

You'll need to win battles to move up from one rank to the next and to eventually move up through the tiers. It starts off pretty easy, with just two victories needed to move up in rank. You can see how close you're getting to moving up in rank by checking the gauge beneath your current tier, like in the image below.

But as you reach higher ranks, you'll need to win more battles to move up through each one. Additionally, if you lose or forfeit enough battles, you can even fall back down to a lower rank! You can't drop into a lower tier, though, so don't worry about losing all your hard work. This penalty also doesn't happen in the Beginner Tier. So don't ever give up—keep trying to climb to the Master Ball Tier!

Tier	Rank
Beginner	1
	2
	3
Poké Ball	4
	5
	6
Great Ball	7
	8
	9
Ultra Ball	10
Master Ball	MAX

1. The chosen battle format
2. Current tier in the chosen battle format
3. Current rank in the chosen battle format
4. Ball style aligns with your tier, while the number of balls shows how you're moving up through the ranks within it

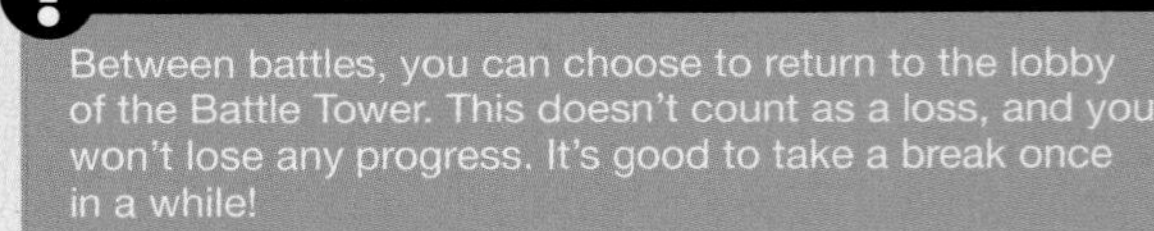

! Between battles, you can choose to return to the lobby of the Battle Tower. This doesn't count as a loss, and you won't lose any progress. It's good to take a break once in a while!

Earn rewards as you climb the Battle Tower

Your rewards for wins at the Battle Tower are much more than just BP to spend in the lobby. You can also get items for multiple wins, reaching new ranks, and reaching new tiers! A few of these are even exclusive rewards that not even BP can buy—like Leon's rare League Card.

Get rewards for racking up wins

As you battle and increase your total number of wins, you'll get a variety of high-level Trainer items as rewards. In the left-hand table below, you can find the rewards that you'll earn as you work your way up to 200 total wins, and you can earn each reward twice—once for the Single Battle format and again for the Double Battle format. After you've won more than 200 battles, the rewards will repeat every 100 wins. For example, you'll get a Bottle Cap at 230 wins and 330 wins. Keep tallying up more wins to collect more of the handy items in the table to the right!

Number of total wins	Rewards up to first 200 wins
10 wins	PP Up
20 wins	Random mint item
30 wins	Bottle Cap
40 wins	PP Max
50 wins	Gold Bottle Cap
100 wins	Lansat Berry
200 wins	Starf Berry

Number of total wins	Rewards after first 200 wins
210, 310, 410...	Random mint item
220, 320, 420...	PP Max
230, 330, 430...	Bottle Cap
240, 340, 440...	Ability Capsule
250, 350, 450...	Lansat Berry
275, 375, 475...	Gold Bottle Cap
300, 400, 500...	Starf Berry

You'll also be able to unlock some backgrounds for your League Card, as you can see on page 302!

Get rewards when reaching new ranks

Each time you increase your rank, you'll be returned to the lobby of the Battle Tower. If it's the first time you've reached that rank, you're in store for some rewards! Generally, the higher your rank, the better the rewards—though there are bonus items to be gained each time you move up a tier, as illustrated in the table to the right.

Rank reached	Rewards	
Rank 2	Rare Candy	3 BP
Rank 3	Rare Candy	3 BP
Rank 4	Rare Candy ×2 Random mint item	Bottle Cap 5 BP
Rank 5	Rare Candy ×2 Random mint item	5 BP
Rank 6	Rare Candy ×2 Random mint item	5 BP
Rank 7	Rare Candy ×3 Random mint item	Bottle Cap 10 BP
Rank 8	Rare Candy ×3 Random mint item	10 BP
Rank 9	Rare Candy ×3 Random mint item	10 BP
Rank 10	Rare Candy ×5 Random mint item Bottle Cap ×2	Ability Capsule 20 BP
Rank MAX	Rare Candy ×10 Random mint item Bottle Cap ×3	Ability Capsule Gold Bottle Cap 50 BP

Remember, you can win each of these rank rewards twice—once for Single Battles and once for Double Battles!

Get rewards after certain milestones

There are a few rewards unique to the Battle Tower that you won't want to miss out on! Most of these are only available once, upon reaching certain new tiers in either the Single Battle or Double Battle format. But the Ribbon (p. 230) reward can be earned as many times as you like—try defeating Leon multiple times in the Master Ball Tier with different Pokémon so they can show off their Ribbons proudly!

Milestone	Rewards
Reach the Poké Ball Tier	Leon's rare League Card Judge function Song selection for Battle Tower
Reach the Master Ball Tier	Battle Tower Uniform
Defeat Leon in the Master Ball Tier	Tower Master Ribbon

The Judge Function

The Judge function is an option in your Boxes to evaluate a Pokémon's stat-growth potential. This is based on the Pokémon's individual strengths (p. 172). While viewing your Boxes, move your cursor over the Pokémon you want to have evaluated, and press ⊕ to open a quick view of its stats. Press ⊕ again to toggle off the regular display of the Pokémon's moves, Ability, and held item and instead view a judgment of its individual strengths!

Victory Station

If you've ever selected the VS option on your X menu, you've visited Victory Station! It's the place to go for online battles if you've got a Nintendo Switch Online membership† (p. 206), as well as the place for hosting your own local wireless tournaments. There's a lot to unpack here, so read on to learn about all the great features Victory Station has got jammed into it as you make your first stop on the way to...well, victory!

Whenever you select VS from the X menu, you'll first see how *Pokémon Sword* and *Pokémon Shield* players around you are stacking up in various things like number of Pokémon caught and number of Pokémon evolved. Whenever you pass other players, your system will pick up data from them about how much they've been battling, catching, evolving, and more. Which version is winning around you? Have you been helping add to the numbers?

The main components of VS

On the lower half of the screen, you've got two choices—Battle Stadium and Live Competition. Here's a quick preview of what each selection can do for you before we cover the many options packed into the Battle Stadium on the next couple of pages.

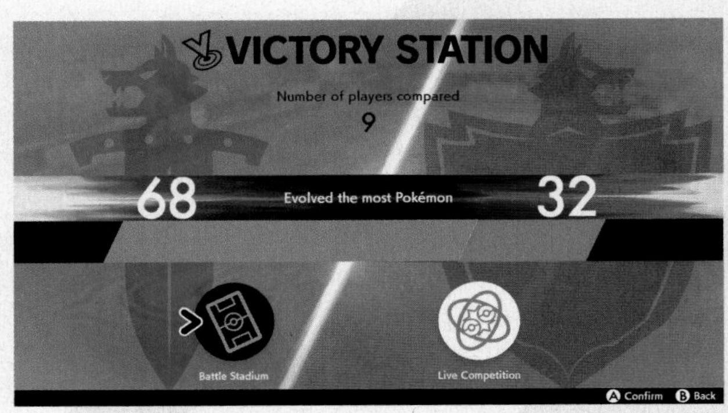

Battle Stadium — INTERNET CONNECTION REQUIRED

This is where you can actively compete with other players or choose to experiment with different teams of Pokémon without affecting your standings. You can also access Rental Teams (p. 204) and download unusual battle rules to use in Live Competitions and Link Battles (p. 300).

Live Competition — LOCAL WIRELESS OK!

You can take part in and host Live Competitions using just local wireless. Live Competitions let you set up your own competitions outside of official events held by The Pokémon Company International. Get some friends together, and give it a try!

Hosting and Joining Live Competitions

Any Trainers who are nearby in the real world can host or battle in a Live Competition. Player-created Live Competitions don't provide any rewards, but they're a fun and easy way for a group of nearby Trainers to see who's the best of the best in battle! One player will have to choose to be the host, and they can name the competition, set battle and time limits, and select battle rules (from defaults or those they've downloaded). Once they do, they can start distributing it. Any players who want to take part will need to get a Digital Player ID. They can get one by choosing to participate in a Live Competition from the Live Competition menu and then selecting **Receive a Digital Player ID** while the host is distributing their competition settings. Once everyone has their Digital Player IDs, they can find their opponents by putting in the same match ID to connect to one another! Match IDs are chosen by the participants, so settle on a 3-digit number together with your opponent.

Battle Stadium

If you're looking for battles that might offer more challenge or tangible rewards than Link Battles, then the Battle Stadium is where you want to head. You'll need to be connected to the internet and have an active Nintendo Switch Online membership† (p. 206), but then you should find lots of real-world Trainers for you to test your skills against. The Battle Stadium has two main options for battles you can do just about anytime—Casual Battles and Ranked Battles.

Traits that Casual Battles and Ranked Battles share

- You can choose **Single Battle** or **Double Battle** format.
- You can only bring **three** Pokémon to Single Battles or **four** to Double Battles.
- Before each match begins, you can change which three or four Pokémon to use.
- You can choose to use Pokémon from either your regular party, a Battle Team (p. 193), or a Rental Team (p. 204).
- Your team's **HP**, **PP**, and **held items** will all be restored after each battle.
- Pokémon over Lv. 50 will **temporarily** be set to Lv. 50.

Unlike with Y-Comm, opponents for all battles in the Battle Stadium are random. You won't be able to choose who you face, so be ready for anything and anyone!

Casual Battles NO REWARDS

Casual Battles are relaxed battles against other Trainers. There are no rewards for winning other than the satisfaction of victory, but there are no penalties for losses either. This makes Casual Battles great for Trainers who just want to enjoy some informal battles with people from all over the world or for those who want to try out a new team of Pokémon to see if they're ready to head into Ranked Battles.

Ranked Battles EARN REWARDS

Ranked Battles are for Trainers who are serious about competitive battling and want to put their best strategies to the test. Winning or losing will affect your rank here, just like it does in the Battle Tower. These ranks, and the tiers they're sorted into, are structured in the same way as the ranks and tiers in the Battle Tower. You can turn back to page 200 to review them! You can move up through tiers based on your success in battle, and you can also earn rewards based on how well you do.

> **!** Typically, you'll be matched against other players within the same tier as you, though not necessarily the same rank. This means you'll be matched with other players of roughly the same skill level as you!

Seasons and Rewards

Ranked Battles are broken into different periods of time called seasons. Whenever a Ranked Battle season ends and a new one begins, every player will drop down two ranks. This way no one can get to the top of the charts and just stay there forever. If you want to stay in the Master Ball Tier, you'll have to keep proving you're still the best of the best by battling other players in Ranked Battles!

You'll be able to see the date when the current season started and the date it will end on when you select Ranked Battles from the Battle Stadium menu. Based on your rank and tier at the end of each season, you'll earn special rewards. These can be things like BP, Bottle Caps, and even Pokémon Eggs that should hatch into great Pokémon specimens!

Build up your rank during a season → Season ends → Earn rewards based on your rank → Your rank goes down by two as a new season starts!

> **!** Even before a season ends, you can also earn other rewards for accomplishments like moving up through ranks or battling a certain number of times. These rewards could include BP, items good for training Pokémon, or items to sell at shops!

Online Competitions

Online Competitions are different from other kinds of online battles, as they aren't always available for you to take part in. There are Official Competitions organized by The Pokémon Company International, and there are Friendly Competitions, which anyone can choose to host.

Official Competitions EARN REWARDS

Official Competitions use a rating system, making them competitive like Ranked Battles, but the rating system itself is quite different. Everyone entered in the competition starts with a rating of 1500. That number will increase or decrease as that player wins or loses battles during the competition period. Competitions do not follow seasons, so their lengths can vary—the same goes for their rewards and their rule sets. You won't know what rewards or rules a competition will have until it's announced, so make sure to stay up-to-date with the latest announcements on Pokémon's official website or through Pokémon HOME (p. 209)! If you've already taken part in an Official Competition, you'll find the results from your most recent competition in your game's Official Competition menu, too.

Friendly Competitions NO REWARDS

If you're interested in competitions that feel a bit more casual but still have interesting rules, then you can either join an ongoing Friendly Competition that someone else is hosting or host your own for others to join. You can also check the results from the last Friendly Competition you joined.

> **!** There's also the Download Rules option in the Battle Stadium menu. If you might want to try battling in a different style, select this option. Any special battle rules currently being distributed will be downloaded, and you'll be able to select them when setting up Link Battles in Y-Comm (p. 300) or Friendly Competitions and Live Competitions here at Victory Station!

Rental Teams

Rental Teams are a great way to see how other people put together formidable teams, especially if you're still just getting the hang of it. When you borrow a Rental Team, you can use it just as you would use one of your Battle Teams (p. 193). You can borrow up to five Rental Teams at a time, so don't hesitate to try out different things!

Renting teams in the game

At the Battle Tower, which you can visit in Wyndon after becoming the Champion, you can borrow some Rental Teams from the generous fellow in the green jacket. But even though you get them at the Battle Tower, that's not the only place you can use them! As you can with your Battle Teams, you can use these teams in Link Battles (p. 300) and in the Battle Stadium (p. 202). Check them out below—or see their details in your game by borrowing them and selecting **Check summary** before choosing the Pokémon to use in a battle!

> The Pokémon on these teams are all Lv. 50, have the best possible individual strengths, and have maximized their base points for two stats. Their Natures, however, are all neutral ones that don't affect stat growth. What Nature would you have given them? Remember, how to train up Pokémon to maximize their strengths was covered back on page 172!

Basic Team

Pokémon	Rillaboom	Cinderace	Inteleon	Gengar	Haxorus	Togekiss
Ability	Overgrow	Blaze	Torrent	Cursed Body	Mold Breaker	Serene Grace
Held item	Sitrus Berry	Life Orb	Blunder Policy	Focus Sash	Lum Berry	Expert Belt
Moves	Drum Beating Wood Hammer Superpower Earthquake	Pyro Ball Zen Headbutt Gunk Shot Iron Head	Snipe Shot Hydro Pump Blizzard Shadow Ball	Shadow Ball Sludge Wave Dazzling Gleam Destiny Bond	Outrage Earthquake Poison Jab Dragon Dance	Air Slash Dazzling Gleam Flamethrower Nasty Plot
Stats with maxed base points	HP, Attack	Attack, Speed	Sp. Atk, Speed	Sp. Atk, Speed	Attack, Speed	Sp. Attack, Speed

This team is built around the final Evolutions of the Pokémon that you could choose as your first partner. If you weren't sure how to raise them to best use their strengths or have been wondering what you might've been able to do with the two Pokémon you didn't choose, give this team a whirl! It's full of solid picks for any Single Battle!

Skill Team

Pokémon	Gyarados	Kommo-o	Falinks	Tyranitar	Duraludon	Grimmsnarl
Ability	Intimidate	Bulletproof	Battle Armor	Sand Stream	Stalwart	Prankster
Held item	Wacan Berry	Sitrus Berry	Focus Sash	Chople Berry	Light Clay	Leftovers
Moves	Waterfall Ice Fang Earthquake Dragon Dance	Clanging Scales Flash Cannon Flamethrower Clangorous Soul	No Retreat Megahorn Close Combat Throat Chop	Stone Edge Crunch Low Kick Dragon Dance	Stealth Rock Light Screen Reflect Steel Beam	Darkest Lariat Spirit Break Drain Punch Bulk Up
Stats with maxed base points	Attack, Speed	Sp. Atk, Speed	Attack, Speed	Attack, Speed	HP, Speed	HP, Attack

Send out Duraludon first to lay some nasty groundwork with Stealth Rock and maybe set up some extra defenses with Light Screen or Reflect. Once that's all in place, consider swapping in Pokémon that can benefit from their stat-boosting moves, like Grimmsnarl with Bulk Up or Gyarados with Dragon Dance, and then knock out everything that comes at you!

Tough Team

Pokémon	Snorlax	Dragapult	Mimikyu	Heat Rotom	Hippowdon	Aegislash
Ability	Immunity	Infiltrator	Disguise	Levitate	Sand Stream	Stance Change
Held item	Sitrus Berry	White Herb	Life Orb	Choice Scarf	Rocky Helmet	Leftovers
Moves	Double-Edge Earthquake Curse Recycle	Dragon Darts Phantom Force Draco Meteor U-turn	Shadow Claw Play Rough Swords Dance Shadow Sneak	Overheat Volt Switch Will-O-Wisp Trick	Earthquake Ice Fang Yawn Slack Off	Shadow Ball Shadow Sneak King's Shield Brick Break
Stats with maxed base points	Attack, Defense	Attack, Speed	Attack, Speed	Sp. Atk, Speed	HP, Defense	HP, Sp. Atk

This heavy-hitting team is full of solid picks that will be ready for just about anything that's thrown at them. They've got a mix of defensive options, favorite damage-dealing moves, and various tricks up their sleeves—like Snorlax recycling its Berry or Dragapult sneaking in a bit of damage before switching out with U-turn.

Rain Team

Pokémon	Pelipper	Ludicolo	Barraskewda	Raichu	Ferrothorn	Seismitoad
Ability	Drizzle	Swift Swim	Swift Swim	Lightning Rod	Iron Barbs	Swift Swim
Held item	Focus Sash	Assault Vest	Life Orb	Bright Powder	Choice Band	Rindo Berry
Moves	Hurricane Scald Tailwind Protect	Energy Ball Scald Ice Beam Fake Out	Liquidation Close Combat Poison Jab Protect	Fake Out Thunder Encore Feint	Power Whip Gyro Ball Iron Head Toxic	Hydro Pump Sludge Bomb Earth Power Muddy Water
Stats with maxed base points	Sp. Atk, Speed	Sp. Atk, Speed	Attack, Speed	Sp. Atk, Speed	HP, Attack	Sp. Atk, Speed

No matter what the forecast, rain teams are here to stay—and for a reason! Change the weather condition to rain, then watch as all your Swift Swim Pokémon get to use their Water-type moves with boosted Speed as well as boosted power from the rain! Use Pelipper to set the scene with its Drizzle Ability and get a nice Tailwind going, and then this team will be ready for action!

Slow Team

Pokémon	Lucario	Oranguru	Hatterene	Torkoal	Dhelmise	Copperajah
Ability	Inner Focus	Inner Focus	Healer	Drought	Steelworker	Sheer Force
Held item	Choice Scarf	Room Service	Mental Herb	Charcoal	Iron Ball	Life Orb
Moves	Final Gambit Crunch Close Combat Quick Guard	Trick Room Instruct Psychic Protect	Trick Room Psychic Mystical Fire Protect	Eruption Heat Wave Solar Beam Protect	Gyro Ball Phantom Force Power Whip Protect	Iron Head High Horsepower Power Whip Protect
Stats with maxed base points	HP, Speed	HP, Sp. Atk	HP, Sp. Atk	HP, Sp. Atk	HP, Attack	HP, Attack

Start out with Lucario and Oranguru, and try putting up a Quick Guard with Lucario as Oranguru sets up Trick Room. As you learned on page 188, Trick Room will really mess with speedy teams you may face, suddenly turning what they thought was their greatest strength into a terrible weakness—as long as they didn't come ready with the Room Service item!

Renting teams from other players

If you have a Nintendo Switch Online membership†, you can also borrow teams that other players have put online. Just open up VS from your X menu, select Battle Stadium, select Rental Teams, and choose **Manage teams you're renting**. If you're connected to the internet, you'll be able to borrow a team of your choosing. Give it a spin—maybe you'll even get a bit of inspiration for yourself!

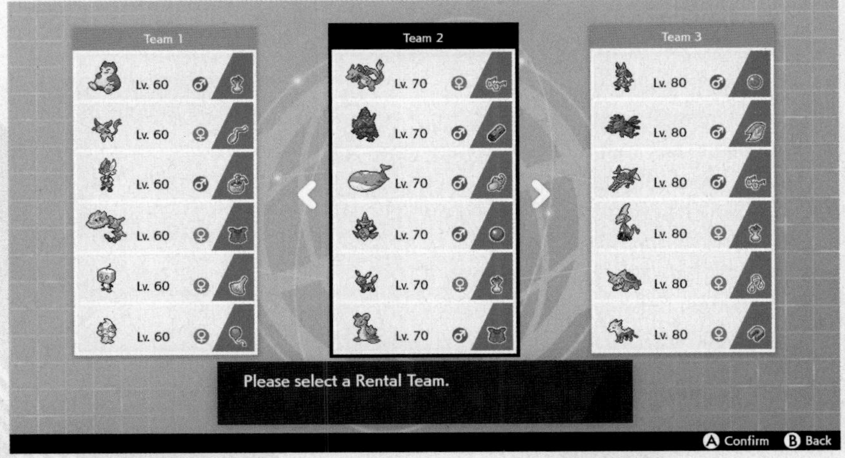

Lending out your own teams

You can also put your teams online for other players to borrow if you've got a Nintendo Switch Online membership†. Ready to show off your latest and greatest team? Follow the same steps as above, but this time, choose to manage the teams you share instead of the ones you rent. Select a Battle Team that you want to share with the world, and upload its info to the internet!

Choosing to share one of your teams won't make it disappear or anything! You can still use it as one of your own Battle Teams. It won't even be locked. It's more like a copy of your team has been saved online—a copy that matches exactly how your team was the moment you uploaded its data. You can feel free to keep modifying your teams as you like.

Nintendo Switch Online

To use all the online features of *Pokémon Sword* and *Pokémon Shield*, you will need a membership for the Nintendo Switch Online service†. Nintendo Switch Online is a paid service that allows you to take full advantage of online play with your Nintendo Switch games and provides benefits, like access to classic games and special offers. You can learn more about the service on Nintendo's official website!

Communication Features that Require Nintendo Switch Online

You will need a Nintendo Switch Online membership† for the following:

- The Battle Stadium in VS, including Ranked Battles, Online Competitions, and Rental Teams (p. 202)
- Finding other players from around the world camping in the Wild Area (p. 295)
- Exchanging stamps and requests on Y-Comm (p. 298) with distant players
- Sharing and downloading League Cards online through Card Codes (p. 308)

Communication Features that Don't Require Nintendo Switch Online

Remember that you can play with other players nearby using local wireless communication for most features. Just get together a few buddies, or hang out in a place with lots of people around and see who else is playing! If you do, you'll find that a Nintendo Switch Online membership† isn't needed for all of the following:

- Receiving Mystery Gifts and updates for your game
- Receiving the latest Wild Area news and special Max Raid Battle distributions
- Live Competitions in VS using local wireless communication
- Finding other players near you who are adventuring and camping in the Wild Area
- Exchanging stamps and requests on Y-Comm with players nearby

Linking your accounts

When you try to access a feature that requires an internet connection, you'll be prompted to link your Nintendo Account to your user profile on your Nintendo Switch system (if you haven't done so already). Your Nintendo Account isn't quite the same thing as a Nintendo Switch Online membership†, but it's a necessary first step. A Nintendo Account can be created for free, and once linked to your system, it allows you to do things like access Nintendo eShop to download demos or purchase digital software.

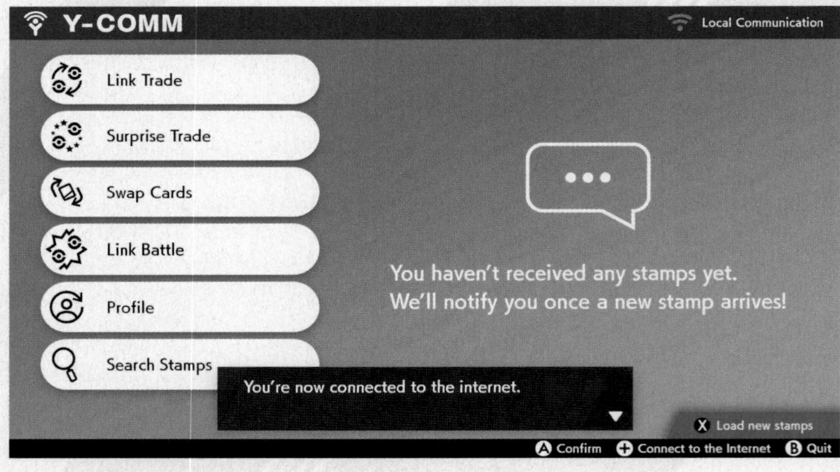

Follow the steps on your Nintendo Switch system to create or sign in to a Nintendo Account and then link to your profile on your Nintendo Switch. If you don't have a Nintendo Account, you can visit Nintendo's official website for the most up-to-date information on how to set one up. Once you have a Nintendo Account, you'll be able to use it on different platforms—and you'll be ready to sign up for a Nintendo Switch Online membership†, if you care to!

†Nintendo Switch Online membership (sold separately) and Nintendo Account required for online play. Not available in all countries. Internet access required for online features. Terms apply. For more information, visit nintendo.com for more details.

Completing Your Pokédex

At the beginning of your adventure, Sonia will add the Pokédex feature to your Rotom Phone. The Pokédex is a handy tool for any Pokémon Trainer—it serves as a database for all the Pokémon you've encountered and caught. It can tell you where their habitats are, show what weather they prefer, and even give recommendations on which of them to catch! There are 400 species of Pokémon you can catch in *Pokémon Sword* and *Pokémon Shield*, so completing your Pokédex won't be easy. Still, catching lots of different Pokémon will help you come up with new teams and strategies, so give it a shot!

Getting familiar with your Pokédex

Of course, if you're going to complete the Pokédex, you should get familiar with it first. Here we'll discuss what features the Pokédex has and how they'll help. For starters, here is what you'll see when you open your Pokédex from the X menu.

1. This section shows the areas in which recommended Pokémon will appear!
2. Here you see how many Pokémon you've obtained and how many you've seen.
3. Here's where you see the currently recommended Pokémon to catch.

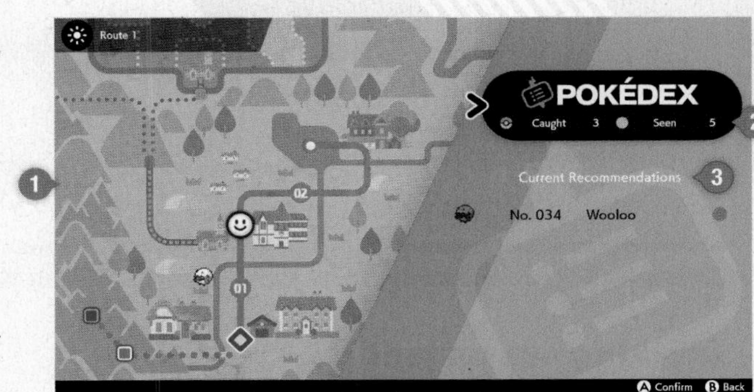

Using the Pokédex menu

You probably noticed the little section at the top right of the screen showing the number of Pokémon you've caught and seen. Select it to open your Pokédex. Here, you'll see detailed pages on each Pokémon you've obtained or encountered.

Every Pokémon you encounter during your adventure—whether it's a wild Pokémon or a Pokémon in another Trainer's party—will be registered to your Pokédex. These are shown as the number of Pokémon seen. This number will increase every time you run into a new species of Pokémon, whether you catch that Pokémon or not.

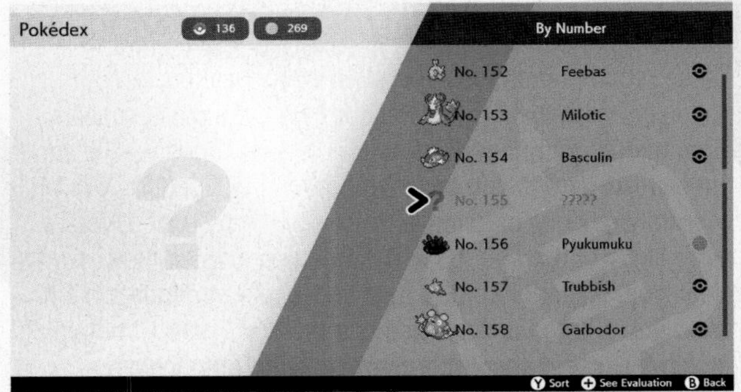

Even if you don't catch a Pokémon, it'll still show up in your Pokédex, but the Pokémon's image in the list will be darkened, and its entry will look something like the below. You'll be able to see what the Pokémon looks like and what type or types it has, and you can check its habitat by pressing Ⓧ, but that's about it.

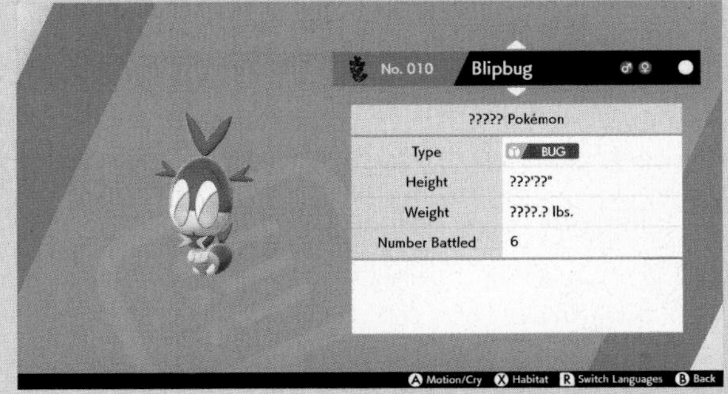

If you later catch a Pokémon you'd registered only as a sighting before, you'll see that a lot of information gets added to its Pokédex entry! You'll be able to see the Pokémon's height and weight, listen to its cry, check its movements, and even read a short paragraph about that species.

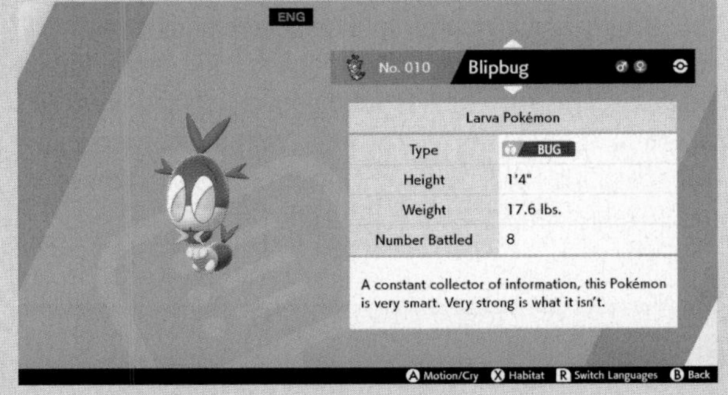

! When viewing your Pokédex, you'll also be able to sort the Pokémon in a variety of ways by pressing Ⓨ. You can also have your Pokédex evaluated by pressing ⊕. The evaluation feature will offer some helpful tips on further filling your Pokédex, so give it a try from time to time!

Different Colors and Forms

Some Pokémon have different color variations or have multiple forms they can take. You'll be able to view these different colors and forms in the Pokédex, too—just use either the Right Stick or Left Stick to scroll through the different forms if the Pokémon has any. Some forms come with their own unique descriptions in the Pokédex, making for interesting reading! Just keep in mind that you'll actually have to catch the Pokémon in those various forms to unlock the Pokédex information. You don't need to worry about differing forms for completing the Pokédex, though—you only need to catch one specimen of each Pokémon, regardless of its form!

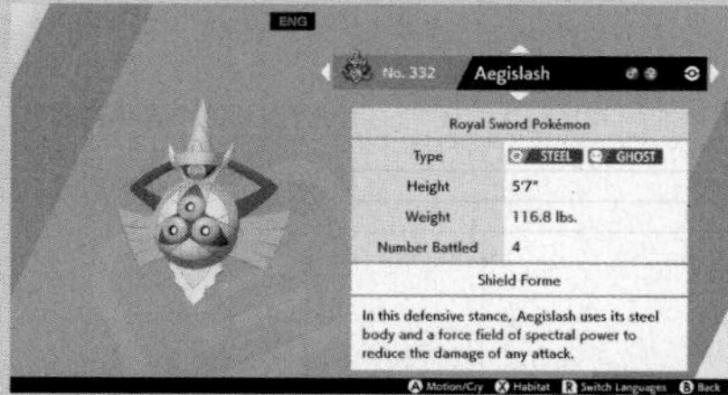

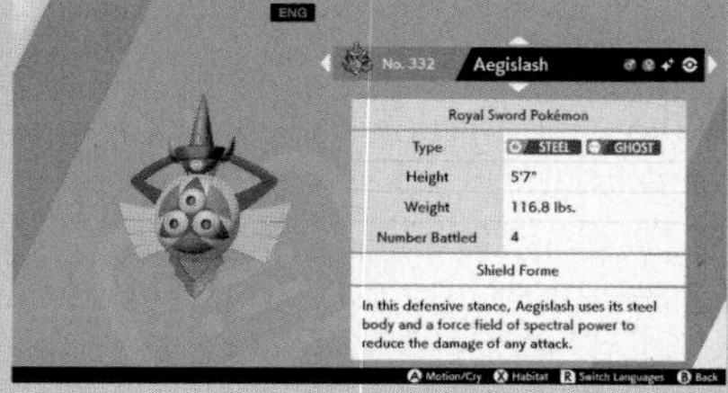

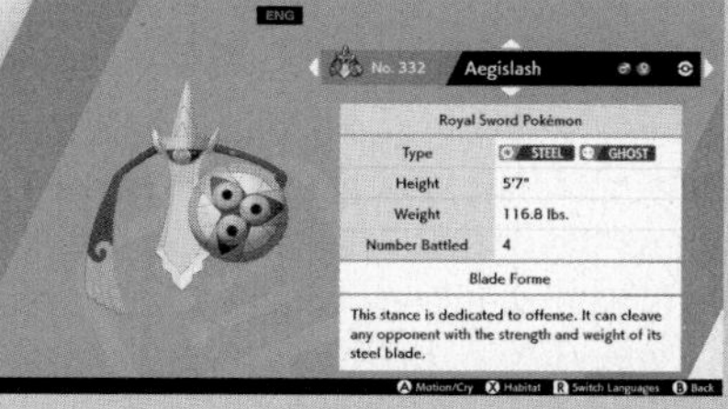

Checking out current recommendations

Another great feature of your high-tech Pokédex is a list of current recommendations for the day, which you can find right below the bubble showing the number of caught and seen Pokémon.

These recommendations are an efficient way to search for Pokémon to complete your Pokédex for a couple of reasons. First, the recommended Pokémon are likely ones you've seen but haven't caught yet, so catching them will generally bring your Pokédex one step closer to completion. Second, you're more likely to run into these Pokémon as long as they're displayed. The habitat map next to the recommendation will show you where the Pokémon can be found nearby, but you'll be more likely to encounter them anywhere they have a chance to appear!

The current recommendations will be refreshed and a new set of up to four Pokémon will be listed if you catch all the currently recommended Pokémon, if you discover new species when you don't have other recommendations, or when the internal clock on your Nintendo Switch changes dates!

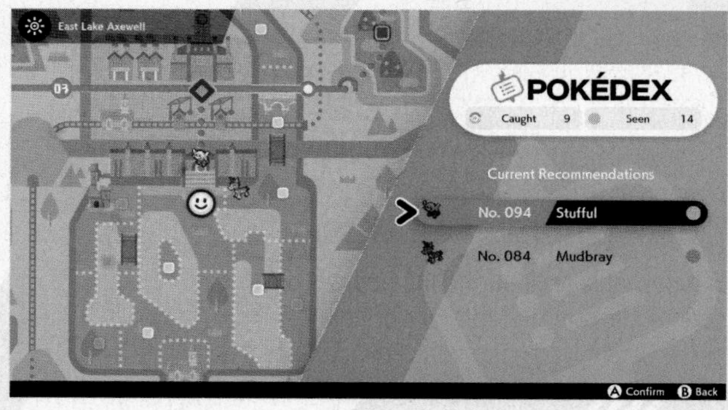

Keep your eyes peeled for Pokémon that have a weather icon next to their Pokédex number. Certain Pokémon only appear during specific weather patterns. If they show up as recommendations, that means it's the right weather to look for them now!

Viewing the habitat map

If you want to know where you'll be able to find certain Pokémon, the habitat map is the place to look! Select the Pokémon you're searching for in the Pokédex, and press ⓧ. This will take you to the habitat map, with showing you which areas the Pokémon can be found in. You can move through Pokémon entries using Ⓛ and Ⓡ.

If you see "Habitat Unknown," then that Pokémon can't be encountered in the wild in the usual ways, such as in the tall grass. You'll need to get it through one of the other methods described in the coming pages.

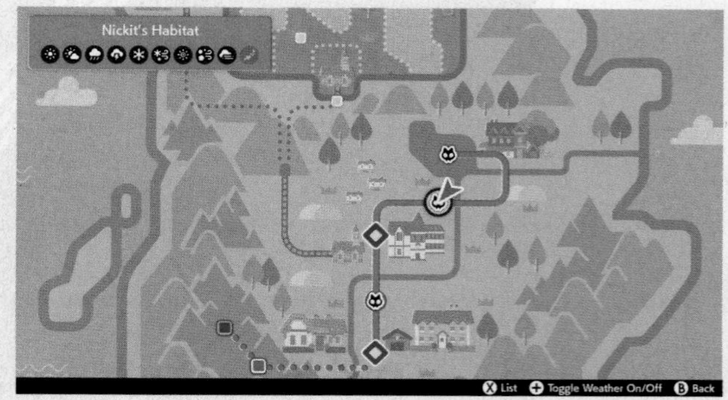

If you look in the top-left corner of each habitat map, you'll see a variety of icons, some highlighted and some not. These show what weather the Pokémon's likely to appear in, with the far-right icon indicating whether you need to go fishing to catch this Pokémon. For more information on the various weather patterns, flip to page 19!

> **!** Being able to see what weather patterns a Pokémon prefers is great, but it won't do you much good unless you can tell what the actual weather is at each location. Luckily, it's very easy to check. While viewing the habitat map, just press ⊕ for a complete view of current weather patterns across the whole Galar region!

Tips for completing your Pokédex

So far we've discussed the basics of how your Pokédex can help you catch every last species you can in the Galar region. But there are a lot of other ways you can speed up completing the Pokédex. Below are some important examples!

Use the right Poké Ball for the situation

There are a variety of different Poké Balls available, each with their own characteristics. There's the normal Poké Ball, which is affordable and perfectly effective early on. There's the Ultra Ball, which will be your go-to once you progress far enough in your adventure. Then there are trickier ones, such as the Quick Ball, which is more likely to catch a Pokémon if you use it as soon as you enter battle, and the Dusk Ball, which is more effective when it's dark around you. Using the right Poké Ball for the situation will increase the likelihood of a successful catch, making it that much easier to fill your Pokédex! For a full list of available Poké Balls and their effects, turn to page 371!

Get your hands on a Catching Charm

Once you make it to Circhester, go into the western building of Hotel Ionia and head up the elevator. On the next floor, enter the room all the way to the left and speak to the man standing by the windows. He'll give you a Catching Charm, which will increase your chances of getting a critical catch—a rare phenomenon in which your Poké Ball is much more likely to successfully catch its target! You should remember this man, because he'll want to see your Pokédex once you've completed it.

Use Y-Comm to trade Pokémon

Trading Pokémon is another good way to make progress on filling your Pokédex. In fact, some Pokémon will only appear in one version of the game, so you'll have to trade in some way to obtain them! The most straightforward way to do this is using the Link Trade option from the Y-Comm menu. You can send out trading requests from here or set up a Link Code to trade with a pal. You'll also be able to engage in Surprise Trades if you're feeling adventurous! For more info on Y-Comm and what you can do, go to page 298.

Completed Your Pokédex? Head Back to Circhester

Remember the man who gave you the Catching Charm? You might recall that he also told you to visit him again once you completed your Pokédex. If you do, he'll give you a certificate recognizing your accomplishment—and a Shiny Charm! The Shiny Charm increases the chances of running into super-rare Shiny Pokémon. Plus, he'll add a special mark to your League Card so the world can know you've completed your Pokédex!

You actually completed your Pokédex!

Keep your eyes peeled for new information on Pokémon HOME

Pokémon HOME is a new service scheduled to be launched in 2020. It will provide a new home for Pokémon you've obtained in earlier games, including *Pokémon: Let's Go, Pikachu!* and *Pokémon: Let's Go, Eevee!* You can bring Pokémon from even older games into Pokémon HOME via *Pokémon Bank*, and many species can then be moved to *Pokémon Sword* and *Pokémon Shield*! You'll also be able to trade Pokémon directly between Pokémon HOME accounts so you can connect with other Trainers and trade for Pokémon you haven't caught yet. Completing your Pokédex has never been easier! For more information on Pokémon HOME, visit Pokémon's official webpage.

Pokémon
HOME

Ways to Obtain Pokémon

If you follow the recommendations in your Pokédex, you'll be well on your way to catching every last species in the Galar region! But there are some tricky ones to find, not to mention Pokémon that don't appear in the wild. To get them all, you may need to complete certain events in the game, evolve other Pokémon species, or try to get them from other players in trades.

In the sections that follow, any Pokémon you can't catch in the wild will be marked with ✣, so pay close attention to these sections if you've been catching all you can and still have missing species. If you need more guidance on how to catch them all or want to learn the details of every Pokémon species and what moves they can learn, check out the official Pokédex published by The Pokémon Company International!

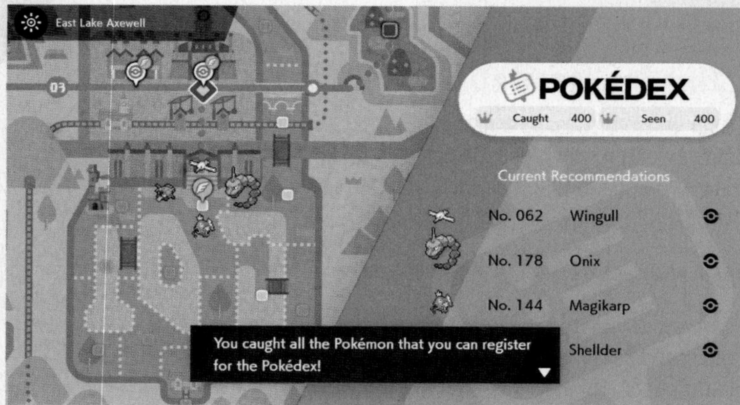

Important tips to remember for filling your Pokédex!

- Pay attention to the recommendations in your Pokédex, as they'll be a great help.
- Watch your X menu for alerts about rare weather conditions in the Wild Area.
- Use the encounter tables in the walkthrough, ticking off species you've already caught.
- Don't rely just on catching wild Pokémon—try to evolve them or find Pokémon Eggs.
- Don't forget that you can trade with other players through Y-Comm (p. 298).

Weather to Watch Out For

Remember that there are particularly rare weather types that can appear in the Wild Area—thunderstorms, blizzards, sandstorms, and fog will trigger an alert on your X menu. There are Pokémon that only appear in some of these weather conditions, so hurry to the Wild Area if you see an alert and try to track one down.

Manectric only appears during thunderstorms.

Mime Jr. only appears in blizzards.

Musharna only appears in heavy fog.

Pokémon you may need to get in events or trades

Regardless which Pokémon you chose for your first partner, you'll have to trade with other players to get the other two. You'll also need to trade for all the version-exclusive species listed on pages 24 and 25 if you hope to complete your Pokédex, though you won't have to obtain all their different forms—they're just nice to have!

001 Grookey ✣

Obtain it in a trade if you didn't pick it as your partner.

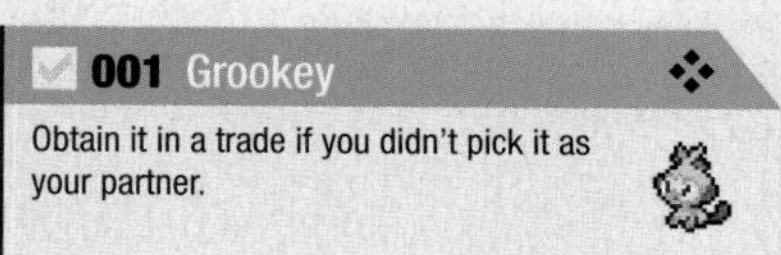

004 Scorbunny ✣

Obtain it in a trade if you didn't pick it as your partner.

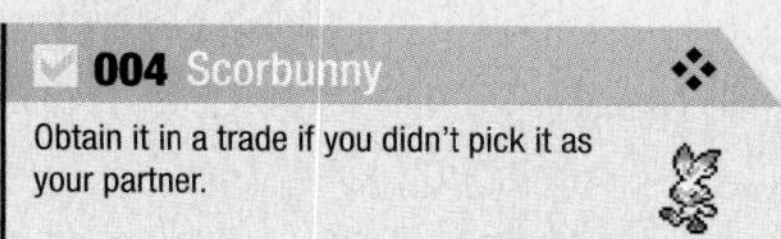

007 Sobble ✣

Obtain it in a trade if you didn't pick it as your partner.

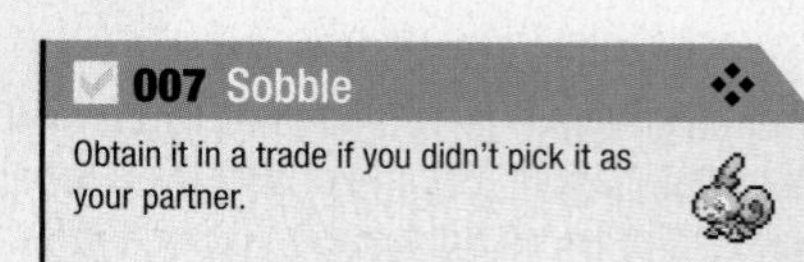

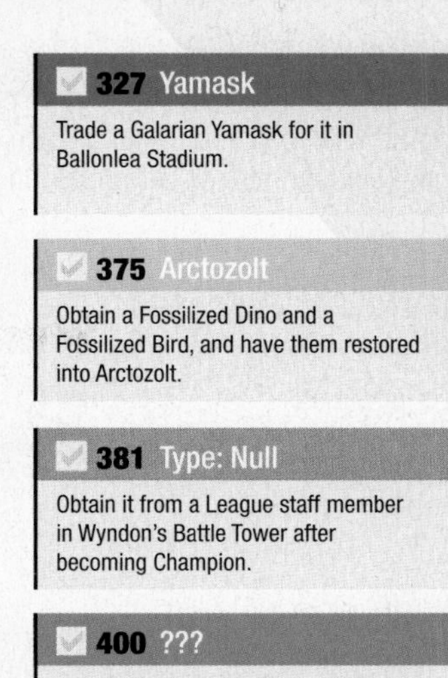
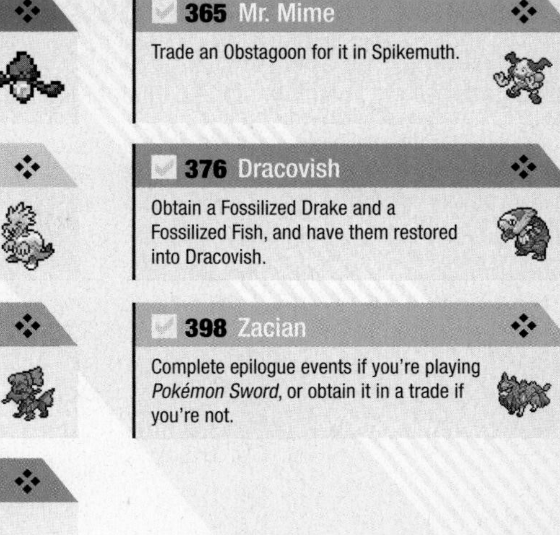

182 Meowth
Trade a Galarian Meowth for it in Turffield Stadium.

327 Yamask
Trade a Galarian Yamask for it in Ballonlea Stadium.

365 Mr. Mime
Trade an Obstagoon for it in Spikemuth.

374 Dracozolt
Obtain a Fossilized Drake and a Fossilized Bird, and have them restored into Dracozolt.

375 Arctozolt
Obtain a Fossilized Dino and a Fossilized Bird, and have them restored into Arctozolt.

376 Dracovish
Obtain a Fossilized Drake and a Fossilized Fish, and have them restored into Dracovish.

377 Arctovish
Obtain a Fossilized Dino and a Fossilized Fish, and have them restored into Arctovish.

381 Type: Null
Obtain it from a League staff member in Wyndon's Battle Tower after becoming Champion.

398 Zacian
Complete epilogue events if you're playing *Pokémon Sword*, or obtain it in a trade if you're not.

399 Zamazenta
Complete epilogue events if you're playing *Pokémon Shield*, or obtain it in a trade if you're not.

400 ???
There's one more Pokémon you'll need to complete your Pokédex, but you'll have to complete the main story to get it!

Pokémon you can only get through level-based Evolution

There are a number of Pokémon species that you simply won't encounter in the wild. If you want to get them for your team or complete your Pokédex, you'll have to obtain an earlier species in the Evolutionary line and evolve it. The Pokémon listed below can only be obtained in this way or by receiving them in a trade from another player. They evolve simply by being leveled up to a certain level or higher.

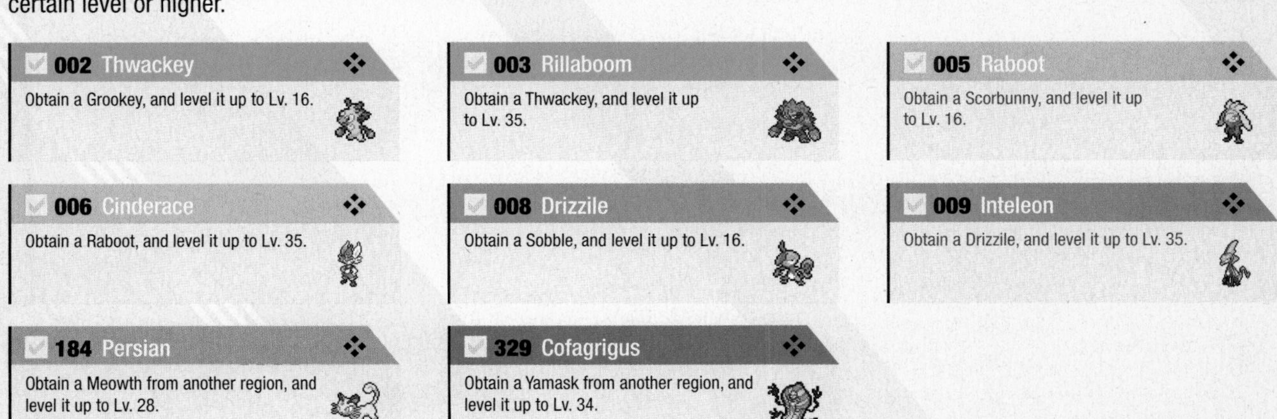

002 Thwackey
Obtain a Grookey, and level it up to Lv. 16.

003 Rillaboom
Obtain a Thwackey, and level it up to Lv. 35.

005 Raboot
Obtain a Scorbunny, and level it up to Lv. 16.

006 Cinderace
Obtain a Raboot, and level it up to Lv. 35.

008 Drizzile
Obtain a Sobble, and level it up to Lv. 16.

009 Inteleon
Obtain a Drizzile, and level it up to Lv. 35.

184 Persian
Obtain a Meowth from another region, and level it up to Lv. 28.

329 Cofagrigus
Obtain a Yamask from another region, and level it up to Lv. 34.

Pokémon You May Want to Get through Evolution

There are also some Pokémon that can be caught in the wild but may be exceedingly rare or only appear in rare weather conditions that are difficult to predict. If you run into one, of course, try to catch it! But always remember that Evolution is another option if you're having a tough time filling your Pokédex just by catching 'em all.

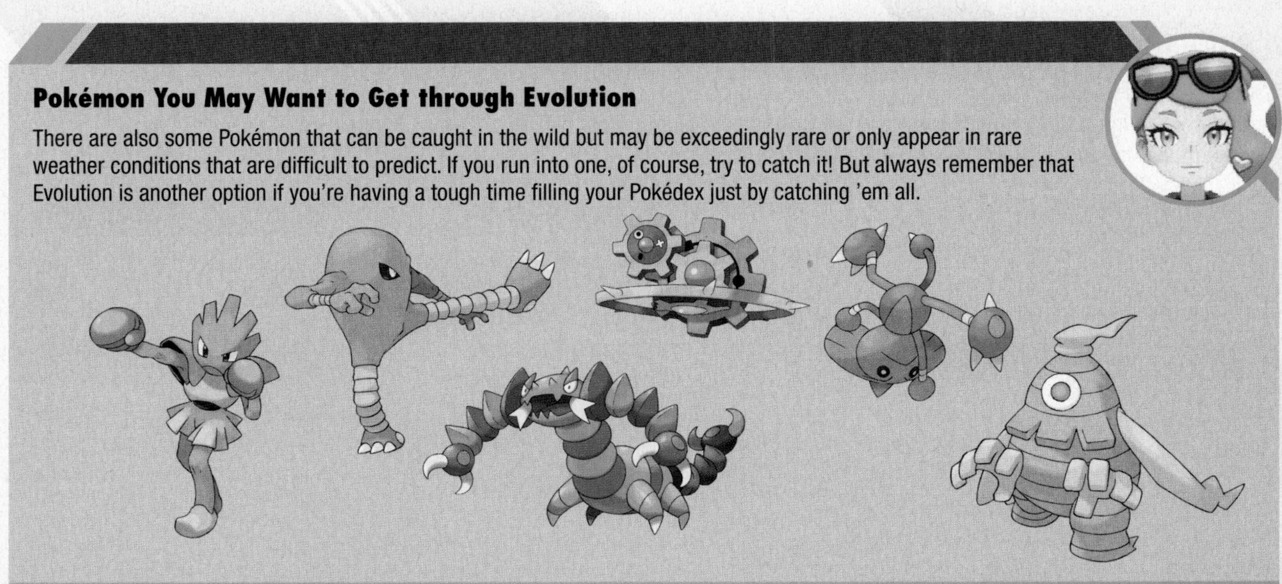

Pokémon that evolve with Evolution stones

If you're having a hard time finding certain Pokémon in the wild, consider getting them through Evolution instead! For some, you'll need certain Evolution stones, though. You can get Evolution stones by completing Poké Jobs, so turn to page 241 if you need to stock up!

Evolution stone	Can be used on...		To evolve it into...	
Fire Stone	068	Vulpix	069	Ninetales
	070	Growlithe	071	Arcanine
	196	Eevee	199	Flareon
Thunder Stone	017	Charjabug	018	Vikavolt
	194	Pikachu	195	Raichu
	196	Eevee	198	Jolteon
Water Stone	037	Lombre	038	Ludicolo
	150	Shellder	151	Cloyster
	196	Eevee	197	Vaporeon
Leaf Stone	040	Nuzleaf	041	Shiftry
	056	Gloom	057	Vileplume
	196	Eevee	202	Leafeon
Ice Stone	196	Eevee	203	Glaceon
	367	Darumaka	368	Darmanitan
Shiny Stone	050	Minccino	051	Cinccino
	060	Roselia	061	Roserade
	258	Togetic	259	Togekiss
Sun Stone	056	Gloom	058	Bellossom
	262	Cottonee	263	Whimsicott
	318	Helioptile	319	Heliolisk
Moon Stone	090	Munna	091	Musharna
	255	Clefairy	256	Clefable
Dusk Stone	288	Lampent	289	Chandelure
	331	Doublade	332	Aegislash
Dawn Stone	079	Snorunt (female)	081	Froslass
	121	Kirlia (male)	123	Gallade

Pokémon that evolve by being traded

Some Pokémon must be traded to trigger their Evolution. A few are even trickier, requiring that the Pokémon also be holding a certain item or meet other conditions when traded. Pokémon you might consider getting through trade-based Evolution, if you're having trouble finding them in the wild, are listed below.

137 Dusknoir

Receive a Dusclops holding a Reaper Cloth in a trade, and it will evolve into Dusknoir.

140 Machamp

Receive a Machoke in a trade, and it will evolve into Machamp.

143 Gengar

Receive a Haunter in a trade, and it will evolve into Gengar.

153 Milotic

Receive a Feebas holding a Prism Scale in a trade, and it will evolve into Milotic.

170 Gigalith

Receive a Boldore in a trade, and it will evolve into Gigalith.

173 Conkeldurr

Receive a Gurdurr in a trade, and it will evolve into Conkeldurr.

179 Steelix
Receive an Onix holding a Metal Coat in a trade, and it will evolve into Steelix.

192 Gourgeist
Receive a Pumpkaboo in a trade, and it will evolve into Gourgeist.

211 Slurpuff
Receive a Swirlix holding a Whipped Dream in a trade, and it will evolve into Slurpuff.

213 Aromatisse
Receive a Spritzee holding a Sachet in a trade, and it will evolve into Aromatisse.

266 Rhyperior
Receive a Rhydon holding a Protector in a trade, and it will evolve into Rhyperior.

274 Escavalier
Trade a Shelmet for a Karrablast, and the Karrablast will evolve into Escavalier.

276 Accelgor
Trade a Karrablast for a Shelmet, and the Shelmet will evolve into Accelgor.

339 Trevenant
Receive a Phantump in a trade, and it will evolve into Trevenant.

Pokémon that evolve when they're friendly

High friendship is another requirement for some Pokémon species to evolve, sometimes with additional conditions. Turn to page 283 to learn more about friendship if you want to get these Pokémon for your Pokédex through Evolution instead of wild encounters!

060 Roselia
Obtain a Budew and level it up with high friendship during the day (in-game) to evolve it into Roselia.

175 Swoobat
Obtain a Woobat and level it up with high friendship to evolve it into Swoobat.

194 Pikachu
Obtain a Pichu and level it up with high friendship to evolve it into Pikachu.

200 Espeon
Obtain an Eevee and level it up with high friendship during the day (in-game) to evolve it into Espeon.

201 Umbreon
Obtain an Eevee and level it up with high friendship at night (in-game) to evolve it into Umbreon.

204 Sylveon
Obtain an Eevee and level it up with high friendship when it knows a Fairy-type move to evolve it into Sylveon.

255 Clefairy
Obtain a Cleffa and level it up with high friendship to evolve it into Clefairy.

258 Togetic
Obtain a Togepi and level it up with high friendship to evolve it into Togetic.

261 Snorlax
Obtain a Munchlax and level it up with high friendship to evolve it into Snorlax.

299 Lucario
Obtain a Riolu and level it up with high friendship during the day (in-game) to evolve it into Lucario.

350 Frosmoth
Obtain a Snom and level it up with high friendship at night (in-game) to evolve it into Frosmoth.

382 Silvally
Obtain a Type: Null and level it up with high friendship to evolve it into Silvally.

! You may find that time acts a bit funny during your main adventure, but after you've become the Champion, it should flow along with your Nintendo Switch system's time settings. Night will fall at 7:00 p.m. each day, and dawn breaks at 6:00 a.m.

Pokémon that evolve when they know certain moves

Some Pokémon must know a certain move in order to evolve. This is generally a move they would naturally learn by leveling up, but if they've forgotten it or you missed your chance for them to learn it, visit Jack in any Pokémon Center (p. 16).

054 Tsareena
Obtain a Steenee and level it up when it knows Stomp to evolve it into Tsareena.

077 Mamoswine
Obtain a Piloswine and level it up when it knows Ancient Power to evolve it into Mamoswine.

204 Sylveon
Obtain an Eevee and level it up with high friendship when it knows a Fairy-type move to evolve it into Sylveon.

253 Sudowoodo
Obtain a Bonsly and level it up when it knows Mimic to evolve it into Sudowoodo.

352 Grapploct
Obtain a Clobbopus and level it up when it knows Taunt to evolve it into Grapploct.

365 Mr. Mime
Obtain a Mime Jr. and level it up in Galar when it knows Mimic to evolve it into Mr. Mime.

Pokémon that evolve in very unusual ways

There are also Pokémon that evolve in such mysterious ways that it's a wonder they ever evolve at all! To complete your Pokédex, try to catch these Pokémon in the wild or refer to the specifics below!

106 Shedinja

Obtain a Nincada and level it up to Lv. 20 when you have an empty space in your party to get Shedinja in addition to Ninjask.

110 Hitmontop

Obtain a Tyrogue and level it up to Lv. 20 with its Attack and Defense equal to evolve it into Hitmontop.

206 Flapple

Obtain an Applin and use a Tart Apple on it to evolve it into Flapple.

291 Malamar

Obtain an Inkay and turn your Nintendo Switch upside down while Inkay is leveling up to Lv. 30 to evolve it into Malamar.

336 Polteageist

Obtain a Sinistea and use either a Chipped Pot or a Cracked Pot on it to evolve it into Polteageist. (Which item triggers Evolution will depend on whether you have a Phony Form Sinistea or an Antique Form Sinistea—try checking the bottom of Sinistea's teacup to see if you can figure it out!)

108 Hitmonlee

Obtain a Tyrogue and level it up to Lv. 20 with its Attack higher than its Defense to evolve it into Hitmonlee.

112 Pangoro

Obtain a Pancham and level it up to Lv. 32 with a Dark-type Pokémon in your party to evolve it into Pangoro.

207 Appletun

Obtain an Applin and use a Sweet Apple on it to evolve it into Appletun.

293 Weavile

Obtain a Sneasel and level it up at night (in-game) when it's holding a Razor Claw to evolve it into Weavile.

355 Mantine

Obtain a Mantyke and level it up with a Remoraid in your party to evolve it into Mantine.

391 Goodra

Obtain a Sliggoo and level it up to Lv. 50 while it's raining to evolve it into Goodra.

109 Hitmonchan

Obtain a Tyrogue and level it up to Lv. 20 with its Defense higher than its Attack to evolve it into Hitmonchan.

186 Alcremie

Obtain a Milcery and give it a Sweet item to hold, then spin around in the field to evolve it into Alcremie—its form will depend on which direction you spin, for how long, and at what time of day.

219 Sirfetch'd

Obtain a Farfetch'd and have it land three critical hits in one battle to evolve it into Sirfetch'd.

328 Runerigus

Obtain a Yamask from the Galar region and let it take damage without fainting over many battles. When it has taken enough total damage, even if you've healed it in between battles, pass under the arch formed by a large stone slab in the Stony Wilderness in the Wild Area. The Yamask will evolve into Runerigus.

Pokémon to hatch from Pokémon Eggs

In general, you'll be able to find Pokémon Eggs that will hatch into the first Pokémon in an Evolutionary line if you follow the steps outlined on page 234. But a few species will only hatch if one of the Pokémon you leave at the Pokémon Nursery is holding a particular incense. You can get the incense you need in Hulbury (p. 69). If you don't seem to have any luck encountering the Pokémon below in the wild, give this method a try!

059 Budew

Hatch an Egg found when you leave a Roselia or a Roserade at the Pokémon Nursery with a Rose Incense.

216 Wynaut

Hatch an Egg found when you leave a Wobbuffet at the Pokémon Nursery with a Lax Incense.

252 Bonsly

Hatch an Egg found when you leave a Sudowoodo at the Pokémon Nursery with a Rock Incense.

260 Munchlax

Hatch an Egg found when you leave a Snorlax at the Pokémon Nursery with a Full Incense.

354 Mantyke

Hatch an Egg found when you leave a Mantine at the Pokémon Nursery with a Wave Incense.

364 Mime Jr.

Hatch an Egg found when you leave a Mr. Mime or a Mr. Rime at the Pokémon Nursery with an Odd Incense.

386 Deino

Hatch an Egg found when you leave a Zweilous or a Hydreigon at the Pokémon Nursery.

! Most Pokémon species can be hatched from Pokémon Eggs without needing to do anything very unusual to find them. You may want to give this method a try to get species for your Pokédex such as Pichu and Cleffa, which are hard to encounter otherwise!

Pokémon you can only encounter in Max Raid Battles

There are some Pokémon you can catch in the wild but only in Max Raid Battles! Scour all of the Pokémon Dens in the Wild Area if you hope to catch these Pokémon for your Pokédex, or else try to obtain them through another method.

No.	Pokémon	May appear in dens with weak pillars of light					May appear in dens with strong pillars of light				
		1★	2★	3★	4★	5★	1★	2★	3★	4★	5★
077	Mamoswine	—	—	—	○	○	—	—	—	○	○
106	Shedinja	—	—	—	—	—	—	—	—	—	○
129	Cherrim	—	—	○	○	○	—	—	○	○	○
160	Centiskorch	—	—	—	○	○	—	—	—	—	○
172	Pichu	○	—	—	—	—	○	—	—	—	—
173	Raichu	—	—	—	—	○	—	—	—	—	—
175	Swoobat	—	—	○	○	○	—	—	○	○	○
173	Alcremie	—	—	—	○	○	—	—	—	—	○
206	Flapple	—	—	—	—	○	—	—	—	—	○
207	Appletun	—	—	—	—	○	—	—	—	—	○
211	Slurpuff	—	—	—	—	○	—	—	○	○	○
213	Aromatisse	—	—	—	—	○	—	—	○	○	○
219	Sirfetch'd	—	—	—	○	○	—	—	—	—	○
225	Scrafty	—	—	○	○	○	—	—	○	○	○
237	Cursola	—	—	—	—	—	—	—	—	○	○
245	Salazzle	—	○	○	—	—	—	—	—	○	○
254	Cleffa	○	—	—	—	—	—	—	—	—	—
257	Togepi	○	—	—	—	—	○	—	—	—	—
263	Whimsicott	—	—	—	—	○	—	—	—	○	○
266	Rhyperior	—	—	—	—	○	—	—	—	—	○
274	Escavalier	—	—	—	—	—	—	—	—	—	○
276	Accelgor	—	—	—	—	—	—	—	—	—	○
291	Malamar	—	—	○	○	○	—	—	—	○	○
311	Toxtricity	—	—	○	○	○	—	—	○	○	○
319	Heliolisk	—	—	○	○	○	—	—	—	○	○
322	Vibrava	—	—	○	○	—	—	—	—	—	○
325	Fraxure	—	—	○	○	—	—	—	—	—	○
328	Runerigus	—	—	○	○	○	—	—	○	○	○
334	Rapidash	—	—	—	—	○	—	—	○	○	○
336	Polteageist	—	—	—	○	○	—	—	—	○	○
339	Trevenant	—	—	—	○	○	—	—	○	○	○
350	Frosmoth	—	—	—	○	○	—	—	○	○	○
366	Mr. Rime	—	—	○	○	○	—	—	—	○	○
368	Darmanitan	—	—	—	—	○	—	—	—	—	○
378	Charmander	—	—	—	—	—	○	○	—	—	—
379	Charmeleon	—	—	—	—	—	—	○	○	—	—
380	Charizard	—	—	—	—	—	—	—	—	—	○
388	Hydreigon	—	—	—	—	○	—	—	—	—	○
389	Goomy	○	○	—	—	—	○	○	—	—	—
390	Sliggoo	—	—	○	○	○	—	—	○	○	○
391	Goodra	—	—	—	○	○	—	—	—	○	○
397	Dragapult	—	—	—	—	○	—	—	—	—	○

And don't forget about version-exclusive Pokémon (p.24)! Some Pokémon are only available in one version or another, so you'll need to trade with other players to get them for your Pokédex!

Gigantamax Pokémon

During your adventures, you may notice that some Pokémon don't just get big when they Dynamax—their appearance changes, too! These Pokémon are Gigantamax Pokémon. They're incredibly rare, but you'll run into them in Pokémon Dens if you're lucky, and they're definitely worth catching. Each has access to a special G-Max Move that has different effects than the regular Max Move it's based on!

> In addition to being powerful additions to your team, Gigantamax Pokémon will have their own entries in your Pokédex! Their Pokédex entries will be added as a separate form of the original Pokémon. While these entries are fun to obtain and read, they don't count toward completing the Pokédex. If you're focusing on that, you don't need to hunt down each and every Gigantamax Pokémon!

Pokémon must have the Gigantamax Factor in order to Gigantamax—and not every specimen does. In other words, a Butterfree you catch in the Galar region will only transform into Gigantamax Butterfree if it has the Gigantamax Factor. Otherwise, your Butterfree will transform into the more common Dynamax Butterfree when you Dynamax it.

The Gigantamax Factor can't be passed on to Eggs, either—leaving a Pokémon with the Gigantamax Factor at the Nursery with another Pokémon will only let you find Eggs for Pokémon that will turn into their normal Dynamax form. On the following pages is a list of all Pokémon species known to date that can sometimes be found with the Gigantamax Factor. Still, this phenomenon is shrouded in mystery, so who knows? There might be other Pokémon out there that can Gigantamax, too...

How to recognize Pokémon with the Gigantamax Factor

If you're lucky enough to get a Pokémon with the Gigantamax Factor for yourself, you won't want to accidentally trade it away or anything! But how do you recognize these Pokémon? When they aren't Dynamaxed in a battle, they will look just like any other specimen you might have caught. But there is one way to tell that they have the Gigantamax Factor, even outside of battle. Check their summary screen! You will see a special mark on a Pokémon that has the Gigantamax Factor.

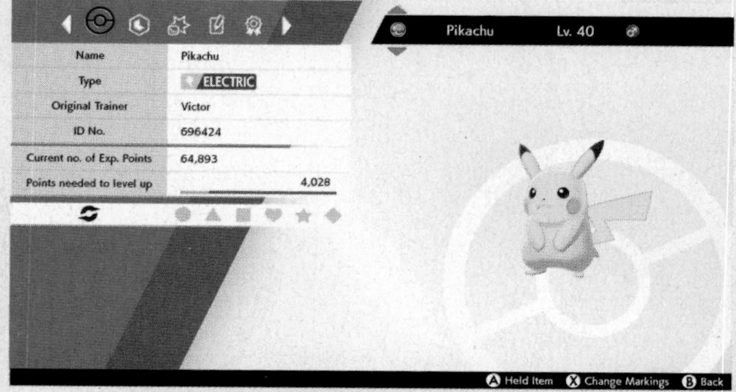

This Pokémon does not have the Gigantamax Factor. It will turn into regular Dynamax Pikachu if you Dynamax it in battle.

This Pokémon *does* have the Gigantamax Factor. It will turn into Gigantamax Pikachu if you Dynamax it in battle.

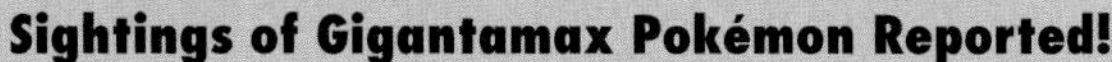

Sightings of Gigantamax Pokémon Reported!

Gigantamax Pokémon are incredibly rare, but we've managed to gather some rumors and reports from Trainers who say they've spotted them in the Wild Area! While it's hard to know if such fantastically rare encounters can be trusted, these reports might just give you an idea of places to start looking. Gather up your Wishing Pieces, use the tips below, and try visiting the dens marked here if you want to try your luck at them. But don't limit your search to only these dens—who knows what other rare finds you might overlook if you do! Here are a few reminders of how to maximize your chances of hitting upon one of those elusive encounters with a Gigantamax Pokémon.

North Wild Area

1. Gigantamax Pokémon will only appear in five-star Max Raid Battles. You can trigger five-star Max Raid Battles once you obtain the Dragon Badge, so don't start expecting to see any before then! You can take part in other Max Raid Battles but only against Dynamax Pokémon. And even in five-star Max Raid Battles, Gigantamax Pokémon are incredibly rare!

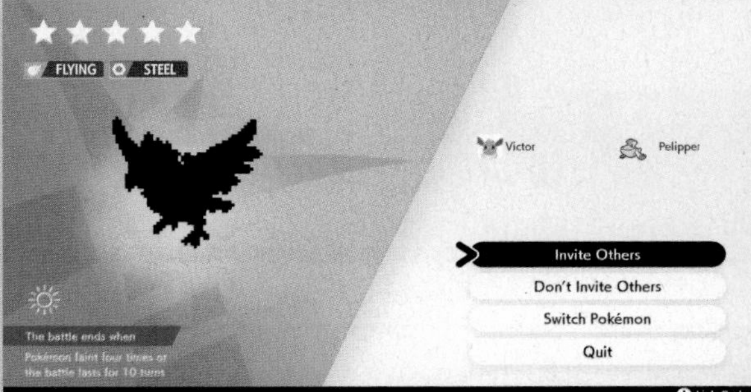

South Wild Area

2. Keep your eyes open for pillars of light that seem more purple in hue, wreathed in swirling energy. Dens emitting this kind of light are more likely to have rare Pokémon hiding in them, including Gigantamax Pokémon! More on page 270.

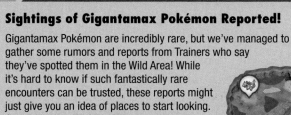

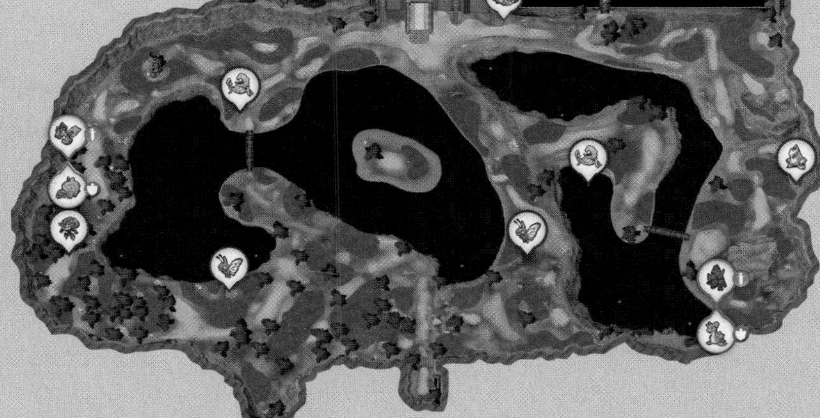

3. Don't be afraid to use Wishing Pieces! Throwing a Wishing Piece into a dormant Pokémon Den will attract a wild Dynamax Pokémon, and it can even attract wild Gigantamax Pokémon if you're incredibly lucky! You can use as many Wishing Pieces as you want in a day, but you can only use Wishing Pieces to lure one Pokémon at a time. If you use a second Wishing Piece before battling the Pokémon lured by the first Wishing Piece, the first Pokémon will go away and you'll lose your chance to battle it!

4. Each day, aim to beat every den that has a pillar of light erupting from it! New dens light up in the Wild Area daily. If you manage to defeat the Dynamax Pokémon in each one, a new set of dens will light up—and when they do, at least one will be guaranteed to contain a rare Pokémon!

Get Three Guaranteed Gigantamax Pokémon!

If you have save data from *Pokémon: Let's Go, Pikachu!* or *Pokémon: Let's Go, Eevee!*, head to the station by the Meetup Spot in the Wild Area! Near the gates to the track, you'll find a girl and a boy who seem interested in the experiences you've shared with Pikachu and Eevee. The girl will give you a Gigantamax Pikachu if you have save data from *Pokémon: Let's Go, Pikachu!* on your Nintendo Switch, while the boy will give you a Gigantamax Eevee if you have save data for *Pokémon: Let's Go, Eevee!*

There's another Pokémon with the Gigantamax Factor that you can obtain. After defeating Leon in the Championship Match, stop by his home—in his room, you'll find a Charmander that has the Gigantamax Factor! Evolve it into Charizard and you'll be able to see its powerful Gigantamax form for yourself!

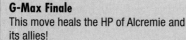

Alcremie

G-Max Finale
This move heals the HP of Alcremie and its allies!

Flapple

Appletun

G-Max Tartness
This move reduces the evasiveness of opponents!

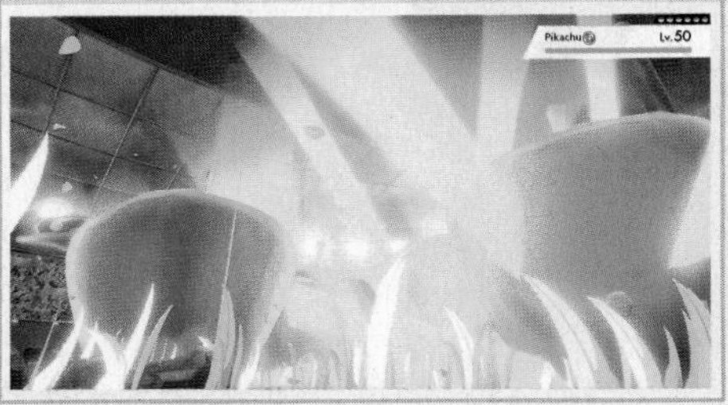

G-Max Sweetness
This move heals the status conditions of Appletun and its allies!

 Butterfree

G-Max Befuddle
This move inflicts the poisoned, paralyzed, or asleep status condition on opponents!

 Centiskorch

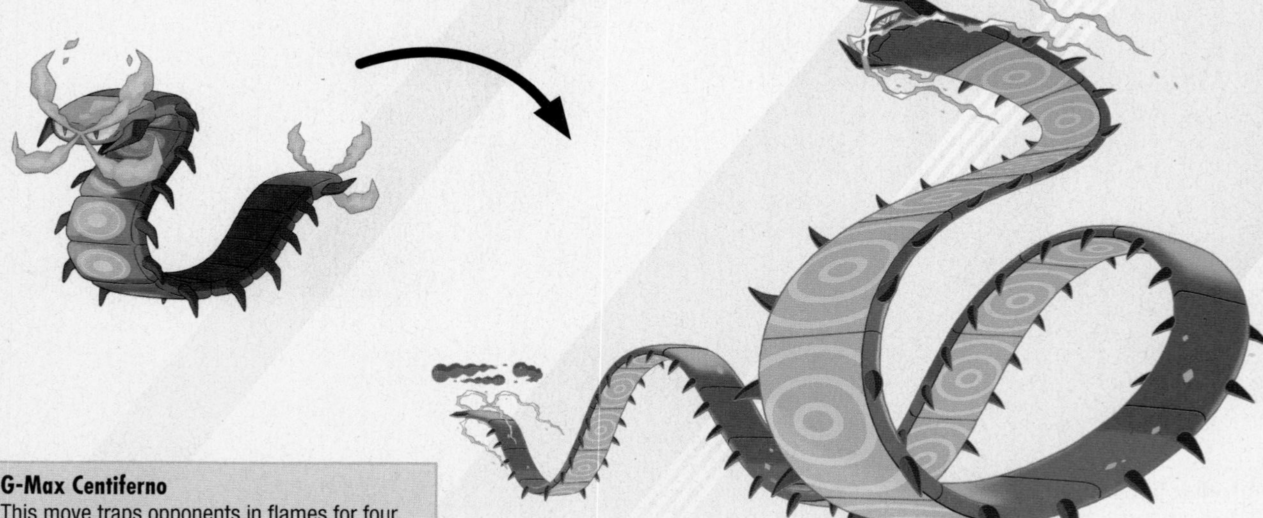

G-Max Centiferno
This move traps opponents in flames for four to five turns!

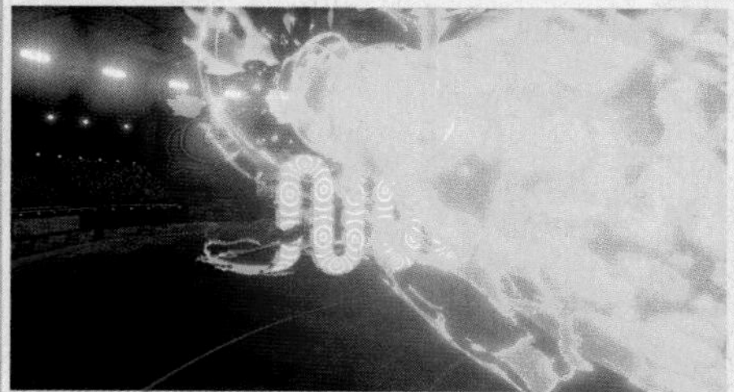

Charizard

G-Max Wildfire
This move continues to deal damage to opponents for four turns!

Coalossal

G-Max Volcalith
This move continues to deal damage to opponents for four turns!

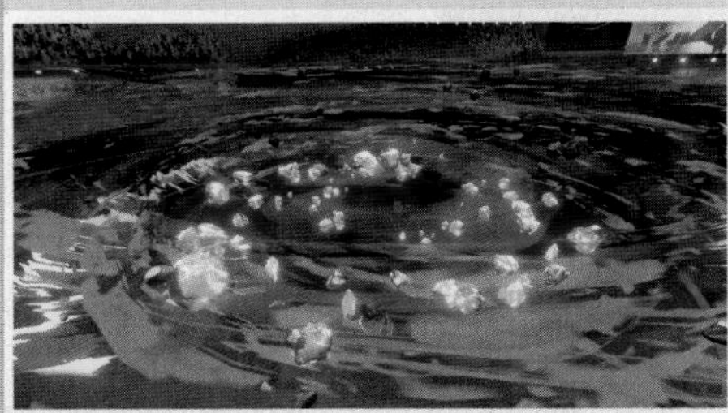

Copperajah

G-Max Steelsurge
This move scatters sharp spikes around the field!

Corviknight

G-Max Wind Rage
This move removes the effects of moves like Light Screen and Reflect!

Drednaw

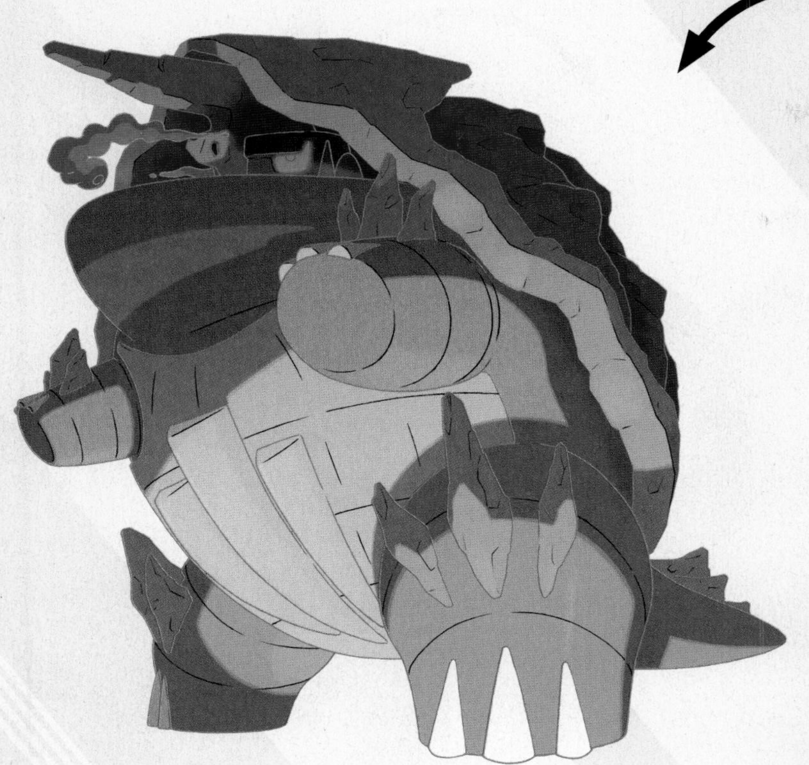

G-Max Stonesurge
This move scatters sharp stones around the field!

Duraludon

G-Max Depletion
This move reduces the PP of opponents' moves by 2!

Eevee

G-Max Cuddle
This move infatuates opponents!

 Garbodor

G-Max Malodor
This move poisons opponents!

Gengar

G-Max Terror
This move prevents opponents from escaping!

Grimmsnarl

G-Max Snooze
This move causes the opponent to fall asleep at the end of the next turn!

Hatterene

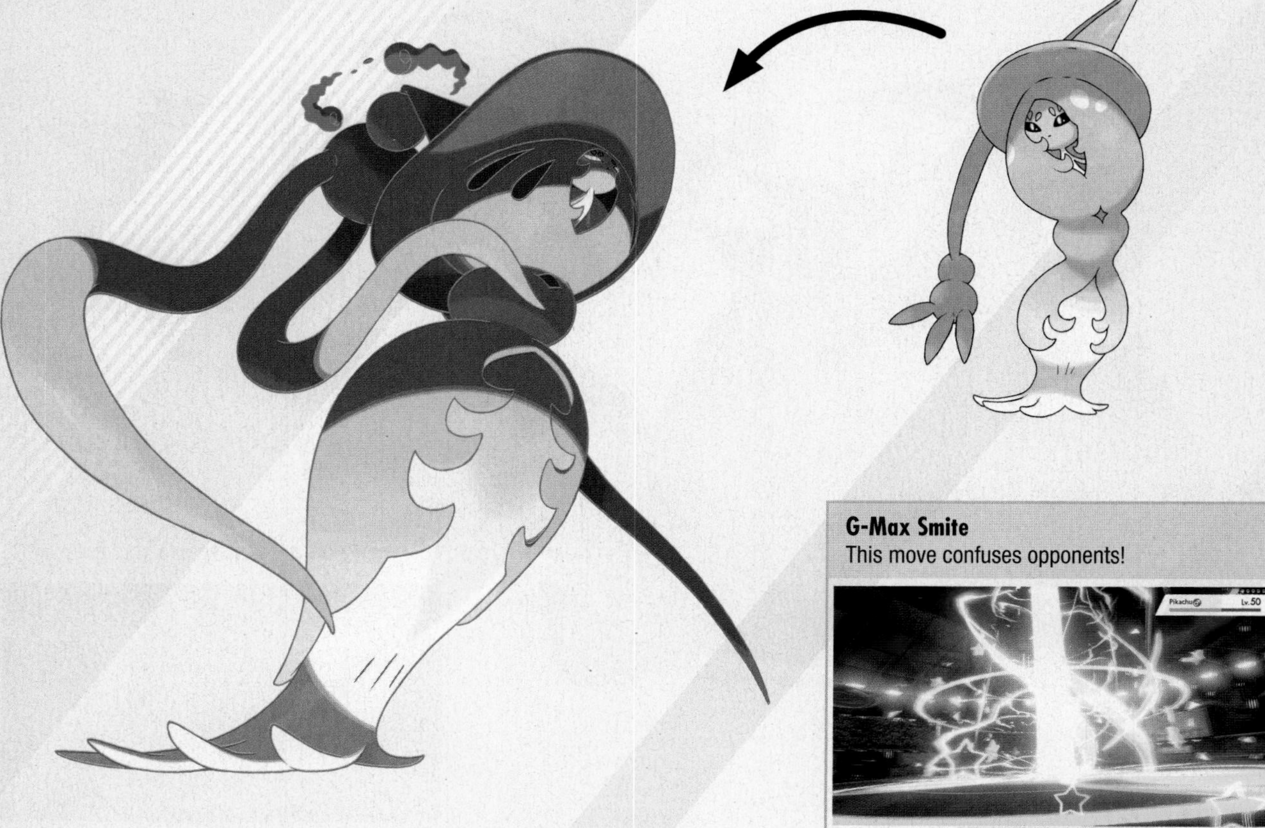

G-Max Smite
This move confuses opponents!

Kingler

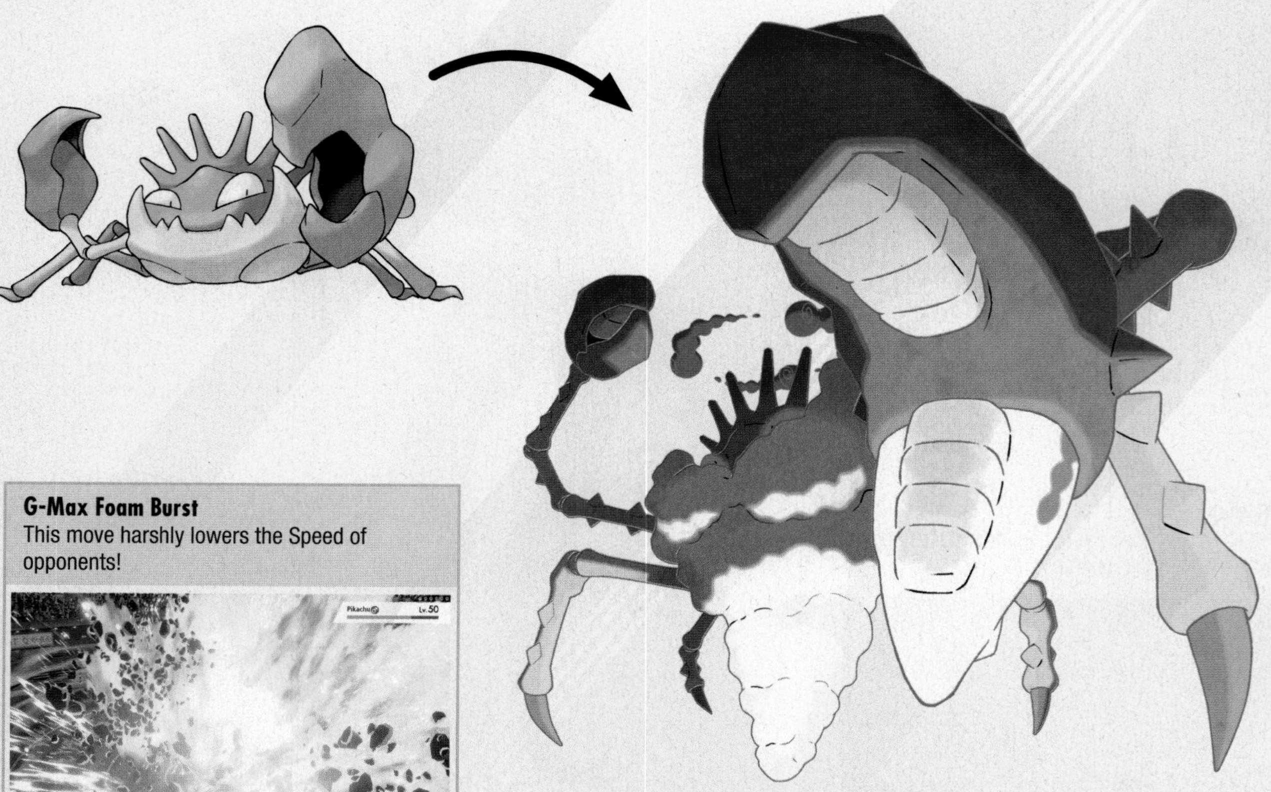

G-Max Foam Burst
This move harshly lowers the Speed of opponents!

Lapras

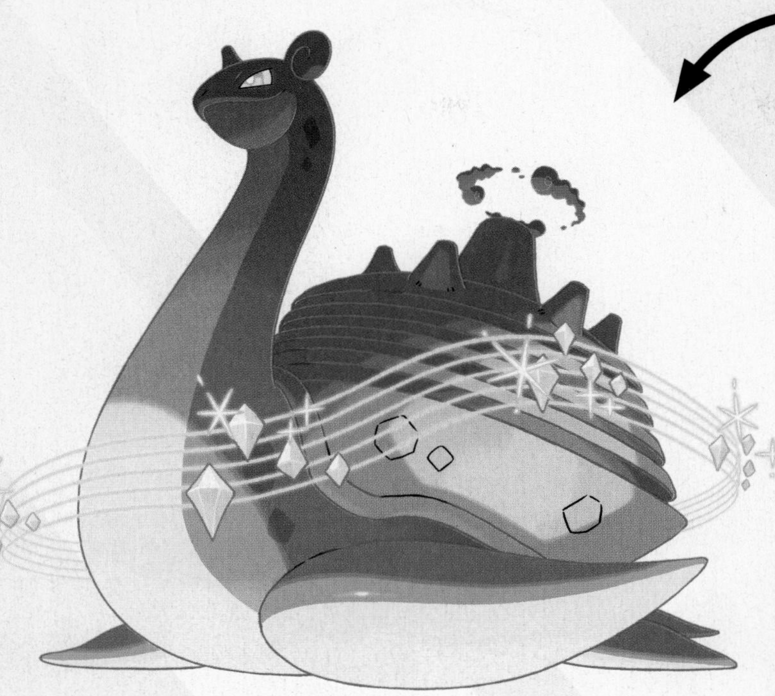

G-Max Resonance
This move reduces incoming damage for five turns!

 Machamp

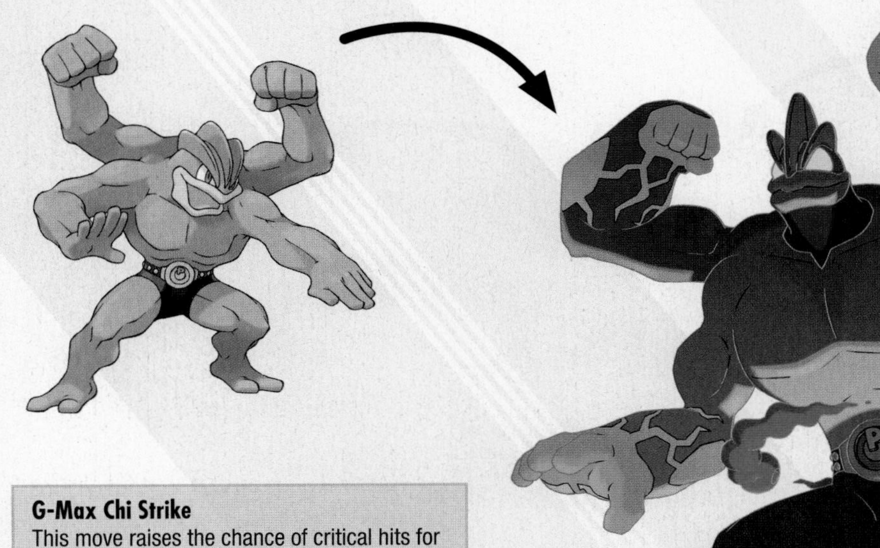

G-Max Chi Strike
This move raises the chance of critical hits for Machamp and its allies!

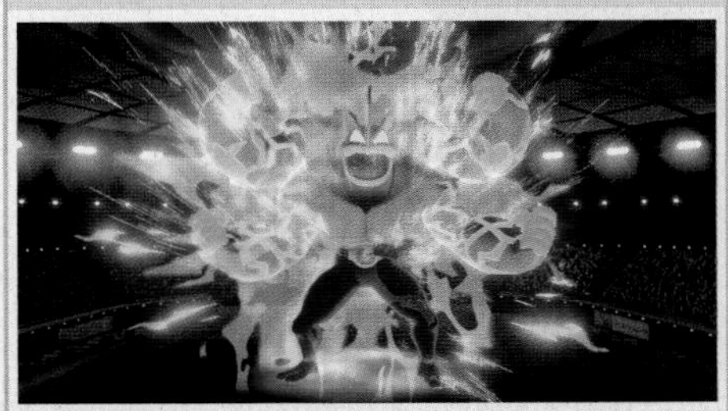

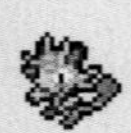

Meowth

G-Max Gold Rush
This move confuses opponents and also awards extra money after the battle!

Orbeetle

G-Max Gravitas
This move increases gravity for five turns!

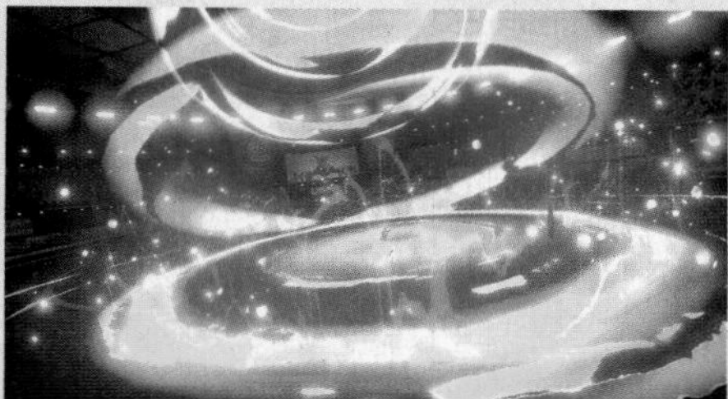

Pikachu

G-Max Volt Crash
This move paralyzes opponents!

 Sandaconda

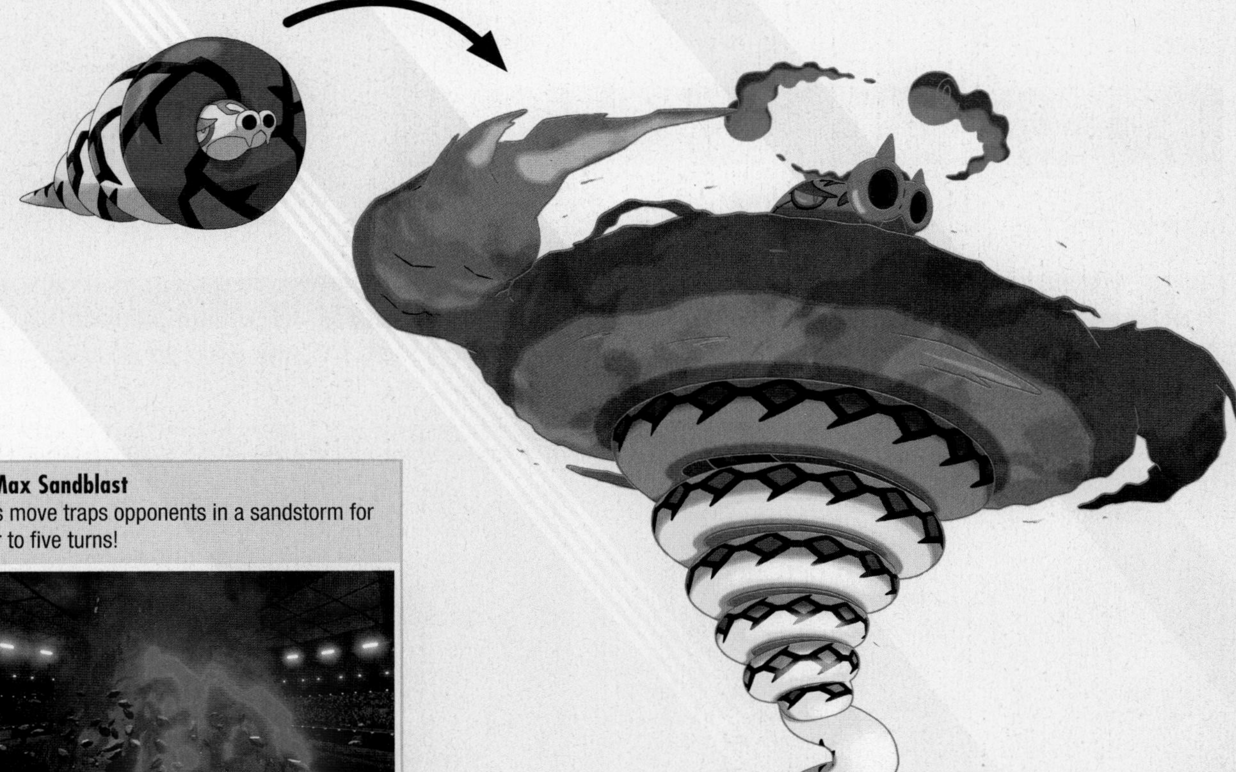

G-Max Sandblast
This move traps opponents in a sandstorm for four to five turns!

Ribbons, Marks, and Special Titles

If you've played another game in the Pokémon series, you may remember that Pokémon can be awarded Ribbons for doing certain things, like defeating the Champion of a region or becoming friendly with their Trainer. Ribbons in *Pokémon Sword* and *Pokémon Shield* have an added perk—they give your Pokémon different titles! Each Ribbon gives a different title, which you can choose to display in battle when you send out that Pokémon.

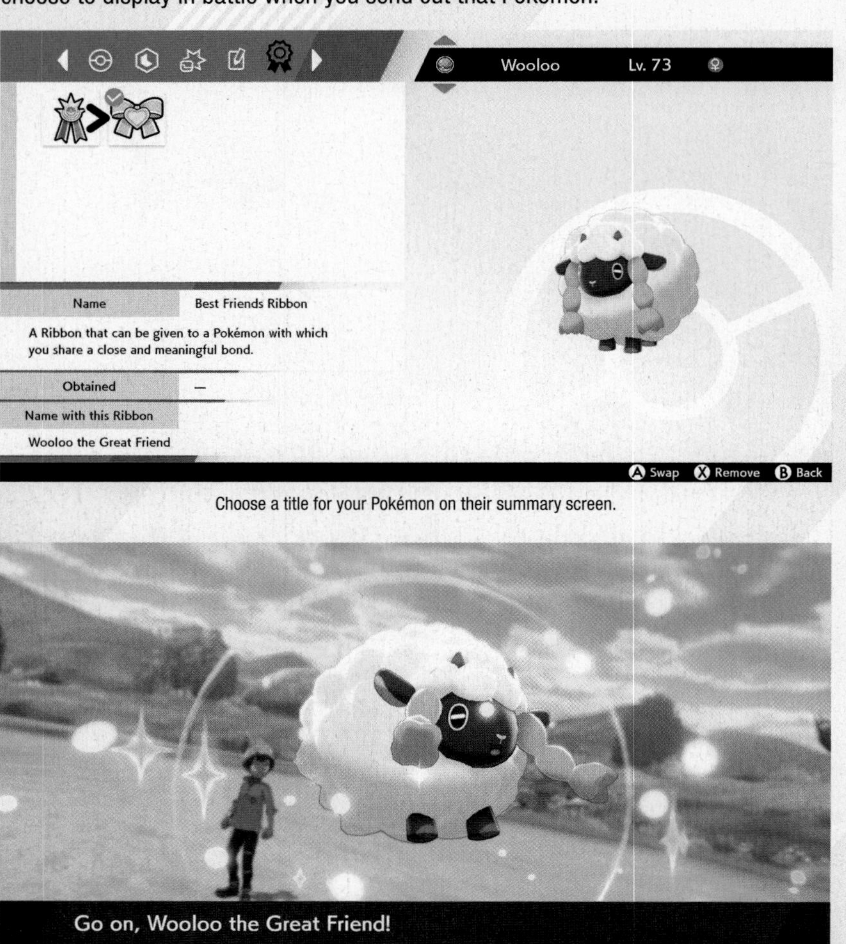

Choose a title for your Pokémon on their summary screen.

It'll display during battle!

Joining Ribbons in the same spot on a Pokémon's status screen are marks. Marks also give special titles and work nearly identically to Ribbons. The difference is in how you get them. Your Pokémon are guaranteed to get certain Ribbons when they accomplish a particular task, but getting marks is based on chance. If you're lucky, Pokémon you catch may have a mark. Which mark they have can change depending on how and when you catch them, too. If you're looking to get a Pokémon with a specific title that you'd like to show off, check out the lists below for each Ribbon and mark—plus the titles they give and how you can get them!

Remember, you can only ever have one title active on a Pokémon. If you choose a new title to use, it'll replace the old one. But you can swap them again as many times as you like!

Ribbons

There are several Ribbons a Pokémon can earn in *Pokémon Sword* and *Pokémon Shield*. If they get one of these Ribbons, they will be able to show off their special title in battle!

Ribbon	Title	How to get it
Galar Champion Ribbon	the Galar Champion	Defeat the Champion with this Pokémon on your team.
Tower Master Ribbon	the Tower Master	Reach Master Ball Tier in the Battle Tower (p. 200), and defeat Leon with this Pokémon on your team.
Master Rank Ribbon	the Rank Master	Win a Ranked Battle (p. 203) against a Master Ball Tier player with this Pokémon on your team.

Ribbon	Title	How to get it
Best Friends Ribbon	the Great Friend	Show a Pokémon with max friendship to a boy in a house in Hammerlocke (p. 82).
Effort Ribbon	the Once Well-Trained	Show a Pokémon with maxed-out base points to a woman in a house in Hammerlocke.

Ribbons from past games

There are also Ribbons that Pokémon could get in past games. With the release of Pokémon HOME (p. 209), you may be able to bring Pokémon with some of these Ribbons to your game and see them shine with the special titles their Ribbons award them. If you have a Pokémon from a past title in the Pokémon series that has a Ribbon, consider trying to bring it to the Galar region!

Some of these Ribbons are available in other, older games as well, but in most cases, only the most recent games are listed as the easiest way to get a Pokémon with one!

Ribbons you could obtain in *Pokémon Ultra Sun, Pokémon Ultra Moon, Pokémon Sun,* or *Pokémon Moon*

Ribbon	Title
Alola Champion Ribbon	the Alola Champion
Battle Royal Master Ribbon	the Royal Master
Battle Tree Great Ribbon	the Tree Victor
Battle Tree Master Ribbon	the Tree Master
Footprint Ribbon	the Strutter

Ribbons you could obtain in *Pokémon Omega Ruby* or *Pokémon Alpha Sapphire*

Ribbon	Title
Hoenn Champion Ribbon	the Hoenn Champion
Contest Star Ribbon	the Shining Star
Coolness Master Ribbon	the Former Star
Beauty Master Ribbon	the Vintage Beauty
Cuteness Master Ribbon	the Former Idol
Cleverness Master Ribbon	the Historic Genius
Toughness Master Ribbon	the Formerly Buff
Gorgeous Ribbon	the Gorgeous
Royal Ribbon	the Royal
Gorgeous Royal Ribbon	the Gorgeous Royal

Ribbons you could obtain in *Pokémon Omega Ruby, Pokémon Alpha Sapphire, Pokémon X,* or *Pokémon Y*

Ribbon	Title
Training Ribbon	the Tried and True
Skillful Battler Ribbon	the Veteran
Expert Battler Ribbon	the Master
Alert Ribbon	the Once Vigilant
Shock Ribbon	the Once Cowardly
Downcast Ribbon	the Once Shaken
Careless Ribbon	the Once Imperfect
Relax Ribbon	the Once Well-Rested
Snooze Ribbon	the Once Sleepy
Smile Ribbon	the Once Cheery

Ribbons you could obtain in *Pokémon X* or *Pokémon Y*

Ribbon	Title
Kalos Champion Ribbon	the Kalos Champion

Ribbons you could obtain by transferring Pokémon with certain older Ribbons to newer games

Ribbon	Title
Contest Memory Ribbon	the Treasured Memory
Battle Memory Ribbon	the Exciting Memory

Ribbons you could obtain in *Pokémon HeartGold* or *Pokémon SoulSilver*

Ribbon	Title
Legend Ribbon	the Living Legend

Ribbons you could obtain in *Pokémon Diamond, Pokémon Pearl,* or *Pokémon Platinum Version*

Ribbon	Title
Sinnoh Champion Ribbon	the Sinnoh Champion

Ribbons you could obtain in *Pokémon FireRed, Pokémon LeafGreen, Pokémon Ruby, Pokémon Sapphire,* or *Pokémon Emerald*

Ribbon	Title
Champion Ribbon	the Champion

Ribbons you could obtain in *Pokémon Ruby, Pokémon Sapphire,* or *Pokémon Emerald*

Ribbon	Title
Artist Ribbon	the Model for Paintings

Ribbons you could obtain from *Pokémon XD: Gale of Darkness* or *Pokémon Colosseum*

Ribbon	Title
National Ribbon	the Triumphant

Ribbon	Title
Earth Ribbon	the 100× Victorious

Ribbons you could obtain through special gifts or events

Ribbon	Title
Event Ribbon	the Festive
Birthday Ribbon	the Best Buddy
Special Ribbon	the Premium

Ribbon	Title
Souvenir Ribbon	the Cherished
Wishing Ribbon	the Wish Granter
Classic Ribbon	the Pokémon Fan

Ribbon	Title
Premier Ribbon	the Celebratory

Marks

Only Pokémon caught in the Galar region can have marks. Since it's mostly random which one a Pokémon has when you catch it (if it even has one at all), it may take you some time to get a Pokémon with the mark and title you're hoping for. Certain marks can only be on Pokémon caught during certain times of day or certain weather, so check the following tables to see how you can try to get each mark. You wouldn't want to spend time catching Pokémon looking for a mark you can't even get at that time or in that weather!

Mark	Title	How to get it
Lunchtime Mark	the Peckish	Pokémon caught after noon (12:00 p.m. to 6:59 p.m.) have a small chance of having this mark.
Dusk Mark	the Dozy	Pokémon caught in the evening (7:00 p.m. to 7:59 p.m.) have a small chance of having this mark.
Sleepy-Time Mark	the Sleepy	Pokémon caught at night (8:00 p.m. to 11:59 p.m.) have a small chance of having this mark.
Dawn Mark	the Early Riser	Pokémon caught in the morning (6:00 a.m. to 11:59 a.m.) have a small chance of having this mark.

Mark	Title	How to get it
Cloudy Mark	the Cloud Watcher	Pokémon caught while it's cloudy have a small chance of having this mark.
Rainy Mark	the Sodden	Pokémon caught while it's raining have a small chance of having this mark.
Stormy Mark	the Thunderstruck	Pokémon caught during a thunderstorm have a small chance of having this mark.
Snowy Mark	the Snow Frolicker	Pokémon caught while it's snowing have a small chance of having this mark.
Blizzard Mark	the Shivering	Pokémon caught during a blizzard have a small chance of having this mark.

Mark	Title	How to get it
Dry Mark	the Parched	Pokémon caught while in harsh sunlight have a small chance of having this mark.
Sandstorm Mark	the Sandswept	Pokémon caught during a sandstorm have a small chance of having this mark.
Misty Mark	the Mist Drifter	Pokémon caught while it's foggy have a small chance of having this mark.

Mark	Title	How to get it
Fishing Mark	the Catch of the Day	Pokémon caught while fishing have a good chance of having this mark.
Curry Mark	the Curry Connoisseur	Pokémon that come to your camp after you've cooked curry will have this mark.
Uncommon Mark	the Sociable	Any Pokémon caught has a small chance of having this mark.

Marks that any Pokémon caught has a very small chance of having

Mark	Title
Rowdy Mark	the Rowdy
Absent-Minded Mark	the Spacey
Jittery Mark	the Anxious
Excited Mark	the Giddy
Charismatic Mark	the Radiant
Calmness Mark	the Serene
Intense Mark	the Feisty
Zoned-Out Mark	the Daydreamer
Joyful Mark	the Joyful
Angry Mark	the Furious

Mark	Title
Smiley Mark	the Beaming
Teary Mark	the Teary-Eyed
Upbeat Mark	the Chipper
Peeved Mark	the Grumpy
Intellectual Mark	the Scholar
Ferocious Mark	the Rampaging
Crafty Mark	the Opportunist
Scowling Mark	the Stern
Kindly Mark	the Kindhearted
Flustered Mark	the Easily Flustered

Mark	Title
Pumped-Up Mark	the Driven
Zero Energy Mark	the Apathetic
Prideful Mark	the Arrogant
Unsure Mark	the Reluctant
Humble Mark	the Humble
Thorny Mark	the Pompous
Vigor Mark	the Lively
Slump Mark	the Worn-Out

Marks that any Pokémon caught has an extremely small chance of having

Mark	Title
Rare Mark	the Recluse

You won't be able to tell if a Pokémon has a mark or not when you encounter it in the wild—the only way to find out is to actually catch it! The Wild Area will always have a variety of weather conditions and plenty of ways to encounter Pokémon, so that's a good place to try to catch Pokémon with marks!

Finding Pokémon Eggs

The Pokémon Nurseries on Route 5 and in the Wild Area are important locations for up-and-coming Trainers. Finding Pokémon Eggs in these places can give you all kinds of benefits! Eggs allow you to obtain more than one of a rare Pokémon species for trading or collecting. They can also help you obtain earlier Evolutions of Pokémon that can't be found in the wild, which is essential if you hope to complete your Galar Pokédex!

Trainers looking for an edge in competitive battles against other players can also use Eggs to obtain Pokémon with preferred Abilities and Natures, great individual strengths, and moves they'd never have in the wild. Read on to find out how you can master this egg-cellent practice of finding Eggs that will hatch into first-rate Pokémon!

Your quick guide to Eggs!

- Leave a male and female Pokémon at the Nursery
  -  Or Ditto and another Pokémon of any gender!
- Check that they share at least one Egg Group
  -  Unless one is Ditto!
- Be sure they aren't in the No Eggs Discovered group
  - Even with Ditto, you won't find an Egg!
- Find Pokémon Eggs after a while
  -  An Oval Charm will sure help!
- Carry the Eggs in your party until they hatch
  -  Use Abilities to speed up hatching!
  -   Riding your bike speeds up hatching, too!

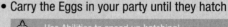

These are just the basics, but read on for all the details you need to know!

How to find and hatch Pokémon Eggs

1. Leave a male and female Pokémon together at a Pokémon Nursery

For most species of Pokémon, both male and female genders exist, though in some cases, all the Pokémon of a species will be of just one gender or their gender will be unknown altogether! The Pokémon Egg Group tables on the pages following this section list the genders of all Pokémon species found in the Galar region. You usually need to leave a male and female Pokémon at a Pokémon Nursery to find a Pokémon Egg, though you can find the Eggs of some gender-unknown Pokémon if you leave them with a Ditto! Much more to come about this special Egg-finding ally below.

2. The two Pokémon you leave at the Nursery should share an Egg Group

Like with types, every Pokémon belongs to at least one Egg Group. The two Pokémon you leave at the Nursery must share at least one Egg Group if you hope to find an Egg while they're there. Once again, the only exception is the uniquely capable Ditto. If you leave Ditto in a Nursery with a Pokémon from any other Egg Group, you'll be able to find Eggs—so long as the other Pokémon isn't from the No Eggs Discovered group. As the group name suggests, no Eggs have ever been found for these Pokémon, so invest your hatching efforts elsewhere.

You can find Ditto in the wild to the west of the Lake of Outrage, which lies in the Wild Area, near Hammerlocke (p. 262). If you're serious about hatching Eggs, Ditto is an absolute must-catch Pokémon! But remember—you won't find any Eggs if you leave two Ditto at the Nursery!

Pokémon Getting Along

After you've dropped off your two Pokémon, the Nursery worker can give you an idea of how likely you are to find an Egg soon—or ever. To up your chances of getting an Egg as soon as possible, try to leave two Pokémon of the same species—especially Pokémon that have different original Trainers. If you get the dreaded last message below, read through steps 1 and 2 again to check what you might've missed!

Nursery worker's judgment	Your outlook for finding Eggs
"They really seem to enjoy each other's company."	Outlook is great!
"They seem to get along all right."	Outlook is just average
"They don't seem very fond of one another."	It's going to take a while
"They don't seem to like playing together at all..."	You'll never find an Egg

The Oval Charm will help you find Pokémon Eggs at the Nursery more quickly, simply by being in your Bag! After you've become the Champion, you can get the Oval Charm by defeating Morimoto at Hotel Ionia in Circhester (p. 106).

Try exploring the vast Wild Area on your bike to hatch Eggs, and you can also look for other Pokémon, rack up Watts (p. 275), or hunt for Max Raid Battles (p. 271) at the same time!

3. Keep the Egg in your party as you travel

Talk to the person who runs the Nursery to pick up your Egg. You'll know they have an Egg for you when their posture changes and it looks like they're thinking about something. To make it hatch, put the Egg in your party while you travel around. If you want to speed up this process, add a Pokémon with the Ability Flame Body or Steam Engine to your party. Any Eggs you're carrying will hatch in half the time, since they've been kept toasty warm! Try catching a Rolycoly along Route 3 or a Carkol in Galar Mine, since they can both have Steam Engine. Carkol's other common Ability is Flame Body, so you really can't go wrong with it! Riding your Rotom Bike will also help shorten the time needed for your Eggs to hatch. Route 5 is an excellent place for this—cycle back and forth across the bridge using your turbo boost (p. 68), and you'll be hatching Eggs like there's no tomorrow!

What will hatch from your Pokémon Egg?

Pokémon Eggs hatch into Lv. 1 Pokémon, and they inherit most of their characteristics from the two Pokémon you leave at the Nursery. A Pokémon Egg will usually hatch into the earliest Evolution of the female Pokémon's species. However, if one of the Pokémon left at the Nursery is a Ditto, the Egg will always be from the same Evolutionary line as the non-Ditto Pokémon. That's true even if the non-Ditto Pokémon is male or gender unknown, unless it's from the No Eggs Discovered group, of course.

Leave a female Sandaconda and a male Duraludon at the Nursery together, and you'll find an Egg that hatches into a Silicobra!

Finding Eggs Using Incense

In an interesting exception to the above rule, Eggs found for just a handful of Pokémon will not hatch into the earliest Evolution of their species without the use of certain incense items. In those cases, you'll have to have one of the Pokémon hold an incense item before you leave it at the Nursery. Take a look at the item list on page 379 to check out these items and which Pokémon they can help you obtain!

Leave a female Snorlax at the Nursery with another Pokémon in its Egg Group or a Ditto. If one of the Pokémon is holding a Full Incense, the Egg you'll find will hatch into a Munchlax!

Eggs inherit their Ability from the female

Like with species, Eggs usually inherit their Ability from the female Pokémon. An Egg is most likely to have the same Ability as the female, but it may also get one of the other regular Abilities that its species can have. An Egg can only inherit a Hidden Ability (p. 182) if the female left at the Nursery has it, though. However, also like with species, if you leave a male or gender-unknown Pokémon at the Nursery with a Ditto, the Egg that hatches will inherit its Ability from the non-Ditto Pokémon.

A female Hattrem with Healer and a male Togedemaru with Iron Barbs will find an Egg that will hatch into a Hatenna and likely have the Healer Ability! (Though it could have Anticipation—another Ability of Hatenna's line!)

Eggs can inherit moves from either Pokémon

Pokémon that hatch from Eggs automatically know some of the basic moves that their species can know at Lv. 1, but they may also know certain moves that they inherit from the two Pokémon left at the Nursery. These can be moves that their species would normally learn at a later level, or they can be rare Egg Moves! Egg Moves are moves that can usually only be inherited by Pokémon as Eggs and cannot be learned by leveling up or from a TM. You can check the full list of Egg Moves for each Pokémon species in an official Pokédex published by The Pokémon Company International.

The Ability Capsule item lets you switch between the two Abilities that a Pokémon species can normally have. Pick up this handy item in exchange for BP at the BP Shop in Wyndon, then use it to swap a Pokémon's Ability to one you'd like it to have or to pass down to an Egg. But remember that an Ability Capsule won't let you switch from a regular Ability to a Hidden Ability, and it won't do anything if the species of the Pokémon you're trying to use it on normally has only one Ability.

Pokémon with brilliant auras may also know Egg Moves! Flip to page 174 to find out more.

Passing on Non-Egg Moves

Egg Moves known by either Pokémon left at the Nursery will always be passed down as long as the Pokémon that hatches can inherit them, but for non-Egg moves, it's not so easy! To pass down a move that the hatched Pokémon would normally learn at a later level, both Pokémon left at the Nursery must know that move. And don't forget—this won't work for moves that the hatched Pokémon species can't learn until it evolves!

Although Egg Moves can usually only be inherited by Pokémon at the time they hatch from Eggs, there's one clever way to teach these moves to a Pokémon you've already raised! If you leave two Pokémon of the same species at the Nursery and one of the Pokémon knows an Egg Move for their species, then the other will learn this move in about the same amount of time it would take them to find an Egg. Make sure the Pokémon you want to pass the Egg Move on to has an empty move slot before you drop them off, and give it a try!

Eggs can inherit their Nature from either Pokémon

Pokémon that hatch from Eggs typically have one of the 25 Natures at random. If you want to choose a specific Nature for your Egg, make sure that one of the Pokémon you leave at the Nursery has that Nature and give it an Everstone to hold. This will guarantee that your Egg will hatch into a Pokémon with the same Nature. Flip to page 365 for the full table of Natures and which stats they affect.

Quiet Nature | Timid Nature | Timid Nature

There are also special mints you can use on your Pokémon to give them the same benefits they could get from a different Nature! These can be bought with BP at the Mint BP Shop in Wyndon (p. 124) or earned in Ranked Battles (p. 203) or the Battle Tower (p. 200).

Eggs can inherit individual strengths from either Pokémon

The two Pokémon you leave at the Nursery will usually pass down a total of three individual strengths (p. 172) to any Eggs found. Which ones are passed down—and from which Pokémon—is usually decided at random. But with the help of certain held items, you can control this process to a certain extent. Leave Pokémon with great individual strengths and the right items at the Nursery, and you'll greatly improve your chances of finding Eggs that are overflowing with potential! All of these items can be obtained in exchange for BP at the BP Shop in the central Pokémon Center in Hammerlocke (p. 80).

Item name	Individual strength passed down
Power Weight	HP of the holder
Power Bracer	Attack of the holder
Power Belt	Defense of the holder
Power Lens	Sp. Atk of the holder
Power Band	Sp. Def of the holder
Power Anklet	Speed of the holder
Destiny Knot	Five individual strengths (rather than the usual three) will be randomly chosen from the two Pokémon left at the Nursery

Eggs can hatch into Pokémon with different forms

Eggs found in Galar will usually hatch into a Pokémon's Galarian form (if it has one), regardless of the form of the Pokémon you left at the Nursery. For example, if you obtain a female Meowth from another region and it finds an Egg in Galar, that Egg will hatch into a Galarian Meowth. If you don't want this to happen, you would need to give that Meowth from another region an Everstone. If a Pokémon is holding an Everstone when you leave it at the Nursery, the Eggs you find will hatch into the same form as the Everstone-holding Pokémon!

Find Shiny Pokémon Faster by Hatching Eggs

If you're hunting for Shiny Pokémon, try leaving two Pokémon caught in different-language versions of the game at the Nursery. There's an increased chance the Pokémon that hatches from the Egg found will be Shiny!

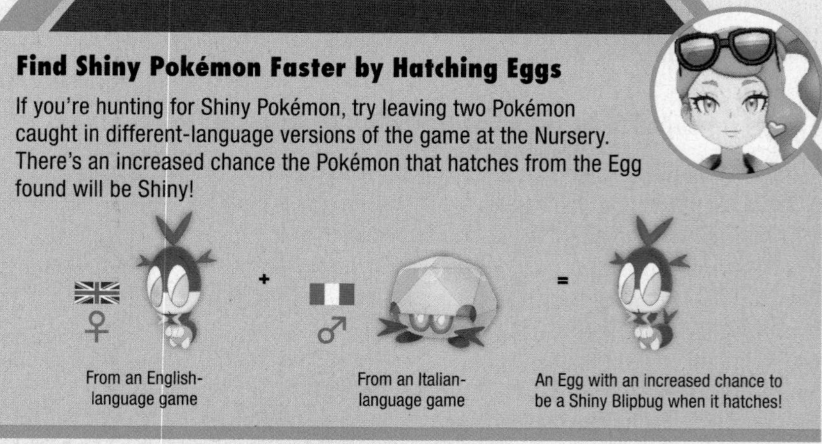

From an English-language game | From an Italian-language game | An Egg with an increased chance to be a Shiny Blipbug when it hatches!

Of all the Pokémon that have Galarian forms, you can only get three of them in different forms within these games.Those three are Meowth, Mr. Mime, and Yamask. But even more forms will become available with the launch of Pokémon HOME (p. 209).

Egg Groups

On the following pages, you'll find tables listing the Egg Groups for all the Pokémon you'll meet in the Galar region. The first column shows their Galar Pokédex number, and you can use this number with the official Galar region Pokédex (sold separately by The Pokémon Company International) for information on where to find each Pokémon. Some Pokémon have multiple forms, whether depending on their Nature (like Toxtricity) or the fact that they might have a regional form (like Meowth). These Pokémon typically have the same Egg Group, so they won't be listed separately. For example, you'll see just one entry for Meowth, even though it can have a different form when it's been brought to Galar from another region.

You'll also see, at the very end, a list of Pokémon in the Egg Group titled No Eggs Discovered. These Pokémon are unique in that you will never be able to find Eggs with them, no matter which Pokémon you pair them with at the Nursery—even Ditto! Just be aware of this so that you don't waste precious time trying to find an unfindable Egg!

> **!** Many Pokémon actually belong to two Egg Groups. For example, Sobble belongs to the Water 1 and Field groups. For these Pokémon, we've listed them under each Egg Group's section—for Sobble, that means you can find it under both the Water 1 Group section and the Field Group section!

Amorphous Group

Amorphous Group Only		
124	Drifloon	♂/♀
125	Drifblim	♂/♀
135	Duskull	♂/♀
136	Dusclops	♂/♀
137	Dusknoir	♂/♀
141	Gastly	♂/♀
142	Haunter	♂/♀
143	Gengar	♂/♀
191	Pumpkaboo	♂/♀
192	Gourgeist	♂/♀
217	Wobbuffet	♂/♀
250	Koffing	♂/♀
251	Weezing	♂/♀
270	Solosis	♂/♀
271	Duosion	♂/♀
272	Reuniclus	♂/♀
287	Litwick	♂/♀
288	Lampent	♂/♀
289	Chandelure	♂/♀
301	Mimikyu	♂/♀
305	Frillish	♂/♀
306	Jellicent	♂/♀
372	Rotom	Unknown

Amorphous Group and Dragon Group		
395	Dreepy	♂/♀
396	Drakloak	♂/♀
397	Dragapult	♂/♀

Amorphous Group and Fairy Group		
185	Milcery	♀ only
186	Alcremie	♀ only

Amorphous Group and Grass Group		
338	Phantump	♂/♀
339	Trevenant	♂/♀

Amorphous Group and Humanlike Group		
120	Ralts	♂/♀
121	Kirlia	♂/♀
122	Gardevoir	♂/♀
123	Gallade	♂ only

Amorphous Group and Mineral Group		
327	Yamask	♂/♀
328	Runerigus	♂/♀
329	Cofagrigus	♂/♀
335	Sinistea	Unknown
336	Polteageist	Unknown

Amorphous Group and Water 1 Group		
226	Stunfisk	♂/♀
230	Shellos	♂/♀
231	Gastrodon	♂/♀
353	Pincurchin	♂/♀

Bug Group

Bug Group Only		
010	Blipbug	♂/♀
011	Dottler	♂/♀
012	Orbeetle	♂/♀
013	Caterpie	♂/♀
014	Metapod	♂/♀
015	Butterfree	♂/♀
016	Grubbin	♂/♀
017	Charjabug	♂/♀
018	Vikavolt	♂/♀
064	Joltik	♂/♀
065	Galvantula	♂/♀
104	Nincada	♂/♀
105	Ninjask	♂/♀
116	Combee	♂/♀
117	Vespiquen	♀ only
159	Sizzlipede	♂/♀
160	Centiskorch	♂/♀
227	Shuckle	♂/♀
273	Karrablast	♂/♀
274	Escavalier	♂/♀
275	Shelmet	♂/♀
276	Accelgor	♂/♀
316	Durant	♂/♀
349	Snom	♂/♀
350	Frosmoth	♂/♀

Bug Group and Dragon Group		
321	Trapinch	♂/♀
322	Vibrava	♂/♀
323	Flygon	♂/♀

Bug Group and Fairy Group		
187	Cutiefly	♂/♀
188	Ribombee	♂/♀

Bug Group and Mineral Group		
086	Dwebble	♂/♀
087	Crustle	♂/♀

Bug Group and Water 1 Group		
214	Dewpider	♂/♀
215	Araquanid	♂/♀

Bug Group and Water 3 Group		
232	Wimpod	♂/♀
233	Golisopod	♂/♀
285	Skorupi	♂/♀
286	Drapion	♂/♀

Ditto Group

Ditto Group Only		
373	Ditto	Unknown

Dragon Group

Dragon Group Only		
386	Deino	♂/♀
387	Zweilous	♂/♀
388	Hydreigon	♂/♀
389	Goomy	♂/♀
390	Sliggoo	♂/♀
391	Goodra	♂/♀
392	Jangmo-o	♂/♀
393	Hakamo-o	♂/♀
394	Kommo-o	♂/♀

Dragon Group and Amorphous Group		
395	Dreepy	♂/♀
396	Drakloak	♂/♀
397	Dragapult	♂/♀

Dragon Group and Bug Group

No.	Pokémon	Gender
321	Trapinch	♂/♀
322	Vibrava	♂/♀
323	Flygon	♂/♀

Dragon Group and Field Group

No.	Pokémon	Gender
224	Scraggy	♂/♀
225	Scrafty	♂/♀
312	Silicobra	♂/♀
313	Sandaconda	♂/♀

Dragon Group and Flying Group

No.	Pokémon	Gender
176	Noibat	♂/♀
177	Noivern	♂/♀

Dragon Group and Grass Group

No.	Pokémon	Gender
205	Applin	♂/♀
206	Flapple	♂/♀
207	Appletun	♂/♀

Dragon Group and Mineral Group

No.	Pokémon	Gender
371	Duraludon	♂/♀

Dragon Group and Monster Group

No.	Pokémon	Gender
244	Salandit	♂/♀
245	Salazzle	♀ only
318	Helioptile	♂/♀
319	Heliolisk	♂/♀
324	Axew	♂/♀
325	Fraxure	♂/♀
326	Haxorus	♂/♀
346	Drampa	♂/♀
347	Turtonator	♂/♀
378	Charmander	♂/♀
379	Charmeleon	♂/♀
380	Charizard	♂/♀

Dragon Group and Water 1 Group

No.	Pokémon	Gender
152	Feebas	♂/♀
153	Milotic	♂/♀

Dragon Group and Water 2 Group

No.	Pokémon	Gender
144	Magikarp	♂/♀
145	Gyarados	♂/♀

Fairy Group

Fairy Group Only

No.	Pokémon	Gender
210	Swirlix	♂/♀
211	Slurpuff	♂/♀
212	Spritzee	♂/♀
213	Aromatisse	♂/♀
241	Hatenna	♀ only
242	Hattrem	♀ only
243	Hatterene	♀ only
255	Clefairy	♂/♀
256	Clefable	♂/♀
337	Indeedee	♂/♀

Fairy Group and Amorphous Group

No.	Pokémon	Gender
185	Milcery	♀ only
186	Alcremie	♀ only

Fairy Group and Bug Group

No.	Pokémon	Gender
187	Cutiefly	♂/♀
188	Ribombee	♂/♀

Fairy Group and Field Group

No.	Pokémon	Gender
194	Pikachu	♂/♀
195	Raichu	♂/♀
295	Mawile	♂/♀
344	Morpeko	♂/♀
348	Togedemaru	♂/♀

Fairy Group and Flying Group

No.	Pokémon	Gender
258	Togetic	♂/♀
259	Togekiss	♂/♀

Fairy Group and Grass Group

No.	Pokémon	Gender
060	Roselia	♂/♀
061	Roserade	♂/♀
128	Cherubi	♂/♀
129	Cherrim	♂/♀
262	Cottonee	♂/♀
263	Whimsicott	♂/♀

Fairy Group and Humanlike Group

No.	Pokémon	Gender
238	Impidimp	♂ only
239	Morgrem	♂ only
240	Grimmsnarl	♂ only

Fairy Group and Mineral Group

No.	Pokémon	Gender
079	Snorunt	♂/♀
080	Glalie	♂/♀
081	Froslass	♀ only
345	Falinks	Unknown

Field Group

Field Group Only

No.	Pokémon	Gender
024	Skwovet	♂/♀
025	Greedent	♂/♀
029	Nickit	♂/♀
030	Thievul	♂/♀
031	Zigzagoon	♂/♀
032	Linoone	♂/♀
033	Obstagoon	♂/♀
034	Wooloo	♂/♀
035	Dubwool	♂/♀
044	Purrloin	♂/♀
045	Liepard	♂/♀
046	Yamper	♂/♀
047	Boltund	♂/♀
048	Bunnelby	♂/♀
049	Diggersby	♂/♀
050	Minccino	♂/♀
051	Cinccino	♂/♀
066	Electrike	♂/♀
067	Manectric	♂/♀
068	Vulpix	♂/♀
069	Ninetales	♂/♀
070	Growlithe	♂/♀
071	Arcanine	♂/♀
075	Swinub	♂/♀
076	Piloswine	♂/♀
077	Mamoswine	♂/♀
084	Mudbray	♂/♀
085	Mudsdale	♂/♀
090	Munna	♂/♀
091	Musharna	♂/♀
094	Stufful	♂/♀
095	Bewear	♂/♀
130	Stunky	♂/♀
131	Skuntank	♂/♀
164	Diglett	♂/♀
165	Dugtrio	♂/♀
166	Drilbur	♂/♀
167	Excadrill	♂/♀
182	Meowth	♂/♀
183	Perrserker	♂/♀
184	Persian	♂/♀
196	Eevee	♂/♀
197	Vaporeon	♂/♀
198	Jolteon	♂/♀
199	Flareon	♂/♀
200	Espeon	♂/♀
201	Umbreon	♂/♀
202	Leafeon	♂/♀
203	Glaceon	♂/♀
204	Sylveon	♂/♀
208	Espurr	♂/♀
209	Meowstic	♂/♀
279	Cubchoo	♂/♀
280	Beartic	♂/♀
292	Sneasel	♂/♀
293	Weavile	♂/♀
300	Torkoal	♂/♀
314	Hippopotas	♂/♀
315	Hippowdon	♂/♀
317	Heatmor	♂/♀
333	Ponyta	♂/♀
334	Rapidash	♂/♀
342	Oranguru	♂/♀
343	Passimian	♂/♀
367	Darumaka	♂/♀
368	Darmanitan	♂/♀

Field Group and Dragon Group

No.	Pokémon	Gender
224	Scraggy	♂/♀
225	Scrafty	♂/♀
312	Silicobra	♂/♀
313	Sandaconda	♂/♀

Field Group and Fairy Group

No.	Pokémon	Gender
194	Pikachu	♂/♀
195	Raichu	♂/♀
295	Mawile	♂/♀
344	Morpeko	♂/♀
348	Togedemaru	♂/♀

Field Group and Flying Group

No.	Pokémon	Gender
174	Woobat	♂/♀
175	Swoobat	♂/♀
218	Farfetch'd	♂/♀
219	Sirfetch'd	♂/♀

Field Group and Grass Group

No.	Pokémon	Gender
001	Grookey	♂/♀
002	Thwackey	♂/♀
003	Rillaboom	♂/♀
039	Seedot	♂/♀
040	Nuzleaf	♂/♀
041	Shiftry	♂/♀

Field Group and Humanlike Group

No.	Pokémon	Gender
004	Scorbunny	♂/♀
005	Raboot	♂/♀
006	Cinderace	♂/♀
111	Pancham	♂/♀
112	Pangoro	♂/♀
299	Lucario	♂/♀

Field Group and Mineral Group

No.	Pokémon	Gender
302	Cufant	♂/♀
303	Copperajah	♂/♀

Field Group and Monster Group

No.	Pokémon	Gender
264	Rhyhorn	♂/♀
265	Rhydon	♂/♀
266	Rhyperior	♂/♀

Field Group and Water 1 Group

No.	Pokémon	Gender
007	Sobble	♂/♀
008	Drizzile	♂/♀
009	Inteleon	♂/♀
078	Delibird	♂/♀
100	Wooper	♂/♀
101	Quagsire	♂/♀
370	Eiscue	♂/♀

Field Group and Water 2 Group

No.	Pokémon	Gender
356	Wailmer	♂/♀
357	Wailord	♂/♀

Flying Group

Flying Group Only

No.	Pokémon	Gender
019	Hoothoot	♂/♀
020	Noctowl	♂/♀
021	Rookidee	♂/♀
022	Corvisquire	♂/♀
023	Corviknight	♂/♀
026	Pidove	♂/♀
027	Tranquill	♂/♀
028	Unfezant	♂/♀
092	Natu	♂/♀
093	Xatu	♂/♀
281	Rufflet	♂ only
282	Braviary	♂ only
283	Vullaby	♀ only
284	Mandibuzz	♀ only
297	Sigilyph	♂/♀

Flying Group and Dragon Group

No.	Pokémon	Gender
176	Noibat	♂/♀
177	Noivern	♂/♀

Flying Group and Fairy Group

No.	Pokémon	Gender
258	Togetic	♂/♀
259	Togekiss	♂/♀

Flying Group and Field Group

No.	Pokémon	Gender
174	Woobat	♂/♀
175	Swoobat	♂/♀
218	Farfetch'd	♂/♀
219	Sirfetch'd	♂/♀

Flying Group and Humanlike Group

No.	Pokémon	Gender
320	Hawlucha	♂/♀

Flying Group and Water 1 Group

No.	Pokémon	Gender
062	Wingull	♂/♀
063	Pelipper	♂/♀
309	Cramorant	♂/♀

Grass Group

Grass Group Only

No.	Pokémon	Gender
052	Bounsweet	♀ only
053	Steenee	♀ only
054	Tsareena	♀ only
055	Oddish	♂/♀
056	Gloom	♂/♀
057	Vileplume	♂/♀
058	Bellossom	♂/♀
126	Gossifleur	♂/♀
127	Eldegoss	♂/♀
296	Maractus	♂/♀
340	Morelull	♂/♀
341	Shiinotic	♂/♀

Grass Group and Amorphous Group

No.	Pokémon	Gender
338	Phantump	♂/♀
339	Trevenant	♂/♀

Grass Group and Dragon Group

No.	Pokémon	Gender
205	Applin	♂/♀
206	Flapple	♂/♀
207	Appletun	♂/♀

Grass Group and Fairy Group

No.	Pokémon	Gender
060	Roselia	♂/♀
061	Roserade	♂/♀
128	Cherubi	♂/♀
129	Cherrim	♂/♀
262	Cottonee	♂/♀
263	Whimsicott	♂/♀

Grass Group and Field Group

No.	Pokémon	Gender
001	Grookey	♂/♀
002	Thwackey	♂/♀
003	Rillaboom	♂/♀
039	Seedot	♂/♀
040	Nuzleaf	♂/♀
041	Shiftry	♂/♀

Grass Group and Mineral Group

No.	Pokémon	Gender
189	Ferroseed	♂/♀
190	Ferrothorn	♂/♀

Grass Group and Monster Group

No.	Pokémon	Gender
096	Snover	♂/♀
097	Abomasnow	♂/♀

Grass Group and Water 1 Group

No.	Pokémon	Gender
036	Lotad	♂/♀
037	Lombre	♂/♀
038	Ludicolo	♂/♀

Humanlike Group

Humanlike Group Only

No.	Pokémon	Gender
108	Hitmonlee	♂ only
109	Hitmonchan	♂ only
110	Hitmontop	♂ only
138	Machop	♂/♀
139	Machoke	♂/♀
140	Machamp	♂/♀
171	Timburr	♂/♀
172	Gurdurr	♂/♀
173	Conkeldurr	♂/♀
222	Croagunk	♂/♀
223	Toxicroak	♂/♀
246	Pawniard	♂/♀
247	Bisharp	♂/♀
248	Throh	♂ only
249	Sawk	♂ only
267	Gothita	♂/♀
268	Gothorita	♂/♀
269	Gothitelle	♂/♀
277	Elgyem	♂/♀
278	Beheeyem	♂/♀
294	Sableye	♂/♀
311	Toxtricity	♂/♀
365	Mr. Mime	♂/♀
366	Mr. Rime	♂/♀

Humanlike Group and Amorphous Group

No.	Pokémon	Gender
120	Ralts	♂/♀
121	Kirlia	♂/♀
122	Gardevoir	♂/♀
123	Gallade	♂ only

Humanlike Group and Fairy Group

No.	Pokémon	Gender
238	Impidimp	♂ only
239	Morgrem	♂ only
240	Grimmsnarl	♂ only

Humanlike Group and Field Group

No.	Pokémon	Gender
004	Scorbunny	♂/♀
005	Raboot	♂/♀
006	Cinderace	♂/♀
111	Pancham	♂/♀
112	Pangoro	♂/♀
299	Lucario	♂/♀

Humanlike Group and Flying Group

No.	Pokémon	Gender
320	Hawlucha	♂/♀

Humanlike Group and Water 1 Group

No.	Pokémon	Gender
351	Clobbopus	♂/♀
352	Grapploct	♂/♀

Mineral Group

Mineral Group Only

No.	Pokémon	Gender
072	Vanillite	♂/♀
073	Vanillish	♂/♀
074	Vanilluxe	♂/♀
082	Baltoy	Unknown
083	Claydol	Unknown
088	Golett	Unknown
089	Golurk	Unknown
106	Shedinja	Unknown
113	Klink	Unknown
114	Klang	Unknown
115	Klinklang	Unknown
118	Bronzor	Unknown
119	Bronzong	Unknown
157	Trubbish	♂/♀
158	Garbodor	♂/♀
161	Rolycoly	♂/♀
162	Carkol	♂/♀
163	Coalossal	♂/♀
168	Roggenrola	♂/♀
169	Boldore	♂/♀
170	Gigalith	♂/♀
178	Onix	♂/♀
179	Steelix	♂/♀
253	Sudowoodo	♂/♀
330	Honedge	♂/♀
331	Doublade	♂/♀
332	Aegislash	♂/♀
360	Dhelmise	Unknown
362	Lunatone	Unknown
363	Solrock	Unknown
369	Stonjourner	♂/♀

Mineral Group and Amorphous Group

No.	Pokémon	Gender
327	Yamask	♂/♀
328	Runerigus	♂/♀
329	Cofagrigus	♂/♀
335	Sinistea	Unknown
336	Polteageist	Unknown

Mineral Group and Bug Group

No.	Pokémon	Gender
086	Dwebble	♂/♀
087	Crustle	♂/♀

ADVANCED TRAINER HANDBOOK

Mineral Group and Dragon Group

No.	Pokémon	Gender
371	Duraludon	♂/♀

Mineral Group and Fairy Group

No.	Pokémon	Gender
079	Snorunt	♂/♀
080	Glalie	♂/♀
081	Froslass	♀ only
345	Falinks	Unknown

Mineral Group and Field Group

No.	Pokémon	Gender
302	Cufant	♂/♀
303	Copperajah	♂/♀

Mineral Group and Grass Group

No.	Pokémon	Gender
189	Ferroseed	♂/♀
190	Ferrothorn	♂/♀

Mineral Group and Monster Group

No.	Pokémon	Gender
358	Bergmite	♂/♀
359	Avalugg	♂/♀

Monster Group

Monster Group Only

No.	Pokémon	Gender
261	Snorlax	♂/♀
383	Larvitar	♂/♀
384	Pupitar	♂/♀
385	Tyranitar	♂/♀

Monster Group and Dragon Group

No.	Pokémon	Gender
244	Salandit	♂/♀
245	Salazzle	♀ only
318	Helioptile	♂/♀
319	Heliolisk	♂/♀
324	Axew	♂/♀
325	Fraxure	♂/♀
326	Haxorus	♂/♀
346	Drampa	♂/♀
347	Turtonator	♂/♀
378	Charmander	♂/♀
379	Charmeleon	♂/♀
380	Charizard	♂/♀

Monster Group and Field Group

No.	Pokémon	Gender
264	Rhyhorn	♂/♀
265	Rhydon	♂/♀
266	Rhyperior	♂/♀

Monster Group and Grass Group

No.	Pokémon	Gender
096	Snover	♂/♀
097	Abomasnow	♂/♀

Monster Group and Mineral Group

No.	Pokémon	Gender
358	Bergmite	♂/♀
359	Avalugg	♂/♀

Monster Group and Water 1 Group

No.	Pokémon	Gender
042	Chewtle	♂/♀
043	Drednaw	♂/♀
361	Lapras	♂/♀

Water 1 Group

Water 1 Group Only

No.	Pokémon	Gender
132	Tympole	♂/♀
133	Palpitoad	♂/♀
134	Seismitoad	♂/♀
156	Pyukumuku	♂/♀
307	Mareanie	♂/♀
308	Toxapex	♂/♀
355	Mantine	♂/♀

Water 1 Group and Amorphous Group

No.	Pokémon	Gender
226	Stunfisk	♂/♀
230	Shellos	♂/♀
231	Gastrodon	♂/♀
353	Pincurchin	♂/♀

Water 1 Group and Bug Group

No.	Pokémon	Gender
214	Dewpider	♂/♀
215	Araquanid	♂/♀

Water 1 Group and Dragon Group

No.	Pokémon	Gender
152	Feebas	♂/♀
153	Milotic	♂/♀

Water 1 Group and Field Group

No.	Pokémon	Gender
007	Sobble	♂/♀
008	Drizzile	♂/♀
009	Inteleon	♂/♀
078	Delibird	♂/♀
100	Wooper	♂/♀
101	Quagsire	♂/♀
370	Eiscue	♂/♀

Water 1 Group and Flying Group

No.	Pokémon	Gender
062	Wingull	♂/♀
063	Pelipper	♂/♀
309	Cramorant	♂/♀

Water 1 Group and Grass Group

No.	Pokémon	Gender
036	Lotad	♂/♀
037	Lombre	♂/♀
038	Ludicolo	♂/♀

Water 1 Group and Humanlike Group

No.	Pokémon	Gender
351	Clobbopus	♂/♀
352	Grapploct	♂/♀

Water 1 Group and Monster Group

No.	Pokémon	Gender
042	Chewtle	♂/♀
043	Drednaw	♂/♀
361	Lapras	♂/♀

Water 1 Group and Water 2 Group

No.	Pokémon	Gender
148	Remoraid	♂/♀
149	Octillery	♂/♀
290	Inkay	♂/♀
291	Malamar	♂/♀

Water 1 Group and Water 3 Group

No.	Pokémon	Gender
102	Corphish	♂/♀
103	Crawdaunt	♂/♀
236	Corsola	♂/♀
237	Cursola	♂/♀

Water 2 Group

Water 2 Group Only

No.	Pokémon	Gender
146	Goldeen	♂/♀
147	Seaking	♂/♀
154	Basculin	♂/♀
155	Wishiwashi	♂/♀
180	Arrokuda	♂/♀
181	Barraskewda	♂/♀
220	Chinchou	♂/♀
221	Lanturn	♂/♀
228	Barboach	♂/♀
229	Whiscash	♂/♀
304	Qwilfish	♂/♀

Water 2 Group and Dragon Group

No.	Pokémon	Gender
144	Magikarp	♂/♀
145	Gyarados	♂/♀

Water 2 Group and Field Group

No.	Pokémon	Gender
356	Wailmer	♂/♀
357	Wailord	♂/♀

Water 2 Group and Water 1 Group

No.	Pokémon	Gender
148	Remoraid	♂/♀
149	Octillery	♂/♀
290	Inkay	♂/♀
291	Malamar	♂/♀

Water 3 Group

Water 3 Group Only

No.	Pokémon	Gender
098	Krabby	♂/♀
099	Kingler	♂/♀
150	Shellder	♂/♀
151	Cloyster	♂/♀
234	Binacle	♂/♀
235	Barbaracle	♂/♀

Water 3 Group and Bug Group

No.	Pokémon	Gender
232	Wimpod	♂/♀
233	Golisopod	♂/♀
285	Skorupi	♂/♀
286	Drapion	♂/♀

Water 3 Group and Water 1 Group

No.	Pokémon	Gender
102	Corphish	♂/♀
103	Crawdaunt	♂/♀
236	Corsola	♂/♀
237	Cursola	♂/♀

No Eggs Discovered

No.	Pokémon	Gender
059	Budew	♂/♀
107	Tyrogue	♂ only
193	Pichu	♂/♀
216	Wynaut	♂/♀
252	Bonsly	♂/♀
254	Cleffa	♂/♀
257	Togepi	♂/♀
260	Munchlax	♂/♀
298	Riolu	♂/♀
310	Toxel	♂/♀
354	Mantyke	♂/♀
364	Mime Jr.	♂/♀
374	Dracozolt	Unknown
375	Arctozolt	Unknown
376	Dracovish	Unknown
377	Arctovish	Unknown
381	Type: Null	Unknown
382	Silvally	Unknown
398	Zacian	Unknown
399	Zamazenta	Unknown
400	???	Unknown

Poké Jobs

When you first reach Motostoke (p. 50), Sonia will introduce you to the Rotomi terminals you'll find in any Pokémon Center. Congratulations! You now have access to all of Rotomi's functions—which includes Poké Jobs!

What are Poké Jobs?

Poké Jobs are special requests for help that come from the various corporations and businesses of the Galar region. You can find a listing of all the Poké Jobs available to you by interacting with Rotomi and selecting the Check Poké Jobs option. Once you do that, you'll be brought to the job postings screen, which looks like this.

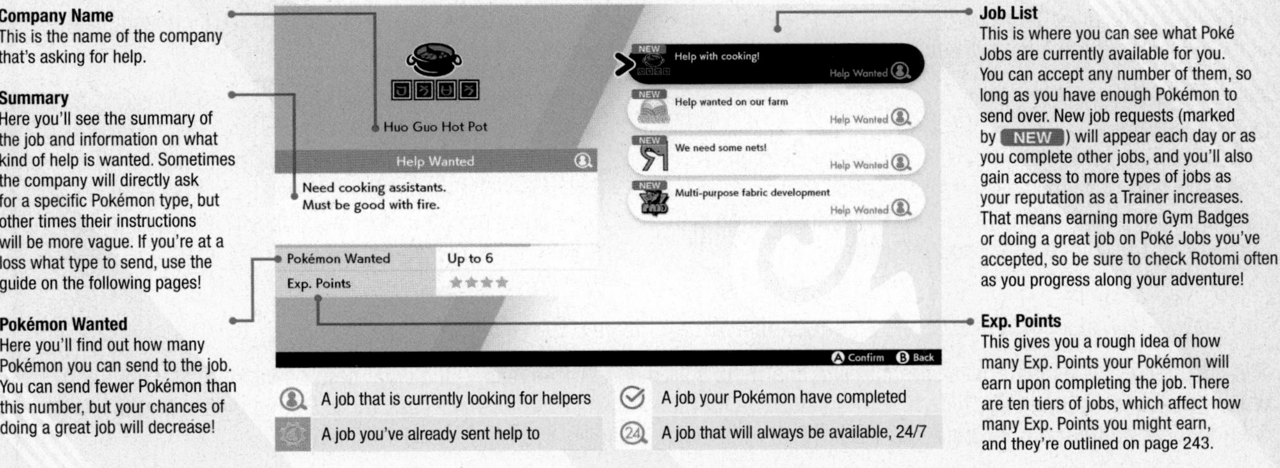

Company Name
This is the name of the company that's asking for help.
Summary
Here you'll see the summary of the job and information on what kind of help is wanted. Sometimes the company will directly ask for a specific Pokémon type, but other times their instructions will be more vague. If you're at a loss what type to send, use the guide on the following pages!
Pokémon Wanted
Here you'll find out how many Pokémon you can send to the job. You can send fewer Pokémon than this number, but your chances of doing a great job will decrease!
Huo Guo Hot Pot
Help Wanted
Need cooking assistants.
Must be good with fire.
Pokémon Wanted
Up to 6
Exp. Points
NEW
Help with cooking!
Help Wanted
NEW
Help wanted on our farm
Help Wanted
NEW
We need some nets!
Help Wanted
NEW
Multi-purpose fabric development
Help Wanted
Confirm
Back
Job List
This is where you can see what Poké Jobs are currently available for you. You can accept any number of them, so long as you have enough Pokémon to send over. New job requests (marked by NEW) will appear each day or as you complete other jobs, and you'll also gain access to more types of jobs as your reputation as a Trainer increases. That means earning more Gym Badges or doing a great job on Poké Jobs you've accepted, so be sure to check Rotomi often as you progress along your adventure!
Exp. Points
This gives you a rough idea of how many Exp. Points your Pokémon will earn upon completing the job. There are ten tiers of jobs, which affect how many Exp. Points you might earn, and they're outlined on page 243.
A job that is currently looking for helpers
A job you've already sent help to
A job your Pokémon have completed
A job that will always be available, 24/7

Accepting a Poké Job

Once you find a job you're interested in, you can select it by pressing Ⓐ and then selecting **Yes**. You'll then be taken to the Pokémon Box screen, where you'll be able to choose which Pokémon you want to send to help out. You can choose as many Pokémon as you want, until you reach the number indicated in the Pokémon Wanted section of the summary. (This number is also shown at the top left of the Box screen.)

This shows the maximum number of Pokémon you can send to the selected job, as well as how many you've selected so far.

!

If you made a mistake or want one of your Pokémon back for a battle, you can always cancel their Poké Job. Just select the job you sent them to, and answer **Yes** when asked if you want to bring them back early. You won't receive any rewards or Exp. Points if you do this, and the job will be removed from the job list (though it should appear again in time), so it's best to be a little careful when sending out your Pokémon!

Choosing the length of time to help

Once you've selected the Pokémon to send over, you'll be prompted to choose how long you want your Pokémon to help out.

In general, the longer your Pokémon help out, the more Exp. Points they'll earn, even compared to other jobs in the same Exp. Point tier. The length of work doesn't affect your chances of success or what rewards you'll receive, though—you're about as likely to do a great job working for one hour as you are for 24 hours! This means if you're more interested in stocking up on items, rather than gaining Exp. Points, it's more efficient to have your Pokémon work for short periods of time.

Once you choose a length of time, your Pokémon will be sent off to begin helping out! At this point, the label on the job posting will change to Pokémon Sent, and all you have to do is wait for the set amount of time to pass.

Also, remember that the lengths of time you choose to send your Pokémon are the actual amounts of time you'll have to wait. If you choose to send your Pokémon to a job for the whole day, those Pokémon will be away until the same time the next day unless you cancel the job! When sending Pokémon over for long periods of time, make sure you choose Pokémon that you don't immediately need on your team.

Completing a job

After the selected time has passed, the job will be marked as completed on the job-selection screen. Select it again to see how your Pokémon did and what kinds of rewards they earned! There are three possible outcomes for finishing a job:

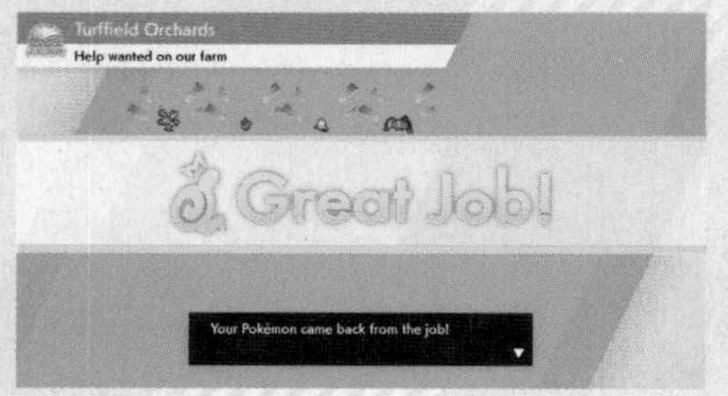

This indicates that the company was very satisfied with your Pokémon's help.

This indicates that your Pokémon helped out well.

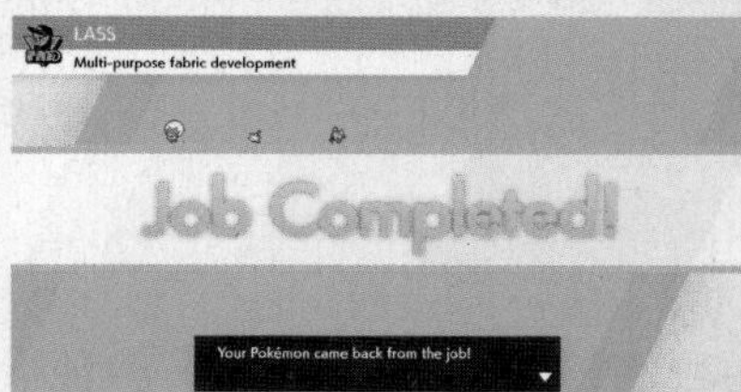

This is the lowest level of completion.

Naturally, you'll get better rewards the better your Pokémon do—better items, more Exp. Points, and so on. So how do you make sure you're maximizing your chances of success? Follow these key rules!

Send the right type!

As mentioned earlier, it's important to select Pokémon of the right type. If a job is asking for Pokémon that are good at burning things, make sure to send Fire types. If a job is asking for help with plants, send Grass types.

Send as many as you can!

It's also important to send the maximum number of allowed Pokémon. The more Pokémon you send, the more likely your chances of success are, if they're the right type of Pokémon for the job!

Let's have a look at an example. Suppose you see the job description pictured below.

The description states that they want cute and charming Pokémon to come help—and what better candidates for cute and charming Pokémon than Fairy types? You can also see that the Pokémon Wanted box says **Up to 5**. This means that if you wanted to guarantee your Pokémon do a great job, you would send over five Fairy-type Pokémon!

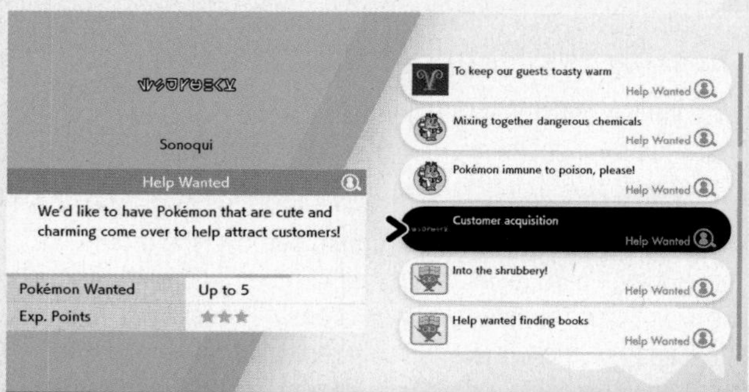

Many jobs are unlocked by earning additional Gym Badges during your Gym Challenge, as you can see in the table on the next page. But that's not the only way you can unlock new work. Doing great work on a job may unlock new jobs, too—and sometimes they'll be from a higher tier than the job you completed! The more you take part in Poké Jobs, the more you'll find that they reward you!

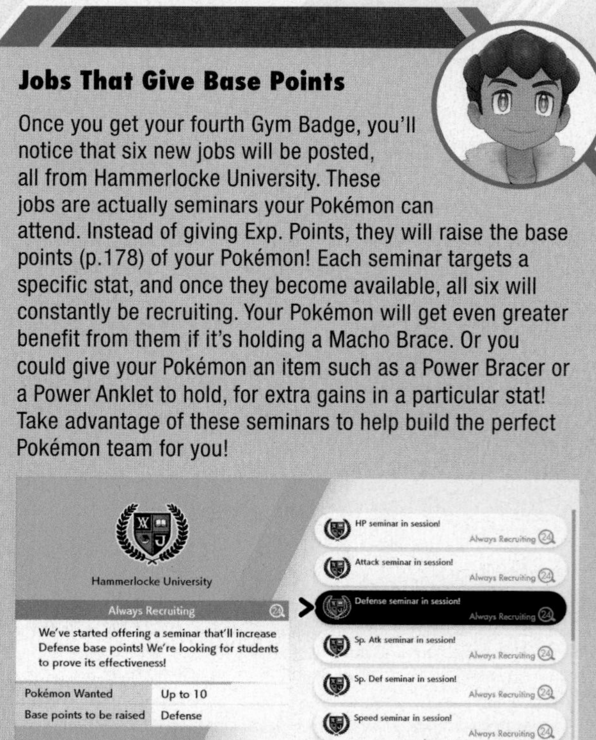

Jobs That Give Base Points

Once you get your fourth Gym Badge, you'll notice that six new jobs will be posted, all from Hammerlocke University. These jobs are actually seminars your Pokémon can attend. Instead of giving Exp. Points, they will raise the base points (p.178) of your Pokémon! Each seminar targets a specific stat, and once they become available, all six will constantly be recruiting. Your Pokémon will get even greater benefit from them if it's holding a Macho Brace. Or you could give your Pokémon an item such as a Power Bracer or a Power Anklet to hold, for extra gains in a particular stat! Take advantage of these seminars to help build the perfect Pokémon team for you!

Poké Job Tiers

You may have previously noticed mentions of job tiers. Now let's dig into them! Jobs have ten levels, which are called tiers, and these tiers affect how many Pokémon you can send on the job, how many Exp. Points those Pokémon can earn, and the kinds of items they may get as a reward! If you want to help your Pokémon level up as quickly as possible, it's safe to say you'll want to always choose the highest-tier job you can find. But if you're on the hunt for a particular item, you might be a bit pickier.

Typical rewards for different tiers of Poké Jobs

LOW ↑ ↓ HIGH

Tier	Max no. of Pokémon	Exp. Point gains	Example rewards for completion	Example rewards for a good job	Example rewards for a great job	General unlock conditions
I	3	★	₽100 1 Heal Ball 1 bottle of Fresh Water	₽200 2 Heal Balls 2 bottles of Fresh Water	₽300 1 Heal Ball 1 bottle of Soda Pop 1 loaf of Bread	Available from the start
II	4	★★	₽200 2 Heal Balls 2 bottles of Fresh Water	₽400 1 Heal Ball 1 bottle of Soda Pop 1 loaf of Bread	₽600 2 Heal Balls 2 bottles of Soda Pop 2 loaves of Bread	Earning the Grass Badge
III	5	★★★	₽300 1 Heal Ball 1 bottle of Soda Pop 1 loaf of Bread	₽600 2 Heal Balls 2 bottles of Soda Pop 2 loaves of Bread	₽900 1 Nest Ball 1 can of Lemonade 1 pack of Sausages 1 Fire Stone 1 Leaf Stone 1 Water Stone	Earning the Water Badge
IV	6	★★★★	₽500 2 Heal Balls 2 bottles of Soda Pop 2 loaves of Bread	₽1,000 1 Nest Ball 1 can of Lemonade 1 pack of Sausages	₽1,500 2 Nest Balls 2 cans of Lemonade 2 packs of Sausages 1 Fire Stone 1 Leaf Stone 1 Water Stone	Earning the Fire Badge
V	7*	★★★★★*	₽1,000 1 Nest Ball 1 can of Lemonade 1 pack of Sausages	₽2,000 2 Nest Balls 2 cans of Lemonade 2 packs of Sausages	₽3,000 1 Repeat Ball 1 Revive 1 box of Packaged Curry 1 Moon Stone 1 Sun Stone 1 Thunder Stone	Earning the Fighting Badge † or Ghost Badge 🛡
VI	8	★★★★★★	₽2,000 2 Nest Balls 2 cans of Lemonade 2 packs of Sausages	₽4,000 1 Repeat Ball 1 Revive 1 box of Packaged Curry	₽6,000 2 Repeat Balls 2 Revives 2 boxes of Packaged Curry 1 Moon Stone 1 Sun Stone 1 Thunder Stone	Earning the Fairy Badge
VII	9	★★★★★★★	₽2,500 1 Repeat Ball 1 Revive 1 box of Packaged Curry	₽5,000 2 Repeat Balls 2 Revives 2 boxes of Packaged Curry	₽7,500 2 Quick Balls 1 Ether 3 Revives 1 wheel of Moomoo Cheese 1 Dusk Stone 1 Shiny Stone	Earning the Rock Badge † or Ice Badge 🛡
VIII	10	★★★★★★★★	₽4,000 2 Repeat Balls 2 Revives 2 boxes of Packaged Curry	₽8,000 2 Quick Balls 2 Ethers 3 Revives 1 wheel of Moomoo Cheese	₽12,000 2 Quick Balls 1 Max Ether 2 wheels of Moomoo Cheese 1 Dusk Stone 1 Shiny Stone	Earning the Dark Badge
IX	30	★★★★★★★★★	₽6,000 1 Quick Ball 1 Ether 1 wheel of Moomoo Cheese 1 Fire Stone 1 Leaf Stone 1 Water Stone	₽12,000 2 Quick Balls 1 Max Ether 2 wheels of Moomoo Cheese 1 Moon Stone 1 Sun Stone 1 Thunder Stone	₽18,000 1 Elixir 1 Max Revive 1 bottle of PP Up 1 Rare Candy	Earning the Dragon Badge
X	30	★★★★★★★★★	1 Everstone	5 Nuggets 6 Nuggets 8 Nuggets	10 Big Nuggets 12 Big Nuggets 15 Big Nuggets	Earning the Dragon Badge

*Except the Hammerlocke University jobs, which accept up to 10 Pokémon and award base points rather than Exp. Points!

Poké Job List

All the Poké Jobs you can unlock are listed here, together with what type of Pokémon each is seeking, so you can maximize your chance of doing a great job on them. Refer to this list if you're feeling stuck!

Understanding each entry

Each of these boxes illustrates a possible job that might be available when you check Poké Jobs at the Rotomi in any Pokémon Center. Here's how to understand what each one is telling you!

Here you'll find the name of the job. This is the same name you'll see in your game when viewing a list of jobs to be done.

On the left side of each entry, you'll see the logo of the company requesting help on a job. Their name is also at the top of each box.

The conditions to unlock each job are here.

This icon indicates that a job is always available. These jobs only appear once you get four Gym Badges.

If you see a type icon here, it will guide you to the type of Pokémon best suited to complete the job, for your chance at maximum rewards!

This circle here shows you which tier the job belongs to, giving you an idea of what sort of rewards you might get.

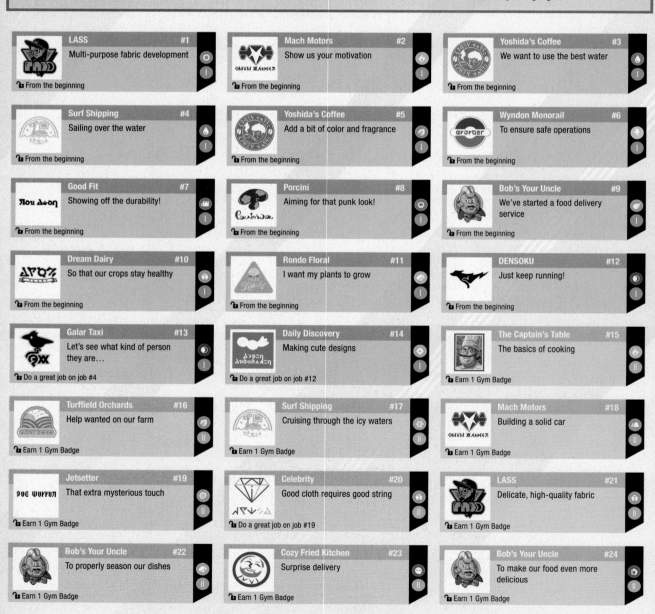

#	Company	Job	Unlock condition	Tier
#1	LASS	Multi-purpose fabric development	From the beginning	I
#2	Mach Motors	Show us your motivation	From the beginning	I
#3	Yoshida's Coffee	We want to use the best water	From the beginning	I
#4	Surf Shipping	Sailing over the water	From the beginning	I
#5	Yoshida's Coffee	Add a bit of color and fragrance	From the beginning	I
#6	Wyndon Monorail	To ensure safe operations	From the beginning	I
#7	Good Fit	Showing off the durability!	From the beginning	I
#8	Porcini	Aiming for that punk look!	From the beginning	I
#9	Bob's Your Uncle	We've started a food delivery service	From the beginning	I
#10	Dream Dairy	So that our crops stay healthy	From the beginning	I
#11	Rondo Floral	I want my plants to grow	From the beginning	I
#12	DENSOKU	Just keep running!	From the beginning	I
#13	Galar Taxi	Let's see what kind of person they are…	Do a great job on job #4	I
#14	Daily Discovery	Making cute designs	Do a great job on job #12	I
#15	The Captain's Table	The basics of cooking	Earn 1 Gym Badge	II
#16	Turffield Orchards	Help wanted on our farm	Earn 1 Gym Badge	II
#17	Surf Shipping	Cruising through the icy waters	Earn 1 Gym Badge	II
#18	Mach Motors	Building a solid car	Earn 1 Gym Badge	II
#19	Jetsetter	That extra mysterious touch	Earn 1 Gym Badge	II
#20	Celebrity	Good cloth requires good string	Do a great job on job #19	II
#21	LASS	Delicate, high-quality fabric	Earn 1 Gym Badge	II
#22	Bob's Your Uncle	To properly season our dishes	Earn 1 Gym Badge	II
#23	Cozy Fried Kitchen	Surprise delivery	Earn 1 Gym Badge	II
#24	Bob's Your Uncle	To make our food even more delicious	Earn 1 Gym Badge	II

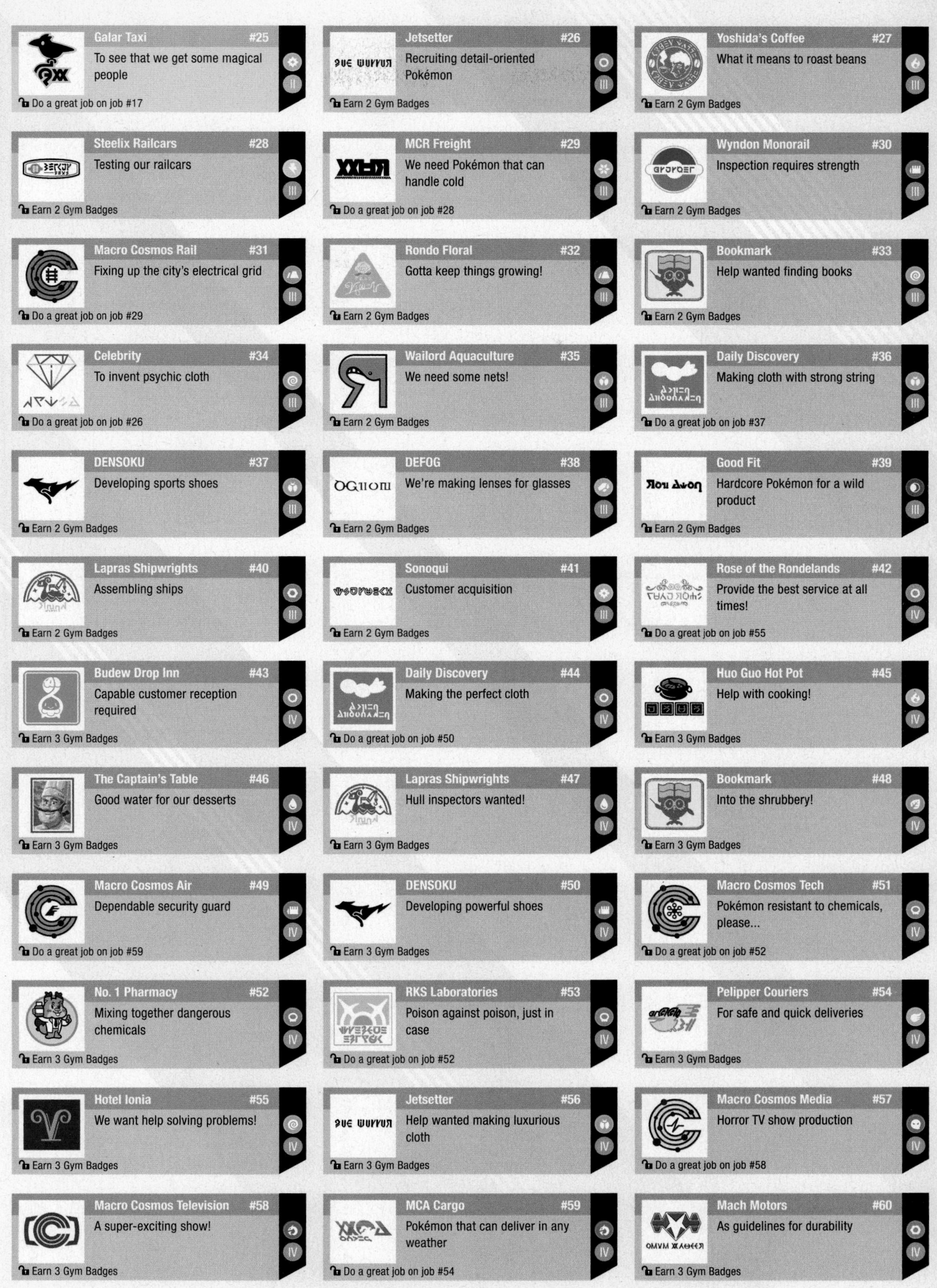

Galar Taxi #25
To see that we get some magical people
Do a great job on job #17
Jetsetter #26
Recruiting detail-oriented Pokémon
Earn 2 Gym Badges
Yoshida's Coffee #27
What it means to roast beans
Earn 2 Gym Badges
Steelix Railcars #28
Testing our railcars
Earn 2 Gym Badges
MCR Freight #29
We need Pokémon that can handle cold
Do a great job on job #28
Wyndon Monorail #30
Inspection requires strength
Earn 2 Gym Badges
Macro Cosmos Rail #31
Fixing up the city's electrical grid
Do a great job on job #29
Rondo Floral #32
Gotta keep things growing!
Earn 2 Gym Badges
Bookmark #33
Help wanted finding books
Earn 2 Gym Badges
Celebrity #34
To invent psychic cloth
Do a great job on job #26
Wailord Aquaculture #35
We need some nets!
Earn 2 Gym Badges
Daily Discovery #36
Making cloth with strong string
Do a great job on job #37
DENSOKU #37
Developing sports shoes
Earn 2 Gym Badges
DEFOG #38
We're making lenses for glasses
Earn 2 Gym Badges
Good Fit #39
Hardcore Pokémon for a wild product
Earn 2 Gym Badges
Lapras Shipwrights #40
Assembling ships
Earn 2 Gym Badges
Sonoqui #41
Customer acquisition
Earn 2 Gym Badges
Rose of the Rondelands #42
Provide the best service at all times!
Do a great job on job #55
Budew Drop Inn #43
Capable customer reception required
Earn 3 Gym Badges
Daily Discovery #44
Making the perfect cloth
Do a great job on job #50
Huo Guo Hot Pot #45
Help with cooking!
Earn 3 Gym Badges
The Captain's Table #46
Good water for our desserts
Earn 3 Gym Badges
Lapras Shipwrights #47
Hull inspectors wanted!
Earn 3 Gym Badges
Bookmark #48
Into the shrubbery!
Earn 3 Gym Badges
Macro Cosmos Air #49
Dependable security guard
Do a great job on job #59
DENSOKU #50
Developing powerful shoes
Earn 3 Gym Badges
Macro Cosmos Tech #51
Pokémon resistant to chemicals, please...
Do a great job on job #52
No. 1 Pharmacy #52
Mixing together dangerous chemicals
Earn 3 Gym Badges
RKS Laboratories #53
Poison against poison, just in case
Do a great job on job #52
Pelipper Couriers #54
For safe and quick deliveries
Earn 3 Gym Badges
Hotel Ionia #55
We want help solving problems!
Earn 3 Gym Badges
Jetsetter #56
Help wanted making luxurious cloth
Earn 3 Gym Badges
Macro Cosmos Media #57
Horror TV show production
Do a great job on job #58
Macro Cosmos Television #58
A super-exciting show!
Earn 3 Gym Badges
MCA Cargo #59
Pokémon that can deliver in any weather
Do a great job on job #54
Mach Motors #60
As guidelines for durability
Earn 3 Gym Badges

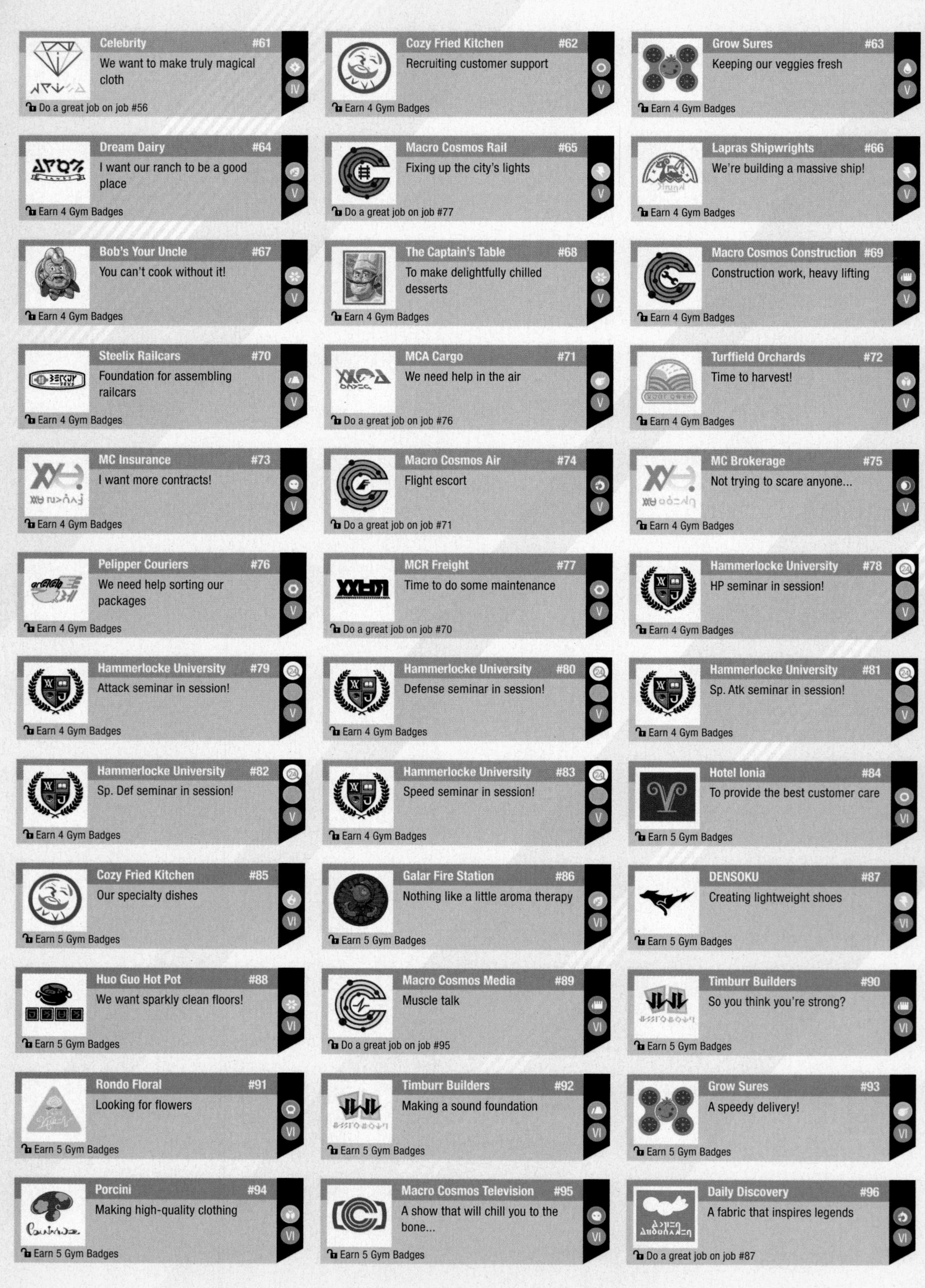

#	Client	Request	Rank	Unlock condition
#61	Celebrity	We want to make truly magical cloth	IV	Do a great job on job #56
#62	Cozy Fried Kitchen	Recruiting customer support	V	Earn 4 Gym Badges
#63	Grow Sures	Keeping our veggies fresh	V	Earn 4 Gym Badges
#64	Dream Dairy	I want our ranch to be a good place	V	Earn 4 Gym Badges
#65	Macro Cosmos Rail	Fixing up the city's lights	V	Do a great job on job #77
#66	Lapras Shipwrights	We're building a massive ship!	V	Earn 4 Gym Badges
#67	Bob's Your Uncle	You can't cook without it!	V	Earn 4 Gym Badges
#68	The Captain's Table	To make delightfully chilled desserts	V	Earn 4 Gym Badges
#69	Macro Cosmos Construction	Construction work, heavy lifting	V	Earn 4 Gym Badges
#70	Steelix Railcars	Foundation for assembling railcars	V	Earn 4 Gym Badges
#71	MCA Cargo	We need help in the air	V	Do a great job on job #76
#72	Turffield Orchards	Time to harvest!	V	Earn 4 Gym Badges
#73	MC Insurance	I want more contracts!	V	Earn 4 Gym Badges
#74	Macro Cosmos Air	Flight escort	V	Do a great job on job #71
#75	MC Brokerage	Not trying to scare anyone...	V	Earn 4 Gym Badges
#76	Pelipper Couriers	We need help sorting our packages	V	Earn 4 Gym Badges
#77	MCR Freight	Time to do some maintenance	V	Do a great job on job #70
#78	Hammerlocke University	HP seminar in session!	V	Earn 4 Gym Badges
#79	Hammerlocke University	Attack seminar in session!	V	Earn 4 Gym Badges
#80	Hammerlocke University	Defense seminar in session!	V	Earn 4 Gym Badges
#81	Hammerlocke University	Sp. Atk seminar in session!	V	Earn 4 Gym Badges
#82	Hammerlocke University	Sp. Def seminar in session!	V	Earn 4 Gym Badges
#83	Hammerlocke University	Speed seminar in session!	V	Earn 4 Gym Badges
#84	Hotel Ionia	To provide the best customer care	VI	Earn 5 Gym Badges
#85	Cozy Fried Kitchen	Our specialty dishes	VI	Earn 5 Gym Badges
#86	Galar Fire Station	Nothing like a little aroma therapy	VI	Earn 5 Gym Badges
#87	DENSOKU	Creating lightweight shoes	VI	Earn 5 Gym Badges
#88	Huo Guo Hot Pot	We want sparkly clean floors!	VI	Earn 5 Gym Badges
#89	Macro Cosmos Media	Muscle talk	VI	Do a great job on job #95
#90	Timburr Builders	So you think you're strong?	VI	Earn 5 Gym Badges
#91	Rondo Floral	Looking for flowers	VI	Earn 5 Gym Badges
#92	Timburr Builders	Making a sound foundation	VI	Earn 5 Gym Badges
#93	Grow Sures	A speedy delivery!	VI	Earn 5 Gym Badges
#94	Porcini	Making high-quality clothing	VI	Earn 5 Gym Badges
#95	Macro Cosmos Television	A show that will chill you to the bone...	VI	Earn 5 Gym Badges
#96	Daily Discovery	A fabric that inspires legends	VI	Do a great job on job #87

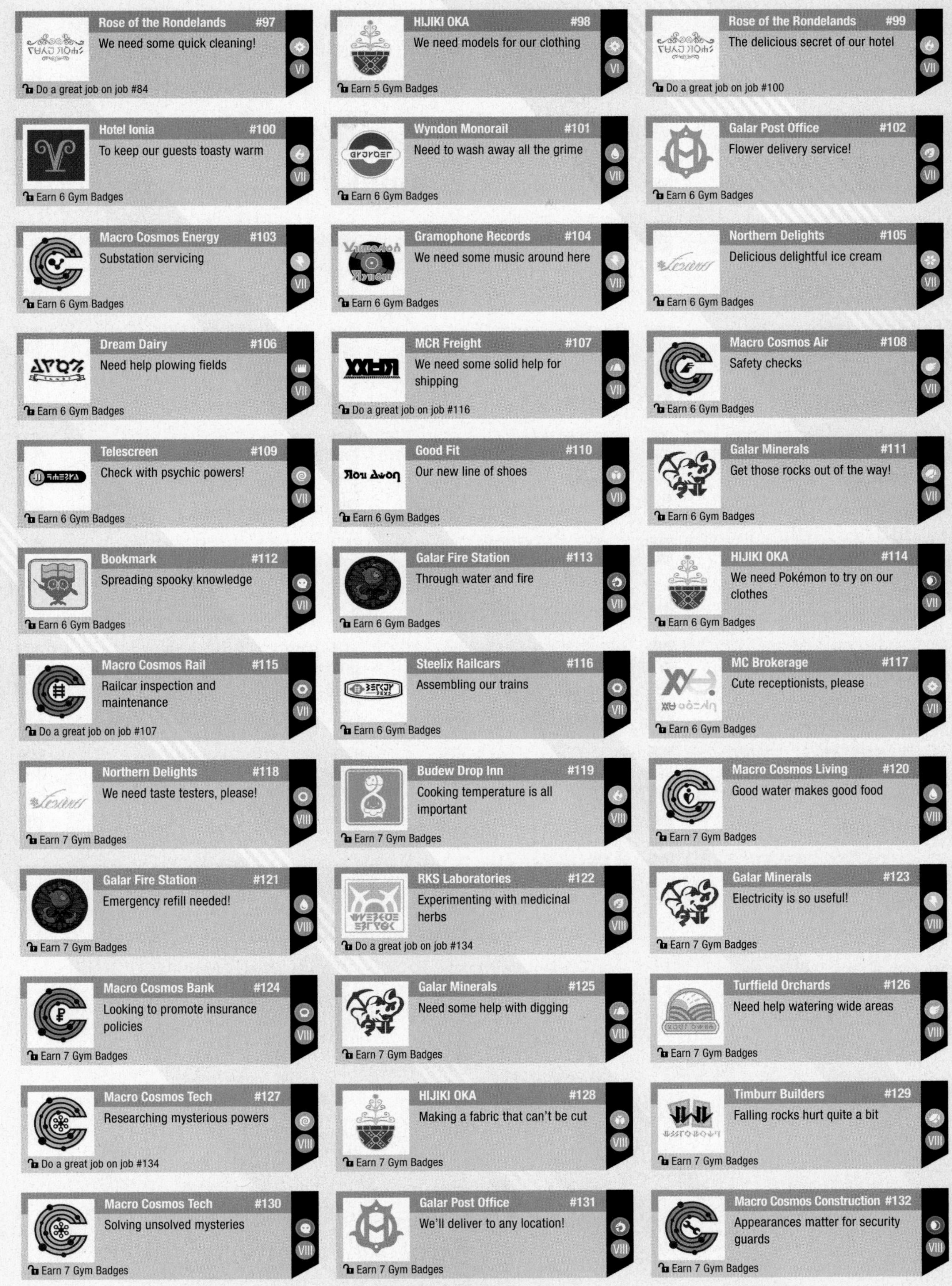

#	Client	Request	Level	Requirement
#97	Rose of the Rondelands	We need some quick cleaning!	VI	Do a great job on job #84
#98	HIJIKI OKA	We need models for our clothing	VI	Earn 5 Gym Badges
#99	Rose of the Rondelands	The delicious secret of our hotel	VII	Do a great job on job #100
#100	Hotel Ionia	To keep our guests toasty warm	VII	Earn 6 Gym Badges
#101	Wyndon Monorail	Need to wash away all the grime	VII	Earn 6 Gym Badges
#102	Galar Post Office	Flower delivery service!	VII	Earn 6 Gym Badges
#103	Macro Cosmos Energy	Substation servicing	VII	Earn 6 Gym Badges
#104	Gramophone Records	We need some music around here	VII	Earn 6 Gym Badges
#105	Northern Delights	Delicious delightful ice cream	VII	Earn 6 Gym Badges
#106	Dream Dairy	Need help plowing fields	VII	Earn 6 Gym Badges
#107	MCR Freight	We need some solid help for shipping	VII	Do a great job on job #116
#108	Macro Cosmos Air	Safety checks	VII	Earn 6 Gym Badges
#109	Telescreen	Check with psychic powers!	VII	Earn 6 Gym Badges
#110	Good Fit	Our new line of shoes	VII	Earn 6 Gym Badges
#111	Galar Minerals	Get those rocks out of the way!	VII	Earn 6 Gym Badges
#112	Bookmark	Spreading spooky knowledge	VII	Earn 6 Gym Badges
#113	Galar Fire Station	Through water and fire	VII	Earn 6 Gym Badges
#114	HIJIKI OKA	We need Pokémon to try on our clothes	VII	Earn 6 Gym Badges
#115	Macro Cosmos Rail	Railcar inspection and maintenance	VII	Do a great job on job #107
#116	Steelix Railcars	Assembling our trains	VII	Earn 6 Gym Badges
#117	MC Brokerage	Cute receptionists, please	VII	Earn 6 Gym Badges
#118	Northern Delights	We need taste testers, please!	VIII	Earn 7 Gym Badges
#119	Budew Drop Inn	Cooking temperature is all important	VIII	Earn 7 Gym Badges
#120	Macro Cosmos Living	Good water makes good food	VIII	Earn 7 Gym Badges
#121	Galar Fire Station	Emergency refill needed!	VIII	Earn 7 Gym Badges
#122	RKS Laboratories	Experimenting with medicinal herbs	VIII	Do a great job on job #134
#123	Galar Minerals	Electricity is so useful!	VIII	Earn 7 Gym Badges
#124	Macro Cosmos Bank	Looking to promote insurance policies	VIII	Earn 7 Gym Badges
#125	Galar Minerals	Need some help with digging	VIII	Earn 7 Gym Badges
#126	Turffield Orchards	Need help watering wide areas	VIII	Earn 7 Gym Badges
#127	Macro Cosmos Tech	Researching mysterious powers	VIII	Do a great job on job #134
#128	HIJIKI OKA	Making a fabric that can't be cut	VIII	Earn 7 Gym Badges
#129	Timburr Builders	Falling rocks hurt quite a bit	VIII	Earn 7 Gym Badges
#130	Macro Cosmos Tech	Solving unsolved mysteries	VIII	Earn 7 Gym Badges
#131	Galar Post Office	We'll deliver to any location!	VIII	Earn 7 Gym Badges
#132	Macro Cosmos Construction	Appearances matter for security guards	VIII	Earn 7 Gym Badges

Client	No.	Job	Unlock condition	
Spikemuth Chamber of Commerce	#133	Nothing too serious	Earn 7 Gym Badges	VIII
No. 1 Pharmacy	#134	Pokémon immune to poison, please!	Earn 7 Gym Badges	VIII
Northern Delights	#135	Making sweets is all about the image!	Earn 7 Gym Badges	VIII
Macro Cosmos Living	#136	Normal help is the best help	Earn 8 Gym Badges	IX
Macro Cosmos Media	#137	Cooking competition show	Do a great job on job #145	IX
Galar Minerals	#138	Removing impurities	Earn 8 Gym Badges	IX
Rondo Floral	#139	Our flowers need help	Earn 8 Gym Badges	IX
Galar Post Office	#140	Our truck needs a wash	Earn 8 Gym Badges	IX
Macro Net	#141	Keep an eye on our network!	Earn 8 Gym Badges	IX
Macro Cosmos Living	#142	Cold delivery	Earn 8 Gym Badges	IX
Bookmark	#143	Help wanted carrying books	Earn 8 Gym Badges	IX
Galar Police Station	#144	Preparing for nature!	Earn 8 Gym Badges	IX
Macro Cosmos Television	#145	A good show about cleaning	Earn 8 Gym Badges	IX
Macro Cosmos Construction	#146	Construction survey	Earn 8 Gym Badges	IX
HIJIKI OKA	#147	Even in the vacuum of space	Earn 8 Gym Badges	IX
Macro Net	#148	To meet our customers' needs!	Earn 8 Gym Badges	IX
Gramophone Records	#149	Recording the cries of bugs	Earn 8 Gym Badges	IX
Macro Cosmos Energy	#150	Pokémon strong against physical attacks	Earn 8 Gym Badges	IX
Telescreen	#151	Handling complaints	Earn 8 Gym Badges	IX
Macro Cosmos Bank	#152	To protect our investments	Earn 8 Gym Badges	IX
Galar Police Station	#153	Preparing for anything!	Earn 8 Gym Badges	IX
Macro Cosmos Bank	#154	A type that can handle danger, please	Earn 8 Gym Badges	IX
Galar Police Station	#155	Preparing for strange things!	Earn 8 Gym Badges	IX
Budew Drop Inn	#156	Cute, fantastical Pokémon wanted	Earn 8 Gym Badges	IX
??????	#157	Top-secret project	Earn 8 Gym Badges	X

If you don't see some of these jobs from the beginning—or after getting a Gym Badge—don't worry! Just accept the jobs that are there, and you'll find new requests will pop up in due time!

The Wild Area

The undeveloped Wild Area is ready to be whatever you want it to be! You can pour hours into your favorite pursuits here, whether they are training up your team, tracking down rare Pokémon, playing with your own Pokémon at your camp, cooking up rare curries with friends, racing for new records in the Rotom Rally, or taking on the thrill of Max Raid Battles! The pages to come will break down the unique things you can do here in greater detail, so start familiarizing yourself with the options that await you in the Wild Area!

Battle and catch Pokémon

There are simply more Pokémon to find in the Wild Area than anywhere else in the Galar region! You can spend hours and hours trying to find them all as the weather changes around you (p. 254).

Find and hatch Eggs

With a Pokémon Nursery right here in the Wild Area—and a nearly endless expanse of space to race across with Eggs in your party—this is a prime place for finding and hatching Pokémon Eggs (p. 234).

Connect with other players

Meet other players exploring the Wild Area. They may give you items, and of course you can connect with them to camp together and reap great rewards for your teams (p. 296).

Meet the people of the Wild Area

It's not only other players you'll meet in the Wild Area—you'll also meet other people who will battle you, sell you rare items for Watts, help you dig up treasures, and more (p. 277).

Want me to dig you up some treasure?
It'll only cost you 500 W!

Max Raid Battles

You'll find Pokémon Dens dotting the lands of the Wild Area. If a den is merely glowing, you'll get nothing but Watts from it if you investigate it. But when a pillar of light is shooting up from a Pokémon Den, you'll be able to jump into a Max Raid Battle against a wild Dynamax Pokémon there, whether you've brought pals with you or not (p. 271)!

Hunt for Gigantamax Pokémon

Incredibly rare and powerful, Gigantamax Pokémon are special forms of Dynamax Pokémon that can use signature G-Max Moves that even regular Dynamax Pokémon can't use (p. 216).

The Rotom Rally

Try to beat the clock in the Rotom Rally, a racing game for those who have a prized Rotom Bike. Try as much as you like to earn Watts and win rewards from the Rotom Rallyists (p. 274)!

Items, Watts, and Watt trading

There are plenty of hidden items to hunt down in the Wild Area day after day (p. 252). And you may notice that you earn Watts after doing other activities in the Wild Area, too. This special currency can be used to buy TRs and other rare items (p. 276).

Yes
No
Hey there! I found a bit of a rare item here in the Wild Area. You want it? Only 100 W!

ADVANCED TRAINER HANDBOOK

Maps of the Wild Area

Use these maps to familiarize yourself with the locations of the Wild Area's most important spots! Pokémon Dens for taking part in Max Raid Battles (p. 271), Berry trees for gathering Berries to use in battles and cooking (p. 290), and fishing spots for reeling in Pokémon with your Fishing Rod are all marked here. You'll also see icons for key people, such as the Camping King (p. 281) and the Rotom Rallyists (p. 276). They provide services you'll likely be coming back to time and again during your adventure.

Love to cook? You've come to the right place!
I've got all the finest ingredients right here!

The hidden items you may find in the Wild Area are covered in the following pages. You'll likely want to return many times to the Wild Area to hunt for them, just as you may want to keep coming back to encounter different Pokémon, because these items may appear over and over somewhat randomly. The items that you can see on the ground in Poké Balls, meanwhile, only appear one time. Once you claim each, that's it. They are listed back where you are first shown each half of the Wild Area. Turn back to pages 46 and 78 if you don't think you've found them all!

ADVANCED TRAINER HANDBOOK

Map Key

 Camping King  Ingredients Seller 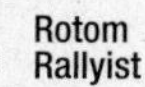 Rotom Rallyist  Digging Duo  Berry Tree  Fishing Spot 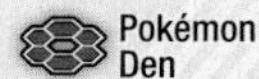 Pokémon Den

South Wild Area

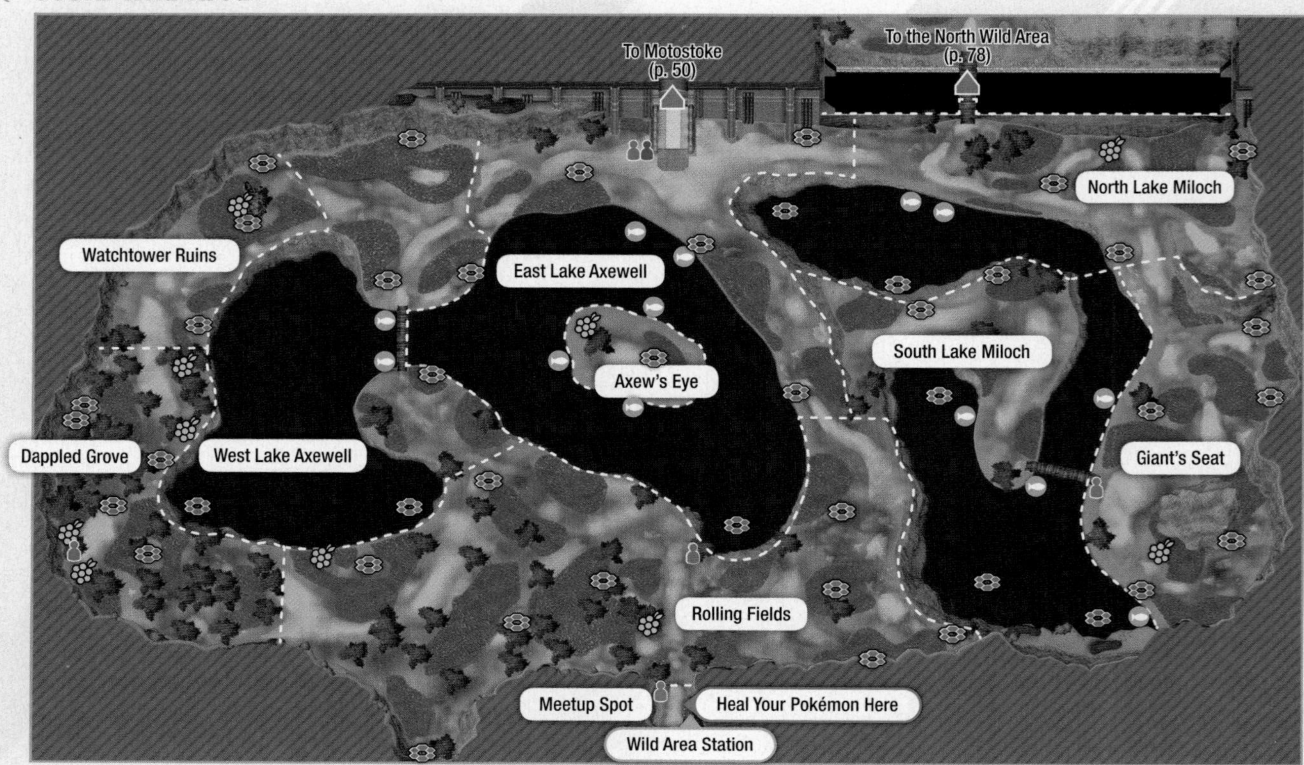

North Wild Area

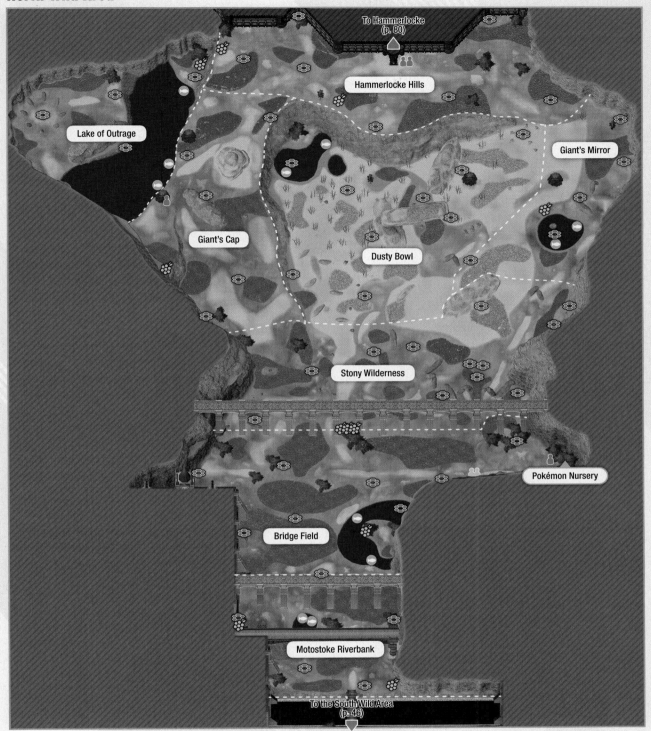

To Hammerlocke (p. 80)
Hammerlocke Hills
Lake of Outrage
Giant's Mirror
Giant's Cap
Dusty Bowl
Stony Wilderness
Pokémon Nursery
Bridge Field
Motostoke Riverbank
To the South Wild Area (p. 46)

Hidden Items in the Wild Area

The Wild Area has more to find than the rare Pokémon listed on the following pages. You can also hunt out hidden items here, coming back regularly to see what new items have appeared. Many of these items can be sold to Poké Mart clerks to help you line your pockets. But you can also often find Poké Balls, healing items, and more. Basically, the Wild Area has most everything you need to support your exploration and adventuring for as long as you want to keep going!

South Wild Area

The most common of items can be found in most zones in the Wild Area, so there's little need to list them again and again. The universal patterns that govern them are simple. For example, pearl items are found in or near almost any body of water, mushroom and apple items often appear under trees, and Honey tends to be found in flower patches. There are also Poké Balls here and there, perhaps where other Trainers lost them after a Pokémon refused to be caught. Pretty Feathers may have drifted down to the ground after shedding from crossing Pokémon, too.

It's the rarer items you'll want to find! For example, you have a tiny chance of finding Wishing Pieces in any zone in the Wild Area. (But they are so rare that you're probably better off collecting Watts so you can trade them for Wishing Pieces instead.) Each zone may also contain unique hidden items, a few of which aren't found anywhere else. Read the tips below and on the next page so you don't miss them!

Rarer finds to look out for in the South Wild Area

- The **Rolling Fields** zone has all the common sorts of items, such as **mushrooms** and **Poké Balls**.
- The **Dappled Grove** is similar, but this zone has **Fancy Apples** (for curry cooking) and a handy **Shed Shell**.
- The **Watchtower Ruins** zone has a **Revive**. Pick it up for when you need to give a Pokémon a pick-me-up.
- Both **West Lake Axewell** and **East Lake Axewell** are lined with **Pungent Roots** and also dotted with **Pearls** and the like.
- Once you can reach **Axew's Eye**, you can get a **Rare Candy** and either a **Tart Apple** or a **Sweet Apple**.
- **North Lake Miloch** has **Revival Herbs** and **Revives**, plus all the usual **Big Pearls** and **Pearl Strings**.
- **South Lake Miloch** is much the same as North Lake Miloch—but it's also the only place in the Wild Area where you can find **Prism Scales**!
- At the **Giant's Seat**, you can find a rare and valuable **Max Revive**. Use it wisely!

North Wild Area

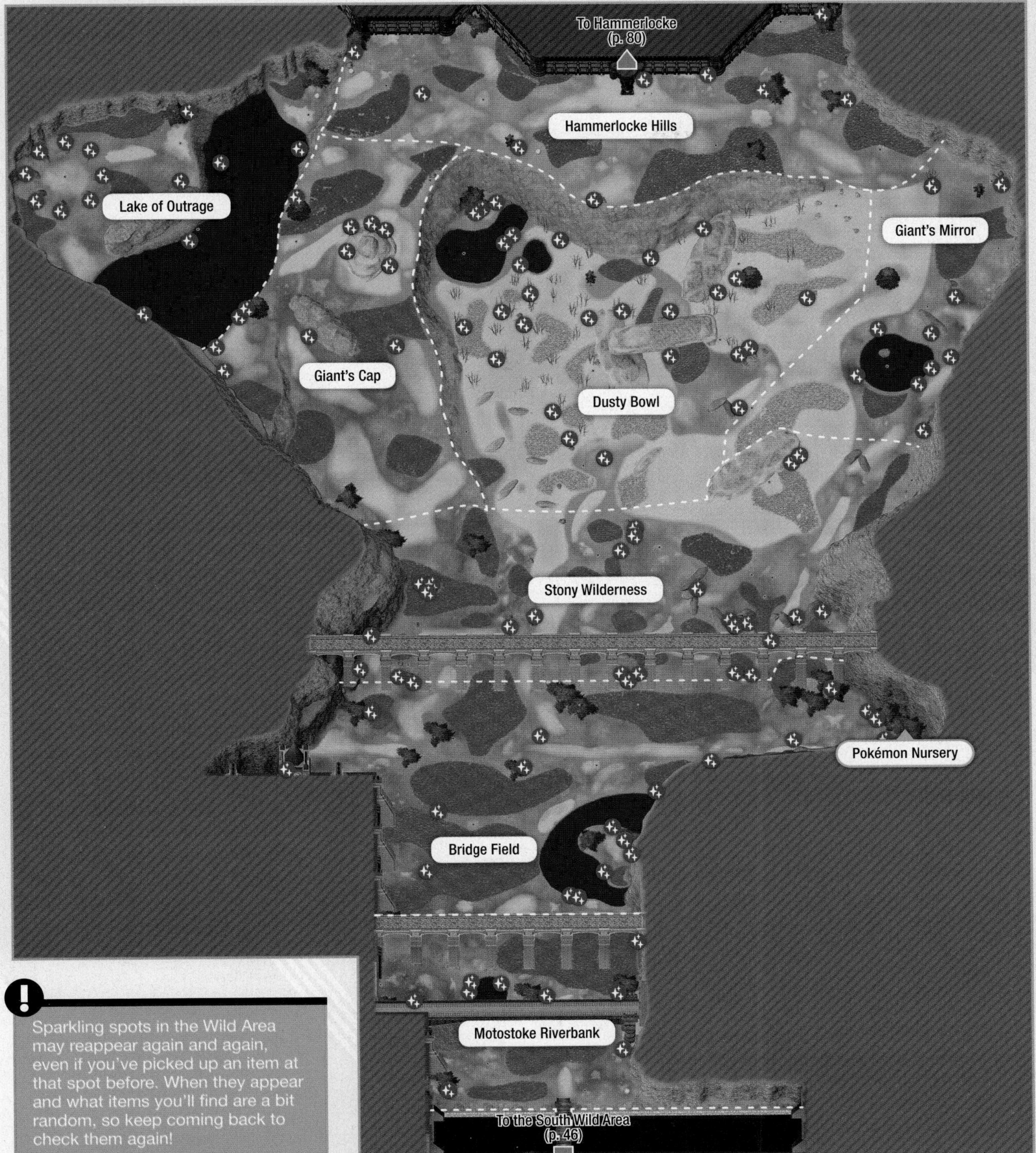

Sparkling spots in the Wild Area may reappear again and again, even if you've picked up an item at that spot before. When they appear and what items you'll find are a bit random, so keep coming back to check them again!

Rarer finds to look out for in the North Wild Area

- The **Motostoke Riverbank** has plenty of plants, like **Pungent Roots** and **Revival Herbs**.
- The **Bridge Field** has **Energy Roots** and **Revival Herbs**—handy if your team is struggling against tough opponents here!
- The **Stony Wilderness** is littered with **Stardust**, **Star Pieces**, and rare **Comet Shards**.
- In the **Dusty Bowl**, you can find **fossilized remains** to restore (p. 87), plus buckets of **Rare Bones** to sell.
- At the **Giant's Mirror**, you'll find stellar items to sell for profit, from **Balm Mushrooms** to **Comet Shards**.
- The **Giant's Cap** is lined with **Large Leeks** for cooking curries, and it has other useful or valuable finds, too!
- Across the **Lake of Outrage**, you can find a whole host of Evolution stones, such as **Dusk Stones** and **Fire Stones**.
- The **Hammerlocke Hills** will reward you with more **restoratives** and **items to sell**. Time to go shopping in the city!

Wild Area Encounters

The Wild Area is a wild paradise for Pokémon and Trainers alike, and you'll find more different species of Pokémon here than anywhere else in the region. Over the following pages, you can check which Pokémon you can encounter in each zone. These can change based on the weather, so visit often, as weather can change quickly in the Galar region. You can use the weather forecast on your Town Map to keep an eye on changing conditions, too. When there is particularly rare weather in the Wild Area (sandstorms, thunderstorms, blizzards, or heavy fog), you'll see it announced when you open your X menu, so watch out for those warnings!

How to read each table

Unlike on the routes you may have been traveling outside the Wild Area, the Pokémon you can encounter here vary greatly based on the current weather! Beside each species' name, you'll find nine columns indicating the rate at which the Pokémon appears in each type of weather.

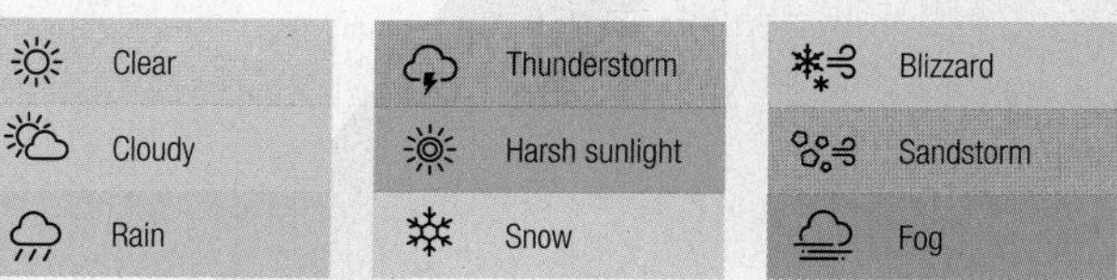

Axew's Eye

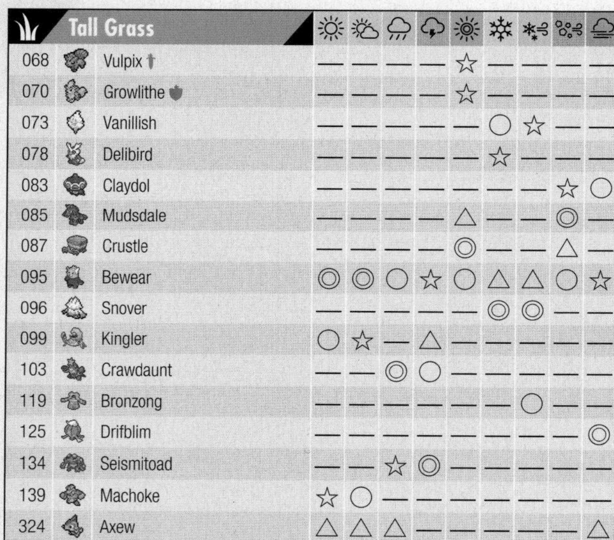

No.	Tall Grass	Clear	Cloudy	Rain	Thunderstorm	Harsh sunlight	Snow	Blizzard	Sandstorm	Fog
068	Vulpix †	—	—	—	—	☆	—	—	—	—
070	Growlithe (Shield)	—	—	—	—	☆	—	—	—	—
073	Vanillish	—	—	—	—	—	○	☆	—	—
078	Delibird	—	—	—	—	—	☆	—	—	—
083	Claydol	—	—	—	—	—	—	—	☆	○
085	Mudsdale	—	—	—	—	△	—	—	◎	—
087	Crustle	—	—	—	—	◎	—	—	△	—
095	Bewear	◎	◎	○	☆	○	△	△	○	☆
096	Snover	—	—	—	—	—	◎	◎	—	—
099	Kingler	○	☆	—	△	—	—	—	—	—
103	Crawdaunt	—	—	◎	○	—	—	—	—	—
119	Bronzong	—	—	—	—	—	—	○	—	—
125	Drifblim	—	—	—	—	—	—	—	—	◎
134	Seismitoad	—	—	☆	◎	—	—	—	—	—
139	Machoke	☆	○	—	—	—	—	—	—	—
324	Axew	△	△	△	—	—	—	—	—	△

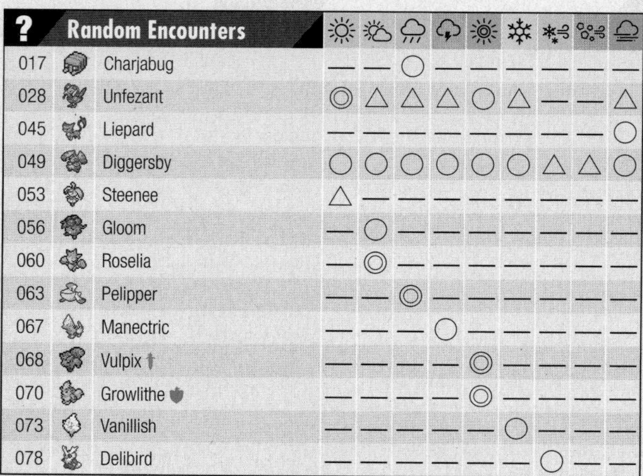

No.	Random Encounters	Clear	Cloudy	Rain	Thunderstorm	Harsh sunlight	Snow	Blizzard	Sandstorm	Fog
017	Charjabug	—	—	○	—	—	—	—	—	—
028	Unfezant	◎	△	△	△	○	△	—	—	△
045	Liepard	—	—	—	—	—	—	—	—	○
049	Diggersby	○	○	○	○	○	○	△	△	○
053	Steenee	△	—	—	—	—	—	—	—	—
056	Gloom	—	○	—	—	—	—	—	—	—
060	Roselia	—	◎	—	—	—	—	—	—	—
063	Pelipper	—	—	◎	—	—	—	—	—	—
067	Manectric	—	—	—	○	—	—	—	—	—
068	Vulpix †	—	—	—	—	◎	—	—	—	—
070	Growlithe (Shield)	—	—	—	—	◎	—	—	—	—
073	Vanillish	—	—	—	—	—	○	—	—	—
078	Delibird	—	—	—	—	—	—	○	—	—

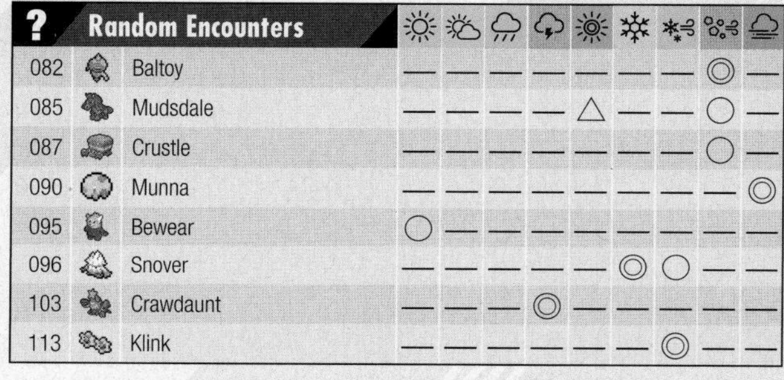

No.	Random Encounters	Clear	Cloudy	Rain	Thunderstorm	Harsh sunlight	Snow	Blizzard	Sandstorm	Fog
082	Baltoy	—	—	—	—	—	—	—	◎	—
085	Mudsdale	—	—	—	—	△	—	—	○	—
087	Crustle	—	—	—	—	—	—	—	○	—
090	Munna	—	—	—	—	—	—	—	—	◎
095	Bewear	○	—	—	—	—	—	—	—	—
096	Snover	—	—	—	—	—	◎	○	—	—
103	Crawdaunt	—	—	—	◎	—	—	—	—	—
113	Klink	—	—	—	—	—	—	◎	—	—

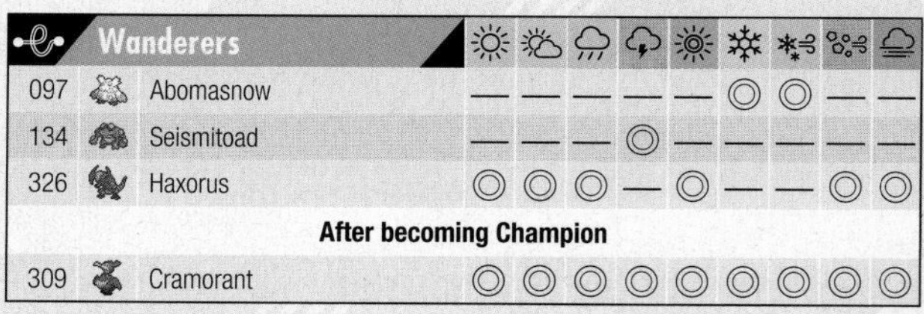

No.	Wanderers	Clear	Cloudy	Rain	Thunderstorm	Harsh sunlight	Snow	Blizzard	Sandstorm	Fog
097	Abomasnow	—	—	—	—	—	◎	◎	—	—
134	Seismitoad	—	—	—	◎	—	—	—	—	—
326	Haxorus	◎	◎	◎	—	◎	—	—	◎	◎
	After becoming Champion									
309	Cramorant	◎	◎	◎	◎	◎	◎	◎	◎	◎

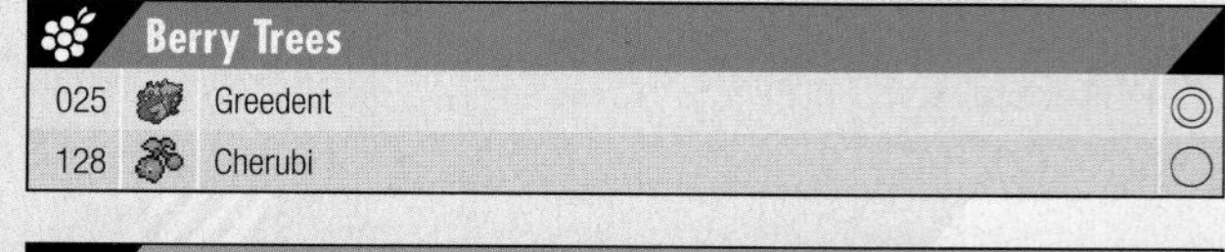

No.	Berry Trees	
025	Greedent	◎
128	Cherubi	○

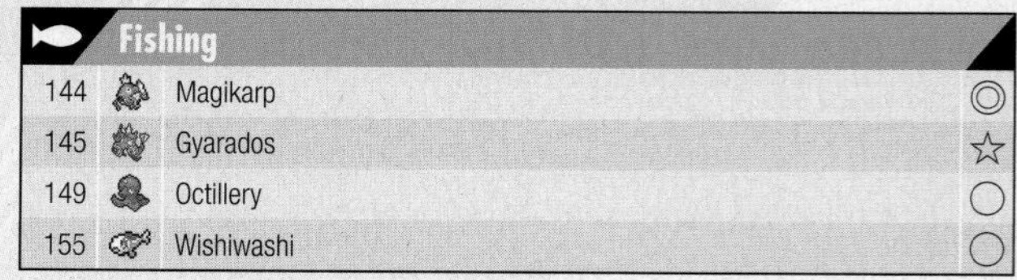

No.	Fishing	
144	Magikarp	◎
145	Gyarados	☆
149	Octillery	○
155	Wishiwashi	○

◎ frequent ○ common △ average ☆ rare ★ almost never — does not appear
† *Pokémon Sword* only (Shield) *Pokémon Shield* only

Bridge Field

No.	Tall Grass	Normal	Overcast	Raining	Thunderstorm	Intense Sun	Snowing	Snowstorm	Sandstorm	Heavy Fog
031	Zigzagoon	○	○	○	○	☆	○	△	○	△
082	Baltoy	—	—	—	—	△	—	—	△	—
090	Munna	—	—	—	—	—	—	—	—	○
094	Stufful	—	—	○	○	—	☆	—	△	☆
118	Bronzor	—	—	△	△	—	—	—	—	—
176	Noibat	△	△	△	△	△	△	☆	△	△
187	Cutiefly	○	○	—	—	○	—	—	—	○
217	Wobbuffet	△	—	—	—	△	—	—	—	—
222	Croagunk 🛡	—	△	—	—	—	—	—	☆	—
224	Scraggy †	—	△	—	—	—	—	—	☆	—
248	Throh 🛡	—	☆	—	—	—	—	—	—	—
249	Sawk †	—	☆	—	—	—	—	—	—	—
252	Bonsly	—	—	—	—	—	—	—	◎	—
277	Elgyem	△	△	—	—	—	—	—	—	○
279	Cubchoo	—	—	—	—	—	◎	○	—	—
292	Sneasel	—	—	—	—	—	△	◎	—	—
296	Maractus	—	—	—	—	○	—	—	—	—
302	Cufant	★	☆	—	—	☆	—	△	—	—
305	Frillish	—	—	—	△	—	—	—	—	—
309	Cramorant	—	—	☆	—	—	—	—	—	—
310	Toxel	☆	—	△	☆	—	—	—	—	—

No.	Random Encounters	Normal	Overcast	Raining	Thunderstorm	Intense Sun	Snowing	Snowstorm	Sandstorm	Heavy Fog
030	Thievul	○	○	—	—	○	○	—	—	☆
045	Liepard	△	—	—	—	—	—	—	—	—
049	Diggersby	—	○	—	—	—	—	—	—	—
072	Vanillite †	—	—	—	—	—	○	—	—	—
072	Vanillite 🛡	—	—	—	—	—	—	△	—	—
133	Palpitoad	△	△	○	○	△	△	△	△	△
162	Carkol	—	—	—	—	△	—	—	—	—
176	Noibat	—	—	—	○	—	—	—	—	—
185	Milcery	—	—	—	—	—	—	—	—	○
189	Ferroseed	☆	☆	☆	☆	☆	☆	☆	☆	☆
217	Wobbuffet	○	—	—	—	—	—	—	—	—
230	Shellos (East Sea)	—	—	○	○	—	—	—	—	—
232	Wimpod	—	—	△	—	—	—	—	—	—
234	Binacle	—	—	○	○	—	—	—	—	—
253	Sudowoodo	—	—	—	—	—	—	—	○	—
257	Togepi	☆	☆	—	—	—	—	—	—	☆
264	Rhyhorn	—	—	—	—	—	—	—	○	—
273	Karrablast	—	○	—	—	—	—	—	—	—
275	Shelmet	—	△	—	—	—	—	—	—	—
277	Elgyem	—	—	—	—	—	—	—	—	○
279	Cubchoo †	—	—	—	—	—	—	○	—	—
279	Cubchoo 🛡	—	—	—	—	—	○	○	—	—
281	Rufflet †	—	—	—	—	—	—	—	○	—
283	Vullaby 🛡	—	—	—	—	—	—	—	○	—
287	Litwick	—	—	—	—	○	—	—	—	○
290	Inkay	○	—	△	△	○	△	○	△	—
292	Sneasel	—	—	—	—	—	○	○	—	—
295	Mawile †	—	—	—	—	—	—	△	—	—

No.	Water Surface	Normal	Overcast	Raining	Thunderstorm	Intense Sun	Snowing	Snowstorm	Sandstorm	Heavy Fog
063	Pelipper	—	—	—	—	◎	—	—	—	—
072	Vanillite	—	—	—	—	—	◎	◎	—	—
074	Vanilluxe	—	—	—	—	—	◎	◎	—	—
145	Gyarados	◎	◎	◎	◎	◎	◎	◎	◎	◎
146	Goldeen	◎	◎	◎	○	○	○	△	○	◎
147	Seaking	◎	◎	—	—	—	—	—	◎	—
221	Lanturn	—	—	—	◎	—	—	—	—	—
290	Inkay	△	△	△	△	△	△	△	△	△
304	Qwilfish	○	◎	◎	◎	◎	△	○	◎	◎
306	Jellicent	—	—	◎	—	—	—	—	—	◎

No.	Flying	Normal	Overcast	Raining	Thunderstorm	Intense Sun	Snowing	Snowstorm	Sandstorm	Heavy Fog
027	Tranquill	☆	△	○	☆	◎	△	○	◎	△
072	Vanillite	—	—	—	—	—	◎	◎	—	—
174	Woobat	○	○	○	○	△	○	☆	○	◎
176	Noibat	◎	◎	◎	◎	○	☆	△	△	○

No.	Wanderers	Normal	Overcast	Raining	Thunderstorm	Intense Sun	Snowing	Snowstorm	Sandstorm	Heavy Fog
020	Noctowl	—	—	—	—	◎	—	—	—	—
025	Greedent	◎	◎	◎	◎	◎	◎	◎	◎	◎
032	Linoone	◎	◎	◎	◎	◎	◎	◎	◎	◎
074	Vanilluxe	—	—	—	—	—	◎	◎	—	—
083	Claydol	—	—	—	—	◎	—	—	◎	—
091	Musharna	—	—	—	—	—	—	—	—	◎
095	Bewear	◎	—	◎	◎	◎	◎	◎	◎	◎
112	Pangoro	—	◎	—	—	◎	—	—	—	—
119	Bronzong	—	—	◎	◎	—	—	—	—	—
123	Gallade	◎	◎	◎	◎	◎	—	—	◎	—
134	Seismitoad	◎	◎	◎	◎	—	—	—	—	◎
177	Noivern	◎	◎	◎	◎	◎	—	◎	◎	◎
188	Ribombee	◎	◎	—	—	◎	—	—	—	◎
190	Ferrothorn	◎	◎	◎	◎	◎	◎	◎	◎	◎
233	Golisopod	◎	—	◎	◎	—	—	—	—	—
265	Rhydon	—	—	—	—	◎	—	—	◎	—
278	Beheeyem	◎	◎	—	—	—	◎	◎	—	◎
280	Beartic	—	—	—	—	—	◎	—	—	—
286	Drapion	—	◎	—	—	—	—	—	—	—
293	Weavile	—	—	—	—	—	—	◎	—	—
301	Mimikyu	—	—	—	—	—	—	—	—	◎
	After becoming Champion									
033	Obstagoon	◎	◎	◎	◎	◎	◎	◎	◎	◎

No.	Berry Trees	
025	Greedent	◎
128	Cherubi	○

No.	Fishing	
043	Drednaw	○
144	Magikarp	○
145	Gyarados	☆
221	Lanturn	○
304	Qwilfish	△

◎ frequent ○ common △ average ☆ rare ★ almost never — does not appear
† *Pokémon Sword* only 🛡 *Pokémon Shield* only

Dappled Grove

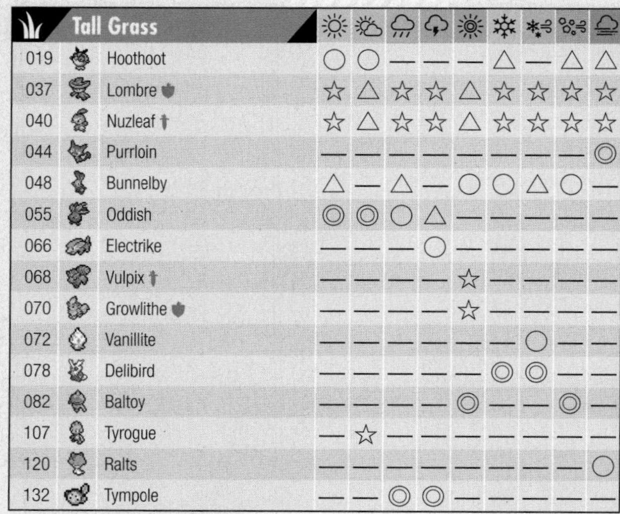

Tall Grass		Normal	Overcast	Rain	Thunderstorm	Intense Sun	Snow	Snowstorm	Sandstorm	Fog
019	Hoothoot	○	○	—	—	—	△	—	△	△
037	Lombre 🛡	☆	△	☆	☆	△	☆	☆	☆	☆
040	Nuzleaf †	☆	△	☆	☆	△	☆	☆	☆	☆
044	Purrloin	—	—	—	—	—	—	—	—	◎
048	Bunnelby	△	—	△	—	○	○	△	○	—
055	Oddish	◎	◎	○	△	—	—	—	—	—
066	Electrike	—	—	—	○	—	—	—	—	—
068	Vulpix †	—	—	—	—	☆	—	—	—	—
070	Growlithe 🛡	—	—	—	—	☆	—	—	—	—
072	Vanillite	—	—	—	—	—	—	○	—	—
078	Delibird	—	—	—	—	—	◎	◎	—	—
082	Baltoy	—	—	—	—	◎	—	—	◎	—
107	Tyrogue	—	☆	—	—	—	—	—	—	—
120	Ralts	—	—	—	—	—	—	—	—	○
132	Tympole	—	—	◎	◎	—	—	—	—	—

Random Encounters		Normal	Overcast	Rain	Thunderstorm	Intense Sun	Snow	Snowstorm	Sandstorm	Fog
016	Grubbin	—	—	○	○	—	—	—	—	—
036	Lotad 🛡	◎	○	○	○	—	—	—	—	○
039	Seedot †	◎	○	○	○	—	—	—	—	○
044	Purrloin	—	—	—	—	—	—	—	—	○
048	Bunnelby	○	—	—	—	○	☆	☆	○	—
052	Bounsweet	☆	—	—	—	—	—	—	☆	—
059	Budew	○	☆	☆	☆	☆	—	—	—	☆
064	Joltik	—	—	—	◎	—	—	—	—	—
068	Vulpix †	—	—	—	—	◎	—	—	—	—
070	Growlithe 🛡	—	—	—	—	◎	—	—	—	—
072	Vanillite	—	—	—	—	—	○	○	—	—

Random Encounters		Normal	Overcast	Rain	Thunderstorm	Intense Sun	Snow	Snowstorm	Sandstorm	Fog
079	Snorunt	—	—	—	—	—	○	◎	—	—
082	Baltoy	—	—	—	—	—	—	—	◎	—
084	Mudbray	—	—	—	—	○	—	—	—	—
088	Golett	—	—	—	—	—	—	—	○	—
094	Stufful	—	◎	—	—	—	—	—	—	—
096	Snover	—	—	—	—	—	◎	—	—	—
113	Klink	—	—	—	—	—	—	○	—	—
120	Ralts	—	—	—	—	—	—	—	—	◎
130	Stunky	—	○	—	—	—	—	—	—	—
132	Tympole	—	—	◎	—	—	—	—	—	—

Wanderers		Normal	Overcast	Rain	Thunderstorm	Intense Sun	Snow	Snowstorm	Sandstorm	Fog
038	Ludicolo 🛡	◎	◎	◎	◎	—	—	—	—	◎
041	Shiftry †	◎	◎	◎	◎	—	—	—	—	◎
057	Vileplume	◎	◎	—	—	—	—	—	—	◎
073	Vanillish	—	—	—	—	—	◎	◎	—	—
083	Claydol	—	—	—	—	◎	—	—	◎	—
095	Bewear	◎	◎	◎	◎	◎	◎	◎	◎	◎
112	Pangoro	—	—	—	—	◎	◎	◎	◎	—
134	Seismitoad	—	—	◎	◎	—	—	—	—	—
After becoming Champion										
012	Orbeetle	◎	◎	◎	◎	◎	◎	◎	◎	◎

Berry Trees		
024	Skwovet	◎
128	Cherubi	○

◎ frequent ○ common △ average ☆ rare ★ almost never — does not appear
† *Pokémon Sword* only 🛡 *Pokémon Shield* only

Dusty Bowl

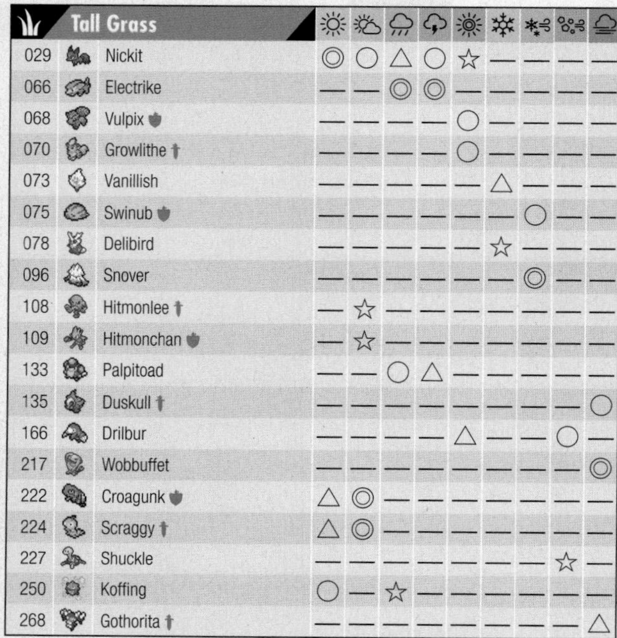

Tall Grass		Normal	Overcast	Rain	Thunderstorm	Intense Sun	Snow	Snowstorm	Sandstorm	Fog
029	Nickit	◎	○	△	○	☆	—	—	—	—
066	Electrike	—	—	◎	◎	—	—	—	—	—
068	Vulpix 🛡	—	—	—	—	○	—	—	—	—
070	Growlithe †	—	—	—	—	○	—	—	—	—
073	Vanillish	—	—	—	—	—	△	—	—	—
075	Swinub 🛡	—	—	—	—	—	—	○	—	—
078	Delibird	—	—	—	—	—	☆	—	—	—
096	Snover	—	—	—	—	—	—	◎	—	—
108	Hitmonlee †	—	☆	—	—	—	—	—	—	—
109	Hitmonchan 🛡	—	☆	—	—	—	—	—	—	—
133	Palpitoad	—	—	○	△	—	—	—	—	—
135	Duskull †	—	—	—	—	—	—	—	—	○
166	Drilbur	—	—	—	—	△	—	—	○	—
217	Wobbuffet	—	—	—	—	—	—	—	—	◎
222	Croagunk 🛡	△	◎	—	—	—	—	—	—	—
224	Scraggy †	△	◎	—	—	—	—	—	—	—
227	Shuckle	—	—	—	—	—	—	—	☆	—
250	Koffing	○	—	☆	—	—	—	—	—	—
268	Gothorita †	—	—	—	—	—	—	—	—	△

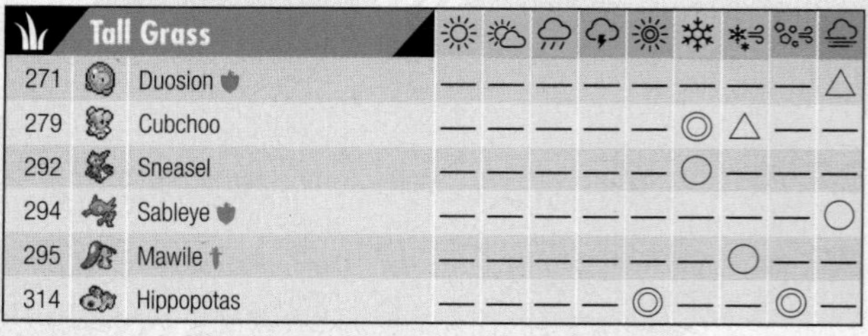

Tall Grass		Normal	Overcast	Rain	Thunderstorm	Intense Sun	Snow	Snowstorm	Sandstorm	Fog
271	Duosion 🛡	—	—	—	—	—	—	—	—	△
279	Cubchoo	—	—	—	—	—	◎	△	—	—
292	Sneasel	—	—	—	—	—	○	—	—	—
294	Sableye 🛡	—	—	—	—	—	—	—	—	○
295	Mawile †	—	—	—	—	—	—	○	—	—
314	Hippopotas	—	—	—	—	◎	—	—	◎	—

Random Encounters		Normal	Overcast	Rain	Thunderstorm	Intense Sun	Snow	Snowstorm	Sandstorm	Fog
017	Charjabug	—	—	—	○	—	—	—	—	—
023	Corviknight	—	—	—	—	—	○	—	—	—
035	Dubwool	○	—	—	—	—	—	—	—	—
043	Drednaw	—	—	—	◎	—	—	—	—	—
047	Boltund	—	—	—	○	—	—	—	—	—
060	Roselia	—	△	—	—	—	—	—	—	—
063	Pelipper	—	—	◎	—	—	—	—	—	—
076	Piloswine	—	—	—	—	—	◎	—	—	—
085	Mudsdale	—	—	—	—	△	—	—	—	—

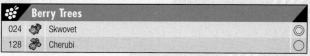

◎ frequent ○ common △ average ☆ rare ★ almost never — does not appear
† *Pokémon Sword* only 🛡 *Pokémon Shield* only

Random Encounters

No.	Pokémon	Normal	Overcast	Rain	Thunderstorm	Intense Sun	Snow	Snowstorm	Sandstorm	Heavy Fog
097	Abomasnow	—	—	—	—	—	○	—	—	—
114	Klang	—	—	—	—	—	—	○	—	—
119	Bronzong	—	—	—	—	—	—	◎	—	—
122	Gardevoir	—	—	—	—	—	—	—	—	☆
127	Eldegoss	◎	○	○	△	—	—	—	○	○
131	Skuntank	—	◎	—	—	—	—	—	—	—
163	Coalossal	—	—	—	—	☆	—	—	—	—
165	Dugtrio	—	—	—	—	—	—	—	◎	—
172	Gurdurr	—	—	—	—	—	△	—	—	—
190	Ferrothorn	—	—	—	—	—	—	△	—	—
205	Applin	△	—	—	—	—	—	—	—	—
209	Meowstic (Male) †	—	—	—	—	—	—	—	—	◎
209	Meowstic (Female) (Shield)	—	—	—	—	—	—	—	—	◎
226	Stunfisk	—	—	—	—	○	—	—	—	—
235	Barbaracle	—	—	○	—	—	—	—	—	—
242	Hattrem	○	○	△	—	—	—	○	△	○
253	Sudowoodo	—	—	—	—	—	—	—	○	—
265	Rhydon	—	—	—	—	◎	—	—	—	—

Water Surface

No.	Pokémon	Normal	Overcast	Rain	Thunderstorm	Intense Sun	Snow	Snowstorm	Sandstorm	Heavy Fog
072	Vanillite	—	—	—	—	—	◎	◎	—	—
145	Gyarados	◎	◎	◎	◎	◎	◎	◎	◎	◎
230	Shellos (East Sea)	◎	◎	◎	◎	◎	○	○	◎	◎
231	Gastrodon (East Sea)	◎	◎	◎	◎	◎	◎	◎	◎	◎
290	Inkay	—	—	—	—	—	○	—	—	—
305	Frillish	○	◎	◎	○	○	—	△	◎	◎

Flying

No.	Pokémon	Normal	Overcast	Rain	Thunderstorm	Intense Sun	Snow	Snowstorm	Sandstorm	Heavy Fog
259	Togekiss	—	—	—	—	—	—	—	—	☆
282	Braviary †	◎	◎	◎	◎	◎	◎	◎	◎	◎
284	Mandibuzz (Shield)	◎	◎	◎	◎	◎	◎	◎	◎	◎

Wanderers

No.	Pokémon	Normal	Overcast	Rain	Thunderstorm	Intense Sun	Snow	Snowstorm	Sandstorm	Heavy Fog
076	Piloswine	—	—	—	—	—	◎	◎	—	—
083	Claydol	—	◎	—	—	◎	—	—	◎	—
085	Mudsdale	◎	—	—	—	◎	—	—	◎	—
089	Golurk	—	◎	◎	◎	—	◎	◎	◎	◎
119	Bronzong	◎	—	◎	◎	—	◎	◎	—	◎
131	Skuntank	—	◎	—	—	—	—	—	—	—
134	Seismitoad	—	—	◎	◎	—	—	—	—	—
136	Dusclops	—	—	—	—	—	—	—	—	◎
170	Gigalith	◎	—	—	—	◎	—	—	—	—
227	Shuckle	◎	◎	◎	◎	◎	◎	◎	◎	◎
235	Barbaracle	—	◎	◎	◎	—	—	—	—	—
253	Sudowoodo	◎	◎	—	—	◎	◎	◎	◎	◎
265	Rhydon	—	—	◎	◎	—	—	—	—	—
297	Sigilyph	—	◎	◎	◎	◎	◎	◎	—	◎
323	Flygon	◎	—	—	—	—	—	—	◎	—
385	Tyranitar (Shield)	◎	—	—	—	◎	◎	◎	◎	◎
394	Kommo-o †	◎	—	—	—	◎	◎	◎	◎	◎
After becoming Champion										
313	Sandaconda	◎	◎	◎	◎	◎	◎	◎	◎	◎

Fishing

No.	Pokémon	
145	Gyarados	☆
181	Barraskewda	◎
221	Lanturn	○
304	Qwilfish	△

◎ frequent ○ common △ average ☆ rare ★ almost never — does not appear
† *Pokémon Sword* only (Shield) *Pokémon Shield* only

East Lake Axewell

Tall Grass

No.	Pokémon	Normal	Overcast	Rain	Thunderstorm	Intense Sun	Snow	Snowstorm	Sandstorm	Heavy Fog
016	Grubbin	—	—	△	—	—	—	—	—	—
052	Bounsweet	△	—	—	—	—	—	—	—	—
055	Oddish	○	△	—	△	—	—	—	—	△
062	Wingull	—	—	◎	—	—	—	—	—	—
066	Electrike	—	—	—	◎	—	—	—	—	—
068	Vulpix †	—	—	—	—	○	—	—	—	—
070	Growlithe (Shield)	—	—	—	—	○	—	—	—	—
079	Snorunt	—	—	—	—	—	☆	◎	—	—
082	Baltoy	—	—	—	—	—	—	—	◎	—
084	Mudbray	—	—	—	—	◎	—	—	○	—
090	Munna	—	—	—	—	—	—	—	—	◎
094	Stufful	◎	◎	○	○	△	○	○	△	○
096	Snover	—	—	—	—	—	◎	—	—	—
111	Pancham	—	○	—	☆	☆	△	△	☆	—

Random Encounters

No.	Pokémon	Normal	Overcast	Rain	Thunderstorm	Intense Sun	Snow	Snowstorm	Sandstorm	Heavy Fog
016	Grubbin	—	—	○	—	—	—	—	—	—
026	Pidove	○	—	—	—	—	—	—	—	—
044	Purrloin	—	—	—	—	—	—	—	—	◎
048	Bunnelby	○	—	—	—	—	—	—	—	—
050	Minccino	—	○	—	—	△	○	○	△	○
055	Oddish	◎	○	○	○	—	—	—	—	—
059	Budew	—	◎	—	—	—	—	—	—	—
062	Wingull	—	—	◎	—	—	—	—	—	—
064	Joltik	—	—	—	◎	—	—	—	—	—
066	Electrike	—	—	—	○	—	—	—	—	—
068	Vulpix †	—	—	—	—	○	—	—	—	—
070	Growlithe (Shield)	—	—	—	—	○	—	—	—	—
072	Vanillite	—	—	—	—	—	—	◎	—	—
079	Snorunt	—	—	—	—	—	◎	—	—	—
082	Baltoy	—	—	—	—	—	—	—	○	—
084	Mudbray	—	—	—	—	◎	—	—	—	—
086	Dwebble	—	—	—	—	—	—	—	◎	—
090	Munna	—	—	—	—	—	—	—	—	○
094	Stufful	☆	☆	☆	☆	☆	☆	☆	☆	☆
096	Snover	—	—	—	—	—	○	○	—	—
178	Onix	—	—	—	—	△	—	—	△	—

◎ frequent ○ common △ average ☆ rare ★ almost never — does not appear
† *Pokémon Sword* only (Shield) *Pokémon Shield* only

East Lake Axewell (continued)

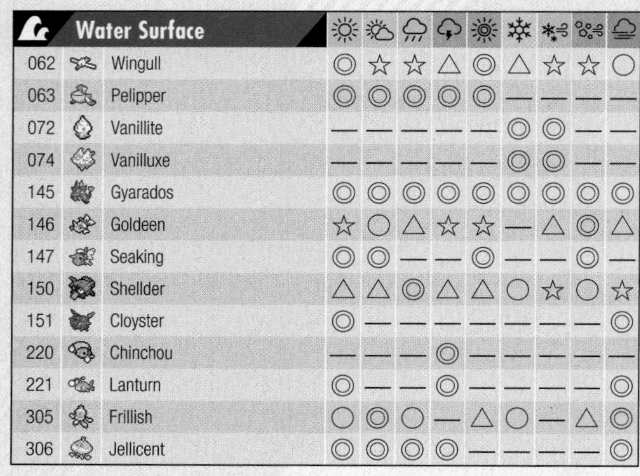

Water Surface		Normal	Overcast	Raining	Thunderstorm	Intense Sun	Snowing	Snowstorm	Sandstorm	Heavy Fog
062	Wingull	◎	☆	☆	△	◎	△	☆	☆	○
063	Pelipper	◎	◎	◎	◎	◎	—	—	—	—
072	Vanillite	—	—	—	—	—	◎	◎	—	—
074	Vanilluxe	—	—	—	—	—	◎	◎	—	—
145	Gyarados	◎	◎	◎	◎	◎	◎	◎	◎	◎
146	Goldeen	☆	○	△	☆	☆	—	△	◎	△
147	Seaking	◎	◎	—	—	◎	—	—	◎	—
150	Shellder	△	△	◎	△	△	○	☆	○	☆
151	Cloyster	◎	—	—	—	—	—	—	—	◎
220	Chinchou	—	—	—	◎	—	—	—	—	—
221	Lanturn	◎	—	—	◎	—	—	—	—	◎
305	Frillish	○	◎	○	—	△	○	—	△	◎
306	Jellicent	◎	◎	◎	◎	—	—	—	—	◎

Flying		Normal	Overcast	Raining	Thunderstorm	Intense Sun	Snowing	Snowstorm	Sandstorm	Heavy Fog
015	Butterfree	○	○	○	○	○	○	○	○	○
026	Pidove	◎	◎	◎	◎	◎	◎	◎	◎	◎

Wanderers		Normal	Overcast	Raining	Thunderstorm	Intense Sun	Snowing	Snowstorm	Sandstorm	Heavy Fog
063	Pelipper	—	—	◎	◎	—	—	—	—	—
076	Piloswine	—	—	—	—	—	◎	◎	—	—
085	Mudsdale	—	—	—	—	◎	—	—	◎	—
093	Xatu	◎	◎	—	—	◎	◎	◎	◎	◎
119	Bronzong	—	—	—	—	—	—	—	—	◎
158	Garbodor	◎	◎	◎	◎	—	—	—	—	—
	After becoming Champion									
251	Weezing	◎	◎	◎	◎	◎	◎	◎	◎	◎

Fishing		
144	Magikarp	◎
146	Goldeen	○
150	Shellder	○
155	Wishiwashi	☆

◎ frequent ○ common △ average ☆ rare ★ almost never — does not appear
† *Pokémon Sword* only ⛊ *Pokémon Shield* only

Giant's Cap

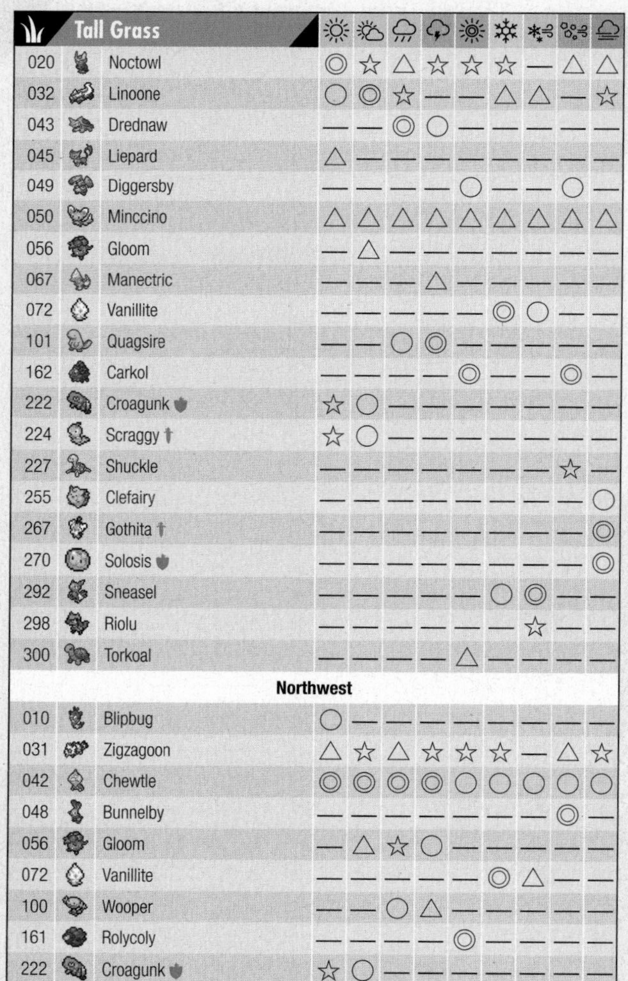

Tall Grass		Normal	Overcast	Raining	Thunderstorm	Intense Sun	Snowing	Snowstorm	Sandstorm	Heavy Fog
020	Noctowl	◎	☆	△	☆	☆	☆	—	△	△
032	Linoone	○	◎	☆	—	—	△	△	—	☆
043	Drednaw	—	—	◎	○	—	—	—	—	—
045	Liepard	△	—	—	—	—	—	—	—	—
049	Diggersby	—	—	—	—	○	—	—	○	—
050	Minccino	△	△	△	△	△	△	△	△	△
056	Gloom	—	△	—	—	—	—	—	—	—
067	Manectric	—	—	—	△	—	—	—	—	—
072	Vanillite	—	—	—	—	—	◎	○	—	—
101	Quagsire	—	—	○	◎	—	—	—	—	—
162	Carkol	—	—	—	—	◎	—	—	◎	—
222	Croagunk ⛊	☆	○	—	—	—	—	—	—	—
224	Scraggy †	☆	○	—	—	—	—	—	—	—
227	Shuckle	—	—	—	—	—	—	—	☆	—
255	Clefairy	—	—	—	—	—	—	—	—	○
267	Gothita †	—	—	—	—	—	—	—	—	◎
270	Solosis ⛊	—	—	—	—	—	—	—	—	◎
292	Sneasel	—	—	—	—	—	○	◎	—	—
298	Riolu	—	—	—	—	—	—	☆	—	—
300	Torkoal	—	—	—	—	△	—	—	—	—
	Northwest									
010	Blipbug	○	—	—	—	—	—	—	—	—
031	Zigzagoon	△	☆	△	☆	☆	☆	—	△	☆
042	Chewtle	◎	◎	◎	◎	○	○	○	○	○
048	Bunnelby	—	—	—	—	—	—	—	◎	—
056	Gloom	—	△	☆	○	—	—	—	—	—
072	Vanillite	—	—	—	—	—	◎	△	—	—
100	Wooper	—	—	○	△	—	—	—	—	—
161	Rolycoly	—	—	—	—	◎	—	—	—	—
222	Croagunk ⛊	☆	○	—	—	—	—	—	—	—

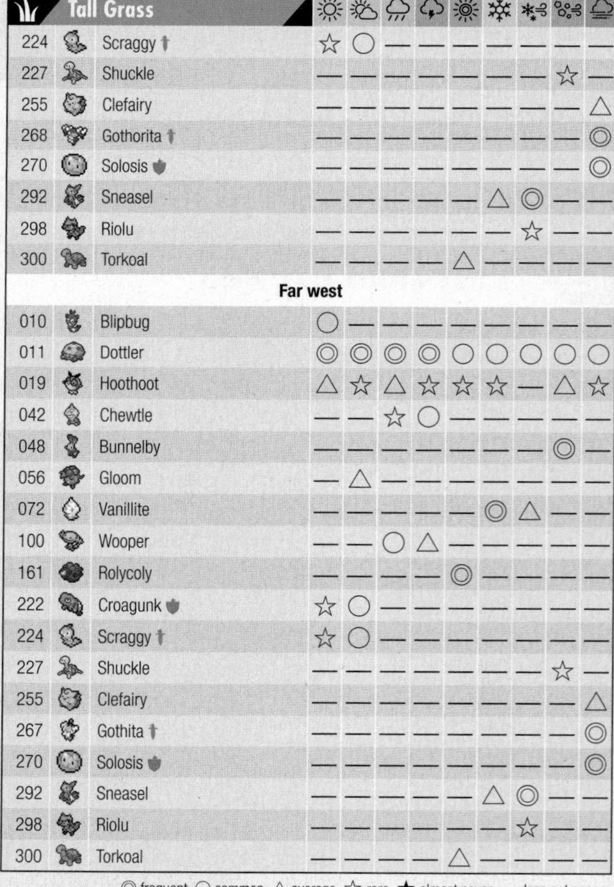

Tall Grass		Normal	Overcast	Raining	Thunderstorm	Intense Sun	Snowing	Snowstorm	Sandstorm	Heavy Fog
224	Scraggy †	☆	○	—	—	—	—	—	—	—
227	Shuckle	—	—	—	—	—	—	—	☆	—
255	Clefairy	—	—	—	—	—	—	—	—	△
268	Gothita †	—	—	—	—	—	—	—	—	◎
270	Solosis ⛊	—	—	—	—	—	—	—	—	◎
292	Sneasel	—	—	—	—	—	△	◎	—	—
298	Riolu	—	—	—	—	—	—	☆	—	—
300	Torkoal	—	—	—	—	△	—	—	—	—
	Far west									
010	Blipbug	○	—	—	—	—	—	—	—	—
011	Dottler	◎	◎	◎	◎	○	○	○	○	○
019	Hoothoot	△	☆	△	☆	☆	☆	—	△	☆
042	Chewtle	—	—	☆	○	—	—	—	—	—
048	Bunnelby	—	—	—	—	—	—	—	◎	—
056	Gloom	—	△	—	—	—	—	—	—	—
072	Vanillite	—	—	—	—	—	◎	△	—	—
100	Wooper	—	—	○	△	—	—	—	—	—
161	Rolycoly	—	—	—	—	◎	—	—	—	—
222	Croagunk ⛊	☆	○	—	—	—	—	—	—	—
224	Scraggy †	☆	○	—	—	—	—	—	—	—
227	Shuckle	—	—	—	—	—	—	—	☆	—
255	Clefairy	—	—	—	—	—	—	—	—	△
267	Gothita †	—	—	—	—	—	—	—	—	◎
270	Solosis ⛊	—	—	—	—	—	—	—	—	◎
292	Sneasel	—	—	—	—	—	△	◎	—	—
298	Riolu	—	—	—	—	—	—	☆	—	—
300	Torkoal	—	—	—	—	△	—	—	—	—

◎ frequent ○ common △ average ☆ rare ★ almost never — does not appear
† *Pokémon Sword* only ⛊ *Pokémon Shield* only

Ground		Clear	Cloudy	Rain	Thunderstorm	Harsh sunlight	Snow	Blizzard	Sandstorm	Fog
161	Rolycoly †	◎	◎	○	○	◎	○	○	◎	◎
161	Rolycoly 🛡	◎	◎	△	△	◎	△	△	◎	◎
169	Boldore †	△	△	△	△	△	△	△	△	△
169	Boldore 🛡	○	○	○	○	○	○	○	○	○
264	Rhyhorn †	○	○	◎	◎	○	◎	◎	○	○
264	Rhyhorn 🛡	△	△	◎	◎	△	◎	◎	△	△

Random Encounters		Clear	Cloudy	Rain	Thunderstorm	Harsh sunlight	Snow	Blizzard	Sandstorm	Fog
011	Dottler	○	○	○	△	—	△	△	△	○
037	Lombre 🛡	◎	—	—	—	—	—	—	—	—
040	Nuzleaf †	◎	—	—	—	—	—	—	—	—
064	Joltik	—	—	—	◎	—	—	—	—	—
078	Delibird	—	—	—	—	—	○	○	—	—
079	Snorunt	—	—	—	—	—	○	◎	—	—
082	Baltoy	—	—	—	—	○	—	—	—	—
084	Mudbray	—	—	—	—	—	—	—	○	—
088	Golett	—	—	—	—	◎	—	—	◎	—
090	Munna	—	○	—	—	—	—	—	—	◎
096	Snover	—	—	—	—	—	◎	—	—	—
127	Eldegoss	○	◎	△	—	—	—	—	—	△
130	Stunky	△	—	—	—	—	—	—	—	—
133	Palpitoad	—	—	◎	—	—	—	—	—	—
135	Duskull	—	—	—	—	—	—	—	—	○
165	Dugtrio	—	—	—	—	△	—	—	—	—
166	Drilbur	—	—	—	—	○	—	—	○	—
230	Shellos (East Sea)	—	—	○	○	—	—	—	—	—
246	Pawniard	—	—	—	—	—	—	○	—	—
273	Karrablast †	—	△	—	—	—	—	—	—	—
275	Shelmet 🛡	—	△	—	—	—	—	—	—	—
310	Toxel	—	—	—	○	—	—	—	—	—

Flying		Clear	Cloudy	Rain	Thunderstorm	Harsh sunlight	Snow	Blizzard	Sandstorm	Fog
362	Lunatone 🛡	◎	◎	◎	◎	◎	◎	◎	◎	◎
363	Solrock †	◎	◎	◎	◎	◎	◎	◎	◎	◎

Wanderers		Clear	Cloudy	Rain	Thunderstorm	Harsh sunlight	Snow	Blizzard	Sandstorm	Fog
012	Orbeetle	◎	◎	◎	◎	◎	◎	◎	◎	◎
023	Corviknight	◎	◎	◎	◎	◎	◎	◎	◎	◎
043	Drednaw	◎	◎	◎	◎	◎	◎	◎	◎	◎
051	Cinccino	◎	◎	—	—	—	—	—	—	◎
065	Galvantula	—	—	—	◎	—	—	—	—	—
080	Glalie	—	—	—	—	—	◎	◎	—	—
134	Seismitoad	—	—	◎	—	—	—	—	—	—
143	Gengar	◎	◎	—	◎	◎	—	◎	◎	◎
167	Excadrill	—	—	—	—	◎	—	—	◎	—
233	Golisopod	—	—	◎	—	—	—	—	—	—
280	Beartic	—	—	—	—	—	◎	—	—	—
331	Doublade	◎	◎	◎	◎	◎	◎	◎	◎	—
332	Aegislash	—	—	—	—	—	—	—	—	◎
After becoming Champion										
163	Coalossal	◎	◎	◎	◎	◎	◎	◎	◎	◎

Berry Trees		
025	Greedent	◎
128	Cherubi	○

Fishing		
098	Krabby	○
102	Corphish	△
145	Gyarados	☆
146	Goldeen	◎

◎ frequent ○ common △ average ☆ rare ★ almost never — does not appear
† *Pokémon Sword* only 🛡 *Pokémon Shield* only

Giant's Mirror

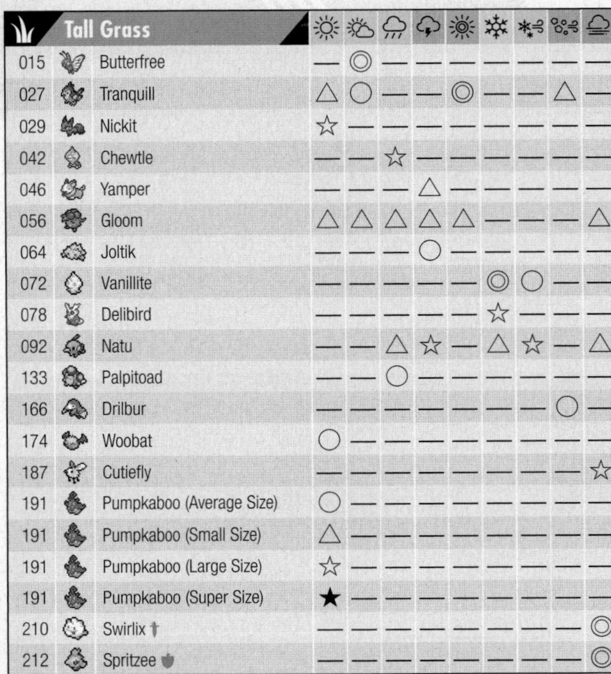

Tall Grass		Clear	Cloudy	Rain	Thunderstorm	Harsh sunlight	Snow	Blizzard	Sandstorm	Fog
015	Butterfree	—	◎	—	—	—	—	—	—	—
027	Tranquill	△	○	—	—	◎	—	—	△	—
029	Nickit	☆	—	—	—	—	—	—	—	—
042	Chewtle	—	—	☆	—	—	—	—	—	—
046	Yamper	—	—	—	△	—	—	—	—	—
056	Gloom	△	△	△	△	△	—	—	—	△
064	Joltik	—	—	—	○	—	—	—	—	—
072	Vanillite	—	—	—	—	—	◎	○	—	—
078	Delibird	—	—	—	—	—	☆	—	—	—
092	Natu	—	—	△	☆	—	△	☆	—	△
133	Palpitoad	—	—	○	—	—	—	—	—	—
166	Drilbur	—	—	—	—	—	—	—	○	—
174	Woobat	○	—	—	—	—	—	—	—	—
187	Cutiefly	—	—	—	—	—	—	—	—	☆
191	Pumpkaboo (Average Size)	○	—	—	—	—	—	—	—	—
191	Pumpkaboo (Small Size)	△	—	—	—	—	—	—	—	—
191	Pumpkaboo (Large Size)	☆	—	—	—	—	—	—	—	—
191	Pumpkaboo (Super Size)	★	—	—	—	—	—	—	—	—
210	Swirlix †	—	—	—	—	—	—	—	—	◎
212	Spritzee 🛡	—	—	—	—	—	—	—	—	◎

Tall Grass		Clear	Cloudy	Rain	Thunderstorm	Harsh sunlight	Snow	Blizzard	Sandstorm	Fog
218	Farfetch'd †	—	☆	—	—	—	—	—	—	—
232	Wimpod	—	—	◎	—	—	—	—	—	—
236	Corsola 🛡	—	☆	—	—	—	—	—	—	—
246	Pawniard	—	—	—	—	—	—	◎	—	—
248	Throh 🛡	—	△	—	—	—	—	—	—	—
249	Sawk †	—	△	—	—	—	—	—	—	—
264	Rhyhorn	—	—	—	—	—	—	—	◎	—
279	Cubchoo	—	—	—	—	—	○	△	—	—
316	Durant †	—	—	—	—	◎	—	—	—	—
316	Durant 🛡	—	—	—	—	☆	—	—	—	—
317	Heatmor †	—	—	—	—	☆	—	—	—	—
317	Heatmor 🛡	—	—	—	—	◎	—	—	—	—
318	Helioptile	—	—	—	◎	—	—	—	—	—
340	Morelull	—	—	—	—	—	—	—	—	○
Parched grass										
029	Nickit	◎	○	△	○	☆	—	—	—	—
066	Electrike	—	—	◎	◎	—	—	—	—	—
068	Vulpix 🛡	—	—	—	—	○	—	—	—	—
070	Growlithe †	—	—	—	—	○	—	—	—	—

◎ frequent ○ common △ average ☆ rare ★ almost never — does not appear
† *Pokémon Sword* only 🛡 *Pokémon Shield* only

Giant's Mirror (continued)

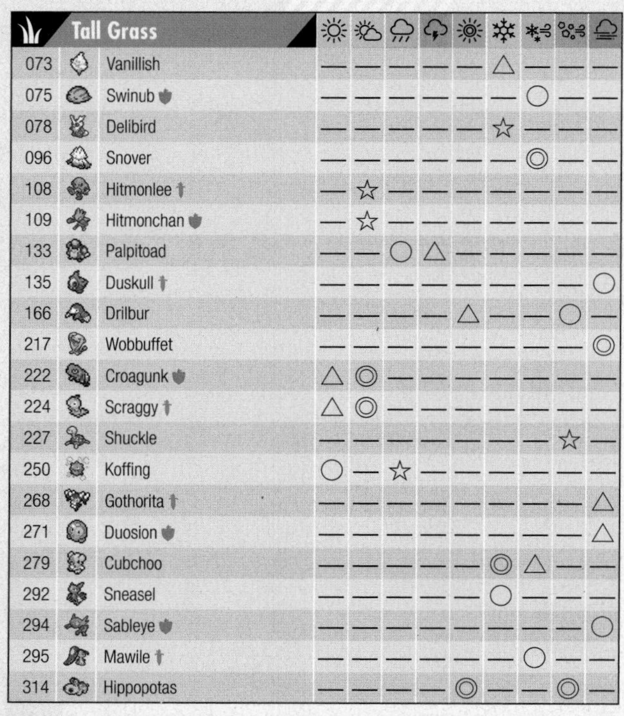

No.	Tall Grass	Normal	Cloudy	Rain	Thunderstorm	Intense Sun	Snow	Blizzard	Sandstorm	Fog
073	Vanillish	—	—	—	—	—	△	—	—	—
075	Swinub 🛡	—	—	—	—	—	—	○	—	—
078	Delibird	—	—	—	—	—	☆	—	—	—
096	Snover	—	—	—	—	—	—	◎	—	—
108	Hitmonlee †	—	☆	—	—	—	—	—	—	—
109	Hitmonchan 🛡	—	☆	—	—	—	—	—	—	—
133	Palpitoad	—	—	○	△	—	—	—	—	—
135	Duskull †	—	—	—	—	—	—	—	—	○
166	Drilbur	—	—	—	—	△	—	—	○	—
217	Wobbuffet	—	—	—	—	—	—	—	—	◎
222	Croagunk 🛡	△	◎	—	—	—	—	—	—	—
224	Scraggy †	△	◎	—	—	—	—	—	—	—
227	Shuckle	—	—	—	—	—	—	—	☆	—
250	Koffing	○	—	☆	—	—	—	—	—	—
268	Gothorita †	—	—	—	—	—	—	—	—	△
271	Duosion 🛡	—	—	—	—	—	—	—	—	△
279	Cubchoo	—	—	—	—	—	◎	△	—	—
292	Sneasel	—	—	—	—	—	○	—	—	—
294	Sableye 🛡	—	—	—	—	—	—	—	—	○
295	Mawile †	—	—	—	—	—	—	○	—	—
314	Hippopotas	—	—	—	—	◎	—	—	◎	—

No.	Ground	Normal	Cloudy	Rain	Thunderstorm	Intense Sun	Snow	Blizzard	Sandstorm	Fog
165	Dugtrio	◎	◎	◎	◎	○	○	○	○	◎
167	Excadrill	○	○	○	○	◎	◎	◎	◎	○
169	Boldore †	△	△	△	△	△	△	△	△	△
169	Boldore 🛡	○	○	○	○	○	○	○	○	○

No.	Random Encounters	Normal	Cloudy	Rain	Thunderstorm	Intense Sun	Snow	Blizzard	Sandstorm	Fog
011	Dottler	○	△	△	—	—	—	—	○	—
049	Diggersby	—	—	—	—	—	—	—	○	—
059	Budew	△	—	—	—	—	—	—	—	—
060	Roselia	—	○	—	—	—	—	—	—	—
064	Joltik	—	—	—	○	—	—	—	—	—
075	Swinub	—	—	—	—	—	○	○	—	—
096	Snover	—	—	—	—	—	○	○	—	—
138	Machop	△	△	△	△	△	△	△	△	△
164	Diglett	—	—	—	—	○	—	—	—	—
185	Milcery	—	—	—	—	—	—	—	—	○
205	Applin	—	—	—	○	—	—	—	—	—
230	Shellos (East Sea)	—	—	○	—	—	—	—	—	—
238	Impidimp	—	—	—	—	—	—	—	—	○

No.	Random Encounters	Normal	Cloudy	Rain	Thunderstorm	Intense Sun	Snow	Blizzard	Sandstorm	Fog
250	Koffing	○	○	○	△	○	△	△	△	○
279	Cubchoo	—	—	—	—	—	○	○	—	—
285	Skorupi	○	○	○	○	○	—	—	—	—
300	Torkoal	—	—	—	—	△	—	—	—	—
301	Mimikyu	—	—	—	—	—	—	—	—	☆
315	Hippowdon	—	—	—	—	—	—	—	○	—

No.	Water Surface	Normal	Cloudy	Rain	Thunderstorm	Intense Sun	Snow	Blizzard	Sandstorm	Fog
072	Vanillite	—	—	—	—	—	◎	◎	—	—
145	Gyarados	◎	◎	◎	◎	◎	◎	◎	◎	◎
230	Shellos (East Sea)	◎	◎	◎	◎	◎	○	○	◎	◎
231	Gastrodon (East Sea)	◎	◎	◎	◎	◎	◎	◎	◎	◎
290	Inkay	—	—	—	—	—	○	—	—	—
305	Frillish	○	◎	◎	○	○	—	△	◎	◎

No.	Flying	Normal	Cloudy	Rain	Thunderstorm	Intense Sun	Snow	Blizzard	Sandstorm	Fog
022	Corvisquire	◎	◎	◎	◎	◎	◎	◎	◎	◎
028	Unfezant	◎	◎	◎	◎	◎	◎	◎	◎	◎

No.	Wanderers	Normal	Cloudy	Rain	Thunderstorm	Intense Sun	Snow	Blizzard	Sandstorm	Fog
028	Unfezant	◎	◎	—	—	◎	—	—	—	—
057	Vileplume	—	◎	◎	◎	—	◎	◎	◎	—
058	Bellossom	◎	—	—	—	◎	—	—	—	◎
093	Xatu	—	—	◎	◎	—	◎	◎	◎	◎
097	Abomasnow	—	—	—	—	—	◎	—	—	—
134	Seismitoad	—	—	◎	—	—	—	—	—	—
140	Machamp	◎	◎	—	◎	◎	—	◎	◎	◎
179	Steelix	◎	◎	◎	◎	◎	◎	◎	◎	◎
	After becoming Champion									
183	Perrserker	◎	◎	◎	◎	◎	◎	◎	◎	◎

No.	Berry Trees	
025	Greedent	◎
128	Cherubi	○

No.	Fishing	
043	Drednaw	◎
145	Gyarados	☆
220	Chinchou	△
307	Mareanie	○

◎ frequent ○ common △ average ☆ rare ★ almost never — does not appear
† *Pokémon Sword* only 🛡 *Pokémon Shield* only

Giant's Seat

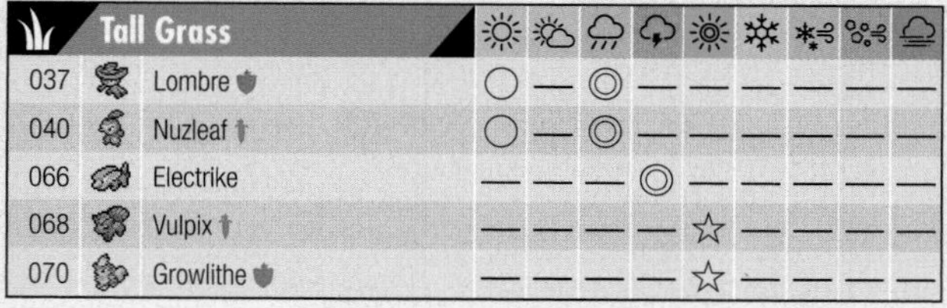

No.	Tall Grass	Normal	Cloudy	Rain	Thunderstorm	Intense Sun	Snow	Blizzard	Sandstorm	Fog
037	Lombre 🛡	○	—	◎	—	—	—	—	—	—
040	Nuzleaf †	○	—	◎	—	—	—	—	—	—
066	Electrike	—	—	—	◎	—	—	—	—	—
068	Vulpix †	—	—	—	—	☆	—	—	—	—
070	Growlithe 🛡	—	—	—	—	☆	—	—	—	—

No.	Tall Grass	Normal	Cloudy	Rain	Thunderstorm	Intense Sun	Snow	Blizzard	Sandstorm	Fog
078	Delibird	—	—	—	—	—	—	☆	—	—
079	Snorunt	—	—	—	—	—	○	○	—	—
084	Mudbray	—	—	—	—	◎	—	—	—	—
088	Golett	—	—	—	—	—	—	—	◎	—

◎ frequent ○ common △ average ☆ rare ★ almost never — does not appear
† *Pokémon Sword* only 🛡 *Pokémon Shield* only

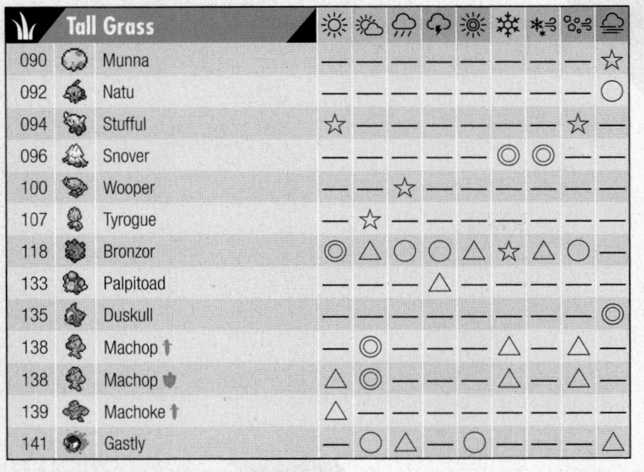

No.	Tall Grass	Normal Weather	Overcast	Raining	Thunderstorm	Intense Sun	Snowing	Snowstorm	Sandstorm	Heavy Fog
090	Munna	—	—	—	—	—	—	—	—	☆
092	Natu	—	—	—	—	—	—	—	—	○
094	Stufful	☆	—	—	—	—	—	—	☆	—
096	Snover	—	—	—	—	—	◎	◎	—	—
100	Wooper	—	—	☆	—	—	—	—	—	—
107	Tyrogue	—	☆	—	—	—	—	—	—	—
118	Bronzor	◎	△	○	○	△	☆	△	○	—
133	Palpitoad	—	—	—	△	—	—	—	—	—
135	Duskull	—	—	—	—	—	—	—	—	◎
138	Machop †	—	◎	—	—	—	△	—	△	—
138	Machop 🛡	△	◎	—	—	—	△	—	△	—
139	Machoke †	△	—	—	—	—	—	—	—	—
141	Gastly	—	○	△	—	○	—	—	—	△

No.	Random Encounters	Normal Weather	Overcast	Raining	Thunderstorm	Intense Sun	Snowing	Snowstorm	Sandstorm	Heavy Fog
027	Tranquill	△	—	—	—	—	—	—	—	—
037	Lombre 🛡	—	—	△	—	—	—	—	—	—
040	Nuzleaf †	—	—	△	—	—	—	—	—	—
045	Liepard	—	—	—	—	—	—	—	—	△
049	Diggersby	○	—	—	—	—	—	—	—	—
067	Manectric	—	—	—	◎	—	—	—	—	—
075	Swinub	—	—	—	—	—	△	△	—	—
078	Delibird	—	—	—	—	—	◎	◎	—	—
085	Mudsdale	—	—	—	—	△	—	—	◎	—
086	Dwebble	—	—	—	—	◎	—	—	△	—
093	Xatu	—	—	—	—	—	—	—	—	◎
095	Bewear †	◎	○	○	○	○	○	☆	○	○
095	Bewear 🛡	◎	○	○	○	○	○	☆	○	☆
101	Quagsire	—	—	◎	—	—	—	—	—	—
103	Crawdaunt	—	—	—	△	—	—	—	—	—
118	Bronzor †	☆	☆	☆	☆	☆	☆	○	☆	☆

No.	Random Encounters	Normal Weather	Overcast	Raining	Thunderstorm	Intense Sun	Snowing	Snowstorm	Sandstorm	Heavy Fog
118	Bronzor 🛡	☆	☆	☆	☆	☆	☆	○	☆	○
139	Machoke	—	◎	—	—	—	—	—	—	—
142	Haunter	—	△	—	—	—	—	—	—	—
178	Onix	○	○	—	—	○	—	—	○	—

No.	Wanderers	Normal Weather	Overcast	Raining	Thunderstorm	Intense Sun	Snowing	Snowstorm	Sandstorm	Heavy Fog
018	Vikavolt	◎	◎	—	—	◎	—	—	◎	—
065	Galvantula	—	—	◎	◎	—	—	—	—	—
080	Glalie	—	—	—	—	—	◎	◎	—	—
085	Mudsdale	—	—	—	—	◎	—	—	—	—
089	Golurk	—	—	—	—	—	—	—	◎	—
091	Musharna	—	—	—	—	—	—	—	—	◎
097	Abomasnow	—	—	—	—	—	◎	◎	—	—
119	Bronzong	—	◎	◎	◎	—	—	—	—	—
136	Dusclops	—	—	—	—	—	—	—	—	◎
179	Steelix	◎	◎	◎	◎	◎	◎	◎	◎	◎
247	Bisharp	◎	◎	◎	◎	◎	◎	◎	◎	◎
265	Rhydon	◎	—	—	—	—	—	—	—	—
	After becoming Champion									
371	Duraludon	◎	◎	◎	◎	◎	◎	◎	◎	◎

No.	Berry Trees	
025	Greedent	◎
128	Cherubi	○

No.	Fishing	
145	Gyarados	△
150	Shellder	◎
151	Cloyster	☆
156	Pyukumuku	○

◎ frequent ○ common △ average ☆ rare ★ almost never — does not appear
† *Pokémon Sword* only 🛡 *Pokémon Shield* only

Hammerlocke Hills

No.	Tall Grass	Normal Weather	Overcast	Raining	Thunderstorm	Intense Sun	Snowing	Snowstorm	Sandstorm	Heavy Fog
079	Snorunt	—	—	—	—	—	○	○	—	—
094	Stufful	○	◎	—	—	—	—	—	—	—
133	Palpitoad	—	—	◎	—	—	—	—	—	—
139	Machoke	☆	△	△	☆	△	—	☆	○	—
141	Gastly	—	—	—	—	—	—	—	—	△
191	Pumpkaboo (Average Size)	☆	☆	☆	○	☆	☆	☆	☆	☆
191	Pumpkaboo (Small Size)	☆	☆	☆	△	☆	☆	☆	☆	☆
191	Pumpkaboo (Large Size)	☆	☆	☆	☆	☆	☆	☆	☆	☆
191	Pumpkaboo (Super Size)	★	★	★	★	★	★	★	★	★
217	Wobbuffet	◎	○	○	○	☆	☆	△	△	—
232	Wimpod	—	—	—	○	—	—	—	—	—
253	Sudowoodo	△	—	—	—	◎	—	—	◎	—
279	Cubchoo	—	—	—	—	—	◎	—	—	—
292	Sneasel	—	—	—	—	—	△	◎	—	—
296	Maractus	—	—	—	—	○	—	—	—	—
321	Trapinch 🛡	—	—	—	—	—	—	—	☆	—
324	Axew †	—	—	—	—	—	—	—	☆	—
330	Honedge	—	—	—	—	—	—	—	—	◎
340	Morelull	—	—	—	—	—	—	—	—	○

No.	Random Encounters	Normal Weather	Overcast	Raining	Thunderstorm	Intense Sun	Snowing	Snowstorm	Sandstorm	Heavy Fog
017	Charjabug	—	—	—	○	—	—	—	—	—
022	Corvisquire	△	—	—	—	—	—	—	—	—
030	Thievul	—	△	—	—	—	—	—	—	—
035	Dubwool	△	—	—	—	—	—	—	—	—
063	Pelipper	—	—	◎	—	—	—	—	—	—
068	Vulpix 🛡	—	—	—	—	◎	—	—	—	—
070	Growlithe †	—	—	—	—	◎	—	—	—	—
072	Vanillite	—	—	—	—	—	—	○	—	—
075	Swinub	—	—	—	—	—	◎	—	—	—
078	Delibird	—	—	—	—	—	△	—	—	—
079	Snorunt	—	—	—	—	—	—	◎	—	—
082	Baltoy	—	—	—	—	○	—	—	—	—
086	Dwebble	—	—	—	—	—	—	—	○	—
113	Klink	△	△	△	△	△	△	△	△	△
139	Machoke	—	○	—	—	—	—	—	—	—
165	Dugtrio	—	—	—	—	—	—	—	◎	—
166	Drilbur	—	—	—	—	—	—	—	△	—
208	Espurr	◎	△	—	△	△	△	—	△	◎

◎ frequent ○ common △ average ☆ rare ★ almost never — does not appear
† *Pokémon Sword* only 🛡 *Pokémon Shield* only

Hammerlocke Hills (continued)

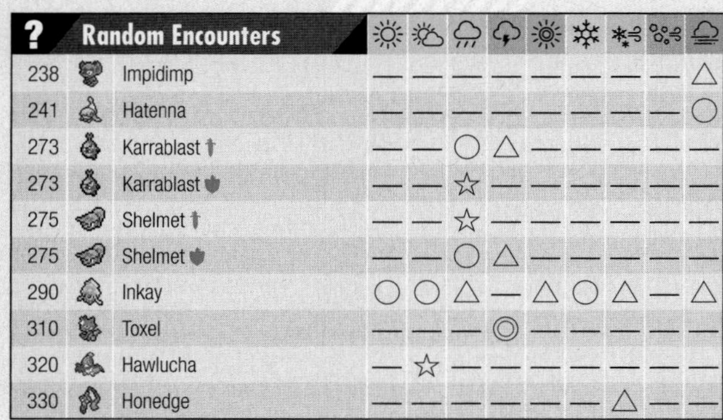

Random Encounters		Normal Weather	Overcast	Raining	Thunderstorm	Intense Sun	Snowing	Snowstorm	Sandstorm	Heavy Fog
238	Impidimp	—	—	—	—	—	—	—	—	△
241	Hatenna	—	—	—	—	—	—	—	—	○
273	Karrablast †	—	—	○	△	—	—	—	—	—
273	Karrablast 🛡	—	—	☆	—	—	—	—	—	—
275	Shelmet †	—	—	☆	—	—	—	—	—	—
275	Shelmet 🛡	—	—	○	△	—	—	—	—	—
290	Inkay	○	○	△	—	△	○	△	—	△
310	Toxel	—	—	—	◎	—	—	—	—	—
320	Hawlucha	—	☆	—	—	—	—	—	—	—
330	Honedge	—	—	—	—	—	—	△	—	—

Wanderers		Normal Weather	Overcast	Raining	Thunderstorm	Intense Sun	Snowing	Snowstorm	Sandstorm	Heavy Fog
023	Corviknight	◎	◎	◎	◎	◎	◎	◎	◎	◎
057	Vileplume	◎	—	◎	◎	◎	—	—	◎	—
061	Roserade	—	◎	—	—	—	—	—	—	◎
097	Abomasnow	—	—	—	—	—	◎	◎	—	—
114	Klang	◎	◎	◎	—	—	◎	—	—	—
115	Klinklang	—	—	—	◎	◎	—	◎	◎	◎
192	Gourgeist (Average Size)	◎	◎	◎	◎	◎	◎	◎	◎	◎
320	Hawlucha	◎	◎	◎	◎	◎	◎	◎	◎	◎
After becoming Champion										
303	Copperajah	◎	◎	◎	◎	◎	◎	◎	◎	◎

Flying		Normal Weather	Overcast	Raining	Thunderstorm	Intense Sun	Snowing	Snowstorm	Sandstorm	Heavy Fog
022	Corvisquire	◎	◎	◎	◎	◎	◎	◎	◎	◎
028	Unfezant	◎	◎	◎	◎	◎	◎	◎	◎	◎

Berry Trees		
025	Greedent	◎
128	Cherubi	○

◎ frequent ○ common △ average ☆ rare ★ almost never — does not appear
† *Pokémon Sword* only 🛡 *Pokémon Shield* only

Lake of Outrage

Tall Grass		Normal Weather	Overcast	Raining	Thunderstorm	Intense Sun	Snowing	Snowstorm	Sandstorm	Heavy Fog
065	Galvantula	—	—	—	○	—	—	—	—	—
069	Ninetales †	—	—	—	—	○	—	—	—	—
071	Arcanine 🛡	—	—	—	—	○	—	—	—	—
074	Vanilluxe	—	—	—	—	—	○	○	—	—
080	Glalie	—	—	—	—	—	○	—	—	—
089	Golurk	○	○	○	○	○	○	△	○	○
097	Abomasnow	—	—	—	—	—	△	—	—	—
110	Hitmontop	—	☆	—	—	—	—	—	—	—
115	Klinklang	—	—	—	—	—	—	○	—	—
134	Seismitoad	—	—	○	—	—	—	—	—	—
158	Garbodor	—	○	—	—	—	—	—	—	—
167	Excadrill	—	—	—	—	—	—	—	○	—
169	Boldore	—	—	—	—	—	—	—	○	—
177	Noivern	—	—	—	○	—	—	—	—	—
215	Araquanid	—	—	○	—	—	—	—	—	—
217	Wobbuffet	—	—	—	—	—	—	—	—	○
233	Golisopod	—	—	△	—	—	—	—	—	—
243	Hatterene	—	—	—	—	—	—	—	—	○
247	Bisharp	—	—	—	—	—	—	○	—	—
251	Weezing	—	△	—	—	—	—	—	—	—
269	Gothitelle †	—	—	—	—	—	—	—	—	△
272	Reuniclus 🛡	—	—	—	—	—	—	—	—	△
278	Beheeyem	○	—	—	—	—	—	—	—	—
282	Braviary †	○	—	—	—	—	—	—	—	—
284	Mandibuzz 🛡	○	—	—	—	—	—	—	—	—
286	Drapion	—	○	—	—	—	—	—	—	—
288	Lampent	—	—	—	—	△	—	—	—	—
297	Sigilyph	△	—	—	—	—	—	—	—	—
303	Copperajah	—	—	—	—	—	—	☆	—	—
316	Durant †	—	—	—	—	○	—	—	—	—
316	Durant 🛡	—	—	—	—	☆	—	—	—	—
317	Heatmor †	—	—	—	—	☆	—	—	—	—

Tall Grass		Normal Weather	Overcast	Raining	Thunderstorm	Intense Sun	Snowing	Snowstorm	Sandstorm	Heavy Fog
317	Heatmor 🛡	—	—	—	—	○	—	—	—	—
323	Flygon †	—	—	—	—	★	—	—	—	—
323	Flygon 🛡	—	—	—	—	☆	—	—	—	—
326	Haxorus †	—	—	—	☆	—	—	—	—	—
326	Haxorus 🛡	—	—	—	★	—	—	—	—	—
344	Morpeko	—	—	—	☆	—	—	—	—	—
358	Bergmite	—	—	—	—	—	☆	—	—	—
372	Rotom	—	—	☆	☆	—	—	—	—	—
373	Ditto	△	△	△	△	△	△	△	△	△
384	Pupitar 🛡	—	—	—	—	—	—	—	☆	—
387	Zweilous †	—	—	—	—	—	—	—	☆	—
396	Drakloak	—	★	★	☆	—	—	—	—	☆

Random Encounters		Normal Weather	Overcast	Raining	Thunderstorm	Intense Sun	Snowing	Snowstorm	Sandstorm	Heavy Fog
012	Orbeetle	△	—	—	—	—	—	—	—	—
023	Corviknight †	◎	○	○	○	○	○	○	○	○
023	Corviknight 🛡	◎	○	○	△	○	○	△	○	○
033	Obstagoon †	○	—	—	—	—	☆	—	—	—
033	Obstagoon 🛡	○	—	—	—	—	—	—	☆	—
043	Drednaw	—	—	—	○	—	—	—	—	—
047	Boltund	—	—	—	○	—	—	—	—	—
063	Pelipper	—	—	○	—	—	—	—	—	—
076	Piloswine	—	—	—	—	—	○	—	—	—
083	Claydol	—	—	—	—	—	—	—	—	○
095	Bewear	○	—	—	—	—	—	—	—	—
101	Quagsire	—	—	△	—	—	—	—	—	—
112	Pangoro	—	△	—	—	—	—	—	—	—
119	Bronzong	—	—	—	—	—	—	—	—	○
122	Gardevoir	—	—	—	—	—	—	—	—	★
131	Skuntank	—	○	—	—	—	—	—	—	—
163	Coalossal	—	—	—	—	○	—	—	—	—

◎ frequent ○ common △ average ☆ rare ★ almost never — does not appear
† *Pokémon Sword* only 🛡 *Pokémon Shield* only

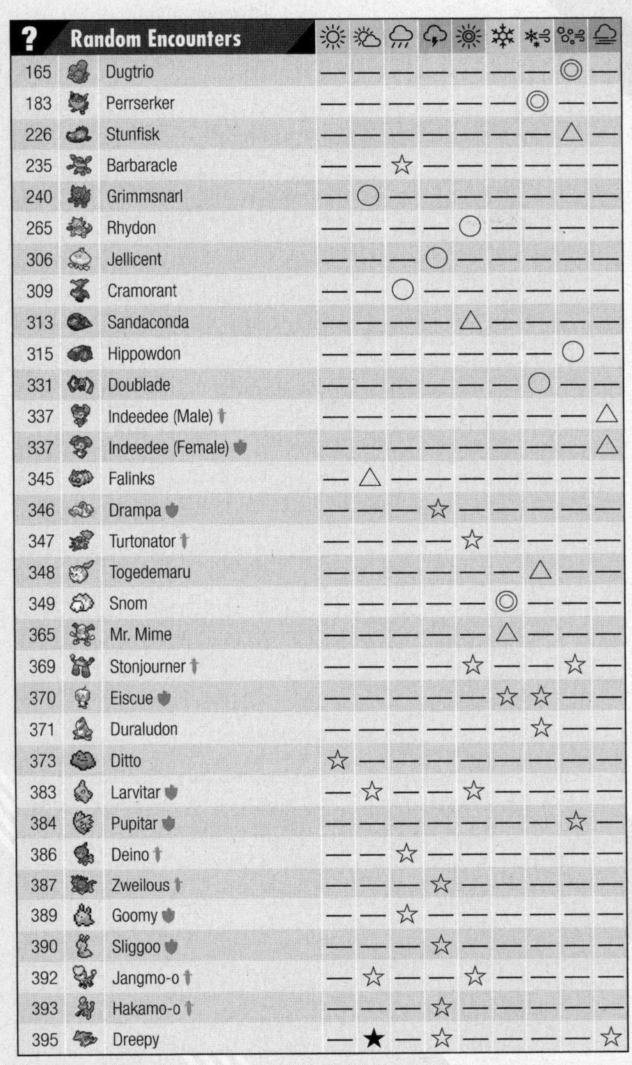

? Random Encounters			☼	⛅	🌧	⛈	☀ (Intense Sun)	❄	❄≋ (Snowstorm)	Sandstorm	Fog
165		Dugtrio	—	—	—	—	—	—	—	◎	—
183		Perrserker	—	—	—	—	—	—	◎	—	—
226		Stunfisk	—	—	—	—	—	—	—	△	—
235		Barbaracle	—	—	☆	—	—	—	—	—	—
240		Grimmsnarl	—	○	—	—	—	—	—	—	—
265		Rhydon	—	—	—	—	○	—	—	—	—
306		Jellicent	—	—	—	○	—	—	—	—	—
309		Cramorant	—	—	○	—	—	—	—	—	—
313		Sandaconda	—	—	—	—	△	—	—	—	—
315		Hippowdon	—	—	—	—	—	—	—	○	—
331		Doublade	—	—	—	—	—	—	○	—	—
337		Indeedee (Male) †	—	—	—	—	—	—	—	—	△
337		Indeedee (Female) 🛡	—	—	—	—	—	—	—	—	△
345		Falinks	—	△	—	—	—	—	—	—	—
346		Drampa 🛡	—	—	—	☆	—	—	—	—	—
347		Turtonator †	—	—	—	—	☆	—	—	—	—
348		Togedemaru	—	—	—	—	—	—	△	—	—
349		Snom	—	—	—	—	—	◎	—	—	—
365		Mr. Mime	—	—	—	—	—	△	—	—	—
369		Stonjourner †	—	—	—	—	☆	—	—	☆	—
370		Eiscue 🛡	—	—	—	—	—	☆	☆	—	—
371		Duraludon	—	—	—	—	—	—	☆	—	—
373		Ditto	☆	—	—	—	—	—	—	—	—
383		Larvitar 🛡	—	☆	—	—	☆	—	—	—	—
384		Pupitar 🛡	—	—	—	—	—	—	—	☆	—
386		Deino †	—	—	☆	—	—	—	—	—	—
387		Zweilous †	—	—	—	☆	—	—	—	—	—
389		Goomy 🛡	—	—	☆	—	—	—	—	—	—
390		Sliggoo 🛡	—	—	—	☆	—	—	—	—	—
392		Jangmo-o †	—	☆	—	—	☆	—	—	—	—
393		Hakamo-o †	—	—	—	☆	—	—	—	—	—
395		Dreepy	—	★	—	☆	—	—	—	—	☆

Water Surface			☼	⛅	🌧	⛈	☀ (Intense Sun)	❄	❄≋ (Snowstorm)	Sandstorm	Fog
063		Pelipper	—	—	—	—	◎	—	—	—	—
072		Vanillite	—	—	—	—	—	◎	◎	—	—
074		Vanilluxe	—	—	—	—	—	◎	◎	—	—
145		Gyarados	◎	◎	◎	◎	◎	◎	◎	◎	—

Water Surface			☼	⛅	🌧	⛈	☀ (Intense Sun)	❄	❄≋ (Snowstorm)	Sandstorm	Fog
147		Seaking	—	◎	—	—	◎	—	—	◎	—
153		Milotic	—	—	—	—	—	—	—	—	◎
181		Barraskewda	☆	☆	☆	☆	☆	☆	☆	☆	☆
221		Lanturn	◎	—	—	◎	—	—	—	—	◎
306		Jellicent	◎	◎	◎	◎	—	—	—	—	◎
354		Mantyke	◎	◎	◎	◎	◎	○	○	◎	◎
355		Mantine	○	◎	◎	○	○	△	△	○	◎
361		Lapras	◎	—	◎	◎	—	◎	◎	—	◎

Wanderers			☼	⛅	🌧	⛈	☀ (Intense Sun)	❄	❄≋ (Snowstorm)	Sandstorm	Fog
122		Gardevoir	◎	—	—	—	—	—	—	—	◎
197		Vaporeon	—	—	◎	—	—	—	—	—	—
198		Jolteon	—	—	—	◎	—	—	—	—	—
199		Flareon	—	—	—	—	◎	—	—	—	—
200		Espeon	—	◎	—	—	—	—	—	—	—
201		Umbreon	—	—	—	—	—	—	—	◎	—
202		Leafeon	◎	—	—	—	—	—	—	—	—
203		Glaceon	—	—	—	—	—	◎	◎	—	—
204		Sylveon	—	—	—	—	—	—	—	—	◎
265		Rhydon	—	—	—	—	—	—	—	◎	—
289		Chandelure	—	—	—	—	◎	—	—	—	—
341		Shiinotic	—	◎	◎	◎	—	—	—	—	—
352		Grapploct	◎	◎	◎	◎	◎	◎	◎	◎	◎
359		Avalugg	—	—	—	—	—	◎	◎	—	—
After becoming Champion											
243		Hatterene	◎	◎	◎	◎	◎	◎	◎	◎	◎

Berry Trees			
025		Greedent	◎
128		Cherubi	☆

Fishing			
145		Gyarados	☆
181		Barraskewda	◎
221		Lanturn	○
304		Qwilfish	△

◎ frequent ○ common △ average ☆ rare ★ almost never — does not appear
† *Pokémon Sword* only 🛡 *Pokémon Shield* only

Motostoke Riverbank

Tall Grass			☼	⛅	🌧	⛈	☀ (Intense Sun)	❄	❄≋ (Snowstorm)	Sandstorm	Fog
021		Rookidee	—	△	—	—	—	—	—	—	—
034		Wooloo	△	—	—	—	—	☆	—	—	—
042		Chewtle †	—	—	△	—	—	—	—	—	—
042		Chewtle 🛡	—	—	△	△	—	—	—	—	—
044		Purrloin †	○	○	○	○	○	○	○	○	○
044		Purrloin 🛡	○	○	○	○	△	○	○	○	○
046		Yamper	—	—	—	◎	—	—	—	—	—
072		Vanillite	—	—	—	—	—	△	○	—	—
126		Gossifleur	○	—	—	—	—	—	—	—	—
135		Duskull	—	—	—	—	—	—	—	—	☆
161		Rolycoly †	—	—	—	—	☆	—	—	△	—
161		Rolycoly 🛡	—	—	—	—	△	—	—	△	—

Tall Grass			☼	⛅	🌧	⛈	☀ (Intense Sun)	❄	❄≋ (Snowstorm)	Sandstorm	Fog
187		Cutiefly	—	○	—	—	—	○	△	—	△
214		Dewpider	—	—	☆	—	—	—	—	—	—
217		Wobbuffet	—	—	—	—	—	—	—	—	○
232		Wimpod	—	—	○	—	—	—	—	—	—
244		Salandit 🛡	—	—	—	—	○	—	—	—	—
246		Pawniard	—	—	—	—	—	—	☆	—	—
248		Throh 🛡	—	☆	—	—	—	—	—	—	—
249		Sawk †	—	☆	—	—	—	—	—	—	—
250		Koffing	—	◎	—	—	—	—	—	—	—
253		Sudowoodo	—	—	—	—	—	—	—	○	—
255		Clefairy	—	—	—	—	—	—	—	—	◎

◎ frequent ○ common △ average ☆ rare ★ almost never — does not appear
† *Pokémon Sword* only 🛡 *Pokémon Shield* only

Motostoke Riverbank (continued)

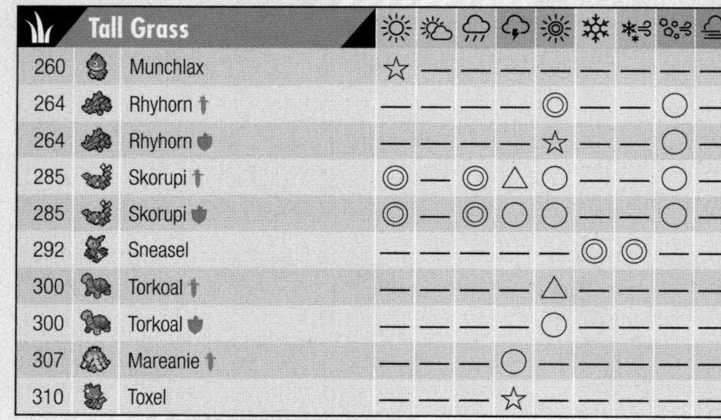

No.	Tall Grass	Normal Weather	Overcast	Raining	Thunderstorm	Intense Sun	Snowing	Snowstorm	Sandstorm	Heavy Fog
260	Munchlax	☆	—	—	—	—	—	—	—	—
264	Rhyhorn †	—	—	—	—	◎	—	—	○	—
264	Rhyhorn 🛡	—	—	—	—	☆	—	—	○	—
285	Skorupi †	◎	—	◎	△	○	—	—	○	—
285	Skorupi 🛡	◎	—	◎	○	○	—	—	○	—
292	Sneasel	—	—	—	—	—	◎	◎	—	—
300	Torkoal †	—	—	—	—	△	—	—	—	—
300	Torkoal 🛡	—	—	—	—	○	—	—	—	—
307	Mareanie †	—	—	—	○	—	—	—	—	—
310	Toxel	—	—	—	☆	—	—	—	—	—

No.	Random Encounters	Normal Weather	Overcast	Raining	Thunderstorm	Intense Sun	Snowing	Snowstorm	Sandstorm	Heavy Fog
020	Noctowl	○	○	—	—	△	△	—	○	△
022	Corvisquire	○	○	○	△	○	○	○	△	○
035	Dubwool	△	△	—	—	—	—	—	—	—
047	Boltund	—	—	—	○	—	—	—	—	—
072	Vanillite	—	—	—	—	—	○	—	—	—
127	Eldegoss	○	—	—	—	—	—	—	—	—
178	Onix	—	—	—	—	—	—	—	○	—
189	Ferroseed	—	—	—	—	—	—	△	—	—
208	Espurr	—	—	—	—	—	—	—	—	○
230	Shellos (East Sea)	—	—	—	○	—	—	—	—	—
232	Wimpod	—	—	—	○	—	—	—	—	—
234	Binacle	—	—	○	—	—	—	—	—	—
246	Pawniard	—	—	—	—	—	—	○	—	—
264	Rhyhorn	—	—	—	—	○	—	—	○	—
273	Karrablast †	—	—	○	—	—	—	—	—	—
273	Karrablast 🛡	—	—	△	—	—	—	—	—	—
275	Shelmet †	—	—	△	—	—	—	—	—	—
275	Shelmet 🛡	—	—	○	—	—	—	—	—	—
277	Elgyem	—	—	—	—	—	—	—	—	○
285	Skorupi	—	○	—	—	—	—	—	—	—
287	Litwick	—	—	—	—	○	—	—	—	—
292	Sneasel	—	—	—	—	—	○	○	—	—
297	Sigilyph	☆	☆	☆	☆	☆	☆	☆	☆	☆

No.	Water Surface	Normal Weather	Overcast	Raining	Thunderstorm	Intense Sun	Snowing	Snowstorm	Sandstorm	Heavy Fog
072	Vanillite	—	—	—	—	—	◎	◎	—	—
154	Basculin (Red-Striped Form) †	◎	◎	◎	○	◎	○	△	○	◎
154	Basculin (Blue-Striped Form) 🛡	◎	◎	◎	○	◎	○	△	○	◎
180	Arrokuda	○	◎	◎	◎	○	△	○	◎	◎
354	Mantyke	☆	☆	☆	☆	☆	☆	☆	☆	☆
356	Wailmer	◎	◎	◎	◎	◎	◎	◎	◎	◎

No.	Wanderers	Normal Weather	Overcast	Raining	Thunderstorm	Intense Sun	Snowing	Snowstorm	Sandstorm	Heavy Fog
023	Corviknight	—	—	◎	◎	◎	◎	◎	◎	—
158	Garbodor	◎	◎	◎	◎	◎	◎	◎	◎	◎
173	Conkeldurr	◎	◎	◎	◎	—	◎	—	—	◎
188	Ribombee	—	◎	—	—	—	◎	◎	—	◎
247	Bisharp	—	—	—	—	—	—	◎	—	—
256	Clefable	—	—	—	—	—	—	—	—	◎
261	Snorlax	◎	◎	◎	◎	◎	◎	◎	◎	—
265	Rhydon	—	—	—	—	◎	—	—	◎	—
286	Drapion	◎	—	◎	◎	◎	—	—	◎	—
297	Sigilyph	◎	◎	◎	◎	◎	◎	◎	◎	◎
After becoming Champion										
127	Eldegoss	◎	◎	◎	◎	◎	◎	◎	◎	◎

No.	Berry Trees	
024	Skwovet	○
025	Greedent	◎

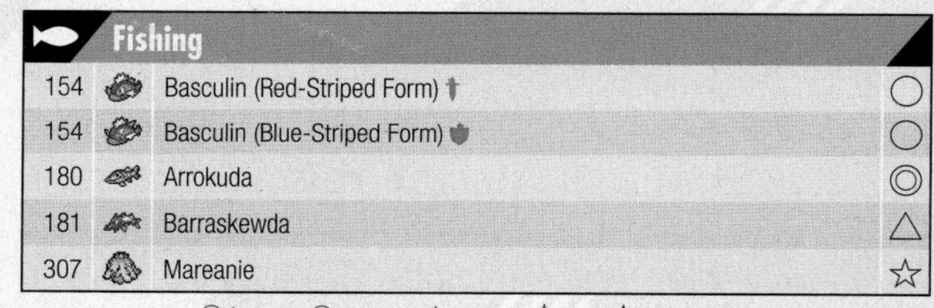

No.	Fishing	
154	Basculin (Red-Striped Form) †	○
154	Basculin (Blue-Striped Form) 🛡	○
180	Arrokuda	◎
181	Barraskewda	△
307	Mareanie	☆

◎ frequent ○ common △ average ☆ rare ★ almost never — does not appear
† *Pokémon Sword* only 🛡 *Pokémon Shield* only

North Lake Miloch

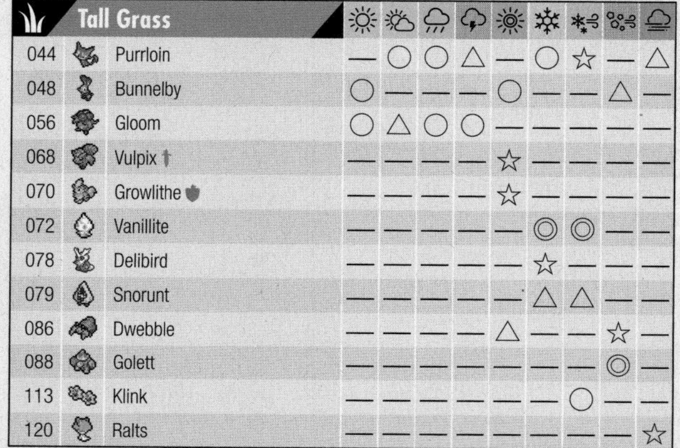

No.	Tall Grass	Normal Weather	Overcast	Raining	Thunderstorm	Intense Sun	Snowing	Snowstorm	Sandstorm	Heavy Fog
044	Purrloin	—	○	○	△	—	○	☆	—	△
048	Bunnelby	○	—	—	—	○	—	—	△	—
056	Gloom	○	△	○	○	—	—	—	—	—
068	Vulpix †	—	—	—	—	☆	—	—	—	—
070	Growlithe 🛡	—	—	—	—	☆	—	—	—	—
072	Vanillite	—	—	—	—	—	◎	◎	—	—
078	Delibird	—	—	—	—	—	☆	—	—	—
079	Snorunt	—	—	—	—	—	△	△	—	—
086	Dwebble	—	—	—	—	△	—	—	☆	—
088	Golett	—	—	—	—	—	—	—	◎	—
113	Klink	—	—	—	—	—	—	○	—	—
120	Ralts	—	—	—	—	—	—	—	—	☆

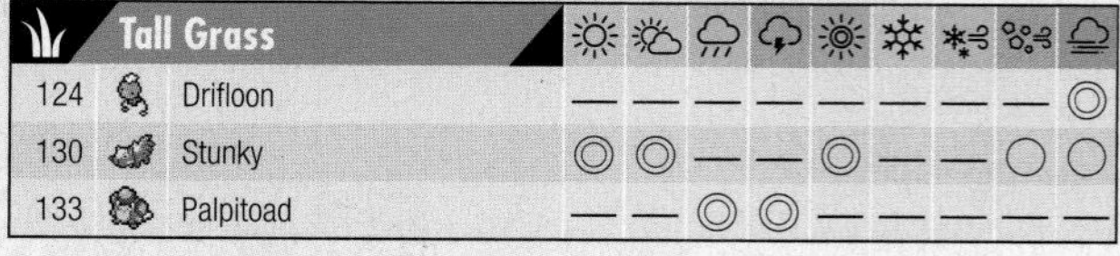

No.	Tall Grass	Normal Weather	Overcast	Raining	Thunderstorm	Intense Sun	Snowing	Snowstorm	Sandstorm	Heavy Fog
124	Drifloon	—	—	—	—	—	—	—	—	◎
130	Stunky	◎	◎	—	—	◎	—	—	○	○
133	Palpitoad	—	—	◎	◎	—	—	—	—	—

No.	Random Encounters	Normal Weather	Overcast	Raining	Thunderstorm	Intense Sun	Snowing	Snowstorm	Sandstorm	Heavy Fog
016	Grubbin	—	—	○	◎	—	—	—	—	—
026	Pidove	○	—	—	—	—	—	—	—	—
049	Diggersby	△	—	—	—	—	—	—	—	—
064	Joltik	—	—	—	○	—	—	—	—	—
078	Delibird	—	—	—	—	—	—	◎	—	—

◎ frequent ○ common △ average ☆ rare ★ almost never — does not appear
† *Pokémon Sword* only 🛡 *Pokémon Shield* only

No.	Random Encounters	Normal Weather	Overcast	Raining	Thunderstorm	Intense Sun	Snowing	Snowstorm	Sandstorm	Heavy Fog
079	Snorunt	—	—	—	—	—	◎	△	—	—
082	Baltoy	—	—	—	—	○	—	—	○	—
084	Mudbray	—	—	—	—	◎	—	—	△	—
086	Dwebble	—	—	—	—	—	—	—	◎	—
092	Natu	—	—	—	—	—	—	—	—	◎
094	Stufful	○	○	△	△	△	△	—	—	○
096	Snover	—	—	—	—	—	○	○	—	—
120	Ralts	—	—	—	—	—	—	—	—	☆
130	Stunky	◎	◎	○	○	○	○	○	○	○
132	Tympole	—	—	◎	—	—	—	—	—	—
138	Machop	—	○	—	—	—	—	—	—	—
141	Gastly	—	△	—	—	—	—	—	—	—

No.	Water Surface	Normal Weather	Overcast	Raining	Thunderstorm	Intense Sun	Snowing	Snowstorm	Sandstorm	Heavy Fog
062	Wingull	○	◎	△	—	☆	△	—	—	☆
063	Pelipper	—	—	◎	—	◎	—	—	—	—
072	Vanillite	—	—	—	—	—	◎	◎	—	—
074	Vanilluxe	—	—	—	—	—	◎	◎	—	—
124	Drifloon	△	☆	—	○	○	☆	○	☆	△
125	Drifblim	◎	◎	—	—	—	—	◎	—	◎
145	Gyarados	—	◎	—	—	◎	—	—	◎	—
146	Goldeen	—	—	○	◎	—	—	—	○	—
147	Seaking	—	—	◎	◎	—	—	—	◎	—
228	Barboach	☆	△	◎	☆	◎	—	☆	◎	○
229	Whiscash	◎	◎	—	◎	◎	—	—	◎	—
305	Frillish	◎	○	☆	△	△	○	△	△	◎

No.	Water Surface	Normal Weather	Overcast	Raining	Thunderstorm	Intense Sun	Snowing	Snowstorm	Sandstorm	Heavy Fog
306	Jellicent	◎	◎	◎	◎	—	—	—	—	◎
361	Lapras	◎	—	◎	◎	—	◎	◎	—	◎

No.	Wanderers	Normal Weather	Overcast	Raining	Thunderstorm	Intense Sun	Snowing	Snowstorm	Sandstorm	Heavy Fog
023	Corviknight	◎	◎	◎	◎	◎	◎	◎	◎	◎
045	Liepard	◎	◎	◎	◎	◎	◎	◎	◎	◎
063	Pelipper	—	—	◎	◎	—	—	—	—	—
073	Vanillish	—	—	—	—	—	◎	◎	—	—
093	Xatu	◎	◎	—	—	◎	◎	◎	◎	◎
125	Drifblim	—	—	—	—	—	—	—	—	◎
131	Skuntank	—	—	◎	—	◎	—	—	◎	—
134	Seismitoad	—	◎	—	◎	—	—	—	—	—
299	Lucario	◎	—	—	—	—	—	—	—	—
	After becoming Champion									
047	Boltund	◎	◎	◎	◎	◎	◎	◎	◎	◎

No.	Berry Trees	
024	Skwovet	◎
128	Cherubi	◎

No.	Fishing	
144	Magikarp	◎
154	Basculin (Red-Striped Form) †	☆
154	Basculin (Blue-Striped Form) 🛡	☆
228	Barboach	◎

◎ frequent ○ common △ average ☆ rare ★ almost never — does not appear
† *Pokémon Sword* only 🛡 *Pokémon Shield* only

Rolling Fields

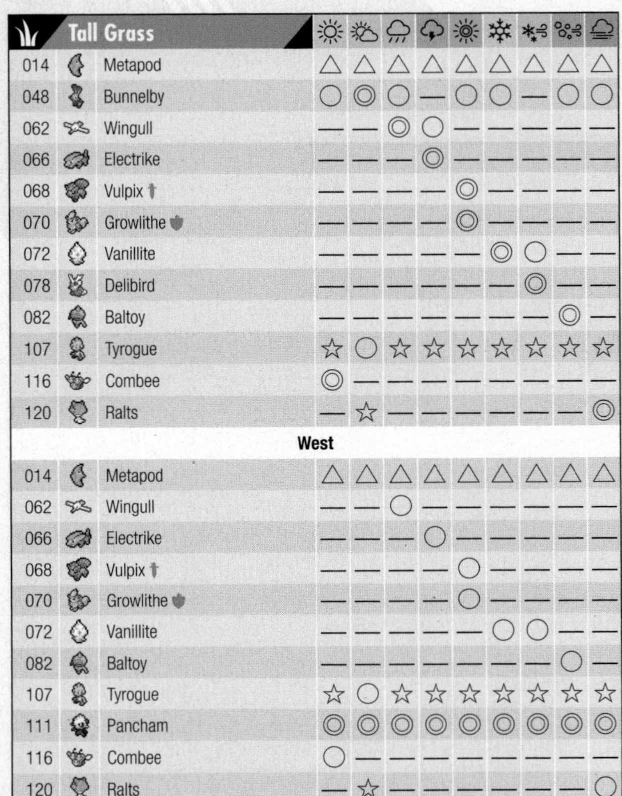

No.	Tall Grass	Normal Weather	Overcast	Raining	Thunderstorm	Intense Sun	Snowing	Snowstorm	Sandstorm	Heavy Fog
014	Metapod	△	△	△	△	△	△	△	△	△
048	Bunnelby	○	◎	○	—	○	○	—	○	○
062	Wingull	—	—	◎	○	—	—	—	—	—
066	Electrike	—	—	—	◎	—	—	—	—	—
068	Vulpix †	—	—	—	—	◎	—	—	—	—
070	Growlithe 🛡	—	—	—	—	◎	—	—	—	—
072	Vanillite	—	—	—	—	—	◎	○	—	—
078	Delibird	—	—	—	—	—	—	◎	—	—
082	Baltoy	—	—	—	—	—	—	—	◎	—
107	Tyrogue	☆	○	☆	☆	☆	☆	☆	☆	☆
116	Combee	◎	—	—	—	—	—	—	—	—
120	Ralts	—	☆	—	—	—	—	—	—	◎
	West									
014	Metapod	△	△	△	△	△	△	△	△	△
062	Wingull	—	—	○	—	—	—	—	—	—
066	Electrike	—	—	—	○	—	—	—	—	—
068	Vulpix †	—	—	—	—	○	—	—	—	—
070	Growlithe 🛡	—	—	—	—	○	—	—	—	—
072	Vanillite	—	—	—	—	—	○	○	—	—
082	Baltoy	—	—	—	—	—	—	—	○	—
107	Tyrogue	☆	○	☆	☆	☆	☆	☆	☆	☆
111	Pancham	◎	◎	◎	◎	◎	◎	◎	◎	◎
116	Combee	○	—	—	—	—	—	—	—	—
120	Ralts	—	☆	—	—	—	—	—	—	○

No.	Ground	Normal Weather	Overcast	Raining	Thunderstorm	Intense Sun	Snowing	Snowstorm	Sandstorm	Heavy Fog
164	Diglett	◎	○	◎	◎	○	◎	◎	○	◎
168	Roggenrola	○	◎	○	○	◎	○	○	◎	○

No.	Random Encounters	Normal Weather	Overcast	Raining	Thunderstorm	Intense Sun	Snowing	Snowstorm	Sandstorm	Heavy Fog
014	Metapod †	☆	☆	☆	☆	—	—	—	—	☆
014	Metapod 🛡	—	☆	☆	☆	—	—	—	—	☆
036	Lotad 🛡	—	—	◎	—	—	—	—	—	—
040	Nuzleaf †	—	—	◎	—	—	—	—	—	—
048	Bunnelby	◎	○	○	○	☆	○	☆	☆	○
050	Minccino †	○	—	—	—	—	☆	—	—	—
050	Minccino 🛡	☆	—	—	—	—	☆	—	—	—
052	Bounsweet	○	—	—	—	—	—	—	—	—
055	Oddish	—	◎	—	—	—	—	—	—	—
059	Budew	—	○	—	—	—	—	—	—	—
062	Wingull	—	—	○	—	—	—	—	—	—
064	Joltik	—	—	—	◎	—	—	—	—	—
066	Electrike	—	—	—	○	—	—	—	—	—
068	Vulpix †	—	—	—	—	○	—	—	—	—
070	Growlithe 🛡	—	—	—	—	○	—	—	—	—
072	Vanillite	—	—	—	—	—	◎	—	—	—
075	Swinub	—	—	—	—	—	○	◎	—	—
078	Delibird	—	—	—	—	—	—	○	—	—

◎ frequent ○ common △ average ☆ rare ★ almost never — does not appear
† *Pokémon Sword* only 🛡 *Pokémon Shield* only

Rolling Fields (continued)

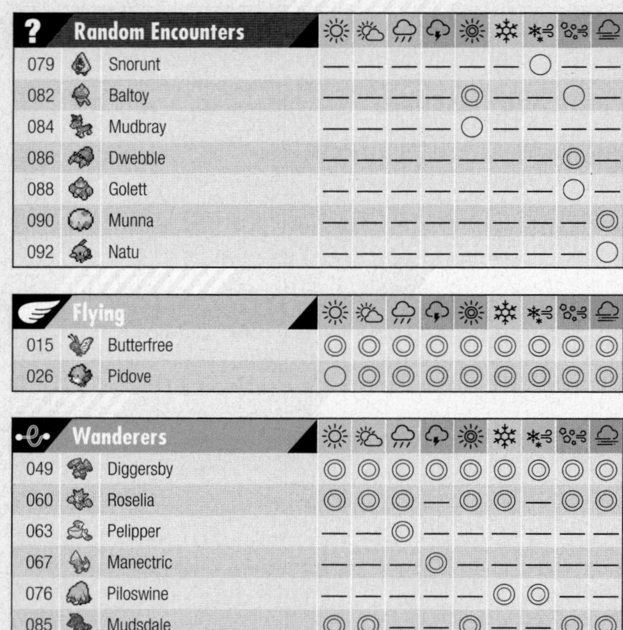

? Random Encounters		Normal	Overcast	Rain	Thunderstorm	Intense Sun	Snow	Snowstorm	Sandstorm	Heavy Fog
079	Snorunt	—	—	—	—	—	—	○	—	—
082	Baltoy	—	—	—	—	◎	—	—	○	—
084	Mudbray	—	—	—	—	○	—	—	—	—
086	Dwebble	—	—	—	—	—	—	—	◎	—
088	Golett	—	—	—	—	—	—	—	○	—
090	Munna	—	—	—	—	—	—	—	—	◎
092	Natu	—	—	—	—	—	—	—	—	○

Flying		Normal	Overcast	Rain	Thunderstorm	Intense Sun	Snow	Snowstorm	Sandstorm	Heavy Fog
015	Butterfree	◎	◎	◎	◎	◎	◎	◎	◎	◎
026	Pidove	○	◎	◎	◎	◎	◎	◎	◎	◎

Wanderers		Normal	Overcast	Rain	Thunderstorm	Intense Sun	Snow	Snowstorm	Sandstorm	Heavy Fog
049	Diggersby	◎	◎	◎	◎	◎	◎	◎	◎	◎
060	Roselia	◎	◎	◎	—	◎	◎	—	◎	◎
063	Pelipper	—	—	◎	—	—	—	—	—	—
067	Manectric	—	—	—	◎	—	—	—	—	—
076	Piloswine	—	—	—	—	—	◎	◎	—	—
085	Mudsdale	◎	◎	—	—	◎	—	—	◎	◎
087	Crustle	—	—	—	—	—	—	—	○	—
105	Ninjask	◎	◎	◎	◎	◎	◎	◎	◎	◎

Wanderers		Normal	Overcast	Rain	Thunderstorm	Intense Sun	Snow	Snowstorm	Sandstorm	Heavy Fog
112	Pangoro	◎	◎	◎	◎	◎	—	—	—	—
117	Vespiquen	◎	—	—	—	—	—	—	—	—
121	Kirlia	—	—	—	—	—	—	—	—	◎
122	Gardevoir	—	—	—	—	—	—	—	—	◎
142	Haunter	—	—	◎	◎	—	—	—	—	—
178	Onix	◎	◎	◎	◎	◎	◎	◎	◎	◎
194	Pikachu	—	—	—	◎	—	—	—	—	—
364	Mime Jr.	—	—	—	—	—	—	◎	—	—
After becoming Champion										
035	Dubwool	◎	◎	◎	◎	◎	◎	◎	◎	◎

Berry Trees		
024	Skwovet	◎
128	Cherubi	○

◎ frequent ○ common △ average ☆ rare ★ almost never — does not appear
† *Pokémon Sword* only ⛊ *Pokémon Shield* only

South Lake Miloch

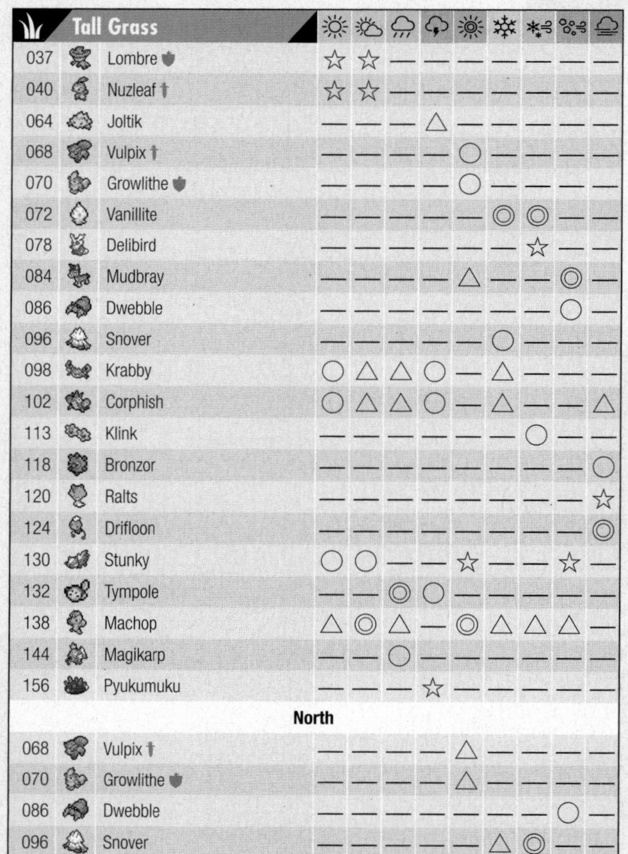

Tall Grass		Normal	Overcast	Rain	Thunderstorm	Intense Sun	Snow	Snowstorm	Sandstorm	Heavy Fog
037	Lombre ⛊	☆	☆	—	—	—	—	—	—	—
040	Nuzleaf †	☆	☆	—	—	—	—	—	—	—
064	Joltik	—	—	—	△	—	—	—	—	—
068	Vulpix †	—	—	—	—	○	—	—	—	—
070	Growlithe ⛊	—	—	—	—	○	—	—	—	—
072	Vanillite	—	—	—	—	—	◎	◎	—	—
078	Delibird	—	—	—	—	—	—	☆	—	—
084	Mudbray	—	—	—	—	△	—	—	◎	—
086	Dwebble	—	—	—	—	—	—	—	○	—
096	Snover	—	—	—	—	—	○	—	—	—
098	Krabby	○	△	△	○	—	△	—	—	—
102	Corphish	○	△	△	○	—	△	—	—	△
113	Klink	—	—	—	—	—	—	○	—	—
118	Bronzor	—	—	—	—	—	—	—	—	○
120	Ralts	—	—	—	—	—	—	—	—	☆
124	Drifloon	—	—	—	—	—	—	—	—	◎
130	Stunky	○	○	—	—	☆	—	—	☆	—
132	Tympole	—	—	◎	○	—	—	—	—	—
138	Machop	△	◎	△	—	◎	△	△	△	—
144	Magikarp	—	—	○	—	—	—	—	—	—
156	Pyukumuku	—	—	—	☆	—	—	—	—	—
North										
068	Vulpix †	—	—	—	—	△	—	—	—	—
070	Growlithe ⛊	—	—	—	—	△	—	—	—	—
086	Dwebble	—	—	—	—	—	—	—	○	—
096	Snover	—	—	—	—	—	△	◎	—	—

Tall Grass		Normal	Overcast	Rain	Thunderstorm	Intense Sun	Snow	Snowstorm	Sandstorm	Heavy Fog
107	Tyrogue	☆	☆	☆	☆	☆	☆	☆	☆	☆
118	Bronzor	—	—	—	—	—	—	—	—	○
130	Stunky	△	○	○	○	—	—	—	—	—
138	Machop	◎	◎	◎	◎	◎	◎	○	◎	◎

? Random Encounters		Normal	Overcast	Rain	Thunderstorm	Intense Sun	Snow	Snowstorm	Sandstorm	Heavy Fog
060	Roselia	—	○	—	—	○	—	—	—	—
062	Wingull	○	—	△	—	—	—	—	—	—
064	Joltik	—	—	—	○	—	—	—	—	—
066	Electrike	—	—	—	◎	—	—	—	—	—
068	Vulpix †	—	—	—	—	○	—	—	—	—
070	Growlithe ⛊	—	—	—	—	○	—	—	—	—
072	Vanillite	—	—	—	—	—	○	—	—	—
079	Snorunt	—	—	—	—	—	◎	—	—	—
082	Baltoy	—	—	—	—	◎	—	—	○	—
092	Natu	—	—	—	—	—	—	—	—	◎
096	Snover	—	—	—	—	—	—	○	—	—
100	Wooper	—	—	—	—	—	—	—	○	—
102	Corphish	△	◎	○	○	—	○	○	—	○
104	Nincada	—	—	—	—	△	—	—	◎	—
107	Tyrogue	—	△	—	—	—	—	—	—	—
113	Klink	—	—	—	—	—	—	◎	—	—
120	Ralts	—	—	—	—	—	—	—	—	△
132	Tympole	○	—	◎	—	—	—	—	△	—
138	Machop	◎	○	○	△	—	△	△	—	○

◎ frequent ○ common △ average ☆ rare ★ almost never — does not appear
† *Pokémon Sword* only ⛊ *Pokémon Shield* only

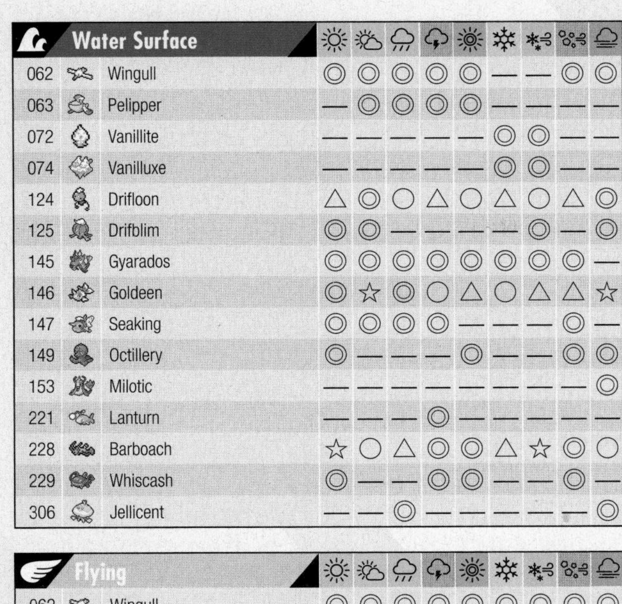

Water Surface		Normal Weather	Overcast	Raining	Thunderstorm	Intense Sun	Snowing	Snowstorm	Sandstorm	Heavy Fog
062	Wingull	◎	◎	◎	◎	◎	—	—	◎	◎
063	Pelipper	—	◎	◎	◎	◎	—	—	—	—
072	Vanillite	—	—	—	—	—	◎	◎	—	—
074	Vanilluxe	—	—	—	—	—	◎	◎	—	—
124	Drifloon	△	◎	○	△	○	△	○	△	◎
125	Drifblim	◎	◎	—	—	—	—	◎	—	◎
145	Gyarados	◎	◎	◎	◎	◎	◎	◎	◎	—
146	Goldeen	◎	☆	◎	○	△	○	△	△	☆
147	Seaking	◎	◎	◎	◎	—	—	—	◎	—
149	Octillery	◎	—	—	—	◎	—	—	◎	◎
153	Milotic	—	—	—	—	—	—	—	—	◎
221	Lanturn	—	—	—	◎	—	—	—	—	—
228	Barboach	☆	○	△	◎	◎	△	☆	◎	○
229	Whiscash	◎	—	—	◎	◎	—	—	◎	—
306	Jellicent	—	—	◎	—	—	—	—	—	◎

Flying		Normal Weather	Overcast	Raining	Thunderstorm	Intense Sun	Snowing	Snowstorm	Sandstorm	Heavy Fog
062	Wingull	◎	◎	◎	◎	◎	◎	◎	◎	◎
124	Drifloon	○	○	○	○	○	○	○	○	○

Wanderers		Normal Weather	Overcast	Raining	Thunderstorm	Intense Sun	Snowing	Snowstorm	Sandstorm	Heavy Fog
065	Galvantula	◎	◎	◎	◎	◎	◎	◎	◎	◎
087	Crustle	—	—	—	—	◎	—	—	—	—
099	Kingler	◎	—	—	◎	—	—	—	—	—
103	Crawdaunt	◎	—	—	◎	—	—	—	—	—
125	Drifblim	—	—	—	—	—	—	—	—	◎
131	Skuntank	◎	◎	—	—	—	◎	◎	◎	◎
133	Palpitoad	—	—	◎	◎	—	—	—	—	—
139	Machoke	◎	◎	◎	◎	◎	◎	◎	◎	◎
After becoming Champion										
030	Thievul	◎	◎	◎	◎	◎	◎	◎	◎	◎

Fishing		
144	Magikarp	◎
148	Remoraid	◎
156	Pyukumuku	★
228	Barboach	△

◎ frequent ○ common △ average ☆ rare ★ almost never — does not appear
† *Pokémon Sword* only 🛡 *Pokémon Shield* only

Stony Wilderness

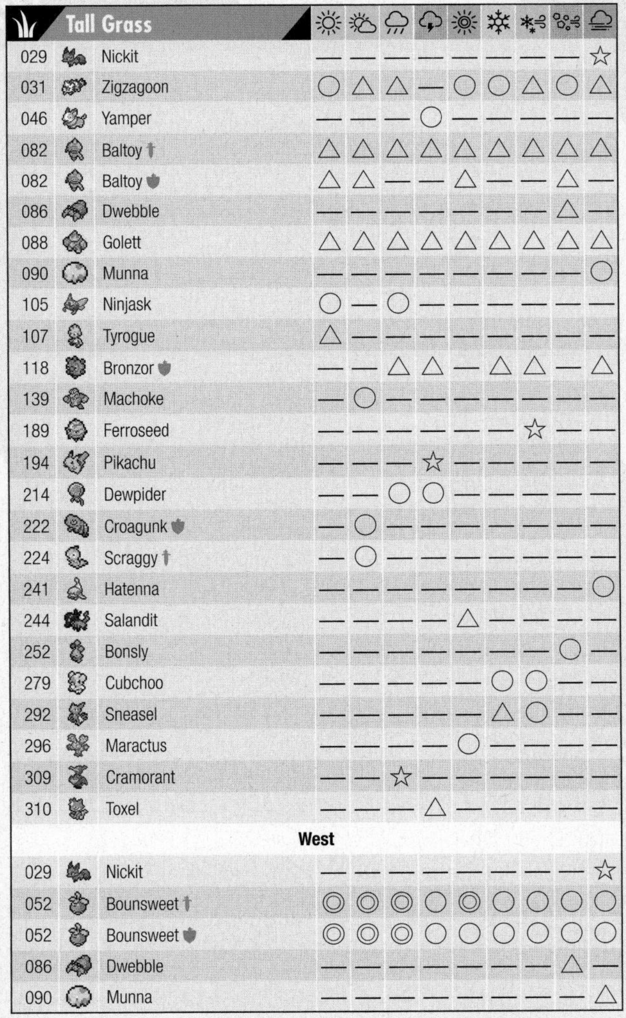

Tall Grass		Normal Weather	Overcast	Raining	Thunderstorm	Intense Sun	Snowing	Snowstorm	Sandstorm	Heavy Fog
029	Nickit	—	—	—	—	—	—	—	—	☆
031	Zigzagoon	○	△	△	—	○	○	△	○	△
046	Yamper	—	—	—	○	—	—	—	—	—
082	Baltoy †	△	△	△	△	△	△	△	△	△
082	Baltoy 🛡	△	△	—	—	△	—	—	△	—
086	Dwebble	—	—	—	—	—	—	—	△	—
088	Golett	△	△	△	△	△	△	△	△	△
090	Munna	—	—	—	—	—	—	—	—	○
105	Ninjask	○	—	○	—	—	—	—	—	—
107	Tyrogue	△	—	—	—	—	—	—	—	—
118	Bronzor 🛡	—	—	△	△	—	△	△	—	△
139	Machoke	—	○	—	—	—	—	—	—	—
189	Ferroseed	—	—	—	—	—	—	☆	—	—
194	Pikachu	—	—	—	☆	—	—	—	—	—
214	Dewpider	—	—	○	○	—	—	—	—	—
222	Croagunk 🛡	—	○	—	—	—	—	—	—	—
224	Scraggy †	—	○	—	—	—	—	—	—	—
241	Hatenna	—	—	—	—	—	—	—	—	○
244	Salandit	—	—	—	—	△	—	—	—	—
252	Bonsly	—	—	—	—	—	—	—	○	—
279	Cubchoo	—	—	—	—	—	○	○	—	—
292	Sneasel	—	—	—	—	—	△	○	—	—
296	Maractus	—	—	—	—	○	—	—	—	—
309	Cramorant	—	—	☆	—	—	—	—	—	—
310	Toxel	—	—	—	△	—	—	—	—	—
West										
029	Nickit	—	—	—	—	—	—	—	—	☆
052	Bounsweet †	◎	◎	◎	○	◎	○	○	○	○
052	Bounsweet 🛡	◎	◎	◎	○	○	○	○	○	○
086	Dwebble	—	—	—	—	—	—	—	△	—
090	Munna	—	—	—	—	—	—	—	—	△

Tall Grass		Normal Weather	Overcast	Raining	Thunderstorm	Intense Sun	Snowing	Snowstorm	Sandstorm	Heavy Fog
107	Tyrogue	△	—	—	—	—	—	—	—	—
138	Machop	○	○	—	—	—	—	—	—	—
189	Ferroseed	—	—	—	—	—	—	☆	—	—
194	Pikachu †	—	—	—	△	—	—	—	—	—
194	Pikachu 🛡	—	—	—	☆	—	—	—	—	—
214	Dewpider	—	—	○	◎	—	—	—	—	—
222	Croagunk 🛡	—	△	—	—	—	—	—	—	—
224	Scraggy †	—	△	—	—	—	—	—	—	—
241	Hatenna	—	—	—	—	—	—	—	—	◎
244	Salandit †	—	—	—	—	☆	—	—	—	—
244	Salandit 🛡	—	—	—	—	△	—	—	—	—
252	Bonsly	—	—	—	—	—	—	—	◎	—
279	Cubchoo	—	—	—	—	—	◎	△	—	—
292	Sneasel	—	—	—	—	—	△	◎	—	—
296	Maractus	—	—	—	—	◎	—	—	—	—
309	Cramorant	—	—	☆	—	—	—	—	—	—
310	Toxel	—	—	—	△	—	—	—	—	—
Parched grass										
029	Nickit	—	—	—	—	—	—	—	—	☆
046	Yamper	—	—	—	◎	—	—	—	—	—
086	Dwebble	◎	△	○	—	○	○	△	○	△
090	Munna	—	—	—	—	—	—	—	—	○
105	Ninjask	○	—	△	—	—	—	—	—	—
107	Tyrogue	△	—	—	—	—	—	—	—	—
139	Machoke	—	◎	—	—	—	—	—	—	—
168	Roggenrola †	—	—	—	—	△	—	—	△	—
168	Roggenrola 🛡	—	—	—	—	—	—	—	△	—
189	Ferroseed	—	—	—	—	—	—	☆	—	—
194	Pikachu	—	—	—	☆	—	—	—	—	—
214	Dewpider	—	—	◎	○	—	—	—	—	—

◎ frequent ○ common △ average ☆ rare ★ almost never — does not appear
† *Pokémon Sword* only 🛡 *Pokémon Shield* only

Stony Wilderness (continued)

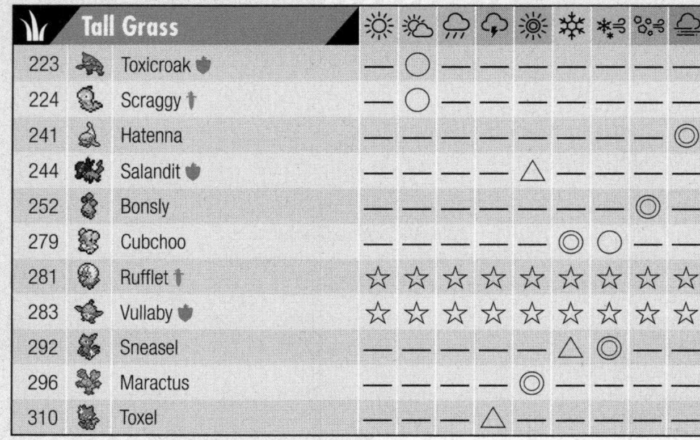

Tall Grass		Normal	Overcast	Raining	Thunderstorm	Intense Sun	Snowing	Snowstorm	Sandstorm	Heavy Fog
223	Toxicroak 🛡	—	○	—	—	—	—	—	—	—
224	Scraggy †	—	○	—	—	—	—	—	—	—
241	Hatenna	—	—	—	—	—	—	—	—	◎
244	Salandit 🛡	—	—	—	—	△	—	—	—	—
252	Bonsly	—	—	—	—	—	—	—	◎	—
279	Cubchoo	—	—	—	—	—	◎	○	—	—
281	Rufflet †	☆	☆	☆	☆	☆	☆	☆	☆	☆
283	Vullaby 🛡	☆	☆	☆	☆	☆	☆	☆	☆	☆
292	Sneasel	—	—	—	—	—	△	◎	—	—
296	Maractus	—	—	—	—	◎	—	—	—	—
310	Toxel	—	—	—	△	—	—	—	—	—

? Random Encounters		Normal	Overcast	Raining	Thunderstorm	Intense Sun	Snowing	Snowstorm	Sandstorm	Heavy Fog
011	Dottler	—	—	—	—	—	—	—	—	○
030	Thievul	—	—	—	—	—	—	—	—	◎
127	Eldegoss	△	—	—	—	—	—	—	—	—
162	Carkol	—	—	—	—	◎	—	—	—	—
166	Drilbur	—	—	—	—	△	—	—	○	—
169	Boldore †	—	—	—	—	—	—	—	○	—
169	Boldore 🛡	◎	—	—	○	○	△	—	◎	—
172	Gurdurr †	◎	—	—	○	○	△	—	—	—
188	Ribombee	○	○	—	—	—	—	—	—	—
194	Pikachu	—	—	△	—	—	—	—	—	—
205	Applin	—	—	—	△	—	—	—	—	—
210	Swirlix †	—	○	—	—	—	—	—	—	—
212	Spritzee 🛡	—	○	—	—	—	—	—	—	—
227	Shuckle	—	—	—	—	—	—	—	△	—
228	Barboach	—	—	◎	—	—	—	—	—	—
230	Shellos (East Sea)	—	—	○	—	—	—	—	—	—
238	Impidimp	○	△	○	○	○	○	△	—	○

? Random Encounters		Normal	Overcast	Raining	Thunderstorm	Intense Sun	Snowing	Snowstorm	Sandstorm	Heavy Fog
246	Pawniard	—	—	—	—	—	—	○	—	—
258	Togetic	—	—	—	—	—	—	—	—	△
262	Cottonee	—	◎	—	—	—	—	—	—	—
264	Rhyhorn †	—	—	—	—	—	—	—	◎	—
264	Rhyhorn 🛡	—	—	—	—	—	—	—	○	—
279	Cubchoo	—	—	—	—	—	◎	○	—	—
292	Sneasel	—	—	—	—	—	○	◎	—	—
310	Toxel	—	—	—	◎	—	—	—	—	—

Flying		Normal	Overcast	Raining	Thunderstorm	Intense Sun	Snowing	Snowstorm	Sandstorm	Heavy Fog
022	Corvisquire	◎	◎	◎	◎	◎	◎	◎	◎	◎
027	Tranquill	◎	◎	◎	◎	◎	◎	◎	◎	◎
297	Sigilyph	◎	◎	◎	◎	◎	◎	◎	◎	◎

Wanderers		Normal	Overcast	Raining	Thunderstorm	Intense Sun	Snowing	Snowstorm	Sandstorm	Heavy Fog
028	Unfezant	—	○	—	—	—	—	—	—	—
054	Tsareena	◎	◎	—	—	◎	◎	◎	◎	◎
083	Claydol	◎	◎	—	—	◎	—	—	◎	—
087	Crustle	◎	◎	—	—	◎	◎	◎	◎	◎
089	Golurk	◎	◎	◎	◎	◎	◎	◎	◎	◎
119	Bronzong	—	—	◎	◎	—	◎	◎	—	◎
137	Dusknoir	◎	◎	◎	◎	◎	◎	◎	◎	◎
215	Araquanid	—	—	◎	◎	—	—	—	—	—
265	Rhydon	◎	◎	◎	◎	◎	◎	◎	◎	◎
297	Sigilyph	◎	—	◎	◎	◎	◎	◎	◎	◎
	After becoming Champion									
240	Grimmsnarl	◎	◎	◎	◎	◎	◎	◎	◎	◎

◎ frequent ○ common △ average ☆ rare ★ almost never — does not appear
† *Pokémon Sword* only 🛡 *Pokémon Shield* only

Watchtower Ruins

Tall Grass		Normal	Overcast	Raining	Thunderstorm	Intense Sun	Snowing	Snowstorm	Sandstorm	Heavy Fog
044	Purrloin	—	—	☆	☆	—	—	△	△	☆
055	Oddish	—	△	—	—	—	—	—	—	—
062	Wingull	—	—	△	—	—	—	—	—	—
068	Vulpix †	—	—	—	—	△	—	—	—	—
070	Growlithe 🛡	—	—	—	—	△	—	—	—	—
078	Delibird	—	—	—	—	—	○	◎	—	—
088	Golett	◎	—	—	—	—	—	—	—	—
120	Ralts	—	—	—	—	—	—	—	—	△
124	Drifloon	△	☆	—	△	◎	◎	—	—	—
135	Duskull	○	◎	◎	○	○	△	—	—	○
141	Gastly	—	○	○	◎	—	—	○	◎	◎
227	Shuckle	—	—	—	—	☆	—	—	○	—

? Random Encounters		Normal	Overcast	Raining	Thunderstorm	Intense Sun	Snowing	Snowstorm	Sandstorm	Heavy Fog
016	Grubbin	—	—	—	○	—	—	—	—	—
026	Pidove	△	—	△	△	—	—	—	△	△
044	Purrloin	—	—	—	—	—	—	—	—	○

? Random Encounters		Normal	Overcast	Raining	Thunderstorm	Intense Sun	Snowing	Snowstorm	Sandstorm	Heavy Fog
052	Bounsweet	○	○	—	—	—	—	—	—	—
062	Wingull	—	—	○	—	—	—	—	—	—
066	Electrike	—	—	—	◎	—	—	—	—	—
068	Vulpix †	—	—	—	—	○	—	—	—	—
070	Growlithe 🛡	—	—	—	—	○	—	—	—	—
079	Snorunt	—	—	—	—	—	◎	○	—	—
086	Dwebble	—	—	—	—	—	—	—	○	—
088	Golett	◎	—	—	—	◎	—	—	◎	—
096	Snover	—	—	—	—	—	○	◎	—	—
124	Drifloon	○	—	—	—	△	△	△	—	—
132	Tympole	—	—	○	—	—	—	—	—	—
135	Duskull	—	◎	◎	○	○	○	○	○	○
138	Machop †	—	○	—	—	—	—	—	—	—
138	Machop 🛡	—	△	—	—	—	—	—	—	—
141	Gastly †	—	△	—	—	—	—	—	—	—
141	Gastly 🛡	—	○	—	—	—	—	—	—	—

◎ frequent ○ common △ average ☆ rare ★ almost never — does not appear
† *Pokémon Sword* only 🛡 *Pokémon Shield* only

Flying		Sun	Overcast	Rain	Thunderstorm	Intense Sun	Snow	Snowstorm	Sandstorm	Fog
174	Woobat	◎	◎	◎	◎	◎	◎	◎	◎	◎
176	Noibat	◎	◎	◎	◎	◎	◎	◎	◎	◎

Wanderers		Sun	Overcast	Rain	Thunderstorm	Intense Sun	Snow	Snowstorm	Sandstorm	Fog
080	Glalie	—	—	—	—	—	◎	◎	—	—
089	Golurk	◎	—	—	—	◎	—	—	◎	—
125	Drifblim	◎	—	—	—	◎	◎	—	—	—
136	Dusclops	—	◎	◎	◎	—	—	—	—	◎
142	Haunter	—	◎	◎	◎	—	—	◎	◎	◎
After becoming Champion										
023	Corviknight	◎	◎	◎	◎	◎	◎	◎	◎	◎

Berry Trees		
024	Skwovet	◎
128	Cherubi	◎

◎ frequent ○ common △ average ☆ rare ★ almost never — does not appear
† *Pokémon Sword* only 🛡 *Pokémon Shield* only

West Lake Axewell

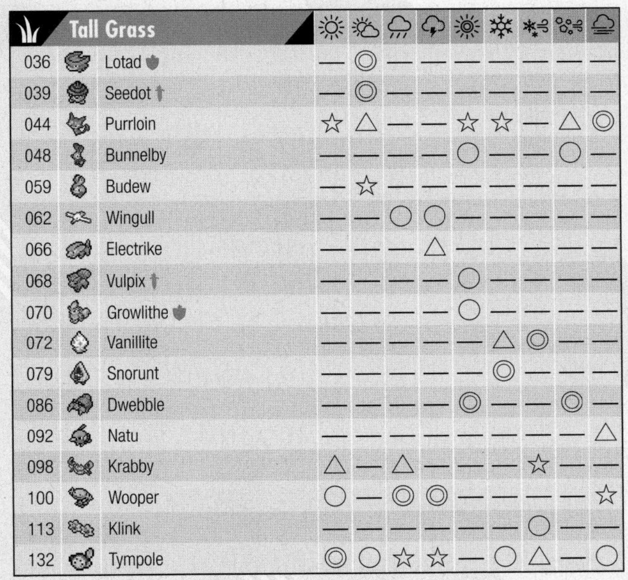

Tall Grass		Sun	Overcast	Rain	Thunderstorm	Intense Sun	Snow	Snowstorm	Sandstorm	Fog
036	Lotad 🛡	—	◎	—	—	—	—	—	—	—
039	Seedot †	—	◎	—	—	—	—	—	—	—
044	Purrloin	☆	△	—	—	☆	☆	—	△	◎
048	Bunnelby	—	—	—	—	○	—	—	○	—
059	Budew	—	☆	—	—	—	—	—	—	—
062	Wingull	—	—	○	○	—	—	—	—	—
066	Electrike	—	—	—	△	—	—	—	—	—
068	Vulpix †	—	—	—	—	○	—	—	—	—
070	Growlithe 🛡	—	—	—	—	○	—	—	—	—
072	Vanillite	—	—	—	—	—	△	◎	—	—
079	Snorunt	—	—	—	—	—	◎	—	—	—
086	Dwebble	—	—	—	—	◎	—	—	◎	—
092	Natu	—	—	—	—	—	—	—	—	△
098	Krabby	△	—	△	—	—	—	☆	—	—
100	Wooper	○	—	◎	◎	—	—	—	—	☆
113	Klink	—	—	—	—	—	—	○	—	—
132	Tympole	◎	○	☆	☆	—	○	△	—	○

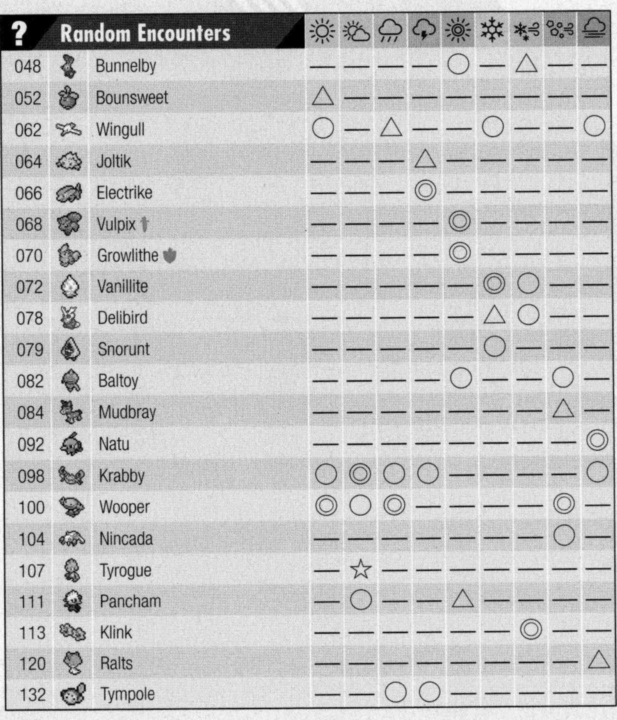

Random Encounters		Sun	Overcast	Rain	Thunderstorm	Intense Sun	Snow	Snowstorm	Sandstorm	Fog
048	Bunnelby	—	—	—	—	○	—	△	—	—
052	Bounsweet	△	—	—	—	—	—	—	—	—
062	Wingull	○	—	△	—	—	○	—	—	○
064	Joltik	—	—	—	△	—	—	—	—	—
066	Electrike	—	—	—	◎	—	—	—	—	—
068	Vulpix †	—	—	—	—	◎	—	—	—	—
070	Growlithe 🛡	—	—	—	—	◎	—	—	—	—
072	Vanillite	—	—	—	—	—	◎	○	—	—
078	Delibird	—	—	—	—	—	△	○	—	—
079	Snorunt	—	—	—	—	—	○	—	—	—
082	Baltoy	—	—	—	—	○	—	—	○	—
084	Mudbray	—	—	—	—	—	—	—	△	—
092	Natu	—	—	—	—	—	—	—	—	◎
098	Krabby	○	◎	○	○	—	—	—	—	○
100	Wooper	◎	○	◎	—	—	—	—	◎	—
104	Nincada	—	—	—	—	—	—	—	○	—
107	Tyrogue	—	☆	—	—	—	—	—	—	—
111	Pancham	—	○	—	—	△	—	—	—	—
113	Klink	—	—	—	—	—	—	◎	—	—
120	Ralts	—	—	—	—	—	—	—	—	△
132	Tympole	—	—	○	○	—	—	—	—	—

Water Surface		Sun	Overcast	Rain	Thunderstorm	Intense Sun	Snow	Snowstorm	Sandstorm	Fog
063	Pelipper	◎	◎	◎	◎	◎	—	—	—	—
072	Vanillite	—	—	—	—	—	◎	◎	—	—
074	Vanilluxe	—	—	—	—	—	◎	◎	—	—
144	Magikarp	☆	△	☆	○	◎	△	△	◎	◎
145	Gyarados	◎	◎	◎	◎	◎	◎	◎	◎	◎
146	Goldeen	○	◎	○	△	△	—	☆	○	○
147	Seaking	◎	◎	—	—	—	—	—	◎	—
148	Remoraid	△	○	△	☆	☆	—	—	△	☆
150	Shellder	—	—	—	—	—	○	—	—	—
151	Cloyster	◎	—	—	—	—	—	—	—	◎
220	Chinchou	—	—	—	◎	—	—	—	—	—
221	Lanturn	—	—	—	◎	—	—	—	—	—
305	Frillish	◎	☆	◎	—	○	☆	△	☆	△
306	Jellicent	—	◎	◎	—	—	—	—	—	◎
352	Grapploct	◎	◎	—	—	◎	◎	◎	◎	◎
361	Lapras	◎	—	◎	◎	—	◎	◎	—	◎

Wanderers		Sun	Overcast	Rain	Thunderstorm	Intense Sun	Snow	Snowstorm	Sandstorm	Fog
049	Diggersby	—	—	—	—	◎	◎	◎	◎	—
063	Pelipper	—	—	◎	◎	—	—	—	—	—
099	Kingler	◎	—	—	—	—	—	—	—	—
101	Quagsire	◎	◎	◎	◎	—	—	—	—	◎
133	Palpitoad	—	◎	—	—	—	◎	◎	◎	◎
After becoming Champion										
043	Drednaw	◎	◎	◎	◎	◎	◎	◎	◎	◎

Fishing		
144	Magikarp	◎
146	Goldeen	○
148	Remoraid	△
155	Wishiwashi	☆

◎ frequent ○ common △ average ☆ rare ★ almost never — does not appear
† *Pokémon Sword* only 🛡 *Pokémon Shield* only

Signals in the Wild Area

If you've spent any time out exploring the Wild Area, you've probably seen a pillar of light or some smoke rising up into the air from a distance. These are signals pointing to exciting activities for you to join. Pillars of light shining out from Pokémon Dens show where you can have a Max Raid Battle, and plumes of smoke mark the camps of other Trainers (p. 296)! If you're interested in either, all you need to do is head straight toward the signal. Your Rotom Bike will come in handy for zipping across the Wild Area, especially if you've upgraded it (p. 276). Yet it's still a long trek across the Wild Area, so check out the tables below to understand what each signal means. That way you can be sure you're on the right path!

The Watchtower Lair

There's one Pokémon Den that's different from the others—the enormous one at the Watchtower Ruins. This one won't ever become active through normal means. You'll need to toss special items into this giant den in order to attract Dynamax Pokémon. These items will only be available through certain events, so make sure to keep your eyes on Pokemon.com for updates!

Light from Pokémon Dens

What the den looks like		What it means
	No light	The den is inactive. Throw a Wishing Piece in it if you want to activate the den!
	Glowing	Checking the den will earn 50 W for most of your adventure. And if you become Champion, you'll find you suddenly get 200 W instead!

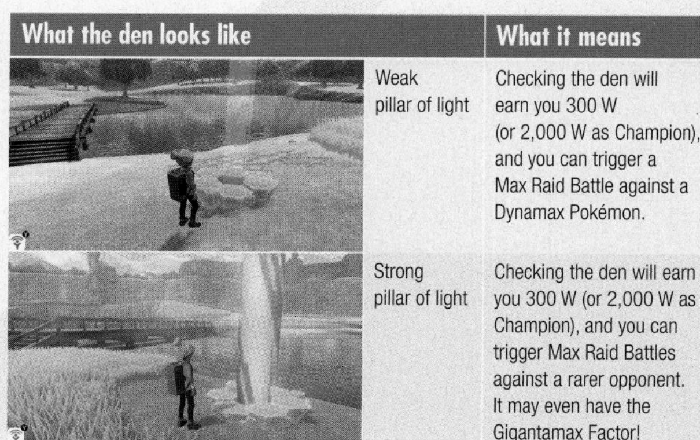

What the den looks like		What it means
	Weak pillar of light	Checking the den will earn you 300 W (or 2,000 W as Champion), and you can trigger a Max Raid Battle against a Dynamax Pokémon.
	Strong pillar of light	Checking the den will earn you 300 W (or 2,000 W as Champion), and you can trigger Max Raid Battles against a rarer opponent. It may even have the Gigantamax Factor!

Smoke from campsites

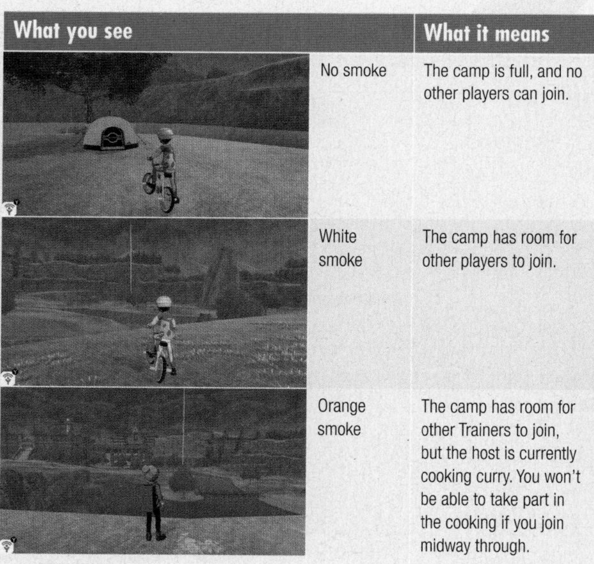

What you see		What it means
	No smoke	The camp is full, and no other players can join.
	White smoke	The camp has room for other players to join.
	Orange smoke	The camp has room for other Trainers to join, but the host is currently cooking curry. You won't be able to take part in the cooking if you join midway through.

More Max Raid Battles

If you love Max Raid Battles or are looking to catch Gigantamax Pokémon, you don't need to worry about running out of chances in a given day. Once you've taken on all the Pokémon Dens emitting pillars of light in the Wild Area, a new set of dens will light up—and at least one should have a strong pillar of light, meaning you'll have a slim chance at finding a Gigantamax Pokémon! You can also go around visiting inactive Pokémon Dens and tossing in Wishing Pieces. Tossing one into a Pokémon Den will attract a Dynamax Pokémon, though it may take a few tries before you get a den with a strong pillar of light. You can stock up on Wishing Pieces from the Rotom Rallyists in exchange for Watts (p. 276)! Which Pokémon Dens are emitting pillars of light will also change at the start of each new day. Your game's time is determined by the internal clock of your Nintendo Switch.

Max Raid Battles

As you advance through the Gym Challenge, you'll come up against Trainers who use Dynamax and even Gigantamax Pokémon, but Max Raid Battles are on another level. The Dynamax Pokémon you'll face down in dens with pillars of light shining out from them are far more challenging than Dynamax Pokémon in Trainer battles!

You'll need a group of four Trainers, each using one of their own Pokémon to battle these fearsome, gigantic Pokémon. You'll also have to strategize around the different ways you can lose these battles and the mysterious barrier that can protect these Pokémon, both features unique to Max Raid Battles.

Max Raid Battle setup

Once you approach an active Pokémon Den and examine it, you'll see a screen like the one below. We'll break down each part of this screen so that you're ready to take on any Dynamax Pokémon you come across.

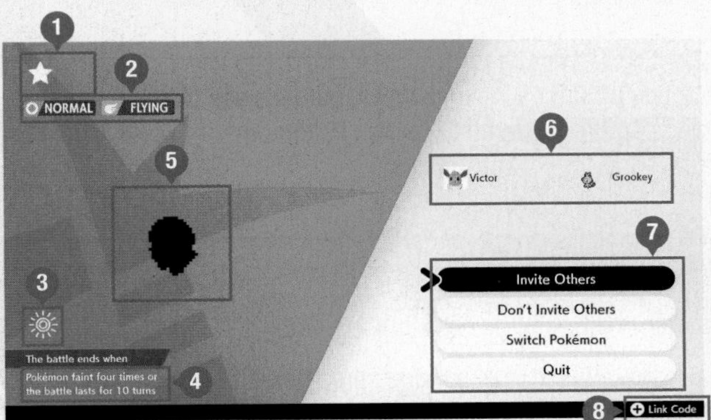

1. The difficulty of the Max Raid Battle
2. The type or types of the Dynamax Pokémon you'll face
3. The current weather
4. The Max Raid Battle's lose conditions
5. The Dynamax Pokémon's silhouette
6. The Trainers and Pokémon that will participate in the Max Raid Battle
7. Max Raid Battle setup options
8. Set or delete a Link Code

Max Raid Battle difficulty

On the setup screen, you'll see a number of stars in the upper-left corner. They show the difficulty of the Dynamax Pokémon you'll face in the Max Raid Battle. Difficulty can range from one star (the lowest) to five stars (the highest). The higher the difficulty, the stronger and rarer the Pokémon you'll have to battle is likely to be. A higher difficulty also means better rewards if you manage to win. When you first arrive in the Wild Area, you'll only find lower-difficulty Max Raid Battles. But as you continue through your Gym Challenge and collect Gym Badges, you'll begin to find higher-difficulty ones. Make sure to come back and check the Wild Area often!

Finding Trainers

Wild Dynamax Pokémon are too tough to face on your own, so you'll need three other Trainers to join you. While you're at the setup screen, you can choose whether or not to invite others to battle with you. If you invite others, Trainers in the real world can join you via either local communication or the internet, depending on your current connection type. By pressing ⊕ on the setup screen, you can set a Link Code, meaning that only Trainers that know the Link Code will be able to join you in the Max Raid Battle.

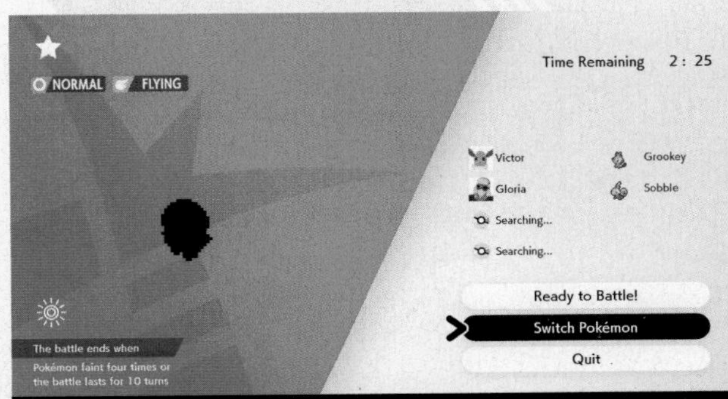

Let other Trainers know you're looking for allies...

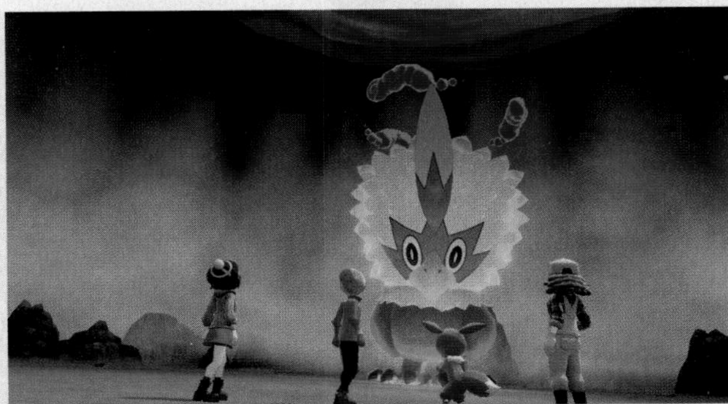

Then they can choose to join you for the Max Raid Battle!

While you wait for other players to join you, you can review the info on the setup screen and swap in a different Pokémon that you want to use from your party or Boxes. You can also choose to start the Max Raid Battle at any time, even if only one or two other Trainers have joined you—or none at all. Any unfilled spots will be filled by in-game Trainers for you. The same thing will happen if you choose not to invite anyone to a Max Raid Battle, so you'll never have to face one alone.

Joining Others' Max Raid Battles

If you're looking to join the Max Raid Battles of other players, try opening your Y-Comm menu (p. 298) and searching for Max Raid Battles. If any come up, move your cursor over to the one you want to join and select it to hop right in. You won't be able to join Max Raid Battles with a rarity higher than your current number of Gym Badges allows, so you may not see very rare Max Raid Battles show up on the Y-Comm menu if you're still collecting Gym Badges!

When relying on in-game Trainers for backup in Max Raid Battles, be warned that the Pokémon that these Trainers use are random, and some of them aren't all that strong. If you're going up against a powerful Dynamax Pokémon, try getting together with some other players you know you can count on in a pinch!

Max Raid Battle rules

By now you've already seen how Max Raid Battles differ from other kinds of battles in some ways, but let's see all the unique rules for these exciting battles to make sure you're ready to battle and capture powerful Dynamax Pokémon!

Things to know about your side

- Each Trainer uses only one Pokémon, and they cannot switch Pokémon after the battle begins.
- If an allied Pokémon faints in battle, it will recover from fainting after one turn of being out of the battle.
- While your Pokémon is out of commission, you can cheer your side on—which may provide some benefits!
- Just like in other kinds of battles, your Pokémon will only stay Dynamaxed for three turns.
- After 10 turns pass or allied Pokémon collectively faint four times, the battle will end.
- Everyone who participates earns rewards and has a shot at catching the opposing Dynamax Pokémon if it is defeated.

Things to know about wild Dynamax Pokémon

- The opposing Dynamax Pokémon may use multiple moves in the same turn.
- The opposing Dynamax Pokémon may summon a mysterious barrier.
- The opposing Dynamax Pokémon may nullify all stat changes and Abilities of other Pokémon.
- The opposing Dynamax Pokémon may use regular moves as well as Max Moves and G-Max Moves.

Using Dynamax in Max Raid Battles

Unlike in other battle formats, you won't be able to Dynamax your Pokémon whenever you like in Max Raid Battles. When a Max Raid Battle starts, one of the four Trainers taking part will be chosen and they will have the chance to Dynamax their Pokémon on that turn. If they choose not to, then the chance will move to another Trainer on the next turn. Once one Trainer has chosen to Dynamax their Pokémon, no other players will be able to do so for the rest of the battle. If you're not able to use Dynamax on a turn, you can see where you are in line by looking at the Dynamax icon on the battle screen.

Three more Trainers have the option to Dynamax their Pokémon before you do.

Two more Trainers have the option to Dynamax their Pokémon before you do.

One more Trainer has the option to Dynamax their Pokémon before you do.

Mysterious barriers and how to break them down

Wild Dynamax Pokémon may summon a barrier of Dynamax energy in front of them at the start of battle or after taking damage. These mysterious barriers need to be destroyed if you want to keep dealing decent damage to your opponent.

While this mysterious barrier is in place, you'll see a meter that's broken into several segments beneath your opponent's HP. Each damage-dealing move that hits the opposing Dynamax Pokémon will deal less damage than usual, but it will also reduce this meter by one segment. Each Max Move (p. 353) or G-Max Move (p. 354) your side uses will take away two segments while also dealing reduced damage. Breaking this barrier won't just let you deal damage normally again—the wild Dynamax Pokémon will also take damage from it shattering, and the Pokémon's Defense and Sp. Def will harshly fall. This will be key to victory!

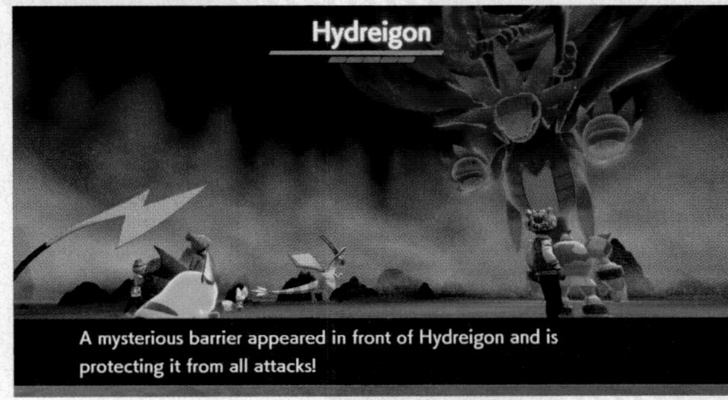

Hydreigon
A mysterious barrier appeared in front of Hydreigon and is protecting it from all attacks!

! A Pokémon behind one of these mysterious barriers won't be affected by status moves, such as Toxic or Thunder Wave, so make sure to bring the barrier down quickly so you can use those helpful supporting moves!

! The strength of the mysterious barrier increases with the difficulty of the Max Raid Battle. You may find that 5★ Dynamax Pokémon can even create barriers twice over the course of a battle! Take this into account, and think carefully about when the optimal moment is to Dynamax your own Pokémon.

Get rewarded for victory

While defeating a Dynamax Pokémon in a Max Raid Battle will always give you the chance to catch that Pokémon, there are other rewards each participant in the battle can earn, too. These include things like Exp. Candies, Berries, or TRs for moves that may likely be the same type as the Dynamax Pokémon you just defeated! Max Raid Battles are a great way to catch some powerful new Pokémon for your team while gathering helpful items and more Exp. Points at the same time!

Item	
Exp. Candy XS	Random TRs
Exp. Candy S	Random Berries
Exp. Candy M	Random treasure items
Exp. Candy L	Rare Candy
Exp. Candy XL	Gigantamix
Dynamax Candy	

! A Pokémon caught from a Max Raid Battle may also have a Hidden Ability (p. 182) or high individual strengths (p. 172). The chances of one of these Pokémon having either of these qualities goes up with difficulty, too!

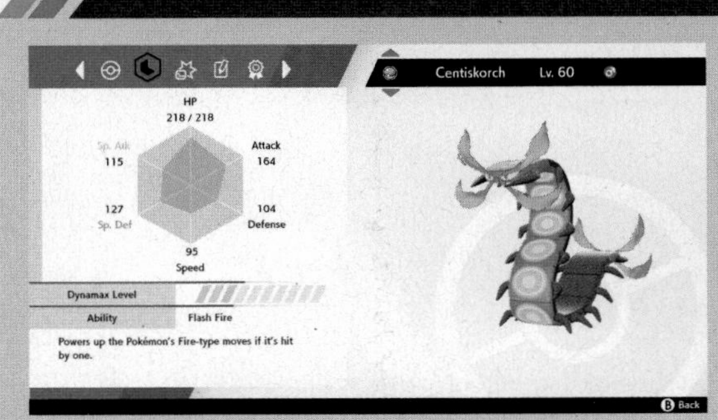

Use Dynamax Candies to Increase Dynamax Level

Dynamax Candies are among the most valuable rewards from Max Raid Battles, as they are the only way to increase a Pokémon's Dynamax Level. Dynamax Levels range from 0 to 10, with 10 being the highest. The higher a Pokémon's Dynamax Level, the greater its maximum HP becomes when it Dynamaxes. High HP can be crucial in battles, so make sure to collect many Dynamax Candies and use them on the Pokémon you plan to Dynamax against tough opponents! You can view a Pokémon's Dynamax Level by checking its summary.

The Rotom Rally

The Rotom Rally is a fun little game available in the Wild Area. You'll race along set courses to try to earn as many points as you can!

Starting up a race

You'll need a bike to participate in the Rotom Rally, of course, but you'll also need to find the various Rotom Rallyists around the Wild Area. Once you've spoken to at least two of them, you'll see that the option to participate in a Rotom Rally becomes available.

There is a total of seven Rotom Rallyists across the Wild Area, but to start with, you should aim to find the ones in the Dappled Grove, in front of Motostoke, and at the Meetup Spot. The others are in areas with very high-level Pokémon, and they can be tricky to reach with a low-level party. Once your party gets stronger, you'll be able to adventure deeper into the Wild Area and unlock all the available courses! The map below shows the location of every Rotom Rallyist, as well as the various courses.

Look for these guys!

The courses are pretty self-explanatory—your goal is to get to the Rotom Rallyist at the location you select as quickly as possible. Once you select a course, the race will begin after a three-second countdown.

!

When starting a race, try pressing Ⓑ, Ⓛ, or Ⓡ just as the number 1 fades away. This will give you a speed boost right off the starting line!

Going for the goal

But wait! You're not going to be able to just go to the goal any way you want! First of all, you have a time limit. See that timer on the top left of the screen? You'll want to reach the goal with as much time left on that timer as possible. If it reaches zero, you'll automatically fail the race.

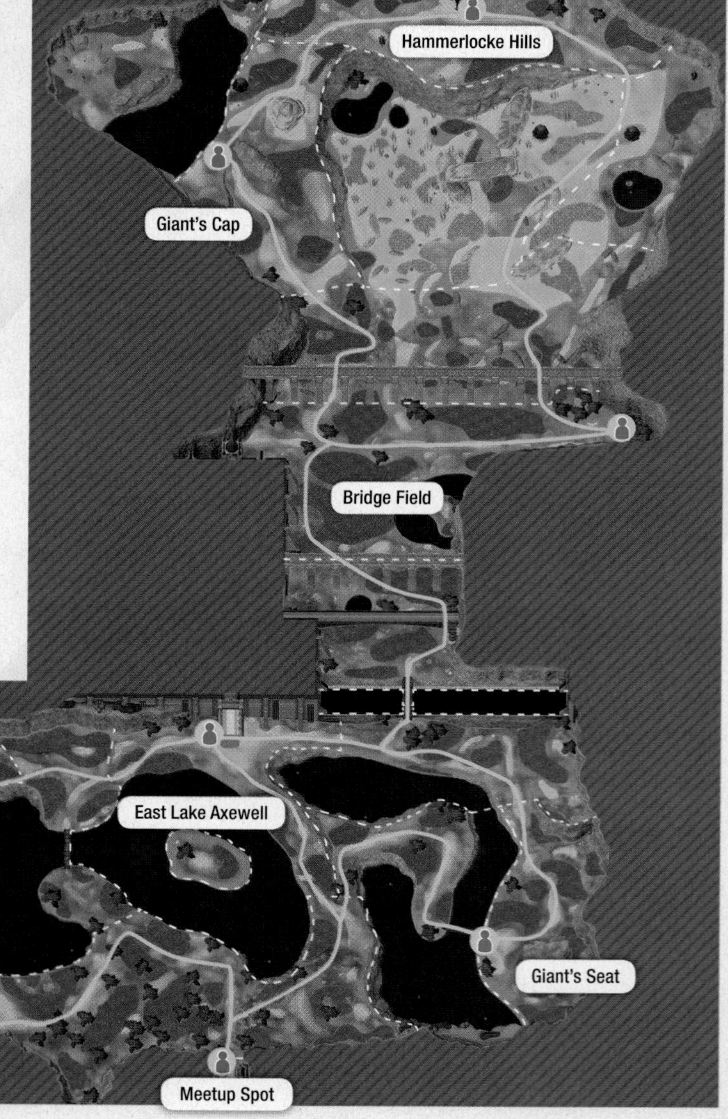

That's where these balloons come into play. While they don't affect your final score directly, they can definitely help improve it. Running into the white balloons will give you a speed boost, while the red balloons will add 15 seconds to the timer! Once you pop a red balloon, a new set of white and red balloons will appear. This will probably happen several times before you reach the goal. The balloons follow a certain path for each course and may be kind of hard to spot when you're first trying out a new run, but don't worry—the yellow lines on the map to the left show the general layout!

> **!** While speed boosts are nice, remember that you don't have to collect all the white balloons along the course—only the red ones are really essential. Keep your eyes peeled for potential shortcuts toward the red balloons, since this may sometimes save more time than speed boosts would. Be careful when cutting through tall grass, though, since wild Pokémon will still appear and could potentially get in your way!

> **!** Watch out for wild Pokémon! Running into one can cause you to spin out and lose precious time. Keep a sharp eye out for any that have wandered onto the course. If you do bump into one, release the Left Stick to reduce spinning!

Rewards from the Rotom Rally

There's more reason to participate in the Rotom Rally than just the thrills, of course. There are a few useful rewards that you can earn for successfully completing a run, plus you'll always earn Watts for popping balloons, even if you don't complete the course. These Watts can be used to purchase various items—as well as upgrades for your bike! The better your score, the more Watts you'll receive, so learn the courses and start earning!

Condition	Reward
Complete a Rotom Rally run for the first time	TM14 Thunder Wave
Obtain a score of 20,000 or higher	TM80 Volt Switch
Complete a total of 11 Rotom Rally runs	Fast Ball

What Are Watts?

Watts are a special currency that you can use for a variety of purposes in the Wild Area. There are lots of ways to earn Watts! Completing Rotom Rallies, checking out Pokémon Dens, and battling Brilliant Pokémon (p. 174) will net you more Watts.

> **!** If you want to earn the most Watts, there are a few things you can do. First of all, be sure to check all the Pokémon Dens that have pillars of light coming out of them. Each one will reward you with 300 W, and you'll usually find several of these dens per day. You don't have to participate in a den's Max Raid Battle to get the Watts, either, so it's a quick and easy way to build up your savings.
>
> You'll also earn more Watts by completing longer Rotom Rally courses. Completing the longest course, which is the one between Hammerlocke and the Meetup Spot, can earn you over 400 W per run if you get used to it! Just keep doing that back and forth, and you'll rack up Watts in no time!

More to do with the Rotom Rallyists

Spend your Watts

Item	Price
Net Ball	50 W
Dive Ball	50 W
Nest Ball	50 W
Repeat Ball	50 W
Timer Ball	50 W
Luxury Ball	100 W
Dusk Ball	50 W
Heal Ball	20 W
Quick Ball	50 W
Wishing Piece	3,000 W

The Rotom Rallyists don't just let you participate in the Rotom Rally—they actually offer a variety of other services, too! For starters, they also serve as Watt Traders, allowing you to spend Watts and purchase valuable items and TRs. Each Rotom Rallyist will offer a different lineup, and these will change every day, but their stock will always include one of the Poké Balls listed to the right—as well as Wishing Pieces and a selection of five TRs. For a full table of the available TRs and their prices, check out page 358.

Get a new cycling outfit

The Rotom Rallyists can also get you a new outfit to wear while you're riding your bike, and they'll do it for free to boot! Just ask for a makeover, and they'll offer an outfit matching the type of the Pokémon at the head of your team. If it has two types, you'll get to choose which one you want for the theme of your outfit! You can change outfits as many times as you like, and you can also swap back to the default Rotom colors if you prefer the classic look.

Upgrade your bike

Another thing you can spend Watts on is upgrading your bike's turbo boost. Just speak to a Rotom Rallyist and select **Improve my bike!**

You can upgrade the turbo boost a total of three times, with each stage costing more Watts. It's worth doing this, though—it shortens the amount of time it takes to charge up your turbo boost, which lets you use it more frequently. When your bike is fully upgraded, the time it takes to charge up a turbo boost will be nearly halved, which can come in handy for the Rotom Rally, too!

Upgrade	Price
First	1,000 W
Second	3,000 W
Third	5,000 W

There's even more to do in the Wild Area. Keep reading to find out who else is out there, waiting to meet you!

People to Meet in the Wild Area

Of course, you're not the only one out enjoying the splendor of nature. Plenty of people from around the Galar region come to explore the Wild Area. Some of them will be willing to trade items they've found for Watts, others might want to battle, and there's even a pair of brothers who'll dig up items for you! Keep reading to find out about the people you can meet in the Wild Area.

Ingredients Sellers

Cooking is a big part of the camping experience in Galar, and for that you'll need Berries and ingredients! Berries you can find on the various Berry trees in the Wild Area and on certain routes, but what about ingredients? Well, you're in luck—there are two Ingredients Sellers right here in the Wild Area! One has set up shop on the south shore of Lake Axewell, in the Rolling Fields, while the other is out in front of Hammerlocke.

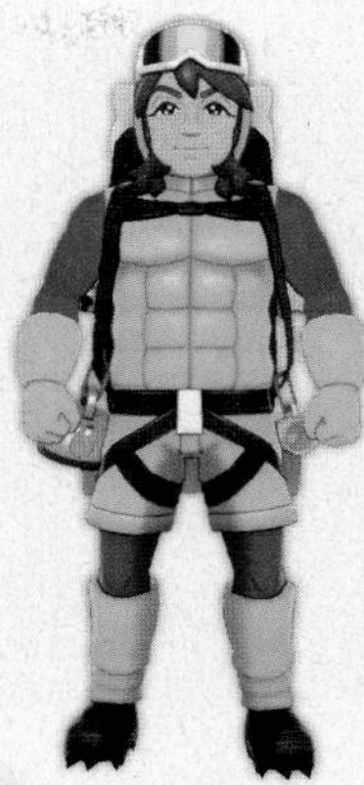

On the south shore of Lake Axewell

Item	Price
Bach's Food Tin	₽950
Bob's Food Tin	₽950
Bread	₽150
Brittle Bones	₽950
Coconut Milk	₽950
Fresh Cream	₽950
Fried Food	₽150
Instant Noodles	₽150
Mixed Mushrooms	₽400
Pack of Potatoes	₽400
Packaged Curry	₽950
Pasta	₽150
Precooked Burger	₽150
Salad Mix	₽400
Sausages	₽400
Spice Mix	₽400
Tin of Beans	₽400

In front of Hammerlocke

Item	Price
Bach's Food Tin	₽950
Bob's Food Tin	₽950
Boiled Egg	₽2,200
Brittle Bones	₽950
Coconut Milk	₽950
Fresh Cream	₽950
Fruit Bunch	₽2,200
Mixed Mushrooms	₽400
Moomoo Cheese	₽2,200
Pack of Potatoes	₽400
Packaged Curry	₽950
Salad Mix	₽400
Sausages	₽400
Smoke-Poke Tail	₽2,200
Spice Mix	₽400
Tin of Beans	₽400

While some of their merchandise overlaps, they both have some unique offerings, too. Their lineup changes every day, and they'll offer a selection of items from the tables above. If you're ever out in the Wild Area and run low on ingredients, just stop by the Ingredients Sellers and they'll get you sorted!

The Camping King

Out in front of Motostoke, you may have noticed a hiker with a distinct yellow outfit. This is the Camping King, an expert on all things camping! The Camping King's all about helping people enjoy camping, and he has several ways of doing so! He can help you change the color of your tent, evaluate your Curry Dex, and even reward you with some new toys for your Pokémon to play with! Learn about all that and more with the guide to becoming a camping expert, which starts on page 280.

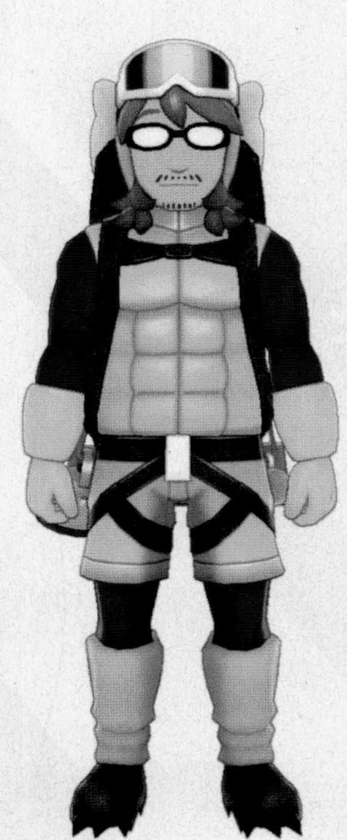

The Digging Duo

The Digging Duo are brothers who excel at digging up items, and they'll happily excavate items for you if you're willing to spend 500 W!

You can find the Digging Duo near the Pokémon Nursery in Bridge Field. As their name implies, there're two of them—one who's got plenty of stamina and one who's got lots of skill. Speak to the one you want to dig for you and pay them the 500 W, and your chosen digger will start digging and handing over every item he finds! The stamina brother can keep going for a long time, while the skilled brother can't dig for very long but can find rare items. Check the tables below to see what each brother can offer!

! Employing the Digging Duo is a good way to get ahold of treasures like Rare Bones and Comet Shards. If you have some Watts to spare but are short on cash, the Digging Duo can help you out! They'll even find various Fossils from time to time, but you should probably hang on to those...

Skill brother

Item	Rarity
Bottle Cap	★
Comet Shard	○
Dawn Stone	△
Dusk Stone	△
Fossilized Bird	○ † ★ 🛡
Fossilized Dino	○ † ★ 🛡
Fossilized Drake	★ † ○ 🛡
Fossilized Fish	★ † ○ 🛡
Gold Bottle Cap*	★
Ice Stone	△
Iron Ball	△
Lagging Tail	△
Light Clay	☆
Metal Coat	△
Moon Stone	△
Normal Gem	☆
Rare Bone	○
Shiny Stone	△
Sticky Barb	☆
Sun Stone	△
Wishing Piece	△

*This is the rarest item here by far. You'll be very lucky indeed if the Digging Duo unearth one for you!

Stamina brother

Item	Rarity
Damp Rock	☆
Dawn Stone	☆
Dusk Stone	☆
Everstone	○
Fire Stone	△
Float Stone	△
Fossilized Bird	△ †
Fossilized Dino	△ †
Fossilized Drake	△ 🛡
Fossilized Fish	△ 🛡
Hard Stone	△
Heat Rock	☆
Ice Stone	☆
Icy Rock	☆
Iron Ball	★
Lagging Tail	★
Leaf Stone	△
Light Clay	☆
Metal Coat	☆
Moon Stone	☆
Normal Gem	★
Rare Bone	○
Shiny Stone	☆
Smooth Rock	☆
Soft Sand	△
Stardust	◎
Star Piece	○
Sticky Barb	★
Sun Stone	△
Thunder Stone	△
Water Stone	△

◎ frequent ○ common △ average
☆ rare ★ almost never
† *Pokémon Sword* only 🛡 *Pokémon Shield* only

Other people exploring the Wild Area

Aside from the folks mentioned in the previous pages, there are plenty of other people who come out to the Wild Area each day to hike or go fishing. You'll find these people pretty much anywhere—in the forests, around lakes, under bridges, and so on—so keep your eyes peeled! You'll generally find about five of these folks around the Wild Area at any given time. After the time on your system reaches midnight, they may move somewhere else—but they'll have something to offer you once more if you search them out again.

Fishers

Fishers appear around the Wild Area and they're not looking for a battle—they're looking to offer you a bargain! In exchange for 100 W, they will happily trade you a special item they've fished up. These are often items you can sell for cash! Considering how much they go for, this is a real steal if you're trying to pad your pockets.

Items Fishers may offer	Rarity
Pearl ×3	○
Big Pearl	○
Big Pearl ×2	△
Big Pearl ×3	△
Pearl String	△
Pearl String ×2	☆
Wishing Piece	☆

◎ frequent ○ common △ average ☆ rare ★ almost never

Hikers

There are also Hikers around in the Wild Area, who will give you items in return for 100 W. The items they give you aren't for money making, though. Instead they'll mostly be items that can help your Pokémon grow stronger. And the size of the Exp. Candies you can receive will grow larger the further you've made it through the Gym Challenge!

Items Hikers may offer	Rarity (Up to 2 Badges)	Rarity (2 to 8 Badges)	Rarity (After becoming Champion)
Exp. Candy XS	○	—	—
Exp. Candy XS ×2	○	—	—
Exp. Candy XS ×3	○	—	—
Exp. Candy XS ×4	△	—	—
Exp. Candy XS ×5	—	○	—
Exp. Candy S	☆	○	○
Exp. Candy S ×2	—	○	○
Exp. Candy S ×3	—	☆	—
Exp. Candy M	—	☆	○
Exp. Candy M ×2	—	—	△
Exp. Candy L	—	—	☆
Wishing Piece	☆	☆	☆
Rare Candy	★	★	★

◎ frequent ○ common △ average ☆ rare ★ almost never — does not appear

Keep Watch for Chloe!

As you wander around the Wild Area, you might run into a Pokémon Breeder who claims she's crazy strong. This is Chloe, and she's definitely no pushover! In fact, you might want to avoid battling her when you first reach the Wild Area. Her team will most likely be higher level than yours at that point, and she uses tricky tactics to boot. If you want to take her on, make sure your team is at least at Lv. 25 or 26! Her team will also get stronger as you progress through the game. They'll jump up in level once when you've earned your Fire Badge and again after you become Champion! But don't worry too much if you can't beat her—she'll heal up your team and let you go on your way rather than send you back to a Pokémon Center.

You are challenged by Pokémon Breeder Chloe!

If you do manage to beat her, though, you'll be rewarded with a hearty amount of prize money. And regardless of whether you win or lose, she'll give you a word of advice on other ways to earn money! Once you defeat her, she'll head off on her way, but she might just pop up again to challenge you another day...

Pokémon Camp

As soon as you get your Camping Gear from your mom early in the game, you'll be ready to set up camp together with your Pokémon. You can camp in all sorts of places across the Galar region, and you'll definitely want to! Camping might seem like just a fun diversion, but it actually offers some serious advantages that any Trainer should know about.

Unlock some really big benefits for battles!

Of course you want to play with your Pokémon, because you adore them! But getting to see your Pokémon be their adorable selves isn't the only reward in store for you. Regular play sessions with your Pokémon not only help your Pokémon grow by granting Exp. Points—they also lead to big effects in battle! Pokémon that feel very friendly toward you thanks to playing together might cure themselves of status conditions in battle, avoid moves, and even hold on to 1 HP when hit with a move that would've made them faint!

Wooloo gathered all its energy to break through its paralysis so you wouldn't worry!

Learn more on page 283!

Save your items, and keep adventuring without interruption!

Filling your Curry Dex is great fun on its own, but mastering the art of cooking delicious curries will also let you restore your Pokémon's HP, heal their status conditions, and even restore PP to their moves. Sure, you could always call a Flying Taxi to go back to the nearest Pokémon Center, but when you're deep in the Wild Area exploring, you may not want to leave and then have to trek back to where you were.

Learn more on page 285!

Get together for some fun with your fellow Trainers!

You're not alone in catching the camping bug! When you're in the Wild Area, you may stumble across the camps of other players if they're playing nearby or if you're connected to the internet! There are also camps along most routes that you can stop by as you travel.

Learn more on page 295!

Setting up your camp

Setting up your camp is easy—once you have your Camping Gear, all you have to do is select Pokémon Camp from your X menu! There are a few restrictions on where you can set up camp, of course. First of all, you obviously can't camp on the water. Your tent is pretty high tech, but it doesn't float! You also won't be able to set up camp during certain activities, such as while you're attempting a Gym mission. Otherwise, you're free to camp pretty much wherever you want—so give it a shot! Once you're ready to leave your camp, just press ⊗, then choose to take down your tent.

! Don't be afraid of inclement weather! You can camp out in any weather at all. In fact, you may find that some of your Pokémon react differently based on the weather. For example, Pokémon with types like Water or Electric love rainy weather, while types like Ghost or Psychic enjoy a good fog.

Change your tent color

Want to show off your camp more? You'll be able to deck out all your camping gear in one of 18 different colors once you find the Camping King—if you've got the right Pokémon! The Camping King hangs around at the steps leading up to Motostoke, and he's always happy to chat with fellow camping fans. If you ask him to change the color of your tent, he'll pick the color he thinks goes well with your lead Pokémon. This color will be based on that Pokémon's type. If that Pokémon happens to have two types, you'll get to choose between two colors. So if you want a particular tent color, put a Pokémon of the right type at the top of your party before talking to the Camping King!

Tent colors you can choose from

The Camping King

You'll want to visit the Camping King for more than just changing the color of your tent. He's also quite the curry fan, and he'll evaluate your Curry Dex as you become a curry-cooking pro. He has rewards for your progress with it, too, which you can learn about on page 294. He'll give you new toys you can use to play with your Pokémon, some rare ingredients to help you complete your Curry Dex, and even some fancy utensils once you've proved yourself as a top curry chef, so search him out in the Wild Area and make yourself a handy new friend!

Playing with Pokémon

One of the great things about camping is that while you're roughing it out in nature, your party Pokémon hop out of their Poké Balls to join you! When you pitch your tent, you'll be able to see the Pokémon in your party walking around and taking in the surrounding scenery. You could just spend a relaxing time watching them interact with each other, but why not play with them? Read on below to learn about the different ways you can play with Pokémon while camping and the goodies you can earn by doing so.

How to play with Pokémon while camping

Once your Pokémon are out having fun in your camp area, you can call them over and interact with them in a number of different ways. You can try talking to them to get an idea of how they're feeling or tell the Pokémon to go and play. Once you've called a Pokémon over, you can also try taking out a toy to play with it. Check the table on the right for the basic controls while camping.

Controls	What they do
L / R	Zoom in
Y / ◀	Take out and change toys / Change hands
X	Open the camping menu
A	Call a Pokémon / Talk to a Pokémon / Talk to a Trainer
Ⓛ / Ⓡ	Move the camera
Ⓛ / Ⓡ (press)	Raise and lower the camera angle
B	Quit camping

Curries can get rid of status conditions, but sometimes all you need to do is call your Pokémon a few times to cure them! If your Pokémon is asleep, for example, just give it a call and eventually it may wake up!

Pokémon Playfulness

You might notice after playing with a Pokémon for a while that it stops chasing after toy balls or reacting to your Poké Toy. When this happens, it means a Pokémon is feeling all played out at the moment and will need a little time before it wants to play again. Trying to play with a Pokémon when it isn't feeling playful won't increase its friendship or get it Exp. Points, either, so give it some time to rest. The Pokémon might also want some curry to eat. You'll know a Pokémon is feeling hungry if you see a curry icon over its head. Cooking and eating curry with a Pokémon is sure to get it energized for some more playtime at your camp!

Use different toys to play with Pokémon

While camping, there are two major types of toys you can use to play with Pokémon—a Poké Toy and toy balls. Both are a lot of fun and can increase your Pokémon's friendship, grant them Exp. Points, and even get you some Watts if you're in the Wild Area. The Poké Toy and toy balls are controlled differently, so look over the table to the right so you know how to use them!

Controls	What they do
Y / ◀	Change toys / Change hands
A / ▶	Throw and pick up toy ball (hold down for a longer throw) / Wave Poké Toy
Ⓛ / Ⓡ	Wave Poké Toy
(motion control)	Throw toy ball / Wave Poké Toy
B	Put toy away

Though you start out with a Poké Toy and a standard toy ball you can use to play with your Pokémon, there are a number of other toy balls you can earn that all behave a little bit differently when you throw them. Some might be heavier, bounce oddly, or even make funny sounds! Each toy ball is given to you by the Camping King (p. 281) after you've cooked enough kinds of curry. Check out the table on the next page to see every available ball and how many new curries you'll need to make in order to get it.

Make sure to call a Pokémon over to you before playing with it. If a Pokémon can't see the toy, it won't respond to it!

Toy	How to get it
Poké Toy	Comes with your Camping Gear (p. 45).
Practice Ball	Comes with your Camping Gear (p. 45).
Fresh Ball	Talk to the Camping King after you've made at least 5 kinds of curry.
Weighted Ball	Talk to the Camping King after you've made at least 10 kinds of curry.
Soothe Ball	Talk to the Camping King after you've made at least 15 kinds of curry.
Mirror Ball	Talk to the Camping King after you've made at least 30 kinds of curry.
Tympole Ball	Talk to the Camping King after you've made at least 50 kinds of curry.
Champion Ball	Talk to the Camping King after you've made at least 80 kinds of curry.

Earn rewards by having fun with your Pokémon friends

Playing with your Pokémon gets them (and you!) all kinds of fun rewards that are sure to help you on your adventure. The three main things you'll get from playing are Exp. Points, Watts, and increased friendship. The more you play with Pokémon while camping, the more of each you'll earn. But remember, if a Pokémon isn't feeling playful, you won't earn anything from playing with it. If one Pokémon isn't feeling up to it at the moment, give it some space and try playing with other Pokémon.

You'll be able to see how many Exp. Points a Pokémon earned while camping when you leave the camp. To see how many Watts you've earned, look at your League Card via the X menu, or talk to someone who's selling something for Watts in the Wild Area. Check the next section to learn about how to check friendship and what it does.

! Pokémon earn Exp. Points from playing based on their level. Higher-level Pokémon will earn more Exp. Points. But playing is still no substitute for proper training in battle, using Exp. Candies, or doing Poké Jobs. If you're looking to level up your Pokémon quickly, earning Exp. Points from camping may not be for you.

Battle Bonuses for Friendly Pokémon

Friendship is the bond between you and your Pokémon. As you spend time traveling, battling, or playing with a Pokémon, its friendship will increase. As that Pokémon grows closer to you, you may notice it behaving a little differently while camping or even during battle! While it's safe to say that raising friendship with your Pokémon is always a good thing, it's also good to know the specifics. Check out the following sections to learn how to check your friendship with your Pokémon and what rewards high friendship can get you!

Growlithe avoided the move in time via your shout!

Checking a Pokémon's friendship

There are a few different ways to check on your friendship with a Pokémon. One of the easiest is to talk to that Pokémon while you're camping. Once you've got your Camping Gear, this is a fast way to see how close you are with your Pokémon, since you can camp almost anywhere. Remember that the Pokémon needs to be in your party for it to come out and play while camping!

Let's chat!
Go play
Never mind
Grookey is eager to play.

You could also stop by the friendship rater in Hammerlocke to check how friendly one of your party Pokémon is with you (p. 82). He'll even give your Pokémon a special ribbon if the two of you have become the best of friends! The friendship rater is the boy in the first house to the right of the southern entrance to Hammerlocke.

Wow, I think you're on your way to becoming real good friends!

To better understand how close you are with your Pokémon and what benefits you may receive, check out the handy table on the next page! Note that you can only grow to the top three ranks of friendship with a Pokémon by spending time together at camp.

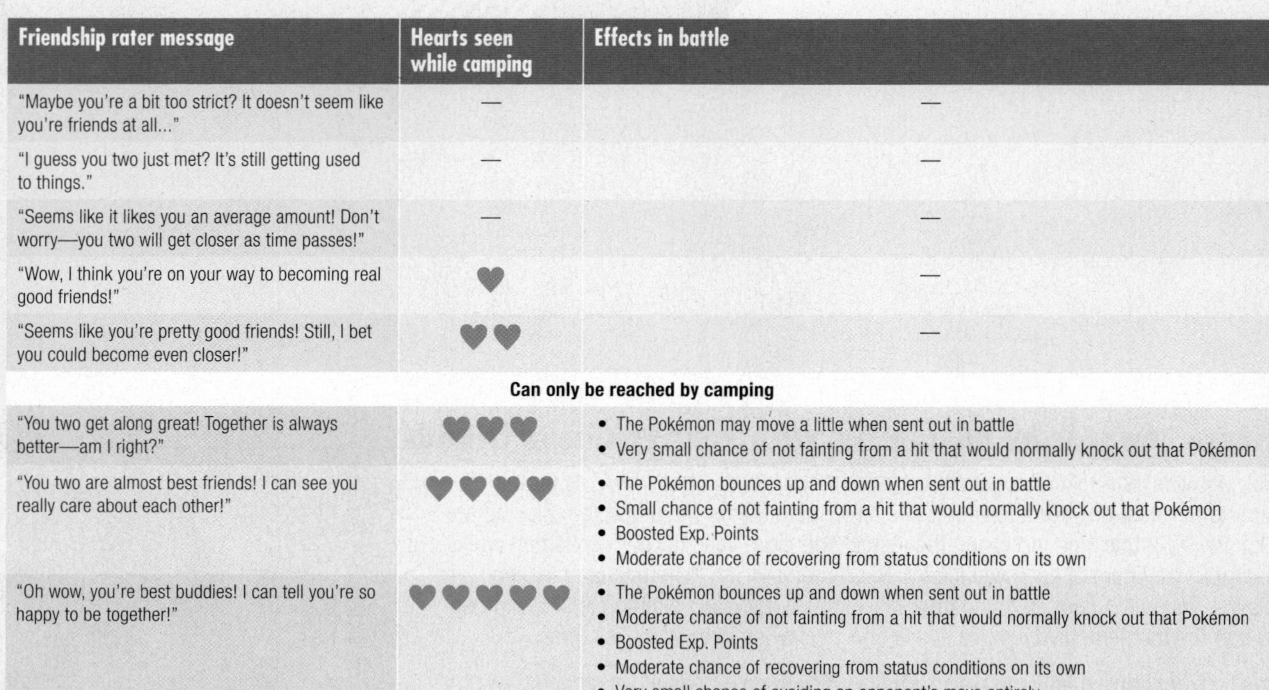

Friendship rater message	Hearts seen while camping	Effects in battle
"Maybe you're a bit too strict? It doesn't seem like you're friends at all..."	—	—
"I guess you two just met? It's still getting used to things."	—	—
"Seems like it likes you an average amount! Don't worry—you two will get closer as time passes!"	—	—
"Wow, I think you're on your way to becoming real good friends!"	♥	—
"Seems like you're pretty good friends! Still, I bet you could become even closer!"	♥♥	—
Can only be reached by camping		
"You two get along great! Together is always better—am I right?"	♥♥♥	• The Pokémon may move a little when sent out in battle • Very small chance of not fainting from a hit that would normally knock out that Pokémon
"You two are almost best friends! I can see you really care about each other!"	♥♥♥♥	• The Pokémon bounces up and down when sent out in battle • Small chance of not fainting from a hit that would normally knock out that Pokémon • Boosted Exp. Points • Moderate chance of recovering from status conditions on its own
"Oh wow, you're best buddies! I can tell you're so happy to be together!"	♥♥♥♥♥	• The Pokémon bounces up and down when sent out in battle • Moderate chance of not fainting from a hit that would normally knock out that Pokémon • Boosted Exp. Points • Moderate chance of recovering from status conditions on its own • Very small chance of avoiding an opponent's move entirely • Increased critical hit ratio

!

As your friendship with a Pokémon increases, it may also find items for you after you cook together at your camp! This first becomes possible when your Pokémon has got at least one ♥!

Increasing and decreasing friendship

There are many different things that can increase friendship (and a few that can decrease your friendship with a Pokémon, too). Some of the ones that increase friendship may be obvious—like playing together with a Pokémon or traveling with it in your party—but there might be a few surprises in the lists below, so check them out!

Give your Pokémon a Soothe Bell to hold if you want to become friends even quicker! It will provide a nice boost to the friendship gains from the methods described here. Get the Soothe Bell from a girl in the same house as the friendship rater (p. 82).

Ways to increase friendship up to 2 ♥s

- Helping your Pokémon level up by earning Exp. Points or by using items on them
- Traveling together with your Pokémon by adding them to your party
- Using items on your Pokémon that boost their stats in battle (p. 187)
- Using items on your Pokémon that help them get permanently stronger (p. 179)
- Having your Pokémon take part in battles against Gym Leaders and other tough Trainers
- Plus all ways of increasing friendship up to 5 ♥s work here, too!

Ways to increase friendship up to 5 ♥s

- Playing with your Pokémon at your camp using toys, especially toy balls
- Breaking up fights by calling a Pokémon over to you when it's bickering with others at your camp
- Cooking curries with your Pokémon, especially if you put in lots of rare Berries

Ways to decrease friendship

- Letting a Pokémon faint (especially when battling a much stronger opponent)
- Using Energy Powder, Heal Powder, an Energy Root, or a Revival Herb on your Pokémon

Cooking Curries

Playing with your Pokémon isn't the only thing you can do while camping. You can also cook up many different kinds of delicious curry for you and your Pokémon to enjoy together out in the open air! Cooking has a few steps and may seem a little challenging at first, but it's a fun way to take a break from your Gym Challenge. It can even help you catch Pokémon or find items!

Gather your Berries and ingredients

Before you can cook anything, you'll need to find certain kinds of items to put in the pot. If you've been playing the game for a while, you've probably found some already—Berries! Berries are one of the two key components you'll be adding to the pot to make your curry. They determine which of the five special tastes—Spicy, Dry, Sweet, Bitter, or Sour—that a curry will be, if any. When you choose Berries that have flavors that balance each other out, the curry will end up without a focus on any of the five tastes. Find Berries by shaking Berry trees! You can learn more about finding Berries on page 290.

The other items you'll want to gather to start your curry cooking are called ingredients. Much like in the real world, ingredients are all different kinds of foodstuffs that you can add to change what kind of curry you get. While Berries affect the flavor of a curry, ingredients affect what kind of curry you're actually making. You can also choose to not add an ingredient if you want a plain curry.

Below you'll find a list of every ingredient you can use for cooking, along with other information, like their rarity and where to find them. Most ingredients can be purchased from two Ingredients Sellers in the Wild Area (p. 277).

Which ingredients they sell will change from day to day, and the rarer ingredients won't be available as often, so it's best to check what's being sold each day. There are also some ingredients that can't be purchased, like Gigantamix, which can only be obtained from Max Raid Battles!

> **!** The more Berries you use in a curry and the rarer those Berries are, the more your friendship will increase with the Pokémon you're camping with!

For example, if you added a loaf of Bread and a Cheri Berry while cooking, you'd get Spicy Toast Curry!

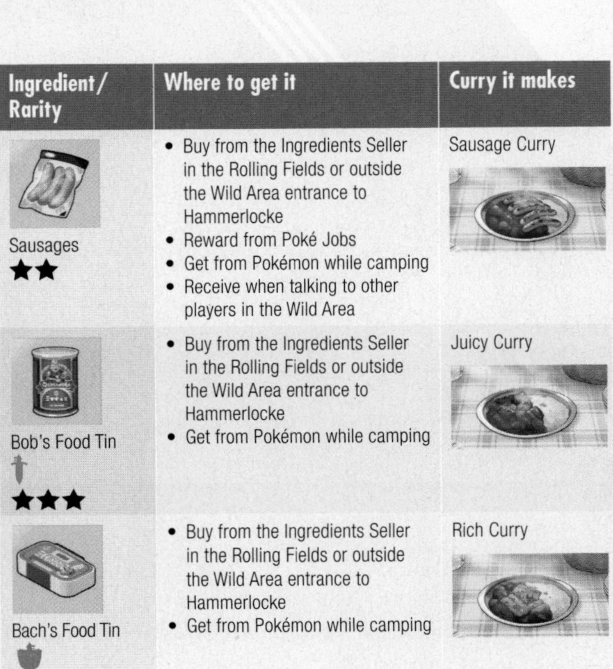

Ingredient/ Rarity	Where to get it	Curry it makes
Sausages ★★	• Buy from the Ingredients Seller in the Rolling Fields or outside the Wild Area entrance to Hammerlocke • Reward from Poké Jobs • Get from Pokémon while camping • Receive when talking to other players in the Wild Area	Sausage Curry
Bob's Food Tin ★★★	• Buy from the Ingredients Seller in the Rolling Fields or outside the Wild Area entrance to Hammerlocke • Get from Pokémon while camping	Juicy Curry
Bach's Food Tin ★★★	• Buy from the Ingredients Seller in the Rolling Fields or outside the Wild Area entrance to Hammerlocke • Get from Pokémon while camping	Rich Curry

The Ingredients Sellers look like Hikers!

Ingredient/ Rarity	Where to get it	Curry it makes
Tin of Beans ★★	• Buy from the Ingredients Seller in the Rolling Fields or outside the Wild Area entrance to Hammerlocke • Get from Pokémon while camping • Receive when talking to other players in the Wild Area	Bean Medley Curry
Bread ★	• Buy from the Ingredients Seller in the Rolling Fields • Reward from Poké Jobs • Get from Pokémon while camping • Receive when talking to other players in the Wild Area	Toast Curry

Ingredient/ Rarity	Where to get it	Curry it makes
Pasta ★	• Buy from the Ingredients Seller in the Rolling Fields • Get from Pokémon while camping • Receive when talking to other players in the Wild Area	Pasta Curry 
Mixed Mushrooms ★★	• Buy from the Ingredients Seller in the Rolling Fields or outside the Wild Area entrance to Hammerlocke • Get from Pokémon while camping • Receive when talking to other players in the Wild Area	Mushroom Medley Curry 
Smoke-Poke Tail ★★★★	• Buy from the Ingredients Seller outside the Wild Area entrance to Hammerlocke • Get from Pokémon while camping	Smoked-Tail Curry 
Large Leek ★★★★	• Find as a hidden item in the Wild Area • Get from Pokémon while camping	Leek Curry 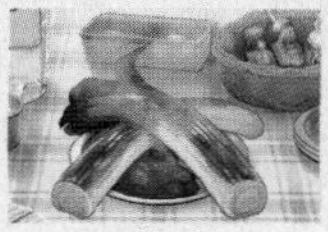
Fancy Apple ★★★★	• Find as a hidden item in the Wild Area • Get from Pokémon while camping	Apple Curry 
Brittle Bones ★★★	• Buy from the Ingredients Seller in the Rolling Fields or outside the Wild Area entrance to Hammerlocke • Get from Pokémon while camping	Bone Curry 
Pack of Potatoes ★★	• Buy from the Ingredients Seller in the Rolling Fields or outside the Wild Area entrance to Hammerlocke • Get from Pokémon while camping	Plenty-of-Potato Curry 
Pungent Root ★★★	• Find as a hidden item in the Wild Area • Get from Pokémon while camping	Herb Medley Curry 
Salad Mix ★★	• Buy from the Ingredients Seller in the Rolling Fields or outside the Wild Area entrance to Hammerlocke • Get from Pokémon while camping • Receive when talking to other players in the Wild Area	Salad Curry   
Fried Food ★	• Buy from the Ingredients Seller in the Rolling Fields • Get from Pokémon while camping • Receive when talking to other players in the Wild Area	Fried-Food Curry 
   Boiled Egg ★★★★	• Buy from the Ingredients Seller outside the Wild Area entrance to Hammerlocke • Get from Pokémon while camping	Boiled-Egg Curry 

Ingredient/ Rarity	Where to get it	Curry it makes
Fruit Bunch ★★★★	• Buy from the Ingredients Seller outside the Wild Area entrance to Hammerlocke • Get from Pokémon while camping	Tropical Curry  
Moomoo Cheese ★★★★	• Buy from the Ingredients Seller outside the Wild Area entrance to Hammerlocke • Reward from Poké Jobs • Get from Pokémon while camping	Cheese-Covered Curry 
Spice Mix ★★	• Buy from the Ingredients Seller in the Rolling Fields or outside the Wild Area entrance to Hammerlocke • Get from Pokémon while camping • Receive when talking to other players in the Wild Area	Seasoned Curry 
Fresh Cream ★★★	• Buy from the Ingredients Seller in the Rolling Fields or outside the Wild Area entrance to Hammerlocke • Get from Pokémon while camping	Whipped-Cream Curry  
Packaged Curry ★★★	• Buy from the Ingredients Seller in the Rolling Fields or outside the Wild Area entrance to Hammerlocke • Reward from Poké Jobs • Get from Pokémon while camping	Decorative Curry 
Coconut Milk ★★★	• Buy from the Ingredients Seller in the Rolling Fields or outside the Wild Area entrance to Hammerlocke • Get from Pokémon while camping	Coconut Curry 
Instant Noodles ★	• Buy from the Ingredients Seller in the Rolling Fields • Get from Pokémon while camping • Receive when talking to other players in the Wild Area	Instant-Noodle Curry  
Precooked Burger ★	• Buy from the Ingredients Seller in the Rolling Fields • Get from Pokémon while camping • Receive when talking to other players in the Wild Area	Burger-Steak Curry  
Gigantamix ★★★★★	• Get as a rare reward for defeating 3★, 4★, and especially 5★ Pokémon in Max Raid Battles	Gigantamax Curry  

Bob's Food Tin and Bach's Food Tin are exclusive to *Pokémon Sword* and *Pokémon Shield* respectively. If you want to complete your Curry Dex, you'll need to trade someone for a Pokémon holding those ingredients, or try your luck when cooking at another player's camp (p. 297)!

The flow of cooking

The curry-making minigame has several steps, each with its own controls. We'll go over each one to make sure you've got the skills you need to create the best-tasting curries in all of Galar!

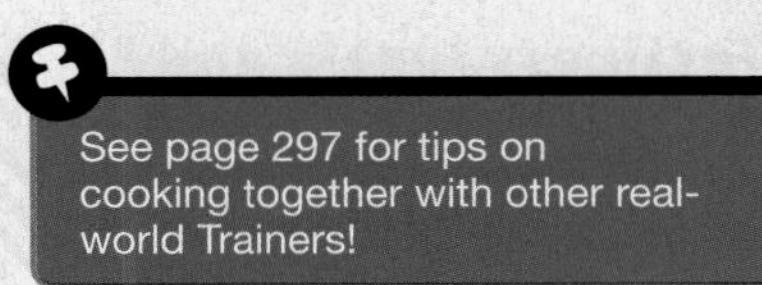
See page 297 for tips on cooking together with other real-world Trainers!

Choose what to put in

The simplest step is choosing what to put in your curry. Open the menu using Ⓧ while camping, and choose the **Cooking** option, then **Start cooking**. As was mentioned before, what you put in your pot changes the kind of curry you'll get. If you're aiming for a specific curry, check the ingredients list on the previous page and the flavors of Berries on the Berry list on page 291. You can choose not to add a key ingredient if you prefer, but you must use at least one Berry.

Controls	What they do
Ⓛ / ▲ / ▼	Scroll through the lists
Ⓐ / ZL / ZR	Choose an ingredient or Berries / Confirm
Ⓑ	Quit cooking / Cancel selection / Put back Berries
L / R	Quickly scroll through the lists
⊕ / ⊖	Skip adding an ingredient / Finish adding Berries

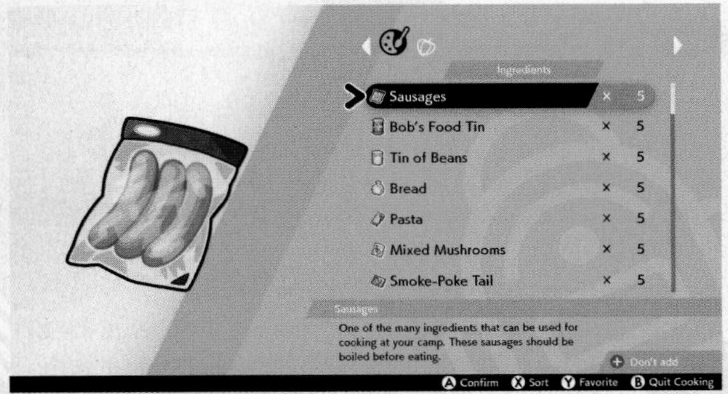

Choose an ingredient first...

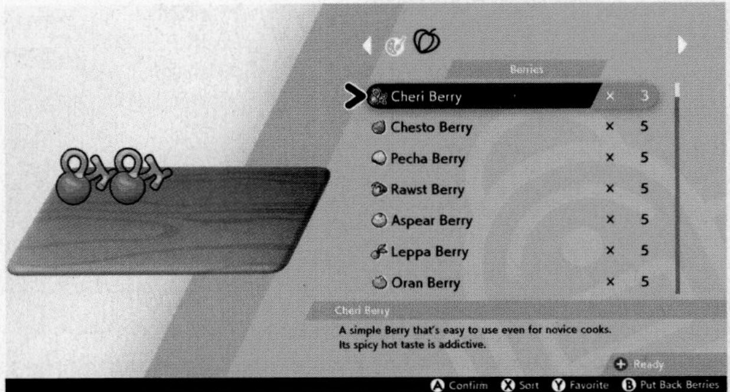

then choose some Berries!

Fan the flames

Now that you've chosen what to put in your pot, it's time to get a fire going. You'll need to build up the heat in order to cook your dish, by fanning the fire with a Magikarp-styled fan. As you fan, you'll see the flames start to rise, and you'll also see more and more steam start to come from the pot. Be sure not to make the flame too hot, or your food might burn!

Controls	What they do
Ⓐ / Wave Joy-Con up and down	Fan the fire

Stir the pot

Once you've got the heat just right, you'll need to stir your dish. Stirring too slow means the curry might be burned, but stirring too fast will make some of the curry fly out of the pot! The trick is to stir at just the right pace.

Controls	What they do
(Ⓛ) / (Ⓡ) / Wave Joy-Con in a circle	Stir the pot

Put your heart into it

Lastly, you need to put your heart into the dish and give it that special something. Watch the yellow ring as it gets smaller and smaller. You'll want to have the heart ball fly into your curry when the yellow ring overlaps the innermost green ring over the pot. This will increase the quality of your dish!

Controls	What they do
Ⓐ / Wave Joy-Con in a throwing motion	Throw heart ball

Tastiness levels and their effects

Now that you know how to cook, it's time for something a little more advanced. Cooking well increases the tastiness level of your dish, which awards you a lot more than just bragging rights. Tastiness is broken up into five levels, and the higher the tastiness level a dish has, the more you and your Pokémon will enjoy it. Most of the benefits of eating curry, like Exp. Points and healing your party Pokémon, will be increased, too! But remember—gains to your Pokémon's friendliness depend on the number and rarity of Berries you use, rather than the level of tastiness.

Taste rating	What it looks like	Effects on Pokémon
Koffing Class		• Very small amount of Exp. Points • Restores 1/4 of HP • Very small increase to sociability
Wobbuffet Class		• Small amount of Exp. Points • Restores 1/2 of HP • Small increase to sociability
Milcery Class		• Medium amount of Exp. Points • Restores all HP and heals all status conditions • Medium increase to sociability
Copperajah Class		• Large amount of Exp. Points • Restores all HP and PP, and heals all status conditions • Large increase to sociability
Charizard Class		• Very large amount of Exp. Points • Restores all HP and PP, and heals all status conditions • Very large increase to sociability

! The number of Exp. Points your Pokémon can get from cooking curries will quickly multiply if you do it together with other players. The more people who take part, the more these Exp. Points will increase! Turn ahead to page 295 for more on camping and cooking with others.

Cooking the greatest dishes

Now that we know all the helpful things a high tastiness level can get you, let's look at what can affect getting a higher or lower tastiness level. Using a rare ingredient and lots of rare Berries will give your curry a tastiness boost, but technique is also key! Just like cooking in the real world, you may not be cooking a perfect Charizard Class-tastiness dish on your first try. But don't be discouraged! Consult the references below and keep practicing, and soon you'll be making the best tasting curry in all of Galar!

Flame level

As you fan the fire to heat up your pot, the fire will grow higher and higher. There's a fine line between the best temperature and burning your food. So if you think you might be fanning too much and your flames are about to get too hot, stop fanning for a moment and let the flame go down a bit. Whenever you aren't fanning, the flame will start to die down.

Flame level	No flame	Low flame	Medium flame	High flame	Too high flame
Effect on tastiness	No increase	Medium increase	Large increase	Very large increase	Tiny increase
What it looks like					

! As you fan or stir, you may notice sparkles coming off of the curry. This is an indicator that you're going at the right speed! The more sparkles you see, the better your curry will end up tasting, so try and maintain a great amount of sparkles!

Stirring speed

Like the level of your flames, stirring also has five levels, and you advance through them by stirring faster and faster. If you stir too fast, your curry will spill. But if you don't stir at all, the curry will burn! Just like fanning, the trick is to stir pretty fast, but not so fast that you spill. If your Joy-Con gives a sharp rumble or you see curry splashing out of the pot, try slowing down or stopping your stirring for a bit.

Stirring level	None	Not stirring enough	Medium amount of stirring	Great amount of stirring	Spilling
Effect on tastiness	No increase	Small increase	Medium increase	Large increase	Small increase

Watch out for signs of spilling!

Heart-ball accuracy

The heart-ball segment is a bit different than the other two. You'll have a much shorter time limit and only one shot to get your throw right. Watch the yellow ring carefully, and throw the heart ball so that it goes through the ring when it overlaps with the innermost green circle. That's all there is to it. A helpful tip is to remember that even after you throw the ball, the yellow ring will continue to shrink. So take that into account when throwing!

Pokémon feel social after cooking

You probably noticed in the last section that one of the bonuses for cooking a tasty dish was an increase in a Pokémon's sociability. While friendship affects the bond between you and your Pokémon, sociability affects how much a Pokémon is willing to interact with other Pokémon. If your Pokémon seem to be happily interacting with one another, it means they're feeling sociable! To get the best gains in sociability, have at least two Pokémon in your camp and cook up some tasty curries together!

Social Pokémon may invite wild Pokémon for you to catch

When your party Pokémon are feeling social, they may interact with one another while camping. But a really high sociability level also gives your Pokémon a chance of drawing the attention of wild Pokémon, bringing them over. This gives you a chance to catch them! The Pokémon attracted to your camp in this way will be the same sorts of Pokémon you'd encounter in the wild in whatever area you're camping in.

Cook and eat some really tasty curries...

Oh...? Impidimp has come to your camp.

and eventually wild Pokémon may come play!

Social Pokémon may give you items

Your own Pokémon may give you items if they feel friendly toward you (p. 284), but other Trainers' Pokémon feel generous when they're sociable! Cook up a curry when camping with other Trainers (p. 297), and their Pokémon may share a little treat. These will tend to be ingredients you can use for more cooking, but there are also a few items you can use in battle or sell for extra pocket money! Check the list below for all the different items a Pokémon may give you.

Gathering Wild Berries

In Galar, you can find certain trees covered with Berries on routes and in the Wild Area. All their locations are labeled on the map on page 293. Give these trees a good shake, and get some Berries for your curry cooking or for you or your Pokémon to use in battles!

The more you shake a tree, the more likely it becomes that a wild Pokémon might leap out for a battle. If you pay close attention to the rumble of your Joy-Con, you may feel that the vibrations grow a bit stronger and closer together as the wild Pokémon gets agitated. Be careful, because even if you defeat or catch that Pokémon, you'll find you've lost some of the Berries that had been gathering on the ground!

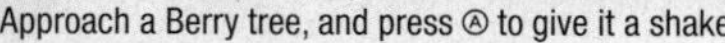

Approach a Berry tree, and press Ⓐ to give it a shake.

Two Persim Berries and one Rawst Berry
fell from the tree!

You'll get one to three Berries every time you shake a tree.

But be careful—shake too many times in a row, and you'll upset that tree's inhabitants!

Generally, you'll lose all of a certain variety of Berries, but if you're really unlucky, you'll lose every single Berry you'd shaken loose! Once you're done harvesting your Berries (or nearby Pokémon steal them), the tree will appear stripped of Berries. But come back the next day, and you'll see a new crop of Berries has appeared on the tree!

The kinds of Berries you can get

In the early stages of your adventure, you'll find basic Berries, such as the Berries that heal status conditions or restore HP or PP, but as you progress in the game and venture out farther, you'll find rarer and more useful Berries. You may also get some Leftovers in addition to Berries from the trees in the Wild Area!

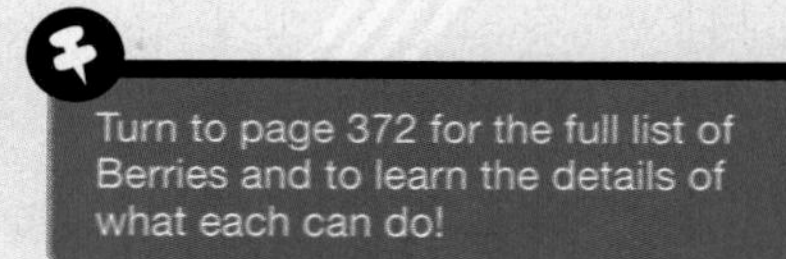
Turn to page 372 for the full list of Berries and to learn the details of what each can do!

Healing Berries

Where to find them: In the South Wild Area, Route 3, and Route 4, among other places

Examples

Cheri Berry (heals paralysis), Pecha Berry (heals poison), Oran Berry (restores HP), Leppa Berry (restores PP)

Stat-boosting Berries

Where to find them: In the North Wild Area, Route 7, and Route 9, among other places

Examples

Liechi Berry (boosts Attack), Ganlon Berry (boosts Defense), Petaya Berry (boosts Sp. Atk), Apicot Berry (boosts Sp. Def)

Base point-lowering Berries

Where to find them: In Bridge Field in the Wild Area and Route 7, among other places

Examples

Pomeg Berry (lowers HP base points), Hondew Berry (lowers Sp. Atk base points), Grepa Berry (lowers Sp. Def base points), Tamato Berry (lowers Speed base points)

Damage-reducing Berries

Where to find them: In the North Wild Area and Route 9, among other places

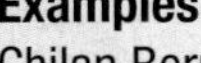

Examples

Chilan Berry (lessens the damage from any Normal-type move), Chople Berry (lessens the damage from a supereffective Fighting-type move), Tanga Berry (lessens the damage from a supereffective Bug-type move), Roseli Berry (lessens the damage from a supereffective Fairy-type move)

HP-restoring Berries that confuse certain Pokémon

Where to find them: Route 7 and Route 9, among other places

Examples

Figy Berry, Wiki Berry, Mago Berry, Aguav Berry

Using Berries for cooking

Berries are important for cooking curries at your camp. Every Berry has its own combination of flavors, as you can see in the following table. When you add different Berries to your cooking, the most intense flavor will determine the taste of the curry. And flavors can add up, too—adding several Berries with a subtle flavor could end up overwhelming one solo Berry with a stronger flavor. If two or more flavors are equally balanced, you end up with a curry that lacks a dominant flavor.

! If you add Gigantamix to a curry, it will always come out as Gigantamax Curry—regardless of the flavors of the Berries you added!

Berry	Rarity	Spicy	Dry	Sweet	Bitter	Sour
Cheri Berry	○	1	—	—	—	—
Chesto Berry	○	—	1	—	—	—
Pecha Berry	○	—	—	1	—	—
Rawst Berry	○	—	—	—	1	—
Aspear Berry	○	—	—	—	—	1
Leppa Berry	○	1	—	1	1	1
Oran Berry	○	1	1	—	1	1
Persim Berry	○	1	1	1	—	1
Lum Berry	○	1	1	1	1	—
Sitrus Berry	○	—	1	1	1	1
Figy Berry	○	2	—	—	—	—
Wiki Berry	○	—	2	—	—	—
Mago Berry	○	—	—	2	—	—
Aguav Berry	○	—	—	—	2	—
Iapapa Berry	○	—	—	—	—	2
Pomeg Berry	○	1	—	1	1	—
Kelpsy Berry	○	—	1	—	1	1
Qualot Berry	○	1	—	1	—	1
Hondew Berry	○	1	1	—	1	—
Grepa Berry	○	—	1	1	—	1
Tamato Berry	○	3	1	—	—	—
Occa Berry	△	2	—	1	—	—
Passho Berry	△	—	2	—	1	—
Wacan Berry	△	—	—	2	—	1
Rindo Berry	△	1	—	—	2	—
Yache Berry	△	—	1	—	—	2
Chople Berry	△	2	—	—	1	—
Kebia Berry	△	—	2	—	—	1
Shuca Berry	△	1	—	2	—	—
Coba Berry	△	—	1	—	2	—

Berry	Rarity	Spicy	Dry	Sweet	Bitter	Sour
Payapa Berry	△	—	—	1	—	2
Tanga Berry	△	3	—	—	—	1
Charti Berry	△	1	3	—	—	—
Kasib Berry	△	—	1	3	—	—
Haban Berry	△	—	—	1	3	—
Colbur Berry	△	—	—	—	1	3
Babiri Berry	△	4	1	—	—	—
Chilan Berry	△	—	4	1	—	—
Liechi Berry	△	5	1	5	—	—
Ganlon Berry	△	—	5	1	5	—
Salac Berry	△	—	—	5	1	5
Petaya Berry	△	5	—	—	5	1
Apicot Berry	△	1	5	—	—	5
Lansat Berry*	☆	5	1	5	1	5
Starf Berry*	☆	5	1	5	1	5
Enigma Berry**	☆	6	1	—	—	—
Micle Berry**	☆	—	6	1	—	—
Custap Berry**	☆	—	—	6	1	—
Jaboca Berry**	☆	—	—	—	6	1
Rowap Berry**	☆	1	—	—	—	6
Roseli Berry	△	—	—	4	1	—
Kee Berry	△	5	5	1	1	1
Maranga Berry	△	1	1	5	5	1

○ Common △ Uncommon ☆ Rare

6-Explosive **5**-Intense **4**-Rich **3**-Moderate **2**-Subtle **1**-Very subtle

*You can get these Berries in the Battle Tower only.
**You can get these Berries via distribution only.

Where to find Berry trees

Number on map	Location	Pokémon you may encounter	Berries you may find
1	Rolling Fields	◎ ○	Oran, Pecha, Cheri
2	Rolling Fields	◎ ○	Cheri, Oran, Persim, Kelpsy
3	Dappled Grove	◎ ○	Oran, Chesto, Pecha, Persim
4	Dappled Grove	◎ ○	Oran, Pecha, Rawst, Chesto, Pomeg
5	Dappled Grove	◎ ○	Chesto, Leppa, Chilan, Rawst, Grepa
6	Dappled Grove	◎ ○	Pecha, Rawst, Oran, Chilan, Apicot
7	Watchtower Ruins	◎ ◎	Sitrus, Leppa, Oran, Cheri, Tamato, Liechi
8	Axew's Eye	◎ ○	Salac, Lum, Kee, Maranga, Kebia, Colbur
9	Giant's Seat	◎ ○	Sitrus, Chesto, Aspear, Leppa, Qualot, Ganlon
10	North Lake Miloch	◎ ◎	Rawst, Persim, Aspear, Hondew, Petaya
11	Route 3	◎ ○	Oran, Pecha, Rawst, Persim
12	Motostoke Riverbank*	◎ ○ △	Sitrus, Leppa, Tanga, Coba, Salac
13	Motostoke Riverbank*	◎ ○ △	Pomeg, Qualot, Grepa, Kelpsy, Hondew, Tamato
14	Bridge Field*	◎ ○	Ganlon, Liechi, Babiri, Roseli, Chople, Kasib
15	Bridge Field*	◎ ○	Hondew, Grepa, Sitrus, Rindo, Aguav
16	Bridge Field*	◎ ○	Pomeg, Tamato, Sitrus, Occa, Figy
17	Bridge Field*	◎ ○	Kelpsy, Qualot, Sitrus, Passho, Wiki
18	Route 4	◎	Cheri, Pecha, Oran, Leppa
19	Route 5	◎	Chesto, Chilan, Cheri, Persim
20	Giant's Mirror*	◎ ○	Kelpsy, Hondew, Tamato, Pomeg, Qualot, Grepa
21	Giant's Cap*	◎ ○	Qualot, Tamato, Lum, Apicot, Ganlon
22	Hammerlocke Hills*	◎ ○	Sitrus, Kelpsy, Hondew, Iapapa, Mago
23	Hammerlocke Hills*	◎ ○	Leppa, Pomeg, Grepa, Wacan, Payapa
24	Lake of Outrage*	◎ ☆	Apicot, Petaya, Haban, Yache, Charti, Shuca
25	Route 6	◎	Sitrus, Rawst, Leppa, Persim
26	Route 7 (south side)	◎	Pomeg, Kelpsy, Qualot, Hondew, Grepa, Tamato, Lum
27	Route 7 (north side)	◎	Aspear, Figy, Mago, Ganlon, Liechi
28	Route 9 (Outer Spikemuth)	◎	Lum, Roseli, Chople, Tanga, Salac
29	Route 9 (Circhester Bay)	◎	Wiki, Aguav, Iapapa, Petaya, Apicot

◎ frequent ○ common △ average ☆ rare

*There is a very slight chance that you can get Leftovers from these trees, too.

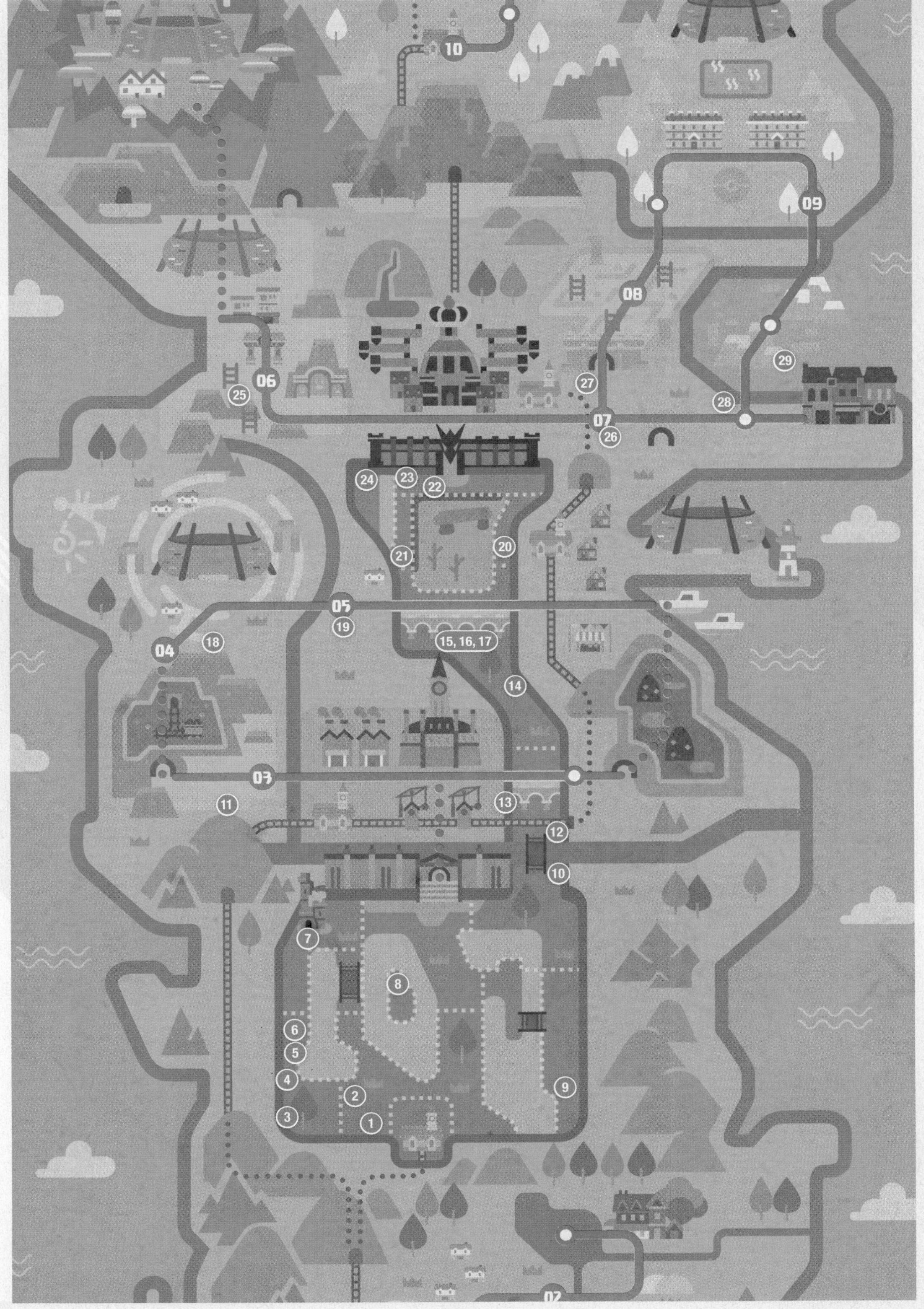

10
09
08
06
25
27
07
26
28
29
24
23
22
21
20
05
19
04
18
15, 16, 17
14
03
11
13
12
10
7
8
6
5
4
2
3
1
9
02

Your Curry Dex

Once you've collected tons of Berries and ingredients, it's time to fill that Curry Dex! Similar to how the Pokédex automatically records information on any Pokémon you see or catch during your adventure, the Curry Dex will record information about any curry that you cook while you're out camping. But unlike your Pokédex, you won't have to wait for anyone to give it to you. After you've cooked your first dish, your Curry Dex will appear under the **Cooking** option when you open the menu by pressing Ⓧ while camping.

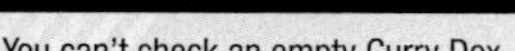
You can't check an empty Curry Dex.

Cook your first curry...

and your Curry Dex will become available!

Using your Curry Dex

Now that we've cooked up our first-ever curry, we can check it out in the Curry Dex! Each entry in this food encyclopedia displays some useful information about that curry. You can read a description of the curry and see what it looks like, including any different sizes that you've cooked. Scroll through the sizes of each dish using Ⓛ and Ⓡ.

Below the curry's description, you'll also see a little medal. It's a record of the highest taste rating you've gotten with that dish. Whenever you make the same dish but get a higher taste rating, that'll become your new personal best record for that curry. If you're truly passionate about cooking while camping, aim for Charizard class in all 151 dishes! Press Ⓨ on any Curry Dex entry for a little extra info. You can see how many times you've made that curry, where you first made it, and which Pokémon you made it with!

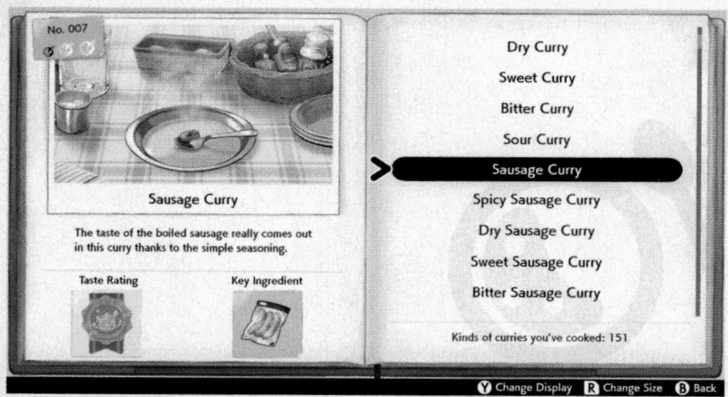

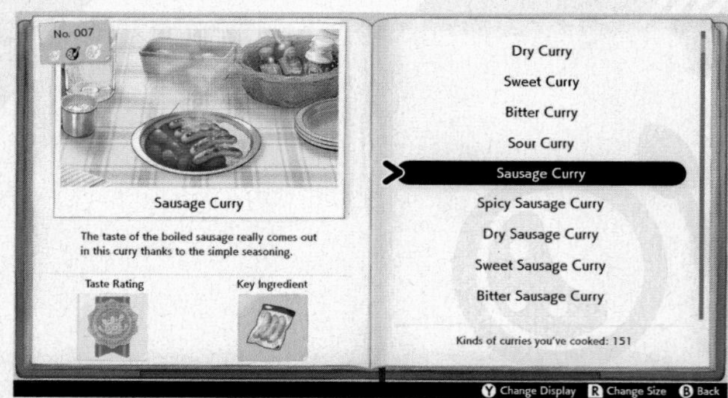

Rewards for filling your Curry Dex

If you manage to cook all 151 curries and fill your Curry Dex, regardless of taste rating, the Camping King (p. 281) will reward you with golden cooking utensils! You can switch between your normal and golden ones by talking to the Camping King.

Reward	How to get it
Sausages ×3	Talk to the Camping King after you've made at least 1 kind of curry.
Fresh Ball	Talk to the Camping King after you've made at least 5 kinds of curry.
Weighted Ball	Talk to the Camping King after you've made at least 10 kinds of curry.
Soothe Ball	Talk to the Camping King after you've made at least 15 kinds of curry.

Reward	How to get it
Mirror Ball	Talk to the Camping King after you've made at least 30 kinds of curry.
Tympole Ball	Talk to the Camping King after you've made at least 50 kinds of curry.
Champion Ball	Talk to the Camping King after you've made at least 80 kinds of curry.
Moomoo Cheese ×3	Talk to the Camping King after you've made at least 110 kinds of curry.

Reward	How to get it
Smoke-Poke Tail ×3	Talk to the Camping King after you've made at least 150 kinds of curry.
Golden Cooking Utensils	Talk to the Camping King after you've made all 151 kinds of curry.

Camping with Others

While you'll always have your trusty team of Pokémon with you when you set up camp, they're not the only ones you can enjoy the great outdoors with. You can camp with the people you come across on many of the routes in the Galar region, and you can camp with other players if you meet up in the Wild Area!

There's plenty to do when visiting the camp of other people and their Pokémon. You might get some helpful camping tips, or sometimes even Berries, from the people you meet if you talk with them. Keep reading to learn about where to find other camps and what you can do there.

Note that when you're visiting other people's camps, only your lead Pokémon will join you for the camping session! If you want to take part in group activities and socialize with other Trainers, visiting other camps you come across may be the easiest way to go. But if you're after Exp. Points, friendship boosts, and other benefits for all of your party Pokémon, set up your own camp for maximum efficiency!

Find people camping all across the Galar region

As you adventure across the routes of the Galar region, you may spot tents set up in various places along your path. These are the tents of other people in Galar who are camping. If you talk to them, you'll be able to visit their camp and do fun activities with them. There's a camp set up on every route except for Route 1 and Route 2.

The camp on Route 3 (p. 56)

The camp on Route 4 (p. 60)

The camp on Route 5 (p. 66)

The camp on Route 6 (p. 85)

The camp on Route 7 (p. 101)

The camp on Route 8 (p. 103)

The camp on Route 9 (p. 112)

The camp on Route 10 (p. 122)

Meet up with other players camping in the Wild Area

Meeting up with other players in the Wild Area can be a little trickier, since they won't always be in the same spots like the campers on routes. You may simply stumble across them or see the plumes of smoke rising from their camps. If you haven't already, you can learn more about such signals if you read up on the Wild Area, starting on page 249.

Choose Where to Camp Carefully

Out in the Wild Area, you can set up your camp just about anywhere (except on the water, of course!), but you might want to put some thought into your location. If you want a good chance at getting some other players to join you at your camp, try setting it up near the entrance to Motostoke or Hammerlocke. Since those cities are both connected to the Wild Area, they're likely to get a lot of player foot traffic—especially since the Camping King is just outside Motostoke and an Ingredients Seller stands just outside the entrance to Hammerlocke!

Talk, cook, and play together

Once you join someone else's camp or someone joins your camp, there are a number of different things you can do with other campers—and even more if those campers are real-world players.

Know those notifications

When camping with other players, there are a few different icons that can pop up, signaling that another player is doing something. You should see a notification appear on the top left of the screen when another player joins or leaves a camp. If you've joined someone else's camp, you'll also receive an invite if the host of the campsite wants to cook with you.

Talking to other campers

If you're curious what other campers have to say about some of the Pokémon at the camp, look over toward them using the Left Stick and press Ⓐ to talk to them. If you're talking to a real-world player, you'll also be able to receive their League Card by then pressing Ⓨ!

Talk to another player while camping together...

and you'll be able to receive their League Card!

Cooking with other campers

You can cook with other campers, whether they're a person met on a route of the Galar region or a real-world player met in the Wild Area. If you're cooking at someone else's camp, you'll only be able to choose what Berries you want to put in. You'll still be able to choose up to 10, but remember that other campers can choose up to 10 Berries as well, and the flavor of the curry will be determined by the combination of all the Berries added. If you're at your own camp with other campers, you'll be able to choose what ingredient you want in the curry as well as what Berries you want to contribute.

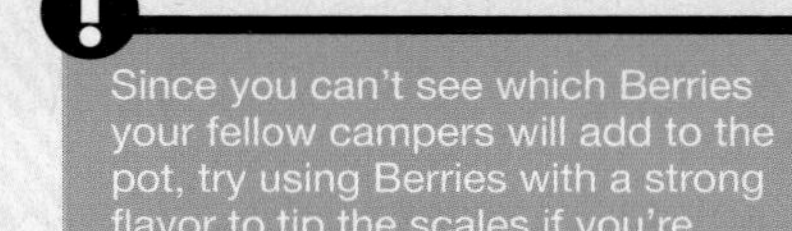

Since you can't see which Berries your fellow campers will add to the pot, try using Berries with a strong flavor to tip the scales if you're hoping for a specific flavor of curry!

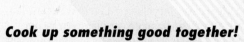

The curry mark appears when a camper wants to cook!

Cook up something good together!

If you're visiting someone else's camp and want to cook, you'll need to make sure to let the host of the camp know! At any of the camps along one of the routes in Galar, just choose the Cooking option like you would if you were camping on your own, and the hosts will never turn you down. But if you're visiting another player's campsite in the Wild Area, you won't get the option to start cooking on your own. Instead, you'll be able to let that player know that you want to cook, and they get to decide if they're in the mood or not.

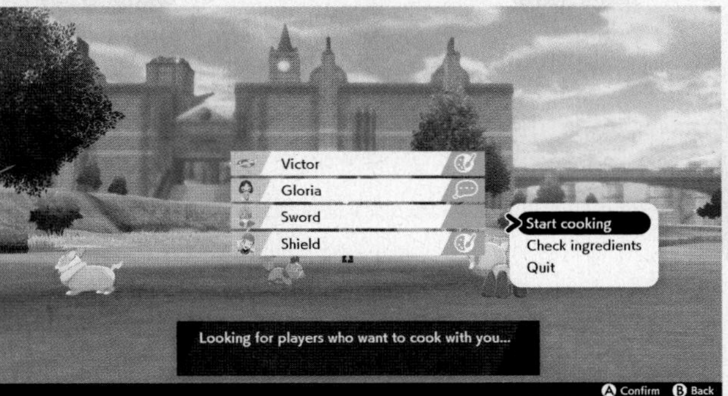

Two players are ready to cook, one is still thinking, and another declined.

Be a good host

If you're the host, you'll be able to see if other players are signaling that they'd like to cook. But even when they aren't, you can always choose the Cooking option like you would normally. Then select "Invite for cooking," and you'll see a new screen pop up that shows who's ready to cook and who's undecided. A next to someone's name means that they've decided to join in the cooking. A next to their name means they're still thinking it over. If there's no icon at all, it means a player declined your offer to cook together. When you start cooking, only the players who have next to their name will join, so be sure that everyone has made their decision before starting. You don't want to leave anyone out!

Work together

Once you actually start the cooking minigame, it works much the same as it does when you cook alone. The only difference is that you'll see other campers fanning the flames, stirring the pot, and pouring their own hearts into the mix, too! You don't need to worry about bumping ladles with them or anything like that, but the taste rating of the dish will depend on how well you all do, so try to work together for the best dish possible! Any Pokémon that partake in the cooking, whether yours or any other camper's, will get the same benefits as when you cook alone.

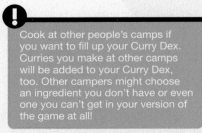

Cook at other people's camps if you want to fill up your Curry Dex. Curries you make at other camps will be added to your Curry Dex, too. Other campers might choose an ingredient you don't have or even one you can't get in your version of the game at all!

Playing with other Pokémon

Playing with Pokémon works just about the same as it does as when you're camping alone. You can still increase the Exp. Points and friendship of your lead Pokémon by playing with it at someone else's camp, and you can also increase the Exp. Points and friendship of the Pokémon of other campers by playing with them! The same goes for other campers playing with your Pokémon!

Welcome to Y-Comm

With Y-Comm, you're always welcome to connect to your fellow Trainers around you—and even around the world! Y-Comm is a communication platform that lets you connect with other players either using local wireless or, if you have a Nintendo Switch Online membership, via the internet. Watch as stamps pop up on your screen as you carry on in your adventure, and you'll never feel alone. Y-Comm will show the latest news from other Trainers, such as their most recent catches or victories, as well as any requests to battle or trade Pokémon or to swap League Cards! There's a handy guide to all the stamps' meanings below, and you'll be able to see details by opening the Y-Comm menu.

If you've played past Pokémon games, you might be familiar with the Global Trade Station (or GTS). There is no GTS in these games. Set up trades with friends when looking for a particular Pokémon, or you can use the Pokémon HOME app (coming early 2020) on your smart device. It'll be your new home for all the Pokémon you've collected during your time as a Trainer!

Nintendo Switch Online

To use online features that connect to the internet—like when you want to play with people living far away—you'll need a Nintendo Switch Online membership (p. 206). Visit Nintendo's website for more information about the service. Even if you haven't signed up for membership, you'll be able to connect with other players using local wireless. So get together with a few buddies or try playing in a place with lots of people around!

Stamps and their meanings

 Looking to have a Single Battle

 Looking to have a Double Battle

 Looking to have a Multi Battle

 Looking for allies for a Max Raid Battle

 In the middle of a Single Battle

 In the middle of a Double Battle

 In the middle of a Multi Battle

 In the middle of a Max Raid Battle

 Won a Single Battle

 Won a Double Battle

 Won a Multi Battle

 Won a Max Raid Battle

 Caught a Pokémon while out adventuring

 Caught a Dynamax Pokémon after a Max Raid Battle

 A Pokémon evolved

 Looking to swap League Cards

 Looking to trade with someone

 Looking for a Surprise Trade

 Just completed a trade

 Trading caused a Pokémon to evolve

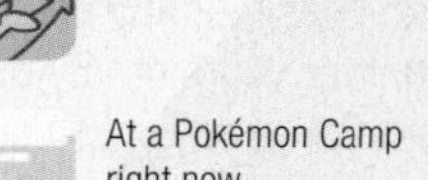 At a Pokémon Camp right now

Made some curry at camp

Did you notice that someone caught a Pokémon you need for your collection? Check the stamp from the Y-Comm menu, and you can see where they were when they caught it—giving you a handy clue to where you might catch it, too!

If you see a bright orange stamp for a Max Raid Battle, like the one shown here, that means it's indicating a battle against a rare Pokémon. Learn all about Max Raid Battles on page 271, as they're your chance to encounter rare and special Pokémon!

Open the Y-Comm menu

Stamps will appear on your main screen, but press Ⓨ and you'll be able to open up the Y-Comm menu to see the details of each—and see stamps of your own that have been sent out to others! This is where you'll want to come if you want to set up a Link Trade or Link Battle, though those aren't the only ways you can interact with other players here!

When you're out on your adventure, new stamps will be displayed as soon as they arrive in your game, which happens whenever it picks up a signal from another player nearby (if you're playing offline) or another player connected to the internet (if you're playing online). But when you've got the Y-Comm menu open, press Ⓧ to load new stamps, if they're available. Press ⊕ or ⊖ to toggle between online or local play. You can also use Ⓛ or Ⓡ to add the sender of a stamp to your block list, if you'd rather not play with them again.

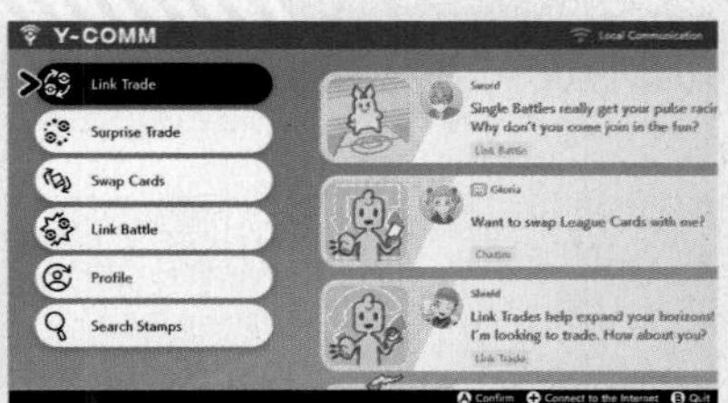

Reading Your Stamps and Making Friends

Press ▶ or use either control stick when viewing the Y-Comm menu to see the complete details of the stamps you've received! There's lots of information to unpack about each one, including that friend icon.

Friends can be added through your Nintendo Switch's HOME Menu if you've linked your user account to a Nintendo Account. Start by selecting your user icon there, then choose **Add Friend**. You'll be able to search for other players who are nearby, ones you've played with before, or those who have shared a friend code with you. Visit Nintendo's support page online if you need more help!

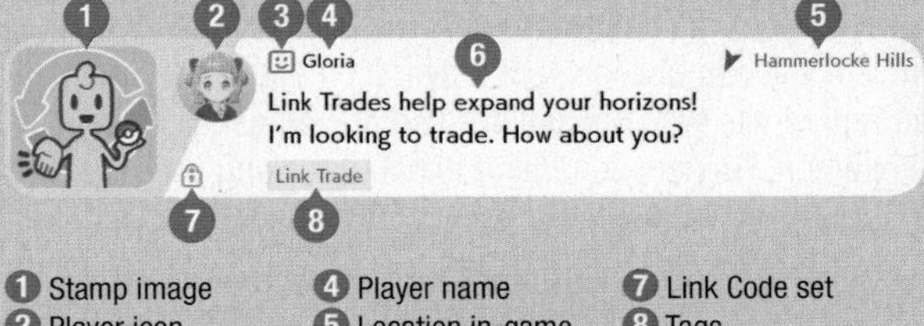

1. Stamp image
2. Player icon
3. Friend icon
4. Player name
5. Location in-game
6. Stamp message
7. Link Code set
8. Tags

Link Trade

Link Trades let you connect to another player to trade Pokémon, with both players able to see what is being offered before they agree to the trade or decide it's not the deal they were looking for. Select a Pokémon from your Boxes or party, see what your trade partner selects, and try to work out a trade you're both happy with!

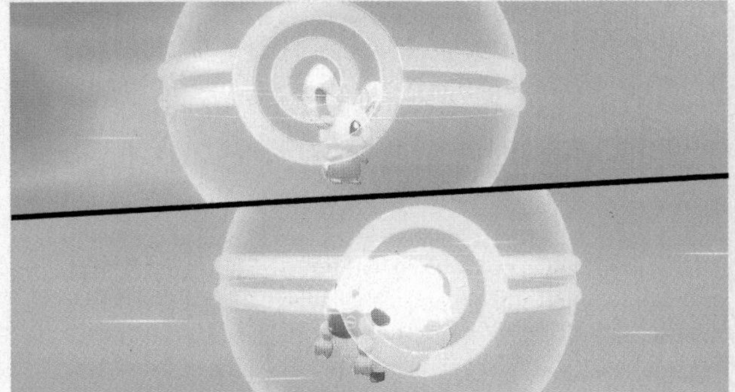

Surprise Trade

A Surprise Trade is just what it sounds like! You choose a Pokémon you're willing to give to another player and send it on its way. When you pass by another player in the real world who has also sent a Pokémon for a Surprise Trade, your Pokémon will be swapped like magic! You never know what you'll get.

Press Ⓨ after receiving this notification to meet your new Pokémon!

! You can only have one request active at a time, so if you're looking for a Surprise Trade, you can't also send out a call for a Link Trade or Link Battle. Consider starting up a Surprise Trade just before you put your system to sleep and tuck it in your bag, especially if you're in a place with a lot of other people nearby. You never know where you'll find a fellow Pokémon Trainer!

Swap Cards

If you're having a blast customizing your League Card and you'd like to show it off to others, then send out a call to swap League Cards with this option! You'll be connected with someone else who's looking to trade, and your collection will soon have another amazing League Card to help fill it out.

Link Battle

Unlike the Ranked Battles or Online Competitions in VS (p. 203), Link Battles don't have any kind of standings, so give them a try whenever you're ready for a friendly match! You can select from Single, Double, or Multi Battles (p. 163). You'll be able to set all Pokémon to Lv. 50, but apart from this, anything goes!

Profile

When you open up the Y-Comm menu for the first time, you might consider making this option one of your first stops. This is where you can change your player icon to one you think best represents you! Choose from among a special selection of Pokémon, Trainers you might encounter along your journey, and familiar logos.

Search Stamps

If you've got a lot of stamps and want to find particular ones, use this option. Filter your many stamps to find just the type you're most interested in at that moment. You can search for stamps from friends or for particular kinds of requests, such as Max Raid Battles or Link Trades.

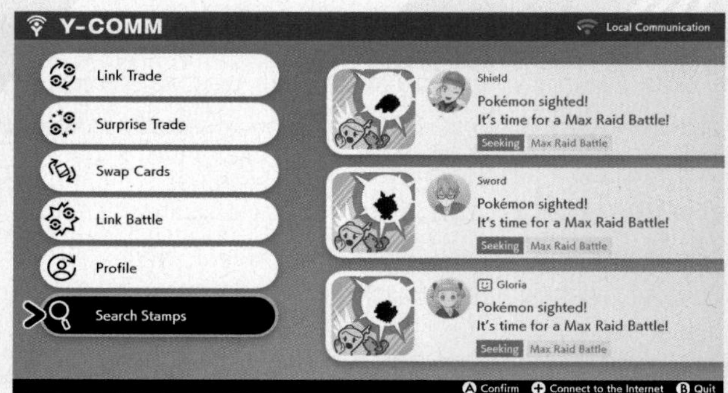

Use Link Codes to Find Friends

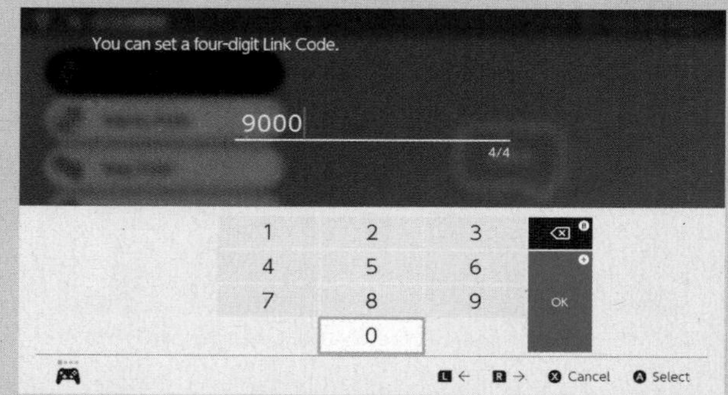

When you send out a call for a Link Trade, for a Link Battle, or to swap cards, you can choose to set a Link Code. This lets you restrict who you connect with, because only someone who enters the same Link Code will be able to respond to your call. If you want to be sure to connect to someone you know, set a Link Code on your request, then share that code with the person you want to connect with. Use this option when you've decided in advance to play with a particular player. You can set a Link Code by pressing ⊕ or ⊖ when you've chosen **Link Battle** or by selecting **Set Link Code** after choosing **Link Trade** or **Swap Cards**.

Wondering how to send out a request for allies for a Max Raid Battle? You'll have to find a Dynamax Pokémon to do that, so turn to page 271 to learn more!

League Cards

Once you reach Motostoke for the first time (p. 50), you'll be introduced to some of the Rotomi's features, including the ability to view and edit your League Card. This card is proof that you're a certified Pokémon Trainer—it will have a picture of you as well as lots of different information about what you've done during your journey.

When you access your League Card from the X menu, you'll first see the front of the card, as well as information about how much money, BP (p. 200), and Watts (p. 275) you've earned. It'll also tell you the highest level of Pokémon that will listen to you if you get it in a trade and what level of Pokémon you can catch. It might look a bit bland at first, but not to worry—you're able to customize how the front of your card looks. From the front view, press L or R to view the back side of your card.

Once you flip your card around, you'll see something like the image on the right. As you can see, it shows your team, your first partner, how many Pokémon you've registered to your Pokédex, and so on.

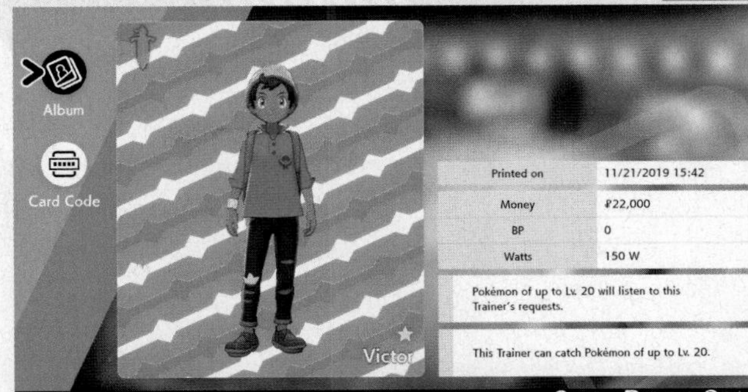

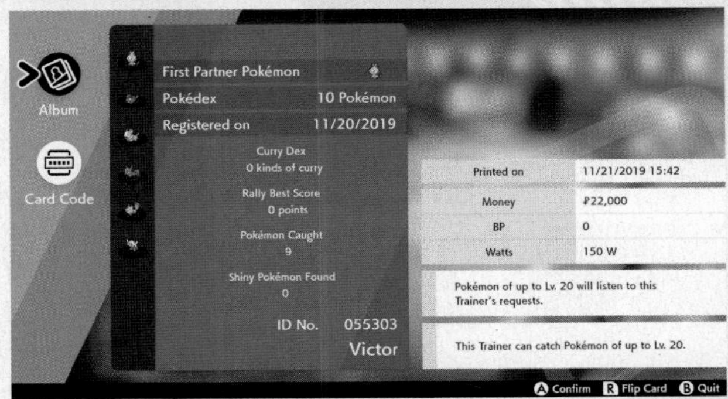

Customizing your League Card

After you first hear about the Rotomi in Motostoke, you'll have access to Rotomi's Card Maker feature. Start it up, and you'll see the screen below. This is where you can customize or update your card with your latest info.

Make a new League Card

Select this option if you want to redesign your card completely. You can change your image, the background, the effect, the frame, and so on. Certain options cost money, but you can give your card a brand-new look and also update your info at the same time.

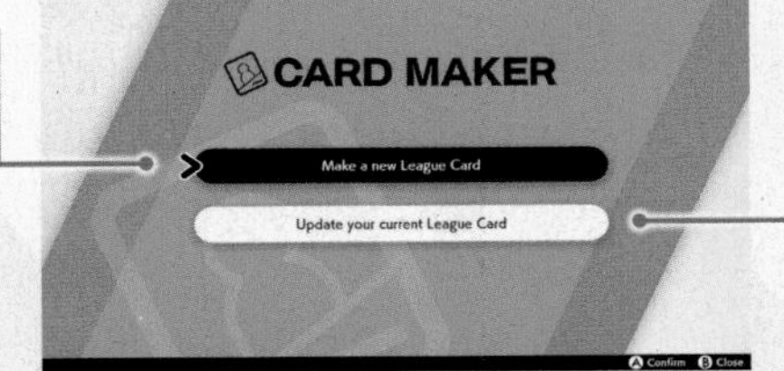

Update your current League Card

This option will only update the information on your card to reflect your latest progress. Your team info, Curry Dex, and so on will all be updated to what you currently have, but the design of the card will not be changed.

This is the screen you'll see once you select **Make a new League Card**. This is where you'll choose your background, plus an effect and frame if you want them—which are all covered on the next pages.

Backgrounds appear behind your character, effects are extra decorations you can add on top of them, and frames go over the whole thing.

Once you're done with these selections, you can press ⊕ / ⊖ or select **To Next Step** to move on.

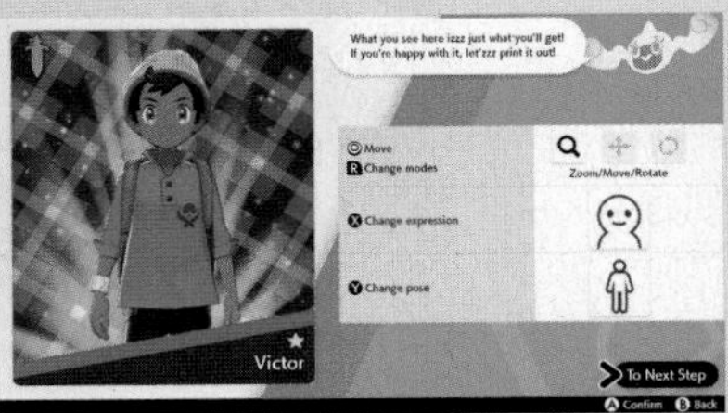

You can zoom in and out, move yourself around, and even rotate to change how you appear on your card. You can also change your expression and pose until you get the perfect shot! The different poses and expressions you can unlock (and how) are covered on the following pages.

Once you're looking picture-perfect, you can confirm your selections and move on to the final screen—coating.

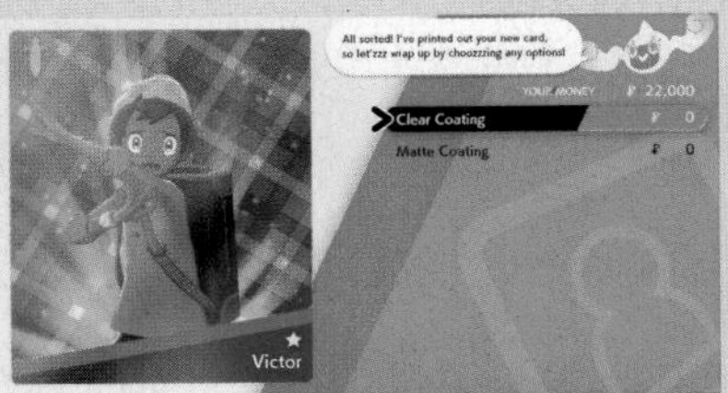

Here's where you'll choose the final touch for your League Card. You can choose whether you want to make your card holographic or not—or even how you want it to sparkle! Keep in mind that some coatings might cost some money, so check the price before making your choice!

You'll see one to five stars near your name—these are an indicator of how far you've advanced in the Gym Challenge!

Customization materials

Below is a comprehensive list of all backgrounds, effects, frames, expressions, poses, and coatings, as well as how to unlock them. Some of these may be a bit tricky to unlock, but that will just make your League Card all the more amazing when you send it to other players!

Backgrounds

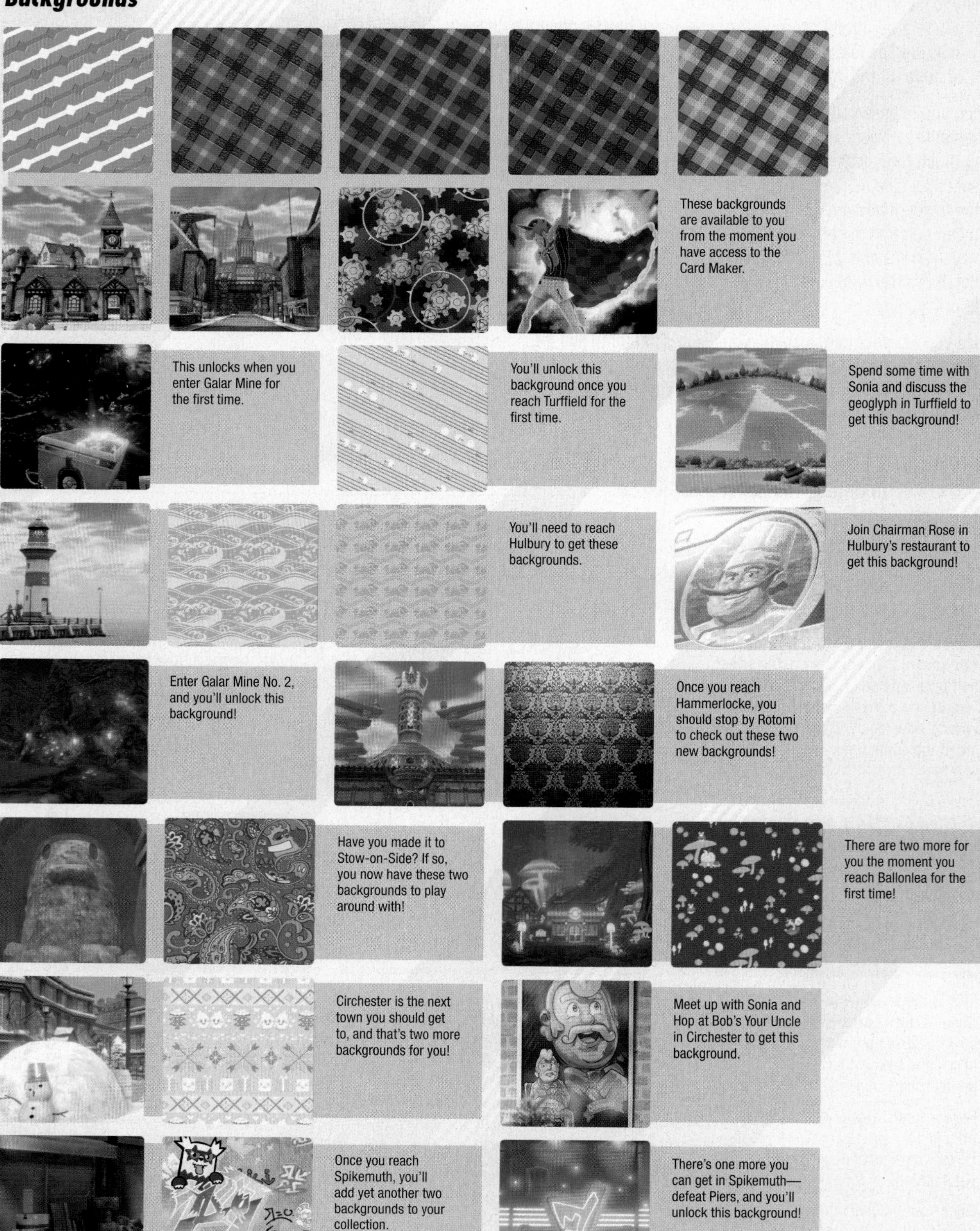

These backgrounds are available to you from the moment you have access to the Card Maker.

This unlocks when you enter Galar Mine for the first time.

You'll unlock this background once you reach Turffield for the first time.

Spend some time with Sonia and discuss the geoglyph in Turffield to get this background!

You'll need to reach Hulbury to get these backgrounds.

Join Chairman Rose in Hulbury's restaurant to get this background!

Enter Galar Mine No. 2, and you'll unlock this background!

Once you reach Hammerlocke, you should stop by Rotomi to check out these two new backgrounds!

Have you made it to Stow-on-Side? If so, you now have these two backgrounds to play around with!

There are two more for you the moment you reach Ballonlea for the first time!

Circhester is the next town you should get to, and that's two more backgrounds for you!

Meet up with Sonia and Hop at Bob's Your Uncle in Circhester to get this background.

Once you reach Spikemuth, you'll add yet another two backgrounds to your collection.

There's one more you can get in Spikemuth—defeat Piers, and you'll unlock this background!

Now it's time to head back to Hammerlocke and face Raihan. Defeat him, and you'll get this background.

These two will unlock the moment you reach Wyndon for the first time!

These three backgrounds will be unlocked when you accomplish something very special—becoming the Champion!

If you have save data from *Pokémon: Let's Go, Pikachu!* on your Nintendo Switch, you'll unlock this background!

If you have save data from *Pokémon: Let's Go, Eevee!* on your Nintendo Switch, you'll unlock this background!

If you have save data from Pokémon Quest on your Nintendo Switch, you'll unlock this background!

Rotomi's a huge help to Trainers, and now you can get a Rotomi-themed background! Make 10 League Cards from scratch to get it!

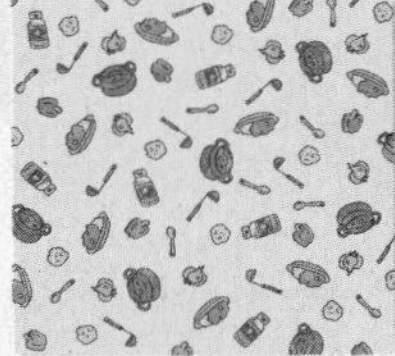

You better get cooking, because you'll need to have filled in 15 curry recipes for your Curry Dex to get this background!

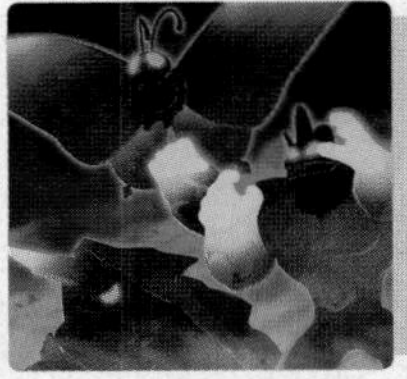

While you're exploring the Wild Area, why not take part in some Max Raid Battles? Participate in 30, and you'll get this background!

If you feel like you need a fresh look, one thing to do is get a new hairstyle at a hair salon. Do that 10 times, and you'll unlock this background!

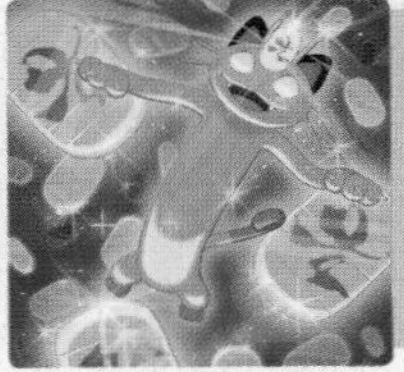

If you've managed to earn a total of ₽1,000,000 over your adventure (even if you spent some of it), you'll get this background!

Receive Ball Guy's League Card (p. 312) to unlock this background!

Begin the epilogue (starting on page 145) to unlock this background!

Defeat the Grass-type Dynamax Pokémon in the epilogue to unlock this background!

Defeat the Water-type Dynamax Pokémon in the epilogue to unlock this background!

Defeat the Fire-type Dynamax Pokémon in the epilogue to unlock this background!

Defeat the Dragon-type Dynamax Pokémon in the epilogue to unlock this background!

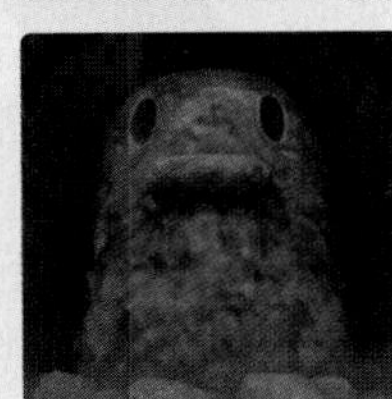

Defeat the Fighting-type Dynamax Pokémon or the Ghost-type Dynamax Pokémon during the epilogue to unlock this background!

Defeat the Rock-type Dynamax Pokémon or the Ice-type Dynamax Pokémon during the epilogue to unlock this background!

Complete the epilogue to unlock this background!

Win 30 Single Battles in the Battle Tower to unlock this background!

Win 50 Double Battles in the Battle Tower to unlock this background!

Win 100 Single Battles in the Battle Tower to unlock this background!

Win 100 Double Battles in the Battle Tower to unlock this background!

Effects

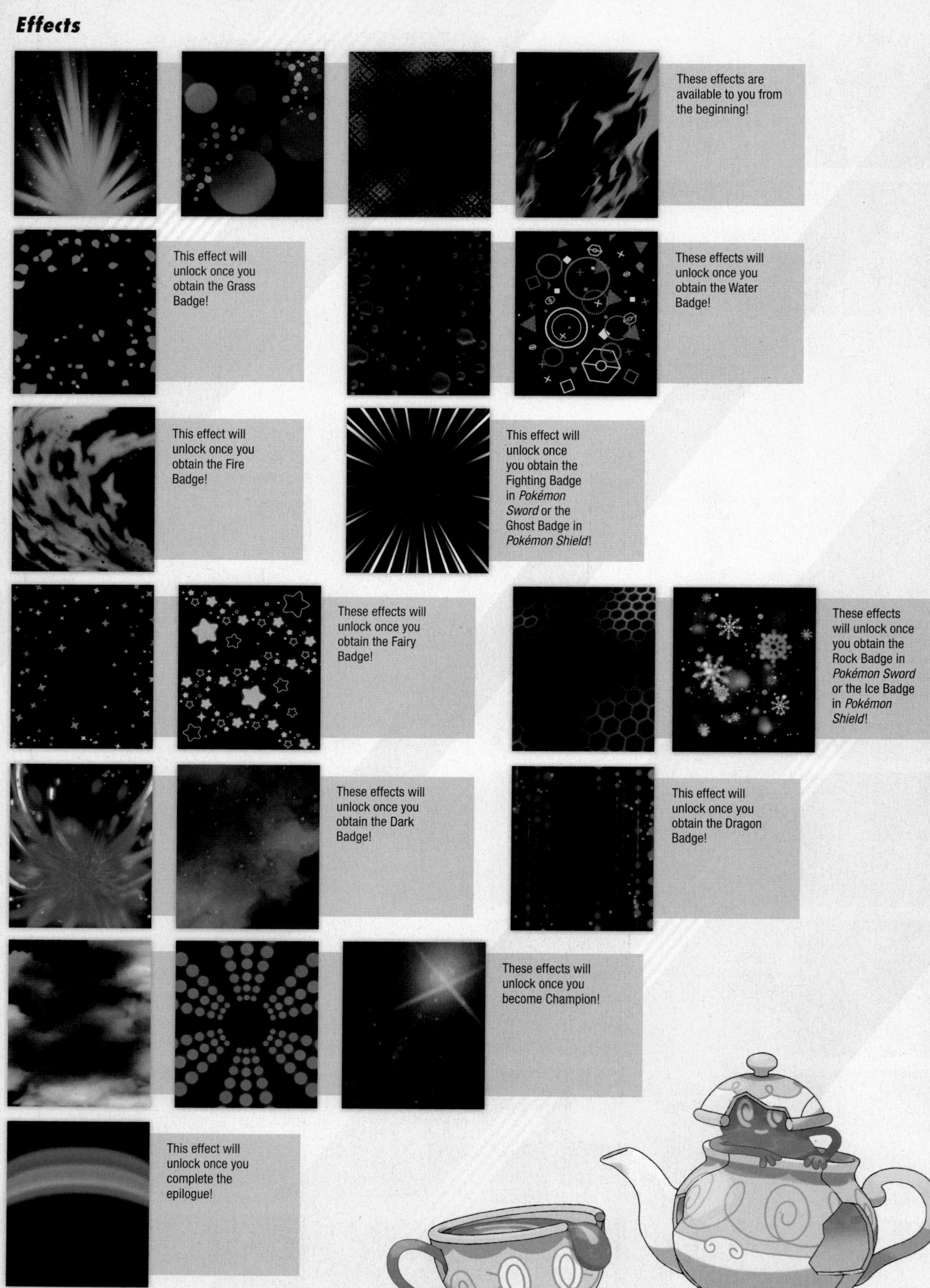

These effects are available to you from the beginning!

This effect will unlock once you obtain the Grass Badge!

These effects will unlock once you obtain the Water Badge!

This effect will unlock once you obtain the Fire Badge!

This effect will unlock once you obtain the Fighting Badge in *Pokémon Sword* or the Ghost Badge in *Pokémon Shield*!

These effects will unlock once you obtain the Fairy Badge!

These effects will unlock once you obtain the Rock Badge in *Pokémon Sword* or the Ice Badge in *Pokémon Shield*!

These effects will unlock once you obtain the Dark Badge!

This effect will unlock once you obtain the Dragon Badge!

These effects will unlock once you become Champion!

This effect will unlock once you complete the epilogue!

Frames

You have these frames from the beginning!

These frames become available once you obtain the Grass Badge!

This frame becomes available once you obtain the Water Badge!

These frames become available once you obtain the Fire Badge!

This frame will become available once you obtain the Rock Badge in *Pokémon Sword* or the Ice Badge in *Pokémon Shield*!

These frames become available once you obtain the Fighting Badge in *Pokémon Sword* or the Ghost Badge in *Pokémon Shield*!

This frame becomes available once you obtain the Dragon Badge!

These frames become available once you obtain the Fairy Badge!

This frame becomes available once you become Champion!

These frames become available once you obtain the Dark Badge!

This frame becomes available if you have save data from *Pokémon: Let's Go, Pikachu!* on your Nintendo Switch!

This frame becomes available if you have save data from *Pokémon: Let's Go, Eevee!* on your Nintendo Switch!

This frame becomes available if you have save data from Pokémon Quest on your Nintendo Switch!

Expressions

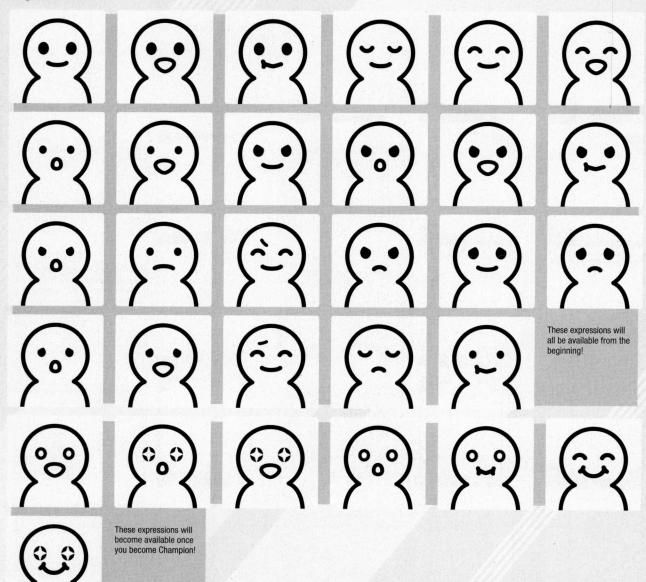

These expressions will all be available from the beginning!

These expressions will become available once you become Champion!

Poses

These poses will become available once you obtain the Fire Badge!

These poses become available once you obtain the Fighting Badge in *Pokémon Sword* or the Ghost Badge in *Pokémon Shield*!

This pose will become available once you obtain the Fairy Badge!

These poses will become available once you obtain the Rock Badge in *Pokémon Sword* or the Ice Badge in *Pokémon Shield*!

This pose will become available once you obtain the Dark Badge!

These poses become available once you obtain the Dragon Badge!

This pose will become available once you become Champion!

Coatings

*

These coatings are available from the beginning!

*The matte coating isn't shiny at all, so you'll only see your card's design on its own!

This coating will become available once you obtain the Grass Badge!

This coating becomes available once you obtain the Fighting Badge in *Pokémon Sword* or the Ghost Badge in *Pokémon Shield*!

These coatings will become available once you obtain the Dark Badge!

These coatings will become available once you become Champion!

This coating will become available once you complete the epilogue!

Your League Card Collection

So now you've got your League Card customized—you found a good background, you gave it a good frame, and you're happy with the photo of yourself. Maybe you even gave it a special shiny coating! But there's more you can do with your League Card than just look at it. You can trade cards with other Trainers and build up a proper League Card Collection!

Swap Card Codes

From the X menu, you can go to the League Card screen, where you'll see the **Card Code** option. Your Card Code is unique to your League Card and is a way to trade cards with other players even when they aren't nearby! To get things started yourself, you can generate your Card Code and share it with a pal. If you're the one receiving a Card Code from another player, choose **Receive a Card** and then enter the code. As long as the other person is still sharing their card, you'll receive a copy!

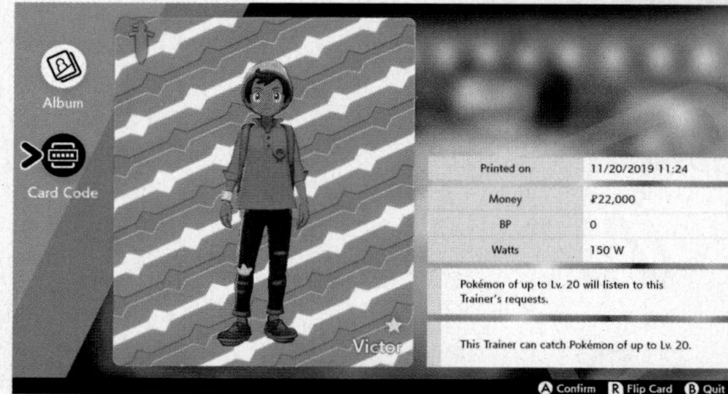

You need to connect to the internet to get cards using a Card Code, which requires a Nintendo Switch Online membership (p. 206).

Trade cards via Y-Comm

One way to trade League Cards on the fly is to use Y-Comm! From the Y-Comm menu, select the **Swap Cards** option and confirm your decision. That's it! You'll automatically swap League Cards with anyone else who is also looking to trade cards nearby or online! Once you successfully complete a trade, you'll get to see the League Card you've received, and it will be added to your album!

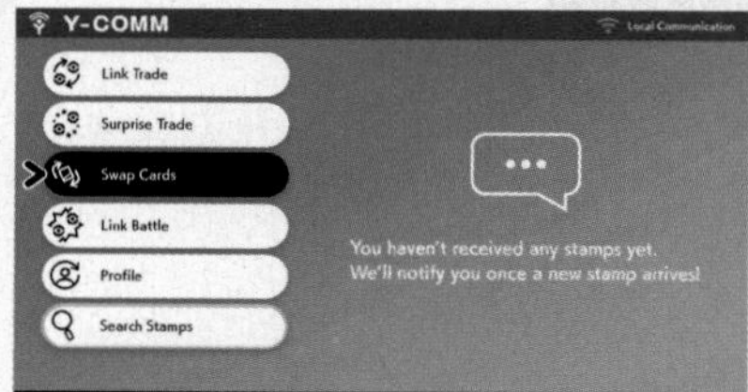

Set Up a Link Code

If you want to trade cards with someone specific, choose **Set Link Code** after selecting **Swap Cards**. If you and another player set the same Link Code, you'll connect with one another, without other connections getting in the way! Learn more about Link Codes on page 300, if you're not sure what they are.

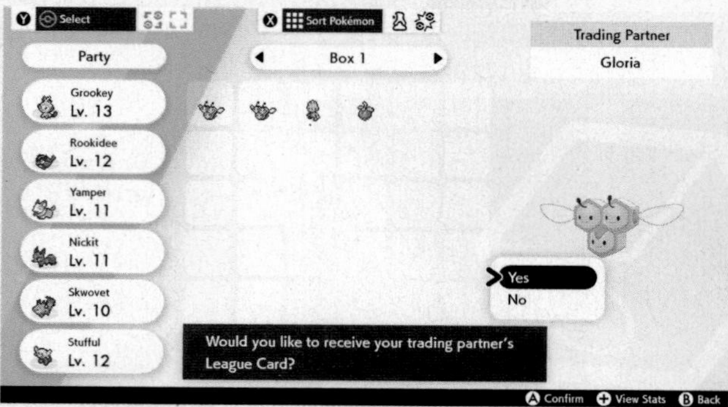

Swap cards after a Link Battle or Link Trade

You'll also be able to receive League Cards after participating in a Link Battle or Link Trade! Once the battle or trade is complete, you'll be asked whether or not you'd like to receive the other Trainer's card. If you want a copy, just accept, and it'll be added to your album!

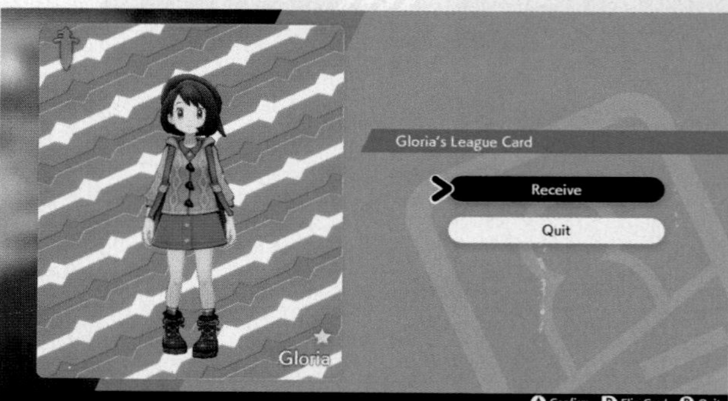

Exchange cards with fellow campers

When you camp together with other players, you'll have the option of viewing their League Card by pressing Ⓨ when talking to them. Once you have a look at their card, you'll have the chance to keep a copy for your collection!

Viewing your collection

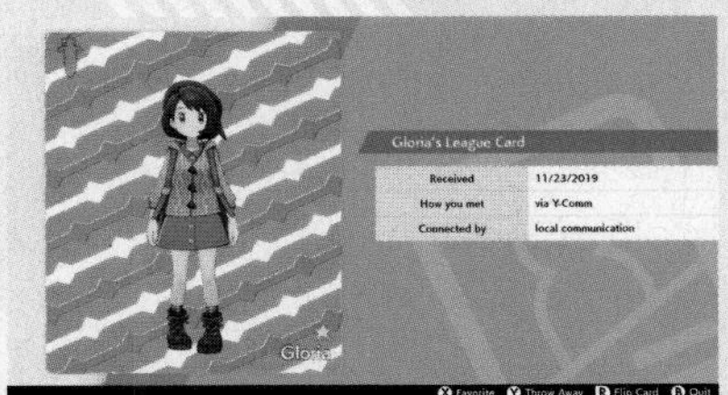

Once you've received League Cards, it's only natural that you'd want to look at your collection from time to time. You can do this by selecting the **Album** option after selecting **League Card** from the X menu. In your album, you'll be able to scroll through all the League Cards you've received.

Select a card from this list to view it, plus see other information, like when and how you received it. If you check the back of another player's card, you'll also see information, like their party composition, their first partner Pokémon, how much progress they've made on their Pokédex, and so on—just like what you'd see on the back of your League Card! If the card belongs to one of the stars covered on the following pages, you'll instead see a fun biographical blurb about them on the back!

! Be aware that your album can only hold 300 cards from other players. Once you hit this number, you'll have to delete cards to make room for new ones. If there are some cards you really don't want to lose, you should favorite them! Your favorite cards can't be selected for deletion, so you won't have to worry about accidentally getting rid of them!

League Cards of Galarian superstars

If you really want your League Card collection to shine, try to collect the cards of all these superstars around the Galar region! Most of them have regular and rare versions, and each comes with different info on the back, filling you in a bit more on the history and personality of these fascinating characters.

Hop's normal League Card
Get it from Hop during the main story

Hop's rare League Card
Battle Hop once more after resolving the events with Sordward and Shielbert after becoming Champion

Marnie's normal League Card
Get it from Marnie during the main story

Marnie's rare League Card
Battle Marnie in Spikemuth after becoming Champion

Milo's normal League Card
Get it from Sonia during the main story

Milo's rare League Card
Go to Turffield Stadium during the events with Sordward and Shielbert after becoming Champion

Nessa's normal League Card
Get it from Nessa during the main story

Nessa's rare League Card
Go to Hulbury Stadium during the events with Sordward and Shielbert after becoming Champion

Kabu's normal League Card
Get it from Marnie during the main story

Kabu's rare League Card
Go to Motostoke Stadium during the events with Sordward and Shielbert after becoming Champion

Bea's normal League Card
Get it from Opal during the main story in *Pokémon Sword*

Bea's rare League Card
Go to Stow-on-Side Stadium during the events with Sordward and Shielbert after becoming Champion in *Pokémon Sword*

Allister's normal League Card
Get it from Opal during the main story in *Pokémon Shield*

Allister's rare League Card
Go to Stow-on-Side Stadium during the events with Sordward and Shielbert after becoming Champion in *Pokémon Shield*

Opal's normal League Card
Get it from Opal during the main story

Opal's rare League Card
Go to Ballonlea Stadium during the events with Sordward and Shielbert after becoming Champion

Gordie's normal League Card
Get it from Hop during the main story in *Pokémon Sword*

Gordie's rare League Card
Go to Circhester Stadium during the events with Sordward and Shielbert after becoming Champion in *Pokémon Sword*

Melony's normal League Card
Get it from Hop during the main story in *Pokémon Shield*

Melony's rare League Card
Go to Circhester Stadium during the events with Sordward and Shielbert after becoming Champion in *Pokémon Shield*

Piers's normal League Card
Get it from Marnie during the main story

Piers's rare League Card
Go to Hammerlocke during the events with Sordward and Shielbert after becoming Champion

Raihan's normal League Card
Get it from Raihan during the main story

Raihan's rare League Card
Go to Hammerlocke Stadium during the events with Sordward and Shielbert after becoming Champion

Leon's normal League Card
Get it from Sonia during the main story

Leon's rare League Card
Beat Leon to reach the Poké Ball Tier in the Battle Tower (p. 200)

Rose's normal League Card
Get it from Oleana during the main story

Rose's rare League Card
Find Oleana in Galar Mine after becoming Champion

Bede's normal League Card
Get it from Bede during the main story

Bede's rare League Card
Go to Ballonlea Stadium during the events with Sordward and Shielbert after becoming Champion

Ball Guy's League Card
Find the Ball Guy in Motostoke after becoming Champion

Customizing Your Character

While you've been able to choose different looks for your character in previous games, there have never been as many options to customize your Trainer as there are in *Pokémon Sword* and *Pokémon Shield*. The next few pages will cover all of the different ways you can customize your look to create a Trainer that's uniquely you!

Get a new do and some glam at salons

There are beauty salons found in Motostoke (p. 50), Hammerlocke (p. 80), Circhester (p. 106), and Wyndon (p. 124), and they all provide the same services for the same prices. Every hair and makeup option is available from the start of your adventure, and there are a lot of them! Check out the lists below for some style inspiration.

Hairstyle choices

Hairstyles

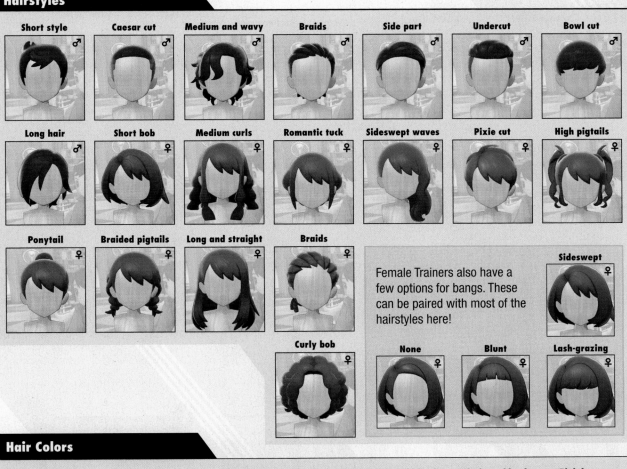

Short style	♂
Caesar cut	♂
Medium and wavy	♂
Braids	♂
Side part	♂
Undercut	♂
Bowl cut	♂
Long hair	♂
Short bob	♀
Medium curls	♀
Romantic tuck	♀
Sideswept waves	♀
Pixie cut	♀
High pigtails	♀
Ponytail	♀
Braided pigtails	♀
Long and straight	♀
Braids	♀
Curly bob	♀

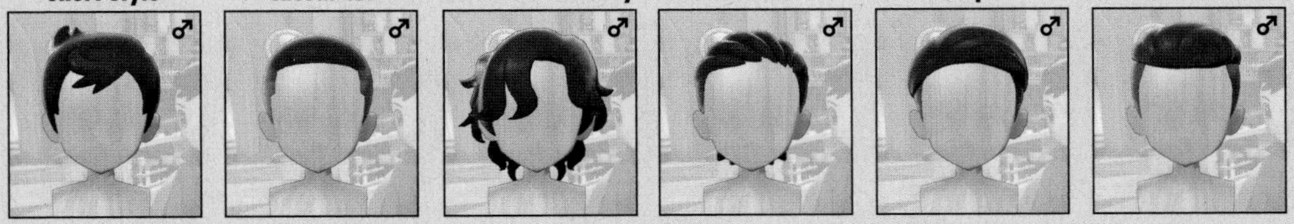

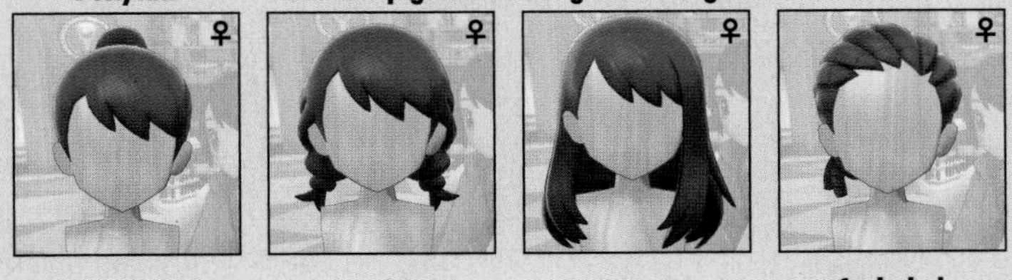

Female Trainers also have a few options for bangs. These can be paired with most of the hairstyles here!

Sideswept	♀
None	♀
Blunt	♀
Lash-grazing	♀

Hair Colors

Makeup

When changing makeup, Trainers can alter the size and color of their eyebrows and add colored contact lenses for a different eye color—or even some wild patterns in their eyes. Female Trainers can also choose a style for their eyelashes and a color for their lips.

Eyebrow Sizes

Normal eyebrows

Thick eyebrows

Thin eyebrows

Eyelash Styles

Natural

Cat-eye extensions

Doll-eye extensions

Contact Colors

Hazel

Gray

Green

Pale blue

Black

Yellow

Pink

Purple

Brown

Ultramarine

Yellow-green

Lavender ice

Poppy red

White

Multicolor swirl

Total dark

Burning passion

Lovely hearts

Star studded

Lip Colors

None

Pale pink

Orange

Pink

Red

Maroon

Blue

Green

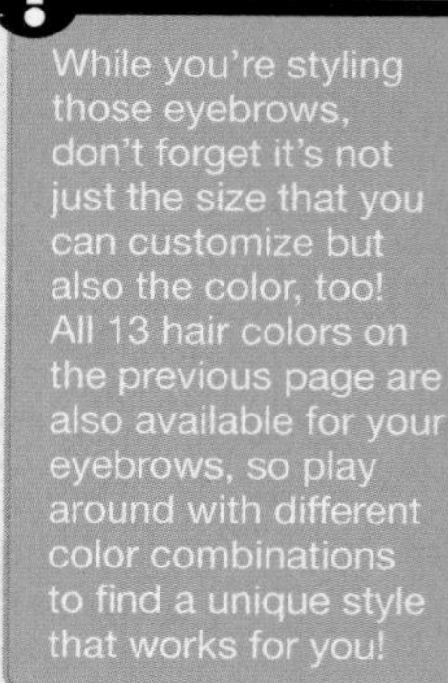

While you're styling those eyebrows, don't forget it's not just the size that you can customize but also the color, too! All 13 hair colors on the previous page are also available for your eyebrows, so play around with different color combinations to find a unique style that works for you!

Outfits You Can Obtain

You can do a lot more than just change your hair and makeup if you want to shake up your look! Boutiques around the Galar region are just waiting to outfit you, as long as you're willing to part with some of your hard-earned cash. You'll be able to show off your great sense of style to the Trainers you meet in the Wild Area or that you battle with via communication features, so don't hesitate to come up with a look that's all your own!

Uniforms

There are a number of amazing uniforms you can obtain if you can't get enough of that sporty style. You'll get 10 uniforms through the course of your main adventure, and eight of them will be from major-division Gyms you defeat during your Gym Challenge. But you can also buy uniforms of all the minor-division Gyms at the uniform shop counter found in stadiums around the region—and obtain a few others in special ways. Starting below, you can see each of the uniform sets you can obtain in your game, together with specifics on how you can get each one. These sets come grouped together, which makes changing into them a breeze, but you can also mix and match any of the parts to create your own unique looks.

The uniform shop is located at these counters

There's more to Galar than its sports tournaments, of course! Boutiques around the region also sell entire lines of different looks, ranging from punk rock to cute and classy. Turn to page 323 for more on these shops.

Challenger Uniform

Get it just before the Gym Challenge opening ceremony

 **Sport Top (Challenger Kit)** ♂ ♀

 **Sport Shorts (Challenger Kit)** ♂ ♀

 **Sport Legwear (Challenger Kit)** ♂ ♀

Sport High-Tops (Challenger Kit) ♂ ♀

 **Sport Glove (Challenger Kit)** ♂ ♀

Grass Uniform 

Get it when you earn your Grass Badge

 **Sport Top (Grass Type)** ♂ ♀ 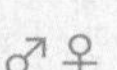

 **Sport Shorts (Grass Type)** ♂ ♀

 **Sport Legwear (Grass Type)** ♂ ♀

 **Sport High-Tops (Grass Type)** ♂ ♀

 **Sport Glove (Grass Type)** ♂ ♀

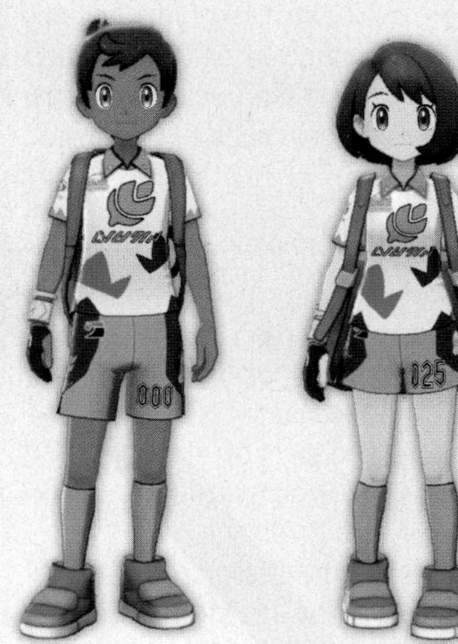

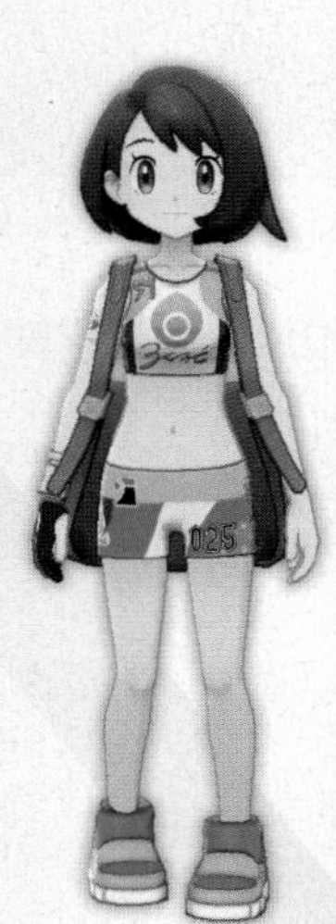

Water Uniform 

Get it when you earn your Water Badge

 **Sport Top (Water Type)** ♂ ♀

 **Sport Shorts (Water Type)** ♂ ♀

 **Sport Legwear (Water Type)** ♂ ♀

 **Sport High-Tops (Water Type)** ♂ ♀

Sport Glove (Water Type) ♂ ♀

Fire Uniform 

Get it when you earn your Fire Badge

 **Sport Top (Fire Type)** ♂ ♀ 

 **Sport Shorts (Fire Type)** ♂ ♀

 **Sport Legwear (Fire Type)** ♂ ♀

 **Sport High-Tops (Fire Type)** ♂ ♀

 **Sport Glove (Fire Type)** ♂ ♀

Ghost Uniform

Get it when you earn your Ghost Badge in *Pokémon Shield*, or buy it at a uniform shop for ₽18,000 in *Pokémon Sword*

- **Sport Top (Ghost Type)** ♂ ♀

- **Sport Shorts (Ghost Type)** ♂ ♀

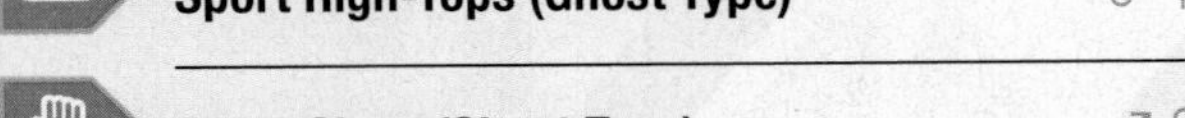

- **Sport Legwear (Ghost Type)** ♂ ♀

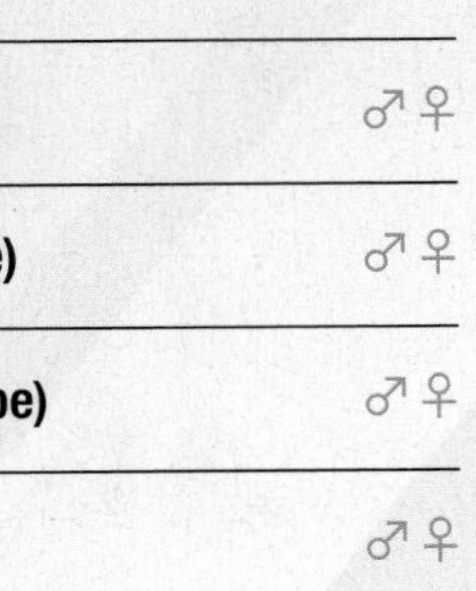

- **Sport High-Tops (Ghost Type)** ♂ ♀
- **Sport Glove (Ghost Type)** ♂ ♀

Fighting Uniform

Get it when you earn your Fighting Badge in *Pokémon Sword*, or buy it at a uniform shop for ₽18,000 in *Pokémon Shield*

- **Sport Top (Fighting Type)** ♂ ♀
- **Sport Shorts (Fighting Type)** ♂ ♀
- **Sport Legwear (Fighting Type)** ♂ ♀
- **Sport High-Tops (Fighting Type)** ♂ ♀
- **Sport Glove (Fighting Type)** ♂ ♀

Fairy Uniform

Get it when you earn your Fairy Badge

- **Sport Top (Fairy Type)** ♂ ♀
- **Sport Shorts (Fairy Type)** ♂ ♀
- **Sport Legwear (Fairy Type)** ♂ ♀

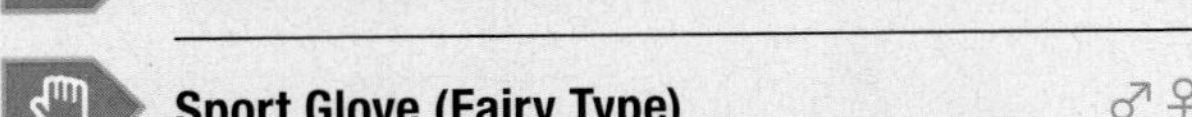

- **Sport High-Tops (Fairy Type)** ♂ ♀
- **Sport Glove (Fairy Type)** ♂ ♀

Rock Uniform

Get it when you earn your Rock Badge in *Pokémon Sword*, or buy it at a uniform shop for ₽18,000 in *Pokémon Shield*

Sport Top (Rock Type) ♂ ♀

Sport Shorts (Rock Type) ♂ ♀

Sport Legwear (Rock Type) ♂ ♀

Sport High-Tops (Rock Type) ♂ ♀

Sport Glove (Rock Type) ♂ ♀

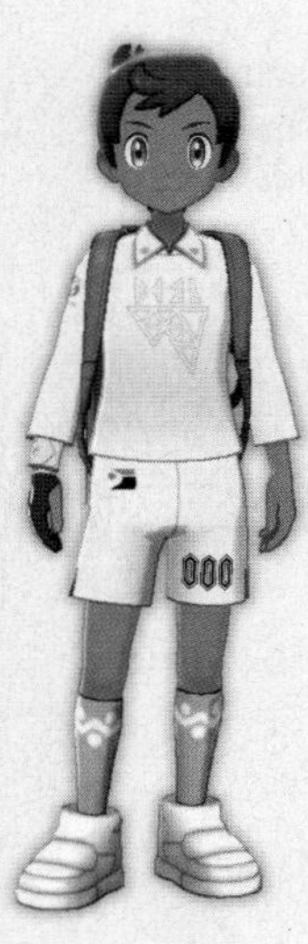

Ice Uniform

Get it when you earn your Ice Badge in *Pokémon Shield*, or buy it at a uniform shop for ₽18,000 in *Pokémon Sword*

Sport Top (Ice Type) ♂ ♀

Sport Shorts (Ice Type) ♂ ♀

Sport Legwear (Ice Type) ♂ ♀

Sport High-Tops (Ice Type) ♂ ♀

Sport Glove (Ice Type) ♂ ♀

Dark Uniform

Get it when you earn your Dark Badge

Sport Top (Dark Type) ♂ ♀

Sport Shorts (Dark Type) ♂ ♀

Sport Legwear (Dark Type) ♂ ♀

Sport High-Tops (Dark Type) ♂ ♀

Sport Glove (Dark Type) ♂ ♀

Dragon Uniform

Get it when you earn your Dragon Badge

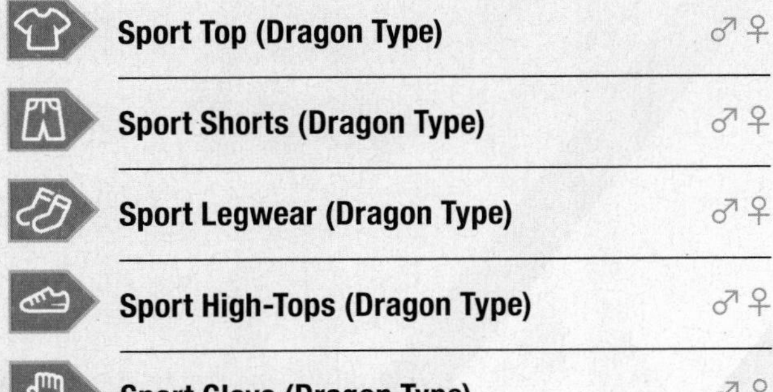

Sport Top (Dragon Type)	♂ ♀
Sport Shorts (Dragon Type)	♂ ♀
Sport Legwear (Dragon Type)	♂ ♀
Sport High-Tops (Dragon Type)	♂ ♀
Sport Glove (Dragon Type)	♂ ♀

Bug Uniform

Buy it at a uniform shop for ₽18,000

Sport Top (Bug Type)	♂ ♀
Sport Shorts (Bug Type)	♂ ♀
Sport Legwear (Bug Type)	♂ ♀
Sport High-Tops (Bug Type)	♂ ♀
Sport Glove (Bug Type)	♂ ♀

Steel Uniform

Buy it at a uniform shop for ₽18,000

Sport Top (Steel Type)	♂ ♀
Sport Shorts (Steel Type)	♂ ♀
Sport Legwear (Steel Type)	♂ ♀
Sport High-Tops (Steel Type)	♂ ♀
Sport Glove (Steel Type)	♂ ♀

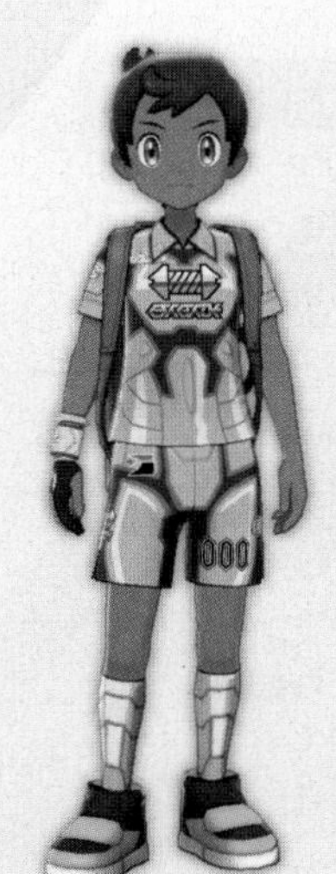

Psychic Uniform

Buy it at a uniform shop for ₽18,000

Sport Top (Psychic Type)	♂ ♀
Sport Shorts (Psychic Type)	♂ ♀
Sport Legwear (Psychic Type)	♂ ♀
Sport High-Tops (Psychic Type)	♂ ♀
Sport Glove (Psychic Type)	♂ ♀

Electric Uniform

Buy it at a uniform shop for ₽18,000

Sport Top (Electric Type)	♂ ♀
Sport Shorts (Electric Type)	♂ ♀
Sport Legwear (Electric Type)	♂ ♀
Sport High-Tops (Electric Type)	♂ ♀
Sport Glove (Electric Type)	♂ ♀

Ground Uniform

Buy it at a uniform shop for ₽18,000

Sport Top (Ground Type)	♂ ♀
Sport Shorts (Ground Type)	♂ ♀
Sport Legwear (Ground Type)	♂ ♀
Sport High-Tops (Ground Type)	♂ ♀
Sport Glove (Ground Type)	♂ ♀

Flying Uniform

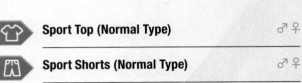

Buy it at a uniform shop for ₽18,000

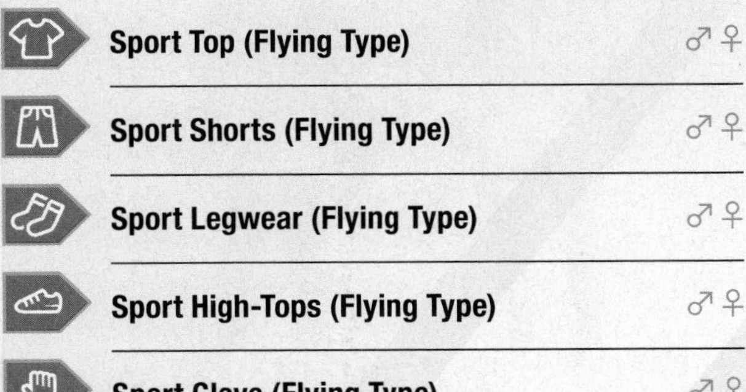

- Sport Top (Flying Type) ♂ ♀
- Sport Shorts (Flying Type) ♂ ♀
- Sport Legwear (Flying Type) ♂ ♀
- Sport High-Tops (Flying Type) ♂ ♀
- Sport Glove (Flying Type) ♂ ♀

Normal Uniform

Buy it at a uniform shop for ₽18,000

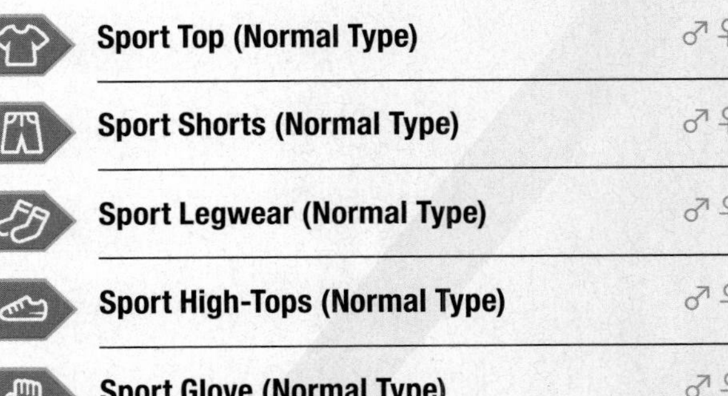

- Sport Top (Normal Type) ♂ ♀
- Sport Shorts (Normal Type) ♂ ♀
- Sport Legwear (Normal Type) ♂ ♀
- Sport High-Tops (Normal Type) ♂ ♀
- Sport Glove (Normal Type) ♂ ♀

Poison Uniform

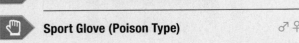

Buy it at a uniform shop for ₽18,000

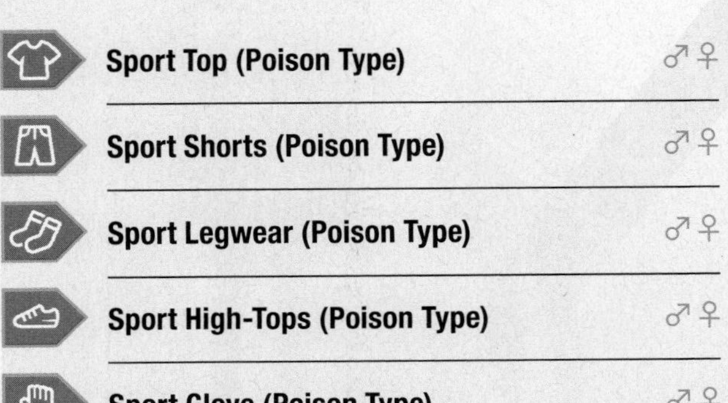

- Sport Top (Poison Type) ♂ ♀
- Sport Shorts (Poison Type) ♂ ♀
- Sport Legwear (Poison Type) ♂ ♀
- Sport High-Tops (Poison Type) ♂ ♀
- Sport Glove (Poison Type) ♂ ♀

Champion Uniform

Get it by becoming the Champion

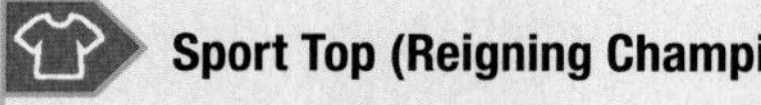

Sport Top (Reigning Champion) ♂ ♀

Sport Shorts (Reigning Champion) ♂ ♀

Sport Legwear (Reigning Champion) ♂ ♀

Sport Glove (Reigning Champion) ♂ ♀

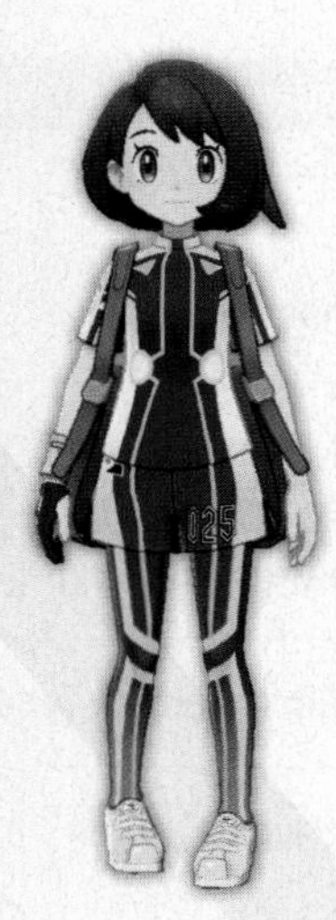

Ranked Battles Uniform

Get it by talking to the person at a BP Shop after taking part in a Link Battle

Sport Top (Ranked Battles) ♂ ♀

Sport Shorts (Ranked Battles) ♂ ♀

Sport Legwear (Ranked Battles) ♂ ♀

Sport Glove (Ranked Battles) ♂ ♀

Battle Tower Uniform

Get it by defeating Leon in the Ultra Ball Tier at the Battle Tower (p. 200)

Sport Top (Battle Tower) ♂ ♀

Sport Shorts (Battle Tower) ♂ ♀

Sport Legwear (Battle Tower) ♂ ♀

Sport Glove (Battle Tower) ♂ ♀

Boutiques

There are five boutiques around the region, with different lineups to support your fashion needs. Whether you go for cute, punk, sporty, or classic styles, these shops will have you covered! If you need a bit of help planning your next shopping spree, you can see the items offered in each shop in the following section. These boutique lineups begin on page 325.

If you need more cash to fuel your shopping habits, remember the tips on page 17!

Wedgehurst boutique (p. 40)

Basic fashion for classic and casual looks

Motostoke boutique (p. 50)

Sporting wear and plenty of preppy plaid

Hammerlocke boutique (p. 80)

Sporting wear, as well as cute clothes

Circhester boutique (p. 106)

Elegant glam grabs and punk rags

Wyndon boutique (p. 124)

Leather, rock-and-roll, and sporting wear to spare

You can get changed in the fitting room in any boutique, even if you don't buy a thing. If you want to adjust your outfit, waltz right into the fitting room like you own the place—no one will stop you! After you change, you'll be asked if you want to update your photo on your League Card. Agree if you'd like to show off your latest style to anyone you swap League Cards with!

Understanding shop lineups

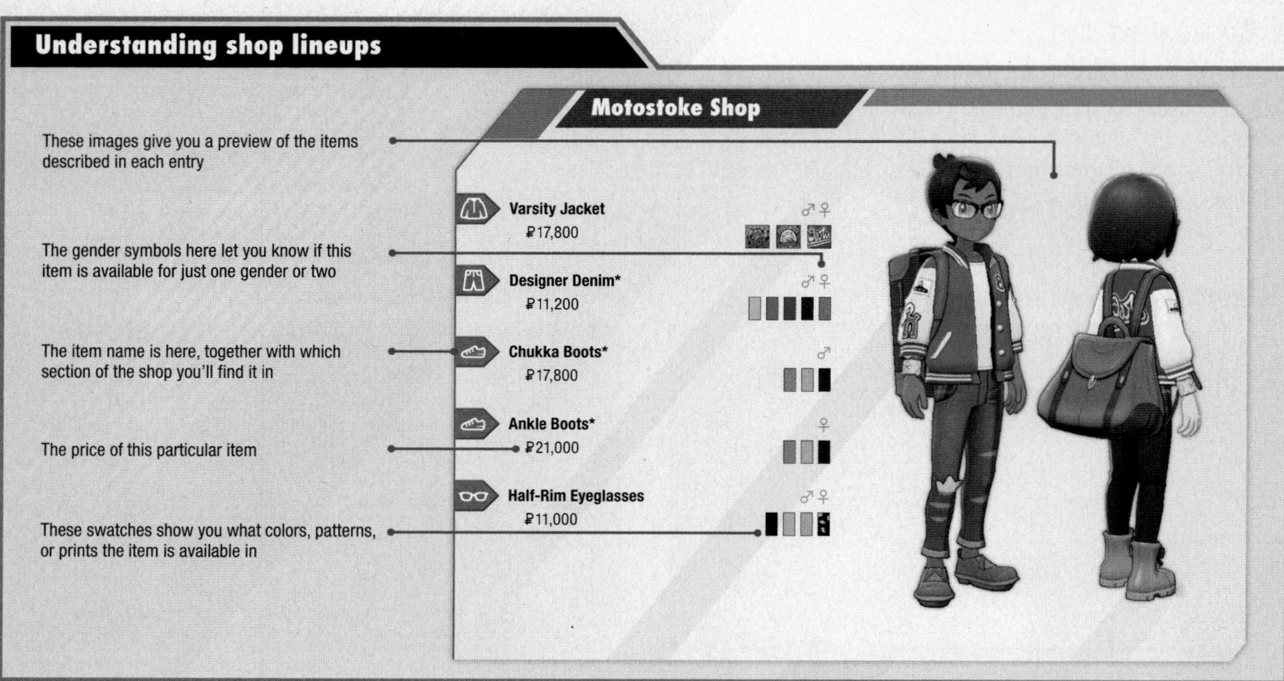

You may find that some items that can appear in multiple colors don't seem to have all their colors show up in their shops. That's because you already have them! The first time you check out a fitting room in any boutique, you should find that you have the following items available to you—whether as an option to put on or as something you're already wearing—depending on the gender you chose at the beginning of the game.

Male Knit Cap (gray), Three-Fourth Sleeves Polo (red), Designer Denim (navy), Trainer Socks (black), Chukka Boots (brown), Leather-Trimmed Bag (brown)

Female Knit Beret (green), Knitted Parka (gray), Simple Shirt Dress (pink), Plaid Socks (green), Ankle Boots (brown), Leather-Trimmed Bag (brown)

Both Square Eyeglasses (red and blue), Simple Gloves (red and blue), Loose Top (white), Striped Top (red and blue), Skinny Trousers (black), High Socks (white and black)

Cycling Outfits

If your passion for personalization extends to your cycling wear, you'll be happy to hear that your Rotom Bike outfit comes in 19 different colors! Speak to a Rotom Rallyist in the Wild Area, then select **A makeover!** to have him change your outfit to match the type of your lead Pokémon. You'll also have the option to switch back to the default Rotom colors if you wish.

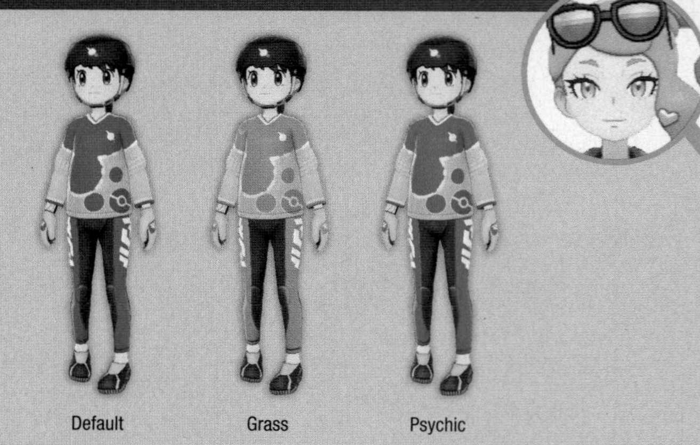

Wedgehurst Shop

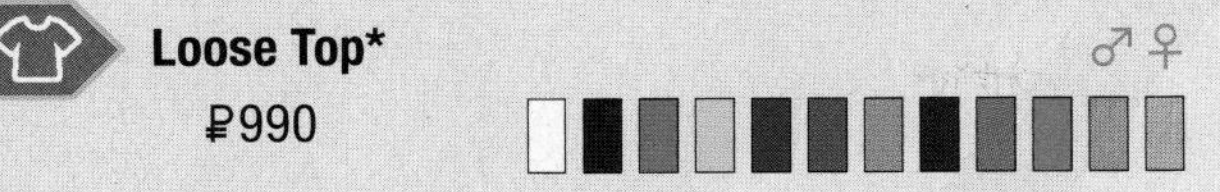

Loose Top* ♂ ♀
₽990

Skinny Trousers* ♂ ♀
₽1,990

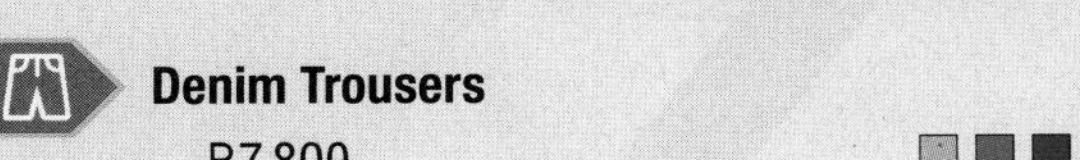

Denim Trousers ♀
₽7,800

Trainer Socks* ♂ ♀
₽350

Loafers ♂ ♀
₽6,740

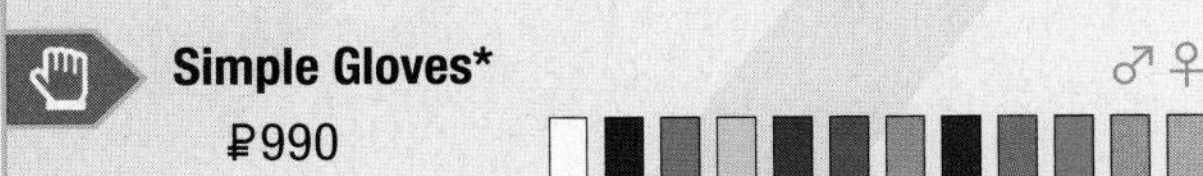

Simple Gloves* ♂ ♀
₽990

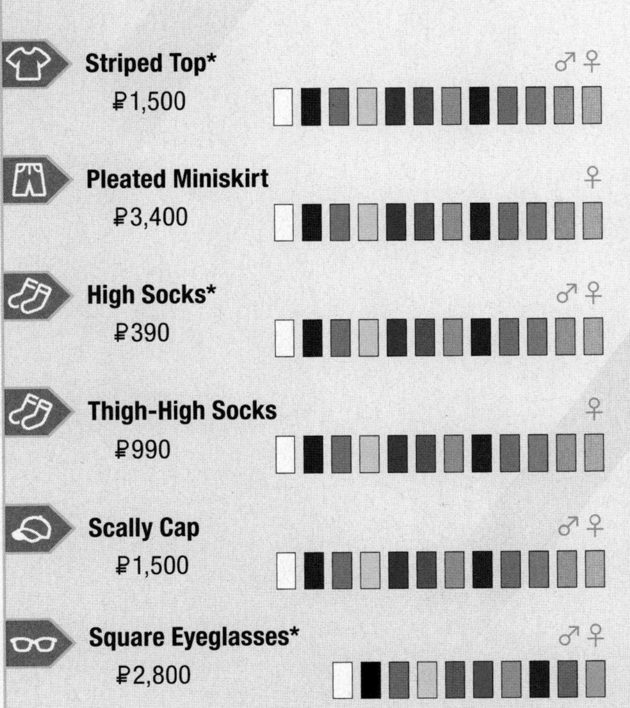

Striped Top* ♂ ♀
₽1,500

Pleated Miniskirt ♀
₽3,400

High Socks* ♂ ♀
₽390

Thigh-High Socks ♀
₽990

Scally Cap ♂ ♀
₽1,500

Square Eyeglasses* ♂ ♀
₽2,800

*Depending on your gender, you may not find some of these colors in the shop, since you own them from the start of your adventure!

Wedgehurst Shop

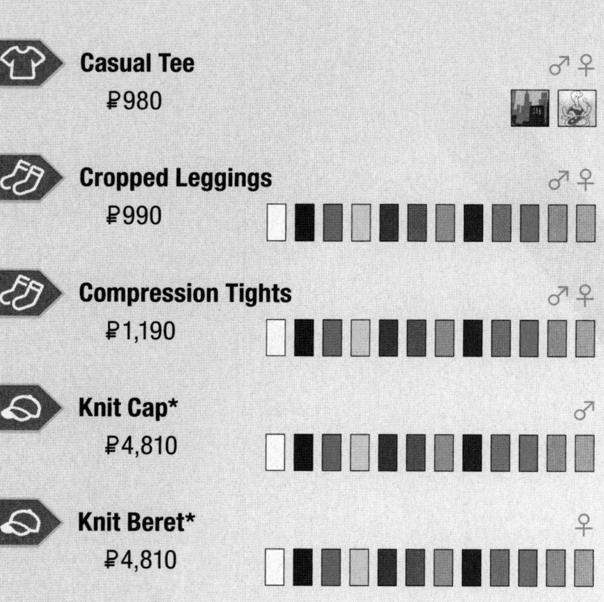

Casual Tee
₽980
♂ ♀
Cropped Leggings
₽990
♂ ♀
Compression Tights
₽1,190
♂ ♀
Knit Cap*
₽4,810
♂
Knit Beret*
₽4,810
♀

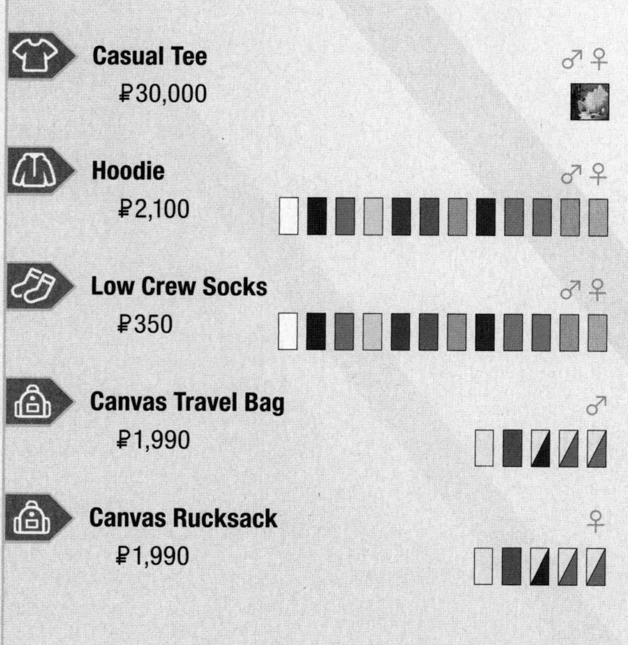

Casual Tee
₽30,000
♂ ♀
Hoodie
₽2,100
♂ ♀
Low Crew Socks
₽350
♂ ♀
Canvas Travel Bag
₽1,990
♂
Canvas Rucksack
₽1,990
♀

Motostoke Shop

Loose Top ♂ ♀
₽1,500

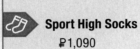

Sport Low Crew Socks ♂ ♀
₽1,020

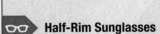

Sport High Socks ♂ ♀
₽1,090

Half-Rim Sunglasses ♂ ♀
₽13,480

Sport Sweatshirt ♂ ♀
₽6,200

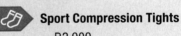

Sport Compression Tights ♂ ♀
₽2,000

Sport Thigh-High Socks ♀
₽1,800

Square Sunglasses ♂ ♀
₽2,800

Motostoke Shop

Tracksuit Jacket ♂ ♀
₽5,000

Trackie Bottoms ♂ ♀
₽4,300

Sport Travel Bag ♂
₽2,900

Sport Rucksack ♀
₽2,900

Sport Cap ♂ ♀
₽2,900

Sport Sunglasses ♂ ♀
₽3,500

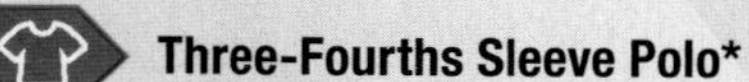

Three-Fourths Sleeve Polo* ♂
₽6,110

Knitted Parka* ♀
₽10,080

Plaid Trousers ♂
₽7,800

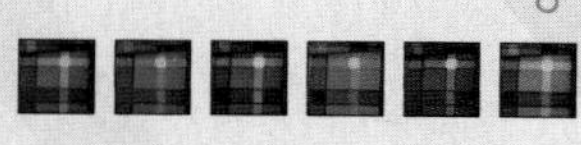

Plaid Pleated Skirt ♀
₽6,950

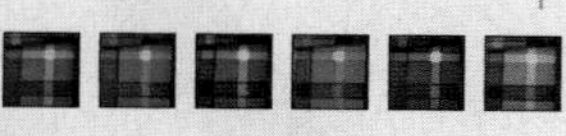

Plaid Socks* ♂ ♀
₽1,000

Plaid Gloves ♂ ♀
₽3,800

ADVANCED TRAINER HANDBOOK

Motostoke Shop

Varsity Jacket ♂ ♀
₽17,800

Designer Denim* ♂ ♀
₽11,200

Chukka Boots* ♂
₽17,800

Ankle Boots* ♀
₽21,000

Half-Rim Eyeglasses ♂ ♀
₽11,000

Hoodie ♂ ♀
₽2,500

Plaid Travel Bag ♂
₽11,120

Plaid Rucksack ♀
₽11,210

*Depending on your gender, you may not find some of these colors in the shop, since you own them from the start of your adventure!

Hammerlocke Shop

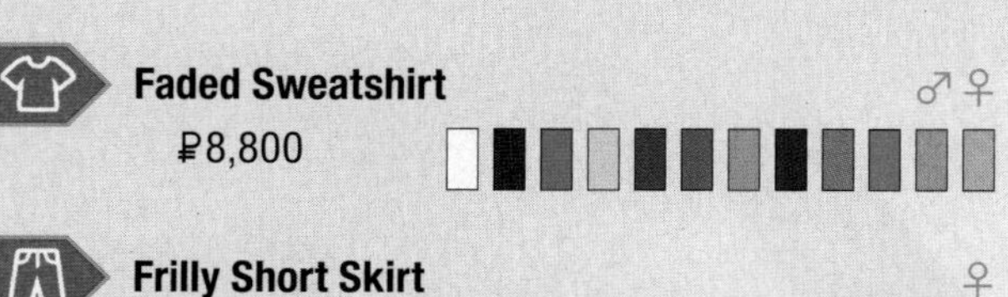

Faded Sweatshirt ♂ ♀
₽8,800

Frilly Short Skirt ♀
₽12,500

Bucket Hat ♂
₽5,100

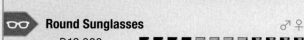

Round Sunglasses ♂ ♀
₽12,000

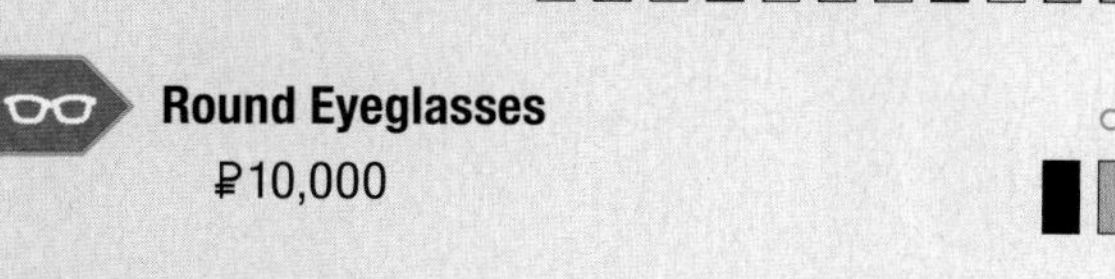

Round Eyeglasses ♂ ♀
₽10,000

Boatneck Sweatshirt ♂ ♀
₽12,800

Zippered Parka ♂ ♀
₽15,000

Frilly Short Skirt ♀
₽15,800

Ribbon Socks ♀
₽1,900

Boater Hat ♀
₽5,800

Hammerlocke Shop

Tracksuit Jacket ♂ ♀
₽10,180

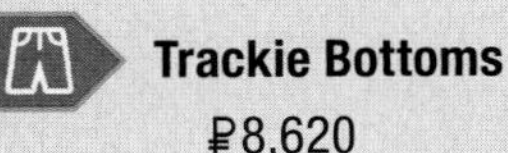

Trackie Bottoms ♂ ♀
₽8,620

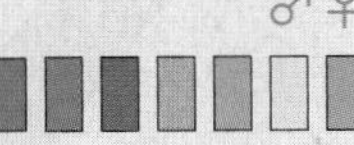

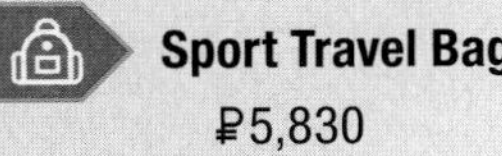

Sport Travel Bag ♂
₽5,830

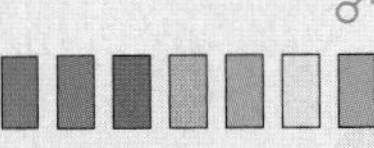

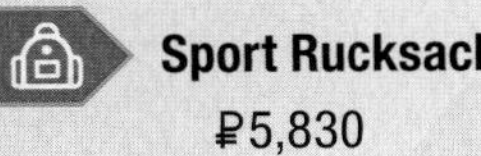

Sport Rucksack ♀
₽5,830

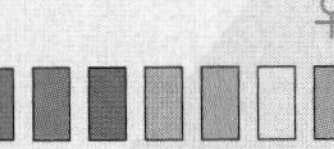

Sport Cap ♂ ♀
₽5,800

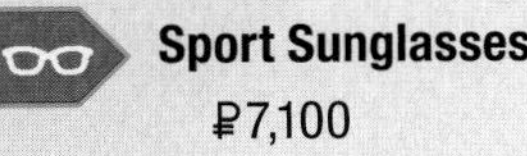

Sport Sunglasses ♂ ♀
₽7,100

Circhester Shop

Torn Top ♂ ♀
₽21,400

Casual Tee ♂ ♀
₽15,800

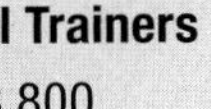

Casual Trainers ♂ ♀
₽13,800

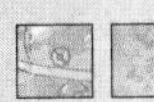

Circhester Shop

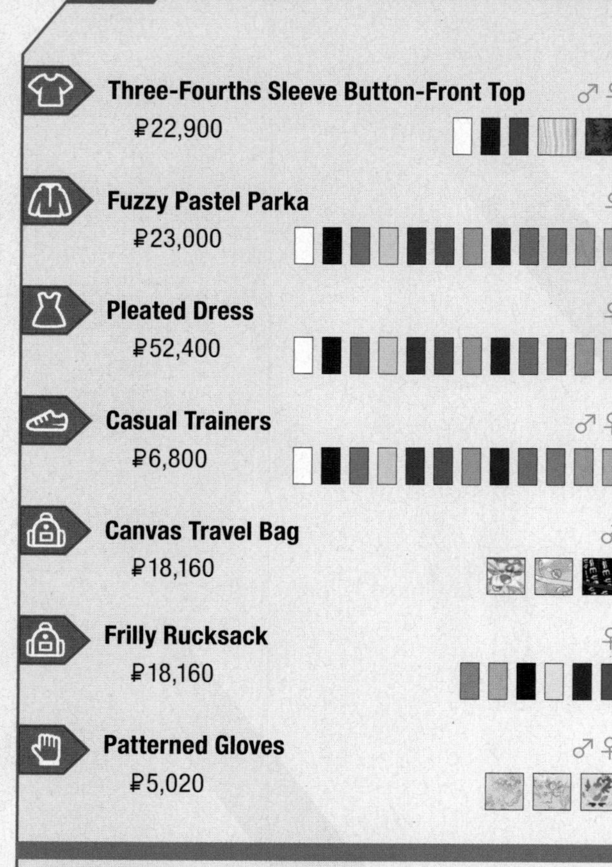

Three-Fourths Sleeve Button-Front Top ♂ ♀
₽22,900

Fuzzy Pastel Parka ♀
₽23,000

Pleated Dress ♀
₽52,400

Casual Trainers ♂ ♀
₽6,800

Canvas Travel Bag ♂
₽18,160

Frilly Rucksack ♀
₽18,160

Patterned Gloves ♂ ♀
₽5,020

Casual Tee ♂ ♀
₽17,000

Satin Varsity Jacket ♂ ♀
₽88,000

Fur-Lined Boots ♀
₽19,200

Trapper Hat ♂ ♀
₽35,800

Wraparound Sunglasses ♂ ♀
₽21,000

Wyndon Shop

Tracksuit Jacket	₽10,180	♂ ♀
Trackie Bottoms	₽8,620	♂ ♀
Sport Travel Bag	₽5,830	♂
Sport Rucksack	₽5,830	♀
Sport Cap	₽5,800	♂ ♀
Sport Sunglasses	₽7,100	♂ ♀

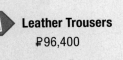

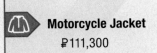

Motorcycle Jacket	₽111,300	♂ ♀
Leather Trousers	₽96,400	♂ ♀
Studded Leather Skirt	₽78,300	♀

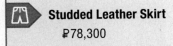

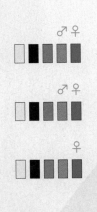

Wyndon Shop

Patterned Leggings ♂ ♀
₽3,200

Damaged Denim Shorts ♀
₽24,000

Creepers ♂ ♀
₽55,500

Leather-Trimmed Bag* ♂ ♀
₽89,000

Knit Beret ♂
₽4,810

Knit Cap ♀
₽4,810

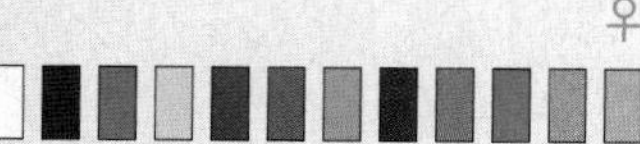

Simple Shirt Dress* ♀
₽13,000

Thigh-High Socks ♀
₽3,100

Loafers ♂ ♀
₽8,400

Studded Leather Case ♂ ♀
₽79,500

Leather Palm Glove ♂ ♀
₽12,000

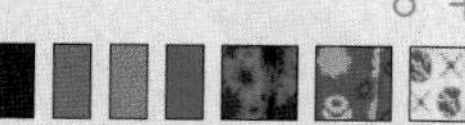

*Depending on your gender, you may not find some of these colors in the shop, since you own them from the start of your adventure!

ADVENTURE DATA

Moves

The following pages list the moves that you might face or use during your adventure in the Galar region. Refer to the keys below to understand what each column tells you. There are some universal rules to keep in mind, too, as you get familiar with all the intricacies of Pokémon battle!

Keep in mind these move universals

- Types can affect what moves do! Turn to the type matchup chart on page 383 to check how
- Priority overrules your Pokémon's Speed stat, so check the priority table on page 352 to learn more
- Moves and status conditions can interact, such as frozen Pokémon being thawed out if they're hit by a Fire-type move
- Moves can become less powerful when targeting multiple Pokémon in Double Battles
- Sound-based moves, like Boomburst or Growl, and certain status moves can bypass Substitute

Different rules for Dynamax Pokémon

- Dynamax Pokémon never flinch because of a move, and they can't be forced to flee or swap out of battle
- They're immune to any move that references a Pokémon's weight (such as Grass Knot, Heat Crash, Heavy Slam, and Low Kick)
- Moves, items, or Abilities that reference how much HP a Pokémon has generally use the Pokémon's pre-Dynamax HP
- Moves that automatically KO an opponent (such as Fissure or Destiny Bond) won't work on Dynamax Pokémon!

Understanding Move Tables

Move	The move's name.
Type	The move's type.
Kind	Whether the move is a physical, special, or status move. **Physical moves** deal damage. They do more damage the higher the user's Attack stat is. They do less damage the higher the target's Defense stat is. **Special moves** deal damage. They do more damage the higher the user's Sp. Atk stat is. They do less damage the higher the target's Sp. Def stat is. **Status moves** affect stats or inflict status conditions—or have various other effects.
Pow.	The move's power. If there is a number here, this move deals damage. If you see a dash (—), the move is either a status move or deals varying amounts of damage. Read the Notes to find out which is the case!
Acc.	The move's accuracy out of a max of 100. If you see a dash (—), the move never misses!
PP	How many times the move can be used before the Pokémon must have its PP restored with an item or at a Pokémon Center.
Range	The number and range of targets the move can affect. Each range is explained in the next key.
DA	A circle means the move's user makes direct contact with the target or targets when the move is used.
Max Move Pow.	The power this move will have when transformed into a Max Move.
Notes	If a move does more than simple damage, any additional effects or other details are listed here!

Range Guide

Normal	The move affects a selected target. If the move is used by a Pokémon during a Double Battle or Max Raid Battle, the move can target any of the other Pokémon (including allies).
Self	The move targets the user.
Self/Ally	The move can target the user or an ally in a Double Battle or Max Raid Battle.
1 Ally	The move affects an ally Pokémon during a Double Battle or Max Raid Battle. It has no effect in a Single Battle.
1 Random	The move affects one of the opposing Pokémon at random in a Double Battle. It affects the opposing Pokémon in a Single Battle or Max Raid Battle.
Many Others	If the move is used during a Double Battle, it will affect both opposing Pokémon. Otherwise, it affects the opposing Pokémon in a Single Battle or Max Raid Battle.
All Others	The move affects all surrounding Pokémon at the same time. If the move is used by a Pokémon during a Double Battle or Max Raid Battle, the move will affect all the other Pokémon (including your ally or allies) simultaneously.
Your Side	The move affects your side of the battlefield. In a Double Battle or a Max Raid Battle, these effects will be felt by the user and any ally Pokémon. Some of these moves affect the battlefield, meaning the move's effects continue even if Pokémon are switched out.
Other Side	The move affects the opponent's side of the battlefield. In a Double Battle, these effects will be felt by both opposing Pokémon. Some of these moves affect the battlefield, meaning the move's effects continue even if Pokémon are switched out.
Both Sides	The move affects the entire battlefield and all Pokémon on it. Since the move affects the battlefield, the move's effects continue even if Pokémon are switched out.
Varies	The move is influenced by things such as the opposing Pokémon using a move, so the effect and range are not fixed.
Your Party	The move affects your entire party, including Pokémon that aren't currently on the battlefield, as well as your allies.
All	The move affects all Pokémon on the battlefield at the time the move is used.

Move	Type	Kind	Pow.	Acc.	PP	Range	DA	Max Move Pow.	Notes
Absorb	Grass	Special	20	100	25	Normal	—	90	Restores the user's HP by an amount equal to 1/2 of the damage dealt to the target.
Acid	Poison	Special	40	100	30	Many Others	—	70	Has a 10% chance of lowering the targets' Sp. Def by 1 stage.
Acid Armor	Poison	Status	—	—	20	Self	—	—	Raises the user's Defense by 2 stages.
Acid Spray	Poison	Special	40	100	20	Normal	—	70	Lowers the target's Sp. Def by 2 stages.
Acrobatics	Flying	Physical	55	100	15	Normal	○	110	This move's power is doubled if the user isn't holding an item.
Acupressure	Normal	Status	—	—	30	Self/Ally	—	—	Raises a random stat by 2 stages. Stats that were already boosted to the max will not be selected.
Aerial Ace	Flying	Physical	60	—	20	Normal	○	110	
After You	Normal	Status	—	—	15	Normal	—	—	Forces the target to use its move immediately after this move is used, regardless of the target's Speed. This move fails if the user doesn't act before the target or if the target was going to use its move right after anyway.
Agility	Psychic	Status	—	—	30	Self	—	—	Raises the user's Speed by 2 stages.
Air Cutter	Flying	Special	60	95	25	Many Others	—	110	This move is more likely than average to deliver a critical hit.
Air Slash	Flying	Special	75	95	15	Normal	—	130	Has a 30% chance of making the target flinch (unable to use moves on that turn).
Ally Switch	Psychic	Status	—	—	15	Self	—	—	A high-priority move. The user switches places with an ally in a Double Battle. This move fails if used in a Single Battle or a Max Raid Battle.
Amnesia	Psychic	Status	—	—	20	Self	—	—	Raises the user's Sp. Def by 2 stages.
Anchor Shot	Steel	Physical	80	100	20	Normal	○	130	The target becomes unable to flee or be switched out of battle.
Ancient Power	Rock	Special	60	100	5	Normal	—	110	Has a 10% chance of raising the user's Attack, Defense, Sp. Atk, Sp. Def, and Speed by 1 stage each.
Apple Acid	Grass	Special	80	100	10	Normal	—	130	Lowers the target's Sp. Def by 1 stage.
Aqua Jet	Water	Physical	40	100	20	Normal	○	90	A high-priority move.
Aqua Ring	Water	Status	—	—	20	Self	—	—	Restores 1/16 of the user's max HP at the end of each turn.
Aqua Tail	Water	Physical	90	90	10	Normal	○	130	
Arm Thrust	Fighting	Physical	15	100	20	Normal	○	70	Attacks 2–5 times in a row in a single turn.
Aromatherapy	Grass	Status	—	—	5	Your Party	—	—	Heals the status conditions of all Pokémon in your party.
Aromatic Mist	Fairy	Status	—	—	20	1 Ally	—	—	Raises one ally's Sp. Def by 1 stage.
Assurance	Dark	Physical	60	100	10	Normal	○	110	This move's power is doubled if the target has already taken some damage on the same turn.
Astonish	Ghost	Physical	30	100	15	Normal	○	90	Has a 30% chance of making the target flinch (unable to use moves on that turn).
Attack Order	Bug	Physical	90	100	15	Normal	—	130	This move is more likely than average to deliver a critical hit.
Attract	Normal	Status	—	100	15	Normal	—	—	Leaves the target unable to attack 50% of the time. This move only works if the user and the target are of different genders.
Aura Sphere	Fighting	Special	80	—	20	Normal	—	90	
Aura Wheel	Electric	Physical	110	100	10	Normal	—	140	This move's type changes depending on the user's form.
Aurora Beam	Ice	Special	65	100	20	Normal	—	120	Has a 10% chance of lowering the target's Attack by 1 stage.
Aurora Veil	Ice	Status	—	—	20	Your Side	—	—	Halves the damage taken by the Pokémon on your side from physical or special moves for 5 turns. This move can only be used when the weather condition is hail. Effects continue even if the user switches out.
Autotomize	Steel	Status	—	—	15	Self	—	—	Raises the user's Speed by 2 stages and lowers its weight by 220 lbs.
Avalanche	Ice	Physical	60	100	10	Normal	○	110	A low-priority move. This move's power is doubled if the user has taken damage from the target on the same turn.
Baby-Doll Eyes	Fairy	Status	—	100	30	Normal	—	—	A high-priority move. Lowers the target's Attack by 1 stage.
Baneful Bunker	Poison	Status	—	—	10	Self	—	—	A high-priority move. The user protects itself from all damage-dealing moves and most status moves on the same turn. If an opposing Pokémon hits the user with a move that makes direct contact, the attacker will be inflicted with the poisoned status condition. This move becomes more likely to fail if used repeatedly. When used against a Max Move, this move will prevent 3/4 of the damage.
Baton Pass	Normal	Status	—	—	40	Self	—	—	The user switches out with another Pokémon in the party and passes along any stat changes.
Beat Up	Dark	Physical	—	100	10	Normal	—	100	Attacks once for each Pokémon in your party, including the user. Does not count Pokémon that have fainted or have status conditions.
Behemoth Bash	Steel	Physical	100	100	5	Normal	○	130	Deals twice the damage if the target is Dynamaxed.
Behemoth Blade	Steel	Physical	100	100	5	Normal	○	130	Deals twice the damage if the target is Dynamaxed.
Belch	Poison	Special	120	90	10	Normal	—	95	This move cannot be selected unless the user has already eaten a held Berry during the current battle.
Belly Drum	Normal	Status	—	—	10	Self	—	—	The user loses 1/2 of its max HP but raises its Attack to the maximum.
Bind	Normal	Physical	15	85	20	Normal	○	90	Inflicts damage equal to 1/8 of the target's max HP at the end of each turn for 4–5 turns. The target cannot flee or be switched out of battle during that time.

Move	Type	Kind	Pow.	Acc.	PP	Range	DA	Max Move Pow.	Notes
Bite	Dark	Physical	60	100	25	Normal	○	110	Has a 30% chance of making the target flinch (unable to use moves on that turn).
Blast Burn	Fire	Special	150	90	5	Normal	—	150	The user cannot act, be switched out, or have items used on it during the next turn.
Blaze Kick	Fire	Physical	85	90	10	Normal	○	130	Has a 10% chance of inflicting the burned status condition on the target. This move is more likely than average to deliver a critical hit.
Blizzard	Ice	Special	110	70	5	Many Others	—	140	Has a 10% chance of inflicting the frozen status condition on the targets. This move is 100% accurate in the hail weather condition.
Block	Normal	Status	—	—	5	Normal	—	—	The target becomes unable to flee or be switched out of battle.
Body Press	Fighting	Physical	80	100	10	Normal	○	90	The user's defenses become its strength. Damage dealt by this move is calculated using the user's Defense rather than the user's Attack.
Body Slam	Normal	Physical	85	100	15	Normal	○	130	Has a 30% chance of inflicting the paralysis status condition on the target. If the target has used Minimize, this move will be a sure hit and its power will be doubled.
Bolt Beak	Electric	Physical	85	100	10	Normal	○	130	This move's power is doubled if the target has not yet used a move on the same turn.
Bone Rush	Ground	Physical	25	90	10	Normal	—	130	Attacks 2–5 times in a row in a single turn.
Boomburst	Normal	Special	140	100	10	All Others	—	140	
Bounce	Flying	Physical	85	85	5	Normal	○	130	This move takes 2 turns. The user flies into the air on the first turn and attacks on the second. Has a 30% chance of inflicting the paralysis status condition on the target.
Branch Poke	Grass	Physical	40	100	40	Normal	○	90	
Brave Bird	Flying	Physical	120	100	15	Normal	○	140	The user also takes 1/3 of the damage dealt to the target.
Breaking Swipe	Dragon	Physical	60	100	15	Many Others	○	110	Lowers opposing Pokémon's Attack by 1 stage.
Brick Break	Fighting	Physical	75	100	15	Normal	○	90	This move is not affected by Aurora Veil or Reflect. It removes the effects of Aurora Veil, Light Screen, and Reflect.
Brine	Water	Special	65	100	10	Normal	—	120	This move's power is doubled if the target's HP is at 1/2 or below.
Brutal Swing	Dark	Physical	60	100	20	All Others	○	110	
Bubble Beam	Water	Special	65	100	20	Normal	—	120	Has a 10% chance of lowering the target's Speed by 1 stage.
Bug Bite	Bug	Physical	60	100	20	Normal	○	110	If the target is holding a Berry, the user eats that Berry and uses its battle effect if it has one.
Bug Buzz	Bug	Special	90	100	10	Normal	—	130	Has a 10% chance of lowering the target's Sp. Def by 1 stage. Strikes the target even if it is using Substitute.
Bulk Up	Fighting	Status	—	—	20	Self	—	—	Raises the user's Attack and Defense by 1 stage each.
Bulldoze	Ground	Physical	60	100	20	All Others	—	110	Lowers the targets' Speed by 1 stage.
Bullet Punch	Steel	Physical	40	100	30	Normal	○	90	A high-priority move.
Bullet Seed	Grass	Physical	25	100	30	Normal	—	130	Attacks 2–5 times in a row in a single turn.
Burn Up	Fire	Special	130	100	5	Normal	—	140	After attacking, the user is no longer Fire type.
Calm Mind	Psychic	Status	—	—	20	Self	—	—	Raises the user's Sp. Atk and Sp. Def by 1 stage each.
Charge	Electric	Status	—	—	20	Self	—	—	Doubles the power of an Electric-type move used by the same user on the next turn. Raises the user's Sp. Def by 1 stage.
Charge Beam	Electric	Special	50	90	10	Normal	—	100	Has a 70% chance of raising the user's Sp. Atk by 1 stage.
Charm	Fairy	Status	—	100	20	Normal	—	—	Lowers the target's Attack by 2 stages.
Circle Throw	Fighting	Physical	60	90	10	Normal	○	80	A low-priority move. Ends battles against wild Pokémon if the target's level is lower than the user's. Forces the target to swap out in a Trainer battle, unless there are no other Pokémon available to battle.
Clanging Scales	Dragon	Special	110	100	5	Many Others	—	140	Lowers the user's Defense by 1 stage.
Clangorous Soul	Dragon	Status	—	100	5	Self	—	—	Raises all of the user's stats by 1 stage but reduces the user's HP by 1/3 of its maximum. If the user's HP is at 1/3 of its maximum or lower, this move fails.
Clear Smog	Poison	Special	50	—	15	Normal	—	75	Eliminates every stat change affecting the target.
Close Combat	Fighting	Physical	120	100	5	Normal	○	95	Lowers the user's Defense and Sp. Def by 1 stage each.
Coil	Poison	Status	—	—	20	Self	—	—	Raises the user's Attack, Defense, and accuracy by 1 stage each.
Confide	Normal	Status	—	—	20	Normal	—	—	Lowers the target's Sp. Atk by 1 stage.
Confuse Ray	Ghost	Status	—	100	10	Normal	—	—	Makes the target confused.
Confusion	Psychic	Special	50	100	25	Normal	—	100	Has a 10% chance of making the target confused.
Copycat	Normal	Status	—	—	20	Self	—	—	The user repeats the last move used in the battle. If the opponent chooses a Max Move, this move will copy the normal version of that move. (For example, if the opponent chooses Max Flare that was formerly Flamethrower, this move will copy Flamethrower.)
Cosmic Power	Psychic	Status	—	—	20	Self	—	—	Raises the user's Defense and Sp. Def by 1 stage each.
Cotton Guard	Grass	Status	—	—	10	Self	—	—	Raises the user's Defense by 3 stages.
Cotton Spore	Grass	Status	—	100	40	Many Others	—	—	Lowers the targets' Speed by 2 stages.

Move	Type	Kind	Pow.	Acc.	PP	Range	DA	Max Move Pow.	Notes
Counter	Fighting	Physical	—	100	20	Varies	○	75	A low-priority move. If the user is hit with a physical move during the same turn, this move inflicts twice the damage taken by the user onto the attacker.
Court Change	Normal	Status	—	100	10	Both Sides	—	—	Swaps the battle effects affecting each side of the battlefield. This includes the effects of moves such as Reflect, Spikes, Tailwind, and others.
Covet	Normal	Physical	60	100	25	Normal	○	110	When the target is holding an item and the user is not, the user can steal that item. When the target is not holding an item, this move will function as a simple damage-dealing move.
Crabhammer	Water	Physical	100	90	10	Normal	○	130	This move is more likely than average to deliver a critical hit.
Crafty Shield	Fairy	Status	—	—	10	Your Side	—	—	A high-priority move. Protects your side from status moves used on the same turn. Does not protect against damage-dealing moves.
Cross Chop	Fighting	Physical	100	80	5	Normal	○	90	This move is more likely than average to deliver a critical hit.
Cross Poison	Poison	Physical	70	100	20	Normal	○	85	Has a 10% chance of inflicting the poisoned status condition on the target. This move is more likely than average to deliver a critical hit.
Crunch	Dark	Physical	80	100	15	Normal	○	130	Has a 20% chance of lowering the target's Defense by 1 stage.
Crush Claw	Normal	Physical	75	95	10	Normal	○	130	Has a 50% chance of lowering the target's Defense by 1 stage.
Curse	Ghost	Status	—	—	10	Varies	—	—	If used by a non-Ghost-type Pokémon, this move lowers the user's Speed by 1 stage and raises its Attack and Defense by 1 stage each. If used by a Ghost-type Pokémon, this move causes the user to lose 1/2 of its max HP but the move lowers the target's HP by 1/4 of its maximum each turn.
Dark Pulse	Dark	Special	80	100	15	Normal	—	130	Has a 20% chance of making the target flinch (unable to use moves on that turn).
Darkest Lariat	Dark	Physical	85	100	10	Normal	○	130	Ignores the stat changes of the target when dealing damage.
Dazzling Gleam	Fairy	Special	80	100	10	Many Others	—	130	
Decorate	Fairy	Status	—	—	15	Normal	—	—	Raises the target's Attack and Sp. Atk by 2 stages each.
Defend Order	Bug	Status	—	—	10	Self	—	—	Raises the user's Defense and Sp. Def by 1 stage each.
Defense Curl	Normal	Status	—	—	40	Self	—	—	Raises the user's Defense by 1 stage.
Defog	Flying	Status	—	—	15	Normal	—	—	Lowers the target's evasiveness by 1 stage. Nullifies Aurora Veil, Light Screen, Mist, Reflect, and Safeguard on the opponents' side. Nullifies Spikes, Stealth Rock, Sticky Web, and Toxic Spikes on both sides. When the target has a substitute, only the effect that lowers evasiveness will fail.
Destiny Bond	Ghost	Status	—	—	5	Self	—	—	If the user faints due to damage caused by an opposing Pokémon, that Pokémon faints as well. This effect lasts until the user's next turn. This move fails if used repeatedly.
Detect	Fighting	Status	—	—	5	Self	—	—	A high-priority move. The user evades all damage-dealing moves and most status moves on the same turn. This move becomes more likely to fail if used repeatedly. When used against a Max Move, this move will prevent 3/4 of the damage.
Dig	Ground	Physical	80	100	10	Normal	○	130	This move takes 2 turns. The user burrows underground on the first turn and attacks on the second.
Disable	Normal	Status	—	100	20	Normal	—	—	Makes the target unable to use its last-used move for 4 turns. This move has no effect against Max Moves.
Disarming Voice	Fairy	Special	40	—	15	Many Others	—	90	
Discharge	Electric	Special	80	100	15	All Others	—	130	Has a 30% chance of inflicting the paralysis status condition on the targets.
Dive	Water	Physical	80	100	10	Normal	○	130	This move takes 2 turns. The user dives deep on the first turn and attacks on the second.
Double Hit	Normal	Physical	35	90	10	Normal	○	120	Attacks twice in a row in a single turn.
Double Kick	Fighting	Physical	30	100	30	Normal	○	80	Attacks twice in a row in a single turn.
Double Team	Normal	Status	—	—	15	Self	—	—	Raises the user's evasiveness by 1 stage.
Double-Edge	Normal	Physical	120	100	15	Normal	○	140	The user also takes 1/3 of the damage dealt to the target.
Draco Meteor	Dragon	Special	130	90	5	Normal	—	140	Lowers the user's Sp. Atk by 2 stages.
Dragon Breath	Dragon	Special	60	100	20	Normal	—	110	Has a 30% chance of inflicting the paralysis status condition on the target.
Dragon Claw	Dragon	Physical	80	100	15	Normal	○	130	
Dragon Dance	Dragon	Status	—	—	20	Self	—	—	Raises the user's Attack and Speed by 1 stage each.
Dragon Darts	Dragon	Physical	50	100	10	Normal	—	130	Attacks twice in a row in a single turn. If there are two opponents, each will be struck once.
Dragon Pulse	Dragon	Special	85	100	10	Normal	—	130	
Dragon Rush	Dragon	Physical	100	75	10	Normal	○	130	Has a 20% chance of making the target flinch (unable to use moves on that turn). If the target has used Minimize, this move will be a sure hit and its power will be doubled.
Dragon Tail	Dragon	Physical	60	90	10	Normal	○	110	A low-priority move. Ends battles against wild Pokémon if the target's level is lower than the user's. Forces the target to swap out in a Trainer battle, unless there are no other Pokémon available to battle.
Drain Punch	Fighting	Physical	75	100	10	Normal	○	90	Restores the user's HP by an amount equal to 1/2 of the damage dealt to the target.
Draining Kiss	Fairy	Special	50	100	10	Normal	○	100	Restores the user's HP by an amount equal to 3/4 of the damage dealt to the target.

Move	Type	Kind	Pow.	Acc.	PP	Range	DA	Max Move Pow.	Notes
Dream Eater	Psychic	Special	100	100	15	Normal	—	130	This move only works when the target is asleep. Restores the user's HP by an amount equal to 1/2 of the damage dealt to the target. This move has no effect against mysterious barriers protecting Dynamax Pokémon.
Drill Peck	Flying	Physical	80	100	20	Normal	○	130	
Drill Run	Ground	Physical	80	95	10	Normal	○	130	This move is more likely than average to deliver a critical hit.
Drum Beating	Grass	Physical	80	100	10	Normal	—	130	Lowers the target's Speed by 1 stage.
Dual Chop	Dragon	Physical	40	90	15	Normal	○	130	Attacks twice in a row in a single turn.
Dynamax Cannon	Dragon	Special	120	100	1	Normal	—	140	Deals twice the damage if the target is Dynamaxed.
Dynamic Punch	Fighting	Physical	100	50	5	Normal	○	90	Makes the target confused.
Earth Power	Ground	Special	90	100	10	Normal	—	130	Has a 10% chance of lowering the target's Sp. Def by 1 stage.
Earthquake	Ground	Physical	100	100	10	All Others	—	130	This move hits against targets that are underground due to using Dig and has doubled power against them.
Echoed Voice	Normal	Special	40	100	15	Normal	—	90	This move's power increases every turn that it is used (max power of 200), no matter which Pokémon uses it. Power returns to normal if no Pokémon uses it in a turn.
Eerie Impulse	Electric	Status	—	100	15	Normal	—	—	Lowers the target's Sp. Atk by 2 stages.
Electric Terrain	Electric	Status	—	—	10	Both Sides	—	—	Electrifies the battlefield for 5 turns. During that time, Pokémon on the ground will be able to do 30% more damage with Electric-type moves and cannot fall asleep.
Electrify	Electric	Status	—	—	20	Normal	—	—	Changes any move used by the target on the same turn into an Electric-type move. This move will have the same effect on Max Moves.
Electro Ball	Electric	Special	—	100	10	Normal	—	130	This move's power becomes greater (max power of 150) the faster the user is compared to the target.
Electroweb	Electric	Special	55	95	15	Many Others	—	110	Lowers the targets' Speed by 1 stage.
Ember	Fire	Special	40	100	25	Normal	—	90	Has a 10% chance of inflicting the burned status condition on the target.
Encore	Normal	Status	—	100	5	Normal	—	—	The target is forced to keep using the last move it used. This effect lasts 3 turns. This move will fail when used against a Dynamax Pokémon. Even if the target was affected by this move before Dynamaxing, the effect will be nullified once it Dynamaxes.
Endeavor	Normal	Physical	—	100	5	Normal	○	130	The target's HP is cut to equal the user's HP. If the target's HP is already lower than the user's, this move will do nothing.
Endure	Normal	Status	—	—	10	Self	—	—	A high-priority move. Leaves the user with 1 HP when hit by a move that would normally knock it out. This move becomes more likely to fail if used repeatedly.
Energy Ball	Grass	Special	90	100	10	Normal	—	130	Has a 10% chance of lowering the target's Sp. Def by 1 stage.
Entrainment	Normal	Status	—	100	15	Normal	—	—	Makes the target's Ability the same as the user's. Fails with certain Abilities, however.
Eruption	Fire	Special	150	100	5	Many Others	—	150	The lower the user's HP, the lower this move's power becomes.
Eternabeam	Dragon	Physical	150	100	5	Normal	—	150	The user cannot act, be switched out, or have items used on it during the next turn.
Explosion	Normal	Physical	250	100	5	All Others	—	150	The user faints after using this move.
Extrasensory	Psychic	Special	80	100	20	Normal	—	130	Has a 10% chance of making the target flinch (unable to use moves on that turn).
Extreme Speed	Normal	Physical	80	100	5	Normal	○	130	A high-priority move.
Facade	Normal	Physical	70	100	20	Normal	○	120	This move's power is doubled if the user has the paralyzed, poisoned, or burned status condition.
Fairy Wind	Fairy	Special	40	100	30	Normal	—	90	
Fake Out	Normal	Physical	40	100	10	Normal	○	90	A high-priority move. Makes the target flinch (unable to use moves on that turn). This move only works if used on the first turn after the user is sent out.
Fake Tears	Dark	Status	—	100	20	Normal	—	—	Lowers the target's Sp. Def by 2 stages.
False Surrender	Dark	Physical	80	—	10	Normal	○	130	
False Swipe	Normal	Physical	40	100	40	Normal	○	90	Always leaves the target with at least 1 HP, even if the damage would have normally made the target faint.
Feather Dance	Flying	Status	—	100	15	Normal	—	—	Lowers the target's Attack by 2 stages.
Feint	Normal	Physical	30	100	10	Normal	—	90	A high-priority move. Strikes even if the target has used a protection move, and removes the protection move's effect.
Fell Stinger	Bug	Physical	50	100	25	Normal	○	100	If the user knocks out an opponent with this move, its Attack is raised by 3 stages.
Final Gambit	Fighting	Special	—	100	5	Normal	—	100	The user faints, and the target takes damage equal to the HP lost by the user. If the move misses or otherwise fails, the user will not faint.
Fire Blast	Fire	Special	110	85	5	Normal	—	140	Has a 10% chance of inflicting the burned status condition on the target.
Fire Fang	Fire	Physical	65	95	15	Normal	○	120	Has a 10% chance of inflicting the burned status condition on the target and a 10% chance of making the target flinch (unable to use moves on that turn).
Fire Lash	Fire	Physical	80	100	15	Normal	○	130	Lowers the target's Defense by 1 stage.

Move	Type	Kind	Pow.	Acc.	PP	Range	DA	Max Move Pow.	Notes
Fire Pledge	Fire	Special	80	100	10	Normal	—	130	When this is combined with Grass Pledge or Water Pledge, the power and effect change. If this is combined with Grass Pledge, the power of this move becomes 150 and it remains a Fire-type move. It will also inflict damage equal to 1/8 of the opposing Pokémon's max HP at the end of each turn for 4 turns, unless they are Fire types. If this is combined with Water Pledge, the power of this move becomes 150 and it becomes a Water-type move. It will also make it more likely that your team's moves will trigger any additional effects they might have for 4 turns.
Fire Punch	Fire	Physical	75	100	15	Normal	○	130	Has a 10% chance of inflicting the burned status condition on the target.
Fire Spin	Fire	Special	35	85	15	Normal	—	90	Inflicts damage equal to 1/8 of the target's max HP at the end of each turn for 4–5 turns. The target cannot flee or be switched out of battle during that time.
First Impression	Bug	Physical	90	100	10	Normal	○	130	A high-priority move. This move only works if used on the first turn after the user is sent out.
Fishious Rend	Water	Physical	85	100	10	Normal	○	130	This move's power is doubled if the target has not yet used a move on the same turn.
Fissure	Ground	Physical	—	30	5	Normal	—	130	The target faints with one hit. The higher the user's level is compared to the target's, the more accurate the move is. If the target's level is higher than the user's, this move fails. If this move hits a Dynamax Pokémon, this move will destroy 2 segments of the mysterious barrier's meter.
Flail	Normal	Physical	—	100	15	Normal	○	130	This move's power becomes greater (max power of 200) the lower the user's HP is.
Flame Charge	Fire	Physical	50	100	20	Normal	○	100	Raises the user's Speed by 1 stage.
Flame Wheel	Fire	Physical	60	100	25	Normal	○	110	Has a 10% chance of inflicting the burned status condition on the target. This move can be used even if the user is frozen and will thaw the user.
Flamethrower	Fire	Special	90	100	15	Normal	—	130	Has a 10% chance of inflicting the burned status condition on the target.
Flare Blitz	Fire	Physical	120	100	15	Normal	○	140	The user also takes 1/3 of the damage dealt to the target. Has a 10% chance of inflicting the burned status condition on the target. This move can be used even if the user is frozen and will thaw the user.
Flash Cannon	Steel	Special	80	100	10	Normal	—	130	Has a 10% chance of lowering the target's Sp. Def by 1 stage.
Flatter	Dark	Status	—	100	15	Normal	—	—	Makes the target confused but also raises its Sp. Atk by 1 stage.
Fling	Dark	Physical	—	100	10	Normal	—	100	The user attacks by throwing its held item at the target. The move's power varies depending on the item. The following items can be thrown to inflict additional effects. Flame Orb: Burned status condition. King's Rock / Razor Fang: Flinching. Light Ball: Paralysis status condition. Mental Herb: Removes Cursed Body, Disable, Encore, infatuation, Taunt, and Torment. Poison Barb: Poisoned status condition. Toxic Orb: Badly poisoned status condition. White Herb: Resets lowered stats.
Flower Shield	Fairy	Status	—	—	10	All	—	—	Raises the Defense of any Grass-type Pokémon on the battlefield by 1 stage.
Fly	Flying	Physical	90	95	15	Normal	○	130	This move takes 2 turns. The user flies into the air on the first turn and attacks on the second.
Flying Press	Fighting	Physical	100	95	10	Normal	○	90	This move is both Fighting type and Flying type. If the target has used Minimize, this move will be a sure hit and its power will be doubled. This move will become Max Knuckle when used by a Dynamax Pokémon.
Focus Blast	Fighting	Special	120	70	5	Normal	—	95	Has a 10% chance of lowering the target's Sp. Def by 1 stage.
Focus Energy	Normal	Status	—	—	30	Self	—	—	Makes the user's future moves more likely than average to deliver critical hits.
Focus Punch	Fighting	Physical	150	100	20	Normal	○	100	A low-priority move. This move fails if the user is hit before this move lands.
Follow Me	Normal	Status	—	—	20	Self	—	—	A high-priority move. Opposing Pokémon aim only at the user for the rest of the turn in which this move is used. This move will cause Dynamax Pokémon to aim only at the user. However, the additional effects of Max Moves will occur as usual.
Force Palm	Fighting	Physical	60	100	10	Normal	○	80	Has a 30% chance of inflicting the paralysis status condition on the target.
Forest's Curse	Grass	Status	—	100	20	Normal	—	—	Gives the target the Grass type in addition to its original type(s).
Foul Play	Dark	Physical	95	100	15	Normal	○	130	The user turns the target's strength against it. Damage dealt by this move is calculated using the target's Attack rather than the user's Attack.
Freeze-Dry	Ice	Special	70	100	20	Normal	—	120	Super effective against Water-type Pokémon. Has a 10% chance of inflicting the frozen status condition on the target.
Frenzy Plant	Grass	Special	150	90	5	Normal	—	150	The user cannot act, be switched out, or have items used on it during the next turn.
Frost Breath	Ice	Special	60	90	10	Normal	—	110	Always delivers a critical hit.
Fury Attack	Normal	Physical	15	85	20	Normal	○	90	Attacks 2–5 times in a row in a single turn.
Fury Cutter	Bug	Physical	40	95	20	Normal	○	90	This move's power is doubled with every successful hit (max power of 320). Power returns to normal once it misses or if another move is selected.
Fury Swipes	Normal	Physical	18	80	15	Normal	○	100	Attacks 2–5 times in a row in a single turn.
Future Sight	Psychic	Special	120	100	10	Normal	—	140	Damage is dealt to the target 2 turns after this move is used.
Gastro Acid	Poison	Status	—	100	10	Normal	—	—	Disables the target's Ability. Fails with certain Abilities, however.
Gear Grind	Steel	Physical	50	85	15	Normal	○	130	Attacks twice in a row in a single turn.

Move	Type	Kind	Pow.	Acc.	PP	Range	DA	Max Move Pow.	Notes
Gear Up	Steel	Status	—	—	20	Your Side	—	—	Raises Attack and Sp. Atk by 1 stage each for any Pokémon on your side with the Plus Ability or Minus Ability.
Giga Drain	Grass	Special	75	100	10	Normal	—	130	Restores the user's HP by an amount equal to 1/2 of the damage dealt to the target.
Giga Impact	Normal	Physical	150	90	5	Normal	○	150	The user cannot act, be switched out, or have items used on it during the next turn.
Glare	Normal	Status	—	100	30	Normal	—	—	Inflicts the paralysis status condition on the target.
Grass Knot	Grass	Special	—	100	20	Normal	○	130	This move's power becomes greater (max power of 120) the heavier the target is. This move has no effect against Dynamax Pokémon.
Grass Pledge	Grass	Special	80	100	10	Normal	—	130	When this is combined with Water Pledge or Fire Pledge, the power and effect change. If this is combined with Water Pledge, the power of this move becomes 150 and it remains a Grass-type move. It will also lower the Speed of opposing Pokémon for 4 turns. If this is combined with Fire Pledge, the power of this move becomes 150 and it becomes a Fire-type move. It will also inflict damage equal to 1/8 of the opposing Pokémon's max HP at the end of each turn for 4 turns, unless they are Fire types.
Grassy Terrain	Grass	Status	—	—	10	Both Sides	—	—	Covers the battlefield with grass for 5 turns. During that time, Pokémon on the ground will be able to do 30% more damage with Grass-type moves and will recover 1/16 of their max HP at the end of each turn. Damage done to Pokémon on the ground by Bulldoze or Earthquake is also halved during this time.
Grav Apple	Grass	Physical	80	100	10	Normal	—	130	Lowers the target's Defense by 1 stage. This move will do 50% more damage when used while the effects of Gravity are present.
Gravity	Psychic	Status	—	—	5	Both Sides	—	—	Airborne Pokémon are grounded. Ground-type moves will now hit Pokémon normally immune to them. Prevents the use of Bounce, Fly, Flying Press, High Jump Kick, Magnet Rise, and Splash. Raises the accuracy of all Pokémon in battle. Lasts 5 turns. Moves that normally would be prevented can still be used as Max Moves by Dynamax Pokémon.
Growl	Normal	Status	—	100	40	Many Others	—	—	Lowers the targets' Attack by 1 stage.
Growth	Normal	Status	—	—	20	Self	—	—	Raises the user's Attack and Sp. Atk by 1 stage each. Raises them by 2 stages when the weather condition is harsh sunlight.
Grudge	Ghost	Status	—	—	5	Self	—	—	Any move that causes the user to faint will have its PP reduced to 0. This move will fail when used against Max Moves.
Guard Split	Psychic	Status	—	—	10	Normal	—	—	The user's and the target's Defense and Sp. Def are each added, then divided equally between them.
Guard Swap	Psychic	Status	—	—	10	Normal	—	—	Swaps the user's and target's stat changes for both Defense and Sp. Def.
Guillotine	Normal	Physical	—	30	5	Normal	○	130	The target faints with one hit. The higher the user's level is compared to the target's, the more accurate the move is. If the target's level is higher than the user's, this move fails. If this move hits a Dynamax Pokémon, this move will destroy 2 segments of the mysterious barrier's meter.
Gunk Shot	Poison	Physical	120	80	5	Normal	—	95	Has a 30% chance of inflicting the poisoned status condition on the target.
Gust	Flying	Special	40	100	35	Normal	—	90	This move hits targets that are in the sky due to using moves such as Bounce or Fly and has doubled power against them.
Gyro Ball	Steel	Physical	—	100	5	Normal	○	130	This move's power becomes greater (max power of 150) the slower the user is compared to the target.
Hail	Ice	Status	—	—	10	Both Sides	—	—	Changes the weather condition to hail for 5 turns. All Pokémon other than Ice types take damage at the end of each turn equal to 1/16 of their max HP.
Hammer Arm	Fighting	Physical	100	90	10	Normal	○	90	Lowers the user's Speed by 1 stage.
Harden	Normal	Status	—	—	30	Self	—	—	Raises the user's Defense by 1 stage.
Haze	Ice	Status	—	—	30	Both Sides	—	—	Eliminates stat changes of all Pokémon in battle.
Head Smash	Rock	Physical	150	80	5	Normal	○	150	The user also takes 1/2 of the damage dealt to the target.
Headbutt	Normal	Physical	70	100	15	Normal	○	120	Has a 30% chance of making the target flinch (unable to use moves on that turn).
Heal Pulse	Psychic	Status	—	—	10	Normal	—	—	Restores 1/2 of the target's max HP.
Healing Wish	Psychic	Status	—	—	10	Self	—	—	The user faints, but the next Pokémon to be switched in will have its HP fully restored and status conditions healed.
Heat Crash	Fire	Physical	—	100	10	Normal	○	130	This move's power becomes greater (max power of 120) the heavier the user is compared to the target. If the target has used Minimize, this move will be a sure hit and its power will be doubled. This move has no effect against Dynamax Pokémon.
Heat Wave	Fire	Special	95	90	10	Many Others	—	130	Has a 10% chance of inflicting the burned status condition on the targets.
Heavy Slam	Steel	Physical	—	100	10	Normal	○	130	This move's power becomes greater (max power of 120) the heavier the user is compared to the target. If the target has used Minimize, this move will be a sure hit and its power will be doubled. This move has no effect against Dynamax Pokémon.
Helping Hand	Normal	Status	—	—	20	1 Ally	—	—	Acts before all other moves on the same turn. Boosts the power of whichever move an ally chooses to use next by 50%.
Hex	Ghost	Special	65	100	10	Normal	—	120	This move's power is doubled if the target has a status condition.
High Horsepower	Ground	Physical	95	95	10	Normal	○	130	

Move	Type	Kind	Pow.	Acc.	PP	Range	DA	Max Move Pow.	Notes
High Jump Kick	Fighting	Physical	130	90	10	Normal	○	95	If this move misses or otherwise fails, the user loses 1/2 of its max HP.
Hone Claws	Dark	Status	—	—	15	Self	—	—	Raises the user's Attack and accuracy by 1 stage each.
Horn Attack	Normal	Physical	65	100	25	Normal	○	120	
Horn Drill	Normal	Physical	—	30	5	Normal	○	130	The target faints with one hit. The higher the user's level is compared to the target's, the more accurate the move is. If the target's level is higher than the user's, this move fails. If this move hits a Dynamax Pokémon, this move will destroy 2 segments of the mysterious barrier's meter.
Horn Leech	Grass	Physical	75	100	10	Normal	○	130	Restores the user's HP by an amount equal to 1/2 of the damage dealt to the target.
Howl	Normal	Status	—	—	40	Your Side	—	—	Raises the user's and ally Pokémon's Attack by 1 stage.
Hurricane	Flying	Special	110	70	10	Normal	—	140	Has a 30% chance of making the target confused. Is 100% accurate in the rain weather condition and 50% accurate in the harsh sunlight weather condition. This move hits targets that are in the sky due to moves such as Bounce or Fly.
Hydro Cannon	Water	Special	150	90	5	Normal	—	150	The user cannot act, be switched out, or have items used on it during the next turn.
Hydro Pump	Water	Special	110	80	5	Normal	—	140	
Hyper Beam	Normal	Special	150	90	5	Normal	—	150	The user cannot act, be switched out, or have items used on it during the next turn.
Hyper Voice	Normal	Special	90	100	10	Many Others	—	130	
Hypnosis	Psychic	Status	—	60	20	Normal	—	—	Inflicts the asleep status condition on the target.
Ice Beam	Ice	Special	90	100	10	Normal	—	130	Has a 10% chance of inflicting the frozen status condition on the target.
Ice Fang	Ice	Physical	65	95	15	Normal	○	120	Has a 10% chance of inflicting the frozen status condition on the target or making the target flinch (unable to use moves on that turn).
Ice Punch	Ice	Physical	75	100	15	Normal	○	130	Has a 10% chance of inflicting the frozen status condition on the target.
Ice Shard	Ice	Physical	40	100	30	Normal	—	90	A high-priority move.
Icicle Crash	Ice	Physical	85	90	10	Normal	—	130	Has a 30% chance of making the target flinch (unable to use moves on that turn).
Icicle Spear	Ice	Physical	25	100	30	Normal	—	130	Attacks 2–5 times in a row in a single turn.
Icy Wind	Ice	Special	55	95	15	Many Others	—	110	Lowers the targets' Speed by 1 stage.
Imprison	Psychic	Status	—	—	10	Self	—	—	Opposing Pokémon are prevented from using any moves that the user also knows. This move will have no effect against Max Moves. Even if the target was affected by this move before Dynamaxing, the effect will be nullified once it Dynamaxes.
Incinerate	Fire	Special	60	100	15	Many Others	—	110	Burns up any Berries being held by the targets, which makes them unusable.
Inferno	Fire	Special	100	50	5	Normal	—	130	Inflicts the burned status condition on the target.
Infestation	Bug	Special	20	100	20	Normal	○	90	Inflicts damage equal to 1/8 of the target's max HP at the end of each turn for 4–5 turns. The target cannot flee or be switched out of battle during that time.
Ingrain	Grass	Status	—	—	20	Self	—	—	Restores 1/16 of the user's max HP at the end of each turn. The user cannot be switched out after using this move. Ground-type moves can now hit the user even if it is normally immune to them.
Instruct	Psychic	Status	—	—	15	Normal	—	—	The target is forced to use the same move it just used. This move fails if the target move is a Max Move.
Iron Defense	Steel	Status	—	—	15	Self	—	—	Raises the user's Defense by 2 stages.
Iron Head	Steel	Physical	80	100	15	Normal	○	130	Has a 30% chance of making the target flinch (unable to use moves on that turn).
Iron Tail	Steel	Physical	100	75	15	Normal	○	130	Has a 30% chance of lowering the target's Defense by 1 stage.
Jaw Lock	Dark	Physical	80	100	10	Normal	○	130	Both the user and target become unable to flee or be switched out of battle.
King's Shield	Steel	Status	—	—	10	Self	—	—	A high-priority move. The user protects itself from all damage-dealing moves used on the same turn. If an opposing Pokémon uses a move that makes direct contact, its Attack will be lowered by 1 stage. This move becomes more likely to fail if used repeatedly. When used against a Max Move, this move will prevent 3/4 of the damage.
Knock Off	Dark	Physical	65	100	20	Normal	○	120	This move's power is increased by 50% if the target is holding an item. The target is forced to drop its held item, but it gets the item back after the battle.
Laser Focus	Normal	Status	—	—	30	Self	—	—	The user's next move will be a critical hit.
Last Resort	Normal	Physical	140	100	5	Normal	○	140	This move fails unless the user has already used each of its other moves at least once.
Lava Plume	Fire	Special	80	100	15	All Others	—	130	Has a 30% chance of inflicting the burned status condition on the targets.
Leaf Blade	Grass	Physical	90	100	15	Normal	○	130	This move is more likely than average to deliver a critical hit.
Leaf Storm	Grass	Special	130	90	5	Normal	—	140	Lowers the user's Sp. Atk by 2 stages.
Leaf Tornado	Grass	Special	65	90	10	Normal	—	120	Has a 50% chance of lowering the target's accuracy by 1 stage.
Leafage	Grass	Physical	40	100	40	Normal	—	90	

Move	Type	Kind	Pow.	Acc.	PP	Range	DA	Max Move Pow.	Notes
Leech Life	Bug	Physical	80	100	10	Normal	○	130	Restores the user's HP by an amount equal to 1/2 of the damage dealt to the target.
Leech Seed	Grass	Status	—	90	10	Normal	—	—	Steals 1/8 of the target's max HP each turn and absorbs it to heal the user. Effects continue even if the user faints or is switched out, with the healing passing to the Pokémon that is switched in.
Leer	Normal	Status	—	100	30	Many Others	—	—	Lowers the targets' Defense by 1 stage.
Lick	Ghost	Physical	30	100	30	Normal	○	90	Has a 30% chance of inflicting the paralysis status condition on the target.
Life Dew	Water	Status	—	100	10	Your Side	—	—	Restores 1/4 of max HP to the user and its ally Pokémon in the battle.
Light Screen	Psychic	Status	—	—	30	Your Side	—	—	Halves the damage Pokémon on your side take from special moves for 5 turns. Effects continue even if the user faints or is switched out.
Liquidation	Water	Physical	85	100	10	Normal	○	130	Has a 20% chance of lowering the target's Defense by 1 stage.
Lock-On	Normal	Status	—	—	5	Normal	—	—	The user's next move against the target will be a sure hit.
Low Kick	Fighting	Physical	—	100	20	Normal	○	100	This move's power becomes greater (max power of 120) the heavier the target is. This move has no effect against Dynamax Pokémon.
Low Sweep	Fighting	Physical	65	100	20	Normal	○	85	Lowers the target's Speed by 1 stage.
Lunge	Bug	Physical	80	100	15	Normal	○	130	Lowers the target's Attack by 1 stage.
Mach Punch	Fighting	Physical	40	100	30	Normal	○	70	A high-priority move.
Magic Coat	Psychic	Status	—	—	15	Self	—	—	A high-priority move. Reflects back moves that attempt to lower the user's stats or inflict status conditions, as well as the effects of moves like Stealth Rock or Taunt.
Magic Powder	Psychic	Status	—	100	20	Normal	—	—	Changes the target's type to Psychic.
Magic Room	Psychic	Status	—	—	10	Both Sides	—	—	No held items will have any effect for 5 turns. Fling cannot be used to throw items while Magic Room is in effect. If Magic Room is used again before its effects end, Magic Room's effects are canceled.
Magical Leaf	Grass	Special	60	—	20	Normal	—	110	
Magnet Rise	Electric	Status	—	—	10	Self	—	—	Makes the user immune to Ground-type moves for 5 turns.
Magnetic Flux	Electric	Status	—	—	20	Your Side	—	—	Raises Defense and Sp. Def by 1 stage each for any Pokémon on your side with the Plus Ability or Minus Ability.
Mean Look	Normal	Status	—	—	5	Normal	—	—	The target becomes unable to flee or be switched out of battle.
Mega Drain	Grass	Special	40	100	15	Normal	—	90	Restores the user's HP by an amount equal to 1/2 of the damage dealt to the target.
Mega Kick	Normal	Physical	120	75	5	Normal	○	140	
Mega Punch	Normal	Physical	80	85	20	Normal	○	130	
Megahorn	Bug	Physical	120	85	10	Normal	○	140	
Memento	Dark	Status	—	100	10	Normal	—	—	The user faints, but the target's Attack and Sp. Atk are lowered by 2 stages each.
Metal Burst	Steel	Physical	—	100	10	Varies	—	100	Targets the opponent that most recently damaged the user with a move. Inflicts 150% of the damage taken.
Metal Claw	Steel	Physical	50	95	35	Normal	○	100	Has a 10% chance of raising the user's Attack by 1 stage.
Metal Sound	Steel	Status	—	85	40	Normal	—	—	Lowers the target's Sp. Def by 2 stages.
Meteor Assault	Fighting	Physical	150	100	5	Normal	—	100	The user cannot act, be switched out, or have items used on it during the next turn.
Meteor Mash	Steel	Physical	90	90	10	Normal	○	130	Has a 20% chance of raising the user's Attack by 1 stage.
Metronome	Normal	Status	—	—	10	Self	—	—	Uses one move randomly chosen from nearly all moves Pokémon can learn.
Mimic	Normal	Status	—	—	10	Normal	—	—	Copies the move the target used on that turn. The copy has the original's max PP and will be retained until the battle ends or the user is switched out. This move fails if the user acts before the target or if it tries to copy Metronome, Struggle, a move that the user already knows, or a Max Move.
Mind Reader	Normal	Status	—	—	5	Normal	—	—	The user's next move against the target will be a sure hit.
Minimize	Normal	Status	—	—	10	Self	—	—	Raises the user's evasiveness by 2 stages. The user will take twice the usual damage, however, if hit by Body Slam, Dragon Rush, Flying Press, Heat Crash, Heavy Slam, or Stomp.
Mirror Coat	Psychic	Special	—	100	20	Varies	—	100	A low-priority move. If the user is hit with a special move during the same turn, this move inflicts twice the damage taken by the user onto the attacker.
Mist	Ice	Status	—	—	30	Your Side	—	—	Protects your side from stat-lowering moves and additional effects for 5 turns.
Misty Terrain	Fairy	Status	—	—	10	Both Sides	—	—	Covers the battlefield with mist for 5 turns. During that time, Pokémon on the ground cannot be afflicted with new status conditions or confusion. Damage done to Pokémon on the ground by Dragon-type moves is also halved during this time.
Moonblast	Fairy	Special	95	100	15	Normal	—	130	Has a 30% chance of lowering the target's Sp. Atk by 1 stage.
Moonlight	Fairy	Status	—	—	5	Self	—	—	Restores 1/2 of the user's max HP in normal weather conditions. Restores 2/3 of the user's max HP in the harsh sunlight weather condition. Restores 1/4 of the user's max HP in the rain/sandstorm/hail weather conditions.

Move	Type	Kind	Pow.	Acc.	PP	Range	DA	Max Move Pow.	Notes
Morning Sun	Normal	Status	—	—	5	Self	—	—	Restores 1/2 of the user's max HP in normal weather conditions. Restores 2/3 of the user's max HP in the harsh sunlight weather condition. Restores 1/4 of the user's max HP in the rain/sandstorm/hail weather conditions.
Mud Shot	Ground	Special	55	95	15	Normal	—	110	Lowers the target's Speed by 1 stage.
Muddy Water	Water	Special	90	85	10	Many Others	—	130	Has a 30% chance of lowering the targets' accuracy by 1 stage.
Mud-Slap	Ground	Special	20	100	10	Normal	—	90	Lowers the target's accuracy by 1 stage.
Multi-Attack	Normal	Physical	120	100	10	Normal	○	95	This move's type changes according to the memory disc that Silvally is holding. This move will become a different Max Move depending on what memory disc is held by the user.
Mystical Fire	Fire	Special	75	100	10	Normal	—	130	Lowers the target's Sp. Atk by 1 stage.
Nasty Plot	Dark	Status	—	—	20	Self	—	—	Raises the user's Sp. Atk by 2 stages.
Nature Power	Normal	Status	—	—	20	Normal	—	—	Turns into a different move depending on the environment. Cave: Power Gem. Dirt/Sand: Earth Power. Grass / Grassy Terrain: Energy Ball. Electric Terrain: Thunderbolt. Indoors / Link Battle: Tri Attack. Misty Terrain: Moonblast. Psychic Terrain: Psychic. Snow/Ice: Ice Beam. Water surface: Hydro Pump. This move will become Max Guard when used by a Dynamax Pokémon.
Night Shade	Ghost	Special	—	100	15	Normal	—	100	Deals a fixed amount of damage equal to the user's level.
Night Slash	Dark	Physical	70	100	15	Normal	○	120	This move is more likely than average to deliver a critical hit.
No Retreat	Fighting	Status	—	—	5	Self	—	—	Raises all of the user's stats by 1 stage but makes it unable to flee or be switched out of battle.
Noble Roar	Normal	Status	—	100	30	Normal	—	—	Lowers the target's Attack and Sp. Atk by 1 stage each.
Nuzzle	Electric	Physical	20	100	20	Normal	○	90	Inflicts the paralysis status condition on the target.
Obstruct	Dark	Status	—	100	10	Self	—	—	A high-priority move. The user protects itself from all damage-dealing moves used on the same turn. If an opposing Pokémon uses a move that makes direct contact, its Defense will be lowered by 2 stages. This move becomes more likely to fail if used repeatedly.
Octazooka	Water	Special	65	85	10	Normal	—	120	Has a 50% chance of lowering the target's accuracy by 1 stage.
Octolock	Fighting	Status	—	100	15	Normal	—	—	Lowers the target's Defense and Sp. Def by 1 stage each turn. The target becomes unable to flee or be switched out of battle. The effect ends if the user leaves the battlefield.
Outrage	Dragon	Physical	120	100	10	1 Random	○	140	Attacks consecutively over 2–3 turns. The user cannot choose other moves during this time, and it becomes confused afterward.
Overdrive	Electric	Special	80	100	10	Many Others	—	130	The sound of the move differs in Amped Form and Low Key Form.
Overheat	Fire	Special	130	90	5	Normal	—	140	Lowers the user's Sp. Atk by 2 stages.
Pain Split	Normal	Status	—	—	20	Normal	—	—	The user's and target's HP are added, then divided equally between them.
Parabolic Charge	Electric	Special	65	100	20	All Others	—	120	Restores the user's HP by an amount equal to 1/2 of the damage dealt to the targets.
Parting Shot	Dark	Status	—	100	20	Normal	—	—	Lowers the target's Attack and Sp. Atk by 1 stage each. After attacking, the user is switched out and another Pokémon from the party is sent onto the battlefield.
Pay Day	Normal	Physical	40	100	20	Normal	—	90	Pays out money after battle. The amount depends on the user's level and the number of times the move was used (₽5 × user's level × times used).
Payback	Dark	Physical	50	100	10	Normal	○	100	This move's power is doubled if the user strikes after the target uses a move or has an item used on it.
Peck	Flying	Physical	35	100	35	Normal	○	90	
Perish Song	Normal	Status	—	—	5	All	—	—	All Pokémon on the battlefield when this move is used will faint after 3 turns unless switched out.
Petal Blizzard	Grass	Physical	90	100	15	All Others	—	130	
Petal Dance	Grass	Special	120	100	10	1 Random	○	140	Attacks consecutively over 2–3 turns. The user cannot choose other moves during this time, and it becomes confused afterward.
Phantom Force	Ghost	Physical	90	100	10	Normal	○	130	This move takes 2 turns. The user disappears on the first turn and attacks on the second. Strikes even if the target has used a protection move and removes the protection move's effect.
Pin Missile	Bug	Physical	25	95	20	Normal	—	130	Attacks 2–5 times in a row in a single turn.
Play Nice	Normal	Status	—	—	20	Normal	—	—	Lowers the target's Attack by 1 stage.
Play Rough	Fairy	Physical	90	90	10	Normal	○	130	Has a 10% chance of lowering the target's Attack by 1 stage.
Pluck	Flying	Physical	60	100	20	Normal	○	110	If the target is holding a Berry, the user eats that Berry and uses its battle effect if it has one.
Poison Fang	Poison	Physical	50	100	15	Normal	○	75	Has a 50% chance of inflicting the badly poisoned status condition on the target.
Poison Gas	Poison	Status	—	90	40	Many Others	—	—	Inflicts the poisoned status condition on the targets.
Poison Jab	Poison	Physical	80	100	20	Normal	○	90	Has a 30% chance of inflicting the poisoned status condition on the target.
Poison Powder	Poison	Status	—	75	35	Normal	—	—	Inflicts the poisoned status condition on the target.
Poison Sting	Poison	Physical	15	100	35	Normal	—	70	Has a 30% chance of inflicting the poisoned status condition on the target.

Move	Type	Kind	Pow.	Acc.	PP	Range	DA	Max Move Pow.	Notes
Poison Tail	Poison	Physical	50	100	25	Normal	○	75	Has a 10% chance of inflicting the poisoned status condition on the target. This move is more likely than average to deliver a critical hit.
Pollen Puff	Bug	Special	90	100	15	Normal	—	130	When targeting an ally, this move restores 1/2 of the ally's max HP. This move becomes a damaging move when transformed into a Max Move.
Pound	Normal	Physical	40	100	35	Normal	○	90	
Powder Snow	Ice	Special	40	100	25	Many Others	—	90	Has a 10% chance of inflicting the frozen status condition on the targets.
Power Gem	Rock	Special	80	100	20	Normal	—	130	
Power Split	Psychic	Status	—	—	10	Normal	—	—	The user's and the target's Attack and Sp. Atk are each added, then divided equally between them.
Power Swap	Psychic	Status	—	—	10	Normal	—	—	Swaps the user's and target's stat changes to both their Attack and Sp. Atk.
Power Trick	Psychic	Status	—	—	10	Self	—	—	Swaps the user's original Attack and Defense stats. (Does not swap stat changes.)
Power Trip	Dark	Physical	20	100	10	Normal	○	130	This move's power increases by 20 (max power of 860) for each stage the user's stats have been boosted.
Power Whip	Grass	Physical	120	85	10	Normal	○	140	
Power-Up Punch	Fighting	Physical	40	100	20	Normal	○	70	Raises the user's Attack by 1 stage.
Present	Normal	Physical	—	90	15	Normal	—	100	This move's power varies between 40 (40% chance), 80 (30% chance), and 120 (10% chance). It also has a 20% chance of restoring 1/4 of the target's max HP. When the healing effect occurs against a Dynamax Pokémon, it won't reduce its mysterious barrier's meter.
Protect	Normal	Status	—	—	10	Self	—	—	A high-priority move. The user protects itself from all damage-dealing moves and most status moves on the same turn. This move becomes more likely to fail if used repeatedly. When used against a Max Move, this move will prevent 3/4 of the damage.
Psybeam	Psychic	Special	65	100	20	Normal	—	120	Has a 10% chance of making the target confused.
Psych Up	Normal	Status	—	—	10	Normal	—	—	Copies the target's stat changes over to the user.
Psychic	Psychic	Special	90	100	10	Normal	—	130	Has a 10% chance of lowering the target's Sp. Def by 1 stage.
Psychic Fangs	Psychic	Physical	85	100	10	Normal	○	130	This move is not affected by Aurora Veil or Reflect. It removes the effects of Aurora Veil, Light Screen, and Reflect.
Psychic Terrain	Psychic	Status	—	—	10	Both Sides	—	—	Covers the battlefield with psychic energy for 5 turns. During that time, Pokémon on the ground will be able to do 30% more damage with Psychic-type moves and will evade high-priority moves.
Psycho Cut	Psychic	Physical	70	100	20	Normal	—	120	This move is more likely than average to deliver a critical hit.
Psycho Shift	Psychic	Status	—	100	10	Normal	—	—	Shifts the user's status condition (paralysis, poisoned, badly poisoned, burned, or asleep) to the target, removing it from the user.
Psyshock	Psychic	Special	80	100	10	Normal	—	130	Damage dealt by this move is calculated using the target's Defense rather than the target's Sp. Def.
Purify	Poison	Status	—	—	20	Normal	—	—	Heals the target's status condition, then restores 1/2 of the user's max HP. This move fails if the target does not have a status condition.
Pyro Ball	Fire	Physical	130	95	10	Normal	—	140	Has a 10% chance of inflicting the burned status condition on the target.
Quash	Dark	Status	—	100	15	Normal	—	—	This move makes the target act last during the current turn. This move fails if the user doesn't act before the target.
Quick Attack	Normal	Physical	40	100	30	Normal	○	90	A high-priority move.
Quick Guard	Fighting	Status	—	—	15	Your Side	—	—	A high-priority move. Protects your side from other high-priority moves used on the same turn.
Quiver Dance	Bug	Status	—	—	20	Self	—	—	Raises the user's Sp. Atk, Sp. Def, and Speed by 1 stage each.
Rage Powder	Bug	Status	—	—	20	Self	—	—	A high-priority move. Opposing Pokémon aim only at the user for the rest of the turn in which this move is used. This move will cause Dynamax Pokémon to aim only at the user. However, the additional effects of Max Moves will occur as usual.
Rain Dance	Water	Status	—	—	5	Both Sides	—	—	Changes the weather condition to rain for 5 turns, boosting the power of Water-type moves by 50% and reducing the power of Fire-type moves by 50%.
Rapid Spin	Normal	Physical	50	100	40	Normal	○	100	Releases the user from moves such as Bind, Leech Seed, and Wrap and removes the effects of moves such as Spikes from the user's side of the battlefield. Also raises the user's Speed by 1 stage.
Razor Leaf	Grass	Physical	55	95	25	Many Others	—	110	This move is more likely than average to deliver a critical hit.
Razor Shell	Water	Physical	75	95	10	Normal	○	130	Has a 50% chance of lowering the target's Defense by 1 stage.
Recover	Normal	Status	—	—	10	Self	—	—	Restores 1/2 of the user's max HP.
Recycle	Normal	Status	—	—	10	Self	—	—	Allows the user to regain a held item it had already used during the battle.
Reflect	Psychic	Status	—	—	20	Your Side	—	—	Halves the damage Pokémon on your side take from physical moves for 5 turns. Effects continue even if the user faints or is switched out.
Reflect Type	Normal	Status	—	—	15	Normal	—	—	The user becomes the same type as the target.
Rest	Psychic	Status	—	—	10	Self	—	—	Fully restores HP and heals status conditions of the user but makes the user sleep for 2 turns.
Retaliate	Normal	Physical	70	100	5	Normal	○	120	This move's power is doubled if an ally fainted during the previous turn.

Move	Type	Kind	Pow.	Acc.	PP	Range	DA	Max Move Pow.	Notes
Revenge	Fighting	Physical	60	100	10	Normal	○	80	A low-priority move. This move's power is doubled if the user has taken damage from the target on the same turn.
Reversal	Fighting	Physical	—	100	15	Normal	○	100	This move's power becomes greater (max power of 200) the lower the user's HP is.
Roar	Normal	Status	—	—	20	Normal	—	—	A low-priority move. Ends battles against wild Pokémon if the target's level is lower than the user's. Forces the target to swap out in a Trainer battle, unless there are no other Pokémon available to battle. This move has no effect against Dynamax Pokémon.
Rock Blast	Rock	Physical	25	90	10	Normal	—	130	Attacks 2–5 times in a row in a single turn.
Rock Polish	Rock	Status	—	—	20	Self	—	—	Raises the user's Speed by 2 stages.
Rock Slide	Rock	Physical	75	90	10	Many Others	—	130	Has a 30% chance of making the targets flinch (unable to use moves on that turn).
Rock Smash	Fighting	Physical	40	100	15	Normal	○	70	Has a 50% chance of lowering the target's Defense by 1 stage.
Rock Throw	Rock	Physical	50	90	15	Normal	—	100	
Rock Tomb	Rock	Physical	60	95	15	Normal	—	110	Lowers the target's Speed by 1 stage.
Rock Wrecker	Rock	Physical	150	90	5	Normal	—	150	The user cannot act, be switched out, or have items used on it during the next turn.
Role Play	Psychic	Status	—	—	10	Normal	—	—	Copies the target's Ability. Fails with certain Abilities, however.
Rollout	Rock	Physical	30	90	20	Normal	○	90	Attacks consecutively over 5 turns or until it misses. The user cannot choose other moves during this time. This move's power is doubled (max power of 480) with every successful hit. This move's power is further doubled if the user has also used Defense Curl.
Roost	Flying	Status	—	—	10	Self	—	—	Restores 1/2 of the user's max HP but takes away the Flying type from the user for that turn.
Round	Normal	Special	60	100	15	Normal	—	110	When multiple Pokémon select this move in a turn, the first one to use it is followed immediately by any allies and the power is doubled for those allies.
Sacred Sword	Fighting	Physical	90	100	15	Normal	○	90	Ignores the stat changes of the target when dealing damage.
Safeguard	Normal	Status	—	—	25	Your Side	—	—	Protects your side from status conditions and confusion for 5 turns. Effects continue even if the user faints or is switched out.
Sand Attack	Ground	Status	—	100	15	Normal	—	—	Lowers the target's accuracy by 1 stage.
Sand Tomb	Ground	Physical	35	85	15	Normal	—	90	Inflicts damage equal to 1/8 of the target's max HP at the end of each turn for 4–5 turns. The target cannot flee or be switched out of battle during that time.
Sandstorm	Rock	Status	—	—	10	Both Sides	—	—	Changes the weather condition to sandstorm for 5 turns, boosting the Sp. Def of Rock-type Pokémon by 50%. All Pokémon other than Ground, Rock, and Steel types take damage at the end of each turn equal to 1/16 of their max HP.
Scald	Water	Special	80	100	15	Normal	—	130	Has a 30% chance of inflicting the burned status condition on the target. This move can be used even if the user is frozen and will thaw the user. This move will also thaw out a frozen target.
Scary Face	Normal	Status	—	100	10	Normal	—	—	Lowers the target's Speed by 2 stages.
Scratch	Normal	Physical	40	100	35	Normal	○	90	
Screech	Normal	Status	—	85	40	Normal	—	—	Lowers the target's Defense by 2 stages.
Seed Bomb	Grass	Physical	80	100	15	Normal	—	130	
Seismic Toss	Fighting	Physical	—	100	20	Normal	○	75	Deals a fixed amount of damage equal to the user's level.
Self-Destruct	Normal	Physical	200	100	5	All Others	—	150	The user faints after using this move.
Shadow Ball	Ghost	Special	80	100	15	Normal	—	130	Has a 20% chance of lowering the target's Sp. Def by 1 stage.
Shadow Claw	Ghost	Physical	70	100	15	Normal	○	120	This move is more likely than average to deliver a critical hit.
Shadow Punch	Ghost	Physical	60	—	20	Normal	○	110	
Shadow Sneak	Ghost	Physical	40	100	30	Normal	○	90	A high-priority move.
Sheer Cold	Ice	Special	—	30	5	Normal	—	130	The target faints with one hit. The higher the user's level is compared to the target's, the more accurate the move is. If the target's level is higher than the user's, this move fails. Accuracy is also lowered when a Pokémon that is not an Ice type uses it. Does not hit Ice-type Pokémon. If this move hits a Dynamax Pokémon, this move will destroy 2 segments of the mysterious barrier's meter.
Shell Smash	Normal	Status	—	—	15	Self	—	—	Lowers the user's Defense and Sp. Def by 1 stage each and raises the user's Attack, Sp. Atk, and Speed by 2 stages each.
Shell Trap	Fire	Special	150	100	5	Many Others	—	150	A low-priority move. Sets a trap at the start of the turn. If the user is hit by a physical move during the same turn, the trap explodes and deals damage.
Shift Gear	Steel	Status	—	—	10	Self	—	—	Raises the user's Speed by 2 stages and Attack by 1 stage.
Shock Wave	Electric	Special	60	—	20	Normal	—	110	
Simple Beam	Normal	Status	—	100	15	Normal	—	—	Changes the target's Ability to Simple. Fails with certain Abilities, however.
Sing	Normal	Status	—	55	15	Normal	—	—	Inflicts the asleep status condition on the target.
Skill Swap	Psychic	Status	—	—	10	Normal	—	—	Swaps the user's and the target's Abilities. Fails with certain Abilities and on Dynamax Pokémon, however.

Move	Type	Kind	Pow.	Acc.	PP	Range	DA	Max Move Pow.	Notes
Skull Bash	Normal	Physical	130	100	10	Normal	○	140	This move takes 2 turns. The user raises its Defense by 1 stage on the first turn and attacks on the second.
Sky Attack	Flying	Physical	140	90	5	Normal	—	140	This move takes 2 turns. The user builds power on the first turn and attacks on the second. Has a 30% chance of making the target flinch (unable to use moves on that turn). This move is more likely than average to deliver a critical hit.
Slack Off	Normal	Status	—	—	10	Self	—	—	Restores 1/2 of the user's max HP.
Slam	Normal	Physical	80	75	20	Normal	○	130	
Slash	Normal	Physical	70	100	20	Normal	○	120	This move is more likely than average to deliver a critical hit.
Sleep Powder	Grass	Status	—	75	15	Normal	—	—	Inflicts the asleep status condition on the target.
Sleep Talk	Normal	Status	—	—	10	Self	—	—	This move only works when the user is asleep. Randomly uses one of the user's other moves.
Sludge	Poison	Special	65	100	20	Normal	—	85	Has a 30% chance of inflicting the poisoned status condition on the target.
Sludge Bomb	Poison	Special	90	100	10	Normal	—	90	Has a 30% chance of inflicting the poisoned status condition on the target.
Sludge Wave	Poison	Special	95	100	10	All Others	—	90	Has a 10% chance of inflicting the poisoned status condition on the targets.
Smack Down	Rock	Physical	50	100	15	Normal	—	100	Makes Ground-type moves able to hit the target even if it is normally immune to them. This move will also bring down Pokémon that are in the sky due to moves such as Bounce or Fly, causing those moves to fail.
Smart Strike	Steel	Physical	70	—	10	Normal	○	120	
Smog	Poison	Special	30	70	20	Normal	—	70	Has a 40% chance of inflicting the poisoned status condition on the target.
Smokescreen	Normal	Status	—	100	20	Normal	—	—	Lowers the target's accuracy by 1 stage.
Snap Trap	Grass	Physical	35	100	15	Normal	○	90	Inflicts damage equal to 1/8 of the target's max HP at the end of each turn for 4–5 turns. The target cannot flee or be switched out of battle during that time.
Snarl	Dark	Special	55	95	15	Many Others	—	110	Lowers the targets' Sp. Atk by 1 stage.
Snipe Shot	Water	Special	80	100	15	Normal	—	130	The user can select a target freely, ignoring the effects of the Ability Storm Drain or the moves Ally Switch, Follow Me, and Rage Powder.
Snore	Normal	Special	50	100	15	Normal	—	100	This move only works when the user is asleep. Has a 30% chance of making the target flinch (unable to use moves on that turn).
Soak	Water	Status	—	100	20	Normal	—	—	Changes the target's type to Water.
Solar Beam	Grass	Special	120	100	10	Normal	—	140	This move takes 2 turns. The user builds power on the first turn and attacks on the second. In the harsh sunlight weather condition, this move only takes 1 turn. In the rain/sandstorm/hail weather conditions, this move's power is halved.
Solar Blade	Grass	Physical	125	100	10	Normal	○	140	This move takes 2 turns. The user builds power on the first turn and attacks on the second. In the harsh sunlight weather condition, this move only takes 1 turn. In the rain/sandstorm/hail weather conditions, this move's power is halved.
Spark	Electric	Physical	65	100	20	Normal	○	120	Has a 30% chance of inflicting the paralysis status condition on the target.
Sparkling Aria	Water	Special	90	100	10	All Others	—	130	Heals targets of the burned status condition.
Speed Swap	Psychic	Status	—	—	10	Normal	—	—	Swaps the user's and the target's Speed.
Spikes	Ground	Status	—	—	20	Other Side	—	—	Damages Pokémon as they are sent out on the opposing side. Can be used up to 2 more times to increase damage. Inflicts damage equal to 1/8 of max HP on first use, 1/6 of max HP on second use, and 1/4 of max HP on third use.
Spiky Shield	Grass	Status	—	—	10	Self	—	—	A high-priority move. The user protects itself from all damage-dealing moves and most status moves on the same turn. If an opposing Pokémon uses a move that makes direct contact, the attacker will be damaged for 1/8 of its max HP. This move becomes more likely to fail if used repeatedly. When used against a Max Move, this move will prevent 3/4 of the damage.
Spirit Break	Fairy	Physical	75	100	15	Normal	○	130	Lowers the target's Sp. Atk by 1 stage.
Spit Up	Normal	Special	—	100	10	Normal	—	100	This move's power becomes greater (max power of 300) the more times the user has used Stockpile. This move fails if the user has not used Stockpile first. If the user's Defense and Sp. Def have been boosted by Stockpile, those boosts are reset.
Spite	Ghost	Status	—	100	10	Normal	—	—	Deducts 4 PP from the last move the target used.
Splash	Normal	Status	—	—	40	Self	—	—	Has no effect.
Spore	Grass	Status	—	100	15	Normal	—	—	Inflicts the asleep status condition on the target.
Stealth Rock	Rock	Status	—	—	20	Other Side	—	—	Damages Pokémon as they are sent out on the opposing side. This damage is Rock type and subject to type matchups.
Steel Beam	Steel	Special	140	95	5	Normal	—	140	The user loses 1/2 of its max HP to deal damage to the target.
Steel Wing	Steel	Physical	70	90	25	Normal	○	120	Has a 10% chance of raising the user's Defense by 1 stage.
Sticky Web	Bug	Status	—	—	20	Other Side	—	—	Lowers the Speed of any Pokémon sent out on the opposing side by 1 stage.
Stockpile	Normal	Status	—	—	20	Self	—	—	Raises the user's Defense and Sp. Def by 1 stage each. Its effect stacks up to three times.

Move	Type	Kind	Pow.	Acc.	PP	Range	DA	Max Move Pow.	Notes
Stomp	Normal	Physical	65	100	20	Normal	○	120	Has a 30% chance of making the target flinch (unable to use moves on that turn). If the target has used Minimize, this move will be a sure hit and its power will be doubled.
Stomping Tantrum	Ground	Physical	75	100	10	Normal	○	130	This move's power is doubled if the user's move missed or otherwise failed during the previous turn.
Stone Edge	Rock	Physical	100	80	5	Normal	—	130	This move is more likely than average to deliver a critical hit.
Stored Power	Psychic	Special	20	100	10	Normal	—	130	This move's power increases by 20 (max power of 860) for each stage the user's stats have been boosted.
Storm Throw	Fighting	Physical	60	100	10	Normal	○	80	Always delivers a critical hit.
Strange Steam	Fairy	Special	90	95	10	Normal	—	130	Has a 20% chance of making the target confused.
Strength	Normal	Physical	80	100	15	Normal	○	130	
Strength Sap	Grass	Status	—	100	10	Normal	—	—	Restores the user's HP by an amount equal to the target's Attack, then lowers the target's Attack by 1 stage.
String Shot	Bug	Status	—	95	40	Many Others	—	—	Lowers the targets' Speed by 2 stages.
Struggle	Normal	Physical	50	—	1	1 Random	○	—	This move becomes available when all other moves are out of PP, and it inflicts damage to the target regardless of type matchup. The user also takes damage equal to 1/4 of its max HP when it uses this move. If a Dynamax Pokémon runs out of PP, it will use Struggle. Struggle will not become a Max Move.
Struggle Bug	Bug	Special	50	100	20	Many Others	—	100	Lowers the targets' Sp. Atk by 1 stage.
Stuff Cheeks	Normal	Status	—	—	10	Self	—	—	If the user is holding a Berry, it eats that Berry and uses its battle effect if it has one. This also raises the user's Defense by 2 stages.
Stun Spore	Grass	Status	—	75	30	Normal	—	—	Inflicts the paralysis status condition on the target.
Submission	Fighting	Physical	80	80	20	Normal	○	90	The user also takes 1/4 of the damage dealt to the target.
Substitute	Normal	Status	—	—	10	Self	—	—	Depletes 1/4 of the user's max HP to create a substitute for the user that protects it from moves that lower stats or inflict status conditions. The substitute also takes damage in the user's place until the substitute runs out of HP. The substitute will disappear if the user Dynamaxes while the substitute is still active.
Sucker Punch	Dark	Physical	70	100	5	Normal	○	120	A high-priority move. Deals damage only if the target's chosen move is a damage-dealing move.
Sunny Day	Fire	Status	—	—	5	Both Sides	—	—	Changes the weather condition to harsh sunlight for 5 turns, boosting the power of Fire-type moves by 50% and reducing the power of Water-type moves by 50%.
Super Fang	Normal	Physical	—	90	10	Normal	○	100	Halves the target's HP.
Superpower	Fighting	Physical	120	100	5	Normal	○	95	Lowers the user's Attack and Defense by 1 stage each.
Supersonic	Normal	Status	—	55	20	Normal	—	—	Makes the target confused.
Surf	Water	Special	90	100	15	All Others	—	130	This move hits and has doubled power against targets that are underwater due to using Dive.
Swagger	Normal	Status	—	85	15	Normal	—	—	Makes the target confused but also raises its Attack by 2 stages.
Swallow	Normal	Status	—	—	10	Self	—	—	Restores the user's HP based on how many times the user has used Stockpile. This move fails if the user has not used Stockpile first. If the user's Defense and Sp. Def have been boosted by Stockpile, those boosts are reset.
Sweet Kiss	Fairy	Status	—	75	10	Normal	—	—	Makes the target confused.
Sweet Scent	Normal	Status	—	100	20	Many Others	—	—	Lowers the targets' evasiveness by 2 stages.
Swift	Normal	Special	60	—	20	Many Others	—	110	
Switcheroo	Dark	Status	—	100	10	Normal	—	—	Swaps the user's and the target's held items.
Swords Dance	Normal	Status	—	—	20	Self	—	—	Raises the user's Attack by 2 stages.
Synthesis	Grass	Status	—	—	5	Self	—	—	Restores 1/2 of the user's max HP in normal weather conditions. Restores 2/3 of the user's max HP in the harsh sunlight weather condition. Restores 1/4 of the user's max HP in the rain/sandstorm/hail weather conditions.
Tackle	Normal	Physical	40	100	35	Normal	○	90	
Tail Slap	Normal	Physical	25	85	10	Normal	○	130	Attacks 2–5 times in a row in a single turn.
Tail Whip	Normal	Status	—	100	30	Many Others	—	—	Lowers the targets' Defense by 1 stage.
Tailwind	Flying	Status	—	—	15	Your Side	—	—	Doubles the Speed of the Pokémon on your side for 4 turns.
Take Down	Normal	Physical	90	85	20	Normal	○	130	The user also takes 1/4 of the damage dealt to the target.
Tar Shot	Rock	Status	—	100	15	Normal	—	—	Lowers the target's Speed by 1 stage and makes it weaker to Fire-type moves, doubling the damage it takes from them.
Taunt	Dark	Status	—	100	20	Normal	—	—	Prevents the target from using status moves for 3 turns.
Tearful Look	Normal	Status	—	—	20	Normal	—	—	Lowers the target's Attack and Sp. Atk by 1 stage each.
Teatime	Normal	Status	—	—	10	All	—	—	Forces all the Pokémon on the battlefield to eat their Berry if they are holding one.
Teeter Dance	Normal	Status	—	100	20	All Others	—	—	Makes all Pokémon on the battlefield confused, except for the user.

Move	Type	Kind	Pow.	Acc.	PP	Range	DA	Max Move Pow.	Notes
Teleport	Psychic	Status	—	—	20	Self	—	—	A low-priority move. This move ends wild Pokémon battles. In a Trainer battle, the user teleports out and another Pokémon from the party is sent onto the battlefield. This move fails if there are no other Pokémon available to battle.
Thief	Dark	Physical	60	100	25	Normal	○	110	When the target is holding an item and the user is not, the user can steal that item. When the target is not holding an item, this move will function as a simple damage-dealing move.
Thrash	Normal	Physical	120	100	10	1 Random	○	140	Attacks consecutively over 2–3 turns. The user cannot choose other moves during this time and becomes confused afterward.
Throat Chop	Dark	Physical	80	100	15	Normal	○	130	The target will not be able to use sound-based moves for 2 turns. Moves that normally would be prevented can still be used as Max Moves by Dynamax Pokémon.
Thunder	Electric	Special	110	70	10	Normal	—	140	Has a 30% chance of inflicting the paralysis status condition on the target. Is 100% accurate in the rain weather condition and 50% accurate in the harsh sunlight weather condition. This move hits targets that are in the sky due to moves such as Bounce or Fly.
Thunder Fang	Electric	Physical	65	95	15	Normal	○	120	Has a 10% chance of inflicting the paralysis status condition on the target or making the target flinch (unable to use moves on that turn).
Thunder Punch	Electric	Physical	75	100	15	Normal	○	130	Has a 10% chance of inflicting the paralysis status condition on the target.
Thunder Shock	Electric	Special	40	100	30	Normal	—	90	Has a 10% chance of inflicting the paralysis status condition on the target.
Thunder Wave	Electric	Status	—	90	20	Normal	—	—	Inflicts the paralysis status condition on the target.
Thunderbolt	Electric	Special	90	100	15	Normal	—	130	Has a 10% chance of inflicting the paralysis status condition on the target.
Tickle	Normal	Status	—	100	20	Normal	—	—	Lowers the target's Attack and Defense by 1 stage each.
Topsy-Turvy	Dark	Status	—	—	20	Normal	—	—	Inverts the effects of any stat changes affecting the target.
Torment	Dark	Status	—	100	15	Normal	—	—	Makes the target unable to use the same move twice in a row. This move will fail when used against a Dynamax Pokémon. Even if the target was affected by this move before Dynamaxing, the effect will be nullified once it Dynamaxes.
Toxic	Poison	Status	—	90	10	Normal	—	—	Inflicts the badly poisoned status condition on the target. This move never misses if used by a Poison-type Pokémon.
Toxic Spikes	Poison	Status	—	—	20	Other Side	—	—	Lays a trap of poison spikes on the opposing side that inflicts the poisoned status condition on Pokémon that switch into battle. Using Toxic Spikes twice inflicts the badly poisoned status condition. This move's effects end if a Poison-type Pokémon switches into battle on the opposing side.
Transform	Normal	Status	—	—	10	Normal	—	—	The user transforms into a copy of the target. The user has the same moves and Ability as the target (all moves have 5 PP).
Tri Attack	Normal	Special	80	100	10	Normal	—	130	Has a 20% chance of inflicting the paralysis, burned, or frozen status condition on the target.
Trick	Psychic	Status	—	100	10	Normal	—	—	Swaps the user's and the target's held items.
Trick Room	Psychic	Status	—	—	5	Both Sides	—	—	Acts after all other moves on the same turn. For 5 turns, Pokémon with lower Speed go first. High-priority moves still go first. If Trick Room is used again before its effects end, Trick Room's effects are canceled.
Trick-or-Treat	Ghost	Status	—	100	20	Normal	—	—	Gives the target the Ghost type in addition to its original type(s).
Triple Kick	Fighting	Physical	10	90	10	Normal	○	80	Attacks 3 times in a row in a single turn. Power increases (max power of 30) each time it hits.
Trop Kick	Grass	Physical	70	100	15	Normal	○	120	Lowers the target's Attack by 1 stage.
Twister	Dragon	Special	40	100	20	Many Others	—	90	Has a 20% chance of making the targets flinch (unable to use moves on that turn). This move hits targets that are in the sky due to moves such as Bounce or Fly and has doubled power against them.
Uproar	Normal	Special	90	100	10	1 Random	—	130	The user makes an uproar for 3 turns. During that time, no Pokémon can fall asleep.
U-turn	Bug	Physical	70	100	20	Normal	○	120	After attacking, the user switches out with another Pokémon in the party.
Vacuum Wave	Fighting	Special	40	100	30	Normal	—	70	A high-priority move.
Venom Drench	Poison	Status	—	100	20	Many Others	—	—	Lowers the Attack, Sp. Atk, and Speed of opposing Pokémon afflicted with the poisoned or badly poisoned status conditions by 1 stage each.
Venoshock	Poison	Special	65	100	10	Normal	—	85	This move's power is doubled if the target has the poisoned or badly poisoned status condition.
Vise Grip	Normal	Physical	55	100	30	Normal	○	110	
Vital Throw	Fighting	Physical	70	—	10	Normal	○	85	A low-priority move.
Volt Switch	Electric	Special	70	100	20	Normal	—	120	After attacking, the user switches out with another Pokémon in the party.
Volt Tackle	Electric	Physical	120	100	15	Normal	○	140	The user also takes 1/3 of the damage dealt to the target. Has a 10% chance of inflicting the paralysis status condition on the target.
Water Gun	Water	Special	40	100	25	Normal	—	90	
Water Pledge	Water	Special	80	100	10	Normal	—	130	When this is combined with Fire Pledge or Grass Pledge, the power and effect change. If this is combined with Fire Pledge, the power of this move becomes 150 and it remains a Water-type move. It will also make it more likely that your team's moves will trigger any additional effects they might have for 4 turns. If this is combined with Grass Pledge, the power of this move becomes 150 and it becomes a Grass-type move. It will also lower the Speed of opposing Pokémon for 4 turns.

Move	Type	Kind	Pow.	Acc.	PP	Range	DA	Max Move Pow.	Notes
Water Pulse	Water	Special	60	100	20	Normal	—	110	Has a 20% chance of making the target confused.
Water Shuriken	Water	Special	15	100	20	Normal	—	90	A high-priority move. Attacks 2–5 times in a row in a single turn.
Water Spout	Water	Special	150	100	5	Many Others	—	150	The lower the user's HP, the lower this move's power becomes.
Waterfall	Water	Physical	80	100	15	Normal	○	130	Has a 20% chance of making the target flinch (unable to use moves on that turn).
Weather Ball	Normal	Special	50	100	10	Normal	—	130	In special weather conditions, this move's type changes and its power is doubled. Harsh sunlight weather condition: Fire type. Rain weather condition: Water type. Hail weather condition: Ice type. Sandstorm weather condition: Rock type. The Max Move this move becomes is determined by the weather condition at the time the move is used.
Whirlpool	Water	Special	35	85	15	Normal	—	90	Inflicts damage equal to 1/8 of the target's max HP at the end of each turn for 4–5 turns. The target cannot flee or be switched out of battle during that time. This move hits and has doubled power against targets that are underwater due to using Dive.
Whirlwind	Normal	Status	—	—	20	Normal	—	—	A low-priority move. Ends battles against wild Pokémon if the target's level is lower than the user's. Forces the target to swap out in a Trainer battle, unless there are no other Pokémon available to battle.
Wide Guard	Rock	Status	—	—	10	Your Side	—	—	A high-priority move. Protects your side from the effects of any moves used on the same turn that target multiple Pokémon.
Wild Charge	Electric	Physical	90	100	15	Normal	○	130	The user also takes 1/4 of the damage dealt to the target.
Will-O-Wisp	Fire	Status	—	85	15	Normal	—	—	Inflicts the burned status condition on the target.
Wing Attack	Flying	Physical	60	100	35	Normal	○	110	
Wish	Normal	Status	—	—	10	Self	—	—	Restores 1/2 of the user's max HP at the end of the next turn. If the user is switched out, the Pokémon that takes its place will be healed instead.
Withdraw	Water	Status	—	—	40	Self	—	—	Raises the user's Defense by 1 stage.
Wonder Room	Psychic	Status	—	—	10	Both Sides	—	—	Each Pokémon has its Defense and Sp. Def stats swapped for 5 turns. If Wonder Room is used again before its effects end, Wonder Room's effects are canceled.
Wood Hammer	Grass	Physical	120	100	15	Normal	○	140	The user also takes 1/3 of the damage dealt to the target.
Work Up	Normal	Status	—	—	30	Self	—	—	Raises the user's Attack and Sp. Atk by 1 stage each.
Worry Seed	Grass	Status	—	100	10	Normal	—	—	Changes the target's Ability to Insomnia. Fails with certain Abilities, however.
Wrap	Normal	Physical	15	90	20	Normal	○	90	Inflicts damage equal to 1/8 of the target's max HP at the end of each turn for 4–5 turns. The target cannot flee or be switched out of battle during that time.
X-Scissor	Bug	Physical	80	100	15	Normal	○	130	
Yawn	Normal	Status	—	—	10	Normal	—	—	Inflicts the asleep status condition on the target at the end of the next turn unless the target switches out.
Zap Cannon	Electric	Special	120	50	5	Normal	—	140	Inflicts the paralysis status condition on the target.
Zen Headbutt	Psychic	Physical	80	90	15	Normal	○	130	Has a 20% chance of making the target flinch (unable to use moves on that turn).
Zing Zap	Electric	Physical	80	100	10	Normal	○	130	Has a 30% chance of making the target flinch (unable to use moves on that turn).

Priority Moves

In addition to all the other factors that affect how moves deal damage, such as their range and their power, there is also priority. Most moves have no priority. That means that for those moves, it is only the Speed stat of the Pokémon in the battle that will decide which move is used first in a turn. If your Pokémon has a higher Speed stat than any other Pokémon on the battlefield, then it'll get to use its move first.

But priority overrules the Speed stat. If a move has higher priority, it will be used first in a turn—no matter how high or low a Pokémon's Speed might be! On the other hand, moves with low priority will be used later in a turn, even if the Pokémon using them would usually be very speedy.

In the table below, you can see how moves fall on these scales of high and low priority. As you move up and down through the rows, you can see how different groups of moves have ever higher or lower priority. For example, if two Pokémon used Extreme Speed and Aqua Jet, the one using Extreme Speed would go first and Aqua Jet second—no matter their Speed. But if the Pokémon used Extreme Speed and Fake Out, then Fake Out would go first, because it's higher in the priority tiers. Study the table below if you want to become a pro at using priority moves!

Remember that there are ways to play with priority and Speed, such as using Trick Room! Turn back to page 188 to learn more.

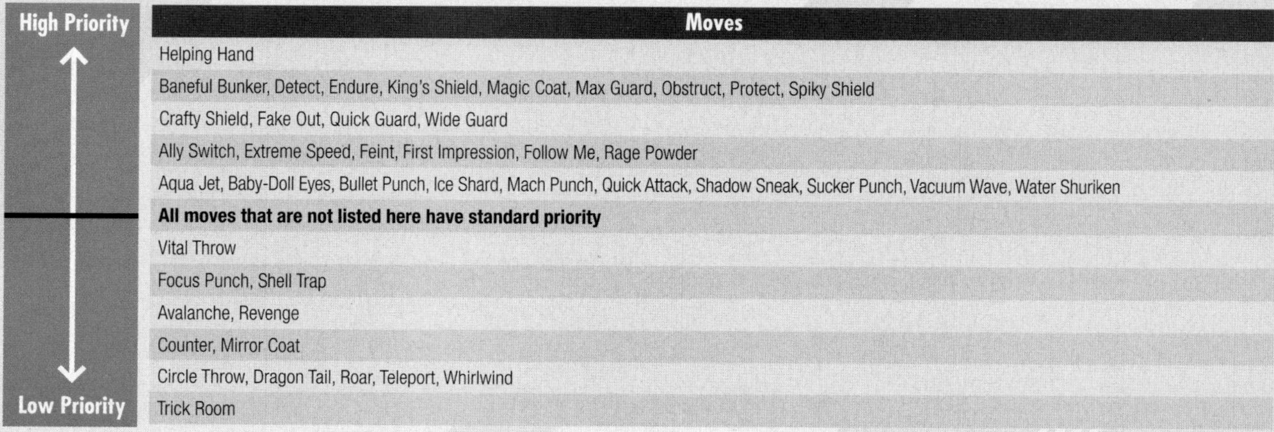

Priority	Moves
High Priority	Helping Hand
	Baneful Bunker, Detect, Endure, King's Shield, Magic Coat, Max Guard, Obstruct, Protect, Spiky Shield
	Crafty Shield, Fake Out, Quick Guard, Wide Guard
	Ally Switch, Extreme Speed, Feint, First Impression, Follow Me, Rage Powder
	Aqua Jet, Baby-Doll Eyes, Bullet Punch, Ice Shard, Mach Punch, Quick Attack, Shadow Sneak, Sucker Punch, Vacuum Wave, Water Shuriken
	All moves that are not listed here have standard priority
	Vital Throw
	Focus Punch, Shell Trap
	Avalanche, Revenge
	Counter, Mirror Coat
	Circle Throw, Dragon Tail, Roar, Teleport, Whirlwind
Low Priority	Trick Room

Max Moves and G-Max Moves

Max Moves

When a Pokémon has Dynamaxed, its moves will all be transformed into awesome Max Moves! The Max Move that each move becomes will be based on two things—the original move's type and its category. Any damage-dealing move will be changed to the Max Move that corresponds to its type. Any status move, regardless of type, will be changed into Max Guard when a Pokémon is Dynamaxed.

The power of a Max Move also varies depending on the original move it is based on. So check the Max Move Pow. column in the regular move tables to see how powerful each move can become when it turns into a Max Move!

Move	Type	Kind	Range	DA	Notes
Max Airstream	Flying	Physical/ Special	Normal	—	Any damage-dealing Flying-type move will turn into this move when used by a Dynamax Pokémon. Raises the user's and ally Pokémon's Speed by 1 stage.
Max Darkness	Dark	Physical/ Special	Normal	—	Any damage-dealing Dark-type move will turn into this move when used by a Dynamax Pokémon. Lowers opposing Pokémon's Sp. Def by 1 stage.
Max Flare	Fire	Physical/ Special	Normal	—	Any damage-dealing Fire-type move will turn into this move when used by a Dynamax Pokémon. Changes the weather condition to harsh sunlight for 5 turns, boosting the power of Fire-type moves by 50% and reducing the power of Water-type moves by 50%.
Max Flutterby	Bug	Physical/ Special	Normal	—	Any damage-dealing Bug-type move will turn into this move when used by a Dynamax Pokémon. Lowers opposing Pokémon's Sp. Atk by 1 stage.
Max Geyser	Water	Physical/ Special	Normal	—	Any damage-dealing Water-type move will turn into this move when used by a Dynamax Pokémon. Changes the weather condition to rain for 5 turns, boosting the power of Water-type moves by 50% and reducing the power of Fire-type moves by 50%.
Max Guard	Normal	Status	Self	—	Any status move will turn into this move when used by a Dynamax Pokémon. The user protects itself from all moves used on the same turn. This move becomes more likely to fail if used repeatedly.
Max Hailstorm	Ice	Physical/ Special	Normal	—	Any damage-dealing Ice-type move will turn into this move when used by a Dynamax Pokémon. Changes the weather condition to hail for 5 turns. All Pokémon other than Ice types take damage at the end of each turn equal to 1/16 of their max HP.
Max Knuckle	Fighting	Physical/ Special	Normal	—	Any damage-dealing Fighting-type move will turn into this move when used by a Dynamax Pokémon. Raises the user's and ally Pokémon's Attack by 1 stage.
Max Lightning	Electric	Physical/ Special	Normal	—	Any damage-dealing Electric-type move will turn into this move when used by a Dynamax Pokémon. Electrifies the battlefield for 5 turns. During that time, Pokémon on the ground will be able to do 50% more damage with Electric-type moves and cannot fall asleep.
Max Mindstorm	Psychic	Physical/ Special	Normal	—	Any damage-dealing Psychic-type move will turn into this move when used by a Dynamax Pokémon. Covers the battlefield with psychic energy for 5 turns. During that time, Pokémon on the ground will be able to do 50% more damage with Psychic-type moves and will evade high-priority moves.
Max Ooze	Poison	Physical/ Special	Normal	—	Any damage-dealing Poison-type move will turn into this move when used by a Dynamax Pokémon. Raises the user's and ally Pokémon's Sp. Atk by 1 stage.
Max Overgrowth	Grass	Physical/ Special	Normal	—	Any damage-dealing Grass-type move will turn into this move when used by a Dynamax Pokémon. Covers the battlefield with grass for 5 turns. During that time, Pokémon on the ground will be able to do 50% more damage with Grass-type moves and will recover 1/16 of their max HP at the end of each turn. Damage done to Pokémon on the ground by Bulldoze or Earthquake is also halved during this time.
Max Phantasm	Ghost	Physical/ Special	Normal	—	Any damage-dealing Ghost-type move will turn into this move when used by a Dynamax Pokémon. Lowers opposing Pokémon's Defense by 1 stage.
Max Quake	Ground	Physical/ Special	Normal	—	Any damage-dealing Ground-type move will turn into this move when used by a Dynamax Pokémon. Raises the user's and ally Pokémon's Sp. Def by 1 stage.
Max Rockfall	Rock	Physical/ Special	Normal	—	Any damage-dealing Rock-type move will turn into this move when used by a Dynamax Pokémon. Changes the weather condition to sandstorm for 5 turns, boosting the Sp. Def of Rock-type Pokémon by 50%. All Pokémon other than Ground, Rock, and Steel types take damage at the end of each turn equal to 1/16 of their max HP.
Max Starfall	Fairy	Physical/ Special	Normal	—	Any damage-dealing Fairy-type move will turn into this move when used by a Dynamax Pokémon. Covers the battlefield with mist for 5 turns. During that time, Pokémon on the ground cannot be afflicted with new status conditions or confusion. Damage done to Pokémon on the ground by Dragon-type moves is also halved during this time.
Max Steelspike	Steel	Physical/ Special	Normal	—	Any damage-dealing Steel-type move will turn into this move when used by a Dynamax Pokémon. Raises the user's and ally Pokémon's Defense by 1 stage.
Max Strike	Normal	Physical/ Special	Normal	—	Any damage-dealing Normal-type move will turn into this move when used by a Dynamax Pokémon. Lowers opposing Pokémon's Speed by 1 stage.
Max Wyrmwind	Dragon	Physical/ Special	Normal	—	Any damage-dealing Dragon-type move will turn into this move when used by a Dynamax Pokémon. Lowers opposing Pokémon's Attack by 1 stage.

G-Max Moves

Remember that even within the Dynamax phenomenon, there is an even rarer phenomenon—Gigantamaxing! If a Pokémon can Gigantamax, it has access to a unique powered-up version of one of the Max Moves! Each of these G-Max Moves has different additional effects than the Max Move it's based on, and these effects only occur for these rare Gigntamax Pokémon.

Move	Pokémon that can use it	Type	Additional effects
G-Max Befuddle	Gigantamax Butterfree	Bug	Inflicts the poison, paralysis, or asleep status condition on all opposing Pokémon.
G-Max Centiferno	Gigantamax Centiskorch	Fire	Inflicts damage equal to 1/8 of max HP to all opponents at the end of each turn for 4–5 turns. Opponents cannot flee or be switched out of battle during that time.
G-Max Chi Strike	Gigantamax Machamp	Fighting	Increases critical hit rates of all ally Pokémon by 2 stages.
G-Max Cuddle	Gigantamax Eevee	Normal	Makes all opposing Pokémon become infatuated, which causes moves to fail 50% of the time.
G-Max Depletion	Gigantamax Duraludon	Dragon	Reduces the PP of the moves used by all opposing Pokémon by 2.
G-Max Finale	Gigantamax Alcremie	Fairy	Restores 1/6 of all ally Pokémon's max HP.
G-Max Foam Burst	Gigantamax Kingler	Water	Decreases the Speed stats of all opposing Pokémon by 2 stages.
G-Max Gold Rush	Gigantamax Meowth	Normal	Pays out money after battle. The amount depends on the user's level and the number of times the move was used. First use: ₽100 × user's level. Second use: ₽300 × user's level. Third use: ₽600 × user's level. Also makes all opposing Pokémon confused.
G-Max Gravitas	Gigantamax Orbeetle	Psychic	Airborne Pokémon are grounded. Ground-type moves will now hit Pokémon normally immune to them. Prevents the use of Bounce, Fly, Flying Press, High Jump Kick, Magnet Rise, and Splash. Raises the accuracy of all Pokémon in battle. Lasts 5 turns.
G-Max Malodor	Gigantamax Garbodor	Poison	Inflicts the poison status condition on all opposing Pokémon.
G-Max Resonance	Gigantamax Lapras	Ice	Reduces damage from physical and special moves for 5 turns.
G-Max Sandblast	Gigantamax Sandaconda	Ground	Inflicts damage equal to 1/8 of max HP to all opponents at the end of each turn for 4–5 turns. Opponents cannot flee or be switched out of battle during that time.
G-Max Smite	Gigantamax Hatterene	Fairy	Makes all opposing Pokémon confused.
G-Max Snooze	Gigantamax Grimmsnarl	Dark	Inflicts the asleep status condition on the target at the end of the next turn unless the target switches out.
G-Max Steelsurge	Gigantamax Copperajah	Steel	Damages Pokémon as they are sent out to the opposing side. This damage is Steel type and subject to type matchups.
G-Max Stonesurge	Gigantamax Drednaw	Water	Damages Pokémon as they are sent out to the opposing side. This damage is Rock type and subject to type matchups.
G-Max Sweetness	Gigantamax Appletun	Grass	Heals the status conditions of all ally Pokémon in battle.
G-Max Tartness	Gigantamax Flapple	Grass	Decreases the evasiveness of all opposing Pokémon by 1 stage.
G-Max Terror	Gigantamax Gengar	Ghost	Prevents all opposing Pokémon from fleeing or being switched out while this Pokémon is in battle.
G-Max Volcalith	Gigantamax Coalossal	Rock	Inflicts damage equal to 1/6 of max HP to all non-Rock-type opponents for 4 turns.
G-Max Volt Crash	Gigantamax Pikachu	Electric	Inflicts the paralysis status condition on all opposing Pokémon.
G-Max Wildfire	Gigantamax Charizard	Fire	Inflicts damage equal to 1/6 of max HP to all non-Fire-type opponents for 4 turns.
G-Max Wind Rage	Gigantamax Corviknight	Flying	Nullifies Aurora Veil, Light Screen, Mist, Reflect, and Safeguard on the opponents' side. Nullifies Spikes, Stealth Rock, Sticky Web, and Toxic Spikes on both sides.

Move Tutors

Pokémon learn many moves by leveling up, evolving, or having TMs or TRs used on them. But sometimes Pokémon can also learn certain moves with the help of a Move Tutor. These special people can teach Pokémon moves they generally wouldn't be able to learn otherwise, so check out the table below if you need help finding a particular tutor!

There may be other Pokémon that can learn these moves once you are able to send them over from Pokémon HOME, available in 2020.

Location	Where to find them	Move	Pokémon that can learn it	Special conditions
Hammerlocke	Down the stairs near the exit to Route 6	Grass Pledge	Grookey, Thwackey, Rillaboom, Silvally	
Hammerlocke	Down the stairs near the exit to Route 6	Fire Pledge	Scorbunny, Raboot, Cinderace, Charmander, Charmeleon, Charizard, Silvally	
Hammerlocke	Down the stairs near the exit to Route 6	Water Pledge	Sobble, Drizzile, Inteleon, Silvally	
Circhester	At the Hero's Bath, on the west side of the pool	Draco Meteor	Any Dragon-type Pokémon, Silvally	
Wyndon	Near the court in the park	Frenzy Plant	Rillaboom	
Wyndon	Near the court in the park	Blast Burn	Cinderace, Charizard	
Wyndon	Near the court in the park	Hydro Cannon	Inteleon	
Motostoke	Near the canals, all the way down the stairs near the east lift	Steel Beam	Any Steel-type Pokémon, Silvally, Zacian, Zamazenta	Become the Champion

ADVENTURE DATA

How to Obtain TMs

TMs are a great way to teach Pokémon moves, since they can be used over and over for as many different Pokémon as you like! All you have to do is track them down, which can be a bit tricky. Some are available in shops, but many can only be found by talking to particular people around the region, meeting certain conditions, or simply finding them lying about in Galar's nooks and crannies!

TM No.	Move	Type	How to obtain	Price
TM00	Mega Punch	Normal	Purchase from a Poké Mart in Hammerlocke (east), which becomes available after you defeat the Fairy-type Gym Leader, Opal	₽10,000
TM01	Mega Kick	Normal	Purchase from a Poké Mart in Hammerlocke (east), which becomes available after you defeat the Fairy-type Gym Leader, Opal	₽40,000
TM02	Pay Day	Normal	Find in Motostoke	—
TM03	Fire Punch	Fire	Purchase from a Poké Mart in Wyndon (stadium front)	₽50,000
TM04	Ice Punch	Ice	Purchase from a Poké Mart in Wyndon (stadium front)	₽50,000
TM05	Thunder Punch	Electric	Purchase from a Poké Mart in Wyndon (stadium front)	₽50,000
TM06	Fly	Flying	Receive from a Flying Taxi driver in the house by the stairs that lead to Stow-on-Side Stadium in Stow-on-Side	—
TM07	Pin Missile	Bug	Find on Route 4	—
TM08	Hyper Beam	Normal	Purchase from a Poké Mart in Wyndon (stadium front)	₽50,000
TM09	Giga Impact	Normal	Purchase from a Poké Mart in Wyndon (stadium front)	₽50,000
TM10	Magical Leaf	Grass	Receive after defeating the Grass-type Gym Leader, Milo	—
TM11	Solar Beam	Grass	Find in Turffield (must have Water Mode for the Rotom Bike)	—
TM12	Solar Blade	Grass	Purchase from a Poké Mart in Wyndon (stadium front)	₽50,000
TM13	Fire Spin	Fire	Purchase from a Poké Mart in Hammerlocke (west)	₽10,000
TM14	Thunder Wave	Electric	Receive after completing a Rotom Rally course for the first time in the Wild Area	—
TM15	Dig	Ground	Find on Route 6	—
TM16	Screech	Normal	Receive from a hiker found upstairs in the eastern building of Circhester's Hotel Ionia (first room to the right of the elevator)	—
TM17	Light Screen	Psychic	Purchase from a Poké Mart in Motostoke (upper level)	₽10,000
TM18	Reflect	Psychic	Purchase from a Poké Mart in Motostoke (upper level)	₽10,000
TM19	Safeguard	Normal	Purchase from a Poké Mart in Motostoke (upper level)	₽10,000
TM20	Self-Destruct	Normal	Purchase from a Pokémon League staff member selling TMs in the Battle Tower (after becoming Champion)	₽100,000
TM21	Rest	Psychic	Find in Ballonlea	—
TM22	Rock Slide	Rock	Find on Route 9	—
TM23	Thief	Dark	Purchase from a Poké Mart in Hammerlocke (west)	₽10,000
TM24	Snore	Normal	Find in Glimwood Tangle	—
TM25	Protect	Normal	Purchase from a Poké Mart in Motostoke (upper level)	₽10,000
TM26	Scary Face	Normal	Find in Galar Mine	—
TM27	Icy Wind	Ice	Receive from a young man in Circhester / Receive after defeating the Ice-type Gym Leader, Melony	—
TM28	Giga Drain	Grass	Purchase from a Pokémon League staff member selling TMs in the Battle Tower (after becoming Champion)	₽100,000
TM29	Charm	Fairy	Find in Hammerlocke	—
TM30	Steel Wing	Steel	Find on Route 6	—
TM31	Attract	Normal	Find on Route 5	—
TM32	Sandstorm	Rock	Purchase from a Poké Mart in Hammerlocke (west)	₽10,000
TM33	Rain Dance	Water	Purchase from a Poké Mart in Hammerlocke (west)	₽10,000
TM34	Sunny Day	Fire	Purchase from a Poké Mart in Hammerlocke (west)	₽10,000
TM35	Hail	Ice	Purchase from a Poké Mart in Hammerlocke (west)	₽10,000
TM36	Whirlpool	Water	Receive after defeating the Water-type Gym Leader, Nessa	—
TM37	Beat Up	Dark	Find on Route 3	—
TM38	Will-O-Wisp	Fire	Receive after defeating the Fire-type Gym Leader, Kabu	—
TM39	Facade	Normal	Find behind one of the pipes on the Motostoke Riverbank in the Wild Area	—
TM40	Swift	Normal	Receive from Hop in front of Wedgehurst Station during the main story	—
TM41	Helping Hand	Normal	Purchase from a Poké Mart in Motostoke (upper level)	₽10,000
TM42	Revenge	Fighting	Receive after defeating the Fighting-type Gym Leader, Bea / Receive from an old lady in Ballonlea	—
TM43	Brick Break	Fighting	Find on Route 8	—
TM44	Imprison	Psychic	Purchase from a Pokémon League staff member selling TMs in the Battle Tower (after becoming Champion)	₽100,000
TM45	Dive	Water	Receive from a female swimmer on the secret beach on Route 9 (Circhester Bay)	—
TM46	Weather Ball	Normal	Purchase from a Poké Mart in Hammerlocke (east), which becomes available after you defeat the Fairy-type Gym Leader, Opal	₽30,000
TM47	Fake Tears	Dark	Receive from a musician found upstairs in the eastern building of Circhester's Hotel Ionia (second hotel room to the right of the elevator)	—

TM No.	Move	Type	How to obtain	Price
TM48	Rock Tomb	Rock	Receive after defeating the Rock-type Gym Leader, Gordie / Receive from a young man in Circhester	—
TM49	Sand Tomb	Ground	Find in Galar Mine No. 2	—
TM50	Bullet Seed	Grass	Purchase from a Poké Mart in Hammerlocke (west)	₽10,000
TM51	Icicle Spear	Ice	Find in Circhester near the Hero's Bath	—
TM52	Bounce	Flying	Purchase from a Pokémon League staff member selling TMs in the Battle Tower (after becoming Champion)	₽100,000
TM53	Mud Shot	Ground	Find in Galar Mine No. 2 (must have Water Mode for the Rotom Bike)	—
TM54	Rock Blast	Rock	Find on Route 3	—
TM55	Brine	Water	Purchase from a Poké Mart in Hammerlocke (west)	₽10,000
TM56	U-turn	Bug	Find in Glimwood Tangle	—
TM57	Payback	Dark	Find on Route 2 behind Professor Magnolia's house	—
TM58	Assurance	Dark	Find on Route 7 near the campsite	—
TM59	Fling	Dark	Purchase from a Pokémon League staff member selling TMs in the Battle Tower (after becoming Champion)	₽100,000
TM60	Power Swap	Psychic	Purchase from a Poké Mart in Wyndon (stadium front)	₽30,000
TM61	Guard Swap	Psychic	Purchase from a Poké Mart in Wyndon (stadium front)	₽30,000
TM62	Speed Swap	Psychic	Purchase from a Poké Mart in Wyndon (stadium front)	₽30,000
TM63	Drain Punch	Fighting	Purchase from a Poké Mart in Wyndon (stadium front)	₽50,000
TM64	Avalanche	Ice	Find on Route 9	—
TM65	Shadow Claw	Ghost	Find across the Lake of Outrage in the Wild Area (must have Water Mode for the Rotom Bike)	—
TM66	Thunder Fang	Electric	Purchase from a Poké Mart in Hammerlocke (east), which becomes available after you defeat the Fairy-type Gym Leader, Opal	₽30,000
TM67	Ice Fang	Ice	Purchase from a Poké Mart in Hammerlocke (east), which becomes available after you defeat the Fairy-type Gym Leader, Opal	₽30,000
TM68	Fire Fang	Fire	Purchase from a Poké Mart in Hammerlocke (east), which becomes available after you defeat the Fairy-type Gym Leader, Opal	₽30,000
TM69	Psycho Cut	Psychic	Find on Route 2 (must have Water Mode for the Rotom Bike)	—
TM70	Trick Room	Psychic	Purchase from a Pokémon League staff member selling TMs in the Battle Tower (after becoming Champion)	₽50,000
TM71	Wonder Room	Psychic	Purchase from a Pokémon League staff member selling TMs in the Battle Tower (after becoming Champion)	₽50,000
TM72	Magic Room	Psychic	Purchase from a Pokémon League staff member selling TMs in the Battle Tower (after becoming Champion)	₽50,000
TM73	Cross Poison	Poison	Find in the Dusty Bowl in the Wild Area (must have Water Mode for the Rotom Bike)	—
TM74	Venoshock	Poison	Find in Stow-on-Side	—
TM75	Low Sweep	Fighting	Find in the Bridge Field in the Wild Area (must have Water Mode for the Rotom Bike)	—
TM76	Round	Normal	Purchase from a Poké Mart in Motostoke (upper level)	₽10,000
TM77	Hex	Ghost	Receive from an old lady in Ballonlea / Receive after defeating the Ghost-type Gym Leader, Allister	—
TM78	Acrobatics	Flying	Receive from an artist in Ballonlea who wants to become a Pokémon (show him a Fire-type Tracksuit Jacket)	—
TM79	Retaliate	Normal	Receive from Sonia in the seafood restaurant in Hulbury during the main story	—
TM80	Volt Switch	Electric	Receive by achieving a very high score in the Rotom Rally in the Wild Area	—
TM81	Bulldoze	Ground	Find near the Giant's Seat in the Wild Area	—
TM82	Electroweb	Electric	Find in Hulbury	—
TM83	Razor Shell	Water	Purchase from a Pokémon League staff member selling TMs in the Battle Tower (after becoming Champion)	₽100,000
TM84	Tail Slap	Normal	Find in a fallen tree on the east side of the Rolling Fields in the Wild Area	—
TM85	Snarl	Dark	Receive after defeating the Dark-type Gym Leader, Piers	—
TM86	Phantom Force	Ghost	Find in the Slumbering Weald when you revisit it	—
TM87	Draining Kiss	Fairy	Receive after defeating the Fairy-type Gym Leader, Opal	—
TM88	Grassy Terrain	Grass	Purchase from a Poké Mart in Hammerlocke (east), which becomes available after you defeat the Fairy-type Gym Leader, Opal	₽20,000
TM89	Misty Terrain	Fairy	Purchase from a Poké Mart in Hammerlocke (east), which becomes available after you defeat the Fairy-type Gym Leader, Opal	₽20,000
TM90	Electric Terrain	Electric	Purchase from a Poké Mart in Hammerlocke (east), which becomes available after you defeat the Fairy-type Gym Leader, Opal	₽20,000
TM91	Psychic Terrain	Psychic	Purchase from a Poké Mart in Hammerlocke (east), which becomes available after you defeat the Fairy-type Gym Leader, Opal	₽20,000
TM92	Mystical Fire	Fire	Purchase from a Pokémon League staff member selling TMs in the Battle Tower (after becoming Champion)	₽100,000
TM93	Eerie Impulse	Electric	Find in Wyndon	—
TM94	False Swipe	Normal	Purchase from a Poké Mart in Motostoke (upper level)	₽10,000
TM95	Air Slash	Flying	Find on Axew's Eye, an island in the Wild Area (must have Water Mode for the Rotom Bike)	—
TM96	Smart Strike	Steel	Find on Route 8	—
TM97	Brutal Swing	Dark	Find in Turffield	—
TM98	Stomping Tantrum	Ground	Find on Route 10 on a side path just over the hill heading toward Wyndon	—
TM99	Breaking Swipe	Dragon	Receive after defeating the Dragon-type Gym Leader, Raihan	—

How to Obtain TRs

There are a couple of ways you can obtain TRs during your adventure. You can receive them as rewards for participating in Max Raid Battles, or you can purchase them from the Watt Trader service offered by the Rotom Rallyists hanging out in the Wild Area. Each Rotom Rallyist offers a different selection of TRs, and their inventories change every day. Visit them all in turn, and if you still can't find a TR you want, just check back with each of them again the next day! The table below shows you all the TRs you can find in the Galar region—plus how many Watts they cost if you want to purchase them.

TR No.	Move	Type	Price
TR00	Swords Dance	Normal	2,000 W
TR01	Body Slam	Normal	3,000 W
TR02	Flamethrower	Fire	5,000 W
TR03	Hydro Pump	Water	8,000 W
TR04	Surf	Water	5,000 W
TR05	Ice Beam	Ice	5,000 W
TR06	Blizzard	Ice	8,000 W
TR07	Low Kick	Fighting	3,000 W
TR08	Thunderbolt	Electric	5,000 W
TR09	Thunder	Electric	8,000 W
TR10	Earthquake	Ground	8,000 W
TR11	Psychic	Psychic	5,000 W
TR12	Agility	Psychic	2,000 W
TR13	Focus Energy	Normal	1,000 W
TR14	Metronome	Normal	1,000 W
TR15	Fire Blast	Fire	8,000 W
TR16	Waterfall	Water	3,000 W
TR17	Amnesia	Psychic	2,000 W
TR18	Leech Life	Bug	3,000 W
TR19	Tri Attack	Normal	2,000 W
TR20	Substitute	Normal	3,000 W
TR21	Reversal	Fighting	2,000 W
TR22	Sludge Bomb	Poison	5,000 W
TR23	Spikes	Ground	2,000 W
TR24	Outrage	Dragon	8,000 W
TR25	Psyshock	Psychic	3,000 W
TR26	Endure	Normal	1,000 W
TR27	Sleep Talk	Normal	2,000 W
TR28	Megahorn	Bug	8,000 W
TR29	Baton Pass	Normal	2,000 W
TR30	Encore	Normal	2,000 W
TR31	Iron Tail	Steel	5,000 W
TR32	Crunch	Dark	3,000 W
TR33	Shadow Ball	Ghost	3,000 W
TR34	Future Sight	Psychic	3,000 W
TR35	Uproar	Normal	3,000 W
TR36	Heat Wave	Fire	5,000 W
TR37	Taunt	Dark	2,000 W
TR38	Trick	Psychic	2,000 W
TR39	Superpower	Fighting	8,000 W
TR40	Skill Swap	Psychic	1,000 W
TR41	Blaze Kick	Fire	3,000 W
TR42	Hyper Voice	Normal	5,000 W
TR43	Overheat	Fire	8,000 W
TR44	Cosmic Power	Psychic	2,000 W
TR45	Muddy Water	Water	5,000 W
TR46	Iron Defense	Steel	2,000 W
TR47	Dragon Claw	Dragon	3,000 W
TR48	Bulk Up	Fighting	2,000 W
TR49	Calm Mind	Psychic	2,000 W
TR50	Leaf Blade	Grass	5,000 W
TR51	Dragon Dance	Dragon	2,000 W
TR52	Gyro Ball	Steel	3,000 W
TR53	Close Combat	Fighting	8,000 W
TR54	Toxic Spikes	Poison	2,000 W
TR55	Flare Blitz	Fire	8,000 W
TR56	Aura Sphere	Fighting	3,000 W
TR57	Poison Jab	Poison	3,000 W
TR58	Dark Pulse	Dark	3,000 W
TR59	Seed Bomb	Grass	3,000 W
TR60	X-Scissor	Bug	3,000 W
TR61	Bug Buzz	Bug	5,000 W
TR62	Dragon Pulse	Dragon	3,000 W
TR63	Power Gem	Rock	3,000 W
TR64	Focus Blast	Fighting	8,000 W
TR65	Energy Ball	Grass	5,000 W
TR66	Brave Bird	Flying	8,000 W
TR67	Earth Power	Ground	5,000 W
TR68	Nasty Plot	Dark	2,000 W
TR69	Zen Headbutt	Psychic	3,000 W
TR70	Flash Cannon	Steel	5,000 W
TR71	Leaf Storm	Grass	8,000 W
TR72	Power Whip	Grass	8,000 W
TR73	Gunk Shot	Poison	8,000 W
TR74	Iron Head	Steel	5,000 W
TR75	Stone Edge	Rock	8,000 W
TR76	Stealth Rock	Rock	3,000 W
TR77	Grass Knot	Grass	3,000 W
TR78	Sludge Wave	Poison	5,000 W
TR79	Heavy Slam	Steel	3,000 W
TR80	Electro Ball	Electric	3,000 W
TR81	Foul Play	Dark	3,000 W
TR82	Stored Power	Psychic	2,000 W
TR83	Ally Switch	Psychic	2,000 W
TR84	Scald	Water	3,000 W
TR85	Work Up	Normal	1,000 W
TR86	Wild Charge	Electric	5,000 W
TR87	Drill Run	Ground	3,000 W
TR88	Heat Crash	Fire	3,000 W
TR89	Hurricane	Flying	8,000 W
TR90	Play Rough	Fairy	5,000 W
TR91	Venom Drench	Poison	2,000 W
TR92	Dazzling Gleam	Fairy	3,000 W
TR93	Darkest Lariat	Dark	5,000 W
TR94	High Horsepower	Ground	5,000 W
TR95	Throat Chop	Dark	3,000 W
TR96	Pollen Puff	Bug	5,000 W
TR97	Psychic Fangs	Psychic	5,000 W
TR98	Liquidation	Water	3,000 W
TR99	Body Press	Fighting	3,000 W

Abilities

Every Pokémon has an Ability, and the table below will help you understand the varied effects Abilities can have! The column titled **Effects in battle** lists how each Ability affects the Pokémon that has it—and sometimes also allies, opponents, or even the entire battlefield! The **Effects outside of battle** column lists the effects that a few Abilities exert on either your party Pokémon or your encounters with wild Pokémon when you're out exploring.

Ability	Effects in battle	Effects outside of battle
Adaptability	Increases the same-type attack bonus from the usual 50% boost in power to 100%.	—
Aftermath	Causes damage to an attacker equal to 1/4 of its max HP if the attacker knocks the Pokémon out using a move that makes direct contact.	—
Analytic	Boosts the power of the Pokémon's moves by 30% if the Pokémon goes last during a turn.	—
Anticipation	Provides a warning if an opposing Pokémon has supereffective moves or one-hit knockout moves. This warning occurs when the Pokémon with this Ability enters the battlefield.	—
Arena Trap	Prevents opposing Pokémon from fleeing or being switched out. Has no effect against Flying- or Ghost-type Pokémon and Pokémon with the Levitate Ability. Pokémon with the Run Away Ability can flee from a Pokémon with Arena Trap, but they will be prevented from switching out.	Makes it more likely you will encounter wild Pokémon if your lead Pokémon has this Ability.
Aroma Veil	Protects the Pokémon's side of the battlefield from the effects of Disable, Encore, Taunt, and Torment. Also protects from infatuation and the effect of the Cursed Body Ability.	—
Ball Fetch	Allows the Pokémon to retrieve a Poké Ball that was used in a battle but failed to catch a wild Pokémon. This effect will only apply to the first Poké Ball used. If the Pokémon is already holding an item, nothing happens.	—
Battery	Boosts the power of special moves used by the Pokémon's allies by 30%.	—
Battle Armor	Prevents opponents' damage-dealing moves from ever delivering a critical hit to the Pokémon.	—
Berserk	Raises the Pokémon's Sp. Atk by 1 stage when the Pokémon takes a hit that causes its HP to drop to 1/2 or less.	—
Big Pecks	Protects the Pokémon from having its Defense lowered by the moves or Abilities of other Pokémon.	—
Blaze	Boosts the power of the Pokémon's Fire-type moves by 50% when the Pokémon's HP drops to 1/3 or less.	—
Bulletproof	Protects the Pokémon from Acid Spray, Aura Sphere, Bullet Seed, Electro Ball, Energy Ball, Focus Blast, Gyro Ball, Octazooka, Pollen Puff, Pyro Ball, Rock Blast, Rock Wrecker, Seed Bomb, Shadow Ball, Sludge Bomb, Weather Ball, and Zap Cannon.	—
Cheek Pouch	Restores 1/3 of the Pokémon's max HP when the Pokémon eats a Berry (in addition to the Berry's usual benefits).	—
Chlorophyll	Doubles the Pokémon's Speed in the harsh sunlight weather condition.	—
Clear Body	Protects the Pokémon from having its stats lowered by the moves or Abilities of other Pokémon.	—
Cloud Nine	Negates the effects of weather conditions for all Pokémon on the battlefield.	—
Competitive	Raises the Pokémon's Sp. Atk by 2 stages whenever any of the Pokémon's stats are lowered due to an opponent's move or Ability.	—
Compound Eyes	Raises the Pokémon's accuracy by 30%.	Makes it more likely that the wild Pokémon you encounter will be holding items if your lead Pokémon has this Ability.
Contrary	Inverts the Pokémon's stat changes to have the opposite effect (lowered stats are instead raised and vice versa).	—
Corrosion	Allows the Pokémon to inflict the poisoned or badly poisoned status condition on Poison types and Steel types.	—
Cotton Down	Scatters cotton fluff around the Pokémon when the Pokémon is hit by a damage-dealing move. This lowers the Speed of all other Pokémon on the battlefield.	—
Cursed Body	Provides a 30% chance of disabling damage-dealing moves used against the Pokémon. Moves disabled this way cannot be used for 4 turns.	—
Cute Charm	Provides a 30% chance of inflicting infatuation on an attacker if the attacker hits the Pokémon with a move that makes direct contact. Gender-unknown Pokémon and Pokémon of the same gender are immune to this effect.	Makes it more likely you will encounter wild Pokémon of the opposite gender if your lead Pokémon has this Ability.
Damp	Prevents all Pokémon on the battlefield from using Explosion or Self-Destruct and nullifies the Aftermath Ability.	—
Dauntless Shield	Raises the Pokémon's Defense by 1 stage when the Pokémon enters the battlefield.	
Defiant	Raises the Pokémon's Attack by 2 stages whenever any of the Pokémon's stats are lowered due to an opponent's move or Ability.	—
Disguise	Protects the Pokémon from most damage the first time it is hit by a damage-dealing move. Then the Pokémon changes to its Busted Form.	—
Drizzle	Triggers the rain weather condition when the Pokémon enters the battlefield. This weather condition lasts for 5 turns.	—
Drought	Triggers the harsh sunlight weather condition when the Pokémon enters the battlefield. This weather condition lasts for 5 turns.	—
Dry Skin	Absorbs Water-type moves, making the Pokémon immune to their damage and effects. Instead, such moves restore 1/4 of the Pokémon's max HP. Restores 1/8 of the Pokémon's max HP at the end of each turn in the rain weather condition. However, this Ability also increases the damage the Pokémon takes from Fire-type moves by 25% and reduces its HP by 1/8 of its maximum at the end of each turn in the harsh sunlight weather condition.	—
Early Bird	Allows the Pokémon to wake more quickly when afflicted with the asleep status condition.	—
Effect Spore	Provides a 30% chance of inflicting the poisoned, paralysis, or asleep status condition on an attacker if the attacker hits the Pokémon with a move that makes direct contact. Grass-type Pokémon are immune to this effect.	—

Ability	Effects in battle	Effects outside of battle
Electric Surge	Triggers Electric Terrain when the Pokémon enters the battlefield. This terrain lasts for 5 turns.	—
Emergency Exit	Causes the Pokémon to automatically switch out of battle when its HP drops to 1/2 or less during a Trainer battle. During a battle with a wild Pokémon, the Pokémon flees when its HP drops to 1/2 or less. This Ability still triggers for Dynamax Pokémon but uses their Dynamax HP as the starting number instead. Does not trigger in Max Raid Battles.	—
Filter	Reduces the damage the Pokémon takes from supereffective moves by 25%.	—
Flame Body	Provides a 30% chance of inflicting the burned status condition on an attacker if the attacker hits the Pokémon with a move that makes direct contact.	Halves the time it takes for Pokémon Eggs to hatch if a Pokémon in your party has this Ability. This effect is not increased by also having other Pokémon with Flame Body or Steam Engine in your party.
Flare Boost	Boosts the power of the Pokémon's special moves by 50% when the Pokémon has the burned status condition.	—
Flash Fire	Absorbs Fire-type moves, making the Pokémon immune to their damage and effects. Also boosts the power of the Pokémon's Fire-type moves by 50% the first time this is triggered in battle.	Makes it more likely you will encounter wild Fire-type Pokémon if your lead Pokémon has this Ability.
Flower Gift	Raises the Pokémon's and the Pokémon's allies' Attack and Sp. Def by 50% each in the harsh sunlight weather condition. Causes Cherrim to change to its Sunshine Form in the harsh sunlight weather condition.	—
Fluffy	Halves the damage the Pokémon takes from moves that make direct contact. Doubles the damage the Pokémon takes from Fire-type moves.	—
Forewarn	Reveals a move an opponent knows when the Pokémon with this Ability enters the battlefield. Damage-dealing moves with high power are prioritized.	—
Friend Guard	Reduces the damage taken by the Pokémon's allies by 25%.	—
Frisk	Identifies opponents' held items when the Pokémon with this Ability enters the battlefield.	—
Gluttony	Held Berries that are normally eaten at very low HP will instead be eaten when the Pokémon's HP drops to 1/2 or less.	—
Gooey	Lowers the Speed of an attacker by 1 stage if the attacker hits the Pokémon with a move that makes direct contact.	—
Gorilla Tactics	Raises the Pokémon's Attack by 1 stage, but the Pokémon can only use the first move it chooses when it enters the battlefield.	—
Gulp Missile	Allows the Pokémon to gulp up prey and change forms when it uses Surf or Dive. If the Pokémon's HP is more than 1/2 of its maximum, the Pokémon will catch an Arrokuda. If the Pokémon's HP is 1/2 of its maximum or below, the Pokémon will catch a Pikachu. When the Pokémon takes damage from an opponent, it will spit out its prey to damage the opponent and also trigger additional effects (Arrokuda: lowers opponent's Defense by 1 stage; Pikachu: inflicts paralysis status condition on the opponent).	—
Guts	Raises the Pokémon's Attack by 50% when the Pokémon is affected by a status condition. Although the burned status condition would usually lower the Pokémon's Attack, the Guts Ability prevents this.	—
Harvest	Provides a 50% chance of restoring one of the Pokémon's used Berries at the end of each turn. This becomes guaranteed in the harsh sunlight weather condition.	Makes it more likely you will encounter wild Grass-type Pokémon if your lead Pokémon has this Ability.
Healer	Provides a 30% chance that an ally Pokémon's status condition will be healed at the end of each turn.	—
Heatproof	Halves the damage the Pokémon takes from Fire-type moves and from the burned status condition.	—
Heavy Metal	Doubles the Pokémon's weight.	—
Honey Gather	Has no effect.	If the Pokémon has no held item, it sometimes finds a jar of Honey after a battle (even if it didn't participate). The chance of finding Honey increases with the Pokémon's level.
Huge Power	Doubles the Pokémon's Attack.	—
Hunger Switch	Causes the Pokémon to change form at the end of each turn, rotating between Full Belly Mode and Hangry Mode.	—
Hustle	Raises the Pokémon's Attack by 50% but lowers the accuracy of the Pokémon's physical moves by 20%.	—
Hydration	Heals the Pokémon's status conditions at the end of each turn in the rain weather condition.	—
Hyper Cutter	Protects the Pokémon from having its Attack lowered by the moves or Abilities of other Pokémon.	—
Ice Body	Restores 1/16 of the Pokémon's max HP at the end of each turn in the hail weather condition. Hail does not damage a Pokémon with this Ability.	—
Ice Face	Protects the Pokémon from damage the first time the Pokémon is hit by a physical move. Then the Pokémon's form changes from Ice Face to Noice Face. Does not protect from special moves. The Pokémon can return to its Ice Face form if the weather condition becomes hail, if it's sent out into battle during hail, or when the battle ends, allowing this Ability to be triggered again.	—
Ice Scales	Halves the damage the Pokémon takes from special moves.	—
Illuminate	Has no effect.	Makes it more likely you will encounter wild Pokémon if your lead Pokémon has this Ability.
Immunity	Protects the Pokémon from the poisoned and badly poisoned status conditions.	—
Imposter	Transforms the Pokémon into a copy of the opponent it is directly facing when it enters the battlefield.	—
Infiltrator	Allows the Pokémon's moves to hit despite Mist, Safeguard, or Substitute. Also prevents damage from being reduced by Aurora Veil, Light Screen, or Reflect.	Makes it less likely you will encounter wild Pokémon if your lead Pokémon has this Ability.
Innards Out	Causes damage to an attacker if the Pokémon with this Ability is knocked out. The attacker's HP is reduced by the same amount of HP as the attacked Pokémon had left before it was knocked out.	—
Inner Focus	Protects the Pokémon from flinching and from the effects of the Intimidate Ability.	—

Ability	Effects in battle	Effects outside of battle
Insomnia	Protects the Pokémon from the asleep status condition.	—
Intimidate	Lowers opponents' Attack by 1 stage when the Pokémon with this Ability enters the battlefield.	—
Intrepid Sword	Raises the Pokémon's Attack by 1 stage when the Pokémon enters the battlefield.	—
Iron Barbs	Causes damage to an attacker equal to 1/8 of its max HP if the attacker hits the Pokémon with a move that makes direct contact.	—
Iron Fist	Boosts the power of the Pokémon's punching moves by 20%. This affects Bullet Punch, Drain Punch, Dynamic Punch, Fire Punch, Focus Punch, Hammer Arm, Ice Punch, Mach Punch, Mega Punch, Meteor Mash, Power-Up Punch, Shadow Punch, and Thunder Punch.	—
Justified	Raises the Pokémon's Attack by 1 stage when the Pokémon is hit by a damage-dealing Dark-type move.	—
Keen Eye	Protects the Pokémon from having its accuracy lowered by opponents' moves. Ignores the effects of opponents' evasiveness-raising moves as well.	—
Klutz	The Pokémon can't use held items in battle, even if it is given an item to hold.	—
Leaf Guard	Protects the Pokémon from status conditions in the harsh sunlight weather condition.	—
Levitate	Gives the Pokémon immunity to damage-dealing Ground-type moves, as well as the effects of Spikes, Sticky Web, Toxic Spikes, and terrains.	—
Light Metal	Halves the Pokémon's weight.	—
Lightning Rod	Draws all Electric-type moves to the Pokémon. Absorbs Electric-type moves, making the Pokémon immune to their damage and effects. Instead, such moves raise the Pokémon's Sp. Atk by 1 stage.	Makes it more likely you will encounter wild Electric-type Pokémon if your lead Pokémon has this Ability.
Limber	Protects the Pokémon from the paralysis status condition.	—
Magic Bounce	Reflects back moves that attempt to lower the Pokémon's stats or inflict status conditions, as well as the effects of moves like Stealth Rock or Taunt.	—
Magic Guard	Protects the Pokémon from any damage not directly dealt by a move. This nullifies the damage from Abilities, weather conditions, status conditions, items, and ongoing move effects (such as Bind or Spikes).	—
Marvel Scale	Raises the Pokémon's Defense by 50% when the Pokémon has a status condition.	—
Merciless	Guarantees that the Pokémon's moves will deliver critical hits as long as the target has the poisoned or badly poisoned status condition.	—
Mimicry	Changes the Pokémon's type depending on the terrain. Electric Terrain: Changes to Electric type. Grassy Terrain: Changes to Grass type. Misty Terrain: Changes to Fairy type. Psychic Terrain: Changes to Psychic type. If the terrain returns to normal, the Pokémon also returns to its regular type.	—
Minus	Raises the Pokémon's Sp. Atk by 50% if an ally has either the Plus or Minus Ability.	—
Mirror Armor	Reflects back any attempt to lower the Pokémon's stats. This does not prevent damage from moves, but additional effects from moves like Breaking Swipe, Mud-Slap, or Psychic are applied to the move's user instead.	—
Misty Surge	Triggers Misty Terrain when the Pokémon enters the battlefield. This terrain lasts for 5 turns.	—
Mold Breaker	Makes the Pokémon's moves ignore the effects of Abilities. For example, Earthquake will hit even Pokémon with the Levitate Ability. Does not nullify Abilities that have effects after a move lands.	—
Moody	Raises one stat by 2 stages and lowers another by 1 stage at the end of each turn. When selecting a stat to raise, this Ability will not select a stat that cannot be raised any higher. The same applies when selecting a stat to lower.	—
Moxie	Raises the Pokémon's Attack by 1 stage when the Pokémon uses a move that knocks out another Pokémon.	—
Mummy	Changes an attacker's Ability if the attacker hits the Pokémon with a move that makes direct contact. That attacker's Ability becomes Mummy. Fails with certain Abilities, however.	—
Natural Cure	Heals the Pokémon's status conditions when the Pokémon is switched out of battle.	—
Neutralizing Gas	Nullifies the Abilities of all other Pokémon on the battlefield and prevents them from being activated. Fails with certain Abilities, however.	—
No Guard	Moves used by or against the Pokémon don't miss.	Makes it more likely you will encounter wild Pokémon if your lead Pokémon has this Ability.
Oblivious	Protects the Pokémon from infatuation, as well as the effects of Taunt and the Intimidate Ability.	—
Overcoat	Protects the Pokémon from taking damage in the hail and sandstorm weather conditions. Also protects it from Cotton Spore, Magic Powder, Poison Powder, Rage Powder, Sleep Powder, Spore, and Stun Spore, as well as the Effect Spore Ability.	—
Overgrow	Boosts the power of the Pokémon's Grass-type moves by 50% when the Pokémon's HP drops to 1/3 or less.	—
Own Tempo	Protects the Pokémon from confusion and from the effects of the Intimidate Ability.	—
Pastel Veil	Protects the Pokémon's side of the battlefield from the poisoned and badly poisoned status conditions.	—
Perish Body	If the Pokémon is hit by a move that makes direct contact, both the Pokémon and the attacker will faint after 3 turns unless switched out.	—
Pickpocket	Allows the Pokémon to steal an attacker's held item if the attacker hits the Pokémon with a move that makes direct contact. If the Pokémon is already holding an item, nothing happens.	—
Pickup	Allows the Pokémon to pick up a held item that an opposing Pokémon used in the same turn. If the Pokémon with this Ability is already holding an item, nothing happens.	If the Pokémon has no held item, it sometimes picks one up after a battle (even if it didn't participate). It picks up different items depending on its level.
Pixilate	Changes the Pokémon's Normal-type moves to Fairy type and boosts their power by 20%. This effect also applies to Max Moves. (Max Strike will become the Fairy-type Max Move, Max Starfall.)	—
Plus	Raises the Pokémon's Sp. Atk by 50% if an ally has either the Plus or Minus Ability.	—
Poison Point	Provides a 30% chance of inflicting the poisoned status condition on an attacker if the attacker hits the Pokémon with a move that makes direct contact.	—

Ability	Effects in battle	Effects outside of battle
Poison Touch	Provides a 30% chance of inflicting the poisoned status condition on a target if the Pokémon with this Ability hits the target with a move that makes direct contact.	—
Power Spot	Boosts the power of moves used by the adjacent Pokémon by 30%.	—
Prankster	Gives higher priority to the Pokémon's status moves. A move affected by this Ability will fail if the target is a Dark-type Pokémon.	—
Pressure	When the Pokémon is targeted by an opponent's move, this Ability causes that move to lose an extra point from its PP.	—
Propeller Tail	Allows the Pokémon to ignore the effects of the Lightning Rod and Storm Drain Abilities, as well as the Ally Switch, Follow Me, and Rage Powder moves.	—
Psychic Surge	Triggers Psychic Terrain when the Pokémon enters the battlefield. This terrain lasts for 5 turns.	—
Punk Rock	Boosts the power of the Pokémon's sound-based moves, such as Boomburst and Overdrive, by 30%. Also halves the damage the Pokémon takes from sound-based moves.	—
Queenly Majesty	Prevents opposing Pokémon from using damage-dealing moves that have high priority.	—
Quick Feet	Raises the Pokémon's Speed by 50% when the Pokémon has a status condition. Although the paralysis status condition would usually lower the Pokémon's Speed, the Quick Feet Ability prevents this.	Makes it less likely you will encounter wild Pokémon if your lead Pokémon has this Ability.
Rain Dish	Restores 1/16 of the Pokémon's max HP at the end of each turn in the rain weather condition.	—
Rattled	Raises the Pokémon's Speed by 1 stage when the Pokémon is hit by a damage-dealing Bug-, Ghost-, or Dark-type move or the Intimidate Ability.	—
Receiver	Copies the Ability of a defeated ally over to the Pokémon, replacing Receiver with that Ability. Fails with certain Abilities, however.	—
Reckless	Boosts the power of any of the Pokémon's moves by 20% if those moves cause recoil damage.	—
Regenerator	Restores 1/3 of the Pokémon's max HP when the Pokémon is switched out of battle.	—
Ripen	Doubles the effect of Berries eaten by the Pokémon. Doubles healing effects, damage reduction, stat changes, friendship gains, and damage dealt to an opponent. Has no effect on Berries that heal status conditions.	—
Rivalry	Boosts the power of the Pokémon's moves by 25% if they are used against a target of the same gender as the Pokémon. If a target is of the opposite gender, moves' power goes down by 25%. No effect when the target's gender is unknown.	—
RKS System	Causes the Pokémon to change its type according to the memory disc it is holding.	—
Rock Head	Protects the Pokémon from recoil damage from moves like Double-Edge and Take Down.	—
Run Away	Allows the Pokémon to always escape from a battle with a wild Pokémon.	—
Sand Force	Boosts the power of the Pokémon's Ground-, Rock-, and Steel-type moves by 30% in the sandstorm weather condition. Sandstorms do not damage a Pokémon with this Ability.	—
Sand Rush	Doubles the Pokémon's Speed in the sandstorm weather condition. Sandstorms do not damage a Pokémon with this Ability.	—
Sand Spit	Triggers the sandstorm weather condition when the Pokémon takes damage. This weather condition lasts for 5 turns.	—
Sand Stream	Triggers the sandstorm weather condition when the Pokémon enters the battlefield. This weather condition lasts for 5 turns.	—
Sand Veil	Lowers the accuracy of moves used on the Pokémon by 20% in the sandstorm weather condition. Sandstorms do not damage a Pokémon with this Ability.	—
Sap Sipper	Absorbs Grass-type moves, making the Pokémon immune to their damage and effects. Instead, such moves raise the Pokémon's Attack by 1 stage.	—
Schooling	Causes the Pokémon to change to its School Form if its level is 20 or greater. It changes back to its Solo Form when its HP drops to 1/4 or less.	—
Scrappy	Allows the Pokémon to hit Ghost-type Pokémon with Normal- and Fighting-type moves. Also protects the Pokémon from the effects of the Intimidate Ability.	—
Screen Cleaner	Nullifies the effects of Aurora Veil, Light Screen, and Reflect for both sides of the battlefield when the Pokémon enters the battlefield.	—
Serene Grace	Doubles the chances of the Pokémon's moves inflicting additional effects.	—
Shadow Tag	Prevents opposing Pokémon from fleeing or switching out. This effect is canceled if an opposing Pokémon also has this Ability.	—
Shed Skin	Provides a 33% chance of healing the Pokémon's status conditions at the end of each turn.	—
Sheer Force	Boosts the power of the Pokémon's moves by 30% if they can have additional effects. However, the additional effects do not trigger.	—
Shell Armor	Prevents opponents' damage-dealing moves from ever delivering a critical hit to the Pokémon.	—
Shield Dust	Protects the Pokémon from the additional effects of moves. However, the Pokémon is still affected by additional effects generated by Max Moves.	—
Simple	Doubles any stat changes affecting the Pokémon.	—
Skill Link	Ensures that the Pokémon's multihit moves always hit the maximum number of times. (Moves that can hit 2–5 times always hit 5 times.)	—
Slush Rush	Doubles the Pokémon's Speed in the hail weather condition. Hail does not damage a Pokémon with this Ability.	—
Sniper	Boosts the power of the Pokémon's critical hits. Power increases by 125% rather than the usual 50%.	—
Snow Cloak	Lowers the accuracy of moves used on the Pokémon by 20% in the hail weather condition. Hail does not damage a Pokémon with this Ability.	—
Snow Warning	Triggers the hail weather condition when the Pokémon enters the battlefield. This weather condition lasts for 5 turns.	—
Solar Power	Raises the Pokémon's Sp. Atk by 50% in the harsh sunlight weather condition. But the Pokémon also loses 1/8 of its max HP at the end of each turn as long as that weather condition continues.	—
Solid Rock	Reduces the damage the Pokémon takes from supereffective moves by 25%.	—
Soundproof	Protects the Pokémon from sound-based moves, such as Clanging Scales and Parting Shot.	—

Ability	Effects in battle	Effects outside of battle
Speed Boost	Raises the Pokémon's Speed by 1 stage at the end of each turn.	—
Stall	Causes the Pokémon to move last each turn.	—
Stalwart	Allows the Pokémon to ignore the effects of the Lightning Rod and Storm Drain Abilities, as well as the Ally Switch, Follow Me, and Rage Powder moves.	—
Stamina	Raises the Pokémon's Defense by 1 stage every time the Pokémon takes damage from a move.	—
Stance Change	Causes the Pokémon to change from its Shield Forme to its Blade Forme when using a damage-dealing move. The Pokémon changes back to Shield Forme if King's Shield is used.	—
Static	Provides a 30% chance of inflicting the paralysis status condition on an attacker if the attacker hits the Pokémon with a move that makes direct contact.	Makes it more likely you will encounter wild Electric-type Pokémon if your lead Pokémon has this Ability.
Steadfast	Raises the Pokémon's Speed by 1 stage every time the Pokémon flinches.	—
Steam Engine	Raises the Pokémon's Speed to the max if the Pokémon is hit by a Fire- or Water-type move.	Halves the time it takes for Pokémon Eggs to hatch if a Pokémon in your party has this Ability. This effect is not increased by also having other Pokémon with Flame Body or Steam Engine in your party.
Steelworker	Boosts the power of the Pokémon's Steel-type moves by 50%.	—
Steely Spirit	Boosts the power of Steel-type moves for the Pokémon and its allies by 50%.	—
Stench	Provides a 10% chance of making targets flinch when the Pokémon hits them with a damage-dealing move.	Makes it less likely you will encounter wild Pokémon if your lead Pokémon has this Ability.
Sticky Hold	Prevents the Pokémon's held item from being removed by other Pokémon's moves or Abilities.	—
Storm Drain	Draws all Water-type moves to the Pokémon. Absorbs Water-type moves, making the Pokémon immune to their damage and effects. Instead, such moves raise the Pokémon's Sp. Atk by 1 stage.	Makes it more likely you will encounter wild Water-type Pokémon if your lead Pokémon has this Ability.
Strong Jaw	Boosts the power of Bite, Crunch, Fire Fang, Fishious Rend, Ice Fang, Jaw Lock, Poison Fang, Psychic Fangs, and Thunder Fang by 50%.	—
Sturdy	Protects the Pokémon from one-hit knockout moves, like Horn Drill and Sheer Cold. If the Pokémon's HP is full, this Ability also leaves the Pokémon with 1 HP if the Pokémon is hit by a move that would normally knock it out.	—
Suction Cups	Protects the Pokémon from being switched out by moves like Dragon Tail, Roar, and Whirlwind and items like Red Card.	—
Super Luck	Makes the Pokémon's moves more likely to deliver a critical hit.	Makes it more likely that the wild Pokémon you encounter will be holding items if your lead Pokémon has this Ability.
Swarm	Boosts the power of the Pokémon's Bug-type moves by 50% when the Pokémon's HP drops to 1/3 or less.	—
Sweet Veil	Protects the Pokémon's side of the battlefield from the asleep status condition.	—
Swift Swim	Doubles the Pokémon's Speed in the rain weather condition.	—
Symbiosis	Causes the Pokémon to give its held item to an ally if that ally uses its own held item.	—
Synchronize	Shares the Pokémon's status conditions. If the Pokémon is inflicted with the poisoned, badly poisoned, paralysis, or burned status condition, the Pokémon that caused the status condition is also afflicted with it.	Guarantees that the wild Pokémon you encounter will have the same Nature as your lead Pokémon if your lead Pokémon has this Ability.
Tangled Feet	Lowers the accuracy of moves used on the Pokémon by 50% if the Pokémon with this Ability is confused.	—
Technician	Boosts the power of the Pokémon's moves by 50% if their power is 60 or less. This effect is triggered for moves of variable power or moves affected by other factors as long as an individual move's power ends up being 60 or less.	—
Telepathy	Prevents the Pokémon from taking damage from allies.	—
Thick Fat	Halves the damage the Pokémon takes from Fire- and Ice-type moves.	—
Tinted Lens	Makes the Pokémon's moves more effective against Pokémon that have a type advantage. (Half damage turns into regular damage, and 1/4 damage turns into half damage.)	—
Torrent	Boosts the power of the Pokémon's Water-type moves by 50% when the Pokémon's HP drops to 1/3 or less.	—
Tough Claws	Boosts the power of the Pokémon's moves by 30% if those moves make direct contact.	—
Trace	Makes the Pokémon's Ability the same as the opponent's. Fails with certain Abilities, however. When the Pokémon is faced with multiple opponents, the Ability of one is chosen at random.	—
Truant	Causes the Pokémon to slack off, making its moves fail every other turn.	—
Unaware	When the Pokémon uses or is the target of a damage-dealing move, the move ignores changes to all opponents' stats except Speed.	—
Unburden	Doubles the Pokémon's Speed if the Pokémon loses or consumes a held item. Its Speed returns to normal if the Pokémon gains a held item again. This Ability has no effect if the Pokémon starts the battle with no held item.	—
Unnerve	Prevents opposing Pokémon from eating Berries they hold.	—
Vital Spirit	Protects the Pokémon from the asleep status condition.	—
Volt Absorb	Absorbs Electric-type moves, making the Pokémon immune to their damage and effects. Instead, such moves restore 1/4 of the Pokémon's max HP.	—
Wandering Spirit	Exchanges the Pokémon's Ability with an attacker's if the attacker hits the Pokémon with a move that makes direct contact. Fails with certain Abilities, however.	—
Water Absorb	Absorbs Water-type moves, making the Pokémon immune to their damage and effects. Instead, such moves restore 1/4 of the Pokémon's max HP.	—

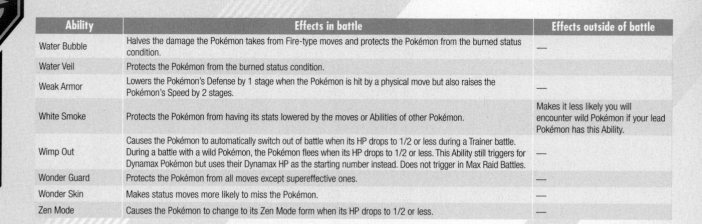

Ability	Effects in battle	Effects outside of battle
Water Bubble	Halves the damage the Pokémon takes from Fire-type moves and protects the Pokémon from the burned status condition.	—
Water Veil	Protects the Pokémon from the burned status condition.	
Weak Armor	Lowers the Pokémon's Defense by 1 stage when the Pokémon is hit by a physical move but also raises the Pokémon's Speed by 2 stages.	—
White Smoke	Protects the Pokémon from having its stats lowered by the moves or Abilities of other Pokémon.	Makes it less likely you will encounter wild Pokémon if your lead Pokémon has this Ability.
Wimp Out	Causes the Pokémon to automatically switch out of battle when its HP drops to 1/2 or less during a Trainer battle. During a battle with a wild Pokémon, the Pokémon flees when its HP drops to 1/2 or less. This Ability still triggers for Dynamax Pokémon but uses their Dynamax HP as the starting number instead. Does not trigger in Max Raid Battles.	—
Wonder Guard	Protects the Pokémon from all moves except supereffective ones.	—
Wonder Skin	Makes status moves more likely to miss the Pokémon.	—
Zen Mode	Causes the Pokémon to change to its Zen Mode form when its HP drops to 1/2 or less.	—

Items Picked Up with the Pickup Ability

The Pickup Ability is a rather handy and interesting Ability to have on your team! A Pokémon with the Pickup Ability sometimes picks up items after a battle ends if they're not already holding an item—even if they didn't take part in the battle themselves! Some of the items they can find are quite rare or valuable, too! If you have a Pokémon with the Pickup Ability, like Zigzagoon or Meowth, be sure to check on it often to see if it's got anything and relieve it of its burden so it'll be ready to find new treasures! The kinds of items it may find will change based on its level, as you can see in the table below.

	Level of Pokémon with the Pickup Ability									
Item	Low									High
Potion	◎									
Tiny Mushroom	○	△								
Repel	△	○								
Super Potion	△	△	○							
Poké Doll	△	△	△	○						
Big Mushroom	☆	△	△							
Super Repel	☆	△	△	△	○					
Full Heal	☆	☆	△	△	△	○				
Revive	☆	☆	☆	△	△	△	○			
Hyper Potion	☆	☆	☆	☆	△	△	△	○		
Ether	★	★	☆	☆	☆					
Max Repel		☆	☆	☆	☆	△	△	△	○	
Moon Stone		☆	☆	☆	☆	☆	☆	☆	△	△
Sun Stone		☆	☆	☆	☆	☆	☆	☆	△	△
Rare Candy		★	★	★	★	☆	☆	☆	☆	☆
Nugget			☆	☆	☆	☆	☆	☆	☆	☆
Max Potion			☆	☆	☆	☆	△	△	△	○
Max Ether			★	★	☆	☆	☆			
PP Up			★	★	★	☆	☆	☆	☆	☆
Big Nugget			★	★	★	★	☆	☆	☆	△
Destiny Knot			★	★	★	★	★	★	★	★
Leftovers			★	★	★	★	★	★	★	★
Mental Herb			★	★	★	★	★	★	★	★
Power Herb			★	★	★	★	★	★	★	★
White Herb			★	★	★	★	★	★	★	★
Balm Mushroom			★	☆	☆	☆	☆	☆	☆	☆
Max Revive				☆	☆	☆	☆	△	△	△
Elixir					★	★	☆	☆	☆	☆
Max Elixir							★	★	☆	☆
Bottle Cap								★	★	★

Very common ◎ > ○ > △ > ☆ > ★ very rare

Natures

Every Pokémon has an innate Nature, which affects how it will react to certain things. This Nature generally makes one of its stats grow more quickly than usual, while another stat will grow slower than usual (p. 173). You can see which stats are affected by each Nature in the table below.

If the Nature your Pokémon started out with isn't helping your Pokémon grow strong in a stat you want, you can help by using a special mint item, like a Jolly Mint or a Modest Mint. You can get these sprigs of mint at the Battle Tower, and they'll change which of your Pokémon's stats get boosted or reduced, just as if your Pokémon had the Nature in that mint's name all along!

Natures can also affect which of the five flavors—Spicy, Dry, Sweet, Bitter, and Sour—are liked and disliked by each Pokémon. When consumed during battle, some healing Berries can confuse Pokémon that don't like their flavor, so this is well worth keeping in mind! Study up on Berry flavors on p. 291, and take note of your Pokémon's Nature when giving them one of these Berries to use.

Nature	Increased stat	Decreased stat	Disliked flavor
Adamant	Attack	Sp. Atk	Dry
Bashful	—	—	—
Bold	Defense	Attack	Spicy
Brave	Attack	Speed	Sweet
Calm	Sp. Def	Attack	Spicy
Careful	Sp. Def	Sp. Atk	Dry
Docile	—	—	—
Gentle	Sp. Def	Defense	Sour
Hardy	—	—	—
Hasty	Speed	Defense	Sour
Impish	Defense	Sp. Atk	Dry
Jolly	Speed	Sp. Atk	Dry
Lax	Defense	Sp. Def	Bitter

Nature	Increased stat	Decreased stat	Disliked flavor
Lonely	Attack	Defense	Sour
Mild	Sp. Atk	Defense	Sour
Modest	Sp. Atk	Attack	Spicy
Naive	Speed	Sp. Def	Bitter
Naughty	Attack	Sp. Def	Bitter
Quiet	Sp. Atk	Speed	Sweet
Quirky	—	—	—
Rash	Sp. Atk	Sp. Def	Bitter
Relaxed	Defense	Speed	Sweet
Sassy	Sp. Def	Speed	Sweet
Serious	—	—	—
Timid	Speed	Attack	Spicy

Characteristics

Each Pokémon also has a characteristic that you can see when you check its summary. Unlike Natures, these characteristics don't have a direct impact on your Pokémon's stats. Instead, they simply give you a clue as to which of your Pokémon's stats might have the highest individual strength. See the table below to get a better idea what each might be telling you!

Stat that grows easily	Characteristic				
HP	Likes to relax	Loves to eat	Nods off a lot	Scatters things often	Takes plenty of siestas
Attack	A little quick tempered	Likes to fight	Likes to thrash about	Proud of its power	Quick tempered
Defense	Capable of taking hits	Good endurance	Good perseverance	Highly persistent	Sturdy body
Sp. Atk	Highly curious	Mischievous	Often lost in thought	Thoroughly cunning	Very finicky
Sp. Def	Hates to lose	Somewhat stubborn	Somewhat vain	Strong willed	Strongly defiant
Speed	Alert to sounds	Impetuous and silly	Likes to run	Quick to flee	Somewhat of a clown

Base Points for Battling Wild Pokémon

When you battle and defeat or catch a wild Pokémon, the Pokémon in your party don't only earn Exp. Points, they also earn one or a few base points for their stats. Which stats those base points apply to is determined by the wild Pokémon's species. Check the table below to see which base points your Pokémon can earn from each of the species you can battle in the Galar region. When a Pokémon has ○ beneath a stat, that means your Pokémon will get some base points for that stat if you defeat or catch it. If the Pokémon has ◎, it will award even more base points for that stat. So look for those marks if you want to get the most base points you can from wild Pokémon encounters!

Dex No.	Name	HP	Atk.	Def.	Sp. Atk	Sp. Def	Speed
010	Blipbug	—	—	—	—	○	—
011	Dottler	—	—	—	—	○	—
012	Orbeetle	—	—	—	—	◎	—
013	Caterpie	○	—	—	—	—	—
014	Metapod	—	—	○	—	—	—
015	Butterfree	—	—	—	○	○	—
016	Grubbin	—	○	—	—	—	—
017	Charjabug	—	—	○	—	—	—
018	Vikavolt	—	—	—	◎	—	—
019	Hoothoot	○	—	—	—	—	—
020	Noctowl	○	—	—	—	—	—
021	Rookidee	—	—	—	—	—	○
022	Corvisquire	—	—	—	—	—	○
023	Corviknight	—	—	◎	—	—	—
024	Skwovet	○	—	—	—	—	—
025	Greedent	○	—	—	—	—	—
026	Pidove	—	○	—	—	—	—
027	Tranquill	—	○	—	—	—	—
028	Unfezant	—	◎	—	—	—	—
029	Nickit	—	—	—	—	○	—
030	Thievul	—	—	—	—	○	—
031	Zigzagoon	—	—	—	—	—	○
032	Linoone	—	—	—	—	—	○
033	Obstagoon	—	—	◎	—	—	—
034	Wooloo	—	—	○	—	—	—
035	Dubwool	—	—	○	—	—	—
036	Lotad	—	—	—	—	○	—
037	Lombre	—	—	—	—	○	—
038	Ludicolo	—	—	—	—	◎	—
039	Seedot	—	—	○	—	—	—
040	Nuzleaf	—	○	—	—	—	—
041	Shiftry	—	◎	—	—	—	—
042	Chewtle	—	○	—	—	—	—
043	Drednaw	—	○	—	—	—	—
044	Purrloin	—	—	—	—	—	○
045	Liepard	—	—	—	—	—	○
046	Yamper	○	—	—	—	—	—
047	Boltund	—	—	—	—	—	○
048	Bunnelby	—	—	—	—	—	○
049	Diggersby	○	—	—	—	—	—
050	Minccino	—	—	—	—	—	○
051	Cinccino	—	—	—	—	—	○
052	Bounsweet	○	—	—	—	—	—
053	Steenee	—	—	—	—	—	○
054	Tsareena	—	◎	—	—	—	—
055	Oddish	—	—	—	○	—	—
056	Gloom	—	—	—	○	—	—
057	Vileplume	—	—	—	◎	—	—
058	Bellossom	—	—	—	—	◎	—
059	Budew	—	—	—	○	—	—
060	Roselia	—	—	—	○	—	—
061	Roserade	—	—	—	◎	—	—
062	Wingull	—	—	—	—	—	○
063	Pelipper	—	—	○	—	—	—
064	Joltik	—	—	—	—	—	○
065	Galvantula	—	—	—	—	—	○
066	Electrike	—	—	—	—	—	○
067	Manectric	—	—	—	—	—	○
068	Vulpix	—	—	—	—	—	○
069	Ninetales	—	—	—	—	○	○
070	Growlithe	—	○	—	—	—	—
071	Arcanine	—	○	—	—	—	—
072	Vanillite	—	—	—	○	—	—
073	Vanillish	—	—	—	○	—	—
074	Vanilluxe	—	—	—	◎	—	—
075	Swinub	—	○	—	—	—	—
076	Piloswine	○	○	—	—	—	—
077	Mamoswine	—	◎	—	—	—	—
078	Delibird	—	—	—	—	—	○
079	Snorunt	○	—	—	—	—	—
080	Glalie	○	—	—	—	—	—
081	Froslass	—	—	—	—	—	○
082	Baltoy	—	—	—	—	○	—
083	Claydol	—	—	—	—	○	—
084	Mudbray	—	○	—	—	—	—
085	Mudsdale	—	○	—	—	—	—
086	Dwebble	—	—	○	—	—	—
087	Crustle	—	—	○	—	—	—
088	Golett	—	○	—	—	—	—
089	Golurk	—	○	—	—	—	—
090	Munna	○	—	—	—	—	—
091	Musharna	○	—	—	—	—	—
092	Natu	—	—	—	○	—	—
093	Xatu	—	—	—	○	—	○
094	Stufful	—	○	—	—	—	—
095	Bewear	—	○	—	—	—	—
096	Snover	—	○	—	—	—	—
097	Abomasnow	—	○	—	○	—	—

Dex No.	Name	HP	Atk.	Def.	Sp. Atk	Sp. Def	Speed
098	Krabby	—	○	—	—	—	—
099	Kingler	—	○	—	—	—	—
100	Wooper	○	—	—	—	—	—
101	Quagsire	○	—	—	—	—	—
102	Corphish	—	○	—	—	—	—
103	Crawdaunt	—	○	—	—	—	—
104	Nincada	—	—	○	—	—	—
105	Ninjask	—	—	—	—	—	○
106	Shedinja	○	—	—	—	—	—
107	Tyrogue	—	○	—	—	—	—
108	Hitmonlee	—	○	—	—	—	—
109	Hitmonchan	—	—	—	—	○	—
110	Hitmontop	—	—	—	—	○	—
111	Pancham	—	○	—	—	—	—
112	Pangoro	—	○	—	—	—	—
113	Klink	—	—	○	—	—	—
114	Klang	—	—	○	—	—	—
115	Klinklang	—	—	◎	—	—	—
116	Combee	—	—	—	—	—	○
117	Vespiquen	—	—	○	—	○	—
118	Bronzor	—	—	○	—	—	—
119	Bronzong	—	—	○	—	○	—
120	Ralts	—	—	—	○	—	—
121	Kirlia	—	—	—	○	—	—
122	Gardevoir	—	—	—	◎	—	—
123	Gallade	—	◎	—	—	—	—
124	Drifloon	○	—	—	—	—	—
125	Drifblim	○	—	—	—	—	—
126	Gossifleur	—	—	—	—	○	—
127	Eldegoss	—	—	—	—	○	—
128	Cherubi	—	—	—	○	—	—
129	Cherrim	—	—	—	○	—	—
130	Stunky	—	—	—	—	—	○
131	Skuntank	○	—	—	—	—	—
132	Tympole	—	—	—	—	—	○
133	Palpitoad	○	—	—	—	—	—
134	Seismitoad	◎	—	—	—	—	—
135	Duskull	—	—	—	—	○	—
136	Dusclops	—	—	○	—	○	—
137	Dusknoir	—	—	○	—	○	—
138	Machop	—	○	—	—	—	—
139	Machoke	—	○	—	—	—	—
140	Machamp	—	◎	—	—	—	—
141	Gastly	—	—	—	○	—	—
142	Haunter	—	—	—	○	—	—
143	Gengar	—	—	—	◎	—	—
144	Magikarp	—	—	—	—	—	○
145	Gyarados	—	○	—	—	—	—
146	Goldeen	—	○	—	—	—	—
147	Seaking	—	○	—	—	—	—
148	Remoraid	—	—	—	○	—	—
149	Octillery	—	○	—	○	—	—
150	Shellder	—	—	○	—	—	—
151	Cloyster	—	—	○	—	—	—

Dex No.	Name	HP	Atk.	Def.	Sp. Atk	Sp. Def	Speed
152	Feebas	—	—	—	—	—	○
153	Milotic	—	—	—	—	○	—
154	Basculin	—	—	—	—	—	○
155	Wishiwashi	○	—	—	—	—	—
156	Pyukumuku	—	—	—	—	○	—
157	Trubbish	—	—	—	—	—	○
158	Garbodor	—	○	—	—	—	—
159	Sizzlipede	—	○	—	—	—	—
160	Centiskorch	—	○	—	—	—	—
161	Rolycoly	—	—	○	—	—	—
162	Carkol	—	—	○	—	—	—
163	Coalossal	—	—	◎	—	—	—
164	Diglett	—	—	—	—	—	○
165	Dugtrio	—	—	—	—	—	○
166	Drilbur	—	○	—	—	—	—
167	Excadrill	—	○	—	—	—	—
168	Roggenrola	—	—	○	—	—	—
169	Boldore	—	○	○	—	—	—
170	Gigalith	—	◎	—	—	—	—
171	Timburr	—	○	—	—	—	—
172	Gurdurr	—	○	—	—	—	—
173	Conkeldurr	—	◎	—	—	—	—
174	Woobat	—	—	—	—	—	○
175	Swoobat	—	—	—	—	—	○
176	Noibat	—	—	—	—	—	○
177	Noivern	—	—	—	—	—	○
178	Onix	—	—	○	—	—	—
179	Steelix	—	—	○	—	—	—
180	Arrokuda	—	—	—	—	—	○
181	Barraskewda	—	—	—	—	—	○
182	Meowth	—	—	—	—	—	○
183	Perrserker	—	○	—	—	—	—
185	Milcery	—	—	—	—	○	—
186	Alcremie	—	—	—	—	○	—
187	Cutiefly	—	—	—	—	—	○
188	Ribombee	—	—	—	—	—	○
189	Ferroseed	—	—	○	—	—	—
190	Ferrothorn	—	—	○	—	—	—
191	Pumpkaboo	—	—	○	—	—	—
192	Gourgeist	—	—	○	—	—	—
193	Pichu	—	—	—	—	—	○
194	Pikachu	—	—	—	—	—	○
195	Raichu	—	—	—	—	—	◎
196	Eevee	—	—	—	—	○	—
197	Vaporeon	○	—	—	—	—	—
198	Jolteon	—	—	—	—	—	○
199	Flareon	—	○	—	—	—	—
200	Espeon	—	—	—	○	—	—
201	Umbreon	—	—	—	—	○	—
202	Leafeon	—	—	○	—	—	—
203	Glaceon	—	—	—	○	—	—
204	Sylveon	—	—	—	—	○	—
205	Applin	—	—	○	—	—	—
206	Flapple	—	○	—	—	—	—

Dex No.	Name	HP	Atk.	Def.	Sp. Atk	Sp. Def	Speed
207	Appletun	○	—	—	—	—	—
208	Espurr	—	—	—	—	—	○
209	Meowstic	—	—	—	—	—	○
210	Swirlix	—	—	○	—	—	—
211	Slurpuff	—	—	○	—	—	—
212	Spritzee	○	—	—	—	—	—
213	Aromatisse	○	—	—	—	—	—
214	Dewpider	—	—	—	—	○	—
215	Araquanid	—	—	—	—	○	—
216	Wynaut	○	—	—	—	—	—
217	Wobbuffet	○	—	—	—	—	—
218	Farfetch'd	—	○	—	—	—	—
219	Sirfetch'd	—	○	—	—	—	—
220	Chinchou	○	—	—	—	—	—
221	Lanturn	○	—	—	—	—	—
222	Croagunk	—	○	—	—	—	—
223	Toxicroak	—	○	—	—	—	—
224	Scraggy	—	○	—	—	—	—
225	Scrafty	—	—	○	—	○	—
226	Stunfisk	○	—	—	—	—	—
227	Shuckle	—	—	○	—	○	—
228	Barboach	○	—	—	—	—	—
229	Whiscash	○	—	—	—	—	—
230	Shellos	○	—	—	—	—	—
231	Gastrodon	○	—	—	—	—	—
232	Wimpod	—	—	—	—	—	○
233	Golisopod	—	—	○	—	—	—
234	Binacle	—	○	—	—	—	—
235	Barbaracle	—	○	—	—	—	—
236	Corsola	—	—	—	—	○	—
237	Cursola	—	—	—	○	—	—
238	Impidimp	—	—	—	○	—	—
239	Morgrem	—	—	—	○	—	—
240	Grimmsnarl	—	◎	—	—	—	—
241	Hatenna	—	—	—	○	—	—
242	Hattrem	—	—	—	○	—	—
243	Hatterene	—	—	—	◎	—	—
244	Salandit	—	—	—	—	—	○
245	Salazzle	—	—	—	—	—	○
246	Pawniard	—	○	—	—	—	—
247	Bisharp	—	○	—	—	—	—
248	Throh	○	—	—	—	—	—
249	Sawk	—	○	—	—	—	—
250	Koffing	—	—	○	—	—	—
251	Weezing	—	—	○	—	—	—
252	Bonsly	—	—	○	—	—	—
253	Sudowoodo	—	—	○	—	—	—
254	Cleffa	—	—	—	—	○	—
255	Clefairy	○	—	—	—	—	—
256	Clefable	◎	—	—	—	—	—
257	Togepi	—	—	—	—	○	—
258	Togetic	—	—	—	—	○	—
259	Togekiss	—	—	—	○	○	—
260	Munchlax	○	—	—	—	—	—
261	Snorlax	○	—	—	—	—	—
262	Cottonee	—	—	—	—	—	○
263	Whimsicott	—	—	—	—	—	○
264	Rhyhorn	—	—	○	—	—	—
265	Rhydon	—	○	—	—	—	—
266	Rhyperior	—	◎	—	—	—	—
267	Gothita	—	—	—	—	○	—
268	Gothorita	—	—	—	—	○	—
269	Gothitelle	—	—	—	—	◎	—
270	Solosis	—	—	—	○	—	—
271	Duosion	—	—	—	○	—	—
272	Reuniclus	—	—	—	◎	—	—
273	Karrablast	—	○	—	—	—	—
274	Escavalier	—	○	—	—	—	—
275	Shelmet	—	—	○	—	—	—
276	Accelgor	—	—	—	—	—	○
277	Elgyem	—	—	—	○	—	—
278	Beheeyem	—	—	—	○	—	—
279	Cubchoo	—	○	—	—	—	—
280	Beartic	—	○	—	—	—	—
281	Rufflet	—	○	—	—	—	—
282	Braviary	—	○	—	—	—	—
283	Vullaby	—	—	○	—	—	—
284	Mandibuzz	—	—	—	○	—	—
285	Skorupi	—	—	○	—	—	—
286	Drapion	—	—	○	—	—	—
287	Litwick	—	—	—	○	—	—
288	Lampent	—	—	—	○	—	—
289	Chandelure	—	—	—	◎	—	—
290	Inkay	—	○	—	—	—	—
291	Malamar	—	○	—	—	—	—
292	Sneasel	—	—	—	—	—	○
293	Weavile	—	○	—	—	—	○
294	Sableye	—	○	○	—	—	—
295	Mawile	—	○	○	—	—	—
296	Maractus	—	—	—	○	—	—
297	Sigilyph	—	—	—	○	—	—
298	Riolu	—	○	—	—	—	—
299	Lucario	—	○	—	○	—	—
300	Torkoal	—	—	○	—	—	—
301	Mimikyu	—	—	—	—	○	—
302	Cufant	—	○	—	—	—	—
303	Copperajah	—	○	—	—	—	—
304	Qwilfish	—	○	—	—	—	—
305	Frillish	—	—	—	—	○	—
306	Jellicent	—	—	—	—	○	—
307	Mareanie	—	—	○	—	—	—
308	Toxapex	—	—	○	—	—	—
309	Cramorant	—	—	—	—	○	—
310	Toxel	—	—	—	○	—	—
311	Toxtricity	—	—	—	○	—	—
312	Silicobra	—	—	○	—	—	—
313	Sandaconda	—	—	○	—	—	—
314	Hippopotas	—	—	○	—	—	—

Dex No.	Name	HP	Atk.	Def.	Sp. Atk	Sp. Def	Speed
315	Hippowdon	—	—	○	—	—	—
316	Durant	—	—	○	—	—	—
317	Heatmor	—	—	—	○	—	—
318	Helioptile	—	—	—	—	—	○
319	Heliolisk	—	—	—	○	—	○
320	Hawlucha	—	○	—	—	—	—
321	Trapinch	—	○	—	—	—	—
322	Vibrava	—	○	—	—	—	○
323	Flygon	—	○	—	—	—	○
324	Axew	—	○	—	—	—	—
325	Fraxure	—	○	—	—	—	—
326	Haxorus	—	◎	—	—	—	—
327	Yamask	—	—	○	—	—	—
328	Runerigus	—	—	○	—	—	—
330	Honedge	—	—	○	—	—	—
331	Doublade	—	—	○	—	—	—
332	Aegislash (Shield Forme)	—	—	○	—	○	—
332	Aegislash (Blade Forme)	—	○	—	○	—	—
333	Ponyta	—	—	—	—	—	○
334	Rapidash	—	—	—	—	—	○
335	Sinistea	—	—	—	○	—	—
336	Polteageist	—	—	—	○	—	—
337	Indeedee (Male)	—	—	—	○	—	—
337	Indeedee (Female)	—	—	—	—	○	—
338	Phantump	—	○	—	—	—	—
339	Trevenant	—	○	—	—	—	—
340	Morelull	—	—	—	—	○	—
341	Shiinotic	—	—	—	—	○	—
342	Oranguru	—	—	—	—	○	—
343	Passimian	—	○	—	—	—	—
344	Morpeko	—	—	—	—	—	○
345	Falinks	—	○	—	—	○	—
346	Drampa	—	—	—	○	—	—
347	Turtonator	—	—	○	—	—	—
348	Togedemaru	—	○	—	—	—	—
349	Snom	—	—	—	○	—	—
350	Frosmoth	—	—	—	○	—	—
351	Clobbopus	—	○	—	—	—	—
352	Grapploct	—	○	—	—	—	—
353	Pincurchin	—	○	—	—	—	—
354	Mantyke	—	—	—	—	○	—
355	Mantine	—	—	—	—	○	—
356	Wailmer	○	—	—	—	—	—
357	Wailord	○	—	—	—	—	—
358	Bergmite	—	—	○	—	—	—
359	Avalugg	—	—	○	—	—	—
360	Dhelmise	—	○	—	—	—	—
361	Lapras	○	—	—	—	—	—
362	Lunatone	—	—	—	○	—	—
363	Solrock	—	○	—	—	—	—
364	Mime Jr.	—	—	—	—	○	—
365	Mr. Mime	—	—	—	—	—	○
366	Mr. Rime	—	—	—	◎	—	—
367	Darumaka	—	○	—	—	—	—
368	Darmanitan (Standard Mode)	—	○	—	—	—	—
368	Darmanitan (Zen Mode)	—	—	—	○	—	—
369	Stonjourner	—	—	○	—	—	—
370	Eiscue	—	—	○	—	—	—
371	Duraludon	—	—	—	○	—	—
372	Rotom	—	—	—	○	—	○
373	Ditto	○	—	—	—	—	—
378	Charmander	—	—	—	—	—	○
379	Charmeleon	—	—	—	○	—	○
380	Charizard	—	—	—	◎	—	—
383	Larvitar	—	○	—	—	—	—
384	Pupitar	—	○	—	—	—	—
385	Tyranitar	—	◎	—	—	—	—
386	Deino	—	○	—	—	—	—
387	Zweilous	—	○	—	—	—	—
388	Hydreigon	—	—	—	◎	—	—
389	Goomy	—	—	—	—	○	—
390	Sliggoo	—	—	—	—	○	—
391	Goodra	—	—	—	—	◎	—
392	Jangmo-o	—	—	○	—	—	—
393	Hakamo-o	—	—	○	—	—	—
394	Kommo-o	—	—	◎	—	—	—
395	Dreepy	—	—	—	—	—	○
396	Drakloak	—	—	—	—	—	○
397	Dragapult	—	—	—	—	—	◎

ADVENTURE DATA

Items

There are many types of items you can collect and use in the Galar region. They tend to fall in certain categories, as you'll find when you open your Bag. On the following pages, items are divided up by the same categories as in your Bag, so you can find the type of item you're looking for based on what you want to do.

Medicine

Name	Description	Main way to obtain
Antidote	A consumable item. If used on a Pokémon, this item will heal the poisoned and badly poisoned status conditions.	Buy at any Poké Mart
Awakening	A consumable item. If used on a Pokémon, this item will heal the asleep status condition.	Buy at any Poké Mart
Berry Juice	A consumable item. If a Pokémon holds this item, it can drink the juice to restore 20 HP during battle when its HP drops to 1/2 of its maximum or lower.	Get as a reward at a Battle Café
Big Malasada	A consumable item. This famous fried bread from the Alola region can be used to heal a Pokémon of any status condition or confusion.	Get as a reward at a Battle Café
Burn Heal	A consumable item. If used on a Pokémon, this item will heal the burned status condition.	Buy at any Poké Mart
Casteliacone	A consumable item. This famous ice cream from Castelia City can be used to heal a Pokémon of any status condition or confusion.	Get as a reward at a Battle Café
Elixir	A consumable item. If used on a Pokémon, this item will restore the PP of all its moves by 10 points each.	Find as a hidden item on Route 8 / Pickup Ability
Energy Powder	A consumable item. If used on a Pokémon, this item will restore the Pokémon's HP by 60 points. However, the very bitter taste will make the Pokémon less friendly.	Buy from the Herb Shop in Hulbury
Energy Root	A consumable item. If used on a Pokémon, this item will restore the Pokémon's HP by 120 points. However, the very bitter taste will make the Pokémon less friendly.	Buy from the Herb Shop in Hulbury
Ether	A consumable item. If used on a Pokémon, this item will restore the PP of one of its moves by 10 points.	Find as a hidden item in Galar Mine or on Route 4 / Pickup Ability
Fresh Water	A consumable item. If used on a Pokémon, this item will restore the Pokémon's HP by 30 points.	Buy from a vending machine in a train station
Full Heal	A consumable item. If used on a Pokémon, this item will heal any status condition or confusion.	Buy at any Poké Mart once you have 6 Gym Badges
Full Restore	A consumable item. If used on a Pokémon, this item will fully restore the Pokémon's HP and cure any status condition or confusion.	Buy at any Poké Mart once you have 8 Gym Badges
Heal Powder	A consumable item. If used on a Pokémon, this item will heal the Pokémon of any status condition or confusion. However, the very bitter taste will make the Pokémon less friendly.	Buy from the Herb Shop in Hulbury
Hyper Potion	A consumable item. If used on a Pokémon, this item will restore the Pokémon's HP by 120 points.	Buy at any Poké Mart once you have 4 Gym Badges
Ice Heal	A consumable item. If used on a Pokémon, this item will heal the frozen status condition.	Buy at any Poké Mart
Lava Cookie	A consumable item. This famous treat from Lavaridge Town can be used to heal a Pokémon of any status condition or confusion.	Get as a reward at a Battle Café
Lemonade	A consumable item. If used on a Pokémon, this item will restore the Pokémon's HP by 70 points.	Buy from a vending machine in a train station
Lumiose Galette	A consumable item. This popular pastry from Lumiose City can be used to heal a Pokémon of any status condition or confusion.	Get as a reward at a Battle Café
Max Elixir	A consumable item. If used on a Pokémon, this item will restore the PP of all its moves completely.	Find as a hidden item on Route 9 / Pickup Ability
Max Ether	A consumable item. If used on a Pokémon, this item will restore the PP of one of its moves completely.	Find as a hidden item on Route 2 / Pickup Ability
Max Potion	A consumable item. If used on a Pokémon, this item will fully restore the Pokémon's HP.	Buy at any Poké Mart once you have 7 Gym Badges
Max Revive	A consumable item. If used on a fainted Pokémon, this item will revive the Pokémon and fully restore its HP.	Find in the Watchtower Ruins in the Wild Area, on Routes 8, 9, or 10, or in Spikemuth / Pickup Ability
Moomoo Milk	A consumable item. If used on a Pokémon, this item will restore the Pokémon's HP by 100 points.	Get as a reward at a Battle Café
Old Gateau	A consumable item. This secret specialty of the Old Chateau can be used to heal a Pokémon of any status condition or confusion.	Get as a reward at a Battle Café
Paralyze Heal	A consumable item. If used on a Pokémon, this item will heal the paralysis status condition.	Buy at any Poké Mart
Pewter Crunchies	A consumable item. This famous snack from Pewter City can be used to heal a Pokémon of any status condition or confusion.	Get as a reward at a Battle Café
Potion	A consumable item. If used on a Pokémon, this item will restore the Pokémon's HP by 20 points.	Buy at any Poké Mart
Rage Candy Bar	A consumable item. This famous snack from Mahogany Town can be used to heal a Pokémon of any status condition or confusion.	Get as a reward at a Battle Café
Revival Herb	A consumable item. It can be used to revive a Pokémon that has fainted. However, the very bitter taste will make the Pokémon less friendly.	Buy from the Herb Shop in Hulbury
Revive	A consumable item. If used on a fainted Pokémon, this item will revive the Pokémon and restore half of its max HP.	Buy at any Poké Mart
Shalour Sable	A consumable item. This famous shortbread from Shalour City can be used to heal a Pokémon of any status condition or confusion.	Get as a reward at a Battle Café
Soda Pop	A consumable item. If used on a Pokémon, this item will restore the Pokémon's HP by 50 points.	Buy from a vending machine in a train station
Super Potion	A consumable item. If used on a Pokémon, this item will restore the Pokémon's HP by 60 points.	Buy at any Poké Mart once you have 1 Gym Badge
Sweet Heart	A consumable item. If used on a Pokémon, this item will restore the Pokémon's HP by 20 points.	Get as a reward at a Battle Café

Poké Balls

	Name	Description	Main way to obtain
	Beast Ball	A type of Poké Ball. It is most effective for catching Ultra Beasts that appear in other regions. It's not very effective at catching regular Pokémon.	Get one from the bargain stall in Stow-on-Side after becoming Champion
	Dive Ball	A type of Poké Ball. It is most effective for catching Pokémon that live in the water or that are encountered on the water's surface.	Get from a Rotom Rallyist in the Wild Area / Buy in Hammerlocke's central Pokémon Center
	Dream Ball	A type of Poké Ball. It is most effective for catching Pokémon when they are asleep.	Get one from the Ball Guy in Wyndon
	Dusk Ball	A type of Poké Ball. It is most effective for catching Pokémon at night or in dark places such as caves.	Get from a Rotom Rallyist in the Wild Area / Buy in Hammerlocke's central Pokémon Center
	Fast Ball	A type of Poké Ball. It is most effective for catching Pokémon that have a high Speed stat.	Get one as a reward after completing a Rotom Rally course for the eleventh time.
	Friend Ball	A type of Poké Ball. It will immediately make a Pokémon caught with it more friendly toward you.	Get one from the Ball Guy in Turffield
	Great Ball	A type of Poké Ball. It is more likely to successfully catch a Pokémon than a basic Poké Ball.	Buy at any Poké Mart once you have 1 Gym Badge
	Heal Ball	A type of Poké Ball. It will fully restore the HP and PP of the Pokémon caught with it and heal any status conditions.	Get from a Rotom Rallyist in the Wild Area / Buy in Motostoke's lower Pokémon Center
	Heavy Ball	A type of Poké Ball. It is most effective for catching Pokémon that weigh a lot.	Get one from the Ball Guy in Stow-on-Side
	Level Ball	A type of Poké Ball. It is most effective for catching Pokémon that are lower in level than your own.	Get one from the Ball Guy in Hammerlocke
	Love Ball	A type of Poké Ball. It is most effective for catching Pokémon that are the same species as and the opposite gender to your active Pokémon.	Get one from the Ball Guy in Ballonlea
	Lure Ball	A type of Poké Ball. It is most effective for catching Pokémon that have been fished up with a fishing rod.	Get one from the Ball Guy in Hulbury
	Luxury Ball	A type of Poké Ball. It makes a Pokémon caught with it quickly become more friendly toward you.	Get from a Rotom Rallyist in the Wild Area / Buy in Wyndon's southern Pokémon Center
	Master Ball	A very rare type of Poké Ball. It is guaranteed to catch any wild Pokémon.	Get one from Professor Magnolia after becoming Champion / Win one in the Loto-ID if you're very lucky
	Moon Ball	A type of Poké Ball. It is most effective for catching Pokémon that can be evolved using a Moon Stone.	Get one from the Ball Guy in Circhester
	Nest Ball	A type of Poké Ball. It is most effective for catching Pokémon of lower levels.	Get from a Rotom Rallyist in the Wild Area / Buy in Motostoke's lower Pokémon Center
	Net Ball	A type of Poké Ball. It is most effective for catching Water- or Bug-type Pokémon.	Get from a Rotom Rallyist in the Wild Area / Buy in Motostoke's lower Pokémon Center
	Poké Ball	A type of Poké Ball. It is the most basic model and is decently successful at catching wild Pokémon.	Buy at any Poké Mart after you meet up with Leon on Route 2
	Premier Ball	A type of Poké Ball made to celebrate a special event of some sort. It is as effective as a basic Poké Ball.	Get one each time you buy 10 Poké Balls at a Poké Mart
	Quick Ball	A type of Poké Ball. It is most effective for catching Pokémon on the first turn in battle.	Get from a Rotom Rallyist in the Wild Area / Buy in Wyndon's southern Pokémon Center
	Repeat Ball	A type of Poké Ball. It is most effective for catching a species of Pokémon that you've caught at least once before.	Get from a Rotom Rallyist in the Wild Area / Buy in Wyndon's southern Pokémon Center
	Timer Ball	A type of Poké Ball. It is most effective for catching Pokémon after many turns have passed in a battle.	Get from a Rotom Rallyist in the Wild Area / Buy in Hammerlocke's central Pokémon Center
	Ultra Ball	A type of Poké Ball. It is more likely to successfully catch a Pokémon than even a Great Ball.	Buy at any Poké Mart once you have 5 Gym Badges

Lists of a few categories of items can be found elsewhere in this guide.

- See the list of TMs and TRs and how to obtain them all on pages 356 and 358.
- Find a list of all the ingredients you can get for cooking on page 285.
- Clothing items don't go directly in your Bag, but you can browse them all starting on page 315.

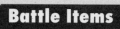

Battle Items

Name	Description	Main way to obtain
Dire Hit	A consumable item. If used on a Pokémon, it becomes much more likely the Pokémon will deliver critical hits.	Buy in Hammerlocke's central Pokémon Center
Guard Spec.	A consumable item. If used during battle, this item will prevent stat reduction among the Trainer's party Pokémon for 5 turns. Cannot be used again until the effect wears off.	Buy in Hammerlocke's central Pokémon Center
Poké Doll	A consumable item. If used in a battle against a wild Pokémon, this item ends the battle instantly.	Buy at any Poké Mart once you have 1 Gym Badge
X Accuracy	A consumable item. If used on a Pokémon during battle, this item will raise the accuracy of the Pokémon by 2 stages.	Buy in Hammerlocke's central Pokémon Center
X Attack	A consumable item. If used on a Pokémon during battle, this item will raise the Attack of the Pokémon by 2 stages.	Buy in Motostoke's lower Pokémon Center
X Defense	A consumable item. If used on a Pokémon during battle, this item will raise the Defense of the Pokémon by 2 stages.	Buy in Motostoke's lower Pokémon Center
X Sp. Atk	A consumable item. If used on a Pokémon during battle, this item will raise the Sp. Atk of the Pokémon by 2 stages.	Buy in Motostoke's lower Pokémon Center
X Sp. Def	A consumable item. If used on a Pokémon during battle, this item will raise the Sp. Def of the Pokémon by 2 stages.	Buy in Motostoke's lower Pokémon Center
X Speed	A consumable item. If used on a Pokémon during battle, this item will raise the Speed of the Pokémon by 2 stages.	Buy in Hammerlocke's central Pokémon Center

Berries

Name	Description	Main way to obtain
Aguav Berry	A consumable item. If a Pokémon holds one, it can eat this Berry to restore some HP when its HP drops to 1/4 of its maximum or lower. It restores 1/3 of max HP but also confuses Pokémon that don't like bitter flavors.	Collect from the Berry tree on Route 9 (Circhester Bay)
Apicot Berry	A consumable item. If a Pokémon holds one, it can eat this Berry to raise its Sp. Def by 1 stage when its HP drops to 1/4 of its maximum or lower.	Collect from the Berry tree at the Lake of Outrage in the Wild Area
Aspear Berry	A consumable item. If a Pokémon holds one, it can eat this Berry to cure itself of the frozen status condition during battle. Using this Berry on a Pokémon directly can also cure the frozen status condition.	Collect from the Berry tree on Route 7 (north side)
Babiri Berry	A consumable item. If a Pokémon holds one, it can eat this Berry to halve the damage taken from one supereffective Steel-type move.	Collect from the Berry tree in the area surrounded by the lake in the Bridge Field in the Wild Area
Charti Berry	A consumable item. If a Pokémon holds one, it can eat this Berry to halve the damage taken from one supereffective Rock-type move.	Collect from the Berry tree at the Lake of Outrage in the Wild Area
Cheri Berry	A consumable item. If a Pokémon holds one, it can eat this Berry to cure itself of the paralysis status condition during battle. Using this Berry on a Pokémon directly can also cure the paralysis status condition.	Buy at Wedgehurst Berry Grocer / Collect from the Berry trees in the Rolling Fields in the Wild Area
Chesto Berry	A consumable item. If a Pokémon holds one, it can eat this Berry to cure itself of the asleep status condition during battle. Using this Berry on a Pokémon directly can also cure the asleep status condition.	Collect from the Berry tree on Route 5
Chilan Berry	A consumable item. If a Pokémon holds one, it can eat this Berry to halve the damage taken from one Normal-type move.	Collect from the Berry trees near West Lake Axewell in the Dappled Grove in the Wild Area
Chople Berry	A consumable item. If a Pokémon holds one, it can eat this Berry to halve the damage taken from one supereffective Fighting-type move.	Collect from the Berry tree on Route 9 (Outer Spikemuth)
Coba Berry	A consumable item. If a Pokémon holds one, it can eat this Berry to halve the damage taken from one supereffective Flying-type move.	Collect from the Berry tree by the river at the Motostoke Riverbank in the Wild Area
Colbur Berry	A consumable item. If a Pokémon holds one, it can eat this Berry to halve the damage taken from one supereffective Dark-type move.	Collect from the Berry tree on Axew's Eye in the Wild Area
Figy Berry	A consumable item. If a Pokémon holds one, it can eat this Berry to restore some HP when its HP drops to 1/4 of its maximum or lower. It restores 1/3 of max HP but also confuses Pokémon that don't like spicy flavors.	Collect from the Berry tree on Route 7 (north side)
Ganlon Berry	A consumable item. If a Pokémon holds one, it can eat this Berry to raise its Defense by 1 stage when its HP drops to 1/4 of its maximum or lower.	Collect from the Berry tree in the area surrounded by the lake in the Bridge Field in the Wild Area
Grepa Berry	A consumable item. If used on a Pokémon, this Berry will make that Pokémon more friendly, but it will also take away base points from its Sp. Def stat.	Collect from the left Berry tree under the bridge in the Bridge Field in the Wild Area
Haban Berry	A consumable item. If a Pokémon holds one, it can eat this Berry to halve the damage taken from one supereffective Dragon-type move.	Collect from the Berry tree at the Lake of Outrage in the Wild Area
Hondew Berry	A consumable item. If used on a Pokémon, this Berry will make that Pokémon more friendly, but it will also take away base points from its Sp. Atk stat.	Collect from the left Berry tree under the bridge in the Bridge Field in the Wild Area
Iapapa Berry	A consumable item. If a Pokémon holds one, it can eat this Berry to restore some HP when its HP drops to 1/4 of its maximum or lower. It restores 1/3 of max HP but also confuses Pokémon that don't like sour flavors.	Collect from the Berry tree on Route 9 (Circhester Bay)
Kasib Berry	A consumable item. If a Pokémon holds one, it can eat this Berry to halve the damage taken from one supereffective Ghost-type move.	Collect from the Berry tree in the area surrounded by the lake in the Bridge Field in the Wild Area
Kebia Berry	A consumable item. If a Pokémon holds one, it can eat this Berry to halve the damage taken from one supereffective Poison-type move.	Collect from the Berry tree on Axew's Eye in the Wild Area
Kee Berry	A consumable item. If a Pokémon holds one, it can eat this Berry to raise its Defense by 1 stage when hit with a physical move.	Collect from the Berry tree on Axew's Eye in the Wild Area

Name	Description	Main way to obtain
Kelpsy Berry	A consumable item. If used on a Pokémon, this Berry will make that Pokémon more friendly, but it will also take away base points from its Attack stat.	Collect from the right Berry tree under the bridge in the Bridge Field in the Wild Area
Lansat Berry	A consumable item. If a Pokémon holds one, it can eat this Berry to make itself more likely to deliver critical hits when its HP drops to 1/4 of its maximum or lower.	Get as a reward at the Battle Tower
Leppa Berry	A consumable item. If a Pokémon holds one, it can eat this Berry to restore 10 points to the PP of one of its moves.	Collect from the Berry tree near the Lake of Outrage on the Hammerlocke Hills in the Wild Area
Liechi Berry	A consumable item. If a Pokémon holds one, it can eat this Berry to raise its Attack by 1 stage when its HP drops to 1/4 of its maximum or lower.	Collect from the Berry tree in the area surrounded by the lake in the Bridge Field in the Wild Area
Lum Berry	A consumable item. If a Pokémon holds one, it can eat this Berry to cure itself of any status condition or confusion during battle.	Collect from the Berry tree on Route 9 (Outer Spikemuth)
Mago Berry	A consumable item. If a Pokémon holds one, it can eat this Berry to restore some HP when its HP drops to 1/4 of its maximum or lower. It restores 1/3 of max HP but also confuses Pokémon that don't like sweet flavors.	Collect from the Berry tree on Route 7 (north side)
Maranga Berry	A consumable item. If a Pokémon holds one, it can eat this Berry to raise its Sp. Def by 1 stage when hit with a special move.	Collect from the Berry tree on Axew's Eye in the Wild Area
Occa Berry	A consumable item. If a Pokémon holds one, it can eat this Berry to halve the damage taken from one supereffective Fire-type move.	Collect from the center Berry tree under the bridge in the Bridge Field in the Wild Area
Oran Berry	A consumable item. If a Pokémon holds one, it can eat this Berry to restore 10 HP when its HP drops to 1/2 of its maximum or lower.	Buy at Wedgehurst Berry Grocer / Collect from the Berry trees in the Rolling Fields in the Wild Area
Passho Berry	A consumable item. If a Pokémon holds one, it can eat this Berry to halve the damage taken from one supereffective Water-type move.	Collect from the right Berry tree in the Bridge Field in the Wild Area
Payapa Berry	A consumable item. If a Pokémon holds one, it can eat this Berry to halve the damage taken from one supereffective Psychic-type move.	Collect from the Berry tree near the Lake of Outrage on the Hammerlocke Hills in the Wild Area
Pecha Berry	A consumable item. If a Pokémon holds one, it can eat this Berry to cure itself of the poisoned or badly poisoned status condition during battle. Using this Berry on a Pokémon directly can also cure the poisoned status condition.	Buy at Wedgehurst Berry Grocer / Collect from the Berry tree near the Meetup Spot in the Rolling Fields in the Wild Area
Persim Berry	A consumable item. If a Pokémon holds one, it can eat this Berry to cure itself of confusion during battle.	Collect from the Berry tree at North Lake Miloch in the Wild Area
Petaya Berry	A consumable item. If a Pokémon holds one, it can eat this Berry to raise its Sp. Atk by 1 stage when its HP drops to 1/4 of its maximum or lower.	Collect from the Berry tree at the Lake of Outrage in the Wild Area
Pomeg Berry	A consumable item. If used on a Pokémon, this Berry will make that Pokémon more friendly, but it will also take away base points from its HP stat.	Collect from the center Berry tree under the bridge in the Bridge Field in the Wild Area
Qualot Berry	A consumable item. If used on a Pokémon, this Berry will make that Pokémon more friendly, but it will also take away base points from its Defense stat.	Collect from the right Berry tree under the bridge in the Bridge Field in the Wild Area
Rawst Berry	A consumable item. If a Pokémon holds one, it can eat this Berry to cure itself of the burned status condition during battle. Using this Berry on a Pokémon directly can also cure the burned status condition.	Collect from the Berry tree at North Lake Miloch in the Wild Area
Rindo Berry	A consumable item. If a Pokémon holds one, it can eat this Berry to halve the damage taken from one supereffective Grass-type move.	Collect from the left Berry tree under the bridge in the Bridge Field in the Wild Area
Roseli Berry	A consumable item. If a Pokémon holds one, it can eat this Berry to halve the damage taken from one supereffective Fairy-type move.	Collect from the Berry tree on Route 9 (Outer Spikemuth)
Salac Berry	A consumable item. If a Pokémon holds one, it can eat this Berry to raise its Speed by 1 stage when its HP drops to 1/4 of its maximum or lower.	Collect from the Berry tree on Axew's Eye in the Wild Area
Shuca Berry	A consumable item. If a Pokémon holds one, it can eat this Berry to halve the damage taken from one supereffective Ground-type move.	Collect from the Berry tree at the Lake of Outrage in the Wild Area
Sitrus Berry	A consumable item. If a Pokémon holds one, it can eat this Berry to restore 1/2 of its max HP when its HP drops to 1/4 of its maximum or lower.	Collect from the Berry tree by the river at the Motostoke Riverbank in the Wild Area
Starf Berry	A consumable item. If a Pokémon holds one, it can eat this Berry to raise one of its stats by 2 stages when its HP drops to 1/4 of its maximum or lower. The stat is selected at random.	Get as a reward at the Battle Tower
Tamato Berry	A consumable item. If used on a Pokémon, this Berry will make that Pokémon more friendly, but it will also take away base points from its Speed stat.	Collect from the center Berry tree under the bridge in the Bridge Field in the Wild Area
Tanga Berry	A consumable item. If a Pokémon holds one, it can eat this Berry to halve the damage taken from one supereffective Bug-type move.	Collect from the Berry tree on Route 9 (Outer Spikemuth)
Wacan Berry	A consumable item. If a Pokémon holds one, it can eat this Berry to halve the damage taken from one supereffective Electric-type move.	Collect from the Berry tree near the Lake of Outrage on the Hammerlocke Hills in the Wild Area
Wiki Berry	A consumable item. If a Pokémon holds one, it can eat this Berry to restore some HP when its HP drops to 1/4 of its maximum or lower. It restores 1/3 of max HP but also confuses Pokémon that don't like dry flavors.	Collect from the Berry tree on Route 9 (Circhester Bay)
Yache Berry	A consumable item. If a Pokémon holds one, it can eat this Berry to halve the damage taken from one supereffective Ice-type move.	Collect from the Berry tree at the Lake of Outrage in the Wild Area

Other Items

Items that can be used to help your Pokémon grow

Name	Description	Main way to obtain
Ability Capsule	A consumable item. Allows a Pokémon of a species that has two possible Abilities (excluding Hidden Abilities) to change its Ability to the one it currently does not have.	Get from the right-hand clerk at the Battle Tower's BP Shop after becoming Champion
Adamant Mint	A consumable item. If used on a Pokémon, this item will cause the Pokémon's Attack to grow more easily while its Sp. Atk will grow more slowly.	Get from the left-hand clerk at the Battle Tower's BP Shop after becoming Champion
Bold Mint	A consumable item. If used on a Pokémon, this item will cause the Pokémon's Defense to grow more easily while its Attack will grow more slowly.	Get from the left-hand clerk at the Battle Tower's BP Shop after becoming Champion
Brave Mint	A consumable item. If used on a Pokémon, this item will cause the Pokémon's Attack to grow more easily while its Speed will grow more slowly.	Get from the left-hand clerk at the Battle Tower's BP Shop after becoming Champion
Calcium	A consumable item. If used on a Pokémon, this item will add base points to the Pokémon's Sp. Atk stat.	Buy in Wyndon's southern Pokémon Center
Calm Mint	A consumable item. If used on a Pokémon, this item will cause the Pokémon's Sp. Def to grow more easily while its Attack will grow more slowly.	Get from the left-hand clerk at the Battle Tower's BP Shop after becoming Champion
Carbos	A consumable item. If used on a Pokémon, this item will add base points to the Pokémon's Speed stat.	Buy in Wyndon's southern Pokémon Center
Careful Mint	A consumable item. If used on a Pokémon, this item will cause the Pokémon's Sp. Def to grow more easily while its Sp. Atk will grow more slowly.	Get from the left-hand clerk at the Battle Tower's BP Shop after becoming Champion
Clever Feather	A consumable item. If used on a Pokémon, this item will add a small number of base points to the Pokémon's Sp. Def stat. It can be used until base points for that stat have been maxed.	Find as a hidden item on the bridge on Route 5 or the bridge in the Motostoke Outskirts
Dynamax Candy	A consumable item. If used on a Pokémon, this item will raise the Pokémon's Dynamax Level by 1.	Find after a Max Raid Battle
Exp. Candy L	A consumable item. If used on a Pokémon, it will award a large amount of Exp. Points.	Find after a Max Raid Battle
Exp. Candy M	A consumable item. If used on a Pokémon, it will award a moderate amount of Exp. Points.	Find after a Max Raid Battle
Exp. Candy S	A consumable item. If used on a Pokémon, it will award a small amount of Exp. Points.	Find after a Max Raid Battle
Exp. Candy XL	A consumable item. If used on a Pokémon, it will award a very large amount of Exp. Points.	Find after a Max Raid Battle
Exp. Candy XS	A consumable item. If used on a Pokémon, it will award a very small amount of Exp. Points.	Find after a Max Raid Battle
Genius Feather	A consumable item. If used on a Pokémon, this item will add a small number of base points to the Pokémon's Sp. Atk stat. It can be used until base points for that stat have been maxed.	Find as a hidden item on the bridge on Route 5 or the bridge in the Motostoke Outskirts
Gentle Mint	A consumable item. If used on a Pokémon, this item will cause the Pokémon's Sp. Def to grow more easily while its Defense will grow more slowly.	Get from the left-hand clerk at the Battle Tower's BP Shop after becoming Champion
Hasty Mint	A consumable item. If used on a Pokémon, this item will cause the Pokémon's Speed to grow more easily while its Defense will grow more slowly.	Get from the left-hand clerk at the Battle Tower's BP Shop after becoming Champion
Health Feather	A consumable item. If used on a Pokémon, this item will add a small number of base points to the Pokémon's HP. It can be used until base points for that stat have been maxed.	Find as a hidden item on the bridge on Route 5 or the bridge in the Motostoke Outskirts
HP Up	A consumable item. If used on a Pokémon, this item will add base points to the Pokémon's HP stat.	Buy in Wyndon's southern Pokémon Center
Impish Mint	A consumable item. If used on a Pokémon, this item will cause the Pokémon's Defense to grow more easily while its Sp. Atk will grow more slowly.	Get from the left-hand clerk at the Battle Tower's BP Shop after becoming Champion
Iron	A consumable item. If used on a Pokémon, this item will add base points to the Pokémon's Defense stat.	Buy in Wyndon's southern Pokémon Center
Jolly Mint	A consumable item. If used on a Pokémon, this item will cause the Pokémon's Speed to grow more easily while its Sp. Atk will grow more slowly.	Get from the left-hand clerk at the Battle Tower's BP Shop after becoming Champion
Lax Mint	A consumable item. If used on a Pokémon, this item will cause the Pokémon's Defense to grow more easily while its Sp. Def will grow more slowly.	Get from the left-hand clerk at the Battle Tower's BP Shop after becoming Champion
Lonely Mint	A consumable item. If used on a Pokémon, this item will cause the Pokémon's Attack to grow more easily while its Defense will grow more slowly.	Get from the left-hand clerk at the Battle Tower's BP Shop after becoming Champion
Macho Brace	A nonconsumable item. If held by a Pokémon, this item will halve the holder's Speed but increase the rate at which it gains base points.	Get from the BP Shop in Hammerlocke's central Pokémon Center
Mild Mint	A consumable item. If used on a Pokémon, this item will cause the Pokémon's Sp. Atk to grow more easily while its Defense will grow more slowly.	Get from the left-hand clerk at the Battle Tower's BP Shop after becoming Champion
Modest Mint	A consumable item. If used on a Pokémon, this item will cause the Pokémon's Sp. Atk to grow more easily while its Attack will grow more slowly.	Get from the left-hand clerk at the Battle Tower's BP Shop after becoming Champion
Muscle Feather	A consumable item. If used on a Pokémon, this item will add a small number of base points to the Pokémon's Attack stat. It can be used until base points for that stat have been maxed.	Find as a hidden item on the bridge on Route 5 or the bridge in the Motostoke Outskirts
Naive Mint	A consumable item. If used on a Pokémon, this item will cause the Pokémon's Speed to grow more easily while its Sp. Def will grow more slowly.	Get from the left-hand clerk at the Battle Tower's BP Shop after becoming Champion
Naughty Mint	A consumable item. If used on a Pokémon, this item will cause the Pokémon's Attack to grow more easily while its Sp. Def will grow more slowly.	Get from the left-hand clerk at the Battle Tower's BP Shop after becoming Champion
Power Anklet	A nonconsumable item. If held by a Pokémon, this item will halve the holder's Speed but increase the rate at which it gains base points for its Speed stat.	Get from the BP Shop in Hammerlocke's central Pokémon Center
Power Band	A nonconsumable item. If held by a Pokémon, this item will halve the holder's Speed but increase the rate at which it gains base points for its Sp. Def stat.	Get from the BP Shop in Hammerlocke's central Pokémon Center
Power Belt	A nonconsumable item. If held by a Pokémon, this item will halve the holder's Speed but increase the rate at which it gains base points for its Defense stat.	Get from the BP Shop in Hammerlocke's central Pokémon Center
Power Bracer	A nonconsumable item. If held by a Pokémon, this item will halve the holder's Speed but increase the rate at which it gains base points for its Attack stat.	Get from the BP Shop in Hammerlocke's central Pokémon Center
Power Lens	A nonconsumable item. If held by a Pokémon, this item will halve the holder's Speed but increase the rate at which it gains base points for its Sp. Atk stat.	Get from the BP Shop in Hammerlocke's central Pokémon Center
Power Weight	A nonconsumable item. If held by a Pokémon, this item will halve the holder's Speed but increase the rate at which it gains base points for its HP stat.	Get from the BP Shop in Hammerlocke's central Pokémon Center
PP Max	A consumable item. If used on a Pokémon, this item can increase the max PP of one of the Pokémon's moves as high as it will go.	Find on Route 2 / Get as a reward at the Battle Tower

Name	Description	Main way to obtain
PP Up	A consumable item. If used on a Pokémon, this item can increase the max PP of one of the Pokémon's moves by a small amount.	Find as a hidden item in the Motostoke Outskirts, on Route 7, or elsewhere
Protein	A consumable item. If used on a Pokémon, this item will add base points to the Pokémon's Attack stat.	Get from the BP Shop in Hammerlocke's central Pokémon Center
Quiet Mint	A consumable item. If used on a Pokémon, this item will cause the Pokémon's Sp. Atk to grow more easily while its Speed will grow more slowly.	Get from the left-hand clerk at the Battle Tower's BP Shop after becoming Champion
Rare Candy	A consumable item. If used on a Pokémon, this item will raise the Pokémon's level by 1.	Get from the BP Shop in Hammerlocke's central Pokémon Center / Get as a reward at a Battle Café
Rash Mint	A consumable item. If used on a Pokémon, this item will cause the Pokémon's Sp. Atk to grow more easily while its Sp. Def will grow more slowly.	Get from the left-hand clerk at the Battle Tower's BP Shop after becoming Champion
Relaxed Mint	A consumable item. If used on a Pokémon, this item will cause the Pokémon's Defense to grow more easily while its Speed will grow more slowly.	Get from the left-hand clerk at the Battle Tower's BP Shop after becoming Champion
Resist Feather	A consumable item. If used on a Pokémon, this item will add a small number of base points to the Pokémon's Defense stat. It can be used until base points for that stat have been maxed.	Find as a hidden item on the bridge on Route 5 or the bridge in the Motostoke Outskirts
Sassy Mint	A consumable item. If used on a Pokémon, this item will cause the Pokémon's Sp. Def to grow more easily while its Speed will grow more slowly.	Get from the left-hand clerk at the Battle Tower's BP Shop after becoming Champion
Serious Mint	A consumable item. If used on a Pokémon, this item will cause the Pokémon's stats to grow at an equal rate.	Get from the left-hand clerk at the Battle Tower's BP Shop after becoming Champion
Swift Feather	A consumable item. If used on a Pokémon, this item will add a small number of base points to the Pokémon's Speed stat. It can be used until base points for that stat have been maxed.	Find as a hidden item on the bridge on Route 5 or the bridge in the Motostoke Outskirts
Timid Mint	A consumable item. If used on a Pokémon, this item will cause the Pokémon's Speed to grow more easily while its Attack will grow more slowly.	Get from the left-hand clerk at the Battle Tower's BP Shop after becoming Champion
Zinc	A consumable item. If used on a Pokémon, this item will add base points to the Pokémon's Sp. Def stat.	Get at Hammerlocke's BP Shop

Items that can be used to influence Pokémon's forms or Evolutions

Name	Description	Main way to obtain
Berry Sweet	A consumable item. It can be used to help Milcery evolve.	Get as a reward at a Battle Café
Bug Memory	A nonconsumable item. If held by Silvally, this item will change Silvally's type to Bug type.	Get Type: Null and all of Silvally's memory discs at the Battle Tower after becoming Champion
Chipped Pot	A consumable item. It can be used to help certain Sinistea evolve.	Buy at the bargain stall in Stow-on-Side
Clover Sweet	A consumable item. It can be used to help Milcery evolve.	Get as a reward at a Battle Café
Cracked Pot	A consumable item. It can be used to help certain Sinistea evolve.	Find in Stow-on-Side / Buy at the bargain stall in Stow-on-Side
Dark Memory	A nonconsumable item. If held by Silvally, this item will change Silvally's type to Dark type.	Get Type: Null and all of Silvally's memory discs at the Battle Tower after becoming Champion
Dawn Stone	A consumable item. It can be used to help Kirlia or Snorunt evolve.	Find as a hidden item at the Lake of Outrage in the Wild Area
Dragon Memory	A nonconsumable item. If held by Silvally, this item will change Silvally's type to Dragon type.	Get Type: Null and all of Silvally's memory discs at the Battle Tower after becoming Champion
Dusk Stone	A consumable item. It can be used to help Lampent or Doublade evolve.	Find as a hidden item at the Lake of Outrage in the Wild Area
Electric Memory	A nonconsumable item. If held by Silvally, this item will change Silvally's type to Electric type.	Get Type: Null and all of Silvally's memory discs at the Battle Tower after becoming Champion
Everstone	A nonconsumable item. If held by a Pokémon, this item will prevent the holder from evolving.	Find as a hidden item in Turffield
Fairy Memory	A nonconsumable item. If held by Silvally, this item will change Silvally's type to Fairy type.	Get Type: Null and all of Silvally's memory discs at the Battle Tower after becoming Champion
Fighting Memory	A nonconsumable item. If held by Silvally, this item will change Silvally's type to Fighting type.	Get Type: Null and all of Silvally's memory discs at the Battle Tower after becoming Champion
Fire Memory	A nonconsumable item. If held by Silvally, this item will change Silvally's type to Fire type.	Get Type: Null and all of Silvally's memory discs at the Battle Tower after becoming Champion
Fire Stone	A consumable item. It can be used to help Vulpix, Growlithe, or Eevee evolve.	Find as a hidden item at the Lake of Outrage in the Wild Area
Flower Sweet	A consumable item. It can be used to help Milcery evolve.	Get as a reward at a Battle Café
Flying Memory	A nonconsumable item. If held by Silvally, this item will change Silvally's type to Flying type.	Get Type: Null and all of Silvally's memory discs at the Battle Tower after becoming Champion
Ghost Memory	A nonconsumable item. If held by Silvally, this item will change Silvally's type to Ghost type.	Get Type: Null and all of Silvally's memory discs at the Battle Tower after becoming Champion
Grass Memory	A nonconsumable item. If held by Silvally, this item will change Silvally's type to Grass type.	Get Type: Null and all of Silvally's memory discs at the Battle Tower after becoming Champion
Ground Memory	A nonconsumable item. If held by Silvally, this item will change Silvally's type to Ground type.	Get Type: Null and all of Silvally's memory discs at the Battle Tower after becoming Champion
Ice Memory	A nonconsumable item. If held by Silvally, this item will change Silvally's type to Ice type.	Get Type: Null and all of Silvally's memory discs at the Battle Tower after becoming Champion
Ice Stone	A consumable item. It can be used to help Eevee evolve.	Find as a hidden item at the Lake of Outrage in the Wild Area
Leaf Stone	A consumable item. It can be used to help Gloom, Eevee, or Nuzleaf evolve.	Find as a hidden item at the Lake of Outrage in the Wild Area
Love Sweet	A consumable item. It can be used to help Milcery evolve.	Get as a reward at a Battle Café
Metal Coat	An item with different uses. It can be used to help Onix evolve. When used in this way, the item will be consumed.	Find as a hidden item in Stow-on-Side

Name	Description	Main way to obtain
Moon Stone	A consumable item. It can be used to help Clefairy or Munna evolve.	Find in the Dusty Bowl in the Wild Area
Poison Memory	A nonconsumable item. If held by Silvally, this item will change Silvally's type to Poison type.	Get Type: Null and all of Silvally's memory discs at the Battle Tower after becoming Champion
Prism Scale	A consumable item. It can be used to help Feebas evolve.	Find as a hidden item on Route 2
Protector	A consumable item. It can be used to help Rhydon evolve.	Find on Route 9 (Circhester Bay)
Psychic Memory	A nonconsumable item. If held by Silvally, this item will change Silvally's type to Psychic type.	Get Type: Null and all of Silvally's memory discs at the Battle Tower after becoming Champion
Razor Claw	An item with different uses. It can be used to help Sneasel evolve. When used in this way, the item will be consumed.	Find as a hidden item in the Dusty Bowl in the Wild Area
Reaper Cloth	A consumable item. It can be used to help Dusclops evolve.	Get by helping deliver an Old Letter for a little girl in Hammerlocke
Ribbon Sweet	A consumable item. It can be used to help Milcery evolve.	Get as a reward at a Battle Café
Rock Memory	A nonconsumable item. If held by Silvally, this item will change Silvally's type to Rock type.	Get Type: Null and all of Silvally's memory discs at the Battle Tower after becoming Champion
Rusted Shield	A nonconsumable item. If held by Zamazenta, this item will change it to its Crowned Shield form.	Obtain during your main adventure
Rusted Sword	A nonconsumable item. If held by Zacian, this item will change it to its Crowned Sword form.	Obtain during your main adventure
Sachet	A consumable item. It can be used to help Spritzee evolve.	Get from the BP Shop in Hammerlocke's central Pokémon Center
Shiny Stone	A consumable item. It can be used to help Togetic, Roselia, and Minccino evolve.	Find as a hidden item at the Lake of Outrage in the Wild Area
Star Sweet	A consumable item. It can be used to help Milcery evolve.	Get as a reward at a Battle Café
Steel Memory	A nonconsumable item. If held by Silvally, this item will change Silvally's type to Steel type.	Get Type: Null and all of Silvally's memory discs at the Battle Tower after becoming Champion
Strawberry Sweet	A consumable item. It can be used to help Milcery evolve.	Find in Hammerlocke / Get as a reward at a Battle Café
Sun Stone	A consumable item. It can be used to help Gloom, Cottonee, or Helioptile evolve.	Find in the Dusty Bowl in the Wild Area
Sweet Apple	A consumable item. It can be used to help Applin evolve.	Get from a guy in Hammerlocke by helping him / Find as a hidden item on Axew's Eye in the Wild Area
Tart Apple	A consumable item. It can be used to help Applin evolve.	Get from a guy in Hammerlocke by helping him / Find as a hidden item on Axew's Eye in the Wild Area
Thunder Stone	A consumable item. It can be used to help Pikachu or Eevee evolve.	Find as a hidden item at the Lake of Outrage in the Wild Area
Water Memory	A nonconsumable item. If held by Silvally, this item will change Silvally's type to Water type.	Get Type: Null and all of Silvally's memory discs at the Battle Tower after becoming Champion
Water Stone	A consumable item. It can be used to help Shellder, Eevee, and Lombre evolve.	Find as a hidden item at the Lake of Outrage in the Wild Area
Whipped Dream	A consumable item. It can be used to help Swirlix evolve.	Get from the BP Shop in Hammerlocke's central Pokémon Center

Items that affect battles and encounters

Name	Description	Main way to obtain
Absorb Bulb	A consumable item. If held by a Pokémon, this item will raise the holder's Sp. Atk by 1 stage if it is hit with a damage-dealing Water-type move.	Find as a hidden item on Route 5
Adrenaline Orb	A consumable item. If held by a Pokémon, this item will boost the holder's Speed when affected by Intimidate.	Get from the right-hand clerk at the Battle Tower's BP Shop after becoming Champion
Air Balloon	A consumable item. If held by a Pokémon, this item will grant immunity to all Ground-type moves until the holder is hit by a damage-dealing move.	Find in Wyndon
Amulet Coin	A nonconsumable item. If a Pokémon holding it appears in battle, this item will double the prize money received from that battle.	Find in the Motostoke Outskirts
Assault Vest	A nonconsumable item. If held by a Pokémon, this item will boost the holder's Sp. Def by 50% but prevent the Pokémon from using status moves.	Find at the Lake of Outrage in the Wild Area
Big Root	A nonconsumable item. If held by a Pokémon, this item will increase the amount of HP restored to the holder by HP-draining moves by 30%.	Find in the Glimwood Tangle
Binding Band	A nonconsumable item. If held by a Pokémon, this item will boost the effectiveness of the holder's binding moves. They will damage the target for 1/6 of its max HP each turn, instead of the regular 1/8.	Buy at the bargain stall in Stow-on-Side
Black Belt	A nonconsumable item. If held by a Pokémon, this item will boost the power of the holder's Fighting-type moves by 20%.	Find as a hidden item on Route 9 (Circhester Bay)
Black Glasses	A nonconsumable item. If held by a Pokémon, this item will boost the power of the holder's Dark-type moves by 20%.	Find in Motostoke
Black Sludge	A nonconsumable item. If held by a Poison-type Pokémon, this item will restore 1/16 of the holder's max HP each turn. If held by any other type, it will cause the holder to lose 1/8 of its max HP each turn.	Find as a hidden item in Wyndon
Blunder Policy	A consumable item. If held by a Pokémon, this item will raise the holder's Speed by 2 stages if one of its moves misses due to low accuracy.	Get from the right-hand clerk at the Battle Tower's BP Shop after becoming Champion
Bright Powder	A nonconsumable item. If held by a Pokémon, this item will lower the accuracy of moves that target the holder.	Find in Glimwood Tangle
Cell Battery	A consumable item. If held by a Pokémon, this item will raise the holder's Attack by 1 stage if it is hit with a damage-dealing Electric-type move.	Find in Wyndon

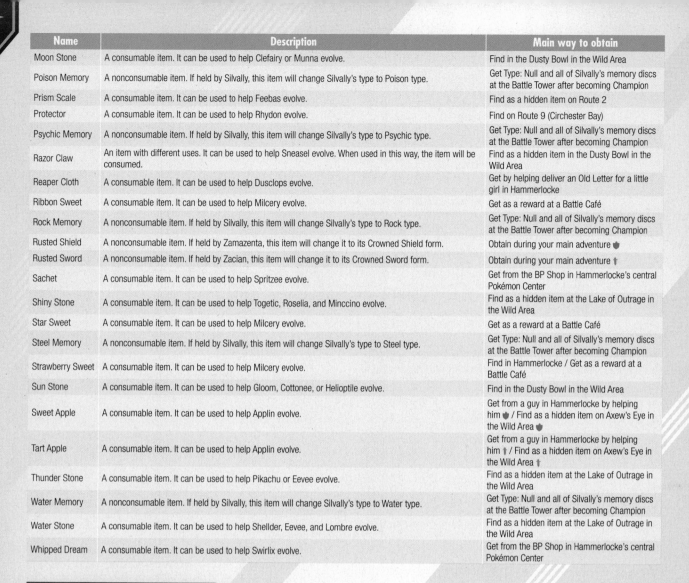

Name	Description	Main way to obtain
Charcoal	A nonconsumable item. If held by a Pokémon, this item will boost the power of the holder's Fire-type moves by 20%.	Receive from Leon in Motostoke if you chose Scorbunny / Buy at the bargain stall in Stow-on-Side
Choice Band	A nonconsumable item. If held by a Pokémon, this item will boost the holder's Attack by 50%. However, the holder will become unable to use any move but the first move it chooses when it enters the battlefield.	Find on Route 2
Choice Scarf	A nonconsumable item. If held by a Pokémon, this item will boost the holder's Speed by 50%. However, the holder will become unable to use any move but the first move it chooses when it enters the battlefield.	Get by helping deliver an Old Letter for a little girl in Hammerlocke
Choice Specs	A nonconsumable item. If held by a Pokémon, this item will boost the holder's Sp. Atk by 50%. However, the holder will become unable to use any move but the first move it chooses when it enters the battlefield.	Find in Spikemuth
Cleanse Tag	A nonconsumable item. If held by the lead Pokémon in your party, this item will reduce wild Pokémon encounters.	Find on Route 4
Damp Rock	A nonconsumable item. If a Pokémon holding this item causes the weather condition to change to rain, the rain will last 8 turns instead of 5.	Get from a gentleman in a house in Hammerlocke
Destiny Knot	A nonconsumable item. If a Pokémon holding this item is afflicted with infatuation, the Pokémon that caused it will also become infatuated.	Get from the BP Shop in Hammerlocke's central Pokémon Center
Dragon Fang	A nonconsumable item. If held by a Pokémon, this item will boost the power of the holder's Dragon-type moves by 20%.	Buy at the bargain stall in Stow-on-Side
Eject Button	A consumable item. If held by a Pokémon, this item will force the holder to switch out of battle if it is hit by a damage-dealing move.	Get from the right-hand clerk at the Battle Tower's BP Shop after becoming Champion
Eject Pack	A consumable item. If held by a Pokémon, this item will force the holder to switch out of battle if any of its stats are lowered.	Get from the right-hand clerk at the Battle Tower's BP Shop after becoming Champion
Electric Seed	A consumable item. If held by a Pokémon, this item will boost the holder's Defense by 1 stage on Electric Terrain.	Find in Wyndon / Sometimes held by wild Togedemaru
Eviolite	A nonconsumable item. If held by a Pokémon, this item will boost the Defense and Sp. Def of the holder by 50% each as long as that Pokémon is still capable of evolving.	Get from a Breeder in a house in Ballonlea
Expert Belt	A nonconsumable item. If held by a Pokémon, this item will boost the power of the holder's supereffective moves by 20%.	Find by solving a riddle in Turffield
Flame Orb	A nonconsumable item. If held by a Pokémon, this item will inflict the burned status condition on the holder.	Get as a reward in a Champion tournament after becoming Champion
Float Stone	A nonconsumable item. If held by a Pokémon, this item will halve the holder's weight.	Get from the Digging Duo in the Wild Area
Focus Band	A nonconsumable item. If held by a Pokémon, this item will give the holder a 10% chance of surviving with 1 HP when it receives damage that would normally cause it to faint.	Sometimes held by wild Machop, Machoke, and Machamp
Focus Sash	A consumable item. If held by a Pokémon with full HP, this item will allow the holder to survive with 1 HP when it receives damage that would normally cause it to faint.	Find at the Lake of Outrage in the Wild Area
Full Incense	A nonconsumable item. If held by a Pokémon, this item will make the holder move later in the turn. It can also be used to help find Pokémon Eggs that hatch into certain species.	Buy from the Incense Merchant in Hulbury
Grassy Seed	A consumable item. If held by a Pokémon, this item will boost the holder's Defense by 1 stage on Grassy Terrain.	Find in Wyndon
Grip Claw	A nonconsumable item. If held by a Pokémon, this item will extend the duration of the holder's moves like Bind and Wrap to 7 turns.	Find in Galar Mine No. 2
Hard Stone	A nonconsumable item. If held by a Pokémon, this item will boost the power of the holder's Rock-type moves by 20%.	Find it as a hidden item in Galar Mine
Heat Rock	A nonconsumable item. If a Pokémon holding this item causes the weather condition to change to harsh sunlight, the harsh sunlight will last 8 turns instead of 5.	Get from a gentleman in a house in Hammerlocke
Heavy-Duty Boots	A nonconsumable item. If held by a Pokémon, this item will protect the holder from the effects of Spikes, Stealth Rock, Sticky Web, and Toxic Spikes.	Find in Galar Mine
Icy Rock	A nonconsumable item. If a Pokémon holding this item causes the weather condition to change to hail, the hail will last 8 turns instead of 5.	Get from a gentleman in a house in Hammerlocke
Iron Ball	A nonconsumable item. If held by a Pokémon, this item will reduce the holder's Speed stat by 50%. If the holder is a Flying-type Pokémon or has the Levitate Ability, it will also lose its immunity to Ground-type moves.	Get from the Digging Duo in the Wild Area
King's Rock	A nonconsumable item. If held by a Pokémon, the holder may cause targets to flinch when dealing damage.	Find on Route 8 / Sometimes held by wild Hawlucha
Lagging Tail	A nonconsumable item. If held by a Pokémon, this item will cause the holder to move later.	Get from the Digging Duo in the Wild Area / Sometimes held by wild Cufant and Copperajah
Lax Incense	A nonconsumable item. If held by a Pokémon, this item will boost the holder's evasiveness. It can also be used to help find Pokémon Eggs that hatch into certain species.	Buy from the Incense Merchant in Hulbury
Leek	A nonconsumable item. If held by a Farfetch'd, this item will make the Farfetch'd much more likely to deliver critical hits.	Sometimes held by wild Farfetch'd and Sirfetch'd
Leftovers	A nonconsumable item. If held by a Pokémon, this item will restore 1/16 of the holder's max HP each turn.	Find at the Giant's Seat in the Wild Area / Get from a Berry tree in the Wild Area
Life Orb	A nonconsumable item. If held by a Pokémon, the holder will lose HP each time it attacks, but the power of its moves will be boosted by 30%.	Find in the Slumbering Weald
Light Ball	A nonconsumable item. If held by a Pikachu, this item will double the Pikachu's Attack and Sp. Atk.	Sometimes held by wild Pikachu
Light Clay	A nonconsumable item. If held by a Pokémon, this item will extend the duration of the moves Aurora Veil, Light Screen, and Reflect by 3 turns.	Find on Route 6
Luck Incense	A nonconsumable item. If a Pokémon holding it appears in battle, this item will double the prize money received from that battle.	Buy from the Incense Merchant in Hulbury
Lucky Egg	A nonconsumable item. If held by a Pokémon, the holder will gain 50% more Exp. Points from battle.	Get from a chef by helping him in Hulbury
Luminous Moss	A consumable item. If held by a Pokémon, this item will raise the holder's Sp. Def by 1 stage if it is hit with a damage-dealing Water-type move.	Find in Glimwood Tangle
Macho Brace	A nonconsumable item. If held by a Pokémon, this item will halve the holder's Speed but increase the rate at which it gains base points.	Get from the BP Shop in Hammerlocke's central Pokémon Center
Magnet	A nonconsumable item. If held by a Pokémon, this item will boost the power of the holder's Electric-type moves by 20%.	Find in Hulbury

Name	Description	Main way to obtain
Max Repel	A consumable item. If you use it, this item will prevent you from encountering lower-level Pokémon in the wild. The effect lasts longer than a Super Repel.	Buy at any Poké Mart once you have 7 Gym Badges
Mental Herb	A consumable item. If held by a Pokémon, the holder will instantly shake off the effects of Attract, Disable, Encore, Taunt, and Torment, as well as Abilities that inflict similar effects.	Find in the Slumbering Weald
Metal Coat	An item with different uses. If held by a Pokémon, this item will boost the power of the holder's Steel-type moves by 20%.	Find as a hidden item in Stow-on-Side
Metal Powder	A nonconsumable item. If held by a Ditto, this item will double the Ditto's Defense.	Sometimes held by wild Ditto
Metronome	A nonconsumable item. If held by a Pokémon, this item will boost the power of a move used consecutively by the holder. The power increases with each use until it reaches the max of 200%.	Buy at the bargain stall in Stow-on-Side
Miracle Seed	A nonconsumable item. If held by a Pokémon, this item will boost the power of the holder's Grass-type moves by 20%.	Receive from Leon in Motostoke if you chose Grookey / Buy at the bargain stall in Stow-on-Side
Misty Seed	A consumable item. If held by a Pokémon, this item will boost the holder's Sp. Def by 1 stage on Misty Terrain.	Find in the Slumbering Weald
Muscle Band	A nonconsumable item. If held by a Pokémon, this item will boost the power of the holder's physical moves by 10%.	Find in Hammerlocke
Mystic Water	A nonconsumable item. If held by a Pokémon, this item will boost the power of the holder's Water-type moves by 20%.	Receive from Leon in Motostoke if you chose Sobble / Buy at the bargain stall in Stow-on-Side
Never-Melt Ice	A nonconsumable item. If held by a Pokémon, this item will boost the power of the holder's Ice-type moves by 20%.	Find as a hidden item on Route 9 (Circhester Bay)
Normal Gem	A consumable item. If held by a Pokémon, this item will boost the power of a Normal-type move used by the holder by 30%.	Find as a hidden item on Route 9 (Circhester Bay)
Odd Incense	A nonconsumable item. If held by a Pokémon, this item will boost the power of the holder's Psychic-type moves by 20%. It can also be used to help find Pokémon Eggs that hatch into certain species.	Buy from the Incense Merchant in Hulbury
Poison Barb	A nonconsumable item. If held by a Pokémon, this item will boost the power of the holder's Poison-type moves by 20%.	Buy at the bargain stall in Stow-on-Side
Power Anklet	A nonconsumable item. If held by a Pokémon, this item will halve the holder's Speed but increase the rate at which it gains base points for its Speed stat.	Get from the BP Shop in Hammerlocke's central Pokémon Center
Power Band	A nonconsumable item. If held by a Pokémon, this item will halve the holder's Speed but increase the rate at which it gains base points for its Sp. Def stat.	Get from the BP Shop in Hammerlocke's central Pokémon Center
Power Belt	A nonconsumable item. If held by a Pokémon, this item will halve the holder's Speed but increase the rate at which it gains base points for its Defense stat.	Get from the BP Shop in Hammerlocke's central Pokémon Center
Power Bracer	A nonconsumable item. If held by a Pokémon, this item will halve the holder's Speed but increase the rate at which it gains base points for its Attack stat.	Get from the BP Shop in Hammerlocke's central Pokémon Center
Power Herb	A consumable item. If held by a Pokémon, the holder will be able to immediately use a move that would normally require one turn to charge.	Get from the right-hand clerk at the Battle Tower's BP Shop after becoming Champion
Power Lens	A nonconsumable item. If held by a Pokémon, this item will halve the holder's Speed but increase the rate at which it gains base points for its Sp. Atk stat.	Get from the BP Shop in Hammerlocke's central Pokémon Center
Power Weight	A nonconsumable item. If held by a Pokémon, this item will halve the holder's Speed but increase the rate at which it gains base points for its HP stat.	Get from the BP Shop in Hammerlocke's central Pokémon Center
Protective Pads	A nonconsumable item. If held by a Pokémon, this item will protect the holder from effects caused by making direct contact with a target.	Buy at the bargain stall in Stow-on-Side
Psychic Seed	A consumable item. If held by a Pokémon, this item will boost the holder's Sp. Def by 1 stage on Psychic Terrain.	Find on Route 2
Pure Incense	A nonconsumable item. If held by the lead Pokémon in your party, this item will reduce wild Pokémon encounters.	Buy from the Incense Merchant in Hulbury
Quick Claw	A nonconsumable item. If held by a Pokémon, this item will occasionally allow the holder to strike with high priority.	Buy at the bargain stall in Stow-on-Side
Quick Powder	A nonconsumable item. If held by a Ditto, this item will double the Ditto's Speed.	Sometimes held by wild Ditto
Razor Claw	An item with different uses. If held by a Pokémon, the holder will become much more likely to deliver critical hits.	Find as a hidden item in the Dusty Bowl in the Wild Area
Red Card	A consumable item. If held by a Pokémon, any other Pokémon that hits the holder with a damage-dealing move will be forced to switch out.	Get from the right-hand clerk at the Battle Tower's BP Shop after becoming Champion
Repel	A consumable item. If you use it, this item will prevent you from encountering lower-level Pokémon in the wild.	Buy at any Poké Mart once you have 3 Gym Badges
Ring Target	A nonconsumable item. If held by a Pokémon, moves that would usually deal no damage to the holder due to type matchups will instead deal regular damage.	Buy at the bargain stall in Stow-on-Side
Rock Incense	A nonconsumable item. If held by a Pokémon, this item will boost the power of the holder's Rock-type moves by 20%. It can also be used to help find Pokémon Eggs that hatch into certain species.	Buy from the Incense Merchant in Hulbury
Rocky Helmet	A nonconsumable item. If held by a Pokémon, any other Pokémon that uses a move that makes direct contact with the holder will lose 1/6 of its max HP.	Find in Stow-on-Side
Room Service	A consumable item. If held by a Pokémon, this item will lower the holder's Speed by 1 stage if Trick Room is used.	Get from the right-hand clerk at the Battle Tower's BP Shop after becoming Champion
Rose Incense	A nonconsumable item. If held by a Pokémon, this item will boost the power of the holder's Grass-type moves by 20%. It can also be used to help find Pokémon Eggs that hatch into certain species.	Buy from the Incense Merchant in Hulbury
Safety Goggles	A nonconsumable item. If held by a Pokémon, the holder will be protected from weather-related damage, certain moves (Cotton Spore, Magic Powder, Poison Powder, Rage Powder, Sleep Powder, Spore, and Stun Spore), and from the Effect Spore Ability.	Find on Route 7
Scope Lens	A nonconsumable item. If held by a Pokémon, it becomes much more likely the holder will deliver critical hits.	Find on Route 9 (Outer Spikemuth)
Sea Incense	A nonconsumable item. If held by a Pokémon, this item will boost the power of the holder's Water-type moves by 20%. It can also be used to help find Pokémon Eggs that hatch into certain species.	Buy from the Incense Merchant in Hulbury
Sharp Beak	A nonconsumable item. If held by a Pokémon, this item will boost the power of the holder's Flying-type moves by 20%.	Find on Route 4
Shed Shell	A nonconsumable item. If held by a Pokémon, this item will allow the holder to switch out even when trapped by the effects of moves or Abilities.	Find on Route 5
Shell Bell	A nonconsumable item. If held by a Pokémon, this item will restore the holder's HP when it hits another Pokémon with a damage-dealing move. The holder will regain HP equal to 1/8 of the damage dealt.	Find in Hulbury

Name	Description	Main way to obtain
Silk Scarf	A nonconsumable item. If held by a Pokémon, this item will boost the power of the holder's Normal-type moves by 20%.	Find in Motostoke
Silver Powder	A nonconsumable item. If held by a Pokémon, this item will boost the power of the holder's Bug-type moves by 20%.	Find on Route 4
Smoke Ball	A nonconsumable item. If held by a Pokémon, this item will allow the holder to run away from wild Pokémon even when trapped by the effects of moves or Abilities.	Find in the Slumbering Weald
Smooth Rock	A nonconsumable item. If a Pokémon holding this item causes the weather condition to change to sandstorm, the sandstorm will last 8 turns instead of 5.	Get from a gentleman in a house in Hammerlocke
Snowball	A consumable item. If held by a Pokémon, this item will raise the holder's Attack by 1 stage if it is hit with a damage-dealing Ice-type move.	Find in Circhester
Soft Sand	A nonconsumable item. If held by a Pokémon, this item will boost the power of the holder's Ground-type moves by 20%.	Find as a hidden item in Galar Mine No. 2
Soothe Bell	A nonconsumable item. If held by a Pokémon, the holder will become friendly more quickly.	Get from a girl in a house in Motostoke
Spell Tag	A nonconsumable item. If held by a Pokémon, this item will boost the power of the holder's Ghost-type moves by 20%.	Buy at the bargain stall in Stow-on-Side
Sticky Barb	A nonconsumable item. If held by a Pokémon, this item will cause the holder to lose 1/8 of its max HP each turn. If another Pokémon uses a move that makes direct contact with the holder, this item will pass to the attacker.	Get from the Digging Duo in the Wild Area
Super Repel	A consumable item. If you use it, this item will prevent you from encountering lower-level Pokémon in the wild. The effect lasts longer than a basic Repel.	Buy at any Poké Mart once you have 5 Gym Badges
Terrain Extender	A nonconsumable item. If held by a Pokémon, any terrain triggered by the holder's moves or Ability will last 8 turns instead of 5.	Find on Route 8
Throat Spray	A consumable item. If held by a Pokémon, this item will raise the holder's Sp. Atk by 1 stage if it uses a sound-based move in battle.	Get from a boy by finding his Minccino in Motostoke
Toxic Orb	A nonconsumable item. If held by a Pokémon, this item will inflict the badly poisoned status condition on the holder during battle.	Get as a reward in a Champion tournament after becoming Champion
Twisted Spoon	A nonconsumable item. If held by a Pokémon, this item will boost the power of the holder's Psychic-type moves by 20%.	Buy at the bargain stall in Stow-on-Side
Utility Umbrella	A nonconsumable item. If held by a Pokémon, this item will negate the effects of both the rain and harsh sunlight weather conditions.	Get from a gentleman in a house in Hammerlocke
Wave Incense	A nonconsumable item. If held by a Pokémon, this item will boost the power of the holder's Water-type moves by 20%. It can also be used to help find Pokémon Eggs that hatch into certain species.	Buy from the Incense Merchant in Hulbury
Weakness Policy	A consumable item. If held by a Pokémon, this item will increase the holder's Attack and Sp. Atk by 2 stages each if the holder is hit with a supereffective move.	Get from the right-hand clerk at the Battle Tower's BP Shop after becoming Champion
White Herb	A consumable item. If held by a Pokémon, this item will restore any lowered stats one time.	Find at the Watchtower Ruins in the Wild Area
Wide Lens	A nonconsumable item. If held by a Pokémon, this item will boost the holder's accuracy by 10%.	Get from Howses by solving a mystery in Circhester's Hotel Ionia
Wise Glasses	A nonconsumable item. If held by a Pokémon, this item will boost the power of the holder's special moves by 10%.	Find in Hammerlocke
Wishing Piece	A consumable item. If you use one at a Pokémon Den, it may attract a wild Dynamax Pokémon.	Get from a Rotom Rallyist in the Wild Area
Zoom Lens	A nonconsumable item. If held by a Pokémon, this item will boost the holder's accuracy by 20% if its targets have already moved that turn.	Find on Route 9 (Circhester Bay)

Items that can be used to help find particular kinds of Pokémon Eggs

Name	Description	Main way to obtain
Destiny Knot	A nonconsumable item. It can be used to help ensure that Pokémon Eggs you find inherit five individual strengths from the Pokémon you leave at the Nursery.	Get from the BP Shop in Hammerlocke's central Pokémon Center
Everstone	A nonconsumable item. It can be used to help ensure that Pokémon Eggs you find inherit regional forms or Natures from the Pokémon you leave at the Nursery.	Find as a hidden item in Turffield
Full Incense	A nonconsumable item. It can be used to help you find a Pokémon Egg that will hatch into a Munchlax.	Buy from the Incense Merchant in Hulbury
Lax Incense	A nonconsumable item. It can be used to help you find a Pokémon Egg that will hatch into a Wynaut.	Buy from the Incense Merchant in Hulbury
Light Ball	A nonconsumable item. It can be used to help you find a Pokémon Egg that will hatch into a Pichu that knows the move Volt Tackle.	Sometimes held by wild Pikachu
Odd Incense	A nonconsumable item. It can be used to help you find a Pokémon Egg that will hatch into a Mime Jr.	Buy from the Incense Merchant in Hulbury
Power Anklet	A nonconsumable item. It can be used to help ensure that Pokémon Eggs you find inherit the Speed individual strength from the Pokémon you leave at the Nursery.	Get from the BP Shop in Hammerlocke's central Pokémon Center
Power Band	A nonconsumable item. It can be used to help ensure that Pokémon Eggs you find inherit the Sp. Def individual strength from the Pokémon you leave at the Nursery.	Get from the BP Shop in Hammerlocke's central Pokémon Center
Power Belt	A nonconsumable item. It can be used to help ensure that Pokémon Eggs you find inherit the Defense individual strength from the Pokémon you leave at the Nursery.	Get from the BP Shop in Hammerlocke's central Pokémon Center
Power Bracer	A nonconsumable item. It can be used to help ensure that Pokémon Eggs you find inherit the Attack individual strength from the Pokémon you leave at the Nursery.	Get from the BP Shop in Hammerlocke's central Pokémon Center
Power Lens	A nonconsumable item. It can be used to help ensure that Pokémon Eggs you find inherit the Sp. Atk individual strength from the Pokémon you leave at the Nursery.	Get from the BP Shop in Hammerlocke's central Pokémon Center
Power Weight	A nonconsumable item. It can be used to help ensure that Pokémon Eggs you find inherit the HP individual strength from the Pokémon you leave at the Nursery.	Get from the BP Shop in Hammerlocke's central Pokémon Center
Rock Incense	A nonconsumable item. It can be used to help you find a Pokémon Egg that will hatch into a Bonsly.	Buy from the Incense Merchant in Hulbury
Rose Incense	A nonconsumable item. It can be used to help you find a Pokémon Egg that will hatch into a Budew.	Buy from the Incense Merchant in Hulbury
Wave Incense	A nonconsumable item. It can be used to help you find a Pokémon Egg that will hatch into a Mantyke.	Buy from the Incense Merchant in Hulbury

Treasures

Name	Description	Main way to obtain
Balm Mushroom	A fragrant mushroom. It can be sold at shops for profit.	Find as a hidden item near trees in the Wild Area
Big Mushroom	A big mushroom. It can be sold at shops for profit.	Find as a hidden item near trees in the Wild Area
Big Nugget	A big nugget of pure gold. It can be sold at shops for profit.	Find on Route 8 or in Wyndon
Big Pearl	A big pearl. It can be sold at shops for profit.	Find as a hidden item near or on the lakes in the Wild Area
Bottle Cap	A beautiful bottle cap that gives off a silver gleam. Use one to have a Lv. 100 Pokémon train up one stat via Hyper Training.	Get from the right-hand clerk at the Battle Tower's BP Shop after becoming Champion
Comet Shard	A shard that fell to the ground when a comet passed by. It can be sold at shops for profit.	Find as a hidden item in the North Wild Area
Fossilized Bird	The fossil of an ancient Pokémon that once soared through the sky. It can be restored, together with another fossil, to obtain certain Pokémon.	Find as a hidden item in the Dusty Bowl in the Wild Area / Get from the Digging Duo in the Wild Area
Fossilized Dino	The fossil of an ancient Pokémon that once lived in the sea. It can be restored, together with another fossil, to obtain certain Pokémon.	Find as a hidden item in the Dusty Bowl in the Wild Area / Get from the Digging Duo in the Wild Area
Fossilized Drake	The fossil of an ancient Pokémon that once roamed the land. It can be restored, together with another fossil, to obtain certain Pokémon.	Find as a hidden item in the Dusty Bowl in the Wild Area / Get from the Digging Duo in the Wild Area
Fossilized Fish	The fossil of an ancient Pokémon that once lived in the sea. It can be restored, together with another fossil, to obtain certain Pokémon.	Find as a hidden item in the Dusty Bowl in the Wild Area / Get from the Digging Duo in the Wild Area
Gold Bottle Cap	A beautiful bottle cap that gives off a golden gleam. Use one to have a Lv. 100 Pokémon train up all six stats via Hyper Training.	Receive as a prize in Ranked Battles at the Battle Tower
Honey	A sweet honey collected by wild Pokémon. It can be sold at shops for profit.	Find as a hidden item in flower patches in the Wild Area
Nugget	A nugget of pure gold. It can be sold at shops for profit.	Find as a hidden item in Motostoke, Hammerlocke, or elsewhere
Pearl	A pretty pearl. It can be sold at shops for profit.	Find as a hidden item near or on the lakes in the Wild Area
Pearl String	A string of large pearls with a silvery sheen. It can be sold at shops for profit.	Find as a hidden item near or on the lakes in the Wild Area
Pretty Feather	A beautiful feather. It can be sold at shops for profit.	Find as a hidden item on the bridge on Route 5 or the bridge in the Motostoke Outskirts
Rare Bone	A rare bone. It can be sold at shops for profit.	Find as a hidden item in the Dusty Bowl or at the Giant's Mirror in the Wild Area
Star Piece	A sparkling red gem. It can be sold at shops for profit.	Find as a hidden item in the North Wild Area
Stardust	Lovely, red-colored sand. It can be sold at shops for profit.	Find as a hidden item in the North Wild Area
Tiny Mushroom	A tiny mushroom. It can be sold at shops for profit.	Find as a hidden item near trees in the Wild Area

Key Items

Name	Description	Main way to obtain
Adventure Guide	A device that automatically collects and records advice during your adventure.	You'll obtain it automatically during your main adventure
Camping Gear	A set of camping gear, including the equipment you need to cook at camp.	You'll obtain it automatically during your main adventure
Catching Charm	A curious charm said to increase the likelihood of catching Pokémon as a critical catch in the wild. Simply possessing one awards a Trainer with its effects.	Get from the game director in Circhester's Hotel Ionia
Dynamax Band	A wristband that allows a Trainer to Dynamax their Pokémon at a Power Spot.	You'll obtain it automatically during your main adventure
Endorsement	A letter you need in order to participate in the Gym Challenge.	You'll obtain it automatically during your main adventure
Escape Rope	A rope that can be used over and over to help you escape from locations like caves or dungeons.	You'll obtain it automatically during your main adventure
Fishing Rod	A fishing rod that allows you to fish up Pokémon living in the water.	You'll obtain it automatically during your main adventure
Hi-tech Earbuds	Strange earbuds that allow you to adjust the volume of various sounds in the Options.	Talk to a man on the street near the eastern record shop in Motostoke
Oval Charm	An oval charm said to increase the chance of Pokémon Eggs being found at the Nursery. Simply possessing one awards a Trainer with its effects.	Get from Morimoto if you defeat him in a battle at Circhester's Hotel Ionia after becoming Champion
Pokémon Box Link	A device that allows you to access your Boxes in the Pokémon storage system even when you're out and about.	You'll obtain it automatically during your main adventure
Rotom Bike	A bike that has been powered up by the Pokémon Rotom. With the right parts, it can run over water as well as on land.	You'll obtain it automatically during your main adventure
Rotom Catalog	A catalog of devices that Rotom like. It can be used to have a Rotom change form.	Get from a Rotom user in Wyndon
Shiny Charm	A shiny charm said to increase the chances of encountering Shiny Pokémon in the wild. Simply possessing one awards a Trainer with its effects.	Get from the game director in Circhester's Hotel Ionia if you complete your Pokédex
Sonia's Book	Professor Sonia's published writings about the Galar region's legends.	Meet Sonia in the Slumbering Weald after becoming Champion
Wishing Star	A stone with a mysterious power. It's said your dreams come true if you find one.	You'll obtain it automatically during your main adventure

Shop Lists

There are many shops to visit around the Galar region, which means plenty of different shopping destinations to keep straight. If you're looking for a particular item, use the tables below to help track down where you can buy it!

!

Don't forget to check out these other shops and ways to obtain items in the Galar region!

- Rotom Rallyists around the Wild Area who also serve as Watt Traders (p. 276)
- The Ingredients Sellers in the Wild Area, along with their daily lineup of ingredients (p. 277)
- The Digging Duo who may dig up some finds for you in the Wild Area (p. 278)
- The various Trainers wandering about the Wild Area who may offer you their finds for Watts (p. 279)
- The fellow selling bargains at the Street Market in Stow-on-Side (p. 89)
- Boutiques in Wedgehurst (p. 40), Motostoke (p. 50), Hammerlocke (p. 80), Circhester (p. 106), and Wyndon (p. 124), as well as uniform shops in most stadiums!

Poké Mart	
Items that are always available	
From the start	
Antidote	₽200
Awakening	₽200
Burn Heal	₽200
Ice Heal	₽200
Paralyze Heal	₽200
Poké Ball*	₽200
Potion	₽200
Revive	₽2,000
After earning 1 Gym Badge	
Great Ball	₽600
Super Potion	₽700
After earning 2 Gym Badges	
Poké Doll	₽300
After earning 3 Gym Badges	
Repel	₽400
After earning 4 Gym Badges	
Hyper Potion	₽1,500
After earning 5 Gym Badges	
Super Repel	₽700
Ultra Ball	₽800
After earning 6 Gym Badges	
Full Heal	₽400
After earning 7 Gym Badges	
Max Potion	₽2,500
Max Repel	₽900
After earning 8 Gym Badges	
Full Restore	₽3,000

*Poké Balls become available after you meet Leon on Route 2.

Poké Mart	
Specialty offerings	
Motostoke (lower level)	
Heal Ball	₽300
Nest Ball	₽1,000
Net Ball	₽1,000
X Attack	₽1,000
X Defense	₽2,000
X Sp. Atk	₽1,000
X Sp. Def	₽2,000
Motostoke (upper level)	
TM17 Light Screen	₽10,000
TM18 Reflect	₽10,000
TM19 Safeguard	₽10,000
TM25 Protect	₽10,000
TM41 Helping Hand	₽10,000
TM76 Round	₽10,000
TM94 False Swipe	₽10,000
Hammerlocke (west)	
TM13 Fire Spin	₽10,000
TM23 Thief	₽10,000
TM32 Sandstorm	₽10,000
TM33 Rain Dance	₽10,000
TM34 Sunny Day	₽10,000
TM35 Hail	₽10,000
TM50 Bullet Seed	₽10,000
TM55 Brine	₽10,000
Hammerlocke (central)	
Dire Hit	₽1,000
Dive Ball	₽1,000
Dusk Ball	₽1,000
Guard Spec.	₽1,500
Timer Ball	₽1,000
X Accuracy	₽1,000
X Speed	₽1,000

Poké Mart	
Hammerlocke (east)	
TM00 Mega Punch	₽10,000
TM01 Mega Kick	₽40,000
TM46 Weather Ball	₽30,000
TM66 Thunder Fang	₽30,000
TM67 Ice Fang	₽30,000
TM68 Fire Fang	₽30,000
TM88 Grassy Terrain	₽20,000
TM89 Misty Terrain	₽20,000
TM90 Electric Terrain	₽20,000
TM91 Psychic Terrain	₽20,000
Wyndon (south)	
Calcium	₽10,000
Carbos	₽10,000
HP Up	₽10,000
Iron	₽10,000
Luxury Ball	₽3,000
Protein	₽10,000
Quick Ball	₽1,000
Repeat Ball	₽1,000
Zinc	₽10,000
Wyndon (stadium front)	
TM03 Fire Punch	₽50,000
TM04 Ice Punch	₽50,000
TM05 Thunder Punch	₽50,000
TM08 Hyper Beam	₽50,000
TM09 Giga Impact	₽50,000
TM12 Solar Blade	₽50,000
TM60 Power Swap	₽30,000
TM61 Guard Swap	₽30,000
TM62 Speed Swap	₽30,000
TM63 Drain Punch	₽50,000

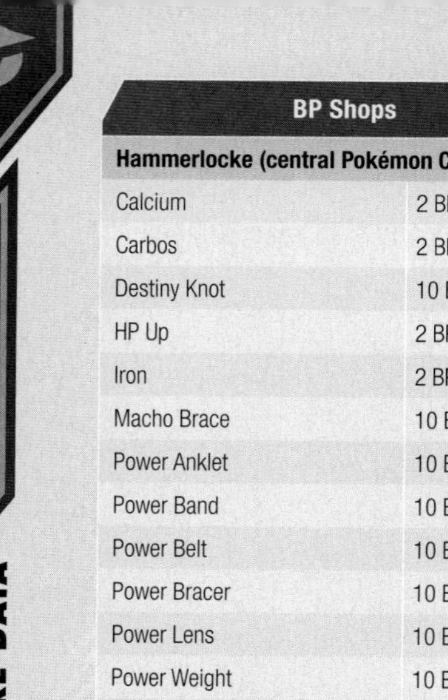

BP Shops

Hammerlocke (central Pokémon Center)	
Calcium	2 BP
Carbos	2 BP
Destiny Knot	10 BP
HP Up	2 BP
Iron	2 BP
Macho Brace	10 BP
Power Anklet	10 BP
Power Band	10 BP
Power Belt	10 BP
Power Bracer	10 BP
Power Lens	10 BP
Power Weight	10 BP
PP Up	10 BP
Protector	10 BP
Protein	2 BP
Rare Candy	20 BP
Razor Claw	10 BP
Reaper Cloth	10 BP
Sachet	10 BP
Whipped Dream	10 BP
Zinc	2 BP
Battle Tower counter (left)	
Adamant Mint	50 BP
Bold Mint	50 BP
Brave Mint	50 BP
Calm Mint	50 BP
Careful Mint	50 BP
Gentle Mint	50 BP
Hasty Mint	50 BP
Impish Mint	50 BP
Jolly Mint	50 BP
Lax Mint	50 BP
Lonely Mint	50 BP
Mild Mint	50 BP
Modest Mint	50 BP
Naive Mint	50 BP
Naughty Mint	50 BP
Quiet Mint	50 BP
Rash Mint	50 BP
Relaxed Mint	50 BP
Sassy Mint	50 BP
Serious Mint	50 BP
Timid Mint	50 BP

BP Shops

Battle Tower counter (right)	
Ability Capsule	50 BP
Absorb Bulb	10 BP
Adrenaline Orb	10 BP
Air Balloon	15 BP
Assault Vest	25 BP
Blunder Policy	20 BP
Bottle Cap	25 BP
Cell Battery	10 BP
Choice Band	25 BP
Choice Scarf	25 BP
Choice Specs	25 BP
Eject Button	20 BP
Eject Pack	20 BP
Focus Sash	15 BP
Life Orb	25 BP
Light Clay	15 BP
Luminous Moss	10 BP
Mental Herb	15 BP
Power Herb	15 BP
Red Card	20 BP
Room Service	15 BP
Snowball	10 BP
Terrain Extender	15 BP
Throat Spray	10 BP
Weakness Policy	20 BP
White Herb	15 BP

Other Shops

Wedgehurst Berry Grocer	
Cheri Berry	₽80
Oran Berry	₽80
Pecha Berry	₽80
Hulbury Incense Merchant	
Full Incense	₽5,000
Lax Incense	₽5,000
Luck Incense	₽11,000
Odd Incense	₽2,000
Pure Incense	₽6,000
Rock Incense	₽2,000
Rose Incense	₽2,000
Sea Incense	₽2,000
Wave Incense	₽2,000
Hulbury Herb Shop	
Energy Powder	₽500
Energy Root	₽1,200
Heal Powder	₽300
Revival Herb	₽2,800
Battle Tower TM seller	
TM20 Self-Destruct	₽100,000
TM28 Giga Drain	₽100,000
TM44 Imprison	₽100,000
TM52 Bounce	₽100,000
TM59 Fling	₽100,000
TM70 Trick Room	₽50,000
TM71 Wonder Room	₽50,000
TM72 Magic Room	₽50,000
TM83 Razor Shell	₽100,000
TM92 Mystical Fire	₽100,000

Vending Machines

Found in train stations	
Fresh Water	₽200
Lemonade	₽350
Soda Pop	₽300

Type Matchup Chart

Remember that all Pokémon—and their moves—have types. Each type has its own strengths and weaknesses, as well as types it will simply deal regular damage to. Damage will be calculated using the Pokémon's stats and the move's power, plus any multiplier caused by the type matchups.

You'll quickly notice that some Pokémon have two types. If a Pokémon has two types, the strengths and weaknesses of the types are both taken into account. They might multiply the damage the Pokémon takes, or they might cancel each other out. Turn back to page 164 for a review!

Type	Effect
	• Immune to damage-dealing Ghost-type moves.
	• Cannot be burned.
	• Immune to Leech Seed. • Immune to powder and spore moves.
	• Cannot be paralyzed.
	• Cannot be frozen. • Take no damage from hail. • Immune to Sheer Cold.
	• Cannot be poisoned or badly poisoned.* • Nullify Toxic Spikes on their side of the battlefield so no other Pokémon will be poisoned when switching in. (If the Poison-type Pokémon is also a Flying type, has the Levitate Ability, or holds an Air Balloon, this nullifying effect will not occur.)
	• Immune to Electric-type moves (including nondamaging moves, such as Thunder Wave). • Take no damage from sandstorms.
	• Immune to Ground-type moves (including nondamaging moves, such as Sand Attack).* • Cannot be damaged or otherwise affected by the effects of moves like Spikes or Sticky Web when switching in.* • Not affected by any terrains.*
	• Take no damage from sandstorms. • Sp. Def goes up in a sandstorm.
	• Immune to Fighting-type moves (including nondamaging moves, such as Octolock) and damage-dealing Normal-type moves.* • Cannot be prevented from fleeing or switching out of battle.
	• Immune to damage-dealing Psychic-type moves. • Immune to the effects of status moves used by Pokémon with the Prankster Ability.
	• Immune to damage-dealing Poison-type moves. • Cannot be poisoned or badly poisoned.* • Take no damage from sandstorms.
	• Immune to damage-dealing Dragon-type moves.

Defending Pokémon's Type (columns) / **Attacking Pokémon's Move Type** (rows)

	NORMAL	FIRE	WATER	GRASS	ELECTRIC	ICE	FIGHTING	POISON	GROUND	FLYING	PSYCHIC	BUG	ROCK	GHOST	DRAGON	DARK	STEEL	FAIRY
NORMAL													▲	×			▲	
FIRE		▲	▲	◉		◉						◉	▲		▲		◉	
WATER		◉	▲	▲					◉				◉		▲			
GRASS		▲	◉	▲				▲	◉	▲		▲	◉		▲		▲	
ELECTRIC			◉	▲	▲				×	◉					▲			
ICE		▲	▲	◉		▲			◉	◉					◉		▲	
FIGHTING	◉					◉		▲		▲	▲	▲	◉	×		◉	◉	▲
POISON				◉				▲	▲				▲	▲			×	◉
GROUND		◉		▲	◉			◉		×		▲	◉				◉	
FLYING				◉	▲		◉					◉	▲				▲	
PSYCHIC							◉	◉			▲					×	▲	
BUG		▲		◉			▲	▲		▲	◉			▲		◉	▲	▲
ROCK		◉				◉	▲		▲	◉		◉					▲	
GHOST	×										◉			◉		▲		
DRAGON															◉		▲	×
DARK							▲				◉			◉		▲		▲
STEEL		▲	▲		▲	◉							◉				▲	◉
FAIRY		▲					◉	▲							◉	◉	▲	

NORMAL	FLYING
FIRE	PSYCHIC
WATER	BUG
GRASS	ROCK
ELECTRIC	GHOST
ICE	DRAGON
FIGHTING	DARK
POISON	STEEL
GROUND	FAIRY

Key

Super effective Moves will do 2× damage.	◉
No weakness or resistance Moves will do the regular amount of damage.	No icon
Not very effective Moves will do ½ damage.	▲
No effect Moves will do no damage.	×

*Some immunities can be negated by moves, Abilities, or items. For example, the Corrosion Ability allows even Poison- or Steel-type Pokémon to be poisoned. Likewise, moves like Smack Down cause Flying-type Pokémon to be grounded, taking away their immunity to Ground-type moves.

Credits

Content & Writing
Jillian Nonaka
Sayuri Munday
Jordan Blanco
Shawn Williams-Brown

Editing Lead
Rei Nakazawa

Editing Support
Kellyn Ballard
Julia Ryer

Additional Research & Fact Checking
Bryson Clark
Isaac Nickerson
Stephan Kim
Irene Mascaró Genestar
Matthieu Béthencourt

Screenshots
Jeff Hines
Robert Colling
Marvin Andrews
Peter Bagley
Steve Stratton (AltaSource Group)

Design Direction & Management
Chris Franc
Kevin Lalli

Lead Designers
Hiromi Kimura
Elisabeth Lariviere
Mark Pedini

Design Support
Justin Gonyea
Dan Stephens

Project Management
Terry Mihashi
Yohei Sugiyama
Hannah Vassallo

Acknowledgments
Heather Dalgleish
Debra Kempker (Piggyback)
Anja Weinbach
Mikiko Ryu
Blaise Selby
Hisato Yamamori
Mayu Todo
Elena Nardo
Kaori Aoki
Bertrand Lecocq
Cyril Schultz
Owen Preece
Pierre Gauthier
Daniel Anscomb

Special Thanks
GAME FREAK inc.
The Pokémon Company

The Pokémon Company
INTERNATIONAL

POKÉMON SWORD & POKÉMON SHIELD
THE OFFICIAL GALAR REGION STRATEGY GUIDE

ISBN: 978-1-604382-04-4 [standard edition]
ISBN: 978-1-604382-06-8 [collector's edition]

Published in the United States by

The Pokémon Company International
10400 NE 4th Street, Suite 2800
Bellevue, WA 98004 USA

3rd Floor Building 10, Chiswick Park
566 Chiswick High Road
London, W4 5XS United Kingdom

Printed in the United States of America.